Pearson School Atlas

CANADA
Confederation: July 1 1867
Capital: Ottawa
Total area: 9 984 670 km²
Area of land: 9 093 507 km²
Area of fresh water: 891 163 km²
Population: 30 007 094
Population density: 3.3/km²
Urban population: 23 908 211
Percent of urban population: 80%

YUKON TERRITORY
Entered Confederation: June 13 1898
Capital: Whitehorse
Total area: 482 443 km²
Percent of total area: 4.8%
Population: 28 674
Percent of total pop'n.: 0.1%
Population density: 0.06/km²
Urban population: 59%

BRITISH COLUMBIA
Entered Confederation: July 20 1871
Capital: Victoria
Total area: 944 735 km²
Percent of total area: 9.5%
Population: 3 907 738
Percent of total pop'n.: 13.0%
Population density: 4.2/km²
Urban population: 85%

ALBERTA
Entered Confederation: September 1 1905
Capital: Edmonton
Total area: 661 848 km²
Percent of total area: 6.6%
Population: 2 974 807
Percent of total pop'n.: 9.9%
Population density: 4.6/km²
Urban population: 81%

SASKATCHEWAN
Entered Confederation: September 1 1905
Capital: Regina
Total area: 651 036 km²
Percent of total area: 6.5%
Population: 978 933
Percent of total pop'n.: 3.3%
Population density: 1.7/km²
Urban population: 64%

MANITOBA
Entered Confederation: July 15 1870
Capital: Winnipeg
Total area: 647 797 km²
Percent of total area: 6.5%
Population: 1 119 583
Percent of total pop'n.: 3.8%
Population density: 2.0/km²
Urban population: 72%

ONTARIO
Entered Confederation: July 1 1867
Capital: Toronto
Total area: 1 076 395 km²
Percent of total area: 10.8%
Population: 11 410 046
Percent of total pop'n.: 38.0%
Population density: 12.4/km²
Urban population: 85%

SCALE 1 : 17 500 000

0 200 400 600 800 km

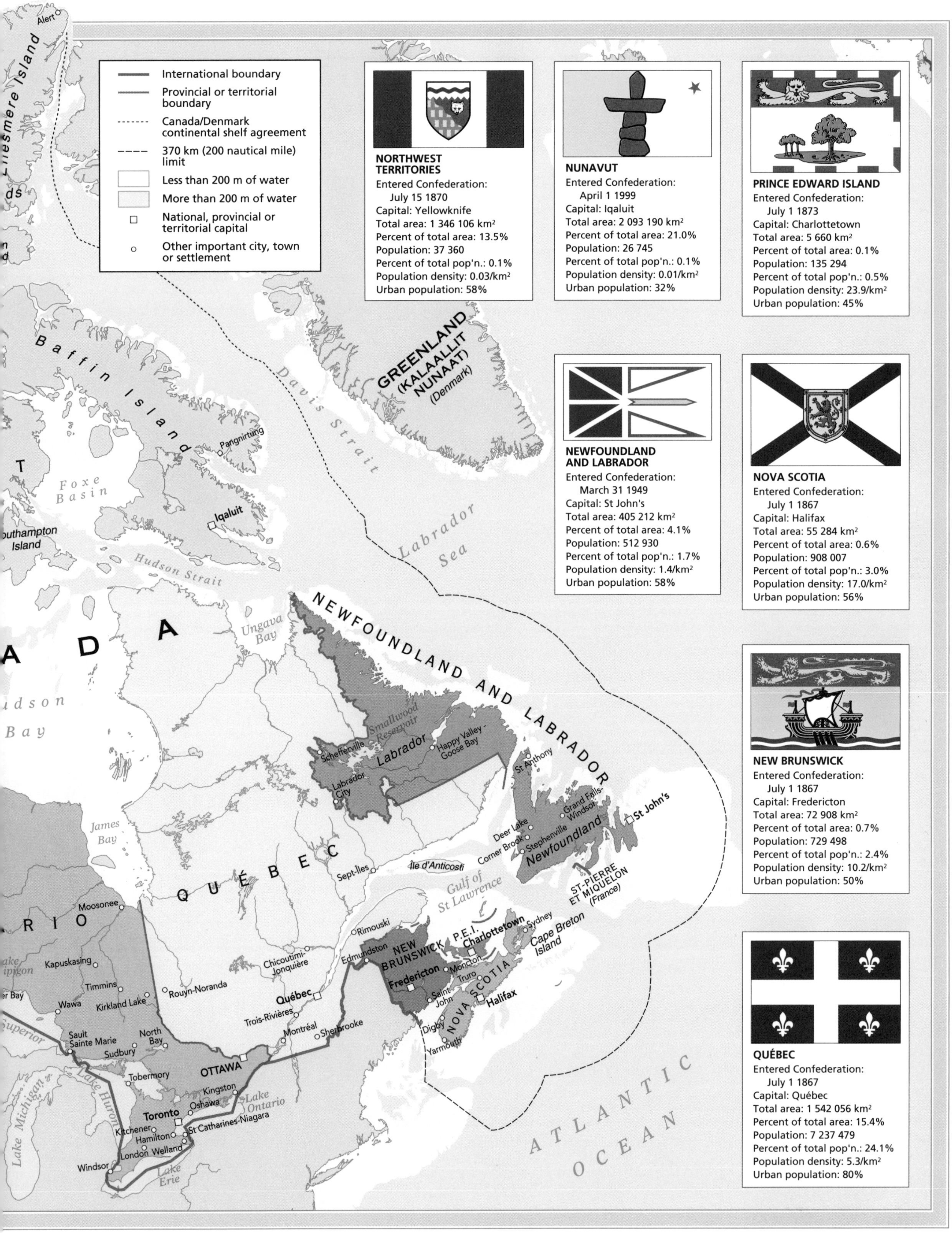

NORTHWEST TERRITORIES
Entered Confederation: July 15 1870
Capital: Yellowknife
Total area: 1 346 106 km²
Percent of total area: 13.5%
Population: 37 360
Percent of total pop'n.: 0.1%
Population density: 0.03/km²
Urban population: 58%

NUNAVUT
Entered Confederation: April 1 1999
Capital: Iqaluit
Total area: 2 093 190 km²
Percent of total area: 21.0%
Population: 26 745
Percent of total pop'n.: 0.1%
Population density: 0.01/km²
Urban population: 32%

PRINCE EDWARD ISLAND
Entered Confederation: July 1 1873
Capital: Charlottetown
Total area: 5 660 km²
Percent of total area: 0.1%
Population: 135 294
Percent of total pop'n.: 0.5%
Population density: 23.9/km²
Urban population: 45%

NEWFOUNDLAND AND LABRADOR
Entered Confederation: March 31 1949
Capital: St John's
Total area: 405 212 km²
Percent of total area: 4.1%
Population: 512 930
Percent of total pop'n.: 1.7%
Population density: 1.4/km²
Urban population: 58%

NOVA SCOTIA
Entered Confederation: July 1 1867
Capital: Halifax
Total area: 55 284 km²
Percent of total area: 0.6%
Population: 908 007
Percent of total pop'n.: 3.0%
Population density: 17.0/km²
Urban population: 56%

NEW BRUNSWICK
Entered Confederation: July 1 1867
Capital: Fredericton
Total area: 72 908 km²
Percent of total area: 0.7%
Population: 729 498
Percent of total pop'n.: 2.4%
Population density: 10.2/km²
Urban population: 50%

QUÉBEC
Entered Confederation: July 1 1867
Capital: Québec
Total area: 1 542 056 km²
Percent of total area: 15.4%
Population: 7 237 479
Percent of total pop'n.: 24.1%
Population density: 5.3/km²
Urban population: 80%

Lambert Conformal Conic projection

Pearson School Atlas

Robert Morrow

Former Curriculum Co-ordinator
Wentworth County Board of Education

PEARSON
Education Canada

Toronto

CONTENTS

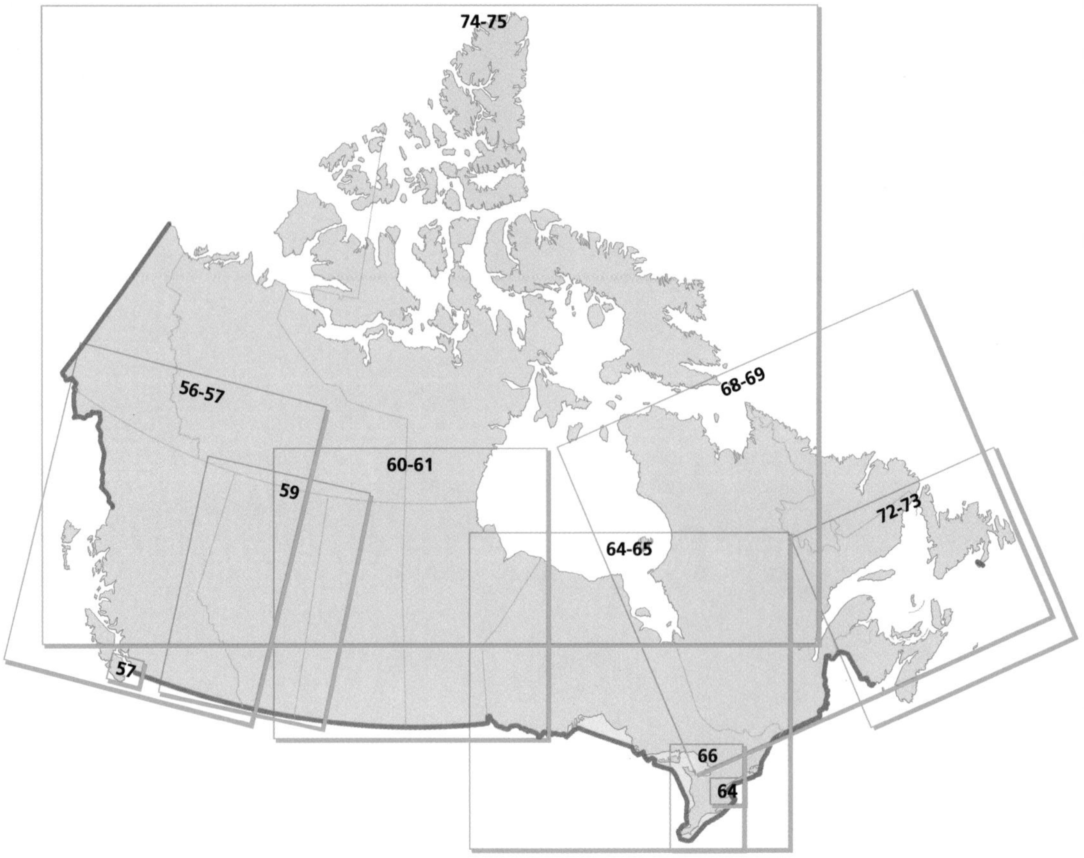
74-75
68-69
56-57
60-61
59
72-73
64-65
57
66
64

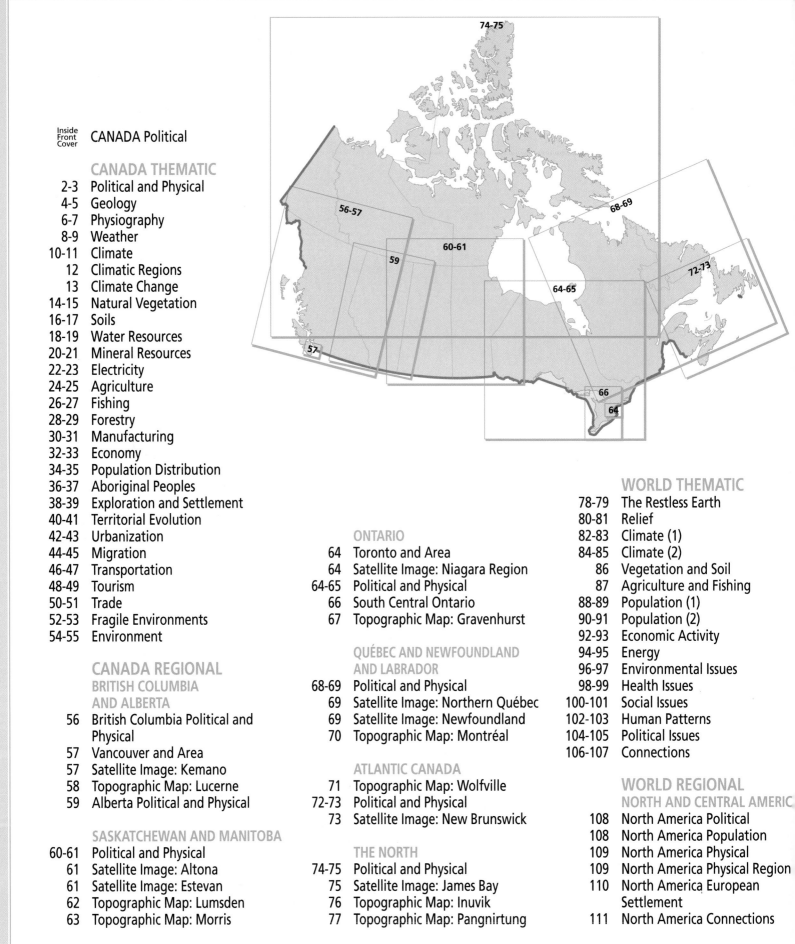

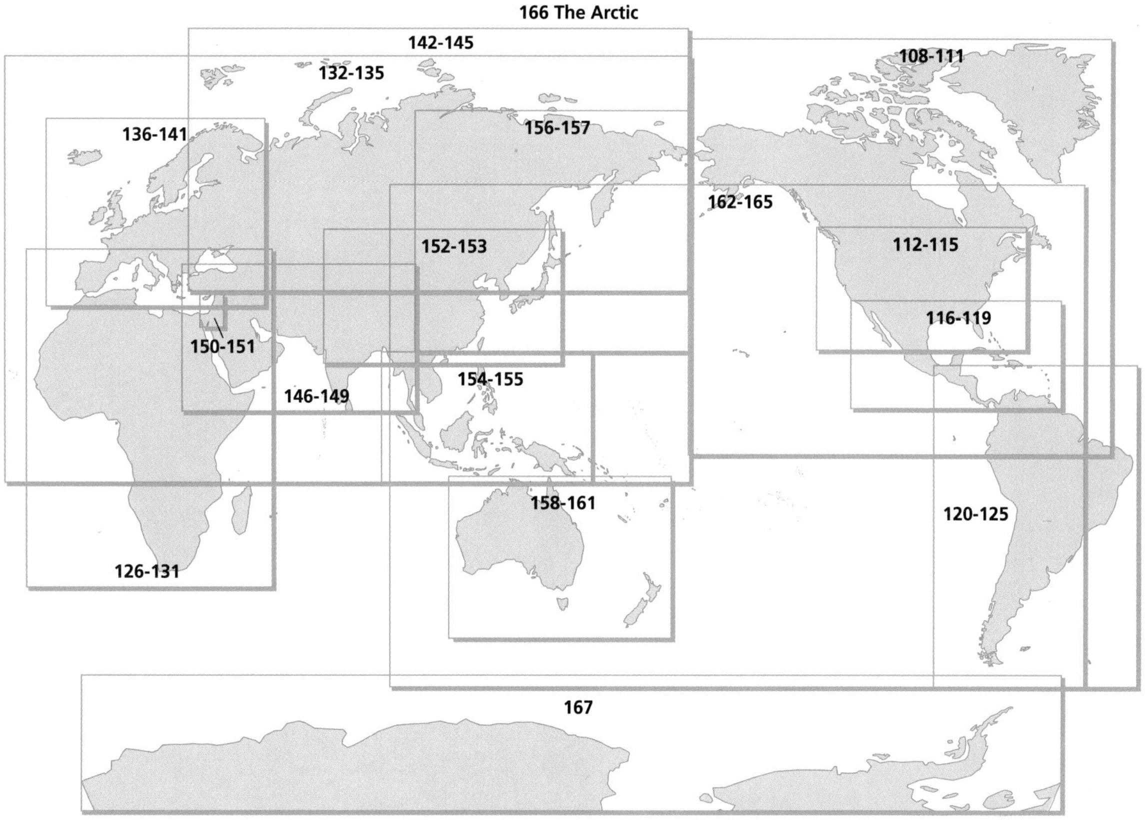
166 The Arctic
142-145
132-135
108-111
136-141
156-157
162-165
152-153
112-115
116-119
150-151
154-155
146-149
158-161
120-125
126-131
167

CANADA Political and Physical

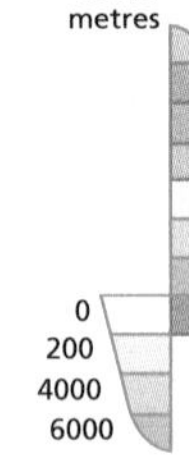

Relief and physical features

Relief metres: 5000, 3000, 2000, 1000, 500, 200, sea level, below sea level; 0, 200, 4000, 6000

5959 ▲ Mountain height (in metres)

Permanent ice

Water features

River

Canal

Lake / Reservoir

Marsh

Communications

Major highway

Other highway

Railway

Airport

Administration

Boundaries

International

Internal

Urban population

over 1 000 000

500 000 - 1 000 000

100 000 - 500 000

25 000 - 100 000

10 000 - 25 000

under 10 000

Square symbols denote national, provincial, territorial or state capital cities.

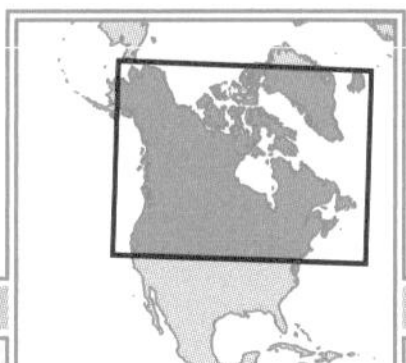

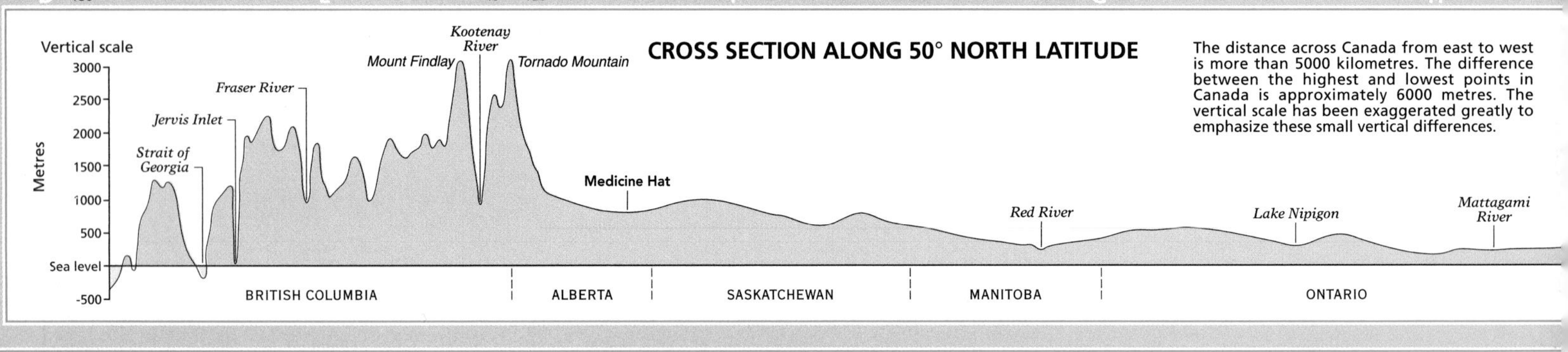

CROSS SECTION ALONG 50° NORTH LATITUDE

The distance across Canada from east to west is more than 5000 kilometres. The difference between the highest and lowest points in Canada is approximately 6000 metres. The vertical scale has been exaggerated greatly to emphasize these small vertical differences.

SCALE 1 : 17 500 000

0 200 400 600 800 km

CROSS SECTION FROM SARNIA TO ST JOHN'S
Vertical scale
Metres
2500
2000
1500
1000
500
Sea level
-500
Sarnia
Niagara Escarpment
Toronto
St Lawrence River
Appalachian Mountains
Saint John River
Northumberland Strait
Gulf of St Lawrence
Burin Peninsula
Placentia Bay
Avalon Peninsula
St John's
ONTARIO
QUÉBEC
MAINE, U.S.A.
NEW BRUNSWICK
P.E.I.
NEWFOUNDLAND
Cape Columbia
Alert
Ellesmere Island
British Empire Range
Nares Strait
Qaanaaq
Cape Parry
Devon Island
Baffin Bay
Bylot Island
Arctic Bay
Borden Peninsula
Mittimatalik
Baffin Island
Clyde River
Home Bay
Penny Icecap
Cape Dyer
Melville Peninsula
Hall Beach
Prince Charles Island
Nettilling Lake
Pangnirtung
Cumberland Sound
Repulse Bay
Foxe Basin
Foxe Channel
Foxe Peninsula
Amadjuak Lake
Iqaluit
Frobisher Bay
Southampton Island
Coral Harbour
Hudson Strait
Resolution Island
Fisher Strait
Coats Island
Mansel Island
Salluit
Péninsule d'Ungava
Kangiqsujuaq
Akpatok Island
Cape Chidley
Ungava Bay
Labrador Sea
Qeqertarsuaq
Qasigiannguit
Davis Strait
Arctic Circle
Sisimiut
Maniitsoq
NUUK
GREENLAND (KALAALLIT NUNAAT) (Denmark)
Paamiut
Ivittuut
Nanortalik
Cape Farewell
NEWFOUNDLAND AND LABRADOR
Kangiqsualujjuaq
Kuujjuaq
Puvurnituq
Ottawa Islands
Hudson Bay
Inukjuak
Nain
Hopedale
Cape Harrison
Smallwood Reservoir
Labrador
Happy Valley-Goose Bay
Port Hope Simpson
Churchill
Schefferville
Belcher Islands
Lac à l'Eau Claire
Caniapiscau
Réservoir La Grande 2
Réservoir La Grande 4
Réservoir La Grande 3
Cape Henrietta Maria
James Bay
Chisasibi
Fort Severn
Labrador City
Gagnon
Réservoir Manicouagan
Havre-St-Pierre
Île d'Anticosti
Strait of Belle Isle
St Anthony
Bonavista
Gander
Grand Falls-Windsor
St John's
Newfoundland
Corner Brook
Cape Race
Channel-Port-aux-Basques
ST-PIERRE ET MIQUELON (France)
Cabot Strait
Gulf of St Lawrence
Sept-Îles
Eastmain
Akimiski Island
Fort Albany
Waskaganish
QUÉBEC
ONTARIO
Moosonee
Lac Mistassini
Mistissini
Chibougamau
Baie-Comeau
Gaspé
Pén. de Gaspé
Rimouski
Rivière-du-Loup
Edmundston
Bathurst
NEW BRUNSWICK
P.E.I.
Charlottetown
Glace Bay
Sydney
Cape Breton Island
Moncton
Truro
NOVA SCOTIA
Halifax
Sable Island
Yarmouth
Cape Sable
Bay of Fundy
Roberval
Chicoutimi-Jonquière
Longlac
Kapuskasing
Lake Nipigon
Timmins
Amos
Val-d'Or
Thunder Bay
Isle Royale
Kirkland Lake
Québec
Montmagny
Presque Isle
Fredericton
Saint John
MAINE
Bangor
Augusta
Portland
Trois-Rivières
Montréal
Sherbrooke
Mount Washington
Chapleau
Lake Superior
Sault Sainte Marie
Sudbury
North Bay
OTTAWA
Cornwall
MICHIGAN
Escanaba
Iron Mountain
Green Bay
Lake Michigan
Lake Huron
Georgian Bay
Traverse City
Cadillac
Owen Sound
Barrie
Peterborough
Kingston
Oshawa
Toronto
St Catharines-Niagara
Hamilton
Burlington
Montpelier
VER.
N.H.
Concord
Boston
MASS.
Lowell
Worcester
Cape Cod
Providence
Bay City
Flint
Sarnia
London
Buffalo
Rochester
Syracuse
Utica
Albany
Springfield
Hartford
CONN.
R.I.
New Haven
NEW YORK
PENN.
Scranton
Bridgeport
New York
Erie
Milwaukee
Grand Rapids
Lansing
Detroit
Windsor
ATLANTIC OCEAN
Rivière Manicouagan
Gulf of St Lawrence
White Bay
Confusion Bay
QUÉBEC
NEWFOUNDLAND

Lambert Conformal Conic projection

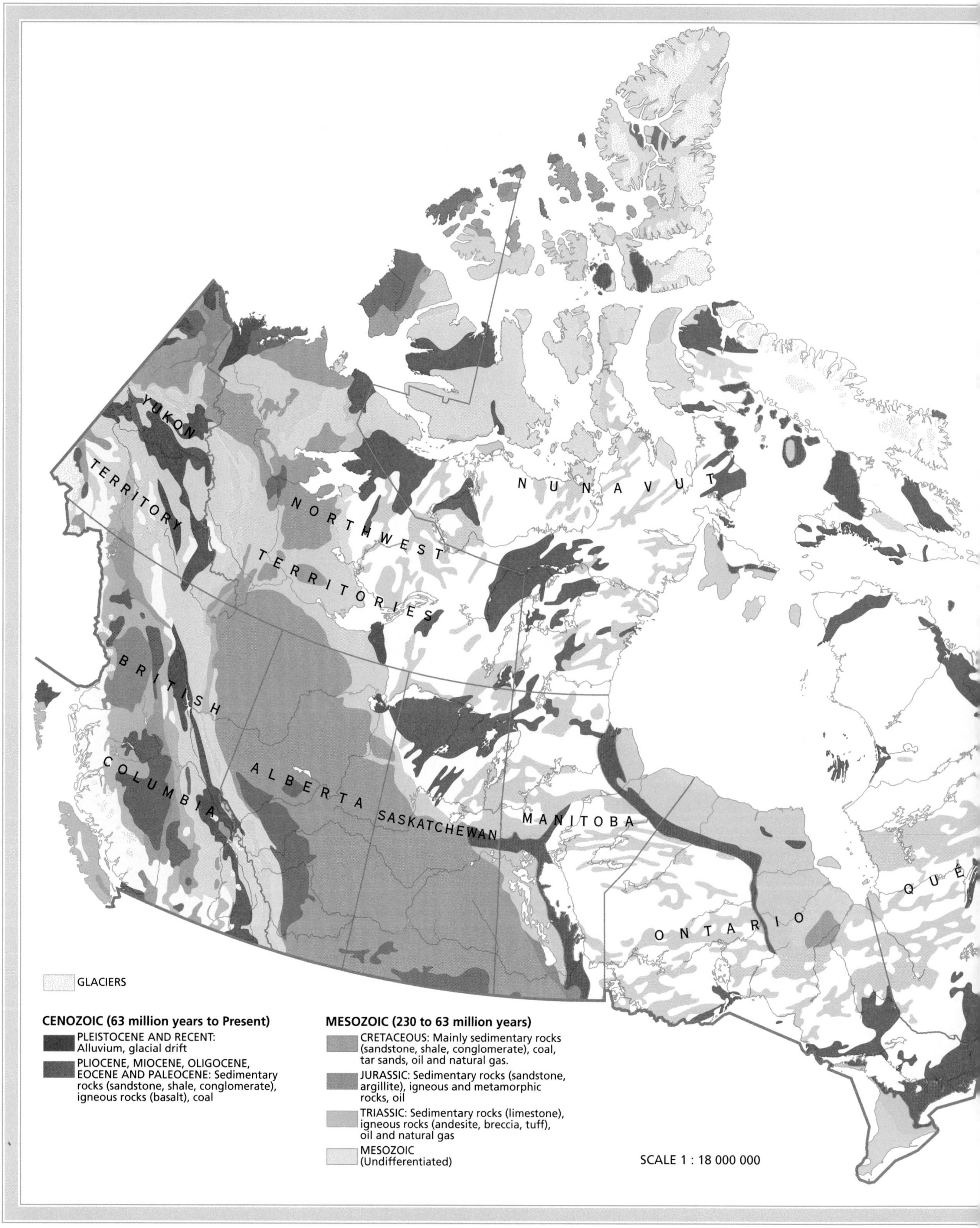
YUKON
TERRITORY
NORTHWEST
TERRITORIES
NUNAVUT
BRITISH
COLUMBIA
ALBERTA
SASKATCHEWAN
MANITOBA
ONTARIO
QUÉ
GLACIERS
CENOZOIC (63 million years to Present)
PLEISTOCENE AND RECENT: Alluvium, glacial drift
PLIOCENE, MIOCENE, OLIGOCENE, EOCENE AND PALEOCENE: Sedimentary rocks (sandstone, shale, conglomerate), igneous rocks (basalt), coal
MESOZOIC (230 to 63 million years)
CRETACEOUS: Mainly sedimentary rocks (sandstone, shale, conglomerate), coal, tar sands, oil and natural gas.
JURASSIC: Sedimentary rocks (sandstone, argillite), igneous and metamorphic rocks, oil
TRIASSIC: Sedimentary rocks (limestone), igneous rocks (andesite, breccia, tuff), oil and natural gas
MESOZOIC (Undifferentiated)
SCALE 1 : 18 000 000

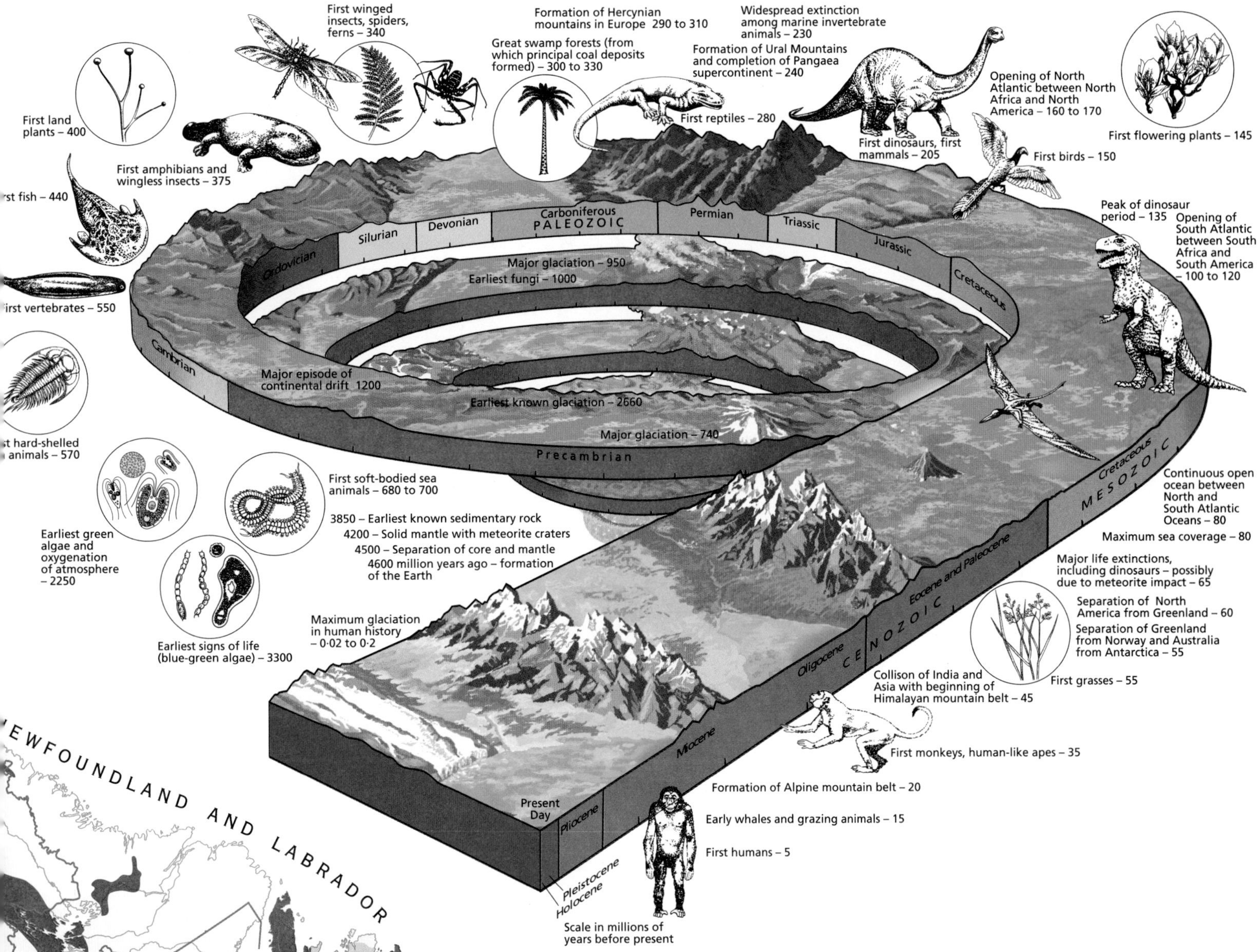

PALEOZOIC (600 to 230 million years)

- PERMIAN AND CARBONIFEROUS: Mainly sedimentary rocks (sandstone, shale, conglomerate, limestone), igneous rocks, coal, gypsum, oil and natural gas
- DEVONIAN: Sedimentary rocks (sandstone, shale, conglomerate, limestone, dolomite), igneous rocks, salt, oil and natural gas
- SILURIAN: Mainly sedimentary rocks (sandstone, shale, limestone, dolomite), some igneous rocks, gypsum, salt, oil and natural gas
- ORDOVICIAN: Sedimentary rocks (sandstone, shale, limestone, dolomite), metamorphic rocks, oil and natural gas
- CAMBRIAN: Sedimentary rocks (sandstone, shale, conglomerate, limestone, dolomite, chert)
- PALEOZOIC (Undifferentiated)

PRECAMBRIAN (Formation of Earth to 600 million years)

- PROTEROZOIC: Sedimentary rocks (sandstone, shale, conglomerate, limestone, dolomite), igneous rocks (basalt, breccia, tuff, greystone), metamorphic rocks (slate, schist, gneiss, quartzite), iron
- ARCHEAN: Sedimentary rocks (sandstone, conglomerate), metamorphic rocks (slate, schist, gneiss, quartzite)

INTRUSIVE ROCKS

- CENOZOIC, MESOZOIC AND PALEOZOIC: Mainly acidic rocks (granite, granodiorite, syenite), some basic rocks (gabbro, serpentine)
- PRECAMBRIAN: Mainly acidic rocks (granite, granodiorite, granite gneiss), some basic rocks (gabbro, diabase)

PHYSIOGRAPHIC REGIONS

Innuitian Region

Arctic Lowlands

Cordilleran Region

Hudson Bay Lowlands

Appalachian Region

Interior Plains

The Canadian Shield

Great Lakes – St Lawrence Lowlands

GLACIATION

GLACIAL EFFECT ON PHYSIOGRAPHY

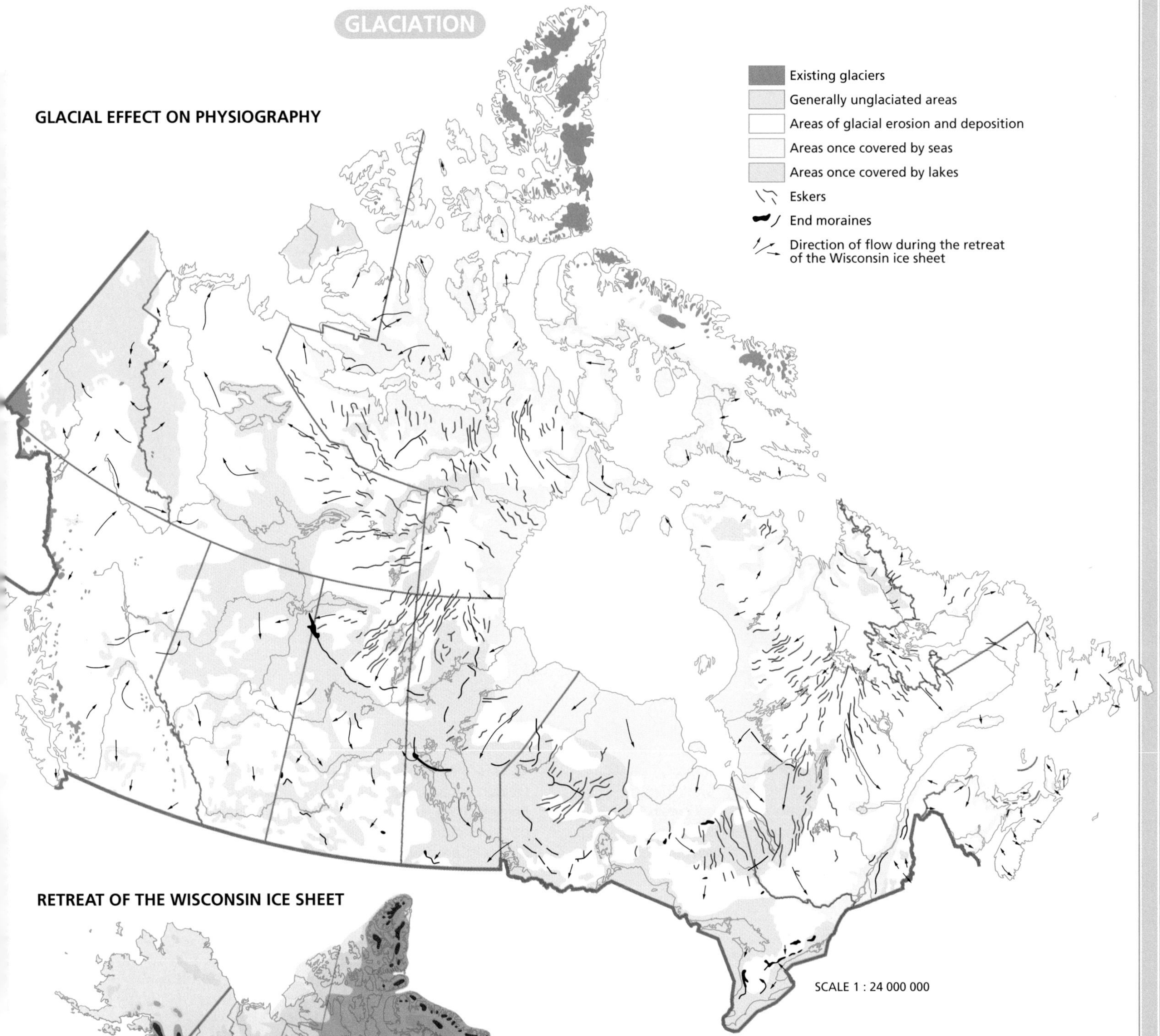

RETREAT OF THE WISCONSIN ICE SHEET

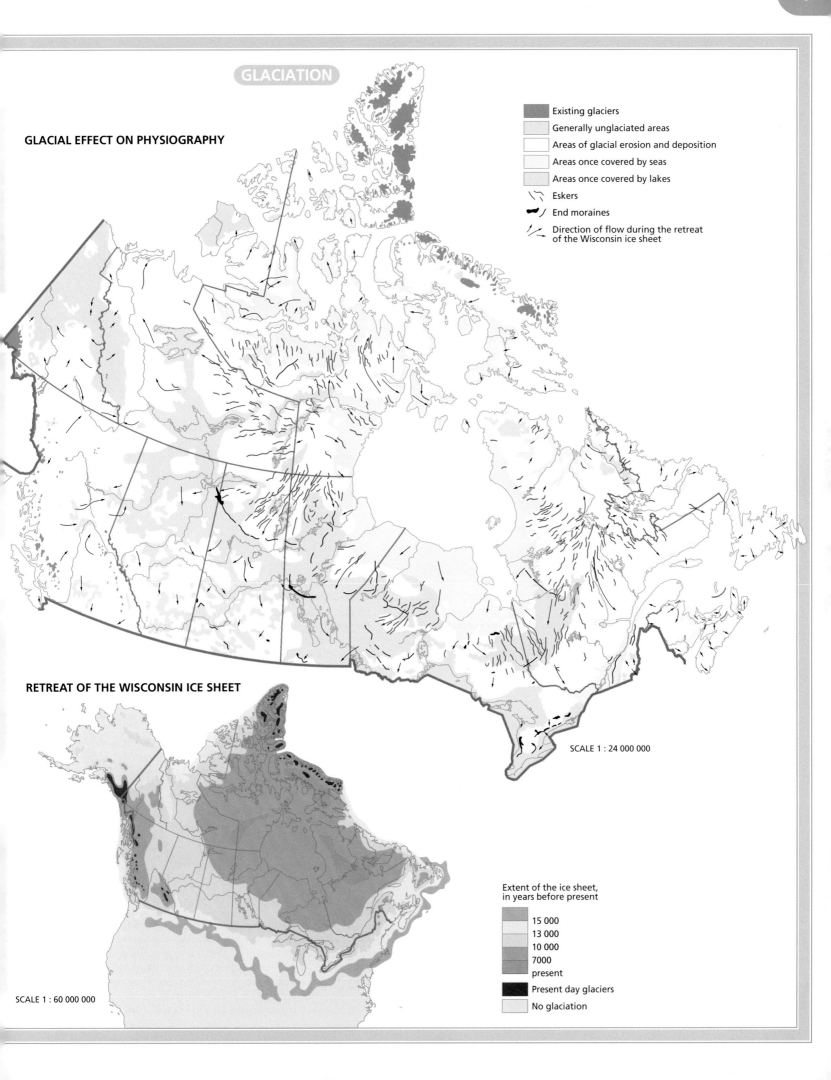

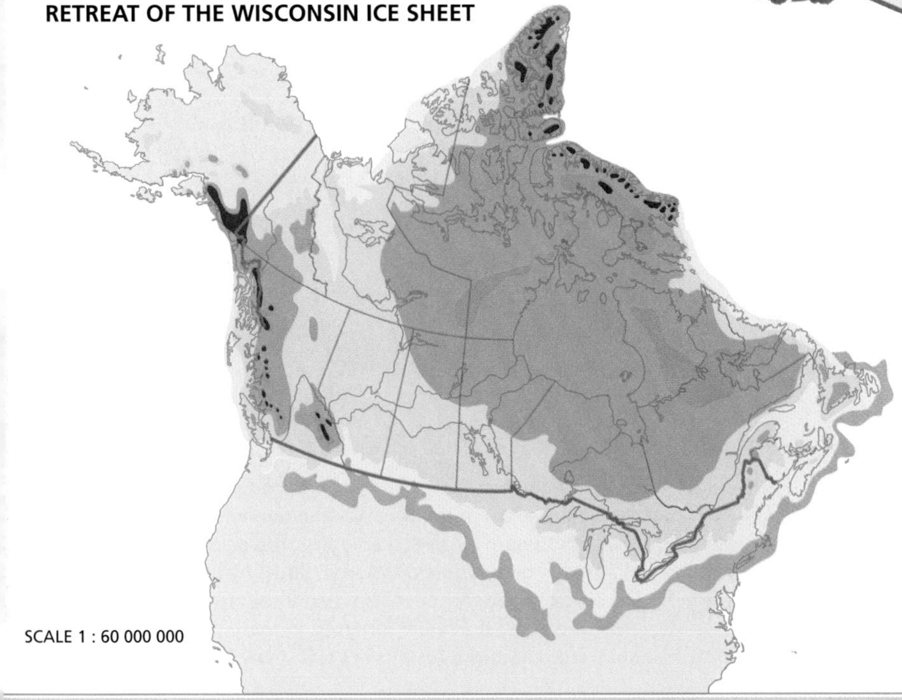

AIR MASSES

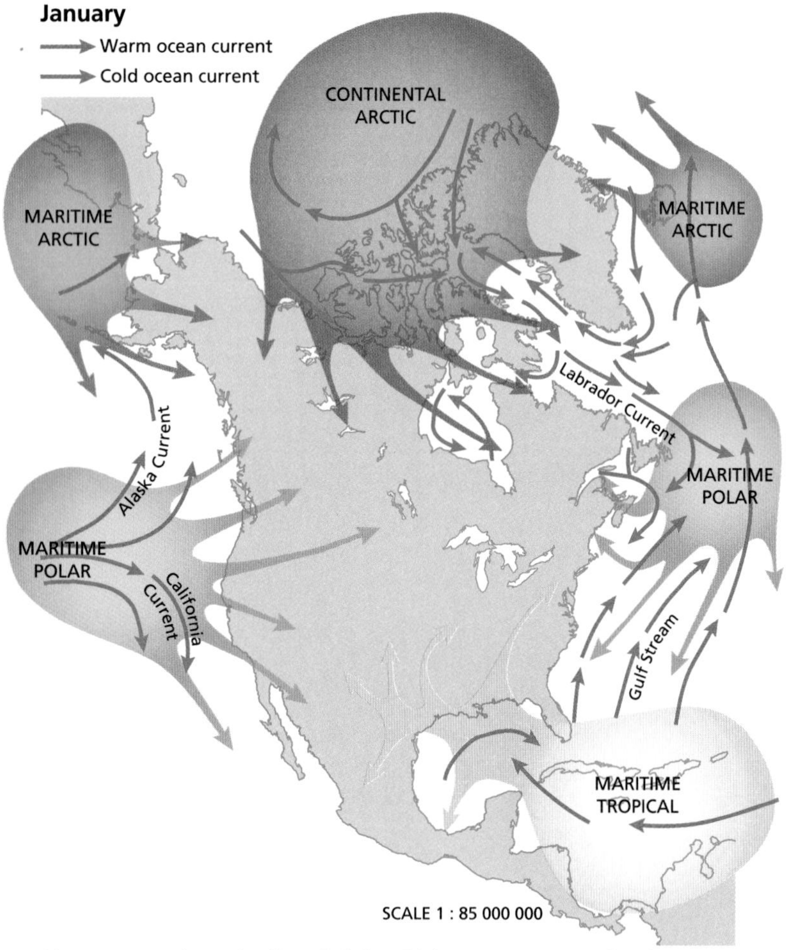

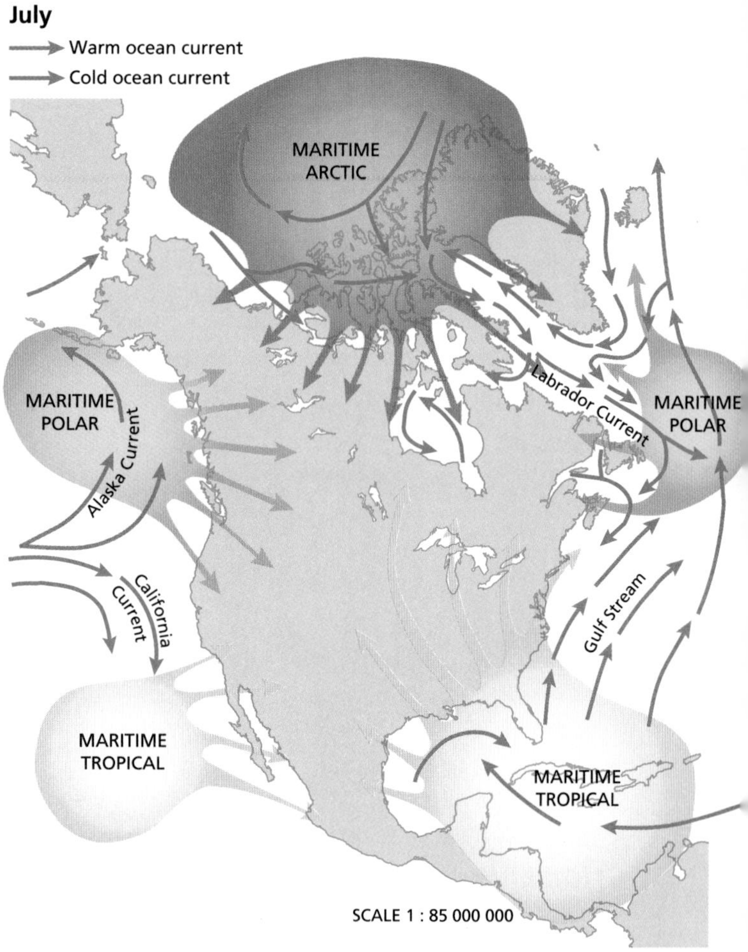

Air masses are large bodies of air in which temperature and moisture conditions are approximately the same throughout the air mass. They take on the characteristics of the areas over which they form. Then, when they move, they take those characteristics to the new areas. Air masses can develop over land or water. In January, the Continental Arctic air mass develops over the northern land and ice-covered areas. It is cold and dry, and brings crisp winter weather further south.

In July, some air masses migrate northward from their January position. The Maritime Tropical air mass becomes much more dominant in eastern Canada, bringing hot, humid weather to areas east of the Rockies. The warm, wet, weather along Canada's west coast is a result of the Maritime Polar air mass moving inland from the Pacific Ocean. However, precipitation is greater in the winter when the Maritime Polar air mass is directly off the west coast.

WEATHER FRONTS

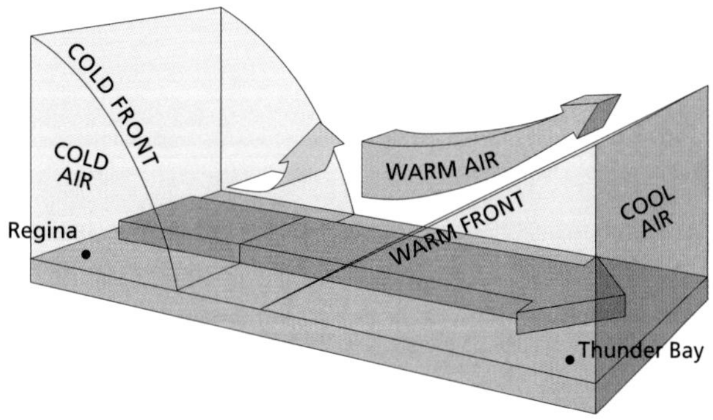

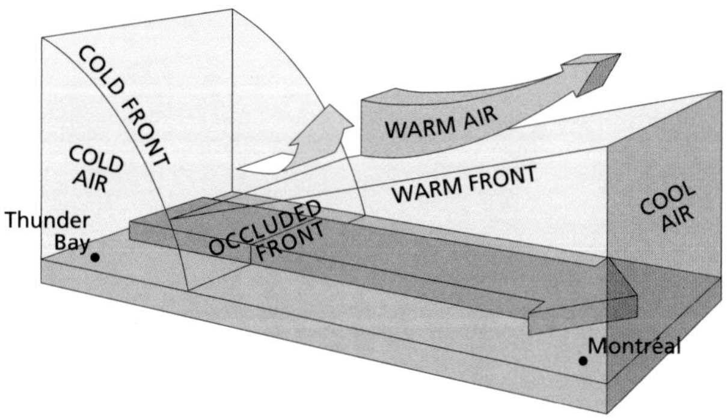

Air masses move in order to equalize atmospheric pressure, moving from high- to low-pressure zones. The line where two masses of air with different characteristics meet is called a *front*. When warm air is moving into an area of cold air, the front is called a warm front. When the reverse is the case, it is called a cold front. Note that cold air burrows *under* warm air, while warm air tends to ride *over* cold air.

A cold front forces the warm air ahead of it to rise quickly, causing heavy precipitation, often in the form of thunderstorms. In contrast, along a warm front warm air rises slowly over the cold air, creating widespread areas of gentle precipitation. Cold fronts move faster than warm fronts. An occluded front occurs when a cold front catches up to a warm front, forcing all the warm air aloft. In this way, an area may go from cool to cold, without experiencing the warm air.

DAYS WITH PRECIPITATION

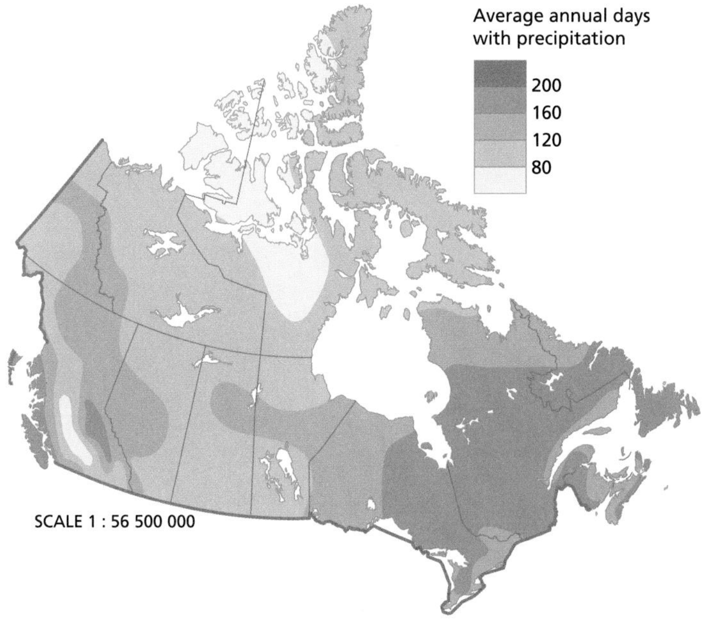

CLOUD COVER

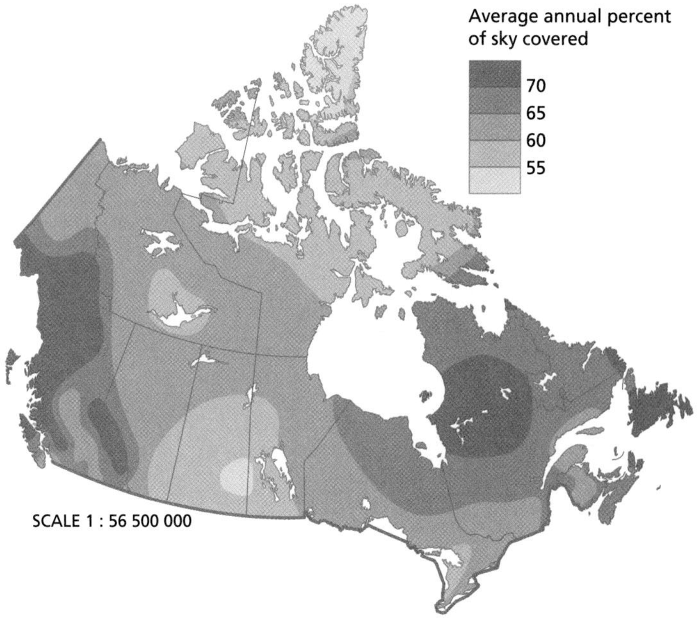

THUNDERSTORMS

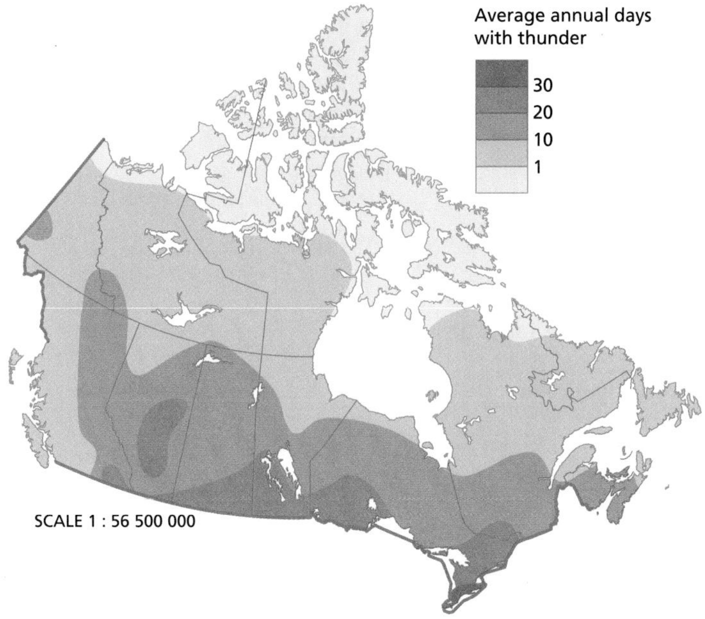

UV INDEX

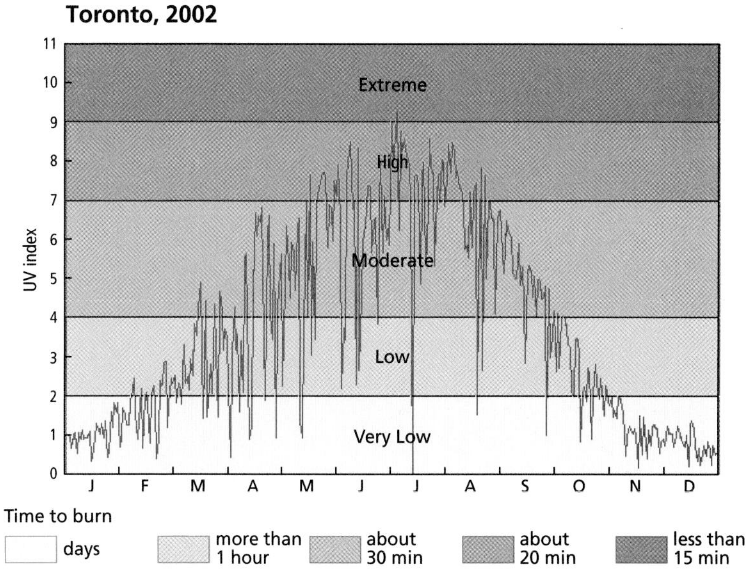

HUMIDITY

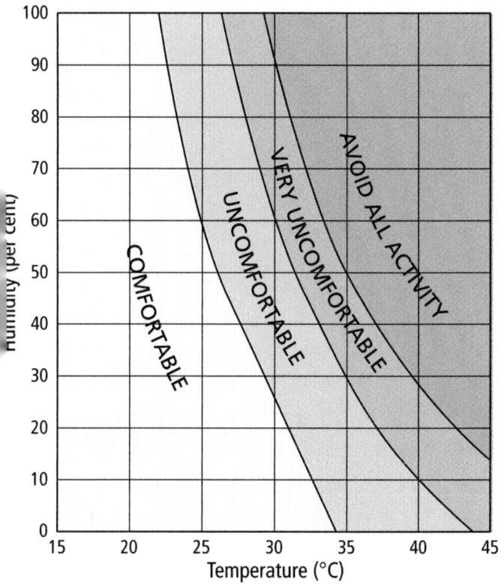

WIND CHILL

Calculation chart

Wind velocity km/h	Air temperature °C						
	5	0	-10	-20	-30	-40	-50
10	3	-3	-15	-27	-39	-51	-63
20	1	-5	-18	-31	-41	-56	-68
30	0	-7	-20	-33	-46	-59	-72
40	-1	-7	-21	-34	-48	-61	-74
50	-1	-8	-22	-35	-49	-63	-76
60	-2	-9	-23	-37	-50	-64	-78
70	-2	-9	-23	-37	-51	-66	-80
80	-3	-10	-24	-38	-52	-67	-81

Thresholds
- Risk of frostbite in prolonged exposure
- Frostbite possible in 10 minutes
- Frostbite possible in 2 minutes

TEMPERATURE

January

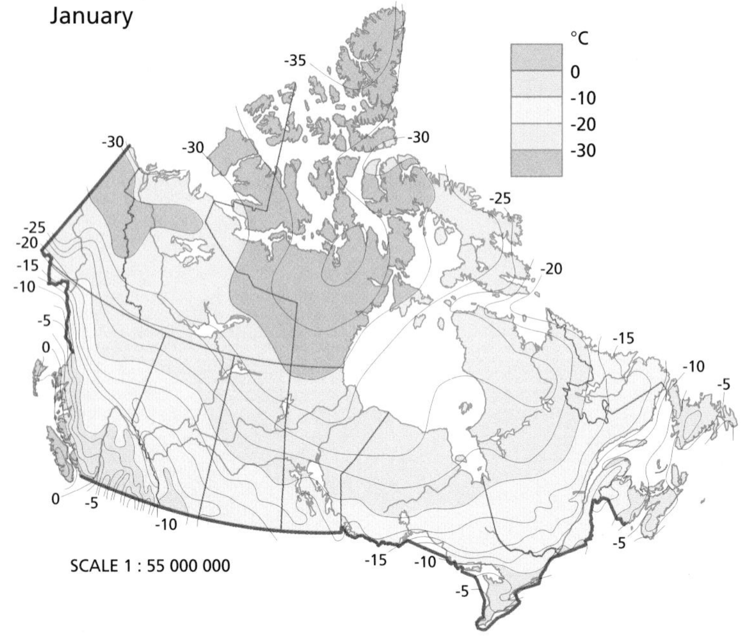

Temperatures across Canada are shown on the maps using isotherms – lines joining places with the same temperature. The temperatures in Canada in January are affected by two conditions: latitude and continentality. Differences occur from north to south, showing the effect of latitude. Differences also occur from the coastal regions towards the centre of the continent, showing the effect of the land mass. Places that are north and in the centre of the land mass (e.g., Baker Lake, Cambridge Bay) are very cold in winter.

July

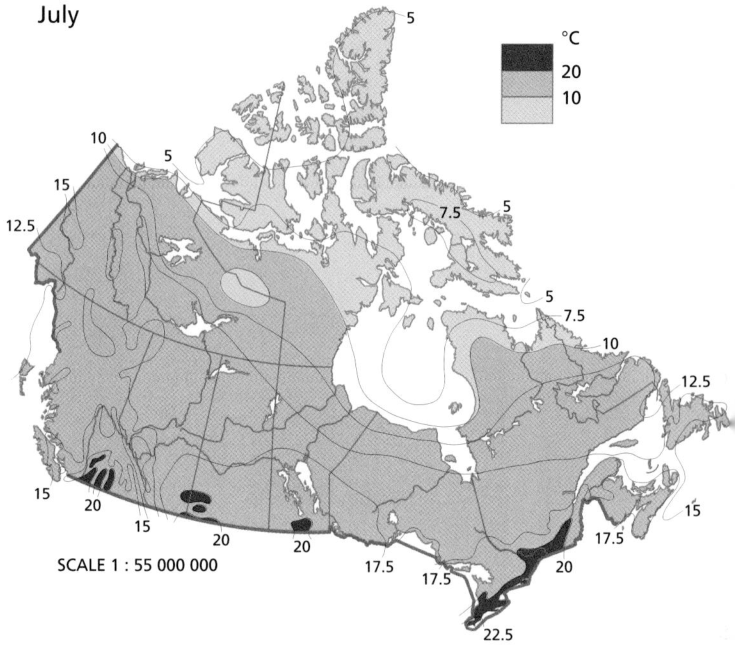

The temperatures in Canada in July reflect the influence of latitude. This is shown by the general east-west trend of the isotherms. Along the coasts, temperatures are moderated by bodies of water. Interior locations have low winter, but relatively high summer, temperatures. This is a true "continental" climate with a wide range of temperature and low precipitation. Canada's highest summer temperatures are in southern Ontario and the southern parts of British Columbia.

PRECIPITATION

Annual precipitation

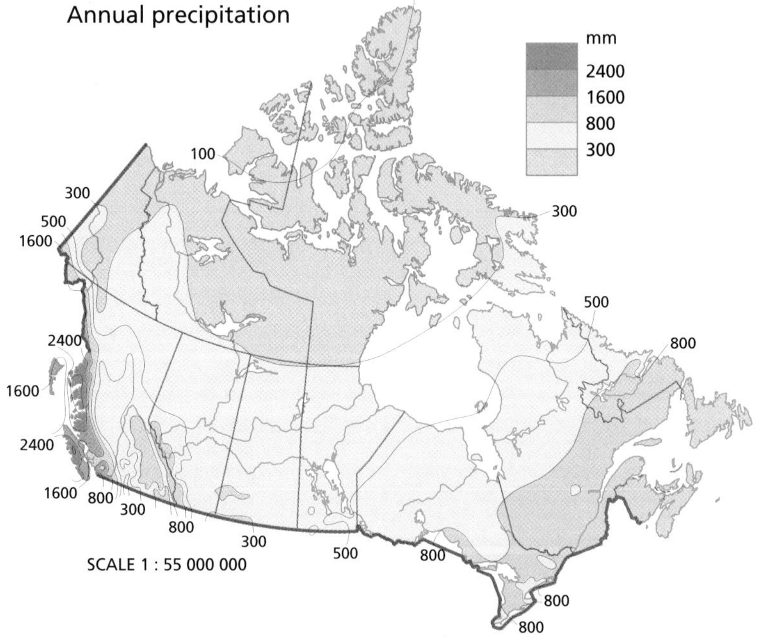

Precipitation includes all forms of moisture. Several factors influence the pattern of precipitation in Canada: bodies of water, prevailing winds, air masses, and relief. The far northern areas are desert-like, with low precipitation. There is little evaporation associated with the low temperatures and, therefore, little precipitation. Heavy precipitation is concentrated in a narrow area along the west coast by the effect of the mountains.

Annual snowfall

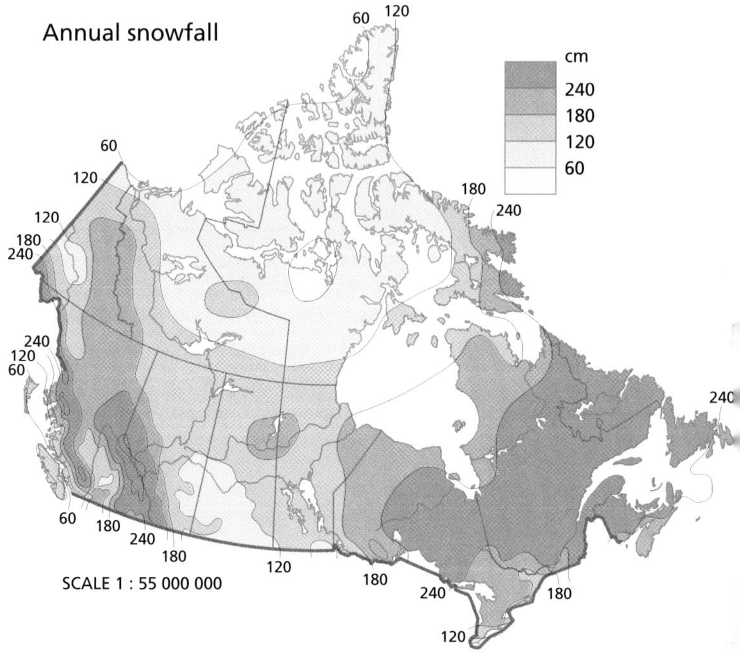

Snowfall is included in the annual precipitation totals. The amount of snowfall is converted to water, using a 10:1 snow-to-moisture ratio. The snowfall map shows the influence of the mountains on precipitation. Moisture-laden air from the Gulf of Mexico mixes with the cooler air across northern Ontario and Québec. There is little actual snowfall in much of the far north – very similar to the amounts received in the southern prairies.

SUNSHINE

Solar radiation

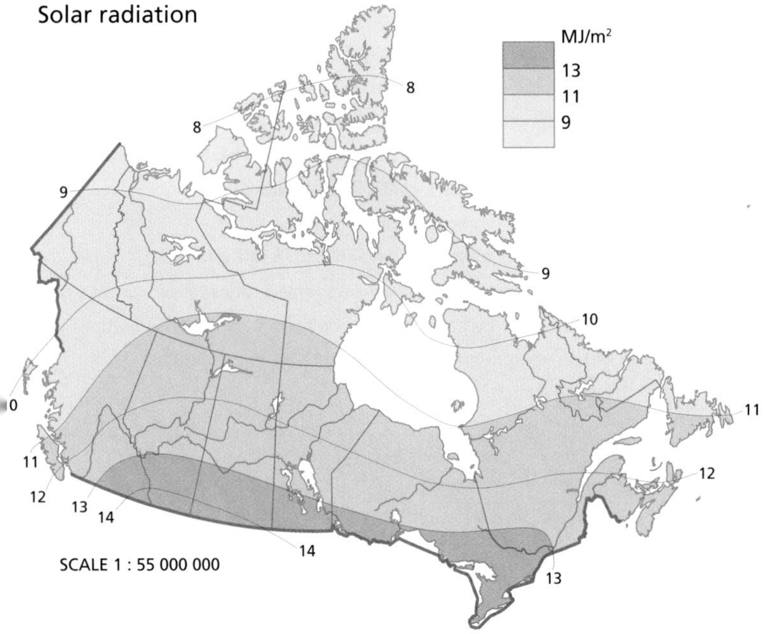

Solar radiation (infrared, visible, and ultraviolet light) is indispensable for life on Earth. The sun heats up the atmosphere and provides sunlight. However, ultraviolet radiation can be very harmful for humans. UV radiation is responsible for most forms of skin cancer. The pattern of solar radiation reflects the influence of cloud cover, latitude, and the angle of the sun's rays as they enter the atmosphere and penetrate to the earth's surface. Solar radiation is measured in megajoules per square metre (MJ/m²).

Bright sunshine hours

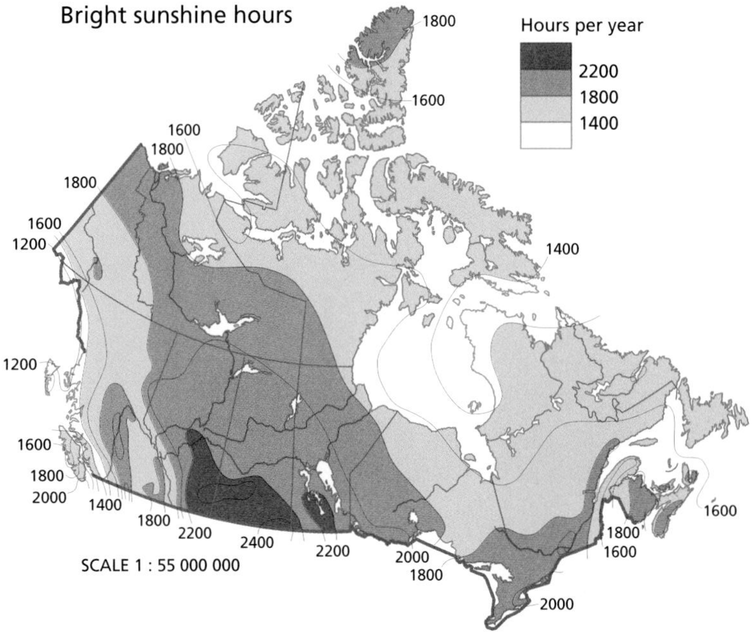

Several factors affect the number of hours of bright sunshine in a given area each year: air masses, cyclonic storms, and number of daylight hours. The southern prairies have the most sunshine hours in a year, reaching more than double the number of hours in some coastal areas of B.C. Estevan, Saskatchewan is Canada's sunshine capital with over 2500 hours of bright sunshine and nearly 3000 hours of clear skies. In contrast, Prince Rupert, B.C. has over 6000 hours of cloudy conditions.

FROST-FREE DAYS

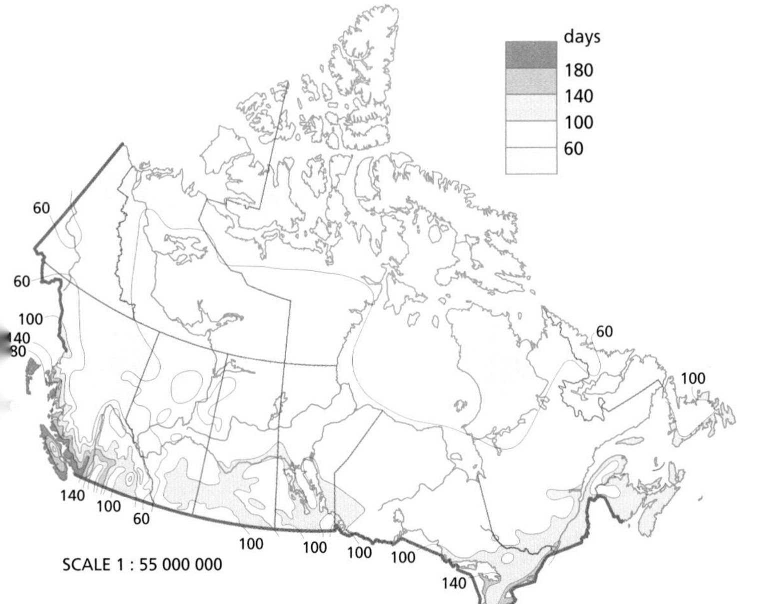

The number of frost-free days is measured from the last frost in the spring to the first frost in the fall. The length of the frost-free period helps to determine planting and harvesting times. However, since these are averages, established over many years of keeping records, the averages cannot be counted upon as a prediction for a specific year. Thompson, Manitoba has the shortest frost-free season in Canada – 64 days.

GROWING SEASON

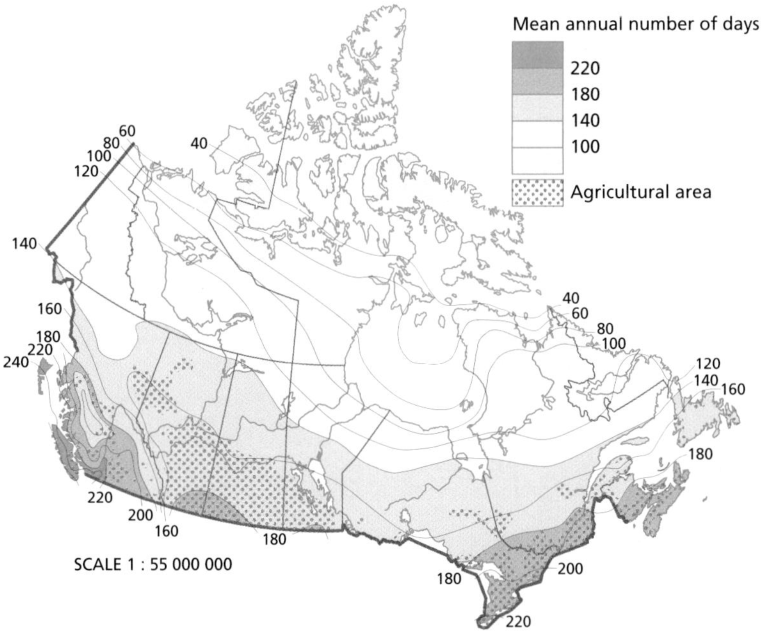

The growing season represents the number of days in the growing season when the temperature exceeds 6°C. When temperatures reach this level, plant growth occurs. There may be days when the temperature reaches 6°C and then falls below the freezing point at night. Consequently, the growing season is longer than the frost-free period. The growing season is longest in southern British Columbia and southwestern Ontario.

CLIMATE REGIONS

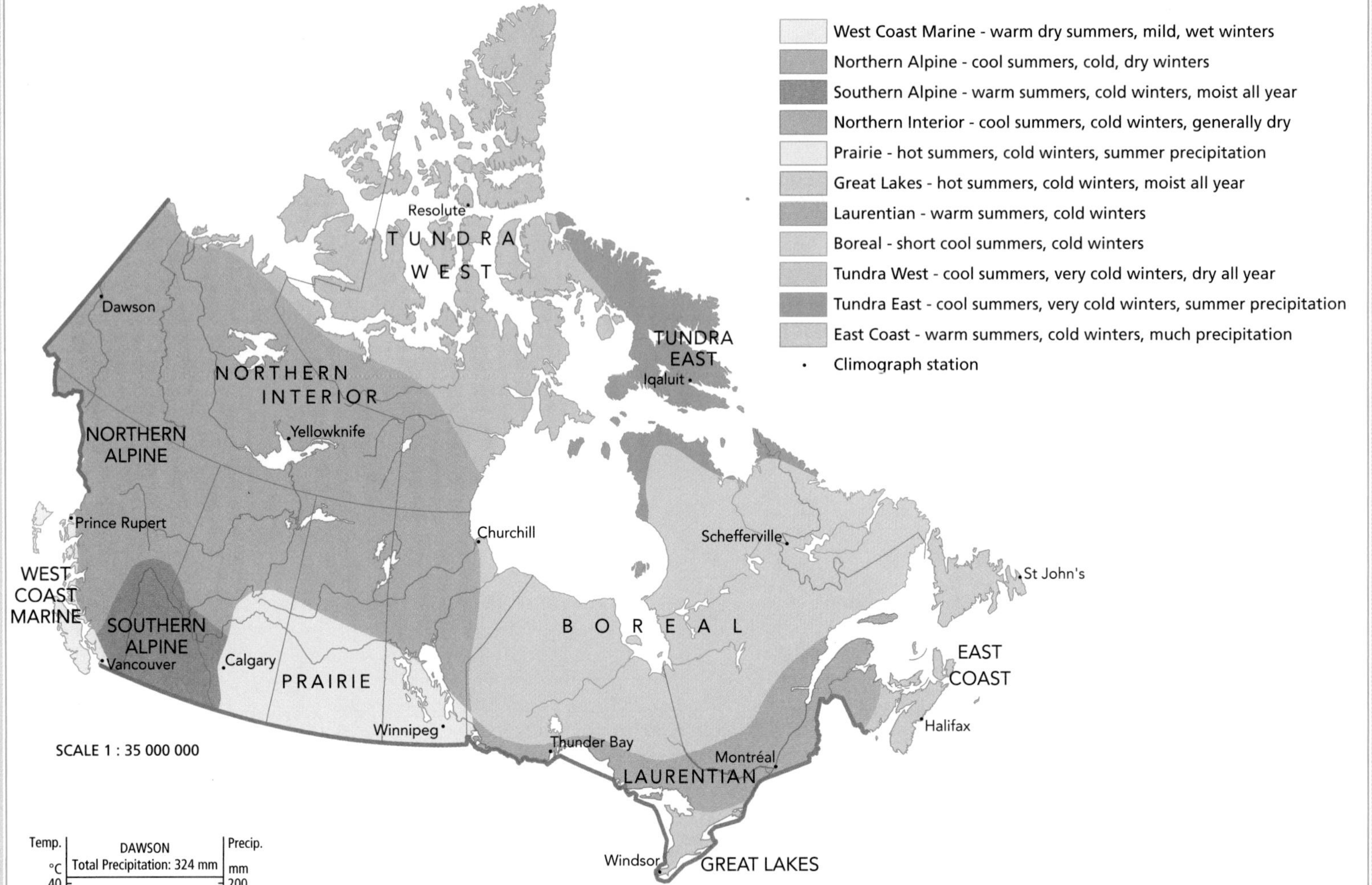
West Coast Marine - warm dry summers, mild, wet winters
Northern Alpine - cool summers, cold, dry winters
Southern Alpine - warm summers, cold winters, moist all year
Northern Interior - cool summers, cold winters, generally dry
Prairie - hot summers, cold winters, summer precipitation
Great Lakes - hot summers, cold winters, moist all year
Laurentian - warm summers, cold winters
Boreal - short cool summers, cold winters
Tundra West - cool summers, very cold winters, dry all year
Tundra East - cool summers, very cold winters, summer precipitation
East Coast - warm summers, cold winters, much precipitation
Climograph station
Resolute
TUNDRA WEST
Dawson
TUNDRA EAST
Iqaluit
NORTHERN INTERIOR
NORTHERN ALPINE
Yellowknife
Prince Rupert
Churchill
Schefferville
St John's
WEST COAST MARINE
SOUTHERN ALPINE
BOREAL
EAST COAST
Vancouver
Calgary
PRAIRIE
Winnipeg
Halifax
Thunder Bay
Montréal
LAURENTIAN
Windsor
GREAT LAKES

SCALE 1 : 35 000 000

CLIMOGRAPHS

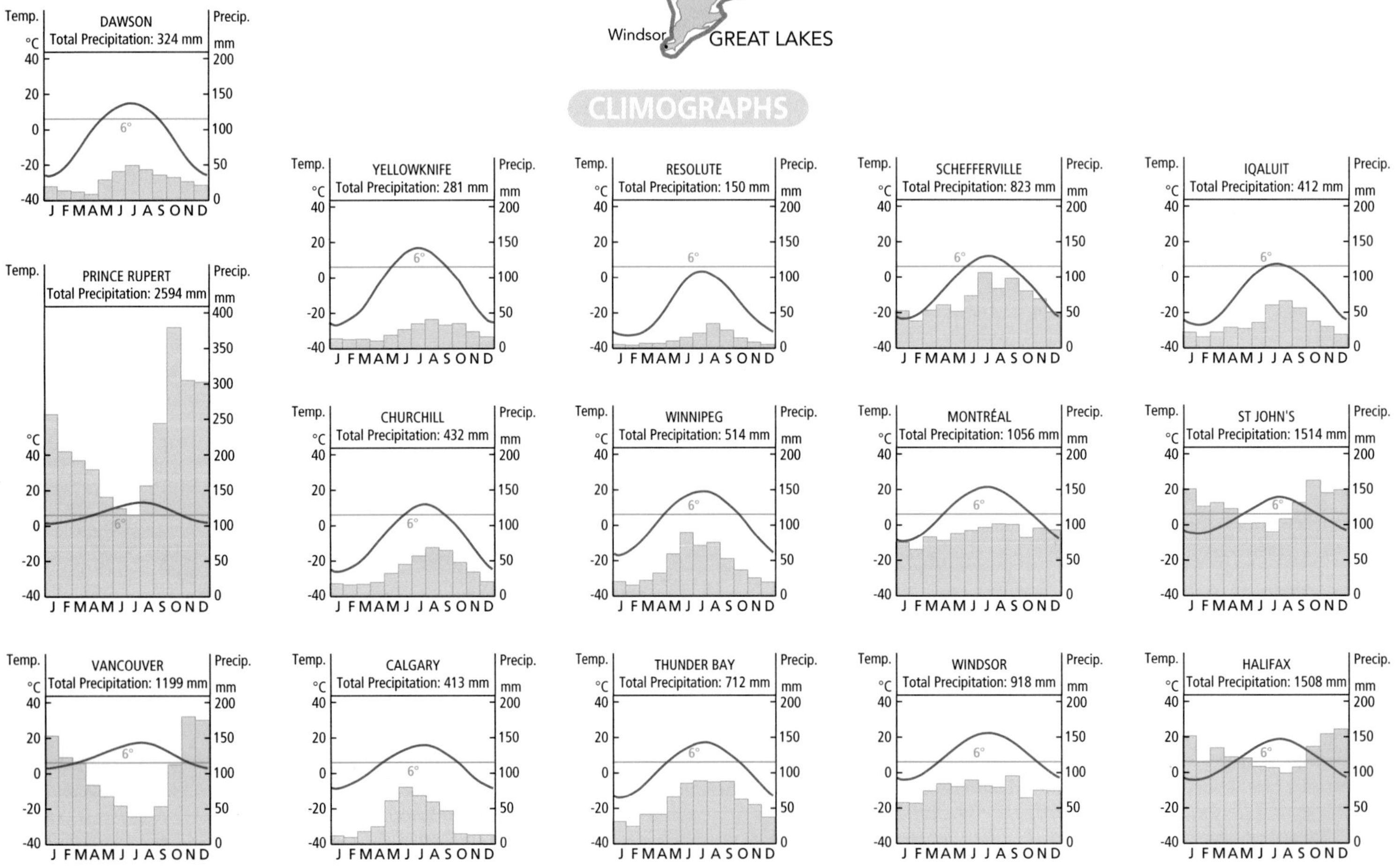
Temp. °C
Precip. mm
DAWSON Total Precipitation: 324 mm
PRINCE RUPERT Total Precipitation: 2594 mm
YELLOWKNIFE Total Precipitation: 281 mm
RESOLUTE Total Precipitation: 150 mm
SCHEFFERVILLE Total Precipitation: 823 mm
IQALUIT Total Precipitation: 412 mm
CHURCHILL Total Precipitation: 432 mm
WINNIPEG Total Precipitation: 514 mm
MONTRÉAL Total Precipitation: 1056 mm
ST JOHN'S Total Precipitation: 1514 mm
VANCOUVER Total Precipitation: 1199 mm
CALGARY Total Precipitation: 413 mm
THUNDER BAY Total Precipitation: 712 mm
WINDSOR Total Precipitation: 918 mm
HALIFAX Total Precipitation: 1508 mm
J F M A M J J A S O N D
6°

GREENHOUSE EFFECT

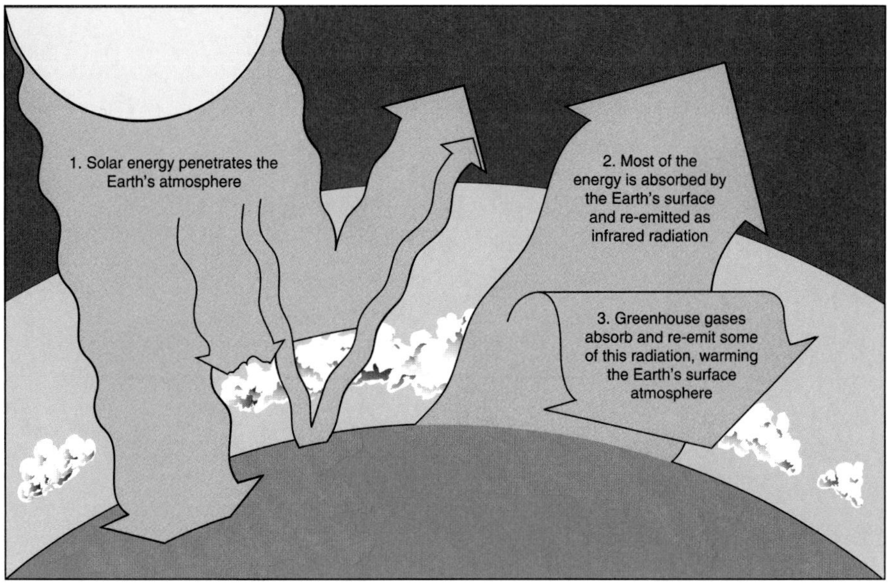

The atmosphere is more than just "air." The mixture of gases that makes up the atmosphere performs many functions and helps to support life. Just as glass in a greenhouse holds heat in, the atmosphere traps heat and keeps it near Earth's surface. For centuries, the atmosphere changed little in temperature, and the balance of gases was suitable for plant, animal, and human survival. In recent years, however, the balance has been disrupted. Fossil fuels for heating and electrical production, gasoline for cars, and manufacturing have added greenhouse gases to the atmosphere. These gases trap the heat and warm the atmosphere. The main greenhouse gases are water vapour (H_20), carbon dioxide (CO_2), methane (CH_4), nitrous oxide (N_2O), ozone (O_3), and halocarbons (CFCs, HFCs, etc.).

OZONE

Total ozone, January 1984

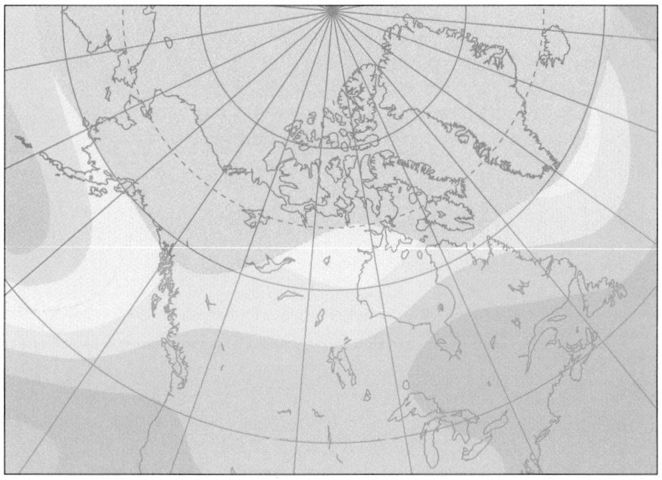

Total ozone, January 2001

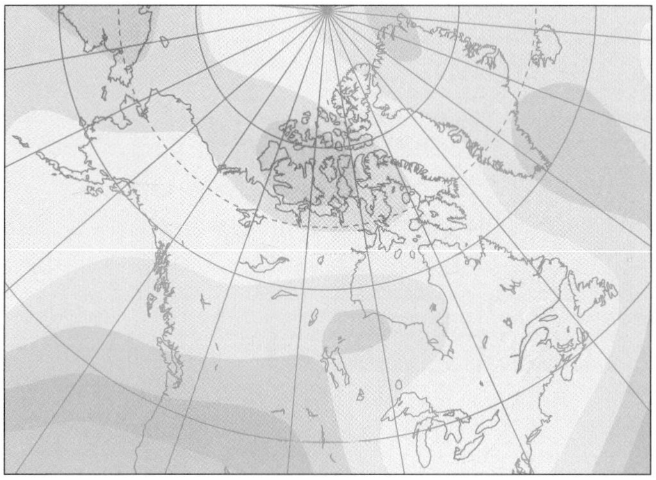

CLIMATE CHANGE IN CANADA

Temperature
Celsius degrees above or below normal

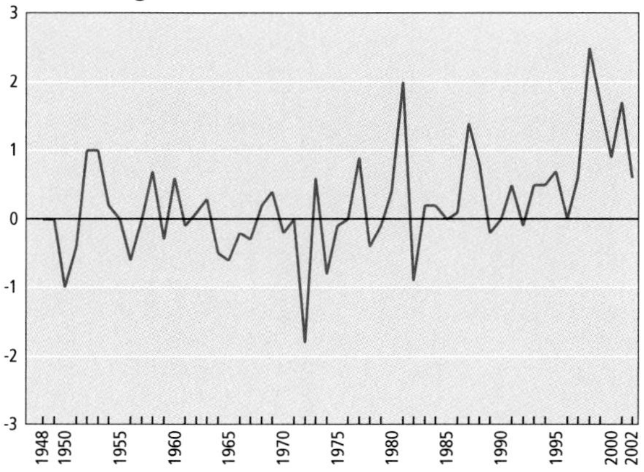

Precipitation
Millimetres above or below normal

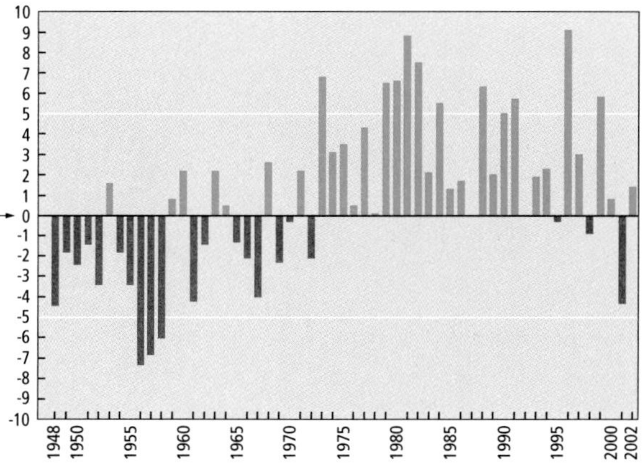

Coastal forest

Parkland

Grassland

VEGETATION AND CHARACTERISTIC FLORA

- **Tundra**
  - Lichen / heath
  - Dwarf shrubs / sedges / lichen / heath
  - Alpine sedges / grasses and shrubs
- **Open woodland** — Scattered needleleaf trees / broadleaf shrubs / heath / grass
- **Bogs** — Moss / sedges / strings of needleleaf trees
- **Boreal forest**
  - Needleleaf trees
  - Mostly needleleaf trees with some broadleaf trees
- **Coastal forest** — Large needleleaf trees
- **Sub-alpine forest** — Needleleaf trees
- **High plateau / Pine forest** — Mostly needleleaf trees with some broadleaf trees and grassland
- **Southeastern mixed forest** — Mixture of broadleaf and needleleaf trees
- **Southern broadleaf forest** — Broadleaf trees
- **Parkland** — Broadleaf or needleleaf trees with patches of grassland
- **Grassland** — Low, medium, and tall grasses
- Glaciers and permanent snow (no vegetation)

SCALE 1 : 18 000 000

Tundra

Boreal forest

Southern broadleaf forest

Southeastern mixed forest

SOIL TYPES

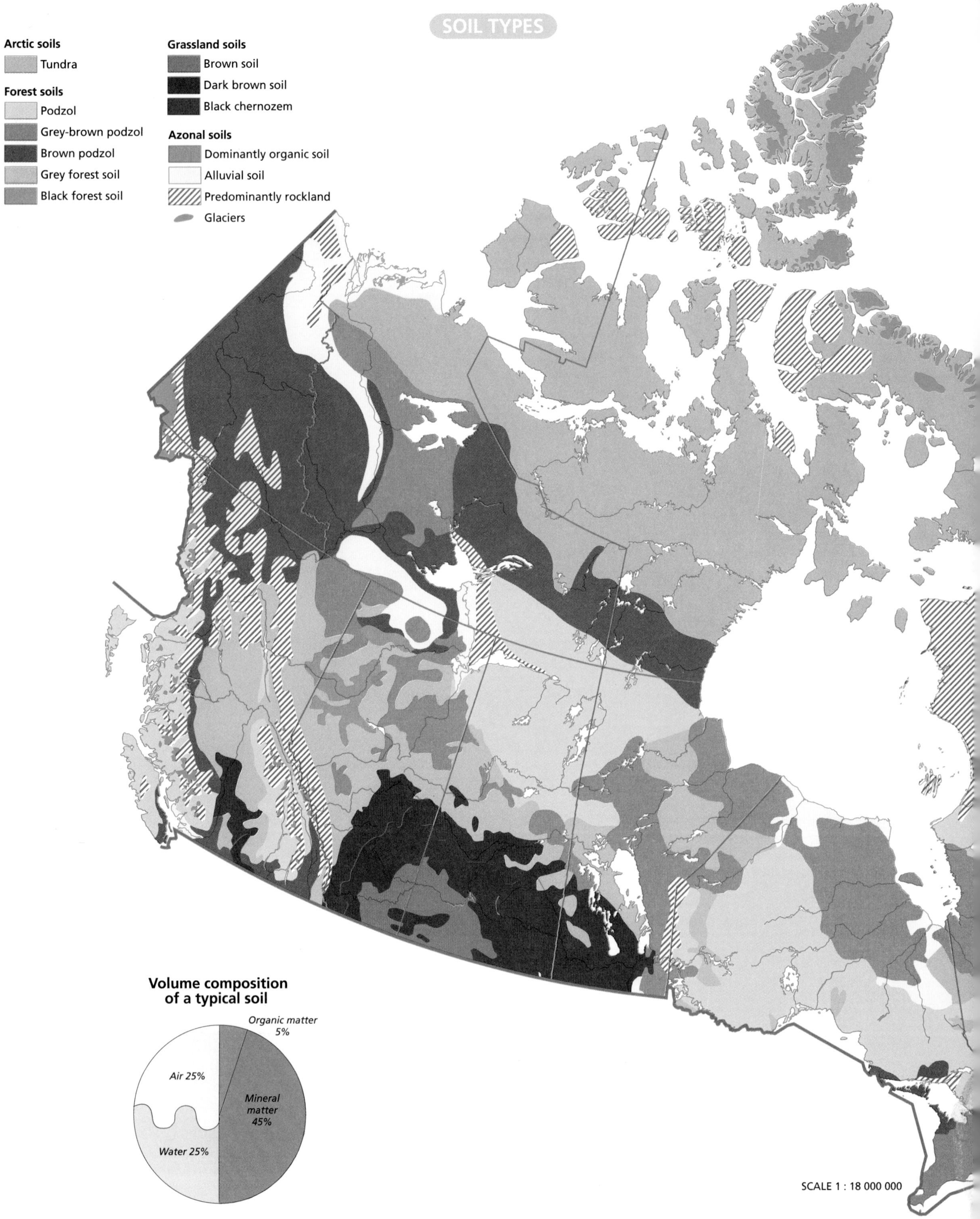
Arctic soils
Tundra
Forest soils
Podzol
Grey-brown podzol
Brown podzol
Grey forest soil
Black forest soil
Grassland soils
Brown soil
Dark brown soil
Black chernozem
Azonal soils
Dominantly organic soil
Alluvial soil
Predominantly rockland
Glaciers
Volume composition of a typical soil
Organic matter 5%
Air 25%
Mineral matter 45%
Water 25%
SCALE 1 : 18 000 000

SOIL CAPABILITY

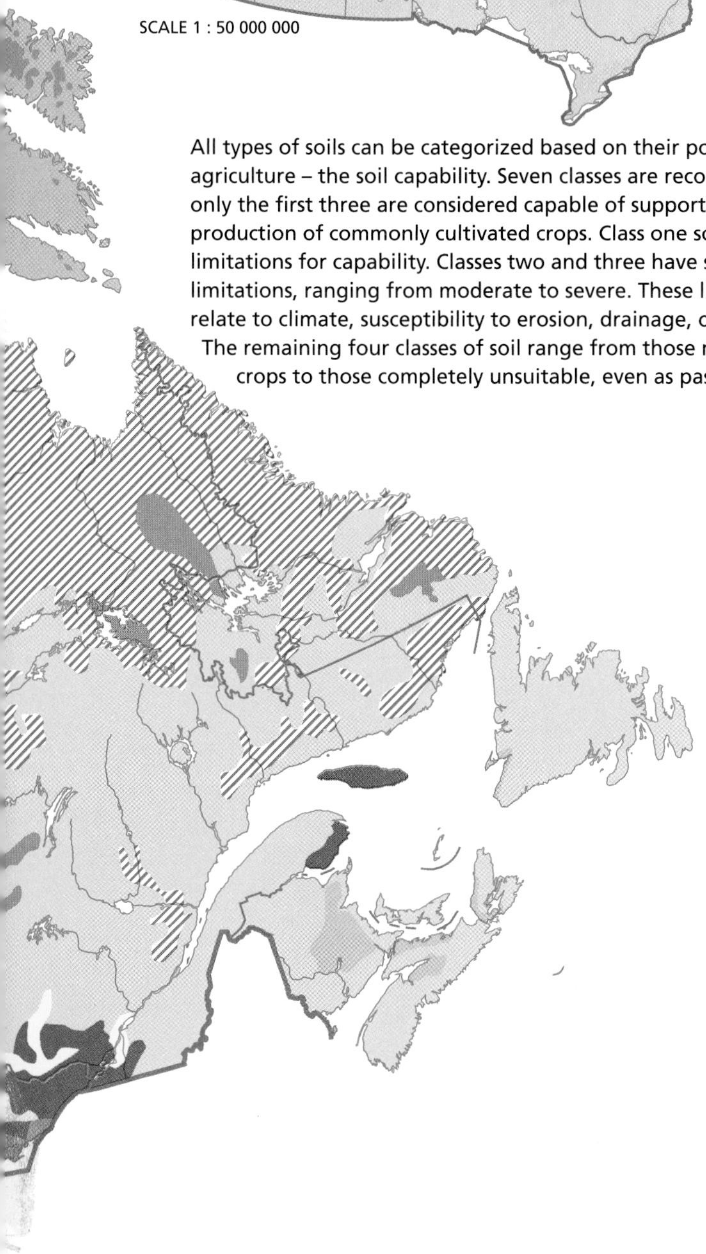

All types of soils can be categorized based on their potential for agriculture – the soil capability. Seven classes are recognized, but only the first three are considered capable of supporting sustained production of commonly cultivated crops. Class one soils have no limitations for capability. Classes two and three have some limitations, ranging from moderate to severe. These limitations may relate to climate, susceptibility to erosion, drainage, or stoniness. The remaining four classes of soil range from those marginal for crops to those completely unsuitable, even as pastureland.

SOIL PROFILES

A typical soil profile

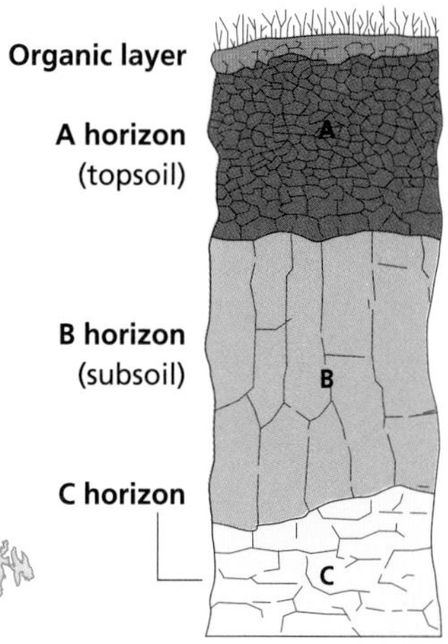

The A horizon is mostly made up of partially decayed organic materials. At the bottom is a modified zone in which water, percolating down, has removed soluble minerals and fine particles.

The B horizon is a combination of mineral and organic material. It contains the soluble minerals and fine particles from the A horizon. It is often possible to identify different layers within this horizon.

The C horizon consists mainly of weathered "parent material," the mineral material from which the soil is made. This can be either bedrock or glacial deposits.

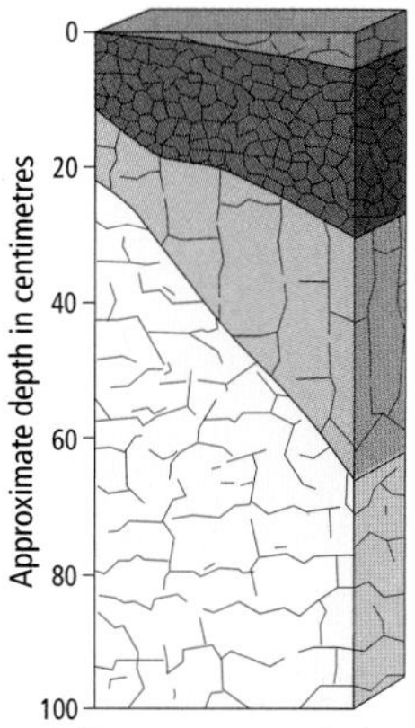

Grey-brown podzol

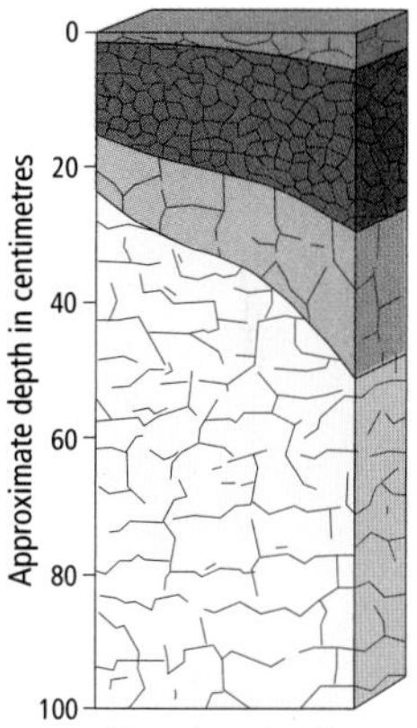

Grey forest soil

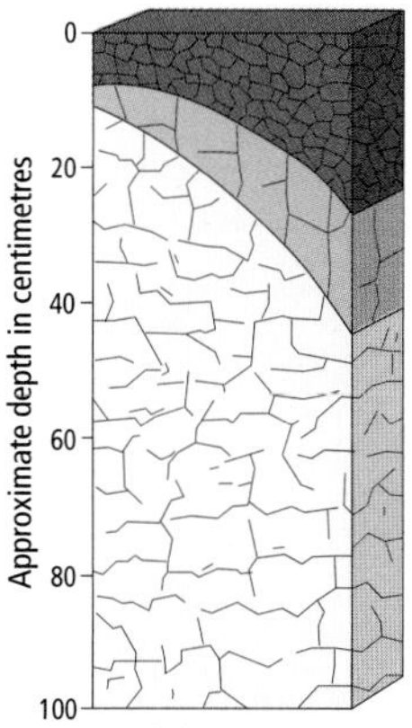

Dark brown soil

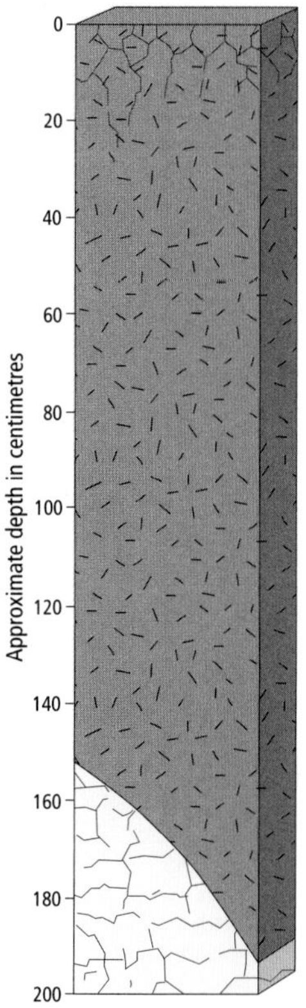

Organic soil

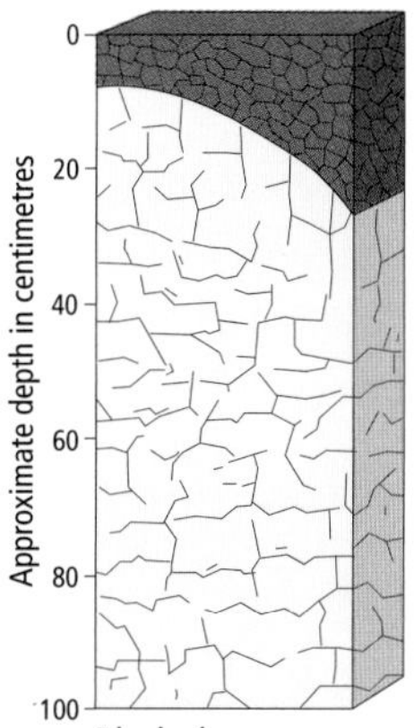

Black chernozem

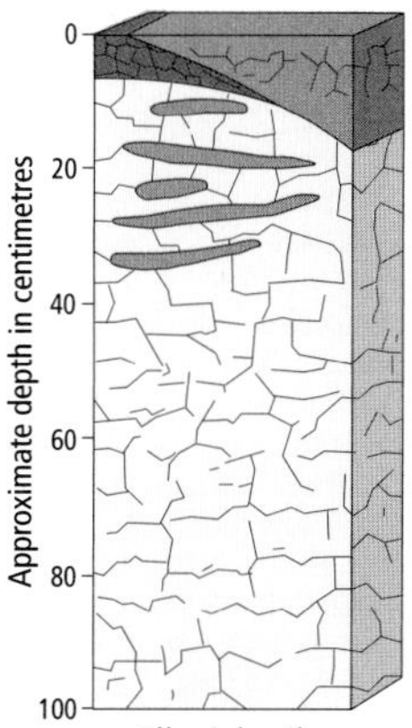

Alluvial soil

DRAINAGE BASINS

- Pacific (1 009 064 km² in Canada)
- Arctic (3 583 265 km² in Canada)
- Hudson Bay (3 860 136 km² in Canada)
- Atlantic (1 520 071 km² in Canada)
- Gulf of Mexico (26 677 km² in Canada)
- Major drainage basin
- Minor drainage basin
- Artificially diverted drainage area
  1 Nechako
  2 Lake St Joseph
  3 Ogoki
  4 Long Lake
- Internal drainage area
- Gauging station

The bar graphs indicate the volume of flow by month at gauging stations on selected rivers.

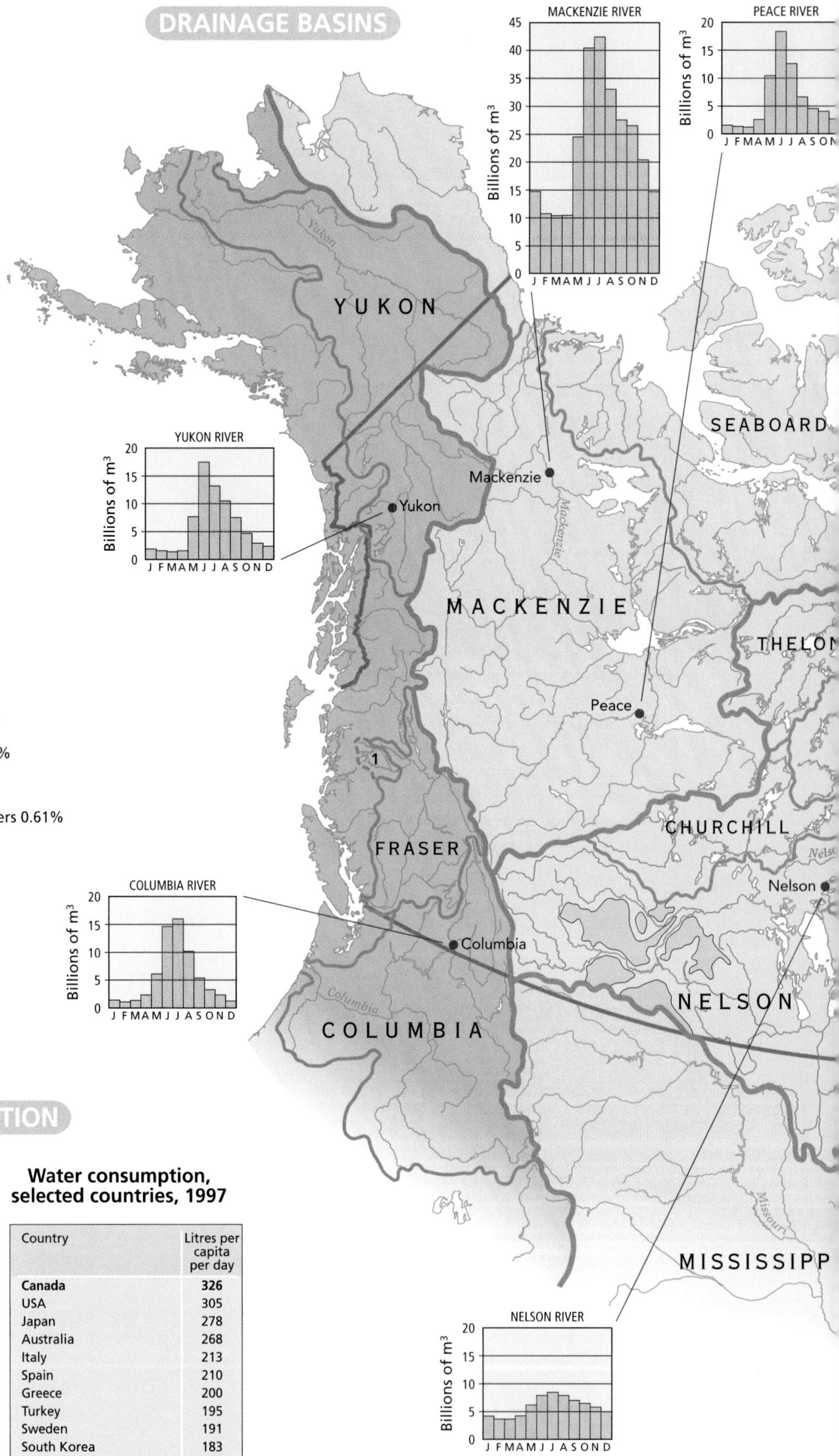

WORLD DISTRIBUTION

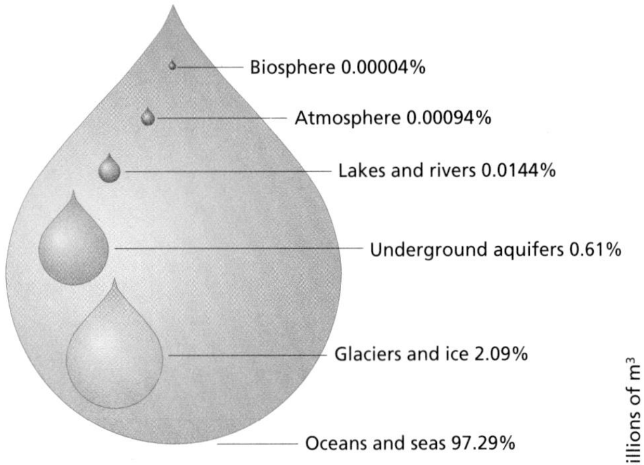

COST AND CONSUMPTION

Cost of water, selected countries

US$ per cubic metre, 1994-1998

Water consumption, selected countries, 1997

Country	Litres per capita per day
Canada	**326**
USA	305
Japan	278
Australia	268
Italy	213
Spain	210
Greece	200
Turkey	195
Sweden	191
South Korea	183
Switzerland	158
UK (England and Wales)	153
Finland	145
Denmark	139
France	137
Austria	135
Netherlands	130
Germany	116

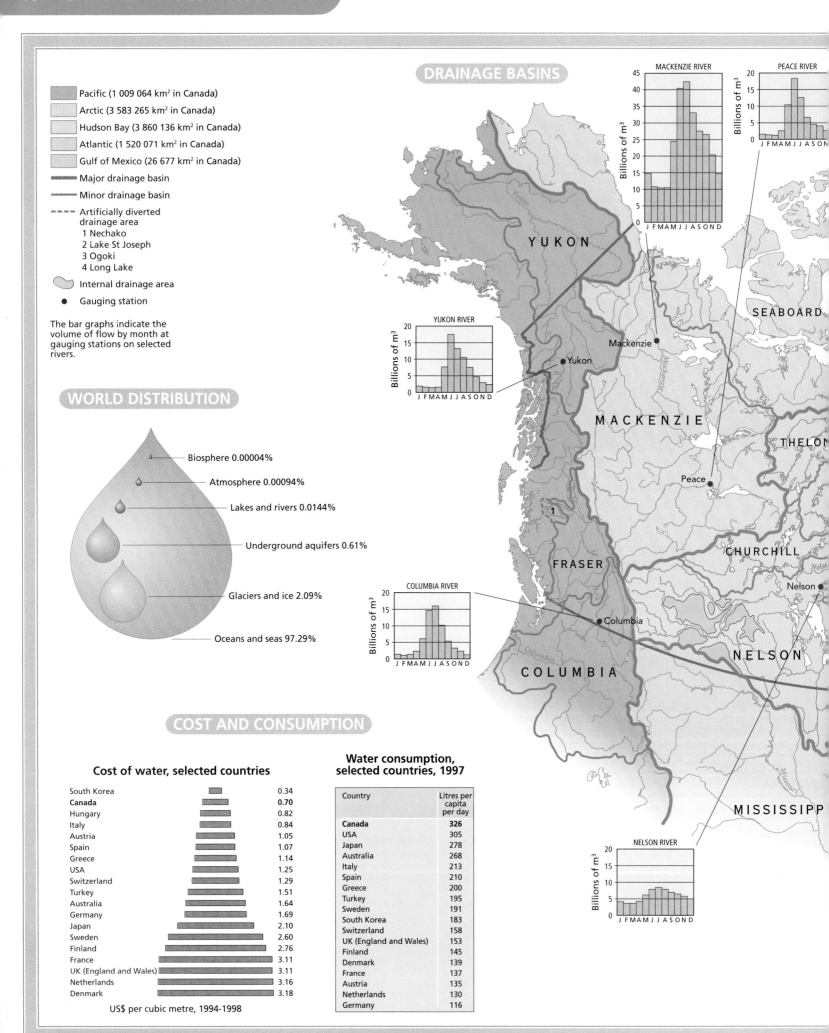

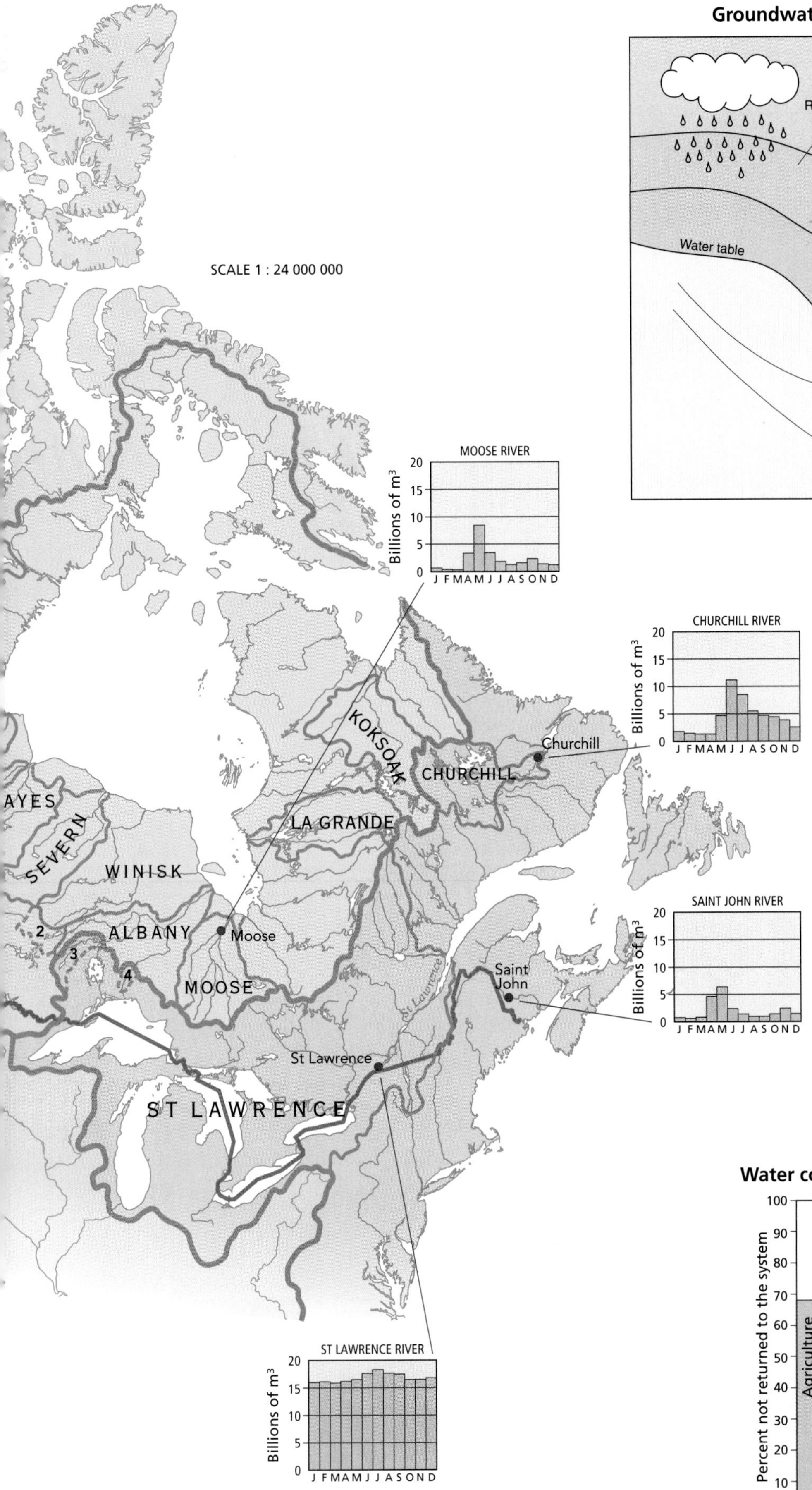

GROUNDWATER

Groundwater contamination from a waste disposal site

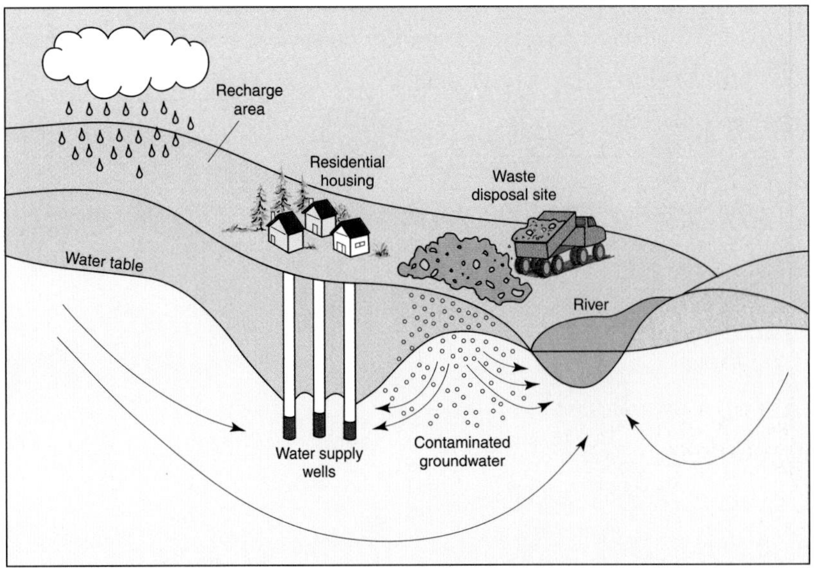

Provincial populations reliant on groundwater

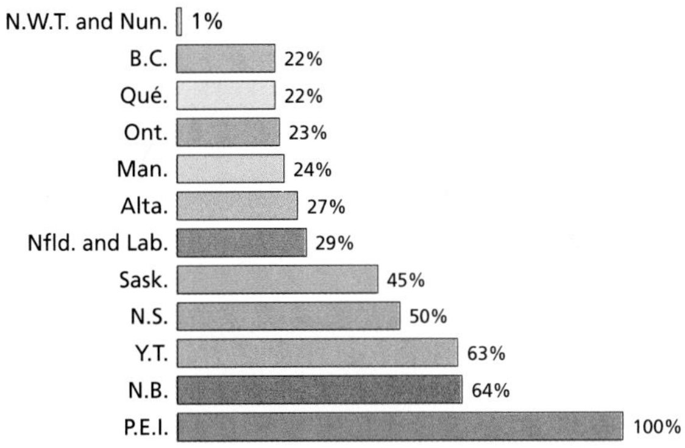

CONSUMPTION AND WITHDRAWAL

Water consumption, 2002

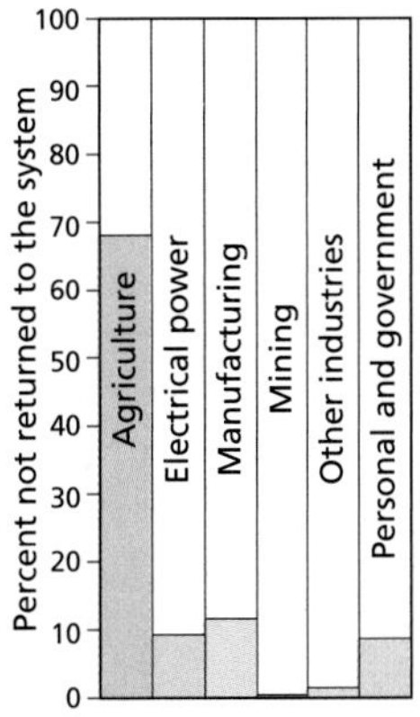

Water withdrawal, 2002

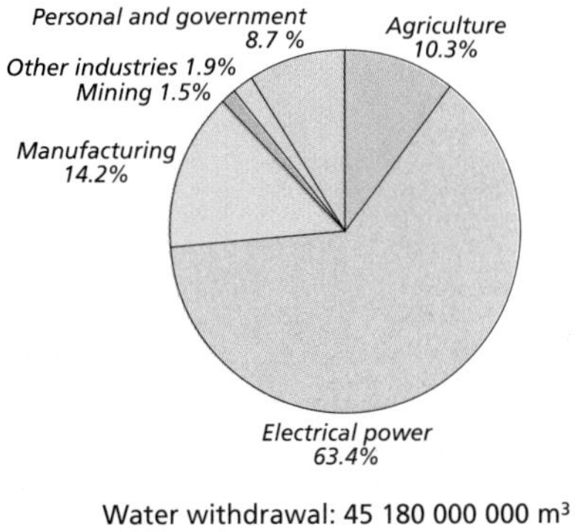

Water withdrawal: 45 180 000 000 m³

CANADA Mineral Resources

METALLIC MINERALS

Iron ore
Lead
Zinc
Copper
Nickel
Silver
Gold
Molybdenum
Cobalt
Landforms
Lowlands or plains
Mountains
Canadian Shield
Continental shelf
Little Cornwallis Island
Nanisivik
Dawson
Contwoyto Lake
Yellowknife
Raglan
Voisey's Bay
Stewart
Endako
Hammerdown
Carol Lake
Mount Wright
Seabee
Thompson
New Britannia
Flin Flon
Logan Lake
Bathurst
Matagami
Sleeping Giant
Red Lake
Dufresnoy
Timmins
Val d'Or
Thunder Bay
Hemlo
Cadillac
Sudbury
SCALE 1 : 35 000 000

NON-METALLIC MINERALS

Potash
Asbestos
Gypsum
Salt
Silica
Diamond
Surface materials
Soil, alluvium, muskeg, bogs and glacial deposits
Bedrock or bedrock outcrops
Ekati
Bruderheim
Lindbergh
Kamloops
Unity
Saskatoon
Vanscoy
Lanigan
Invermere
Allan
Canal Flats
Rocanville
Amaranth
Winnipeg
Fischells
Îles de la Madeleine
Amherst
Pugwash
Sussex
Wentworth
Upper Musquodoboit
Asbestos
Ormstown
Goderich
Caledonia
Windsor
SCALE 1 : 35 000 000

FUEL MINERALS

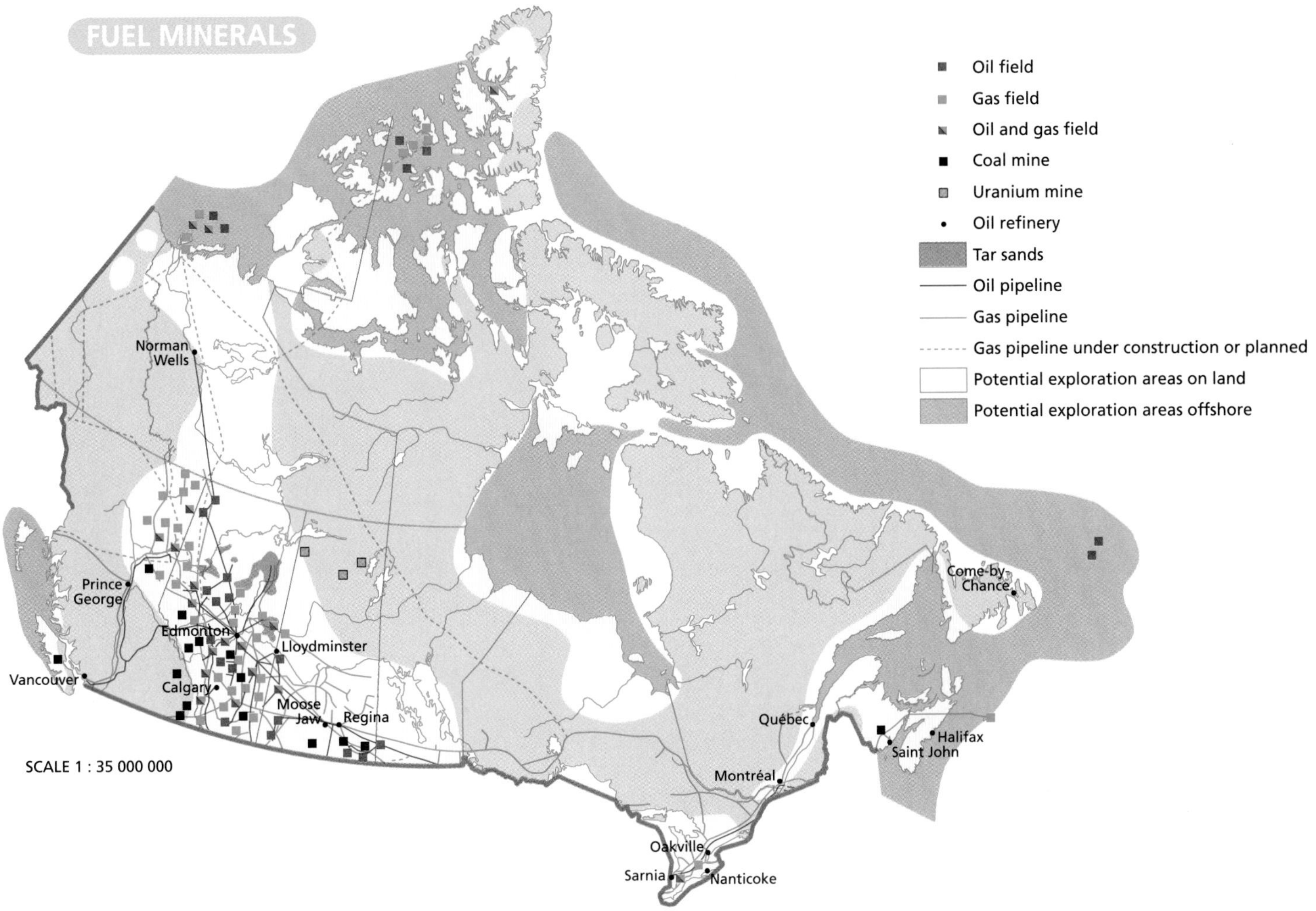

SCALE 1 : 35 000 000

MINERALS : ECONOMIC VALUE

Production, 2001

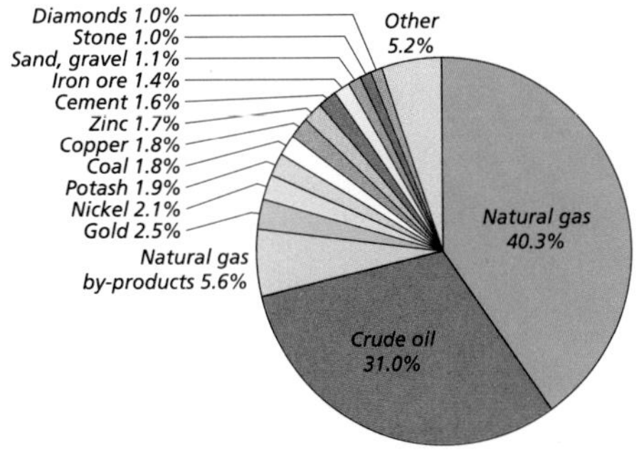

Total : $ 83 782 386 000

Exports, 2001 including fabricated minerals

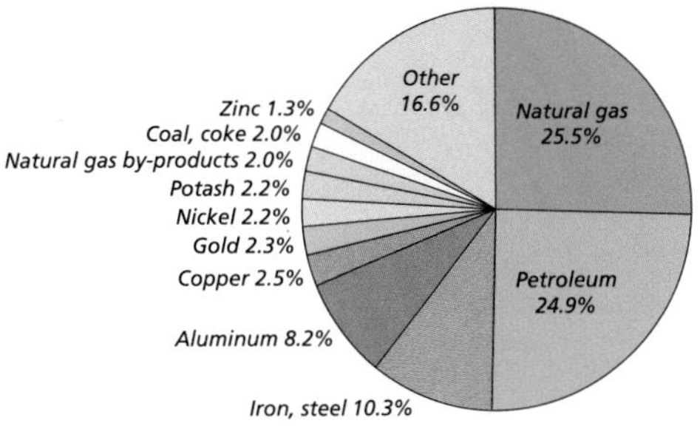

Total : $ 100 173 155 000

Provincial share, 2001

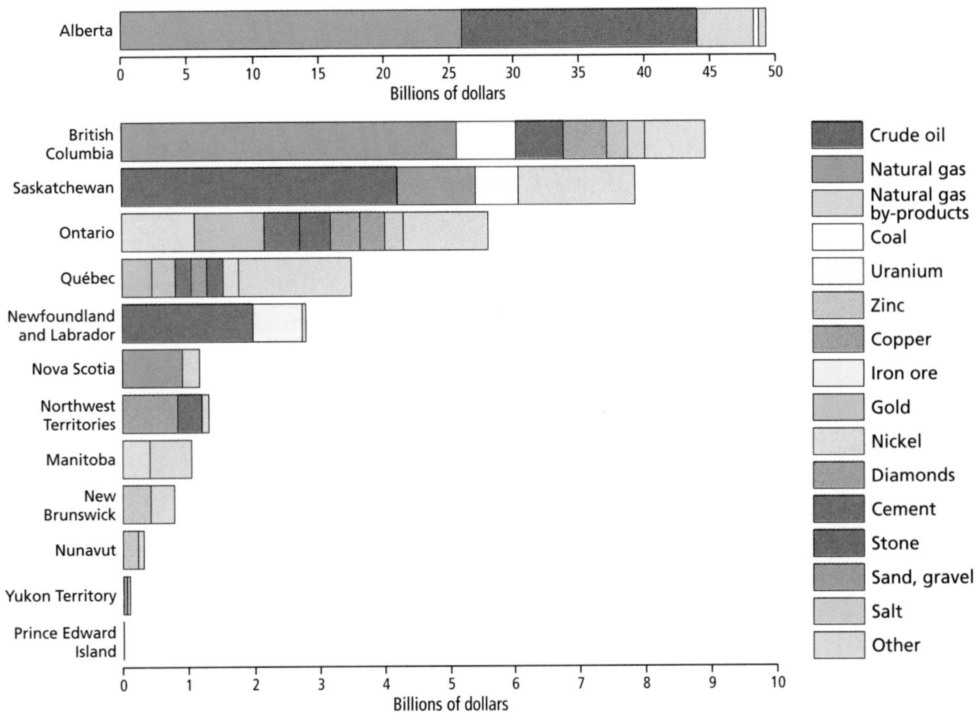

ELECTRICITY GENERATION

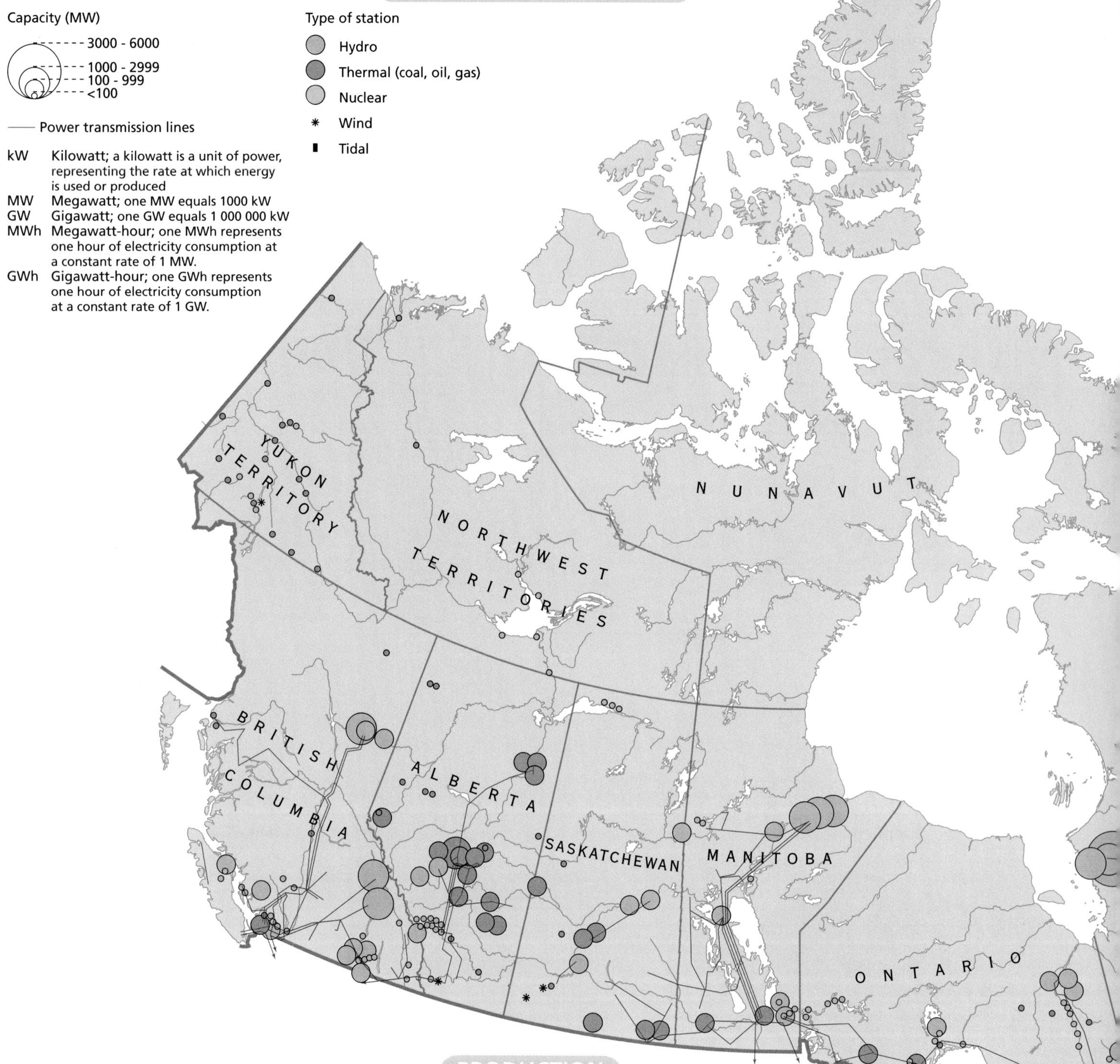

PRODUCTION

Primary energy sources, 2001

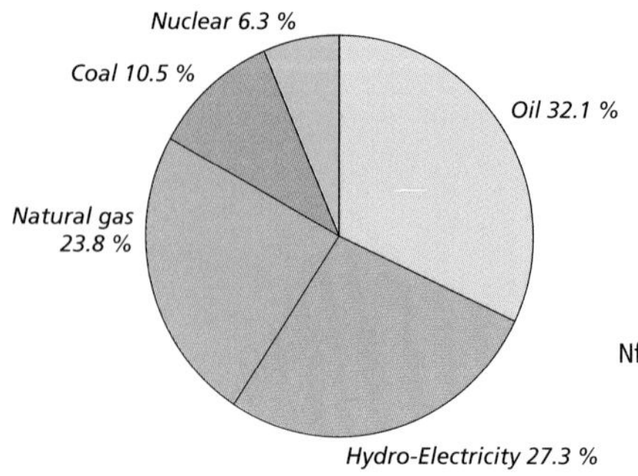

Electrical Energy Production

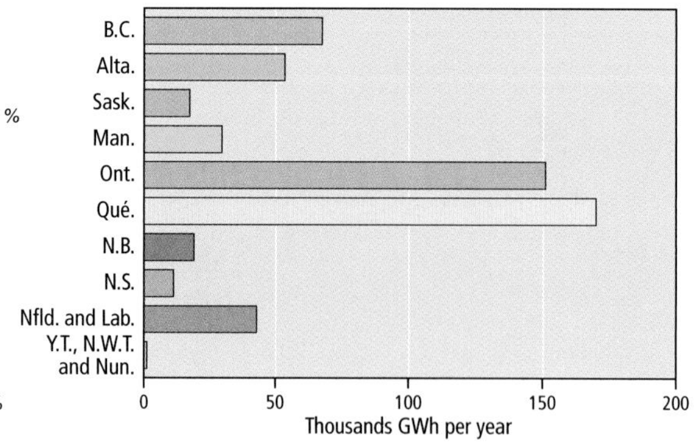

Electricity generation by fuel type, 1999

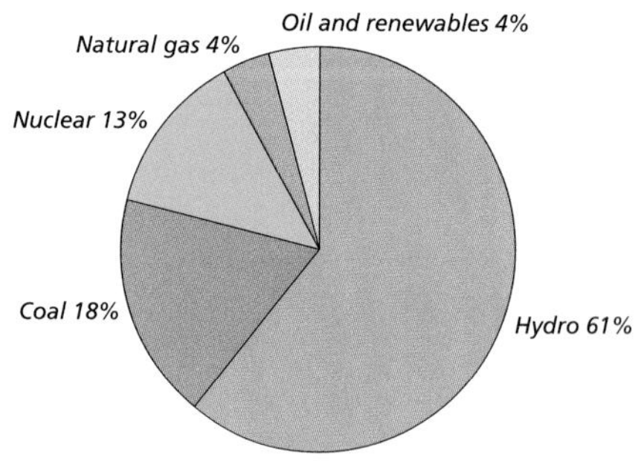

CONSUMPTION

Electricity consumption, 2000

Country	Average annual per capita (kWh)
Iceland	26 220
Norway	25 182
Canada	**16 967**
Kuwait	16 393
Sweden	15 659
Finland	15 285
Luxembourg	15 320
Qatar	14 991
USA	13 843
United Arab Emirates	12 095
Australia	10 052
New Zealand	9 155
Bahrain	8 510
Japan	8 331
Taiwan	8 316
Belgium	8 244
Switzerland	7 843
Singapore	7 467
Brunei	7 437
France	7 302
Austria	7 004
Germany	6 684

Monthly residential electricity costs *

City	Monthly cost in dollars
Winnipeg	98
Montréal	100
Vancouver	101
Ottawa	121
St John's	136
Regina	154
Moncton	154
Halifax	156
Toronto	160
Charlottetown	170
Edmonton	185

* Based on 1000 kWh per month, 2002

Electricity demand, 2001

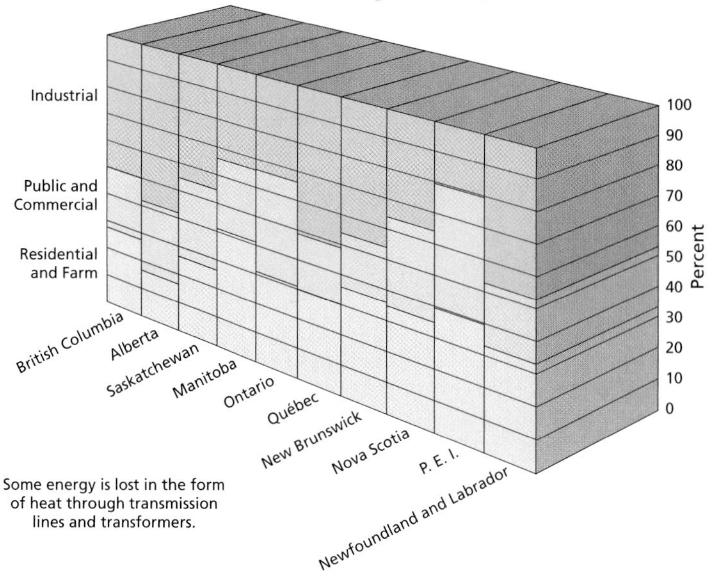

Some energy is lost in the form of heat through transmission lines and transformers.

TRADE

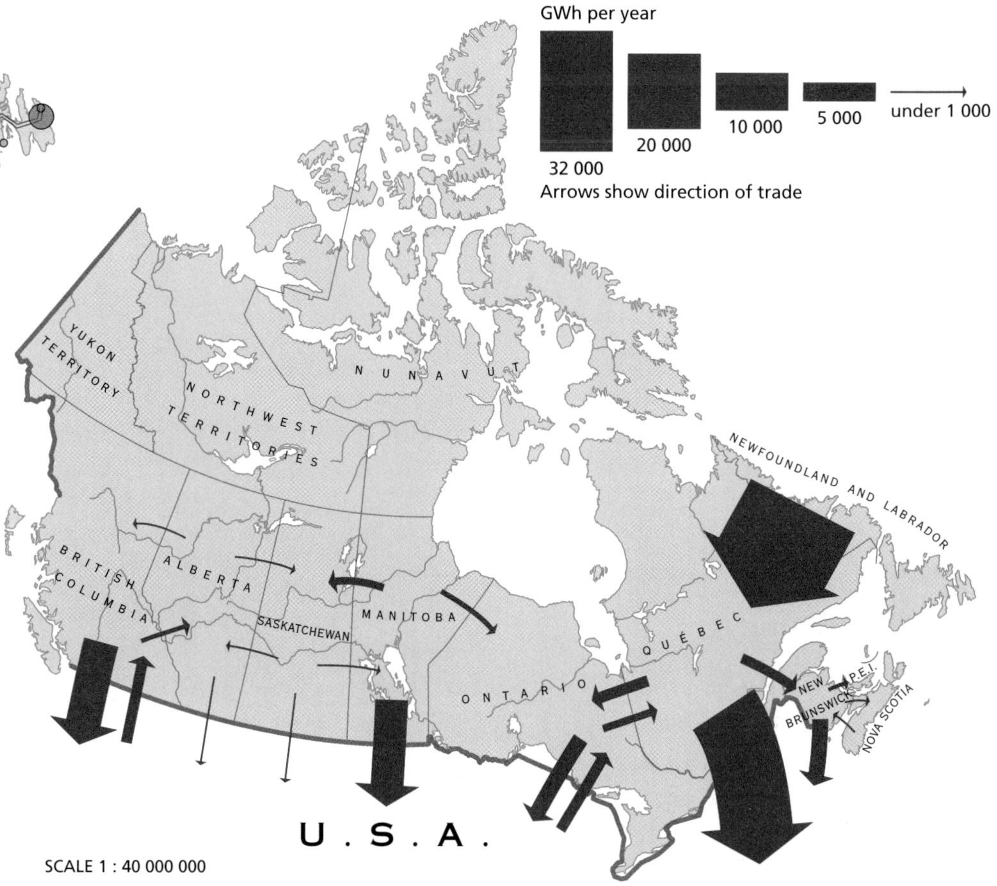

GROWING DEGREE DAYS

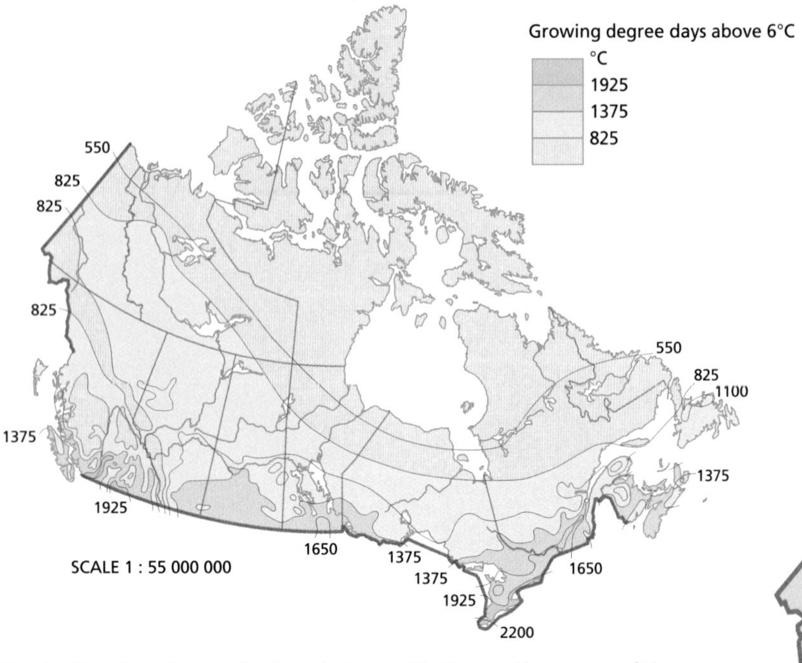

Productive Canadian agriculture is focused in the southern part of the prairies and in southern Québec and Ontario. Some products are associated with specific regions – wheat with Saskatchewan – but many areas practise "mixed" farming, involving both crops and livestock. Although there are only 250 000 farms in Canada, they are generally large and mechanized. The average value of a farm in Canada is more than $1 million. Many farmers use sophisticated technology, such as GPS, to assist with efficient and effective production.

Markets have a strong influence on agriculture. Near large urban markets, the diversity of agriculture is increased to meet the demands. Exports are particularly important to Canadian farmers, and account for close to half of all agricultural income.

Environmentally friendly land management practices have gained popularity in recent years and are now used on more than half the land tilled in Canada. Conservation tillage minimizes the number of passes farmers make over their fields. This decreases fuel costs and reduces carbon dioxide emissions.

TYPES OF FARMING

THE CHANGING FARM

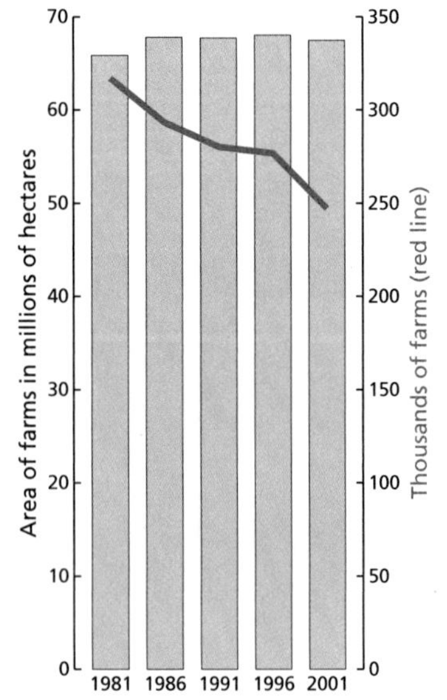

IMPORTS AND EXPORTS

Value of agricultural imports, 2000

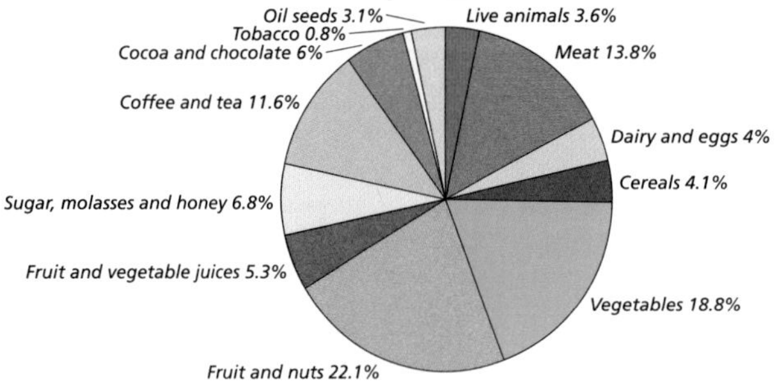

Total : $ 7 239 815 000

Value of agricultural exports, 2000

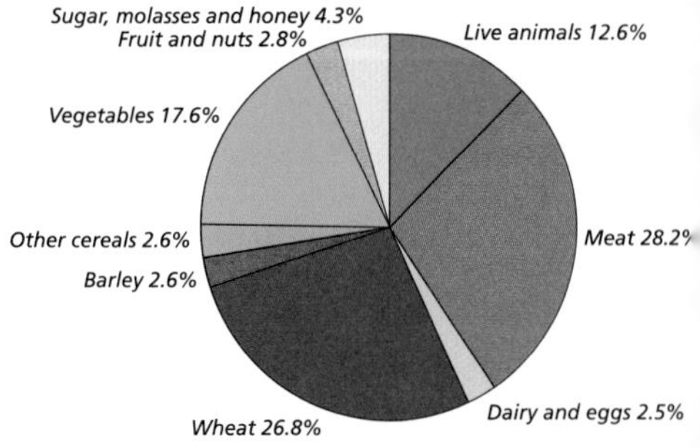

Total : $ 9 259 308 000

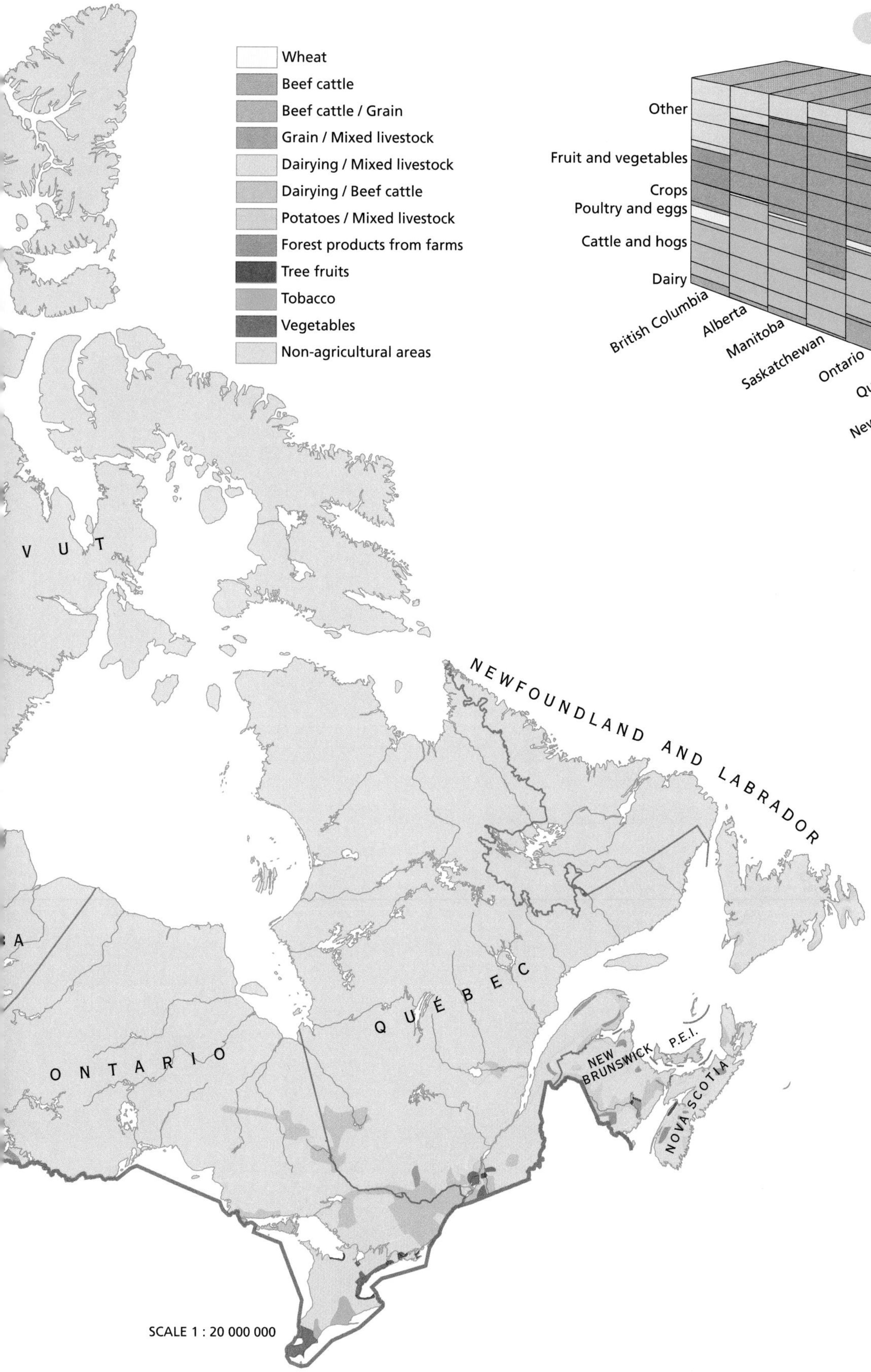

Wheat
Beef cattle
Beef cattle / Grain
Grain / Mixed livestock
Dairying / Mixed livestock
Dairying / Beef cattle
Potatoes / Mixed livestock
Forest products from farms
Tree fruits
Tobacco
Vegetables
Non-agricultural areas
V U T
NEWFOUNDLAND AND LABRADOR
QUÉBEC
ONTARIO
NEW BRUNSWICK
P.E.I.
NOVA SCOTIA
SCALE 1 : 20 000 000

TYPE OF FARM

2001

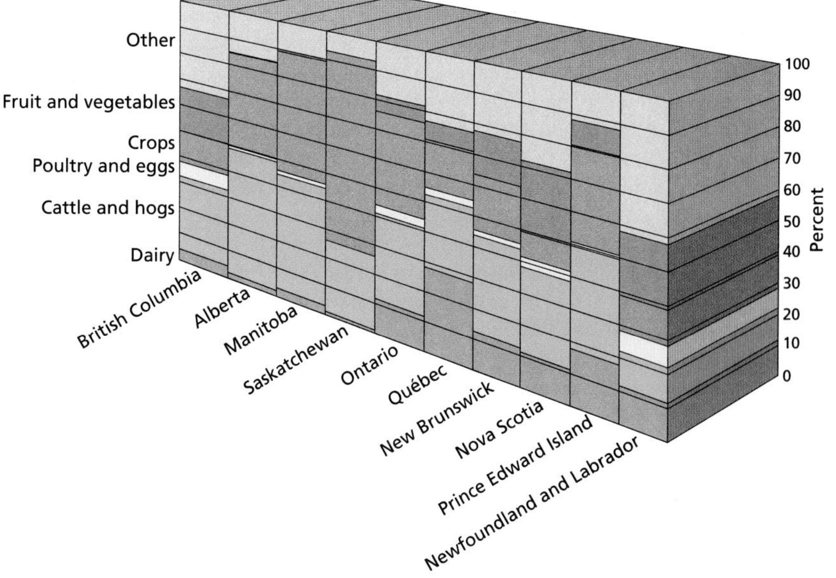

Other
Fruit and vegetables
Crops
Poultry and eggs
Cattle and hogs
Dairy
British Columbia
Alberta
Manitoba
Saskatchewan
Ontario
Québec
New Brunswick
Nova Scotia
Prince Edward Island
Newfoundland and Labrador
100
90
80
70
60
50
40
30
20
10
0
Percent

FARM RECEIPTS

2001

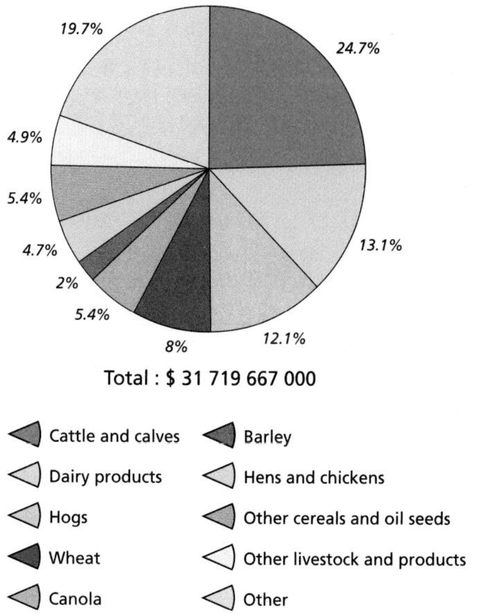

24.7%
13.1%
12.1%
8%
5.4%
2%
4.7%
5.4%
4.9%
19.7%
Total : $ 31 719 667 000
Cattle and calves
Dairy products
Hogs
Wheat
Canola
Barley
Hens and chickens
Other cereals and oil seeds
Other livestock and products
Other

Surrounded by oceans on three sides, and home to the Great Lakes, it is not surprising that Canada has one of the world's most valuable commercial fishing industries, worth almost $5 billion a year. Canada is a major exporter of seafood and seafood products. Approximately 500 000 tonnes with a value of $4 billion are exported annually. The United States, Japan, and Europe are the most important markets. In the Pacific fishery, top catches are hake, Pacific herring (harvested for roe), rockfish and salmon. Value leaders are clams, halibut, shrimp, rockfish, and salmon. Aquaculture has become a significant element in the west coast fishery, with a value of more than $500 million in recent years. Aquaculture accounts for 10 percent of the total Canadian production of fish and shellfish. Canada is one of the world's main suppliers of farmed salmon (Atlantic, Chinook, and Coho). Trout, steelhead, and Arctic char are also raised. The east coast fishery has focused on cod and other groundfish. However, in recent years, top catches were herring (harvested for its roe), shrimp, snow crab, scallops, cod, and lobster. The value leaders are crab, shrimp, and cod. Lobster continues to be Canada's most valuable seafood product, worth over $500 million.

Unfortunately, pollution in inland waters and in coastal areas has resulted in declines in the fish population and has raised health concerns. The destruction of spawning beds and the construction of dams has affected fish habitats. Weather, ocean conditions, and overharvesting by other nations just outside Canada's territorial waters have added to the problems faced by the fishing industry. In 2003, the northern cod fishery was closed down due to overfishing of the stock and habitat destruction. This has resulted in unemployment in this industry, affecting the economy of provinces such as Newfoundland and Labrador.

FISH HABITATS : WEST COAST

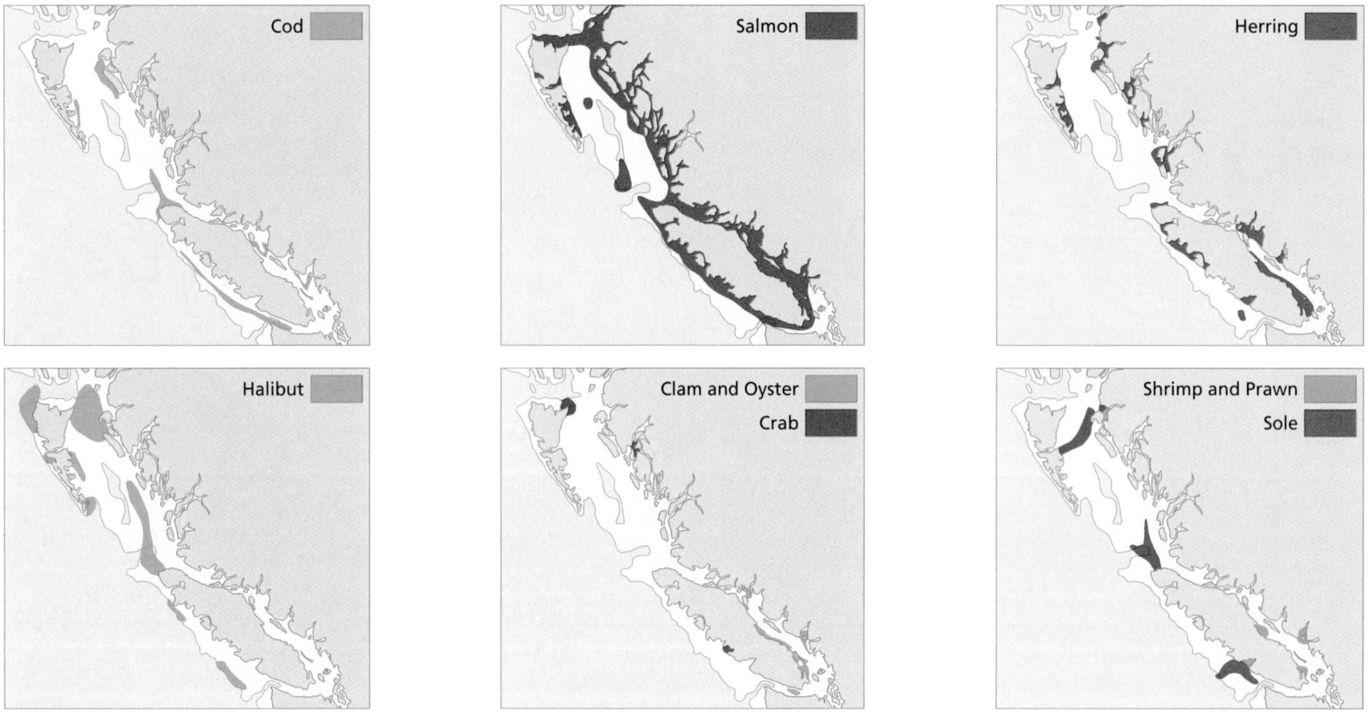

VOLUME AND VALUE OF CATCH

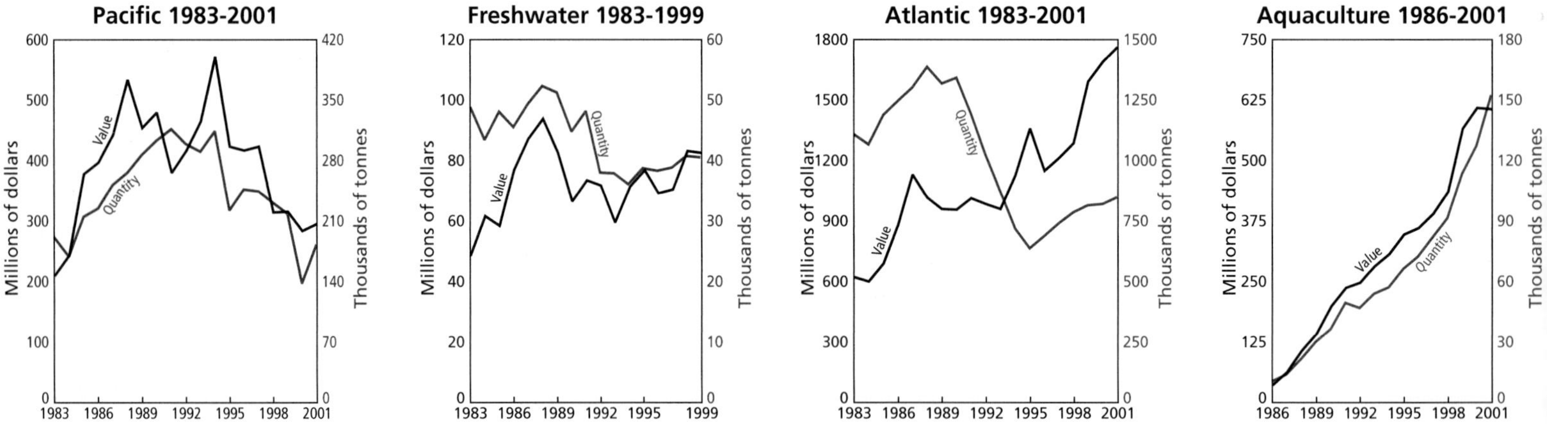

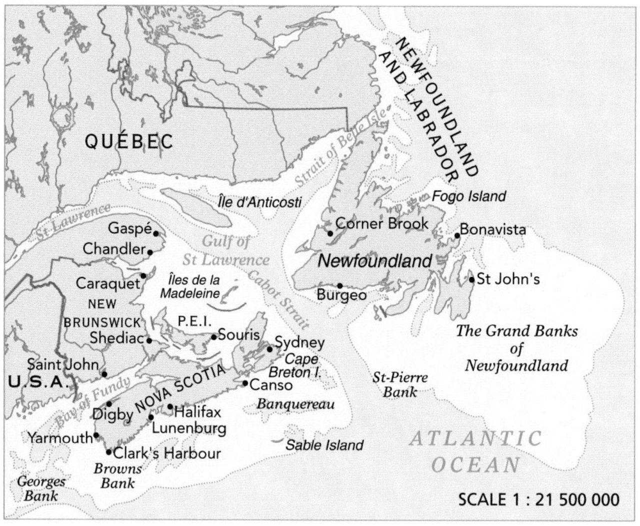

WORLD COMPARISON

Major fishing countries, 2000

Country	Fish production tonnes	Country	Fish production tonnes
1 China	43 069 240	16 Denmark	1 577 698
2 Peru	10 665 420	17 Malaysia	1 441 018
3 Japan	5 752 178	18 Mexico	1 368 021
4 India	5 689 468	19 Spain	1 289 081
5 USA	5 173 583	20 Myanmar	1 168 638
6 Indonesia	4 928 545	**21 Canada**	**1 116 902**
7 Chile	4 691 747	22 Argentina	919 509
8 Russian Fed.	4 047 659	23 United Kingdom	898 776
9 Thailand	3 630 578	24 Morocco	898 467
10 Norway	3 191 335	25 France	864 673
11 Philippines	2 280 512	26 Brazil	847 268
12 South Korea	2 146 393	27 Egypt	724 407
13 Iceland	1 986 145	28 Ecuador	654 658
14 Vietnam	1 952 145	29 South Africa	647 763
15 Bangladesh	1 661 385	30 New Zealand	646 964

Total world fish production : 130 433 800 tonnes

FISH HABITATS : EAST COAST

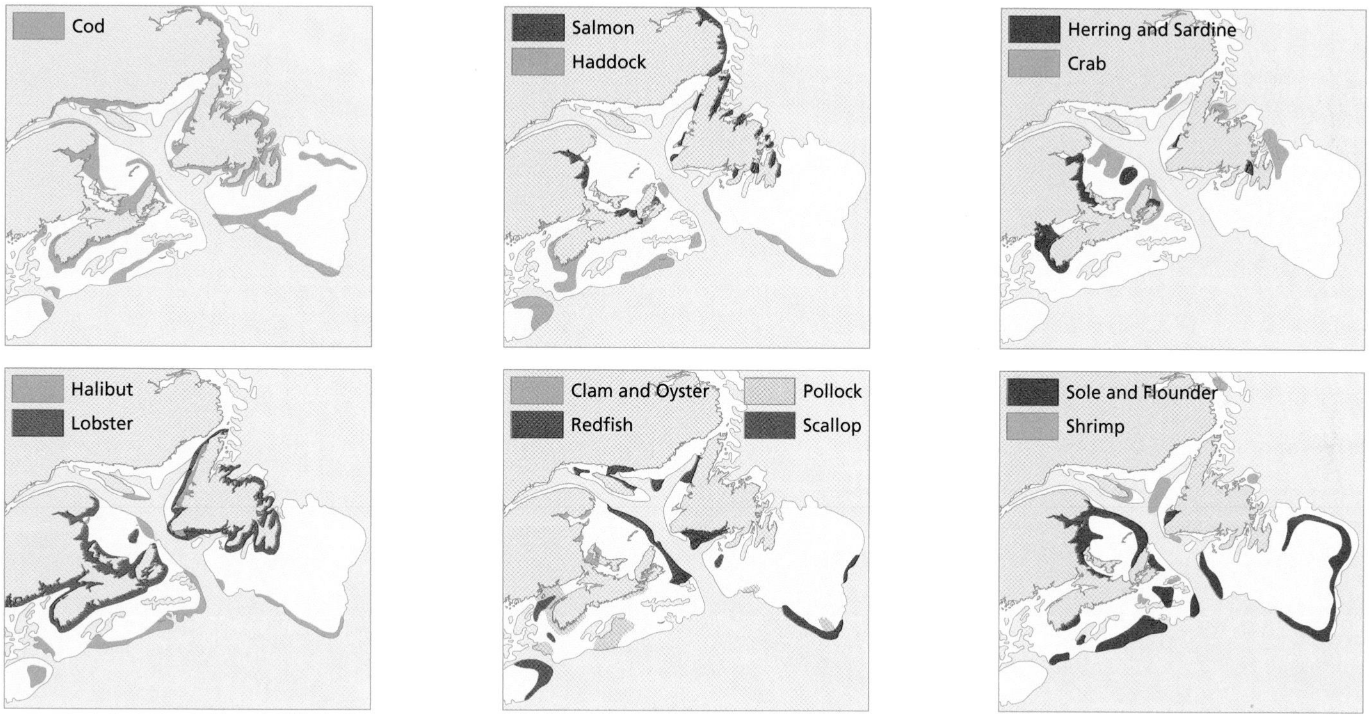

EMPLOYMENT

Number employed

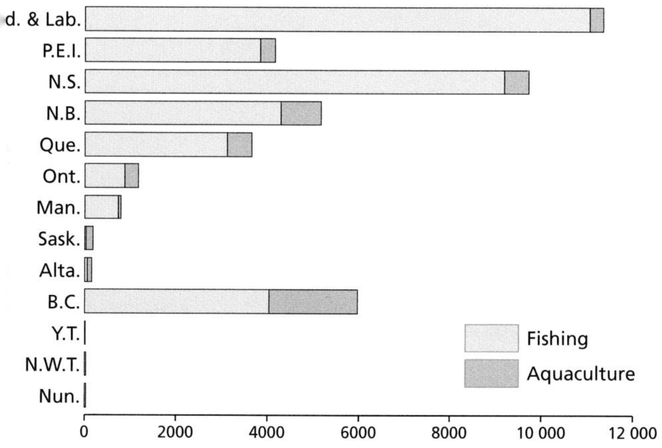

VOLUME AND VALUE

Volume 2001: 1 030 666 tonnes

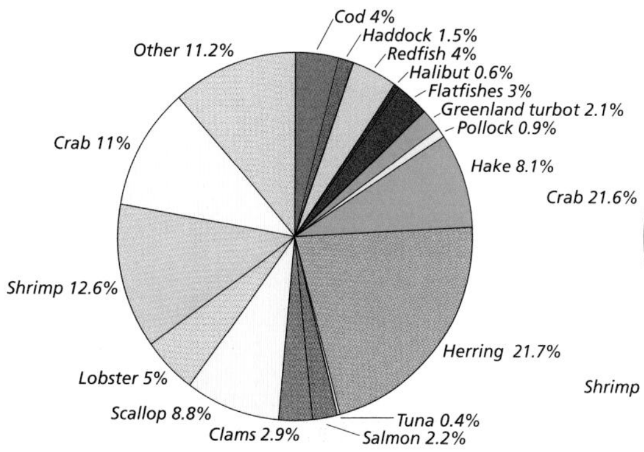

Landed value 2001: $ 2 056 977 000

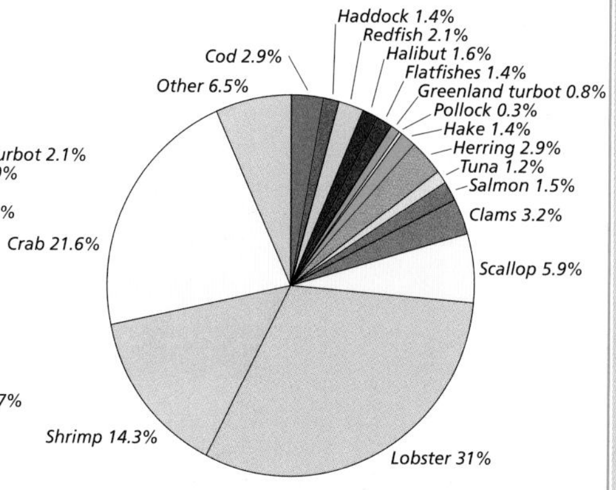

Forest regions and principal tree species

Non-productive forest	Boreal–forest and barren ground	Black Spruce, White Spruce, Tamarack
	Boreal–forest and grassland	Trembling Aspen, Willow, Bur Oak
Productive forest	Boreal–predominantly forest	Black Spruce, White Spruce, Balsam Fir, Jack Pine, White Birch, Trembling Aspen
	Subalpine	Alpine Fir, Engelmann Spruce, Lodgepole Pine
	Montane	Douglas Fir, Lodgepole Pine, Ponderosa Pine, Trembling Aspen
	Coast	Western Red Cedar, Western Hemlock, Douglas Fir, Sitka Spruce
	Columbia	Western Red Cedar, Western Hemlock, Douglas Fir
	Deciduous	Beech, Maple, Black Walnut, Hickory, Oak
	Great Lakes-St Lawrence	Eastern White Pine, Eastern Hemlock, Red Pine, Yellow Birch, Maple, Oak
	Acadian	Red Spruce, Balsam Fir, Maple, Yellow Birch
	Non-forested land	No major tree species

Each symbol represents one pulp and paper mill with a production capacity of 300 t (tonnes) or more per day

Forest tenures granted to private companies

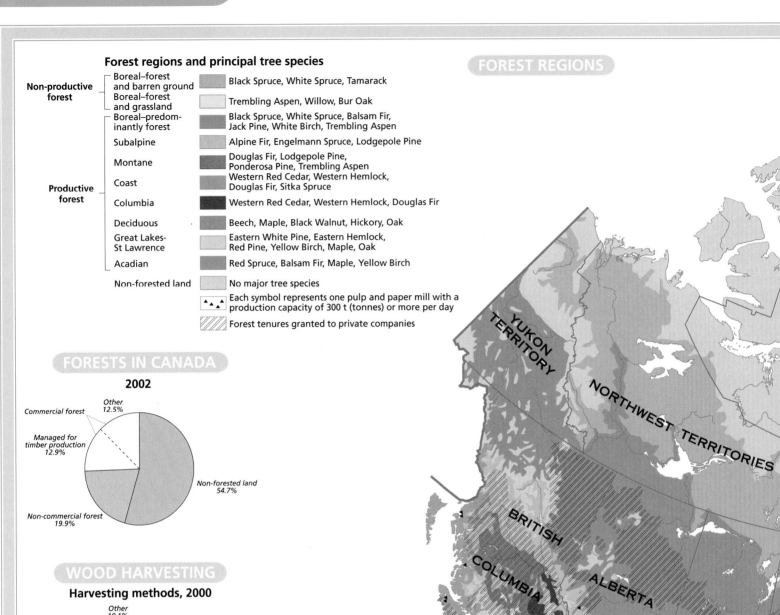

FOREST REGIONS

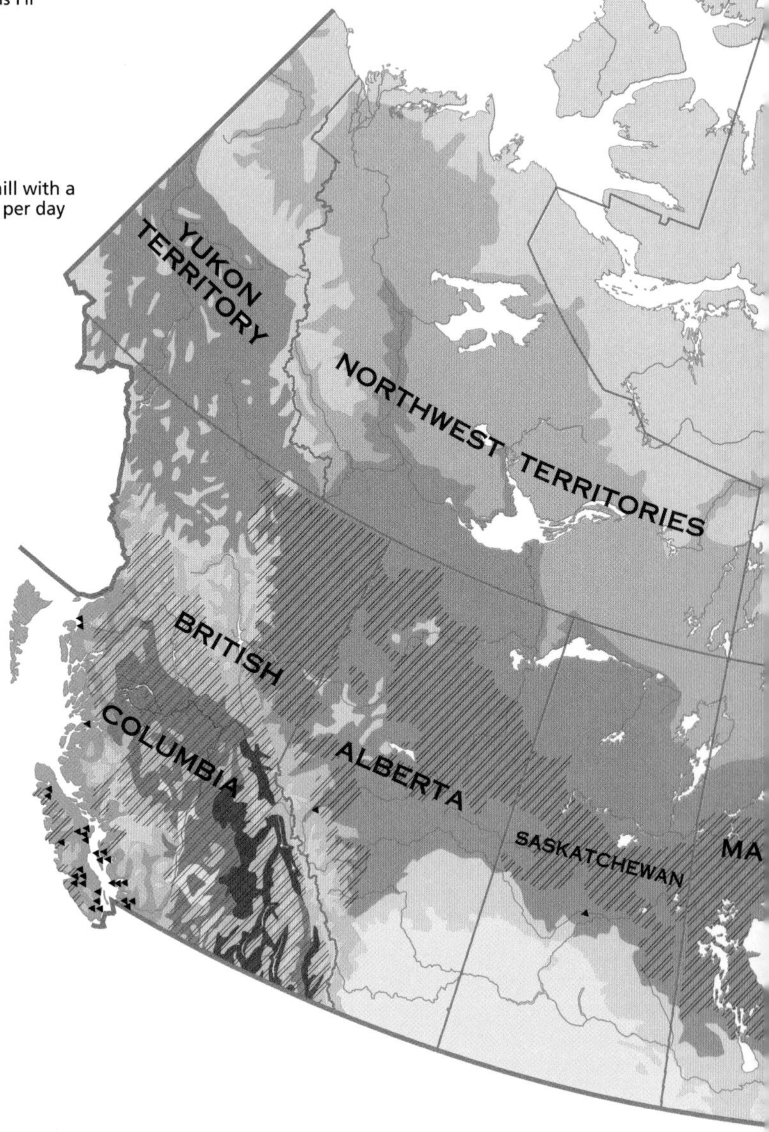

FORESTS IN CANADA

2002

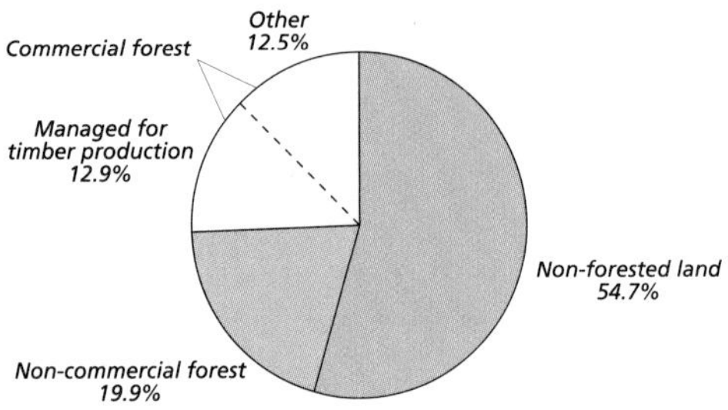

WOOD HARVESTING

Harvesting methods, 2000

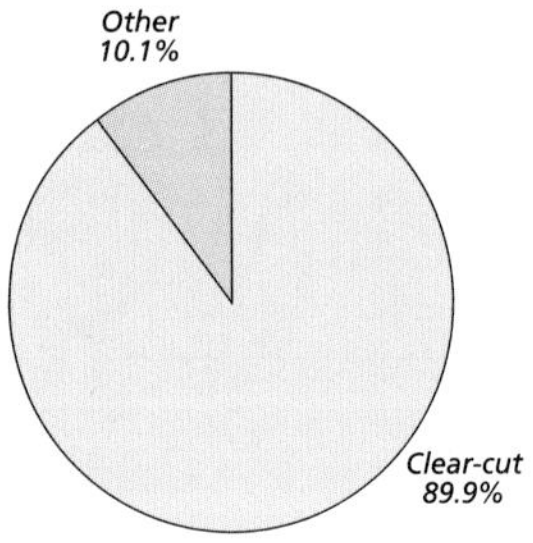

Total harvested : 1 027 711 hectares

FORESTED LAND

Provincial share, 2002

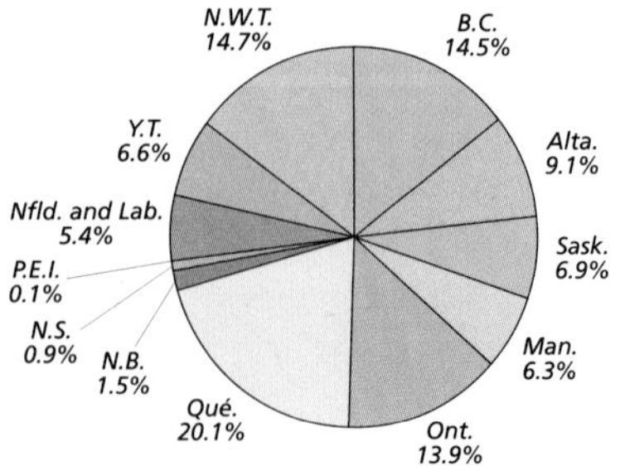

Total : 417 600 000 hectares

FOREST LOSS

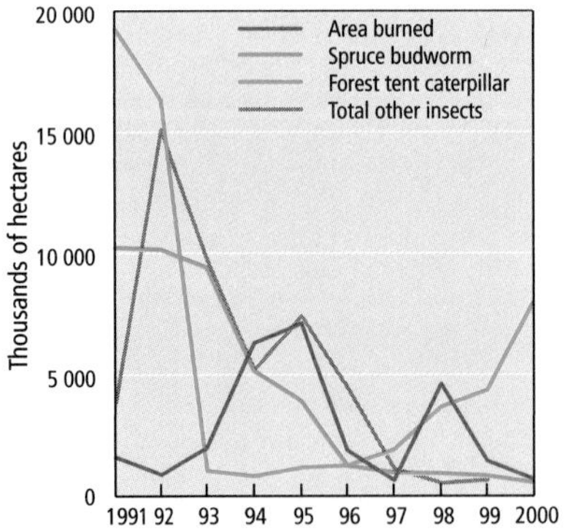

WORLD EXPORTS

Export of forest products, 2001

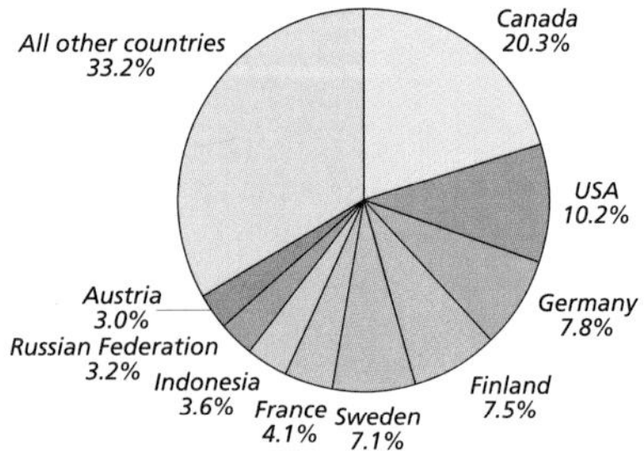

Total : US$ 141 489 359 000

PRODUCTION BY REGION

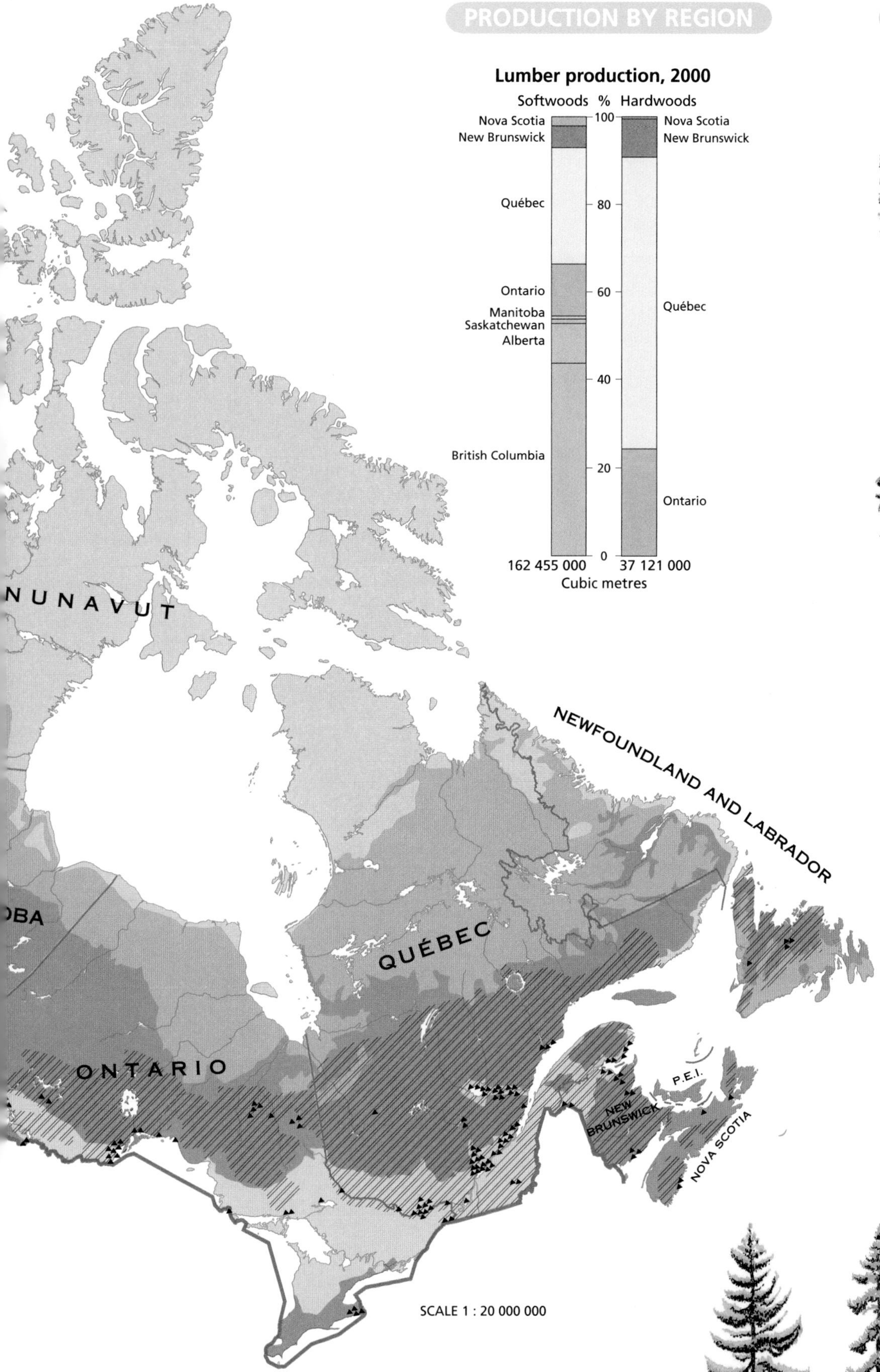

PRINCIPAL FOREST SPECIES

Note: Trees are not drawn to a common scale. The names of hardwood trees are shown in red, softwood trees in black.

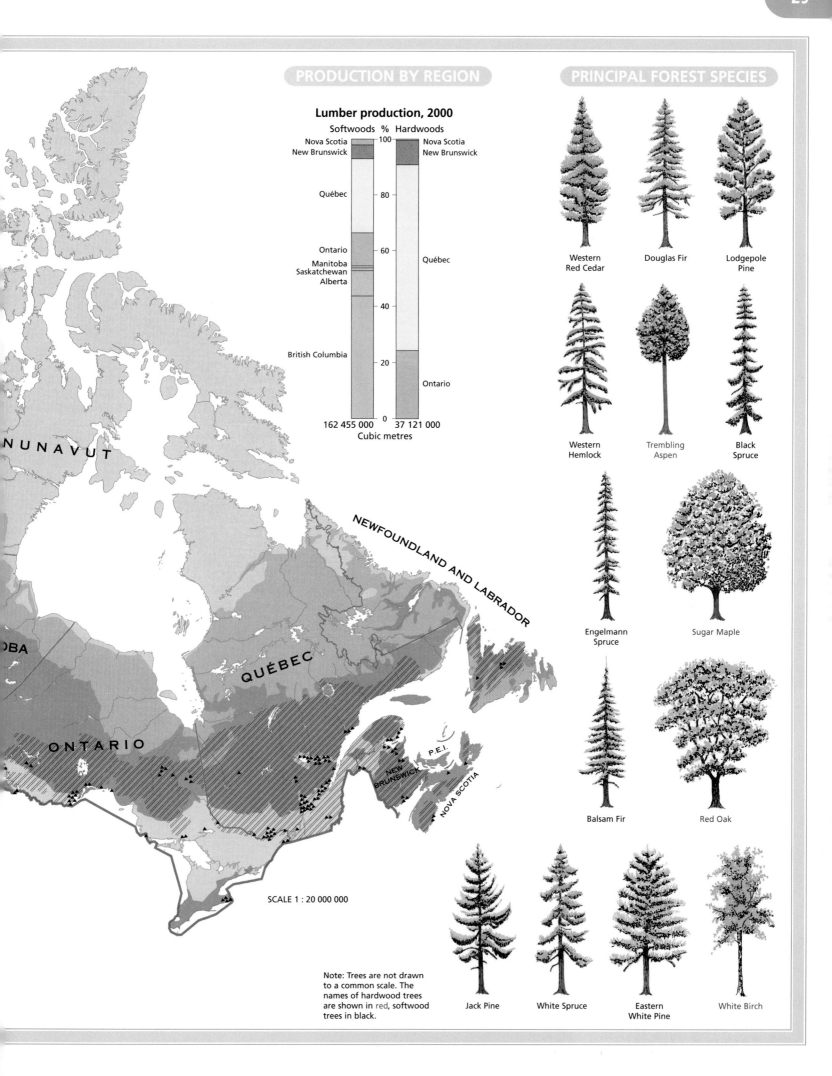

MANUFACTURING

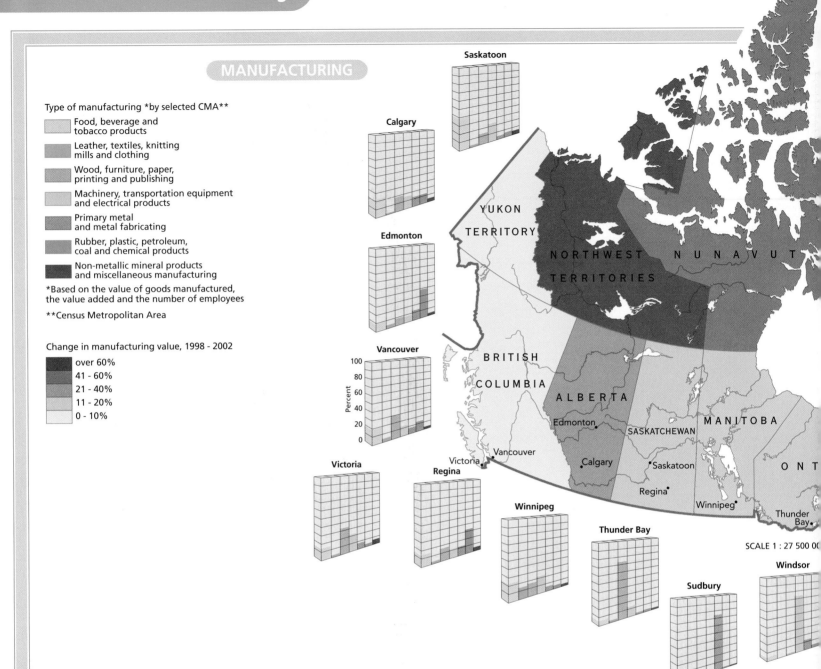

Type of manufacturing *by selected CMA**

- Food, beverage and tobacco products
- Leather, textiles, knitting mills and clothing
- Wood, furniture, paper, printing and publishing
- Machinery, transportation equipment and electrical products
- Primary metal and metal fabricating
- Rubber, plastic, petroleum, coal and chemical products
- Non-metallic mineral products and miscellaneous manufacturing

*Based on the value of goods manufactured, the value added and the number of employees

**Census Metropolitan Area

Change in manufacturing value, 1998 - 2002

- over 60%
- 41 - 60%
- 21 - 40%
- 11 - 20%
- 0 - 10%

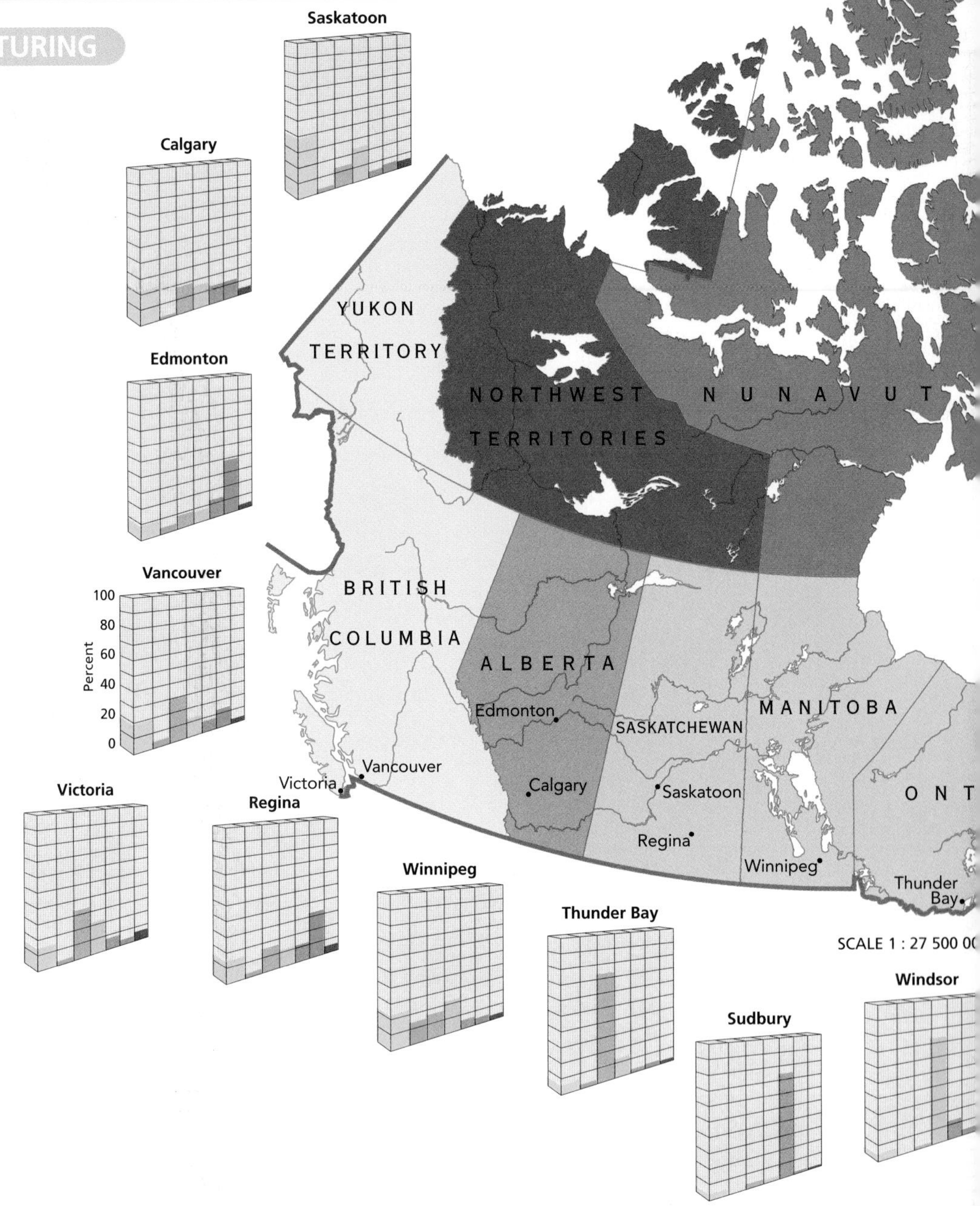

MANUFACTURING SHIPMENTS

Value by province, 2002

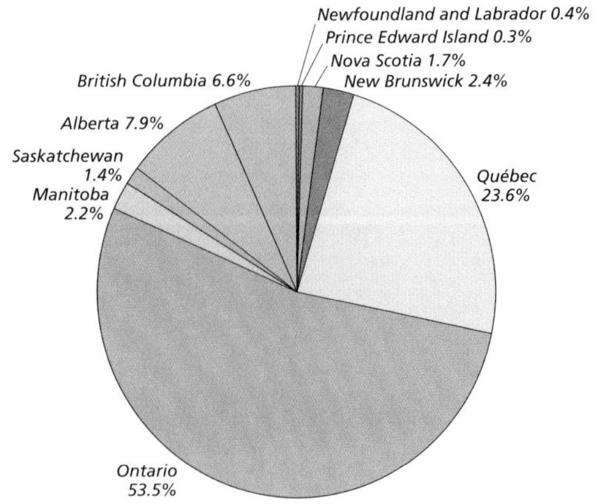

Total : $ 518 504 900 000

Value, 1990 - 2002

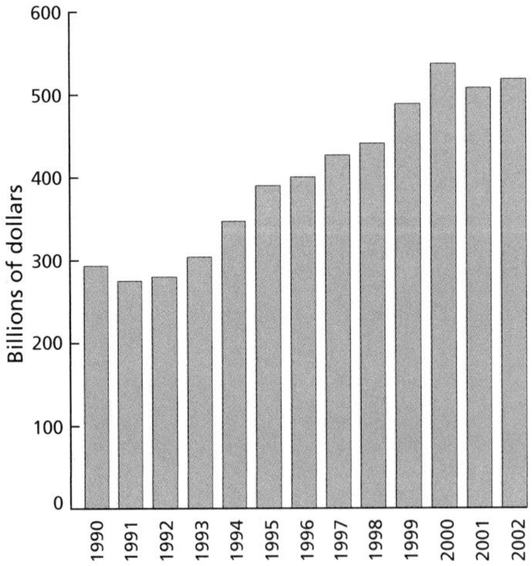

EXPORTS

Manufactured goods, 2002

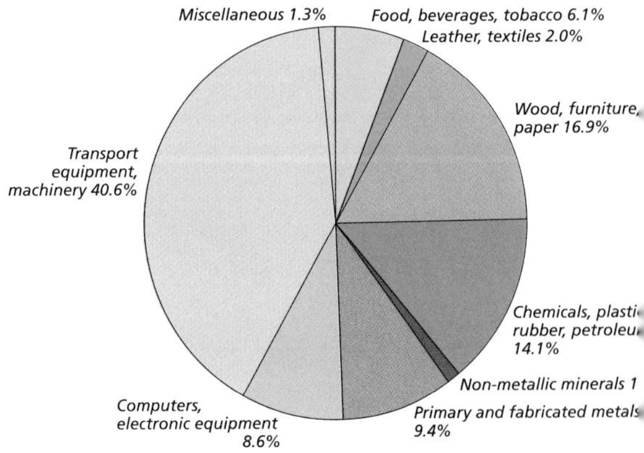

Total : $ 305 058 957 000

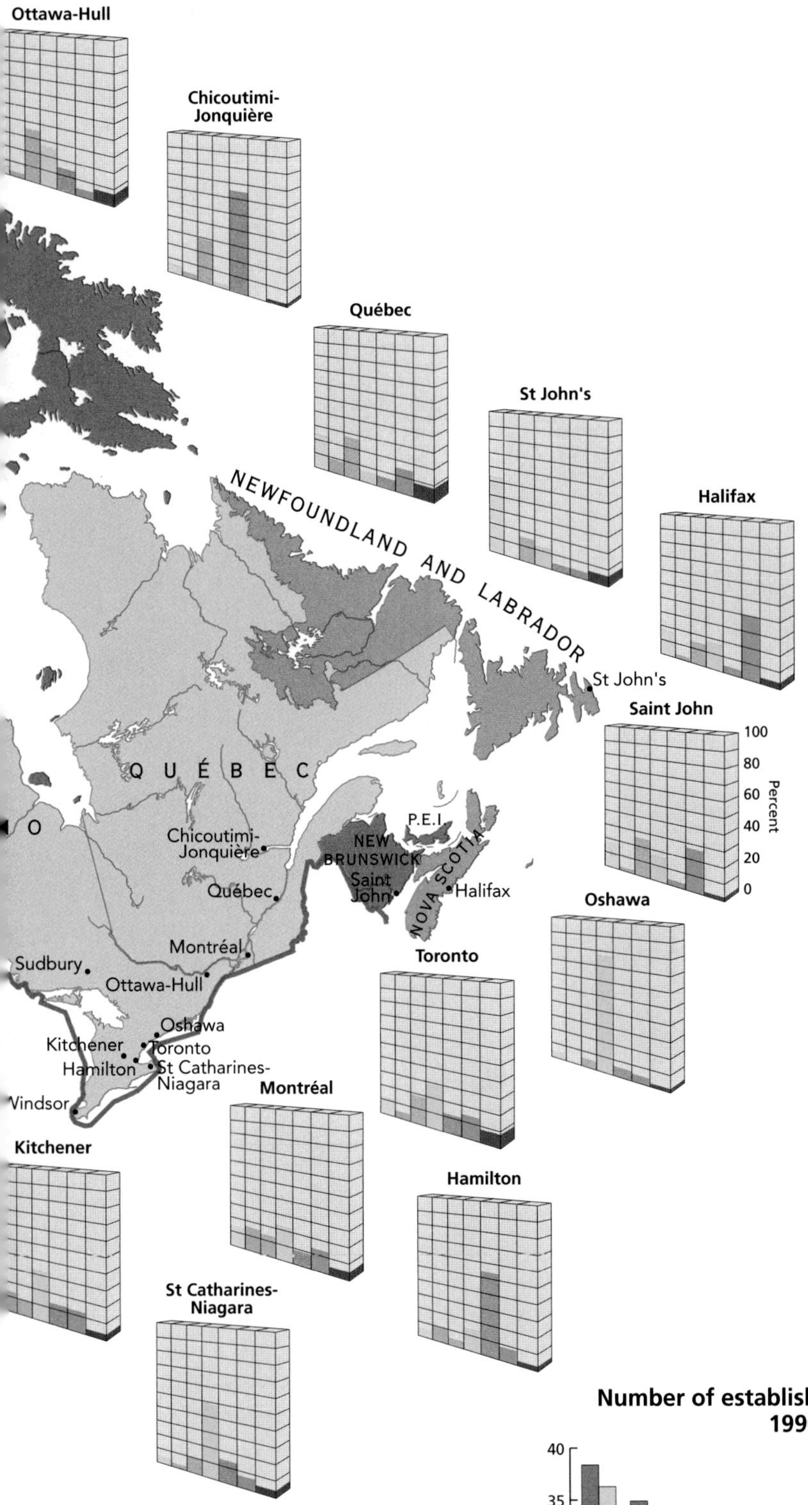

ESTABLISHMENTS AND EMPLOYEES

Type of manufacturing	Number of establishments	Number of employees per establishment
Food Manufacturing	3 467	63
Beverage and Tobacco Products	227	154
Textile Mills	374	71
Textile Product Mills	422	42
Clothing Manufacturing	1 342	63
Leather and Allied Products	176	62
Wood Products	2 144	68
Paper Manufacturing	663	156
Printing and Related Support Activities	2 623	31
Petroleum and Coal Products	204	63
Chemical Manufacturing	1 274	73
Plastics and Rubber Products	1 436	80
Non-Metallic Mineral Products	1 354	34
Primary Metal Manufacturing	478	196
Fabricated Metal Products	4 283	39
Machinery Manufacturing	2 653	50
Computer and Electronic Products	956	101
Electrical Equipment, Appliance and Component Manufacturing	605	87
Transportation Equipment	1 332	182
Furniture and Related Products	1 748	49
Miscellaneous Manufacturing	2 061	25
All Manufacturing	**29 822**	**64**

Number of establishments and employees, 1990 - 1999

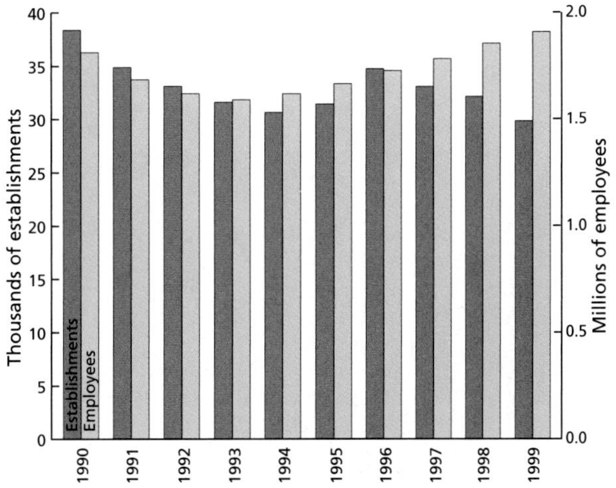

Average annual salary, 1990 - 1999

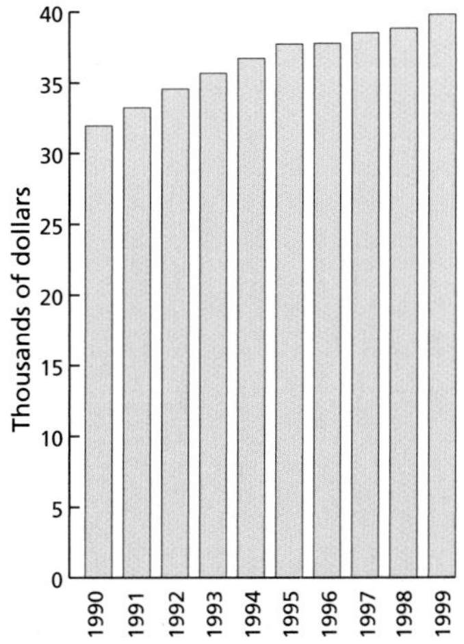

GROSS DOMESTIC PRODUCT BY REGION

GDP per capita, 2001

GDP by province, 2001

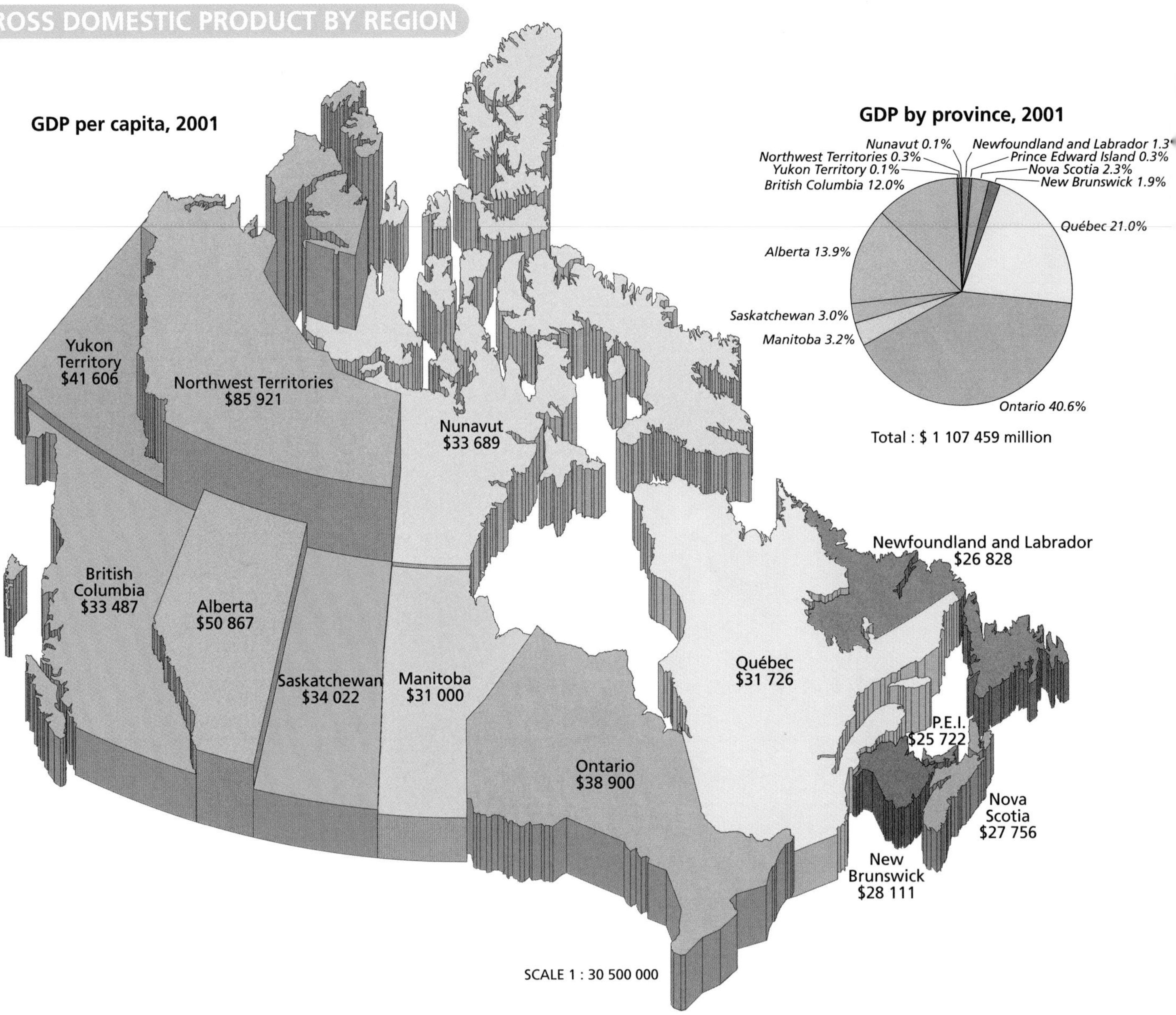

Total : $ 1 107 459 million

EARNINGS

Average weekly earnings, 2001

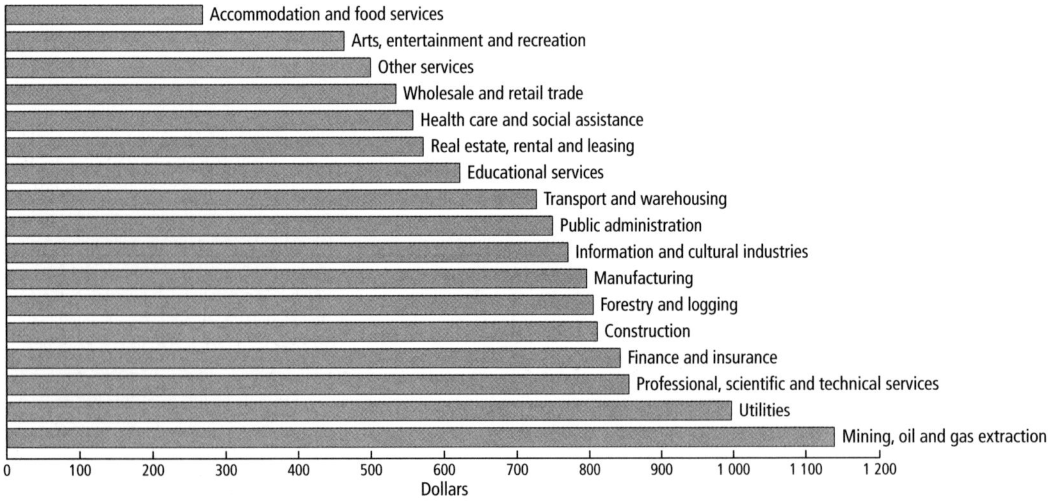

Earnings by educational level, 2001

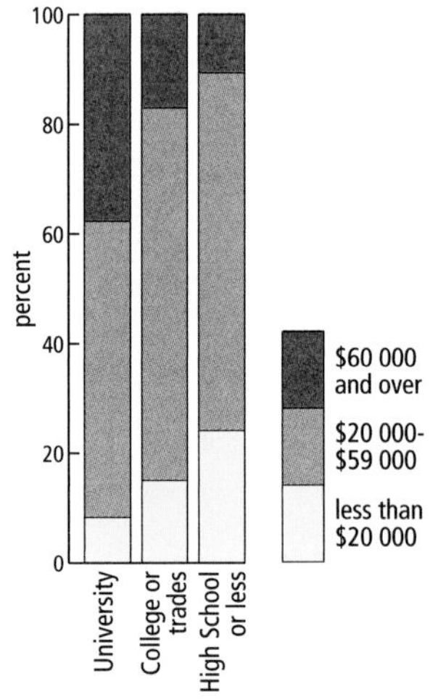

GROSS DOMESTIC PRODUCT BY INDUSTRY

2001

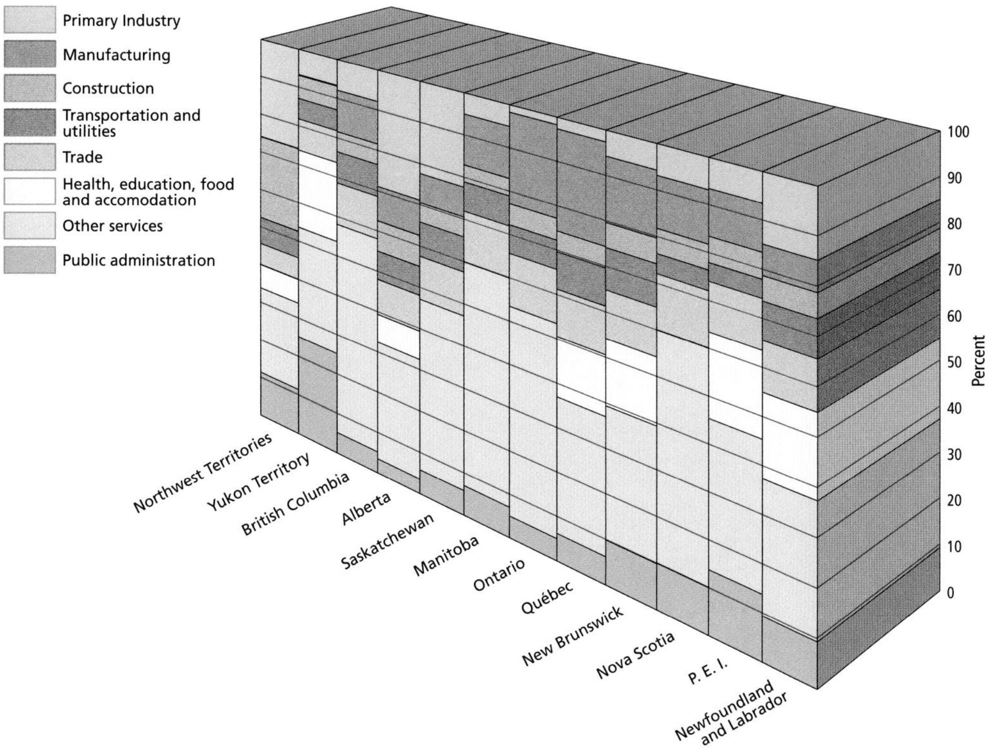

EMPLOYMENT

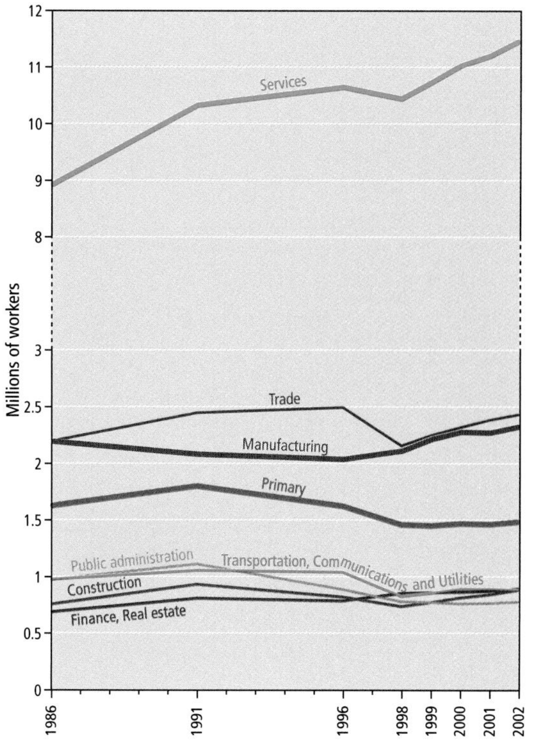

LABOUR FORCE

Males and females in the labour force, percent

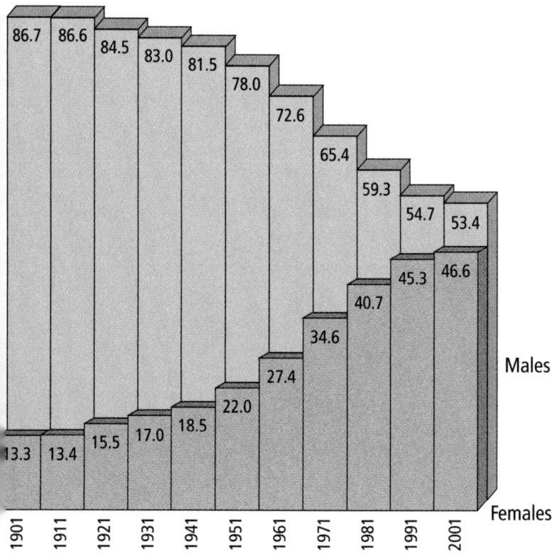

Average annual earnings of males and females

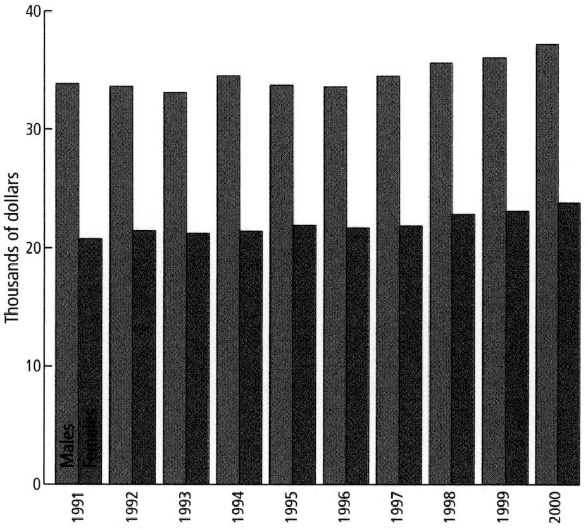

Composition of the labour force by sector, 2001

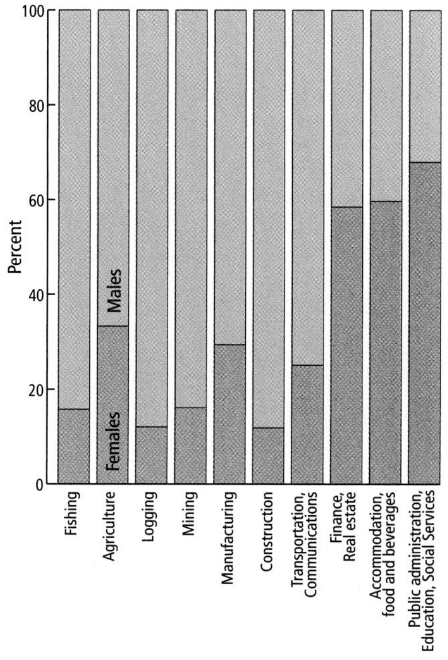

POPULATION DISTRIBUTION

Population distribution 2001

One dot represents 200 people

Population distribution 1871

One dot represents 200 people

Population distribution 1911

One dot represents 200 people

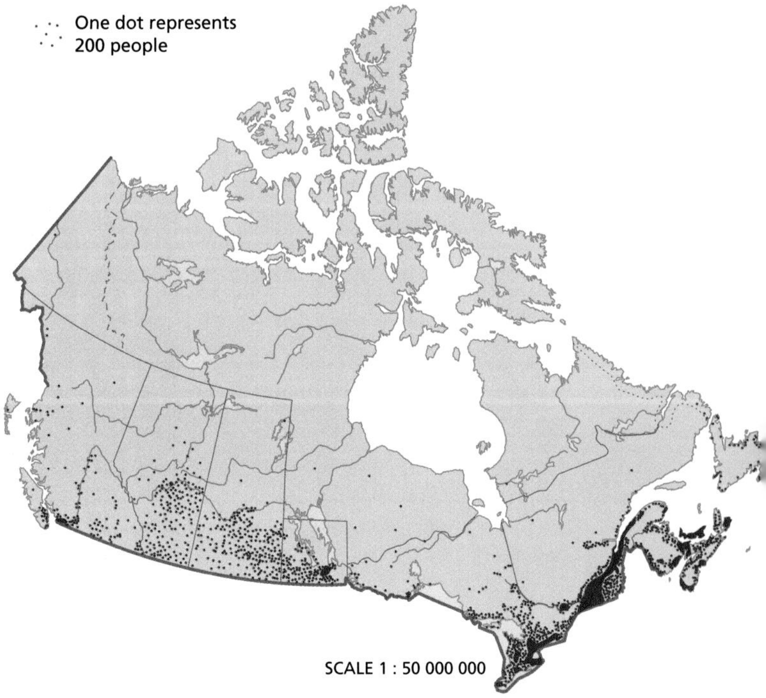

POPULATION PYRAMIDS

2001

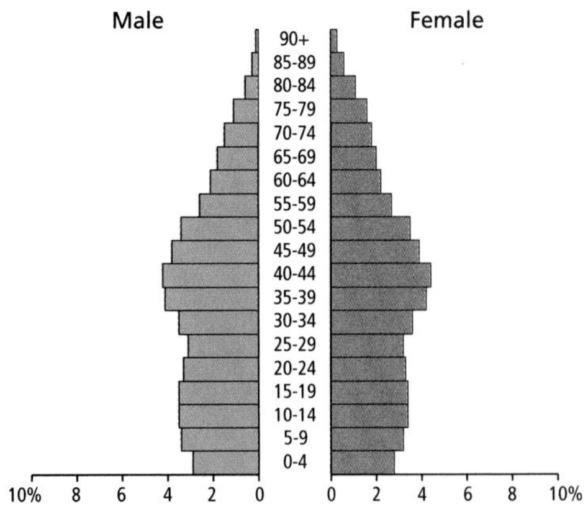

1911

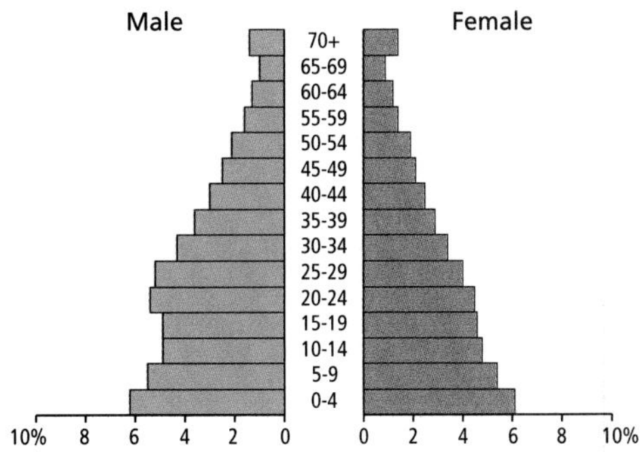

1871

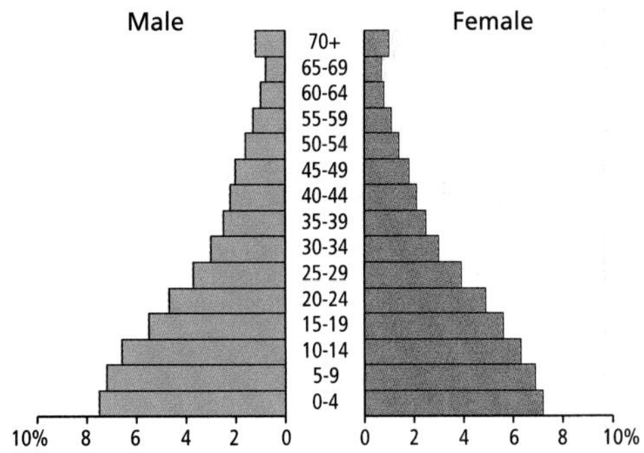

POPULATION BY PROVINCE AND TERRITORY

1871

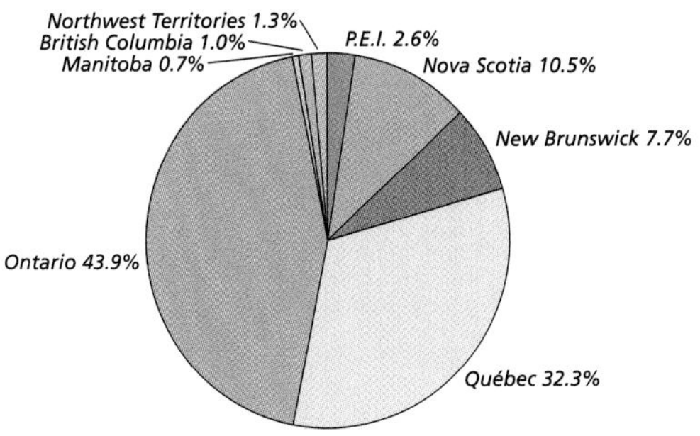

Total : 3 689 257

1911

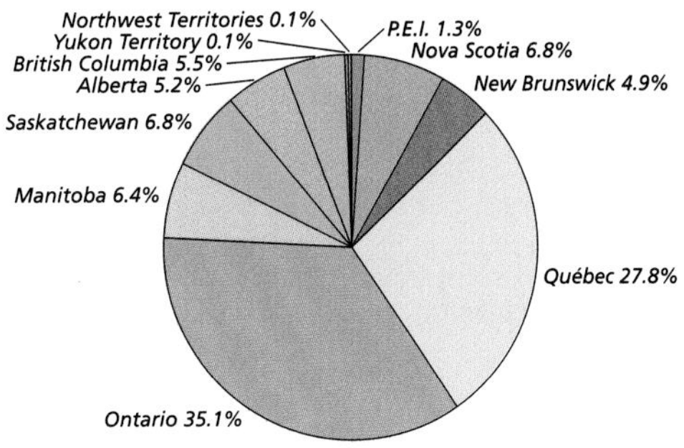

Total : 7 206 643

2001

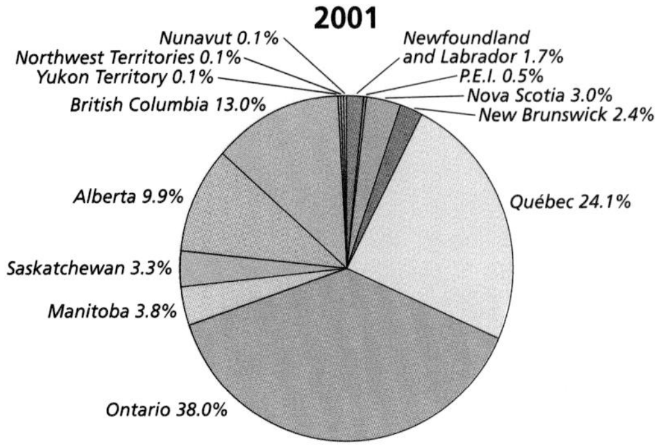

Total : 30 007 094

FIRST NATIONS IN MAJOR CITIES

Populations, 2001

City	Total population	First Nations population	Métis population
Toronto	4 682 897	13 780	5 100
Montréal	3 426 350	6 100	3 670
Vancouver	1 986 965	22 700	12 505
Ottawa-Hull	1 063 664	7 555	4 690
Calgary	951 395	10 155	10 580
Edmonton	937 845	18 260	21 060
Quebéc	682 757	3 020	875
Winnipeg	671 274	22 955	31 390
Hamilton	662 401	5 605	1 185
London	432 451	4 415	980
Kitchener	414 284	2 115	865
St Cath.-Niagara	377 009	3 370	1 335
Halifax	359 183	2 350	800
Saskatoon	225 927	11 290	8 305
Regina	192 800	9 200	5 995
Fredericton	81 346	2 225	270

ABORIGINAL PEOPLES BY PROVINCE AND TERRITORY

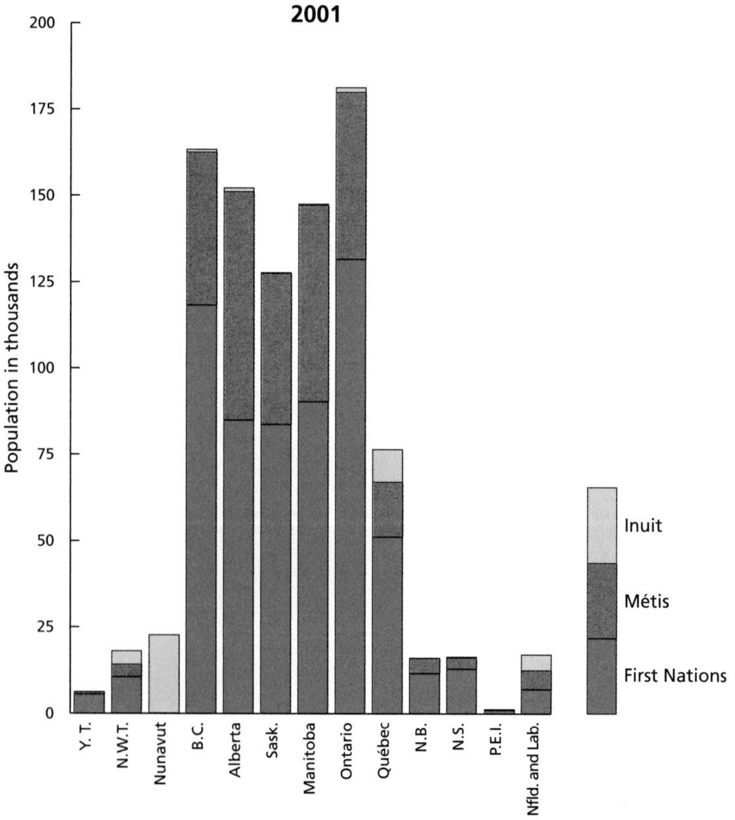

LANGUAGE AND DISTRIBUTION

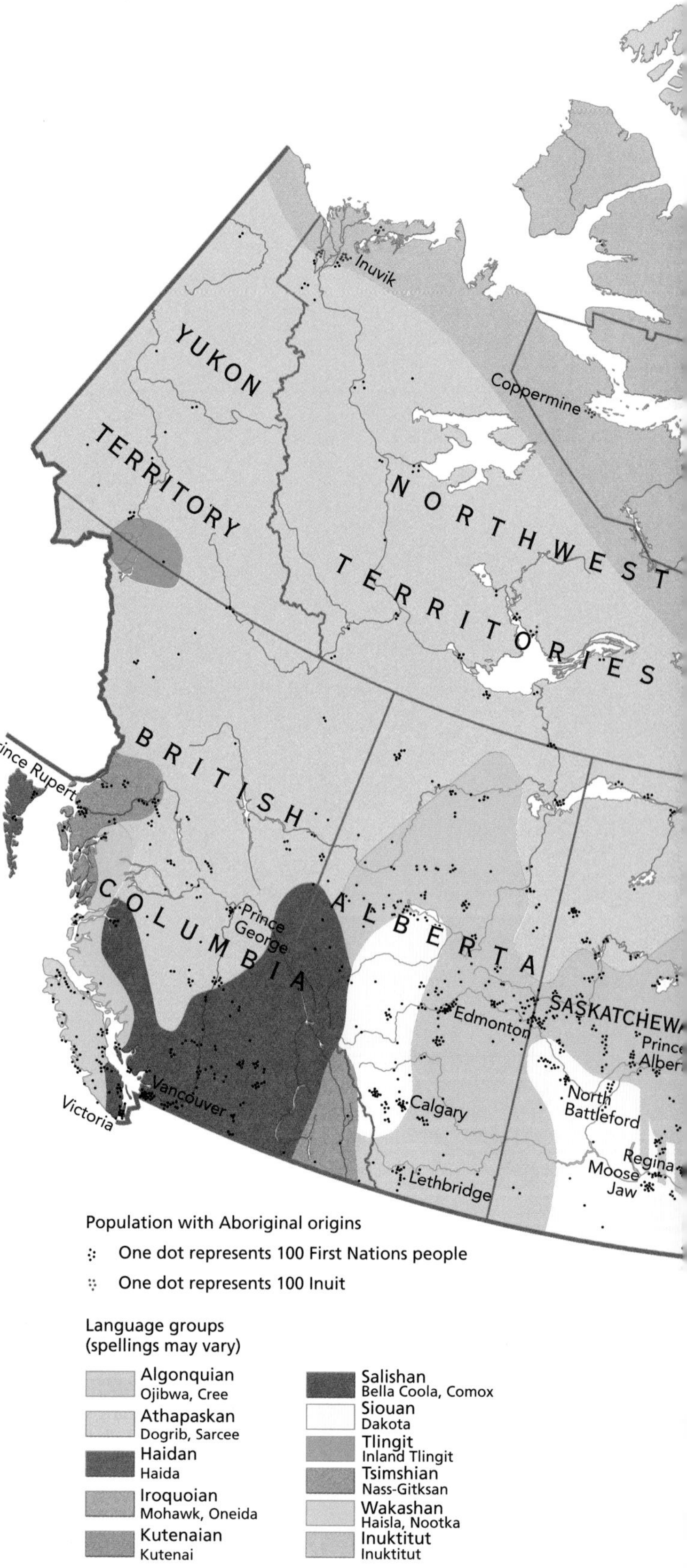

LANGUAGES

Speakers of First Nations languages, 2001

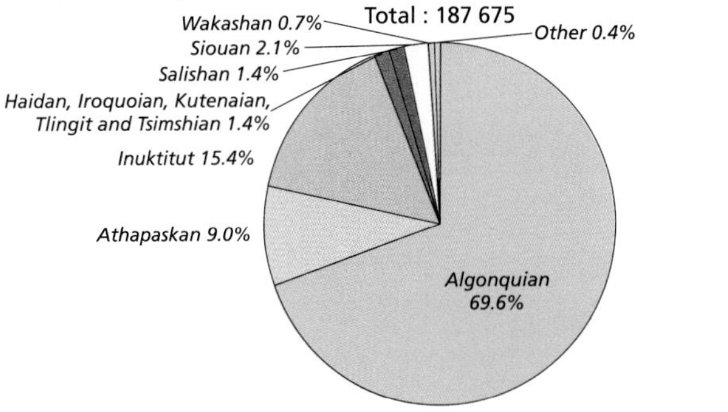

RESERVES

Population living on reserves, 2001

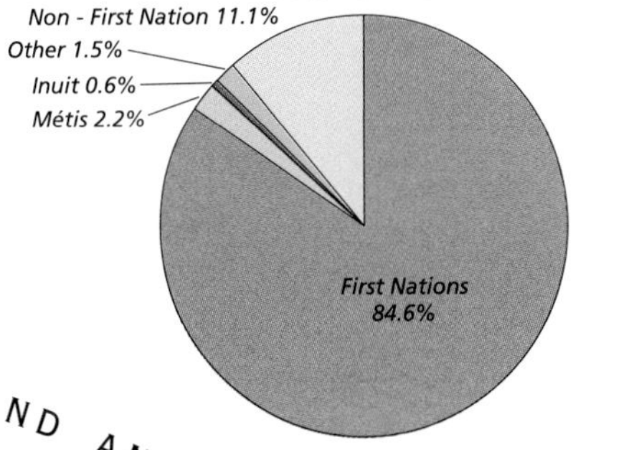

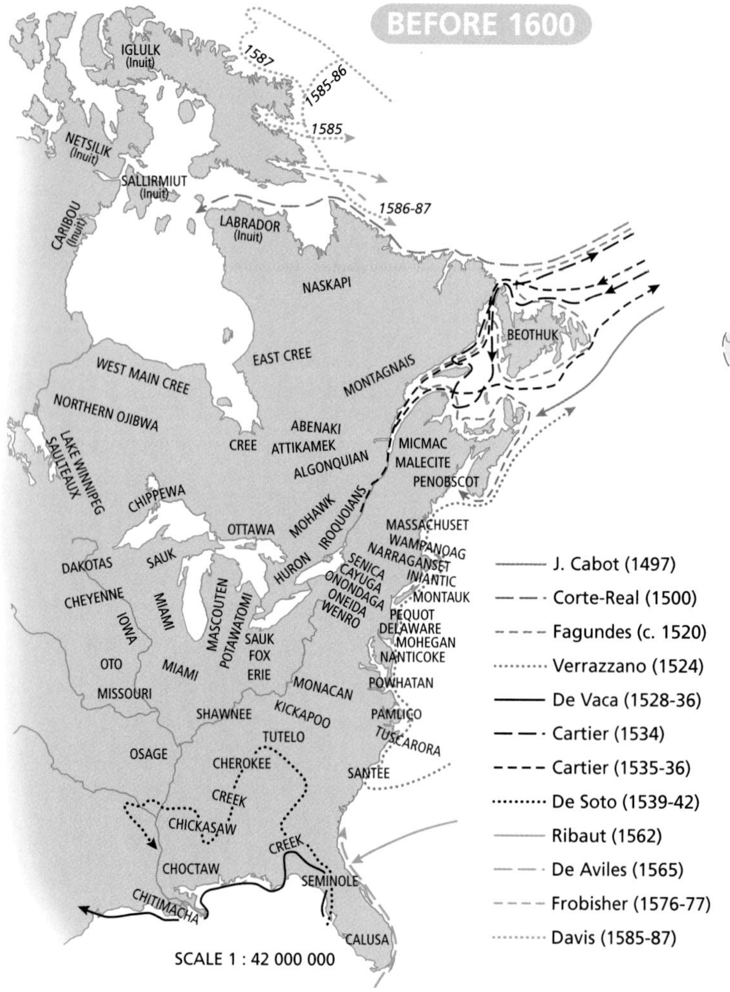
BEFORE 1600
IGLULK (Inuit)
NETSILIK (Inuit)
SALLIRMIUT (Inuit)
CARIBOU (Inuit)
LABRADOR (Inuit)
1587
1585-86
1585
1586-87
NASKAPI
BEOTHUK
EAST CREE
WEST MAIN CREE
MONTAGNAIS
NORTHERN OJIBWA
ABENAKI
CREE
ATTIKAMEK
ALGONQUIAN
MICMAC
MALECITE
PENOBSCOT
LAKE WINNIPEG SAULTEAUX
CHIPPEWA
MOHAWK
IROQUOIANS
OTTAWA
MASSACHUSET
WAMPANOAG
NARRAGANSET
NIANTIC
MONTAUK
PEQUOT
DELAWARE
MOHEGAN
NANTICOKE
SENECA
CAYUGA
ONONDAGA
ONEIDA
WENRO
HURON
DAKOTAS
SAUK
CHEYENNE
IOWA
MIAMI
MASCOUTEN
POTAWATOMI
SAUK
FOX
ERIE
OTO
MIAMI
MISSOURI
MONACAN
POWHATAN
SHAWNEE
KICKAPOO
PAMLICO
TUTELO
TUSCARORA
OSAGE
CHEROKEE
SANTEE
CREEK
CHICKASAW
CREEK
CHOCTAW
SEMINOLE
CHITIMACHA
CALUSA
SCALE 1 : 42 000 000
J. Cabot (1497)
Corte-Real (1500)
Fagundes (c. 1520)
Verrazzano (1524)
De Vaca (1528-36)
Cartier (1534)
Cartier (1535-36)
De Soto (1539-42)
Ribaut (1562)
De Aviles (1565)
Frobisher (1576-77)
Davis (1585-87)

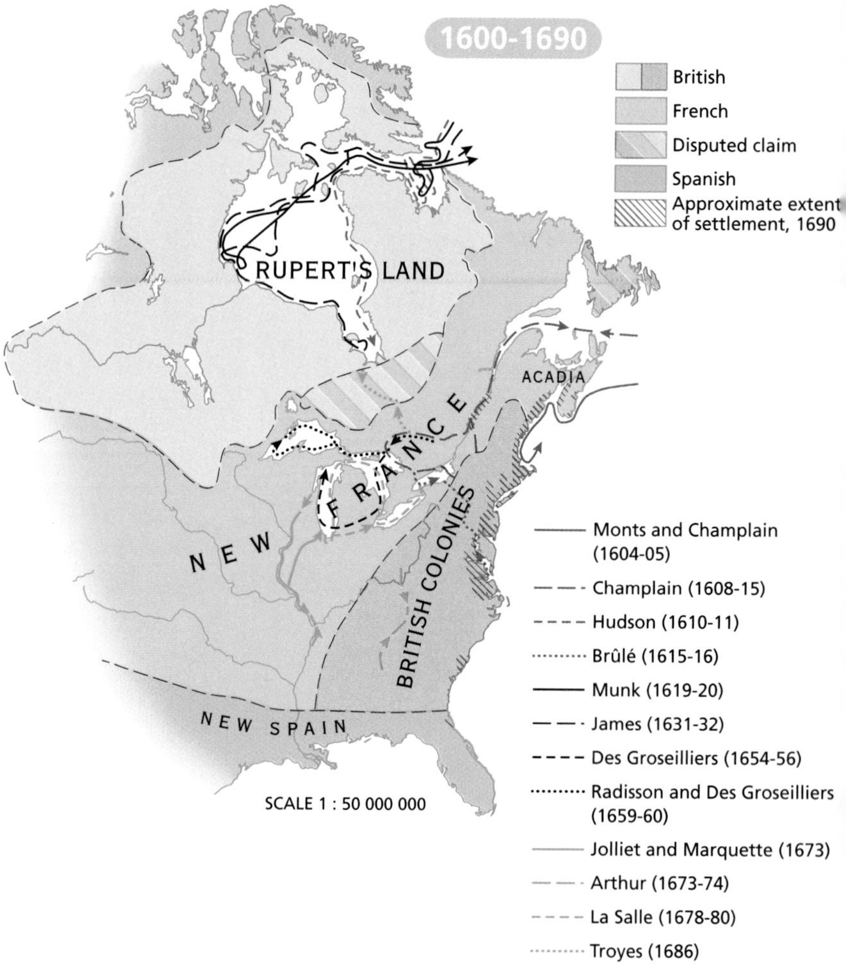
1600-1690
British
French
Disputed claim
Spanish
Approximate extent of settlement, 1690
RUPERT'S LAND
ACADIA
NEW FRANCE
BRITISH COLONIES
NEW SPAIN
SCALE 1 : 50 000 000
Monts and Champlain (1604-05)
Champlain (1608-15)
Hudson (1610-11)
Brûlé (1615-16)
Munk (1619-20)
James (1631-32)
Des Groseilliers (1654-56)
Radisson and Des Groseilliers (1659-60)
Jolliet and Marquette (1673)
Arthur (1673-74)
La Salle (1678-80)
Troyes (1686)

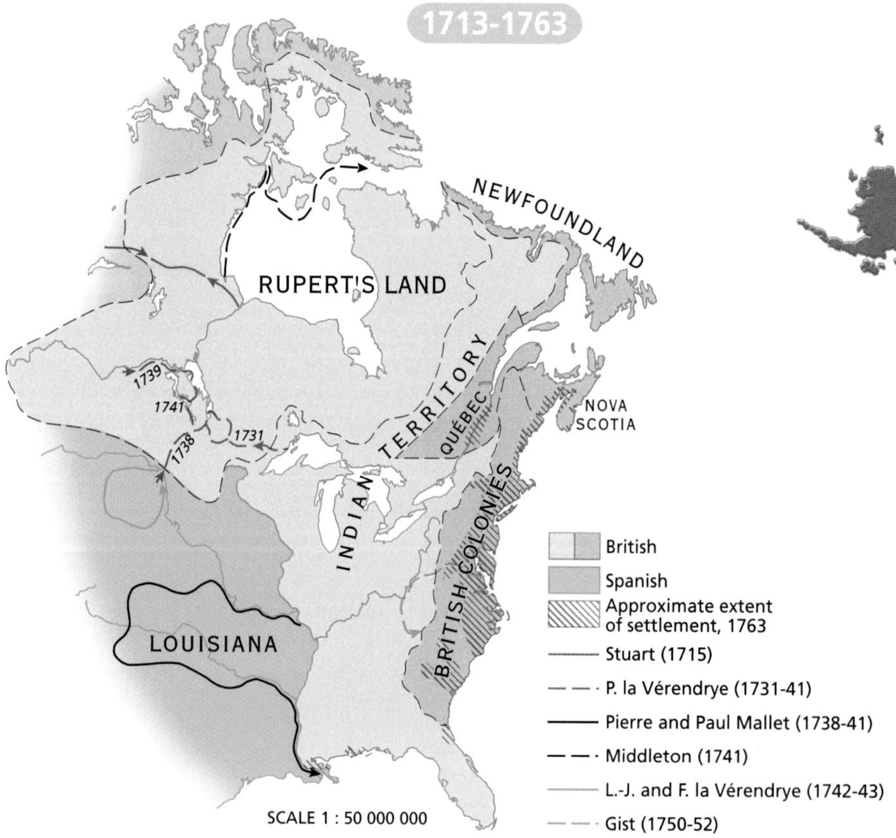
1713-1763
NEWFOUNDLAND
RUPERT'S LAND
1739
1741
1738
1731
INDIAN TERRITORY
QUÉBEC
NOVA SCOTIA
BRITISH COLONIES
LOUISIANA
SCALE 1 : 50 000 000
British
Spanish
Approximate extent of settlement, 1763
Stuart (1715)
P. la Vérendrye (1731-41)
Pierre and Paul Mallet (1738-41)
Middleton (1741)
L.-J. and F. la Vérendrye (1742-43)
Gist (1750-52)

1784-1825
British
American
Joint occupation
Spanish
Russian
Approximate extent of settlement, 1825
ALASKA
THE NORTH-WESTERN TERRITORY
NEWFOUNDLAND
RUPERT'S LAND
LOWER CANADA
P.E.I.
N.B.
NOVA SCOTIA
OREGON TERRITORY
UPPER CANADA
UNITED STATES
MEXICO
SCALE 1 : 64 000 000

ARCTIC EXPLORATION

- Davis (1585, 1586, 1587)
- Baffin and Bylot (1616)
- Parry (1819-20, 1821-22)
- Franklin (1819-22, 1845-47)
- Franklin and Richardson (1825-27)
- Back (1833-34)
- M'Clure (1850-54)
- Sverdrup (1898-1902)
- Peary (1898-1902, 1905-06, 1908-09)
- Amundsen (1903-06)
- Stefansson (1913-18)

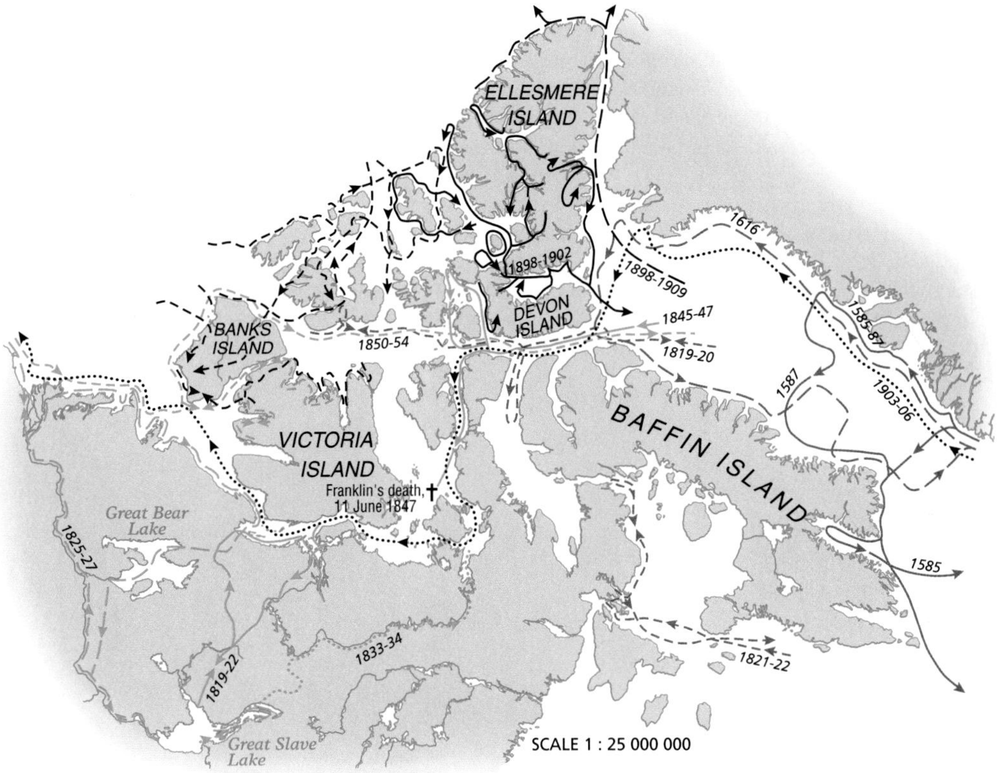

WESTERN EXPLORATION

- Bering (1741)
- Henday (1754-55)
- Hearne (1770, 1771, 1772)
- Perez (1774)
- Cook (1778-79)
- Mackenzie (1789, 1793)
- Vancouver (1792, 1793, 1794)
- Thompson (1792-1812)
- Fraser (1806, 1808)
- Simpson (1824-25, 1841)
- Campbell (1840, 1843, 1851)
- Tyrrell (1892-94, 1898)

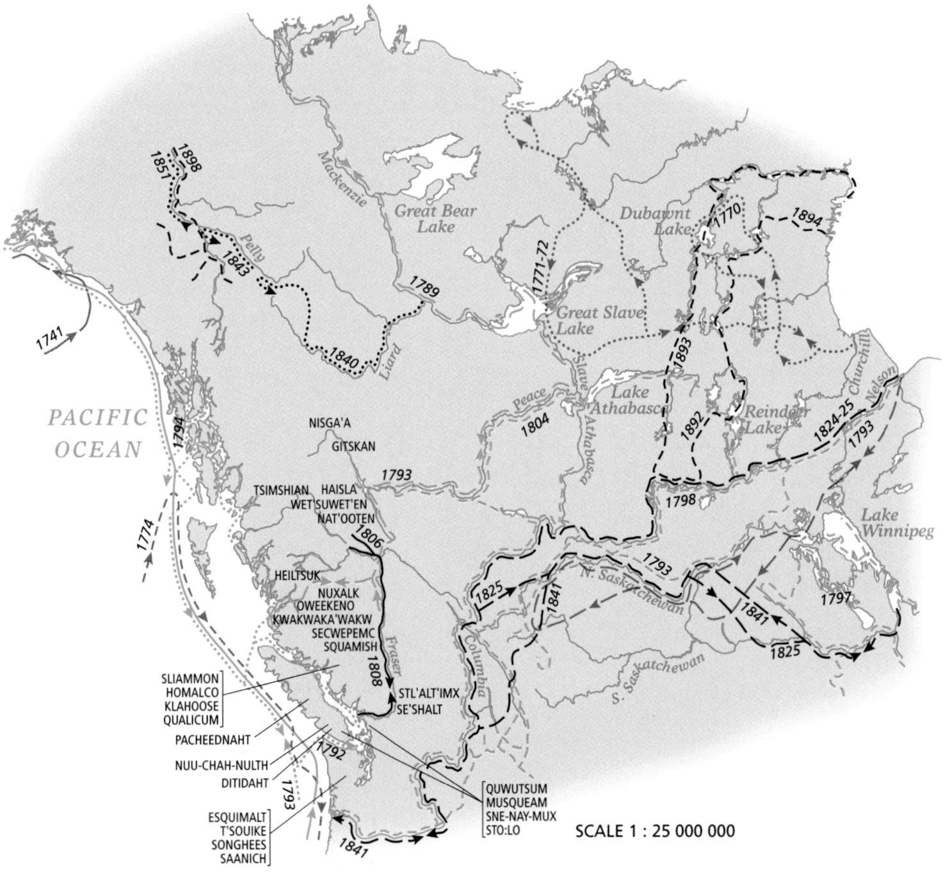

This series of maps illustrates the evolution of the provincial, territorial, and international boundaries of Canada. The series begins in 1866, before Confederation (below) and then proceeds in chronological sequence, working from top to bottom of the four columns of Canadian maps. At Confederation, New Brunswick and Nova Scotia joined with Upper and Lower Canada (renamed Ontario and Québec) to create the Dominion of Canada. Based on a promise to provide a railway link with the east, British Columbia joined Confederation in 1871. Prince Edward Island was added in 1873. Territories were changed to provinces as settlement expanded westward in the early part of the 20th century. By 1912, the country had developed a "look" which is quite similar to that of the current map except for the boundary between Quebec and Labrador, which was established by the Imperial Privy Council in 1927. However, it was not until 1949 that the tenth province – known then as Newfoundland and now as Newfoundland and Labrador – joined Confederation.

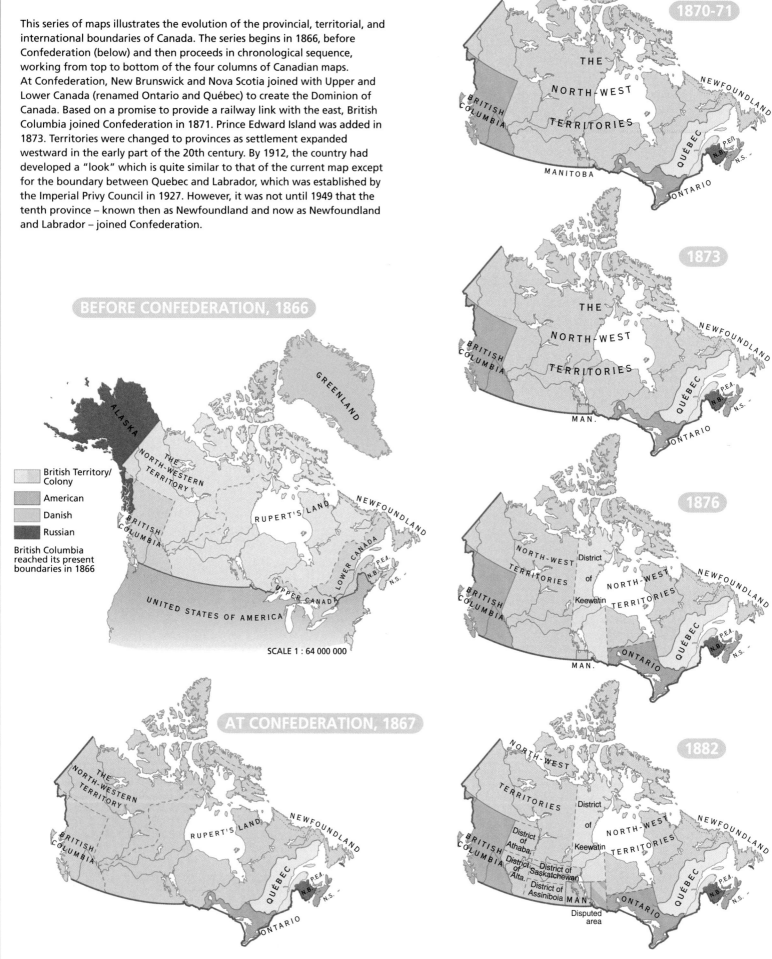

1870-71

1873

BEFORE CONFEDERATION, 1866

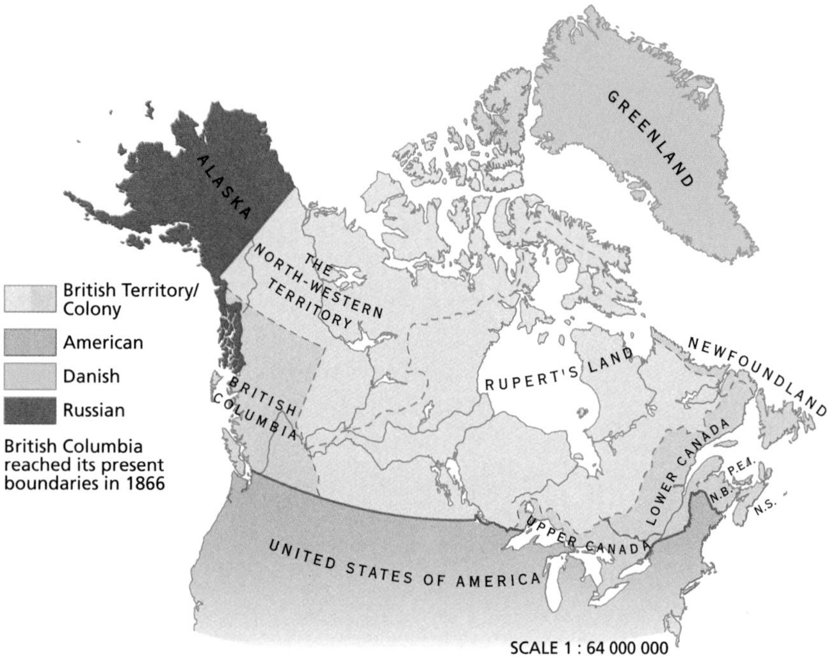

1876

AT CONFEDERATION, 1867

1882

The Canada map (2001) illustrates several changes from 1949, including the extension of the boundaries into the Arctic Ocean as well as all waters within 370 km (200 nautical miles) of Canada's shoreline. On January 1, 1997, Nunavut was created as a territory separate from the Northwest Territories. On December 6, 2001, Newfoundland officially changed its name to Newfoundland and Labrador. Its two-letter postal abbreviation was changed from NF to NL on October 21, 2002.

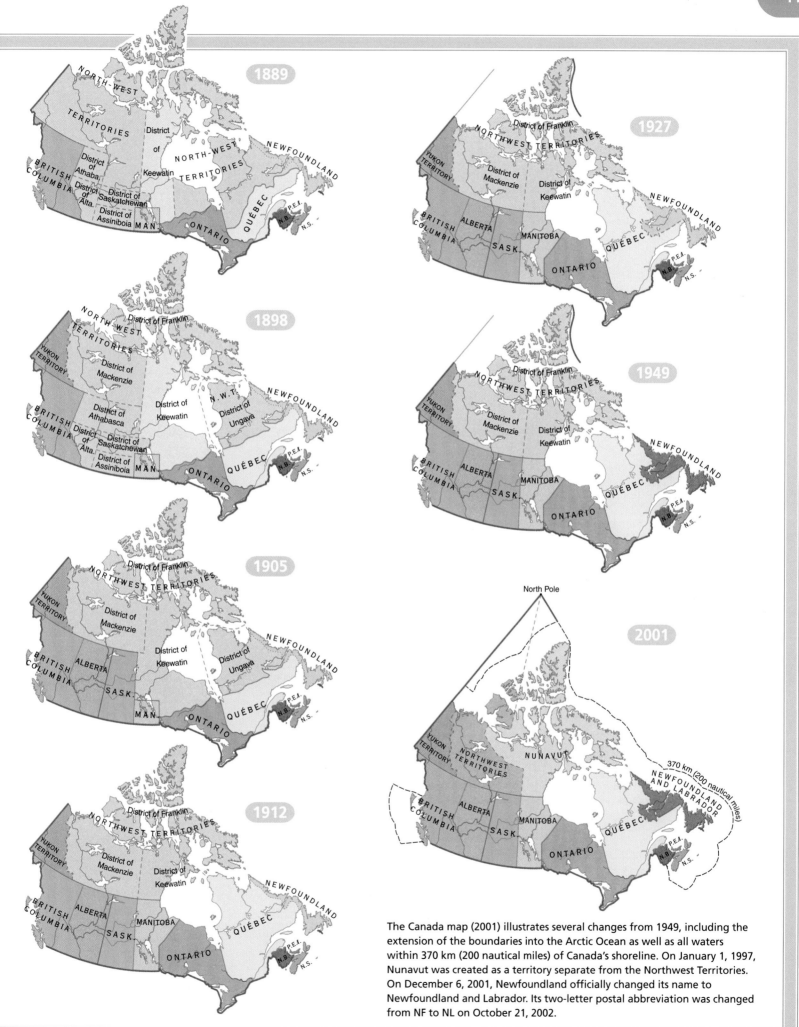

URBANIZATION

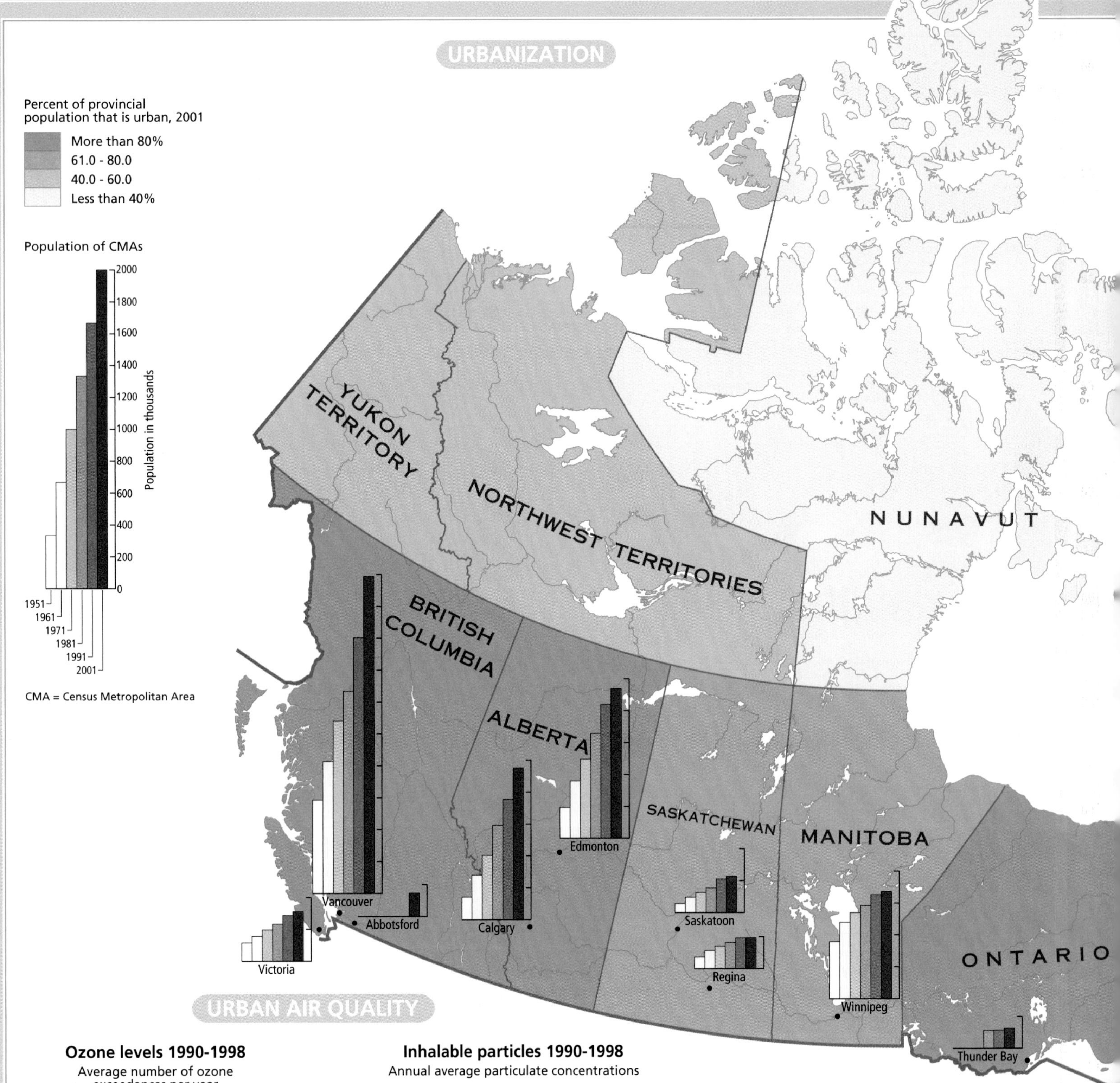

SCALE 1 : 18 000 000

URBAN AIR QUALITY

Ozone levels 1990-1998

Average number of ozone exceedances per year

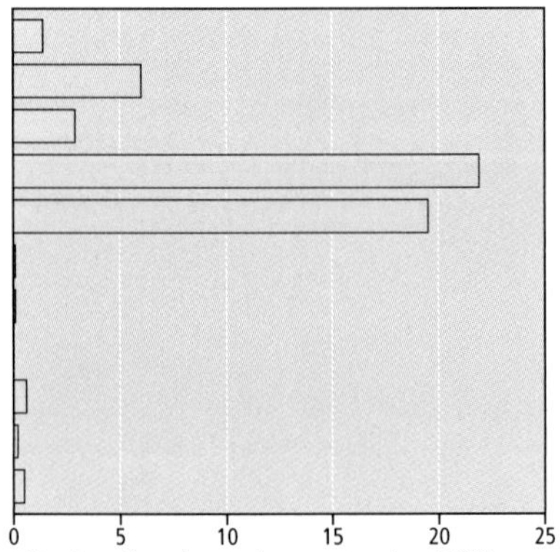

* Figures for 1990 – 2000

Inhalable particles 1990-1998

Annual average particulate concentrations

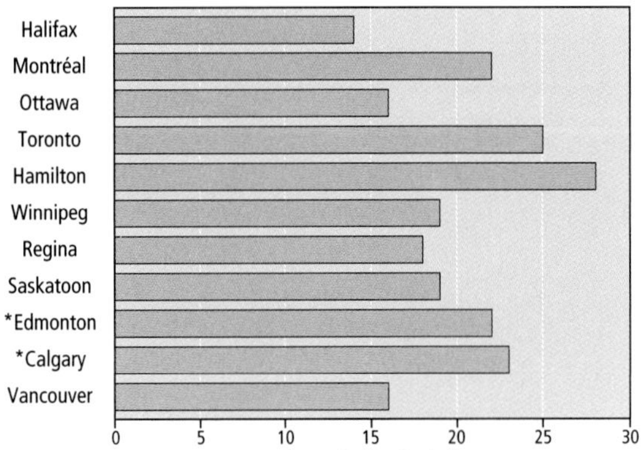

* Figures for 1990 – 2000

URBAN AND RURAL POPULATION

Urban and rural population

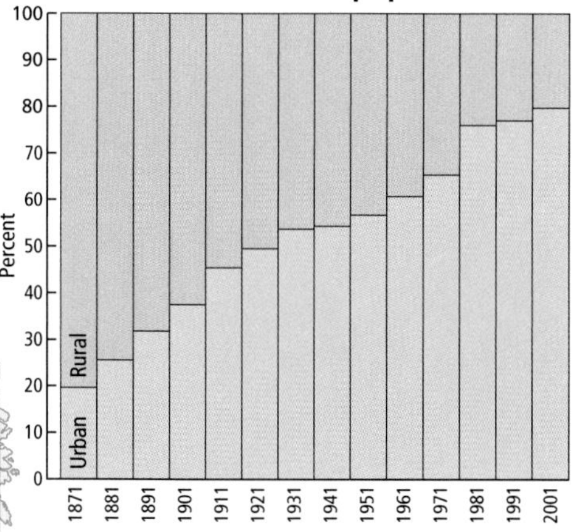

Urban population comparisons, 2000

Country	Percent urban population
Singapore	100
Kuwait	98
Belgium	97
Qatar	93
Iceland	93
Luxembourg	92
Bahrain	92
Uruguay	91
Malta	91
Israel	91
United Kingdom	90
Lebanon	90
Netherlands	89
The Bahamas	89
Argentina	89
Libya	88
Germany	88
Venezuela	87
New Zealand	87
United Arab Emirates	86
Saudi Arabia	86

Urban population changes

Urban centre	1996 population	2001 population	Percent change
Calgary (Alta.)	821 628	951 395	15.8
Oshawa (Ont.)	268 773	296 298	10.2
Toronto (Ont.)	4 263 759	4 682 897	9.8
Edmonton (Alta.)	862 597	937 845	8.7
Vancouver (B.C.)	1 831 665	1 986 965	8.5
Kitchener (Ont.)	382 940	414 284	8.2
Abbotsford (B.C.)	136 480	147 370	8.0
Windsor (Ont.)	286 811	307 877	7.3
Ottawa-Hull (Ont./Qué.)	998 718	1 063 664	6.5
Hamilton (Ont.)	624 360	662 401	6.1
Halifax (N.S.)	342 966	359 183	4.7
London (Ont.)	416 546	432 451	3.8
Saskatoon (Sask.)	219 056	225 927	3.1
Montréal (Qué.)	3 326 447	3 426 350	3.0
Sherbrooke (Qué.)	149 569	153 811	2.8
Victoria (B.C.)	304 287	311 902	2.5
Kingston (Ont.)	144 528	146 838	1.6
Québec (Qué.)	671 889	682 757	1.6
St Catharines-Niagara (Ont.)	372 406	377 009	1.2
Winnipeg (Man.)	667 093	671 274	0.6
Regina (Sask.)	193 652	192 800	-0.4
St John's (Nfld. and Lab.)	174 051	172 918	-0.7
Trois-Rivières (Qué.)	139 956	137 507	-1.7
Saint John (N.B.)	125 705	122 678	-2.4
Chicoutimi-Jonquière (Qué.)	160 454	154 938	-3.4
Thunder Bay (Ont.)	126 643	121 986	-3.7
Greater Sudbury (Ont.)	165 618	155 601	-6.0

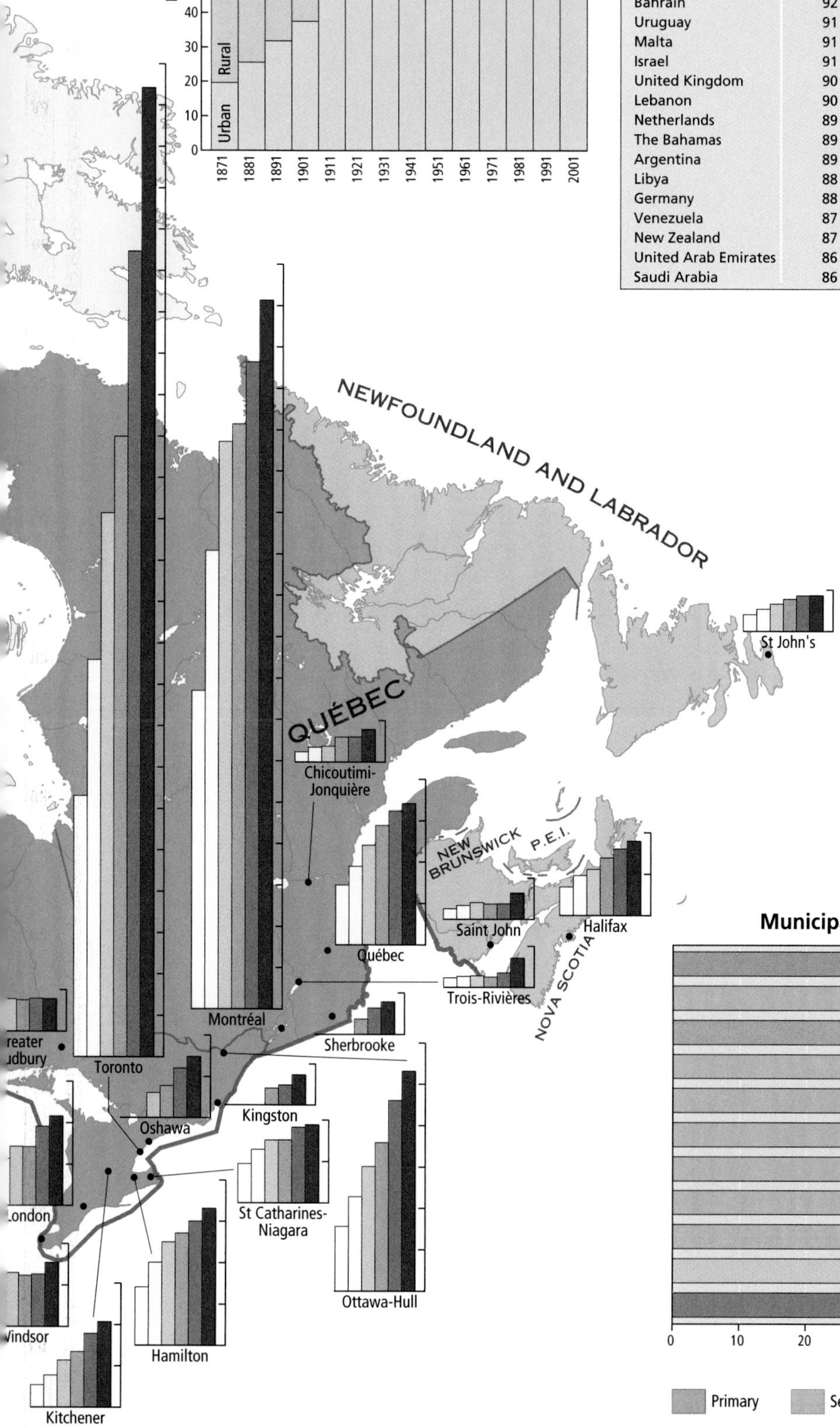

SEWAGE TREATMENT

Cities use a variety of methods to treat sewage. Primary treatment is a physical process that involves screening and settling, and removes approximately 60 percent of solids and 40 percent of organic materials. Sludge is "skimmed" off and disposed of in a variety of ways. Secondary treatment is a biological treatment, using bacteria to break down almost 90 percent of the dissolved organics in the waste. A few urban centres use filters and chemical processes to remove organics, inorganics, and heavy metals in the tertiary treatment stage of sewage treatment.

Municipal sewage treatment, selected cities, 1999

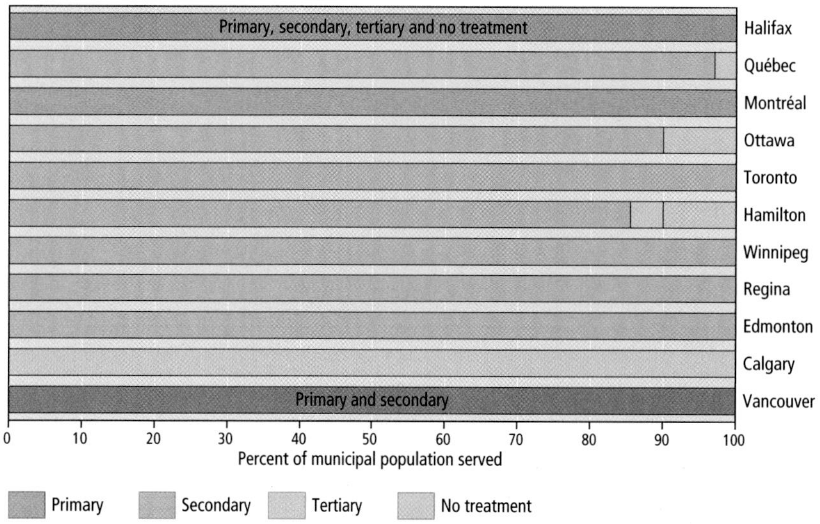

IMMIGRATION 1901-1911

NORTHERN
EUROPE
CANADA
BRITISH
ISLES
RUSSIA
EUROPE
UNITED STATES
OF
AMERICA
ASIA
AFRICA
SOUTH
AMERICA
AUSTRALASIA
Share of immigrants to
Canada by percent
More than 25%
15.0 - 25.0
5.0 - 14.9
1.0 - 4.9
Less than 1%
SCALE 1 : 140 000 000

IMMIGRATION 1991-2001

NORTHERN
EUROPE
RUSSIAN FEDERATION
CANADA
U.K.
EASTERN
EUROPE
WESTERN
EUROPE
SOUTHERN EUROPE
UNITED STATES
OF
AMERICA
ASIA
CENTRAL AMERICA
AND THE CARIBBEAN
AFRICA
SOUTH
AMERICA
OCEANIA
Share of immigrants to
Canada by percent
50.0 - 59.9%
5.0 - 9.9
1.0 - 4.9
Less than 1%
SCALE 1 : 140 000 000

DESTINATIONS OF IMMIGRANTS

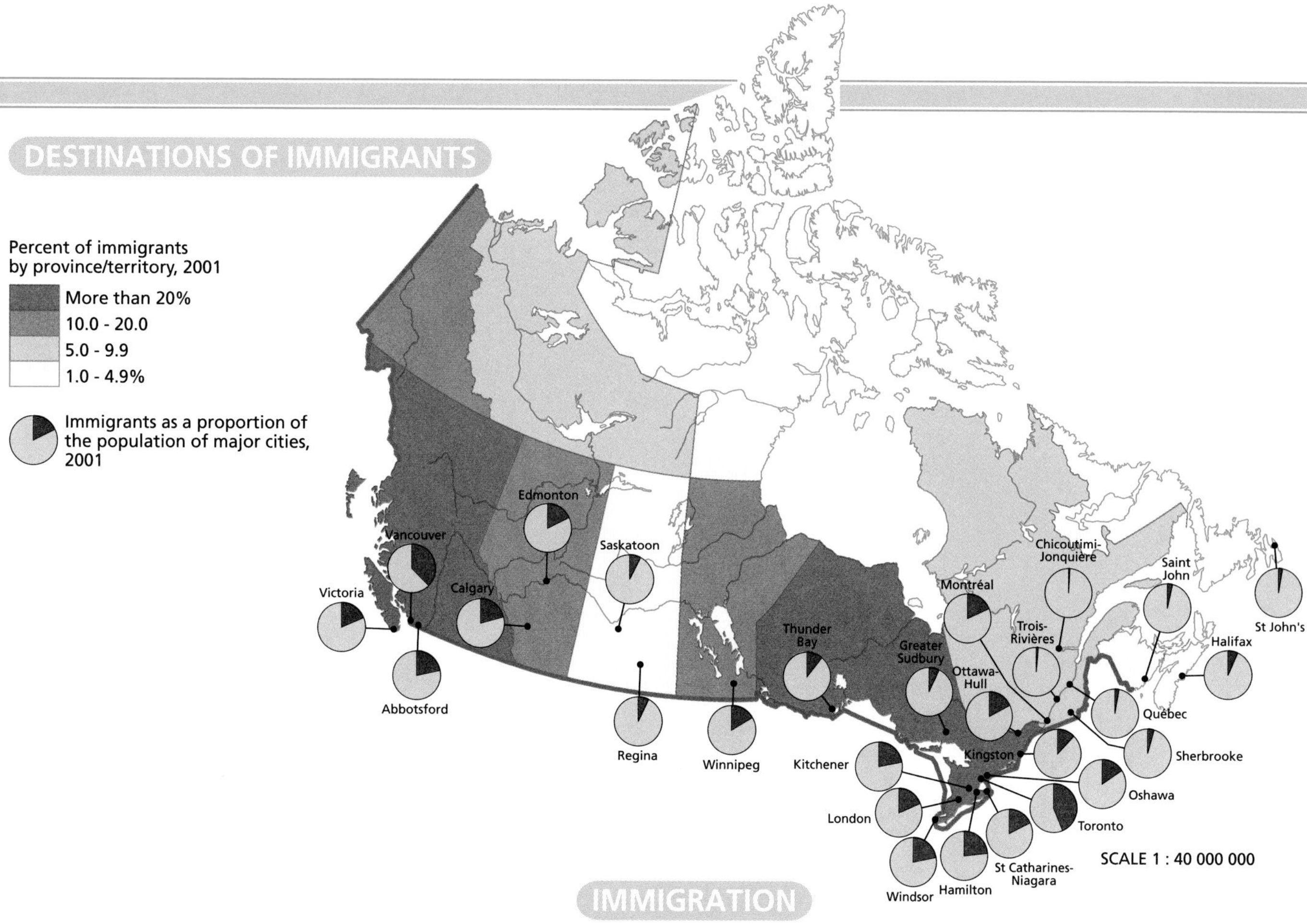

IMMIGRATION

Annual immigration, 1870-2001

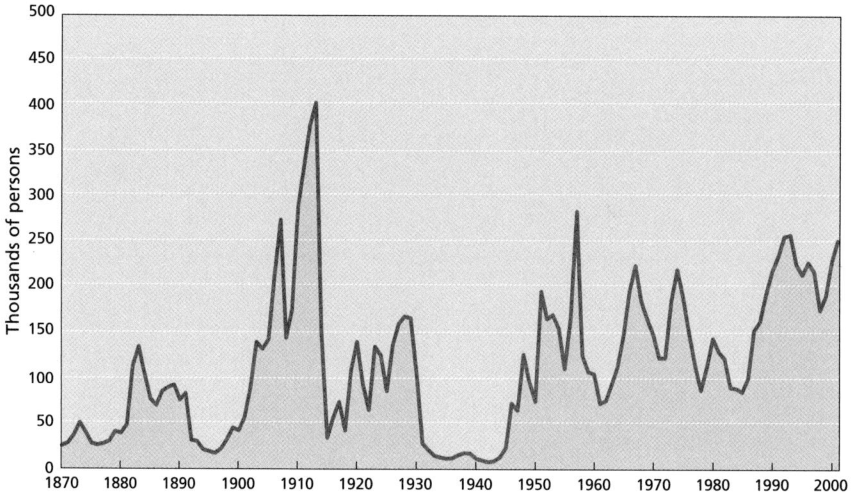

Origin of immigrants, 1971-2001

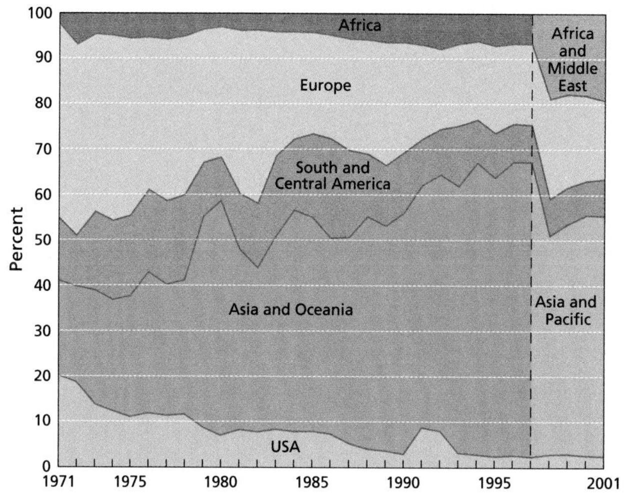

MIGRATION

Inter-provincial migration 1996-2001

Destination of migrants	Source of migrants												
	N. & L.	P.E.I.	N.S.	N.B.	QUÉ.	ONT.	MAN.	SASK.	ALTA.	B.C.	Y.T.	N.W.T.	NUN.
Newfoundland & Labrador	-	300	2 680	900	860	6 555	365	215	2 175	1 590	85	200	145
Prince Edward Island	910	-	1 740	1 110	395	2 350	90	105	570	495	0	110	20
Nova Scotia	6 745	1 855	-	8 140	3 340	18 220	1 720	990	5 305	6 055	155	270	205
New Brunswick	2 215	1 085	6 925	-	5 630	9 945	910	410	2 785	2 335	150	115	135
Québec	1 005	260	3 035	6 220	-	36 690	1 940	965	3 960	7 745	145	145	310
Ontario	17 555	2 375	22 135	14 080	80 505	-	15 225	8 850	32 275	46 955	775	1 205	565
Manitoba	720	85	1 520	980	1 860	12 800	-	6 850	8 755	8 260	140	425	205
Saskatchewan	790	80	890	550	965	5 290	7 275	-	16 260	9 540	270	585	110
Alberta	13 755	1 305	9 900	6 605	11 820	44 045	20 780	37 645	-	89 685	2 130	4 105	450
British Columbia	2 370	375	4 825	2 220	13 705	52 830	12 280	10 820	48 335	-	2 450	1 260	255
Yukon Territory	125	0	110	30	170	565	95	230	580	1 605	-	190	35
Northwest Territories	550	25	300	125	225	770	325	355	1 600	900	145	-	415
Nunavut	370	20	230	90	280	545	185	95	210	165	25	300	-

ETHNICITY

Ethnic composition of Canada, 2001

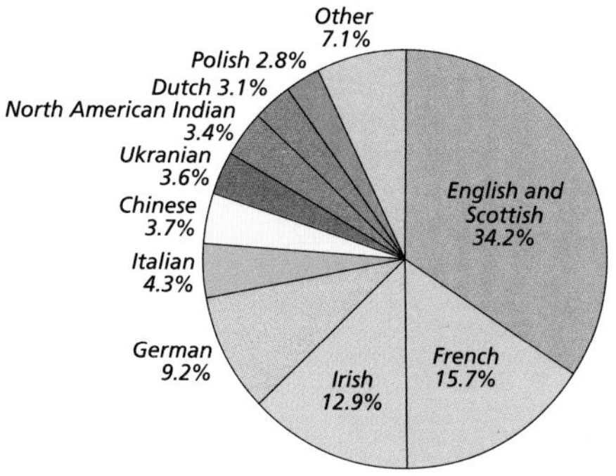

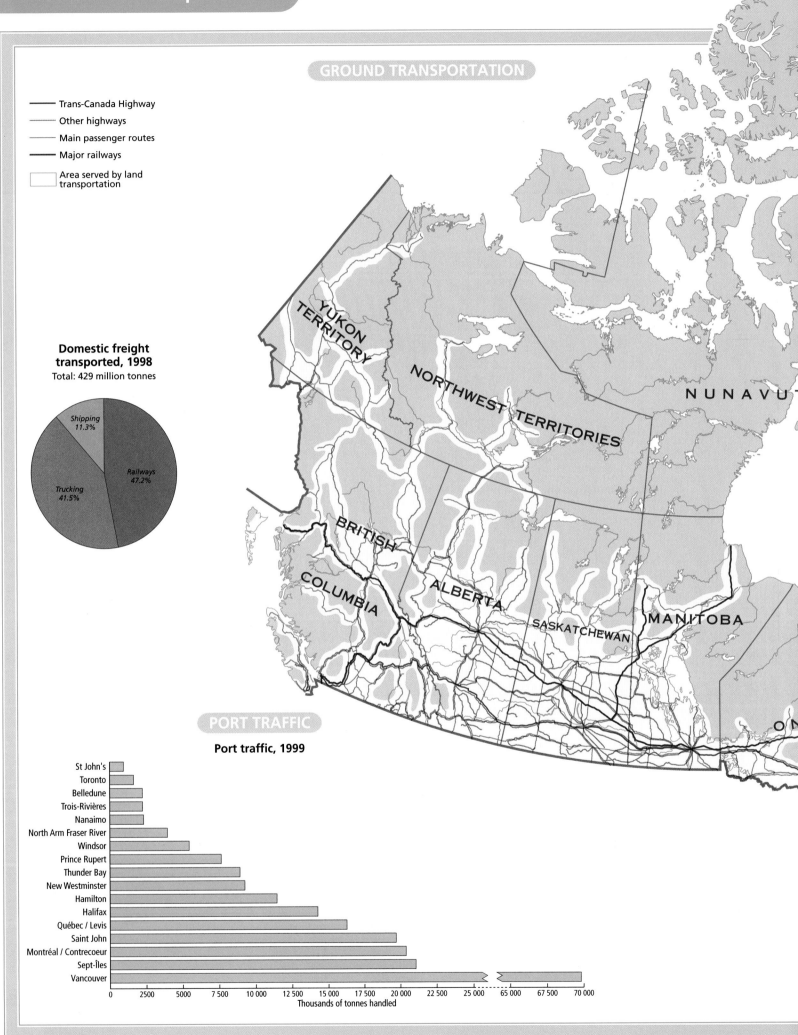

GROUND TRANSPORTATION

- Trans-Canada Highway
- Other highways
- Main passenger routes
- Major railways
- Area served by land transportation

Domestic freight transported, 1998
Total: 429 million tonnes

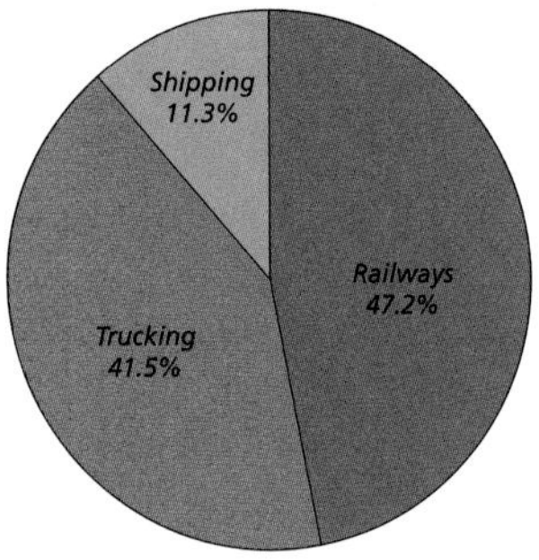

PORT TRAFFIC

Port traffic, 1999

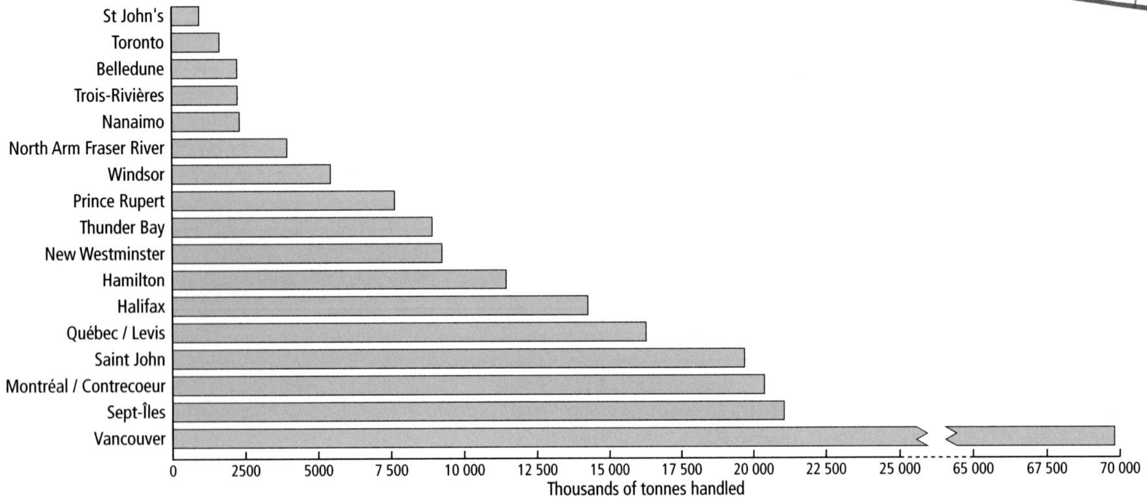

AIR TRAVEL

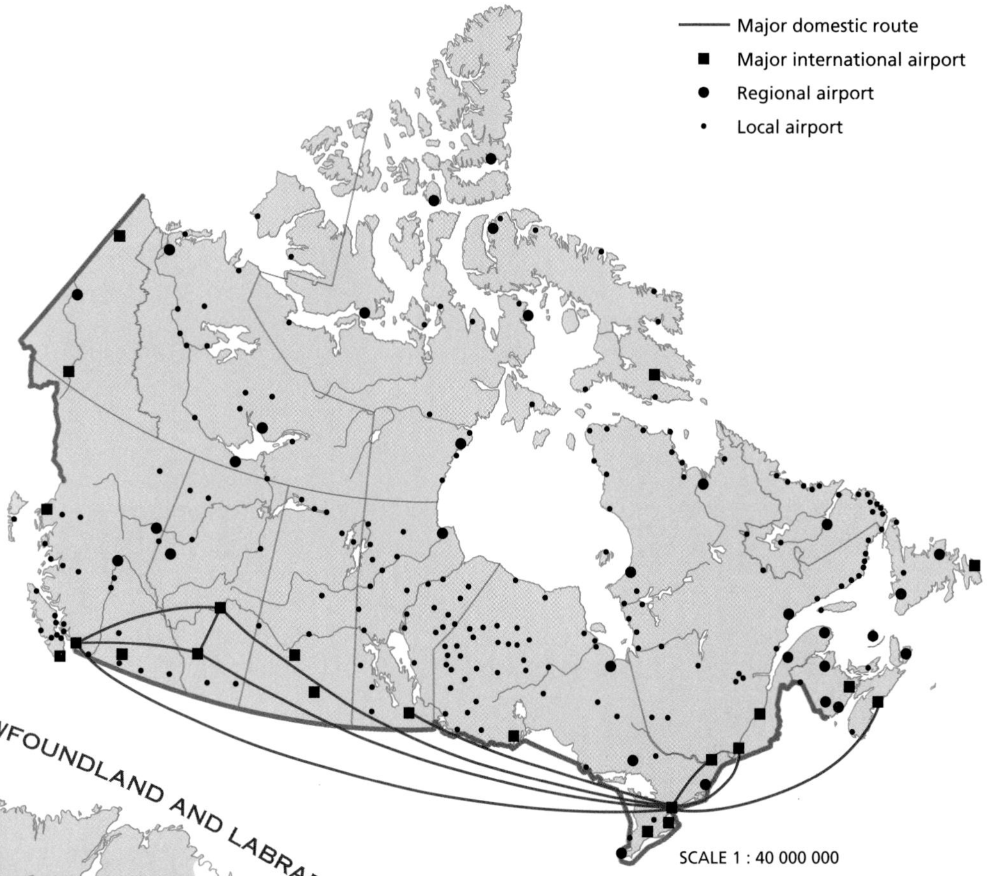

SCALE 1 : 40 000 000

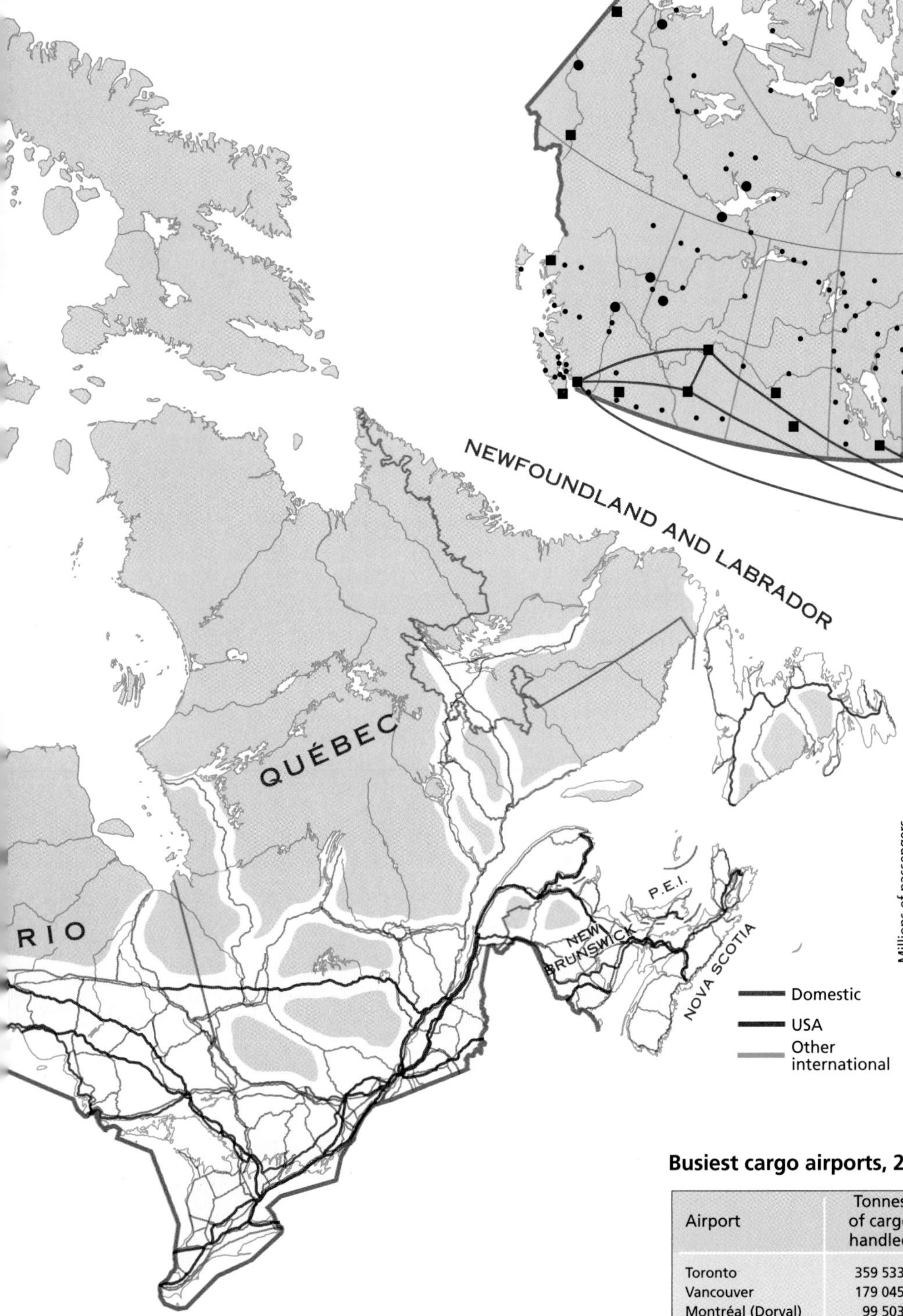

SCALE 1 : 18 000 000

Trends in air travel

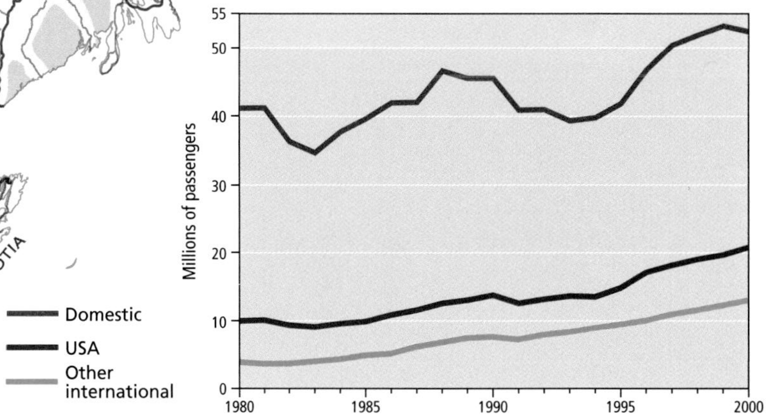

Busiest cargo airports, 2000

Airport	Tonnes of cargo handled
Toronto	359 533
Vancouver	179 045
Montréal (Dorval)	99 503
Calgary	57 576
Montréal (Mirabel)	41 048
Halifax	16 457
Winnipeg	11 016
Edmonton Inter'l	9 960
Ottawa	7 298

Busiest passenger airports, 2000

Airport	Number of passengers	Number of flights
Toronto	27 027 000	422 995
Vancouver	15 162 000	337 495
Montréal (Dorval)	8 301 000	209 732
Calgary	8 143 000	231 913
Edmonton Inter'l	3 867 000	97 737
Ottawa	3 304 000	138 001
Winnipeg	2 751 000	137 036
Halifax	2 695 000	92 015
Montréal (Mirabel)	1 270 000	39 913

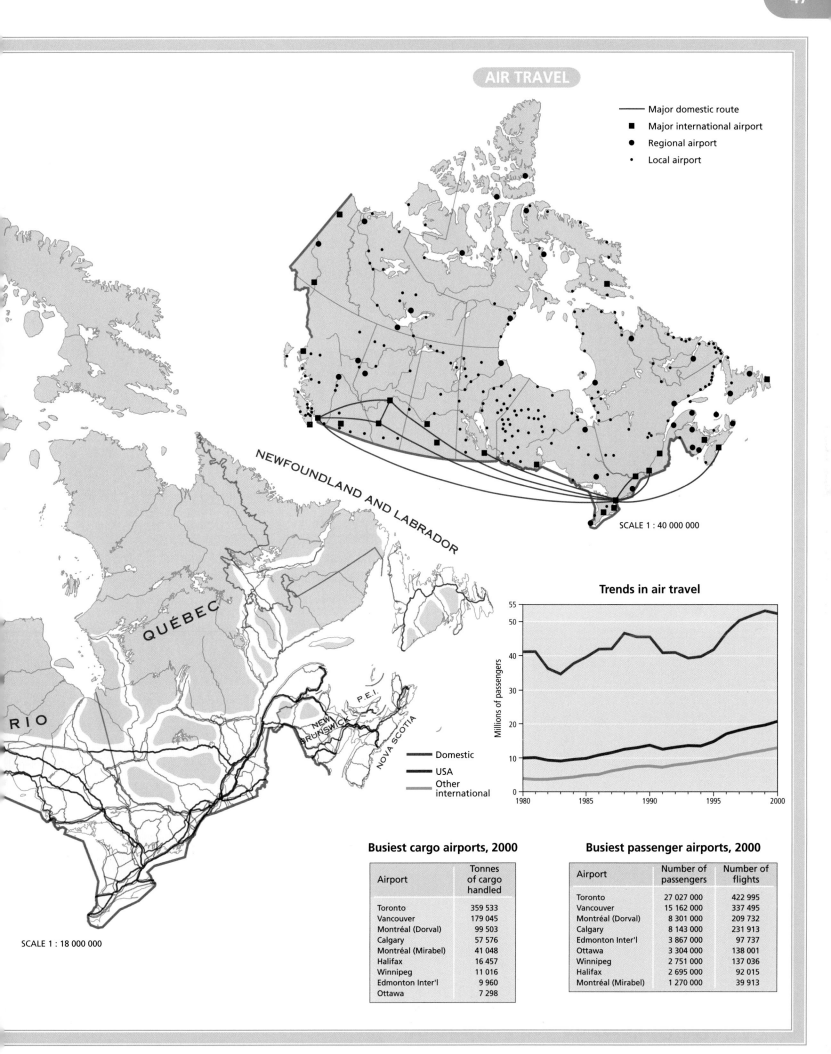

INTERNATIONAL DESTINATIONS

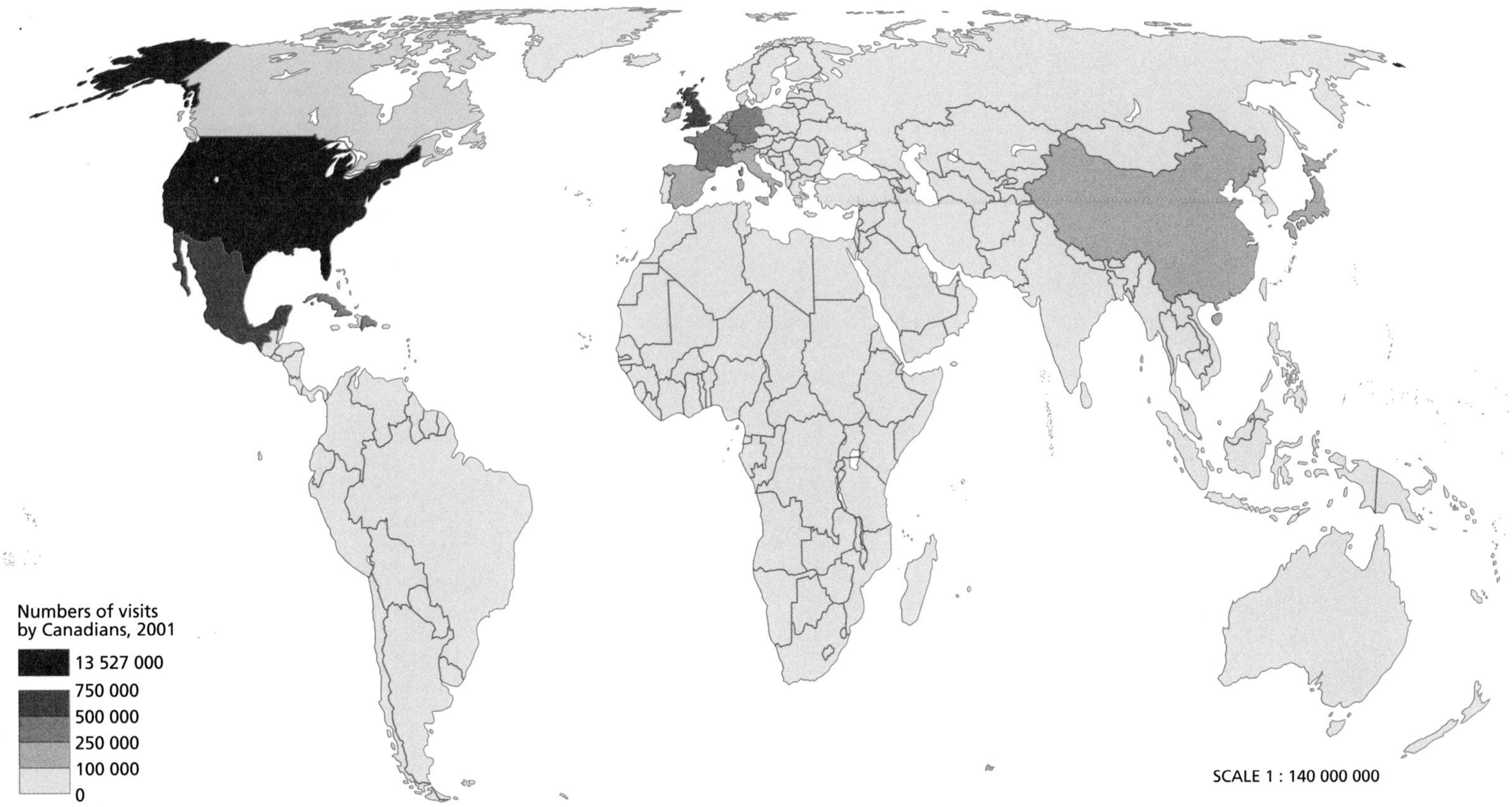

TRENDS IN TRAVEL

Overnight Person Trips by Canadians

Year	Foreign	Domestic	Total
2001	19 697 000	73 859 000	93 556 000
2000	19 663 000	83 438 000	103 101 000
1999	19 367 000	85 862 000	105 229 000
1998	18 828 000	83 961 000	102 789 000
1997	17 636 000	65 727 000	83 363 000
1996	17 285 000	80 885 000	98 170 000
1995	16 932 000	-	-
1994	15 972 000	76 599 000	92 571 000
1993	15 105 000	-	-
1992	14 741 000	84 043 000	98 784 000
1991	14 912 000	-	-
1990	15 210 000	78 326 000	93 536 000
1989	15 111 000	-	-
1988	15 485 000	79 460 000	94 945 000

International Tourist Arrivals in Canada

Year	United States of America	Overseas tourists					Total overseas	Total arrivals
		UK	Japan	France	Germany	Other countries		
2001	15 590 000	826 000	410 000	356 000	337 000	2 105 000	4 034 000	19 624 000
2000	15 225 000	866 000	500 000	404 000	385 000	2 238 000	4 393 000	19 618 000
1999	15 180 000	780 000	516 000	414 000	393 000	2 084 000	4 187 000	19 367 000
1998	14 893 000	747 000	484 000	402 000	379 000	1 923 000	3 935 000	18 828 000
1997	13 401 000	734 000	566 000	439 000	398 000	2 097 000	4 234 000	17 636 000
1996	12 909 000	691 000	648 000	460 000	447 000	2 131 000	4 377 000	17 285 000
1995	13 005 000	641 000	589 000	430 000	421 000	1 846 000	3 927 000	16 932 000
1994	12 542 000	577 000	481 000	410 000	367 000	1 594 000	3 429 000	15 972 000
1993	12 024 000	562 000	408 000	361 000	339 000	1 411 000	3 081 000	15 105 000
1992	11 819 000	536 000	392 000	310 000	290 000	1 394 000	2 922 000	14 741 000
1991	12 003 000	530 000	393 000	307 000	273 000	1 406 000	2 909 000	14 912 000
1990	12 252 000	553 000	411 000	259 000	253 000	1 482 000	2 958 000	15 210 000
1989	12 184 000	561 000	387 000	243 000	263 000	1 473 000	2 927 000	15 111 000
1988	12 763 000	527 000	324 000	230 000	263 000	1 378 000	2 722 000	15 485 000

INTERNATIONAL VISITORS

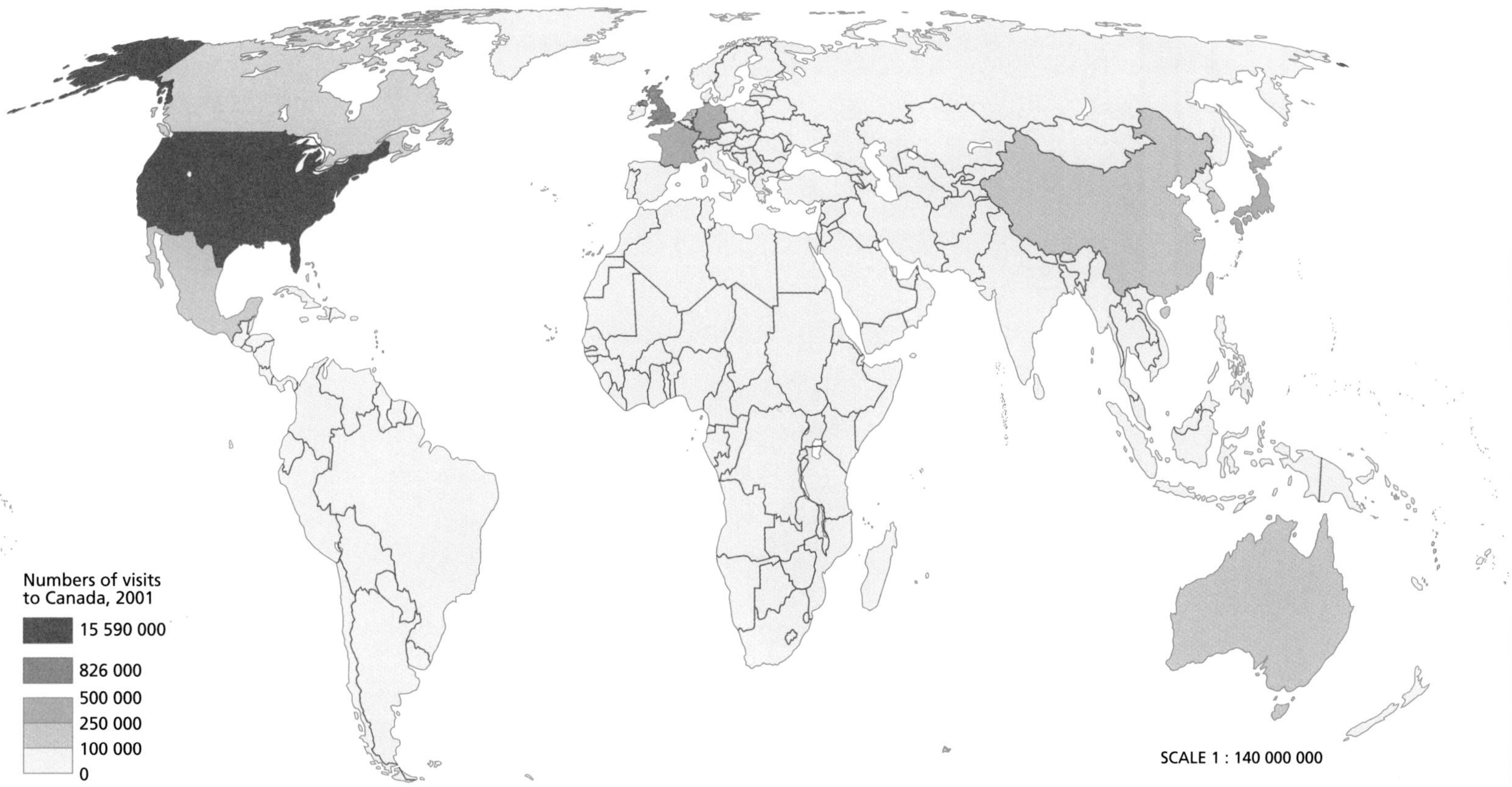

TOP INTERNATIONAL DESTINATIONS AND EARNERS

World's Top 15 Tourism Destinations, 2001

Rank 2001	Country	International tourist arrivals (thousands)		Percent change 2001/2000	Market share (percent) 2001
		2000	2001		
1	France	75 600	76 600	1.2	11.0
2	Spain	49 700	49 500	3.4	7.1
3	USA	50 900	45 500	-10.7	6.6
4	Italy	41 200	39 100	-5.2	5.6
5	China	31 200	33 200	6.2	4.8
6	United Kingdom	25 200	22 800	-9.4	3.3
7	Russian Federation	21 200	-	-	-
8	Mexico	20 600	19 800	-4.0	2.9
9	**Canada**	**19 700**	**19 700**	**0.2**	**2.8**
10	Austria	18 000	18 200	1.1	2.6
11	Germany	19 000	17 900	-5.9	2.6
12	Hungary	15 600	15 300	-1.5	2.2
13	Poland	17 400	15 000	-13.8	2.2
14	Hong Kong (China)	13 100	13 700	5.1	2.0
15	Greece	13 100	-	-	-

World's Top 15 Tourism Earners, 2001

Rank 2001	Country	International tourist receipts (US$ millions)		Percent change 2001/2000	Market share (percent) 2001
		2000	2001		
1	USA	82 000	72 300	-11.9	15.6
2	Spain	31 500	32 900	4.5	7.1
3	France	30 800	30 000	-2.5	6.5
4	Italy	27 500	25 800	-6.2	5.6
5	China	16 200	17 800	9.7	3.8
6	Germany	18 500	17 200	-6.8	3.7
7	United Kingdom	19 500	16 300	-16.7	3.5
8	**Canada**	**10 700**	**10 800**	**0.7**	**2.3**
9	Austria	9 900	10 100	1.9	2.2
10	Greece	9 200	-	-	-
11	Turkey	7 600	8 900	17.0	1.9
12	Mexico	8 300	8 400	1.3	1.8
13	Hong Kong (China)	7 900	8 200	4.5	1.8
14	Australia	8 500	7 600	-9.8	1.6
15	Switzerland	7 500	7 600	1.6	1.6

DOMESTIC TRAVEL

		2001	2000	Percent change
Intraprovincial	Same day	67 266 000	75 148 000	-10.5
	Overnight	58 284 000	66 441 000	-12.3
Interprovincial	Same day	3 078 000	3 520 000	-12.6
	Overnight	15 575 000	16 997 000	-8.4
Total	Same day	70 344 000	78 668 000	-10.6
	Overnight	73 859 000	83 438 000	-11.5
Grand total		144 203 000	162 106 000	-11.0

EXPORTS FROM CANADA

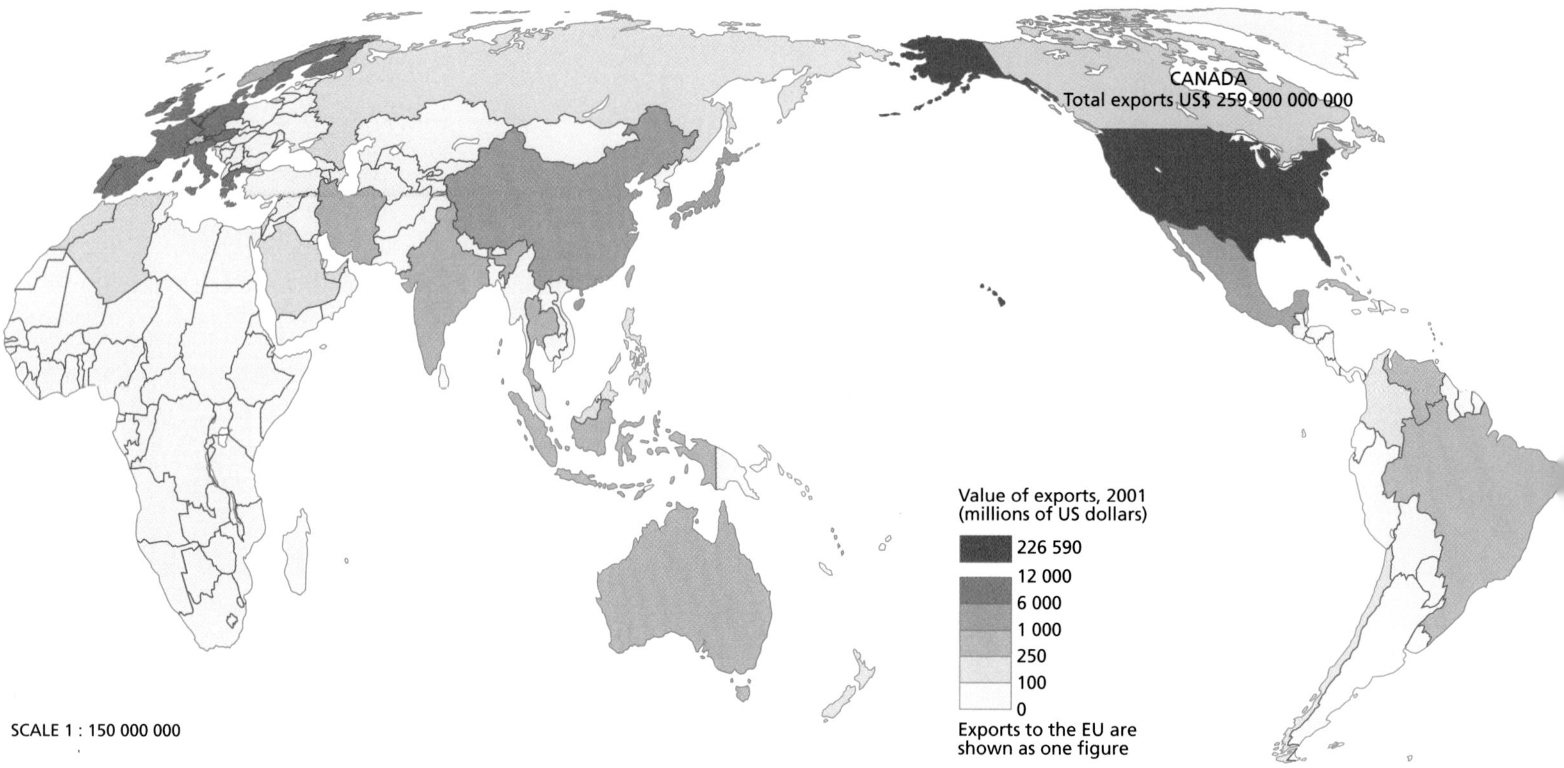

Highest Trade Partners (Exports), 2001

Country	Millions of US dollars
USA	226 590
European Union	11 800
Japan	5 280
China	3 370
Mexico	1 750
South Korea	1 280
Australia	690
Taiwan	640
Norway	640
Brazil	590

Types of Exports, Main Trading Partners, 2001

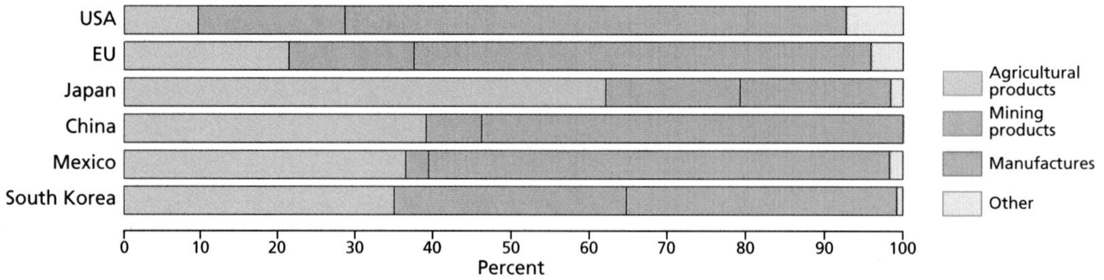

WORLD EXPORTS

Exports by Type, Selected Countries (% of Total Share), 2001

Country	Food, beverages and tobacco		Crude materials		Fuels		Animal and vegetable oils		Chemicals		Manufactured goods		Machinery and transport		Miscellaneous manufactured goods		Other	
	1990	2001	1990	2001	1990	2001	1990	2001	1990	2001	1990	2001	1990	2001	1990	2001	1990	2001
Australia	20.1	20.0	27.0	20.1	19.3	21.5	0.3	0.3	2.6	4.6	12.6	11.7	8.3	11.7	2.6	3.8	7.2	6.3
Canada	7.8	6.8	13.8	7.4	10.0	14.1	0.1	0.2	5.3	5.8	16.0	14.4	37.2	38.2	3.7	6.5	6.1	6.6
China [1]	6.5	3.7	2.5	1.4	2.8	1.9	0.1	0.1	5.4	4.9	17.8	15.4	22.4	37.4	41.8	34.8	0.7	0.4
Egypt [2]	7.9	9.5	8.8	6.7	39.2	40.5	0.1	0.3	4.6	7.7	30.1	18.4	0.5	1.3	8.8	8.5	0.0	7.1
France	15.0	10.5	3.4	1.8	2.3	2.5	0.2	0.2	13.5	15.9	17.3	13.9	37.3	45.0	10.6	10.1	0.4	0.1
Italy	5.9	5.9	1.1	1.0	2.3	1.9	0.4	0.4	6.6	9.7	21.8	20.5	37.5	37.7	23.2	21.2	1.2	1.7
Japan	0.6	0.7	0.7	0.8	0.4	0.4	0.1	0.1	5.5	7.6	11.9	10.2	70.7	67.2	8.5	8.8	1.6	4.2
Mexico [3]	11.4	4.9	4.2	1.1	37.4	9.7	0.1	0.1	6.7	3.2	11.3	8.3	25.1	59.0	3.4	13.6	0.4	0.1
Norway	8.0	6.1	3.5	1.3	39.8	61.6	0.2	0.1	7.3	2.8	21.2	9.6	16.3	11.2	3.6	2.7	0.1	4.6
Saudi Arabia [4]	0.6	0.5	0.2	0.2	91.7	88.8	0.1	0.1	5.0	7.1	1.2	1.6	0.9	1.3	0.3	0.3	0.0	0.1
UK	7.0	4.8	2.2	1.2	5.2	7.8	0.1	0.1	13.1	14.1	15.8	12.9	41.9	47.4	13.9	11.4	0.8	0.3
USA	9.5	6.4	6.9	3.8	3.1	1.8	0.3	0.2	10.1	11.3	8.6	9.1	46.5	51.3	11.0	12.1	4.0	4.0

1 China - 1992 data   2 Egypt - 1994 data   3 Mexico - 2000 data   4 Saudi Arabia - 1991 data

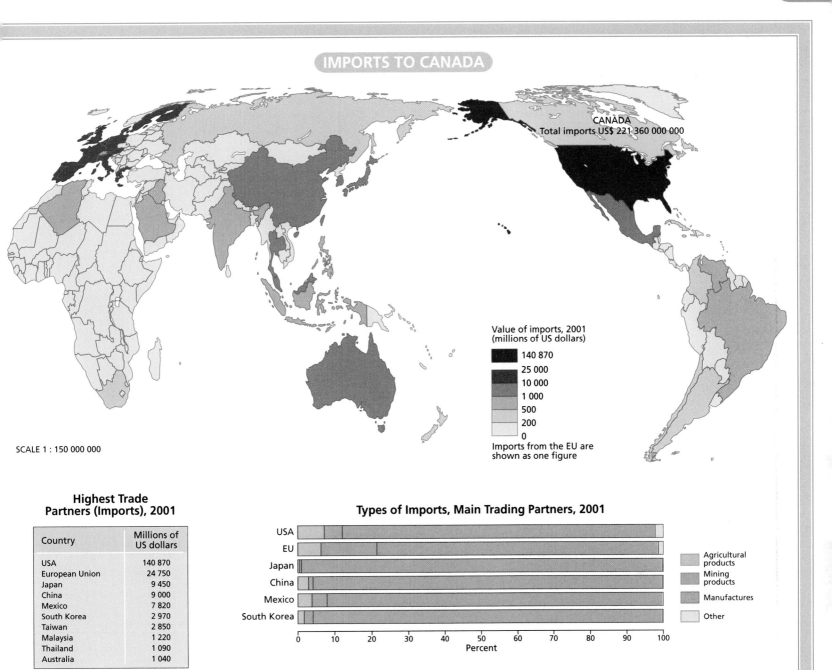

IMPORTS TO CANADA

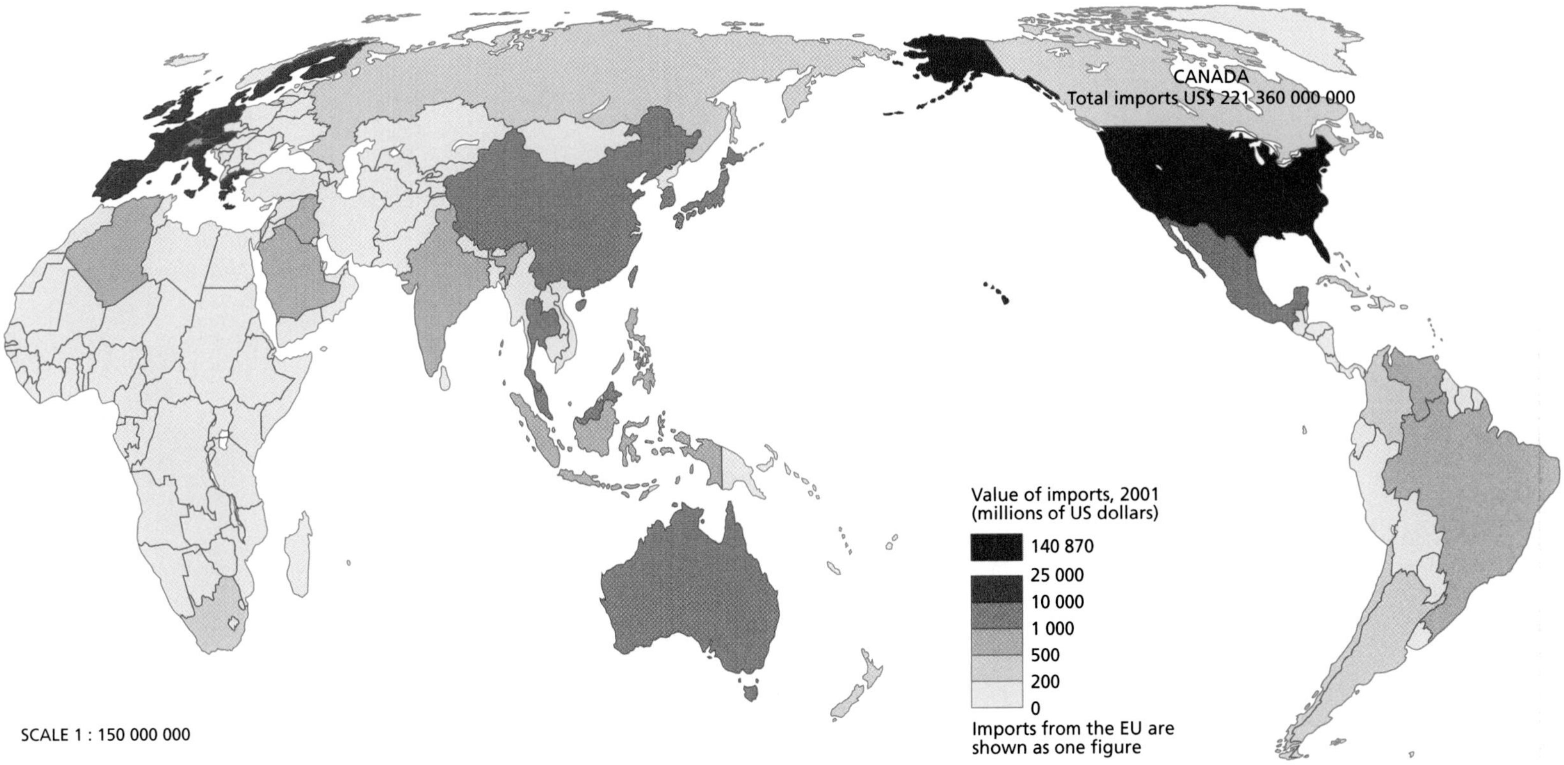

SCALE 1 : 150 000 000

Highest Trade Partners (Imports), 2001

Country	Millions of US dollars
USA	140 870
European Union	24 750
Japan	9 450
China	9 000
Mexico	7 820
South Korea	2 970
Taiwan	2 850
Malaysia	1 220
Thailand	1 090
Australia	1 040

Types of Imports, Main Trading Partners, 2001

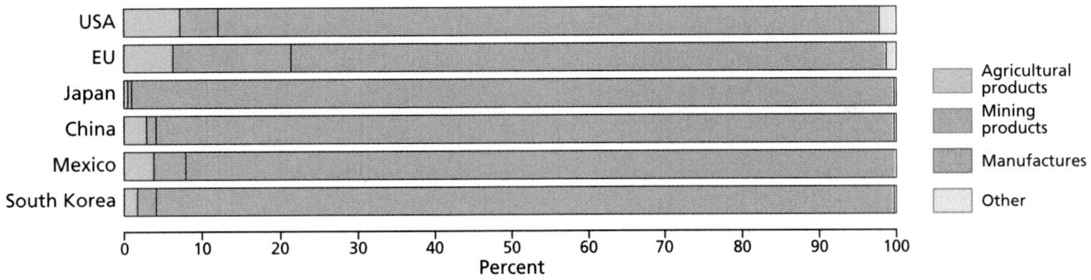

WORLD IMPORTS

Imports by Type, Selected Countries (% of Total Share), 2001

Country	Food, beverages and tobacco		Crude materials		Fuels		Animal and vegetable oils		Chemicals		Manufactured goods		Machinery and transport		Miscellaneous manufactured goods		Other	
	1990	2001	1990	2001	1990	2001	1990	2001	1990	2001	1990	2001	1990	2001	1990	2001	1990	2001
Australia	4.7	4.6	2.8	1.5	5.7	8.5	0.3	0.2	10.3	12.4	15.4	11.9	45.1	44.5	13.9	14.5	1.8	1.9
Canada	5.9	5.4	3.4	2.8	6.3	5.6	0.1	0.1	6.6	9.3	12.6	12.6	50.2	49.7	12.0	12.1	2.9	2.4
China [1]	5.5	3.1	4.0	5.6	2.9	4.8	0.3	0.3	9.6	9.8	22.2	16.7	33.9	43.8	19.2	15.3	2.4	0.6
Egypt [2]	25.1	23.8	7.5	7.6	1.4	5.0	2.0	1.4	12.2	12.1	18.9	16.4	29.1	22.0	3.8	4.5	0.0	7.2
France	9.3	7.8	4.0	2.6	9.6	9.5	0.3	0.3	10.7	12.7	17.7	14.3	34.1	38.6	14.0	14.1	0.3	0.1
Italy	11.1	8.0	7.7	5.3	10.5	9.2	0.7	0.5	11.1	12.3	16.4	15.2	30.1	33.2	7.9	10.5	4.5	5.8
Japan	13.5	12.4	12.7	6.5	24.2	20.1	0.1	0.2	6.5	7.2	12.6	8.7	15.4	27.3	12.4	15.9	2.6	1.7
Mexico [3]	12.3	3.8	6.4	2.5	3.8	2.9	1.2	0.3	10.3	8.2	13.1	17.5	33.4	50.3	8.6	11.9	10.9	2.6
Norway	5.4	6.4	7.3	7.0	3.7	4.1	0.2	0.4	8.5	9.3	17.9	14.7	40.9	42.1	16.0	15.2	0.1	0.8
Saudi Arabia [4]	12.3	14.7	1.8	2.0	0.3	0.2	0.4	0.5	8.6	9.8	19.6	16.6	40.4	42.0	11.4	11.3	5.2	2.9
UK	9.9	7.5	4.6	2.7	4.7	4.3	0.3	0.2	8.8	9.9	17.8	14.9	38.3	45.0	15.0	15.1	0.6	0.4
USA	5.6	4.3	3.1	1.9	13.3	10.9	0.2	0.1	4.5	6.9	12.2	11.0	41.4	43.1	16.5	17.5	3.2	4.3

1 China - 1992 data   2 Egypt - 1994 data   3 Mexico - 2000 data   4 Saudi Arabia - 1991 data

AT RISK

Species at risk

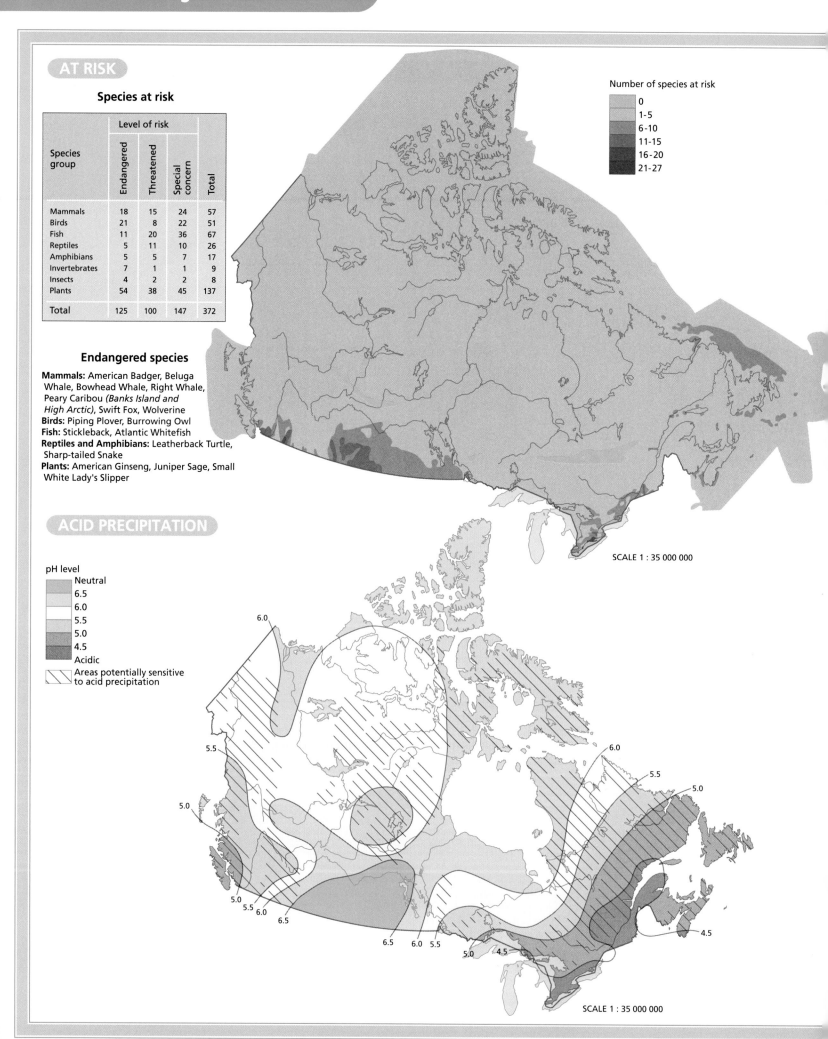

Species group	Level of risk: Endangered	Threatened	Special concern	Total
Mammals	18	15	24	57
Birds	21	8	22	51
Fish	11	20	36	67
Reptiles	5	11	10	26
Amphibians	5	5	7	17
Invertebrates	7	1	1	9
Insects	4	2	2	8
Plants	54	38	45	137
Total	125	100	147	372

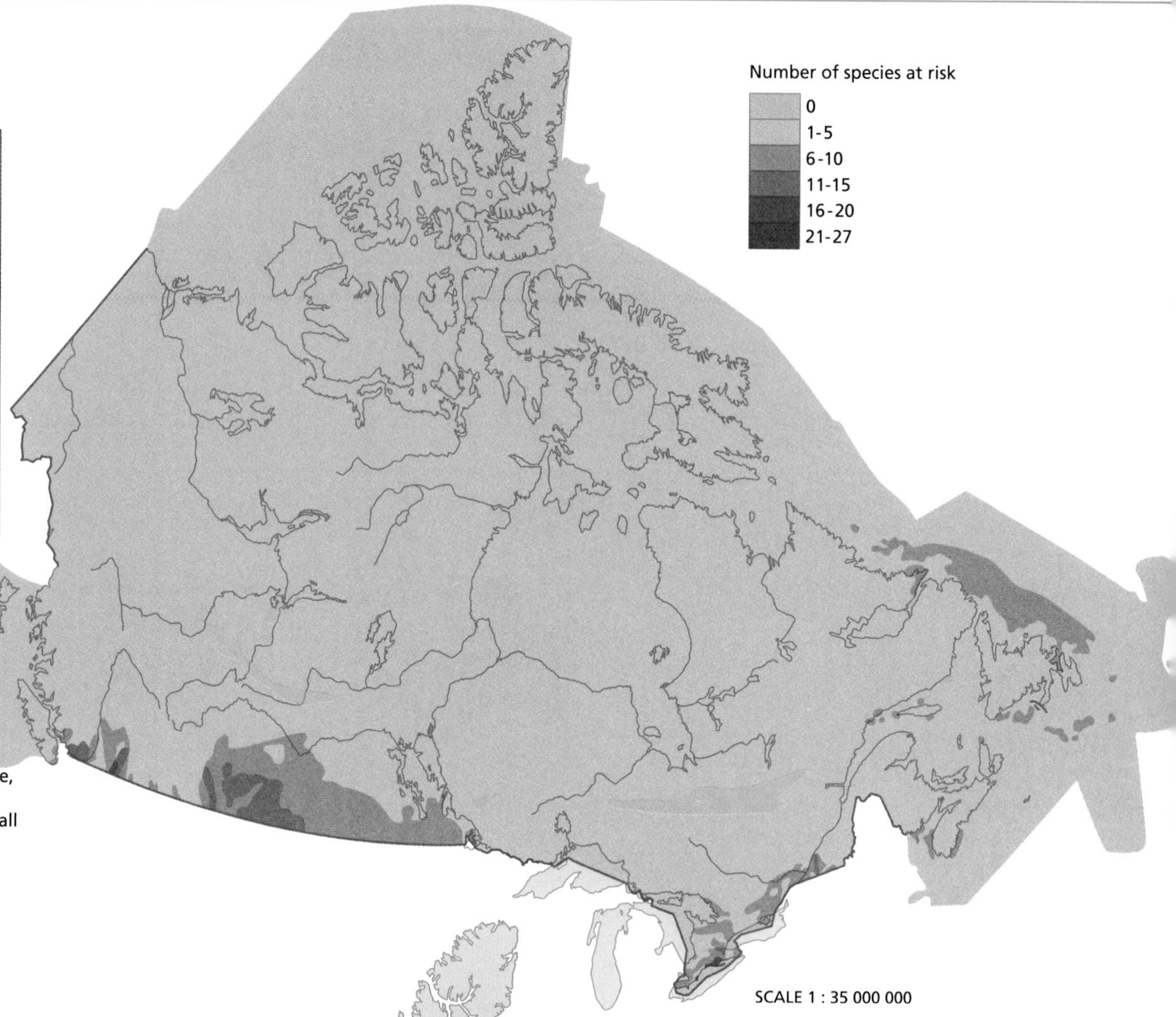

Endangered species

Mammals: American Badger, Beluga Whale, Bowhead Whale, Right Whale, Peary Caribou *(Banks Island and High Arctic)*, Swift Fox, Wolverine
Birds: Piping Plover, Burrowing Owl
Fish: Stickleback, Atlantic Whitefish
Reptiles and Amphibians: Leatherback Turtle, Sharp-tailed Snake
Plants: American Ginseng, Juniper Sage, Small White Lady's Slipper

ACID PRECIPITATION

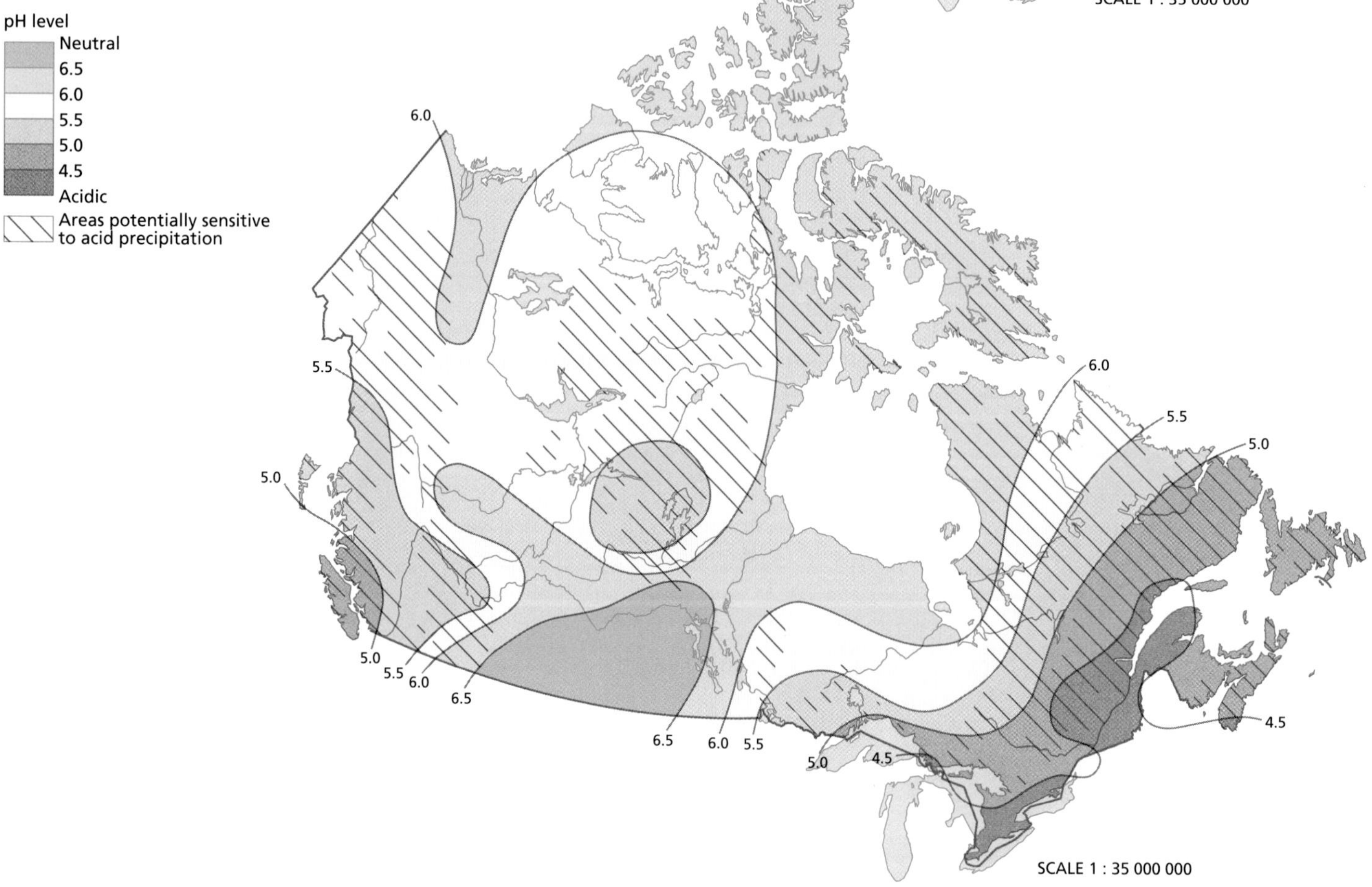

GREENHOUSE GAS EMISSIONS

Canada
(692 Mt)

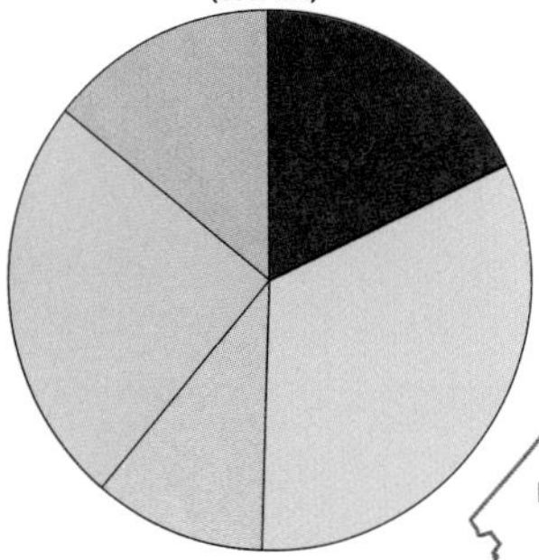

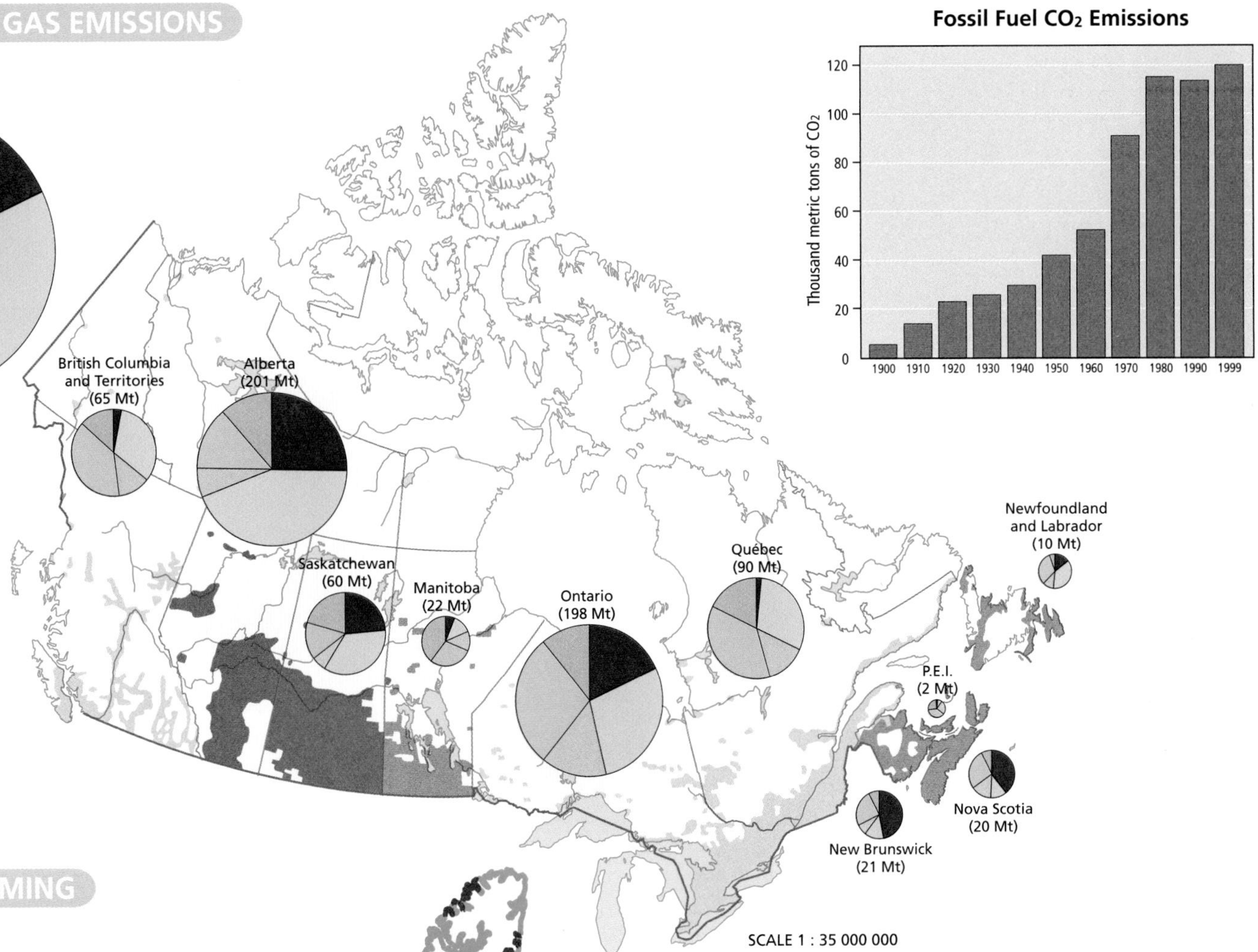

SCALE 1 : 35 000 000

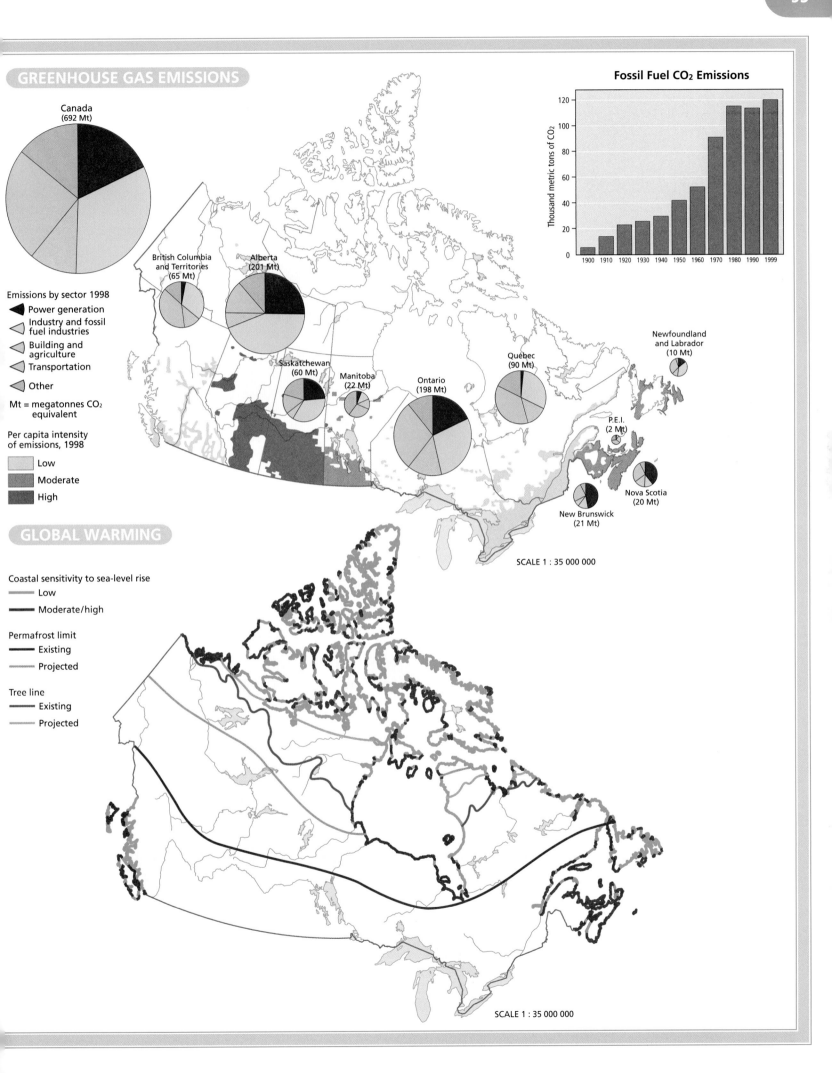

Emissions by sector 1998
- Power generation
- Industry and fossil fuel industries
- Building and agriculture
- Transportation
- Other

Mt = megatonnes CO_2 equivalent

Per capita intensity of emissions, 1998
- Low
- Moderate
- High

GLOBAL WARMING

Coastal sensitivity to sea-level rise
- Low
- Moderate/high

Permafrost limit
- Existing
- Projected

Tree line
- Existing
- Projected

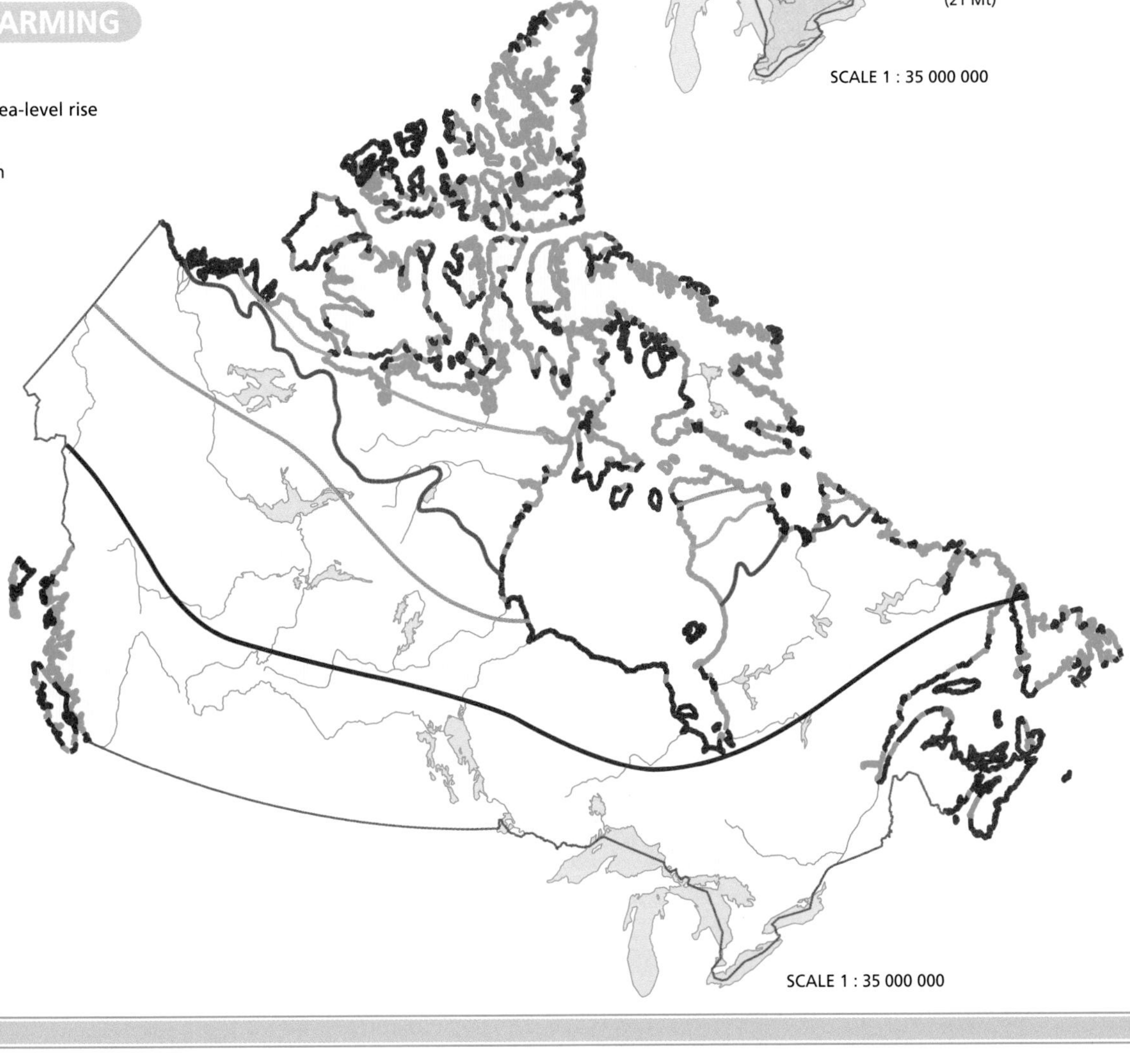

SCALE 1 : 35 000 000

ECOZONES

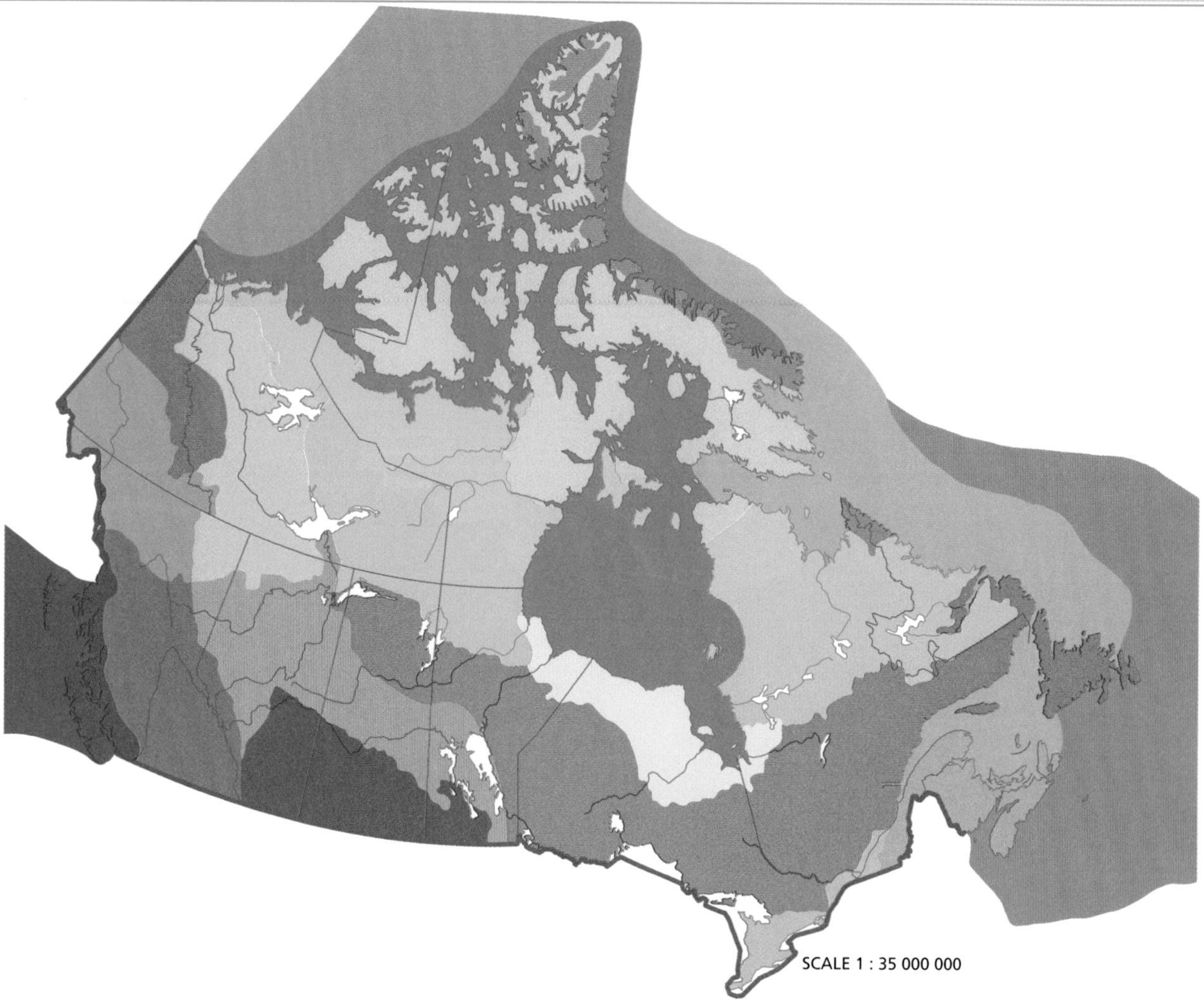

Land ecozones
- Arctic Cordillera
- Northern Arctic
- Southern Arctic
- Taiga Plains
- Taiga Shield
- Boreal Shield
- Atlantic Maritime
- Mixedwood Plains
- Boreal Plains
- Prairies
- Taiga Cordillera
- Boreal Cordillera
- Pacific Maritime
- Montane Cordillera
- Hudson Plains

Marine ecozones
- Arctic Basin
- Pacific
- Atlantic
- Northwest Atlantic
- Arctic Archipelago

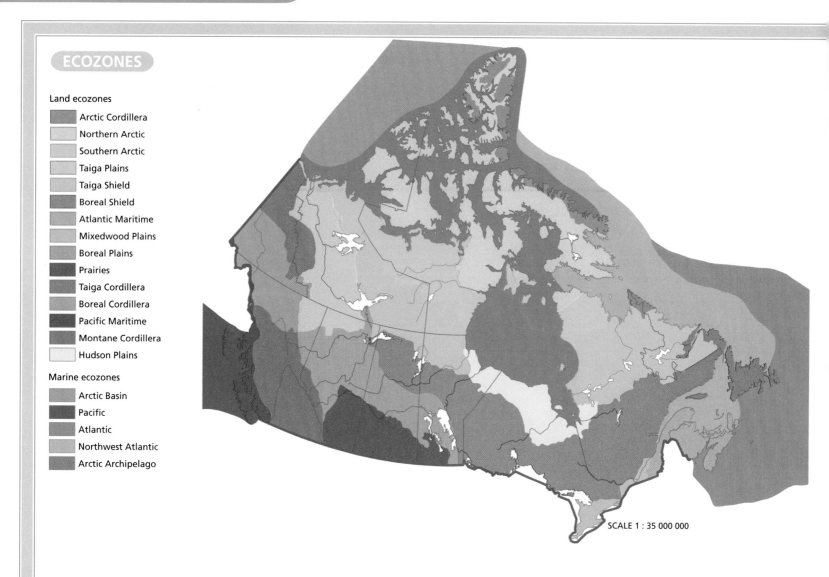

EFFECTS ON THE LAND

Major influences on forest ecosystems

ECOZONE	Fire	Insects, Disease	Harvesting	Change to other use	Transport corridors	Pollution
Boreal Cordillera	✓			✓	✓	
Pacific Maritime		✓	✓	✓	✓	✓
Montane Cordillera	✓	✓	✓	✓	✓	
Boreal Plains	✓		✓	✓	✓	
Taiga Plains	✓				✓	
Taiga Shield	✓					
Boreal Shield	✓	✓	✓	✓		✓
Mixedwood Plains		✓		✓		✓
Atlantic Maritime	✓	✓	✓	✓		✓

Major influences on farmland

	Prairies	Pacific Maritime	Montane Cordillera	Boreal Plains	Boreal Shield	Mixedwood Plains	Atlantic Maritime	
Loss of organic matter	■	■	■	■		■	□	Loss of soil quality
Nutrient content			■	■		□	□	
Acidification	■	■	■	■		□		
Salinization				■				
Erosion	■	■	■	■	□	■	■	
Compaction	■	■		□				
Farm to urban	■	□	□	□		■	□	Change in land use
Wetland to farm			■	■		■	□	
Monoculture	□		□	■		■	□	Farming practices
Fertilizer use	■	■	■	■		■	■	
Pesticide use	■	■	■	■	□	■	□	

■ Primary importance
□ Secondary importance

PROTECTING THE ENVIRONMENT

National Park attendance

National park	Attendance 1990	Attendance * 2001-2002
Banff, Alta.	4 030 000	4 687 378
Jasper, Alta.	1 310 000	1 947 286
Kootenay, B.C.	1 160 000	1 590 596
Yoho, B.C.	680 000	1 371 105
Prince Edward Island, P.E.I.	810 000	927 625
Pacific Rim, B.C.	600 000	644 841
Glacier, B.C.	160 000	} 566 679
Mount Revelstoke, B.C.	160 000	
Saguenay - St Lawrence, Qué.	no data	442 182
Fathom Five, Ont.	no data	435 794
Waterton Lakes, Alta.	350 000	413 515
Riding Mountain, Man.	390 000	411 267
Cape Breton Highlands, N.S.	570 000	366 617
Point Pelee, Ont.	460 000	331 244
Fundy, N.B.	230 000	249 314
Terra Nova, Nfld.	170 000	248 746
Kouchibouguac, N.B.	180 000	242 388
Prince Albert, Sask.	190 000	230 530
Bruce Peninsula, Ont.	3 500	212 457
Elk Island, Alta.	300 000	211 547
La Mauricie, Qué.	280 000	196 786
Forillon, Qué.	210 000	180 320
Gros Morne, Nfld.	98 000	118 071
Georgian Bay Islands, Ont.	49 000	91 331
Kejimkujik, N.S.	170 000	66 472
St Lawrence Islands, Ont.	85 000	65 603
Kluane, Y.T.	69 000	59 517
Archipélago de Mingan, Qué.	25 000	32 269
Pukaskwa, Ont.	15 000	8 488
Nahanni, N.W.T.	1 300	6 918
Grasslands, Sask.	no data	6 773
Gwaii Haanas Reserve, B.C.	no data	2 331
Wood Buffalo, Alta. - N.W.T.	6 600	1 305
Auyuittuq, Nun.	350	413
Quttinirpaaq (Ellesmere Island), Nun.	230	192
Ivvavik, Y.T.	99	165
Aulavik, N.W.T.	no data	88
Wapusk, Man.	no data	no data
Tuktut Nogait, N.W.T.	no data	no data
Sirmilik, Nun.	no data	no data
Yuntut, Y.T.	no data	no data

* Fiscal year

Protected space by ecozone

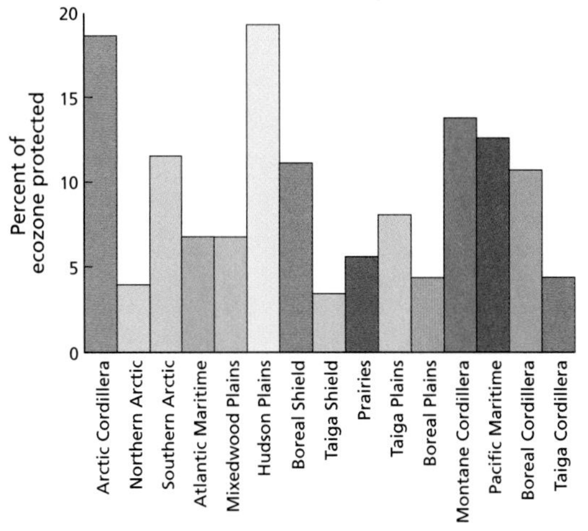

Relief and physical features
Relief metres
5000
3000
2000
1000
500
200
sea level
below sea level
0
200
4000
6000
5959 Mountain height (in metres)
Permanent ice
Water features
River
Lake / Reservoir
Marsh
Communications
Major highway
Other highway
Railway
Ferry route (inset only)
Airport
Administration
Boundaries
International
Internal
National park
Settlement
Urban area
Urban population
Over 1 000 000
500 000 - 1 000 000
100 000 - 500 000
25 000 - 100 000
10 000 - 25 000
under 10 000
Square symbols denote provincial, territorial or state capital cities.
YUKON TERRITORY
BRITISH COLUMBIA
ALASKA
U.S.A.
ROCKY MOUNTAINS
COAST MOUNTAINS
Cassiar Mountains
Skeena Mountains
Omineca Mountains
Cariboo Mountains
Columbia Mountains
Selwyn Mountains
Mackenzie Mountains
Logan Mountains
Pelly Mountains
Anvil Range
St Elias Mountains
Horn Mountains
Babine Range
Dawson Range
Mt Logan 5959
Mount Fairweather 4670
Fox Mountain 2404
Mount Sir James MacBrien 2762
Devil's Paw 2616
Mount Edziza 2787
Kate's Needle 3049
Mount Pattullo 2729
Mount Lloyd George 2972
Sentinel Peak 2515
Mount Robson 3954
Kalone Peak 2557
Mount Waddington 4042
Golden Hinde 2201
Mount Garibaldi 2678
Mount Baker 3285
Glacier Peak 3213
Mt Olympus 2428
Mount Columbia 3747
KLUANE NATIONAL PARK
NAHANNI NATIONAL PARK
GLACIER BAY NATIONAL PARK AND PRESERVE
ADMIRALTY ISLAND NATIONAL MONUMENT - KOOTZNOOWOO WILDERNESS
MISTY FIORDS NATIONAL MONUMENT WILDERNESS
GWAII HAANAS NATIONAL PARK RESERVE
PACIFIC RIM NATIONAL PARK
OLYMPIC NATIONAL PARK
JASPER NATIONAL PARK
GLACIER NATIONAL PARK
Liard Plateau
Stikine Plateau
Fraser Plateau
Alexander Archipelago
Chichagof Island
Admiralty Island
Baranof Island
Kupreanof Island
Prince of Wales Island
Revillagigedo Island
Dall Island
Graham Island
Moresby Island
Queen Charlotte Islands
Banks Island
Pitt Island
Princess Royal Island
Vancouver Island
Nootka Island
Dixon Entrance
Hecate Strait
Queen Charlotte Sound
Queen Charlotte Strait
Strait of Georgia
Juan de Fuca Strait
PACIFIC OCEAN
Cape St James
Cape Scott
Cape Flattery
White Pass
Yellowhead Pass
Whitehorse
Carmacks
Faro
Ross River
Haines Junction
Dawson
Carcross
Watson Lake
Fort Nelson
Fort St John
Dawson Creek
Grande Prairie
Prince George
Prince Rupert
Terrace
Kitimat
Quesnel
Williams Lake
Kamloops
Kelowna
Vernon
Penticton
Vancouver
Victoria
Nanaimo
Abbotsford
Chilliwack
Bellingham
Seattle
Bellevue
Renton
Everett
Juneau
Sitka
Ketchikan
Skagway
Haines
Fort Simpson
Fort Liard
Fort Providence
Hay River
Masset
Port Hardy
Campbell River
Courtenay
Port Alberni
Tofino
Bella Coola
Smithers
Hazelton
Stewart
Dease Lake
Telegraph Creek
Mackenzie
Valemount
McBride
Revelstoke
Whistler
Squamish
Hope
Lillooet
Merritt
Salmon Arm
Port Angeles
Wenatchee
Okanogan
WASHINGTON
Liard
Stikine
Skeena
Nass
Fraser
Peace
Finlay
Williston Lake
Babine Lake
Stuart Lake
Takla Lake
François Lake
Ootsa Lake
Quesnel Lake
Shuswap Lake
Okanagan Lake
Kootenay Lake
Atlin Lake
Teslin Lake
Kluane Lake
Lake Laberge
Great Slave Lake
Mills Lake
Trout Lake
Bistcho Lake
Clear Hills
Caribou Mountains
140°
136°
132°
128°
124°
120°
116°
60°
56°
52°
48°
SCALE 1 : 6 500 000
0
100
200
300
400 km

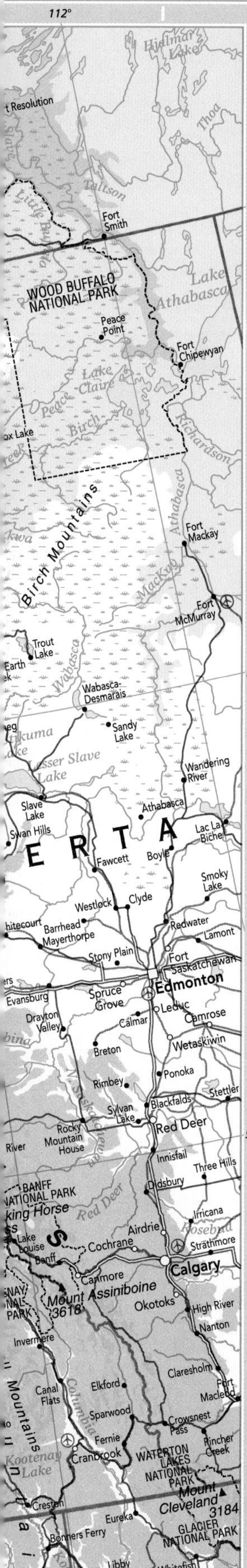

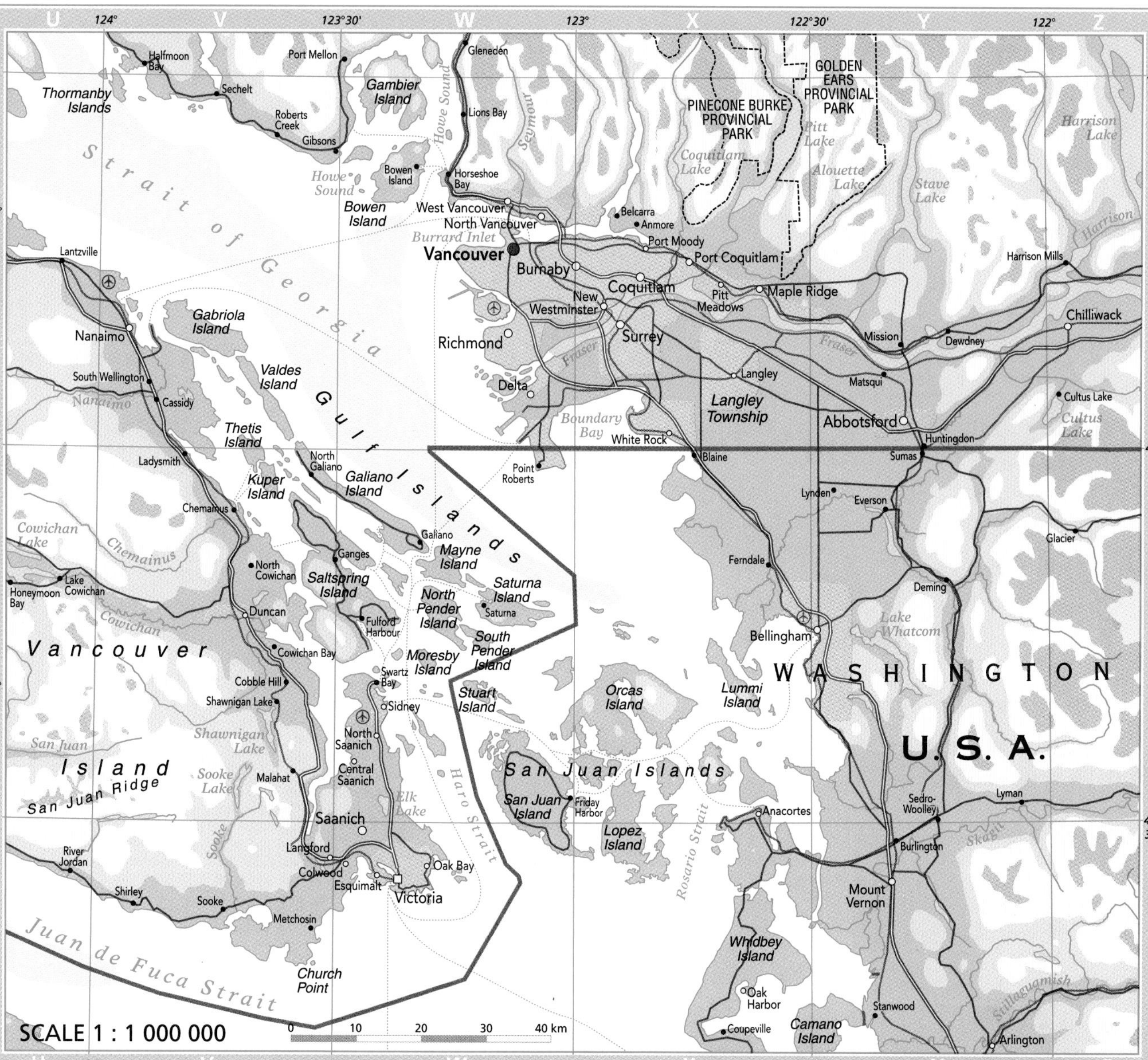

A Landsat image of the Kemano area in western British Columbia, just east of the Queen Charlotte Islands. The Coast Mountains, deep river valleys, fjord coastline, and clear-cut forested blocks are clearly visible.

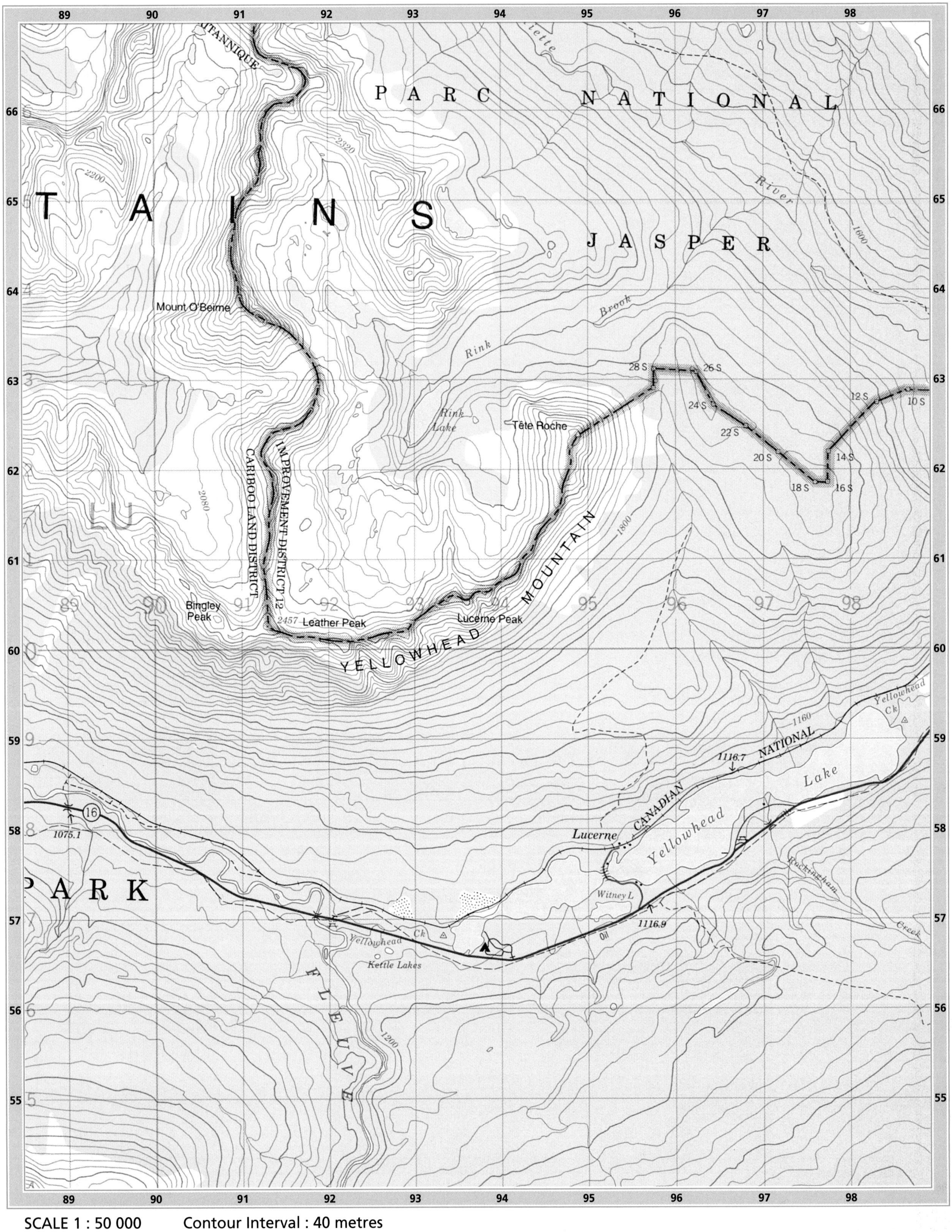
PARC NATIONAL
JASPER
TAINS
LU
PARK
Mount O'Beirne
Bingley Peak
2457 Leather Peak
Lucerne Peak
Tête Roche
Rink Lake
Rink Brook
River
CARIBOO LAND DISTRICT
IMPROVEMENT DISTRICT 12
YELLOWHEAD MOUNTAIN
Lucerne
CANADIAN NATIONAL
Yellowhead Lake
Yellowhead Ck
Witney L
Kettle Lakes
Rockingham Creek
FLEUVE
1075.1
1116.7
1116.9
2320
2200
2080
1800
1600
1160
1200
28 S
26 S
24 S
22 S
20 S
18 S
16 S
14 S
12 S
10 S
16
Oil

SCALE 1 : 50 000 Contour Interval : 40 metres

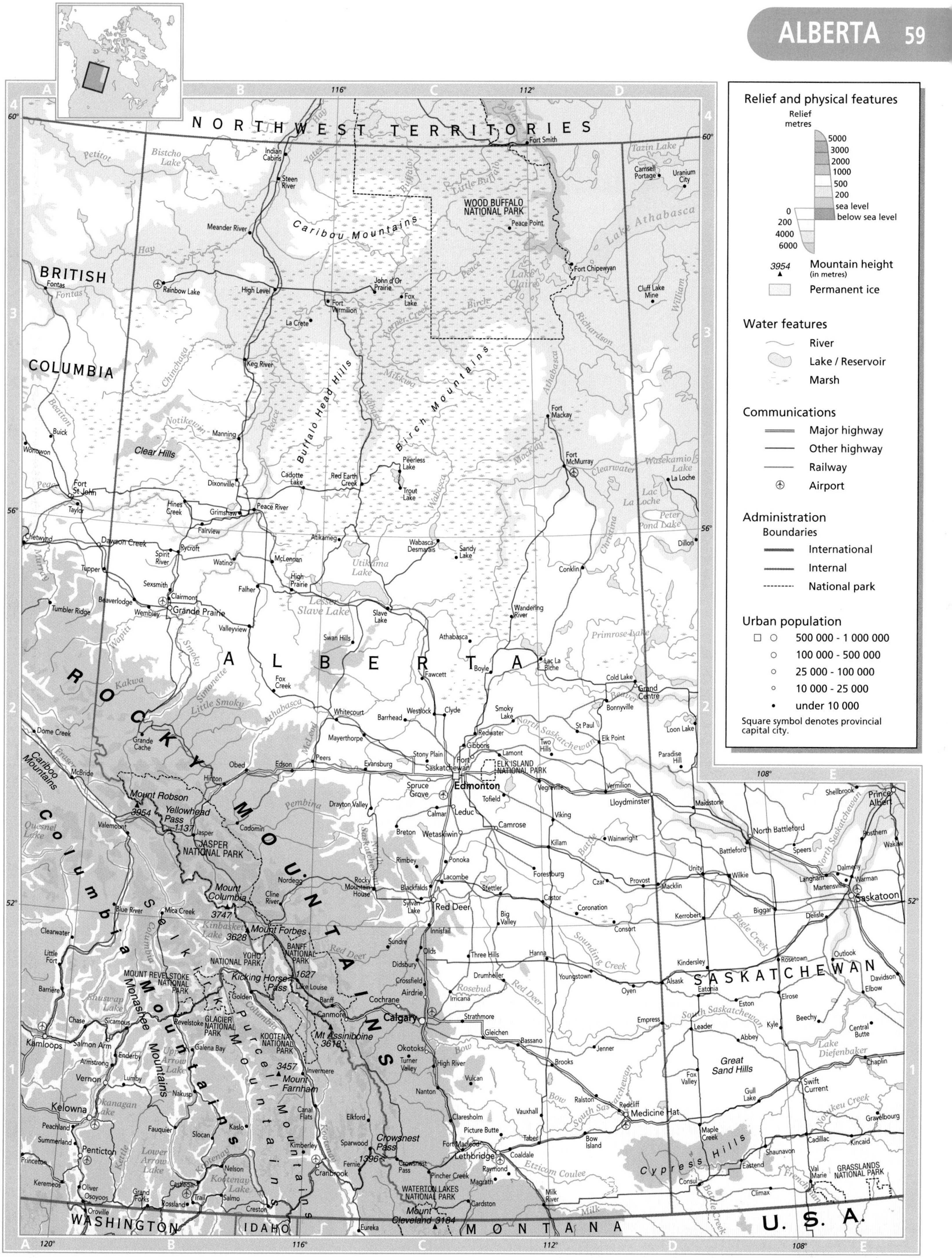

SCALE 1 : 5 000 000

0 50 100 150 200 km

Conic Equidistant projection

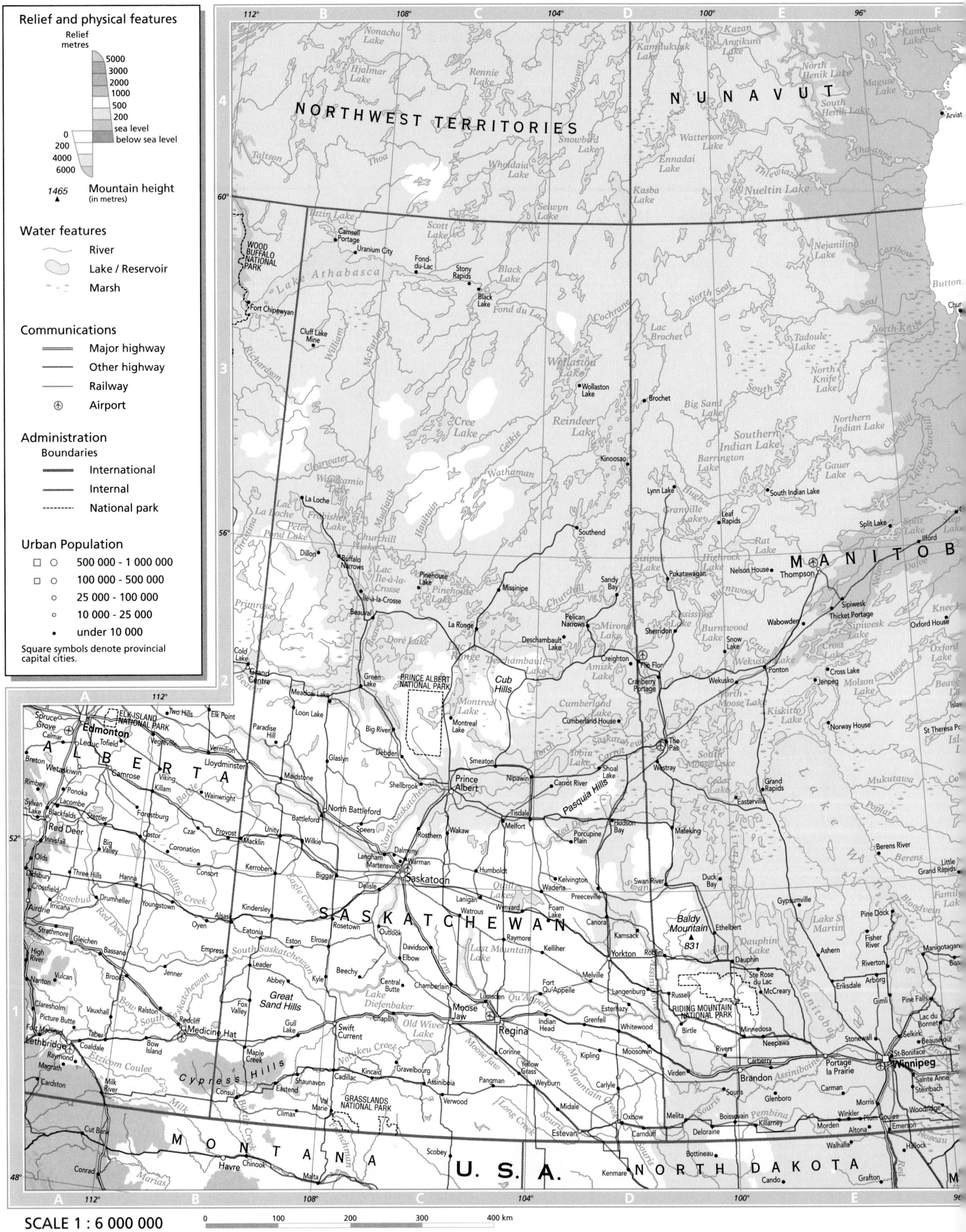
Relief and physical features
Relief metres
5000
3000
2000
1000
500
200
0
sea level
below sea level
200
4000
6000
1465 Mountain height (in metres)
Water features
River
Lake / Reservoir
Marsh
Communications
Major highway
Other highway
Railway
Airport
Administration
Boundaries
International
Internal
National park
Urban Population
500 000 - 1 000 000
100 000 - 500 000
25 000 - 100 000
10 000 - 25 000
under 10 000
Square symbols denote provincial capital cities.
NORTHWEST TERRITORIES
NUNAVUT
MANITOBA
SASKATCHEWAN
ALBERTA
MONTANA
NORTH DAKOTA
U. S. A.
WOOD BUFFALO NATIONAL PARK
PRINCE ALBERT NATIONAL PARK
ELK ISLAND NATIONAL PARK
RIDING MOUNTAIN NATIONAL PARK
GRASSLANDS NATIONAL PARK
Lake Athabasca
Wollaston Lake
Reindeer Lake
Southern Indian Lake
Cree Lake
Nueltin Lake
Lake Winnipeg
Lake Manitoba
Lake Winnipegosis
Cypress Hills
Great Sand Hills
Pasquia Hills
Cub Hills
Baldy Mountain
831
Edmonton
Red Deer
Lethbridge
Medicine Hat
Saskatoon
Regina
Moose Jaw
Prince Albert
North Battleford
Swift Current
Yorkton
Lloydminster
Brandon
Winnipeg
Portage la Prairie
Thompson
Flin Flon
The Pas
Dauphin
Estevan
Uranium City
La Ronge
Churchill
Nelson
Saskatchewan
South Saskatchewan
North Saskatchewan
Assiniboine
Qu'Appelle
Souris
Red
Milk
112°
108°
104°
100°
96°
60°
56°
52°
48°

SCALE 1 : 6 000 000

0 100 200 300 400 km

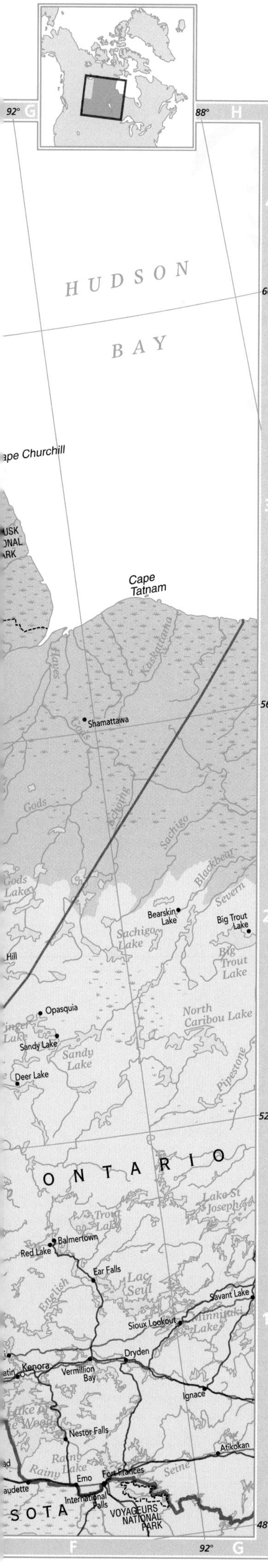

This is a "seasonal image" near Altona, Manitoba, combining data collected by space shuttle Endeavour in April and October. Red represents April data; green represents October data, and blue shows the ratio between the two data sets. This rich farmland is important for wheat, barley, canola, corn, sunflowers, and sugar beets.

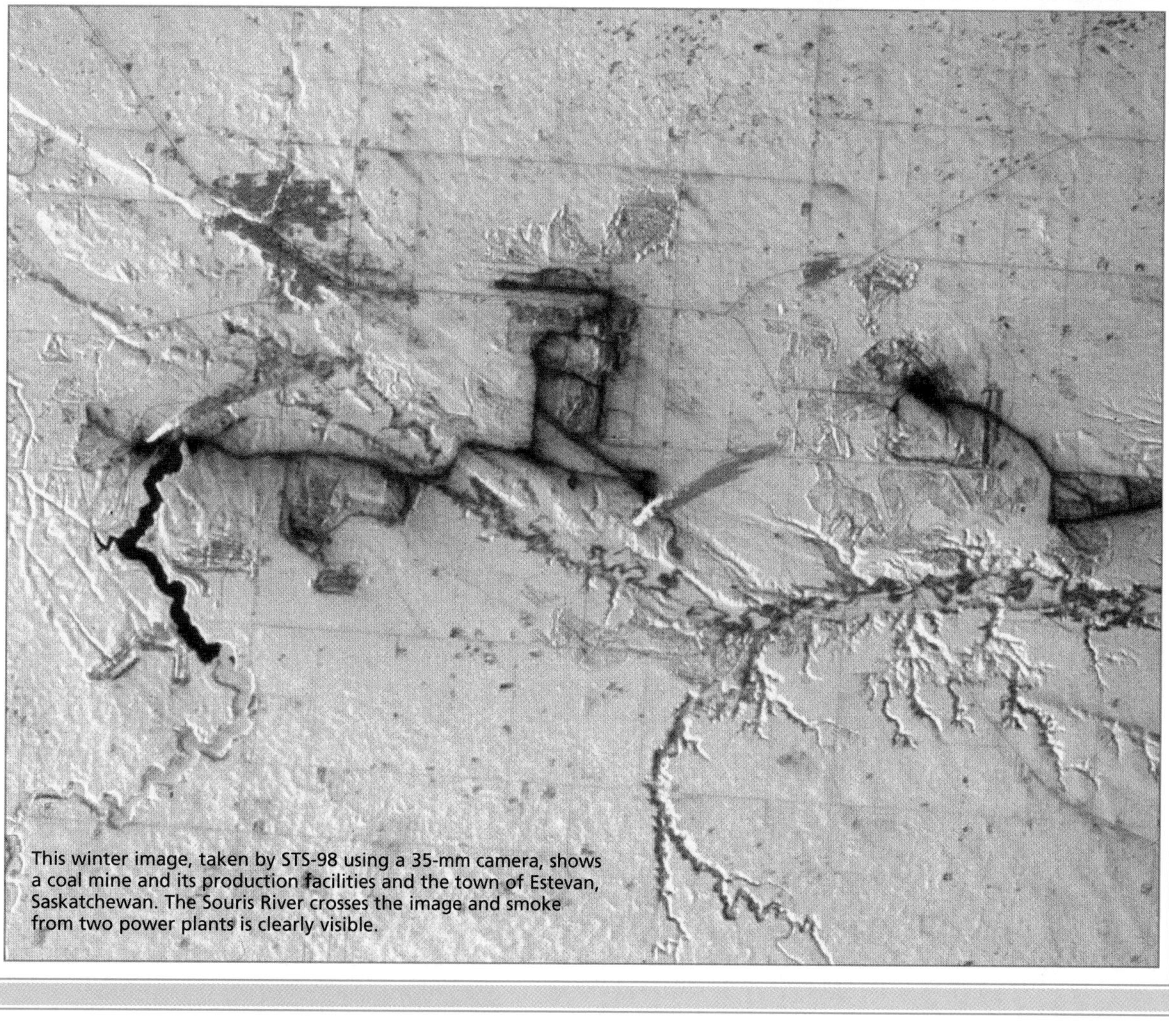

This winter image, taken by STS-98 using a 35-mm camera, shows a coal mine and its production facilities and the town of Estevan, Saskatchewan. The Souris River crosses the image and smoke from two power plants is clearly visible.

Conic Equidistant projection

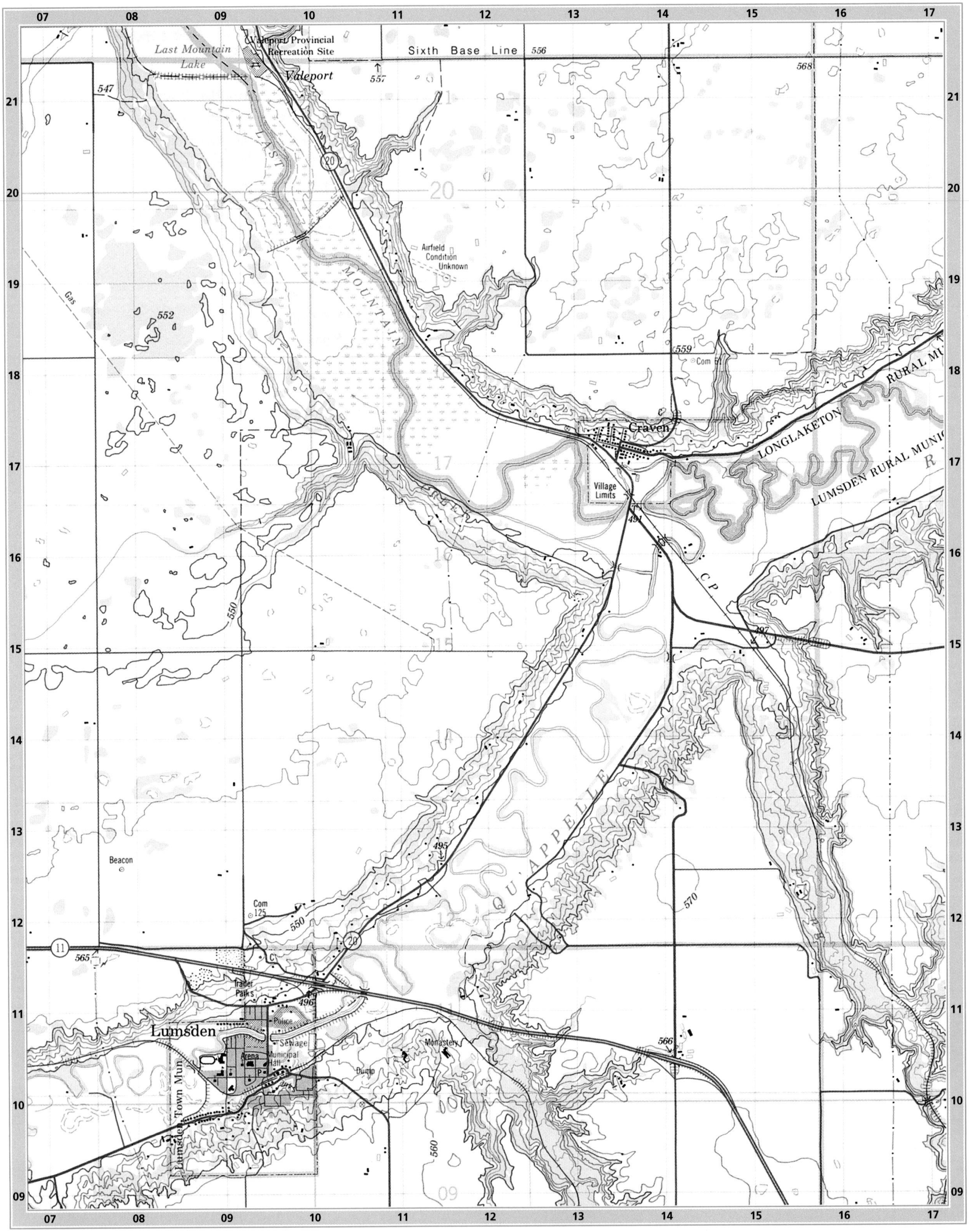
Last Mountain Lake
Valeport Provincial Recreation Site
Valeport
Sixth Base Line
LAST MOUNTAIN
Airfield Condition Unknown
Gas
Craven
Village Limits
LONGLAKETON RURAL MUN
LUMSDEN RURAL MUNIC
CP
QU'APPELLE
Beacon
Com 125
Trailer Parks
Lumsden
Police
Sewage
Arena
Municipal Hall
Monastery
Dump
Lumsden Town Mun

SCALE 1 : 50 000   Contour Interval : 10 metres

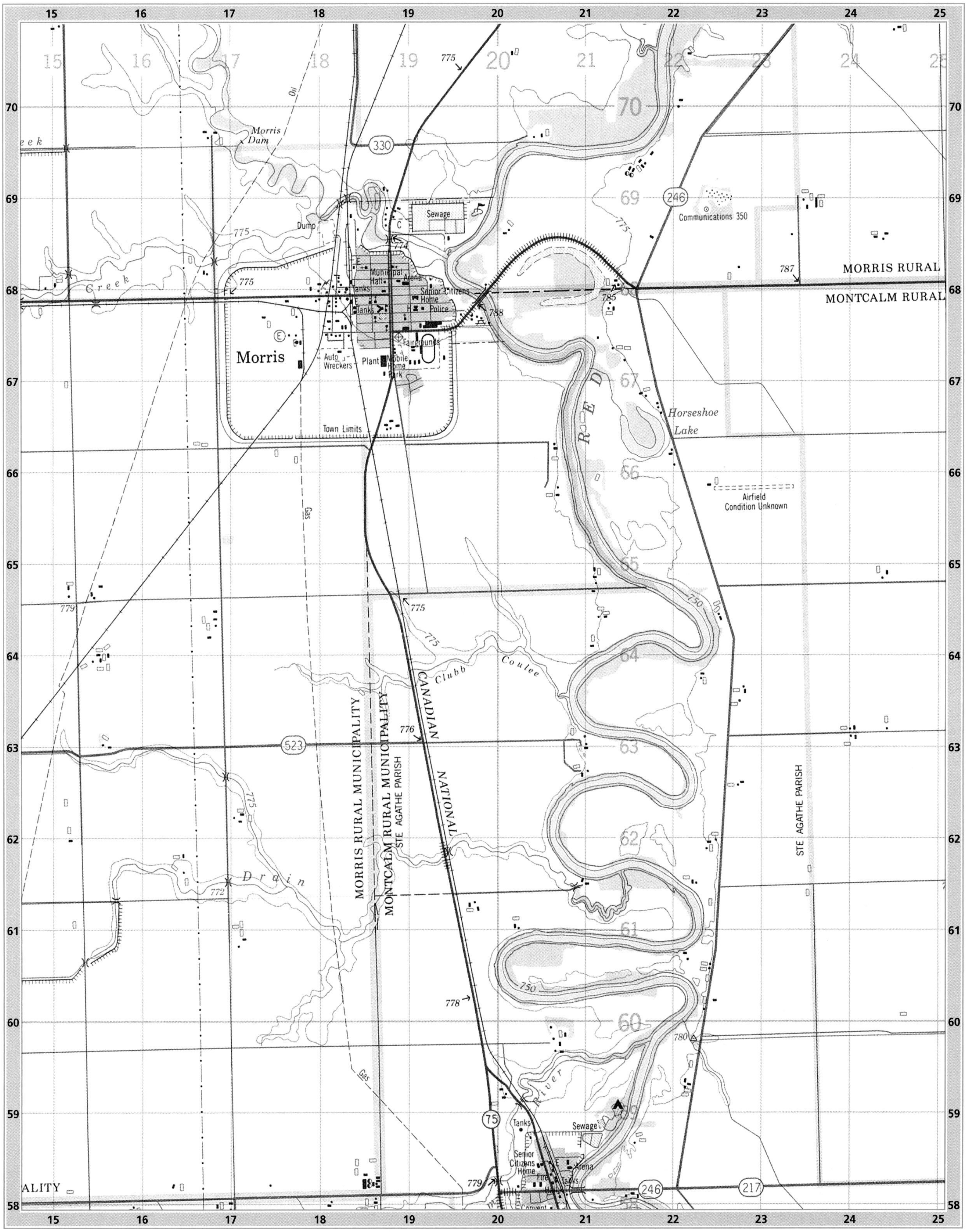
Morris
Morris Dam
Dump
Sewage
Municipal Hall
Arena
Tanks
Senior Citizens Home
Police
Fairgrounds
Auto Wreckers
Plant
Mobile Home Park
Town Limits
Creek
Oil
Gas
330
246
523
75
217
Communications 350
MORRIS RURAL
MONTCALM RURAL
Horseshoe Lake
RED
River
Airfield Condition Unknown
Clubb Coulee
Drain
CANADIAN NATIONAL
MORRIS RURAL MUNICIPALITY
MONTCALM RURAL MUNICIPALITY
STE AGATHE PARISH
Tanks
Sewage
Senior Citizens Home
Fire
Arena
Convent
ALITY

SCALE 1 : 50 000 Contour Interval : 25 feet

The Niagara River, dividing Canada from the United States, and both the Horseshoe and American falls are visible in this digital image taken from the International Space Station at an altitude of almost 400 kilometres.

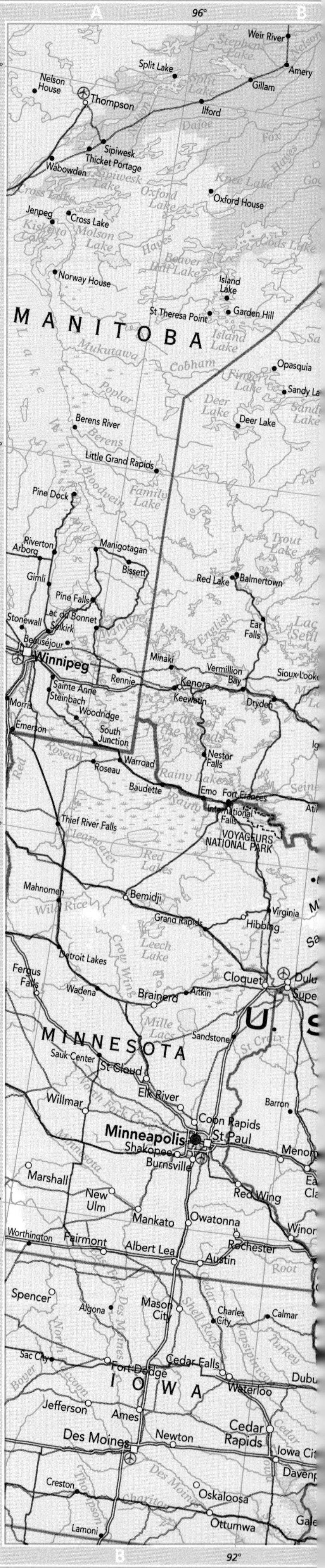

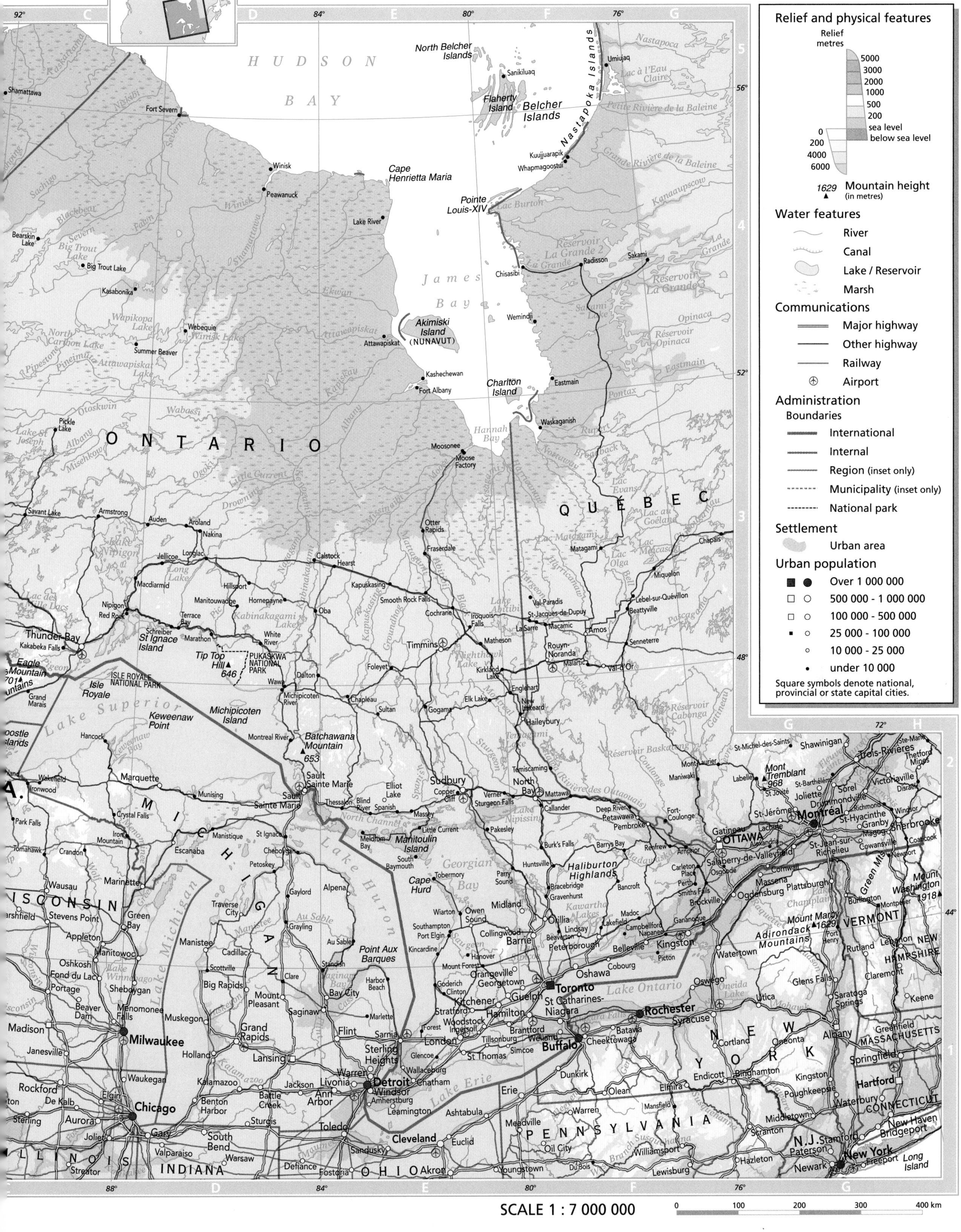
Relief and physical features
Relief metres
5000
3000
2000
1000
500
200
sea level
below sea level
0
200
4000
6000
1629 Mountain height (in metres)
Water features
River
Canal
Lake / Reservoir
Marsh
Communications
Major highway
Other highway
Railway
Airport
Administration
Boundaries
International
Internal
Region (inset only)
Municipality (inset only)
National park
Settlement
Urban area
Urban population
Over 1 000 000
500 000 - 1 000 000
100 000 - 500 000
25 000 - 100 000
10 000 - 25 000
under 10 000
Square symbols denote national, provincial or state capital cities.
HUDSON BAY
James Bay
ONTARIO
QUÉBEC
MICHIGAN
WISCONSIN
ILLINOIS
INDIANA
OHIO
PENNSYLVANIA
NEW YORK
VERMONT
NEW HAMPSHIRE
MASSACHUSETTS
CONNECTICUT
N.J.
Lake Superior
Lake Michigan
Lake Huron
Lake Erie
Lake Ontario
Georgian Bay
Belcher Islands
Flaherty Island
North Belcher Islands
Nastapoka Islands
Akimiski Island (NUNAVUT)
Charlton Island
Cape Henrietta Maria
Pointe Louis-XIV
Manitoulin Island
Isle Royale
ISLE ROYALE NATIONAL PARK
PUKASKWA NATIONAL PARK
St Ignace Island
Michipicoten Island
Keweenaw Point
Tip Top Hill 646
Batchawana Mountain 653
Mont Tremblant 968
Mount Marcy 1629
Mount Washington 1918
Haliburton Highlands
Adirondack Mountains
Fort Severn
Winisk
Peawanuck
Lake River
Attawapiskat
Kashechewan
Fort Albany
Moosonee
Moose Factory
Big Trout Lake
Kasabonika
Webequie
Summer Beaver
Pickle Lake
Savant Lake
Armstrong
Auden
Nakina
Longlac
Geraldton
Hearst
Kapuskasing
Cochrane
Timmins
Iroquois Falls
Kirkland Lake
New Liskeard
Haileybury
Temiscaming
Thunder Bay
Nipigon
Marathon
Wawa
Chapleau
Sault Sainte Marie
Elliot Lake
Sudbury
North Bay
Mattawa
Pembroke
Huntsville
Parry Sound
Bracebridge
Orillia
Barrie
Owen Sound
Peterborough
Belleville
Kingston
Brockville
Cornwall
OTTAWA
Toronto
Oshawa
Hamilton
St Catharines-Niagara
Kitchener
Guelph
Brantford
London
Sarnia
Windsor
Chatham
Leamington
Rouyn-Noranda
Val-d'Or
Amos
Chibougamau
Matagami
Radisson
Chisasibi
Wemindji
Eastmain
Waskaganish
Kuujjuarapik
Whapmagoostui
Umiujaq
Sanikiluaq
Gatineau
Montréal
Trois-Rivières
Shawinigan
Sherbrooke
Granby
St-Jérôme
Detroit
Chicago
Milwaukee
Cleveland
Buffalo
Rochester
Syracuse
Albany
New York
Hartford
Springfield
Marquette
Green Bay
Lansing
Grand Rapids
Flint
Saginaw
Toledo
Erie
Binghamton
SCALE 1 : 7 000 000
0 100 200 300 400 km

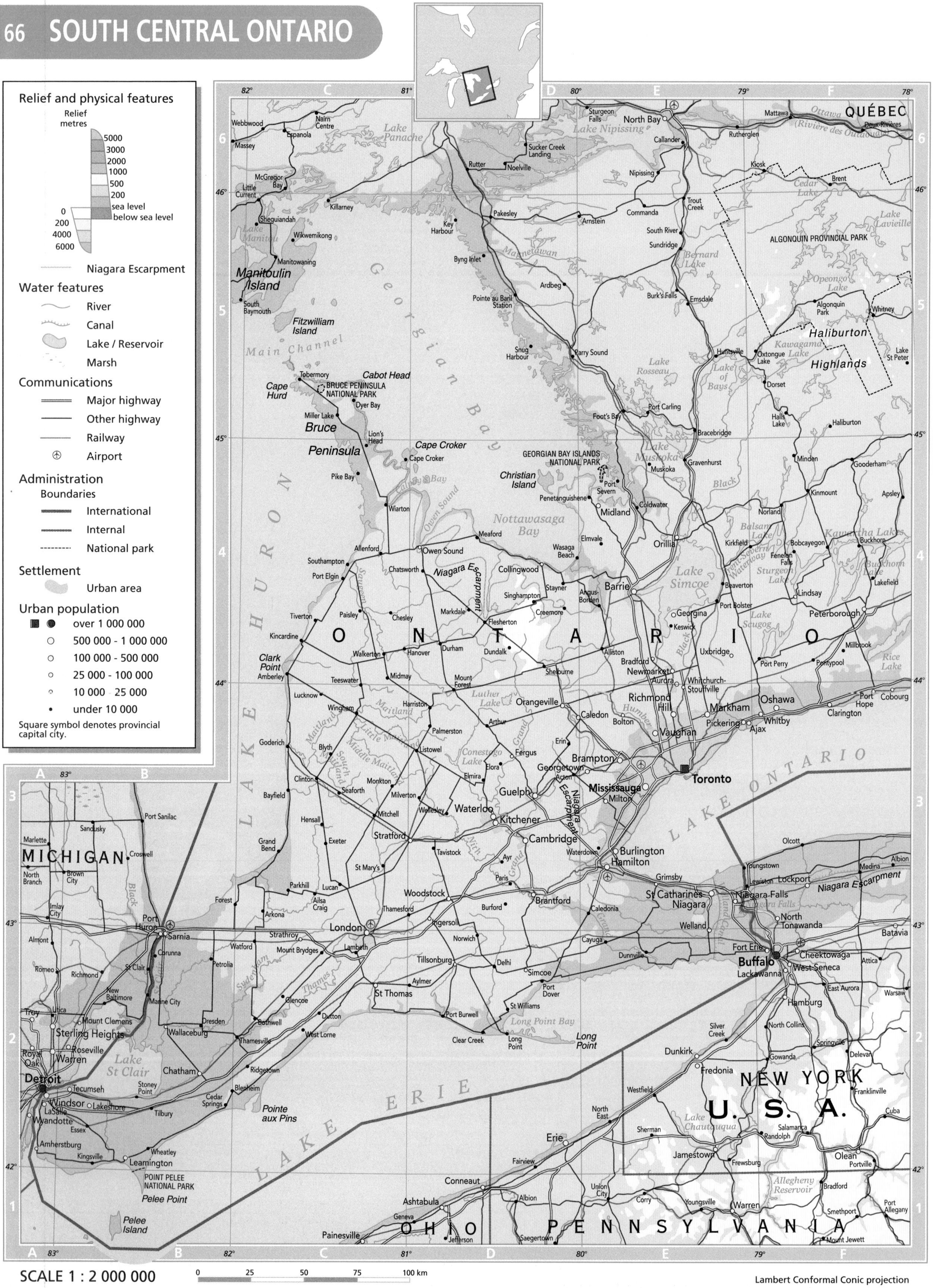

SCALE 1 : 2 000 000

Lambert Conformal Conic projection

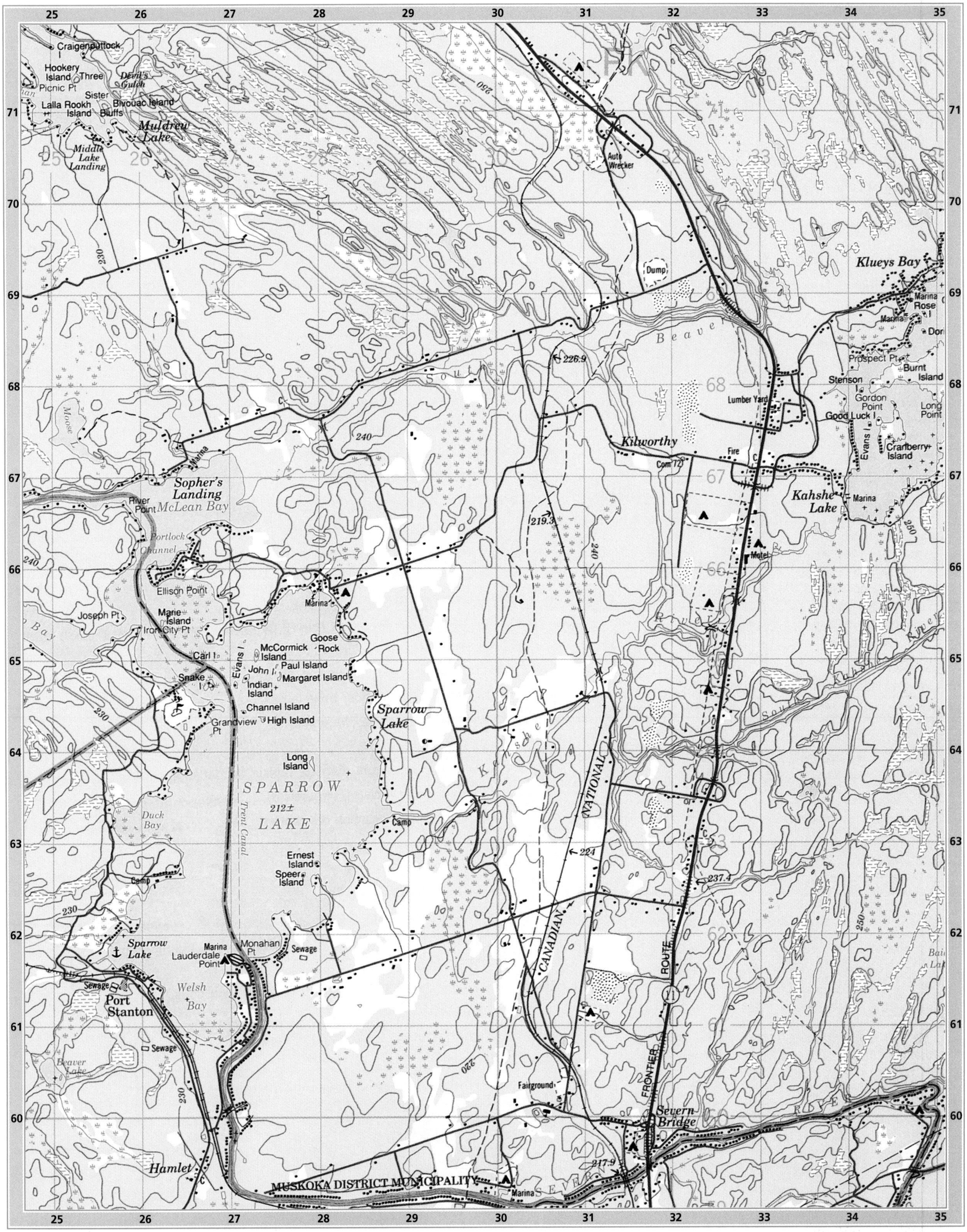
Craigenputtock
Hookery Island
Three
Devil's Gulch
Picnic Pt
Sister
Lalla Rookh Island
Bivouac Island
Bluffs
Muldrew Lake
Middle Lake Landing
Auto Wrecker
Dump
Klueys Bay
Marina
Rose I
Beaver
South
Prospect Pt
Burnt Island
Stenson
Gordon Point
Long Point
Lumber Yard
Good Luck I
Kilworthy
Fire
Com 72
Evans I
Cranberry Island
Kahshe Lake
Marina
Sopher's Landing
River Point
McLean Bay
Portlock Channel
Motel
Ellison Point
Joseph Pt
Marie Island
Iron City Pt
Marina
Goose Rock
McCormick Island
Carl I
John I
Paul Island
Margaret Island
Snake I
Evans I
Indian Island
Channel Island
Grandview Pt
High Island
Sparrow Lake
Long Island
SPARROW LAKE
212±
Trent Canal
Duck Bay
Camp
Ernest Island
Speer Island
Camp
CANADIAN NATIONAL
FRONTIER ROUTE 11
Sparrow Lake
Marina
Lauderdale Point
Monahan Pt
Sewage
Sewage
Port Stanton
Welsh Bay
Sewage
Beaver Lake
Fairground
Severn Bridge
Hamlet
MUSKOKA DISTRICT MUNICIPALITY
Marina
226.9
219.3
224
237.4
217.9

SCALE 1 : 50 000 Contour Interval : 10 metres

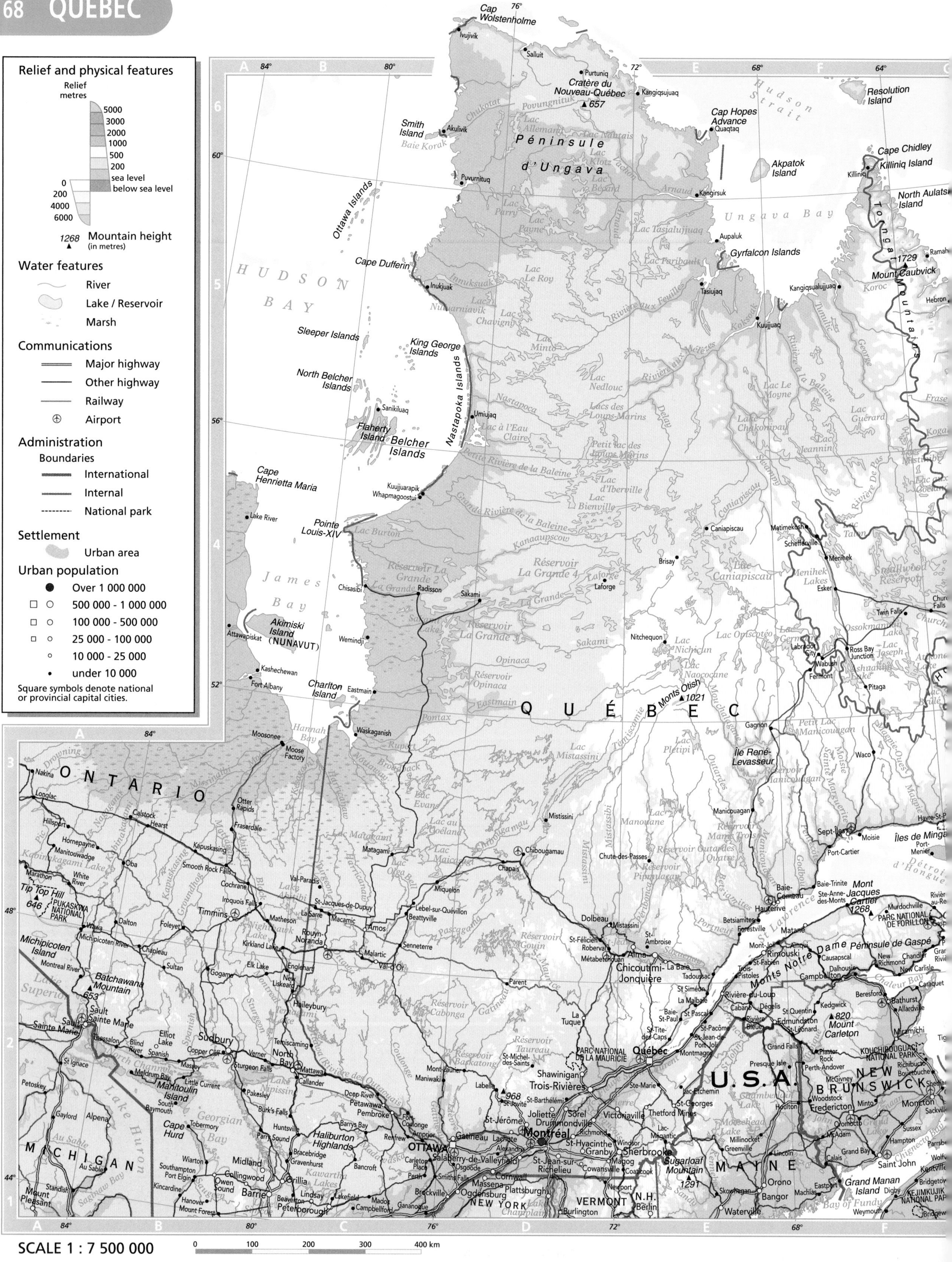
Relief and physical features
Relief metres
5000
3000
2000
1000
500
200
0
sea level
below sea level
200
4000
6000
1268
Mountain height (in metres)
Water features
River
Lake / Reservoir
Marsh
Communications
Major highway
Other highway
Railway
Airport
Administration
Boundaries
International
Internal
National park
Settlement
Urban area
Urban population
Over 1 000 000
500 000 - 1 000 000
100 000 - 500 000
25 000 - 100 000
10 000 - 25 000
under 10 000
Square symbols denote national or provincial capital cities.
Cap Wolstenholme
Ivujivik
Salluit
Purtuniq
Cratère du Nouveau-Québec
657
Kangiqsujuaq
Hudson Strait
Resolution Island
Cap Hopes Advance
Quaqtaq
Smith Island
Akulivik
Baie Korak
Péninsule d'Ungava
Akpatok Island
Cape Chidley
Killiniq Island
Puvurnituq
Kangirsuk
North Aulatsivik Island
Ottawa Islands
Ungava Bay
Torngat Mountains
Aupaluk
Gyrfalcon Islands
1729
Mount Caubvick
Cape Dufferin
HUDSON BAY
Inukjuak
Tasiujaq
Kangiqsualujjuaq
Hebron
Sleeper Islands
King George Islands
Kuujjuaq
North Belcher Islands
Nastapoka Islands
Sanikiluaq
Flaherty Island
Belcher Islands
Umiujaq
Cape Henrietta Maria
Kuujjuarapik
Whapmagoostui
Lake River
Pointe Louis-XIV
Caniapiscau
Matimekosh
Schefferville
Réservoir La Grande 4
Réservoir La Grande 2
Brisay
Laforge
Menihek
James Bay
Chisasibi
Radisson
Sakami
Akimiski Island (NUNAVUT)
Attawapiskat
Wemindji
Nitchequon
Twin Falls
Labrador City
Wabush
Ross Bay Junction
Fermont
Pitaga
Kashechewan
Fort Albany
Charlton Island
Eastmain
Monts Otish
1021
QUÉBEC
Gagnon
Moosonee
Moose Factory
Waskaganish
Hannah Bay
Île René-Levasseur
Waco
ONTARIO
Nakina
Longlac
Otter Rapids
Hearst
Calstock
Mistissini
Manicouagan
Havre-St-Pierre
Sept-Îles
Moisie
Îles de Mingan
Port-Cartier
Fraserdale
Kapuskasing
Matagami
Chibougamau
Chapais
Chute-des-Passes
Hornepayne
Manitouwadge
Smooth Rock Falls
Oba
Marathon
White River
Tip Top Hill
646
PUKASKWA NATIONAL PARK
Cochrane
Iroquois Falls
Val-Paradis
Miquelon
Lebel-sur-Quévillon
Beattyville
Baie-Comeau
Hauterive
Baie-Trinite
Ste-Anne-des-Monts
Mont Jacques Cartier
1268
Murdochville
PARC NATIONAL DE FORILLON
Timmins
Dalton
Matheson
St-Jacques-de-Dupuy
La Sarre
Macamic
Amos
Rouyn-Noranda
Dolbeau
Mistassini
Betsiamites
Forestville
Matane
Michipicoten Island
Wawa
Michipicoten River
Foleyet
Chapleau
Kirkland Lake
Malartic
Val-d'Or
Senneterre
St-Félicien
Roberval
Métabetchouan
Alma
St-Ambroise
Chicoutimi-Jonquière
La Baie
Mont-Joli
Rimouski
St-Fabien
Péninsule de Gaspé
Causapscal
Montreal River
Sultan
Elk Lake
Englehart
New Liskeard
Gogama
Parent
Tadoussac
Trois-Pistoles
Monts Notre Dame
Dalhousie
Campbellton
New Richmond
Carleton
New Carlisle
Batchawana Mountain
653
Haileybury
St Siméon
La Malbaie
Rivière-du-Loup
Cabano
Dégelis
Kedgwick
Beresford
Bathurst
Caraquet
Sault Sainte Marie
Sudbury
Elliot Lake
Blind River
Spanish
Copper Cliff
Verner
North Bay
Temiscaming
La Tuque
Baie-St-Paul
St Pascal
St-Tite-des-Caps
St-Pacôme
Edmundston
St-Léonard
820 Mount Carleton
Miramichi
Grand Falls
Plaster Rock
Perth-Andover
Presque Isle
KOUCHIBOUGUAC NATIONAL PARK
St Ignace
Massey
Sturgeon Falls
Mattawa
Callander
PARC NATIONAL DE LA MAURICIE
Québec
St-Jean-Port-Joli
Montmagny
Mont-Laurier
Maniwaki
Shawinigan
Trois-Rivières
Ste-Marie
Lac-Etchemin
U.S.A.
NEW BRUNSWICK
Petoskey
Meldrum Bay
Little Current
Manitoulin Island
South Baymouth
Pakesley
Deep River
Petawawa
Pembroke
Labelle
968
St-Barthélémi
Joliette
Sorel
Drummondville
Victoriaville
Thetford Mines
St-Georges
Woodstock
Fredericton
McGivney
Minto
Moncton
Sackville
Gaylord
Alpena
Cape Hurd
Tobermory
Burk's Falls
Huntsville
Barrys Bay
Fort Coulonge
Renfrew
Arnprior
St-Jérôme
Montréal
Richmond
St-Hyacinthe
Windsor
Sherbrooke
Lac-Mégantic
Oromocto
Sussex
Hampton
Saint John
MICHIGAN
Lake Huron
Georgian Bay
Parry Sound
Haliburton Highlands
Bracebridge
Gravenhurst
OTTAWA
Carleton Place
Gatineau
Lachute
Alexandria
Salaberry-de-Valleyfield
Granby
Magog
Sugarloaf Mountain
1291
Millinocket
Greenville
Lincoln
Calais
Grand Bay
MAINE
Wiarton
Southampton
Port Elgin
Owen Sound
Collingwood
Midland
Orillia
Bancroft
Perth
Smiths Falls
Cornwall
Massena
St-Jean-sur-Richelieu
Cowansville
Coaticook
Orono
Eastport
Grand Manan Island
Digby
KEJIMKUJIK NATIONAL PARK
Kincardine
Hanover
Mount Forest
Barrie
Beaverton
Lindsay
Peterborough
Lakefield
Madoc
Campbellford
Gananoque
Brockville
Ogdensburg
Plattsburgh
NEW YORK
Burlington
VERMONT
Newport
N.H.
Berlin
Skowhegan
Bangor
Machias
Waterville
Bay of Fundy
Weymouth
Bridgewater
Mount Pleasant
Standish
Au Sable
Saginaw Bay

SCALE 1 : 7 500 000

0 100 200 300 400 km

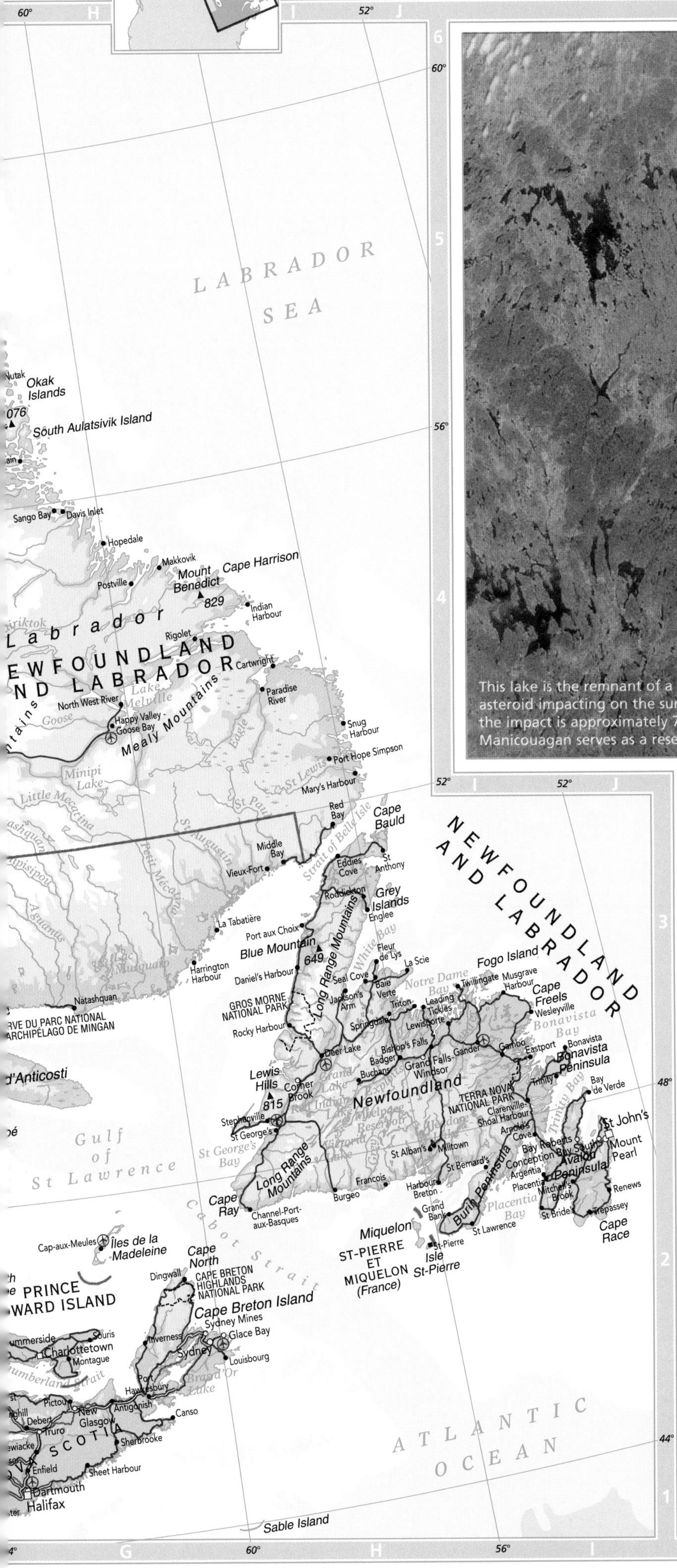

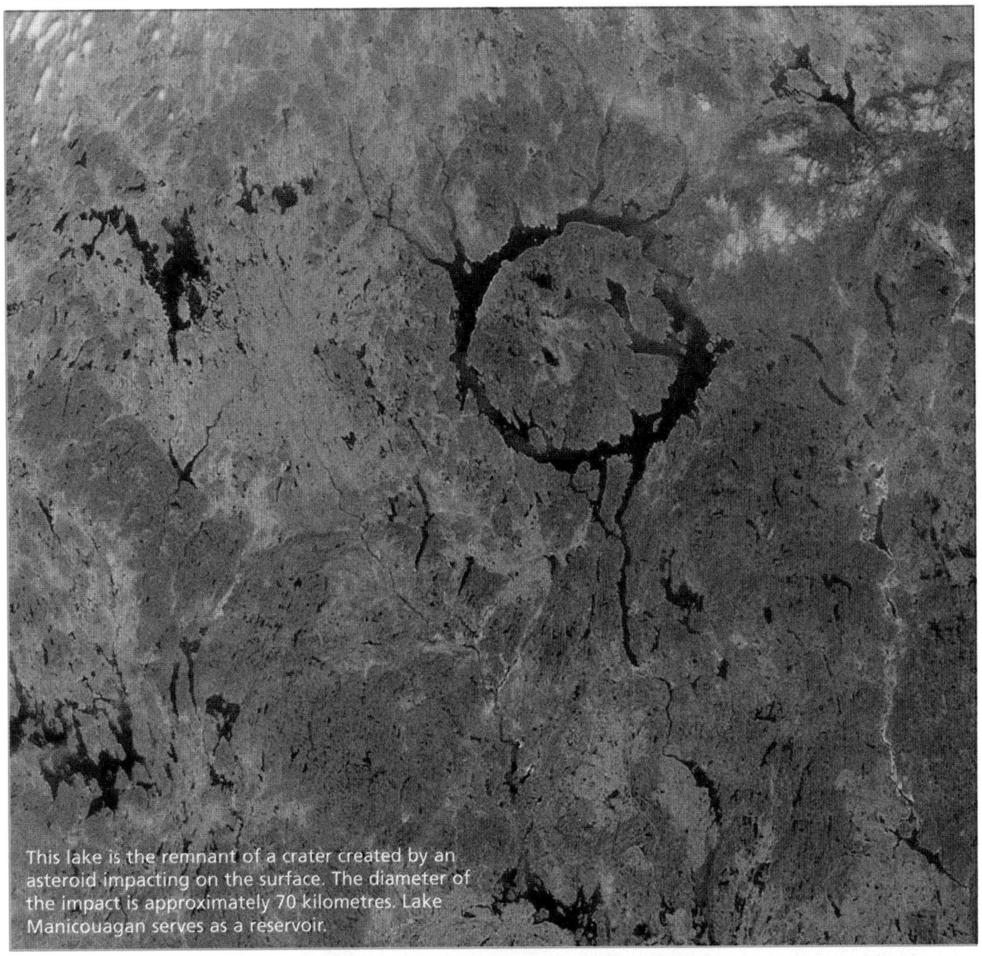

This lake is the remnant of a crater created by an asteroid impacting on the surface. The diameter of the impact is approximately 70 kilometres. Lake Manicouagan serves as a reservoir.

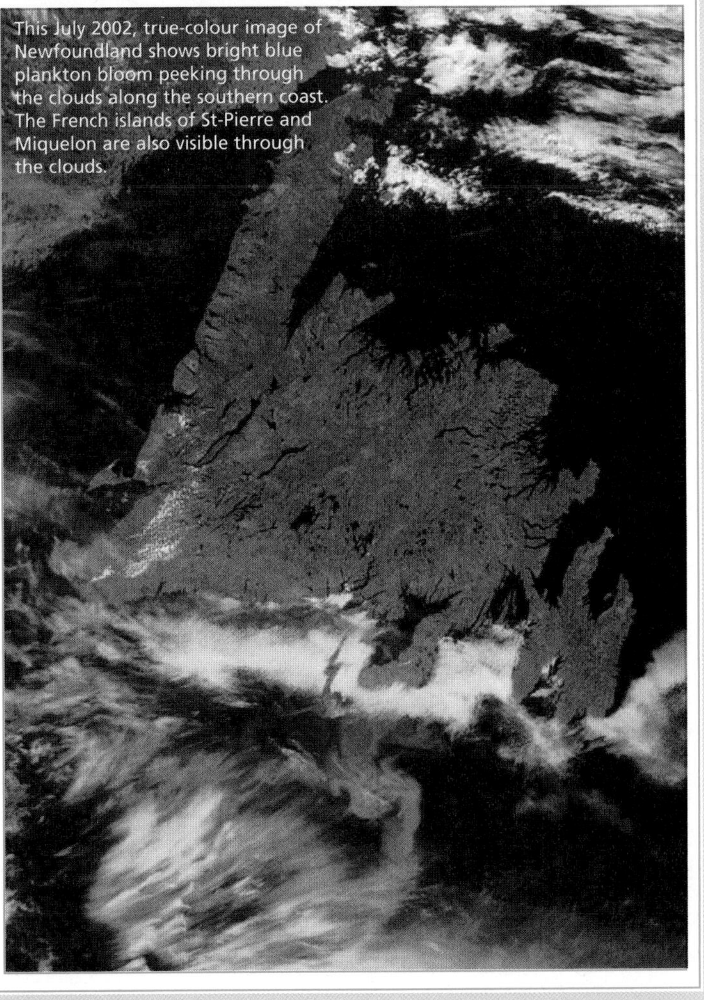

This July 2002, true-colour image of Newfoundland shows bright blue plankton bloom peeking through the clouds along the southern coast. The French islands of St-Pierre and Miquelon are also visible through the clouds.

Conic Equidistant projection

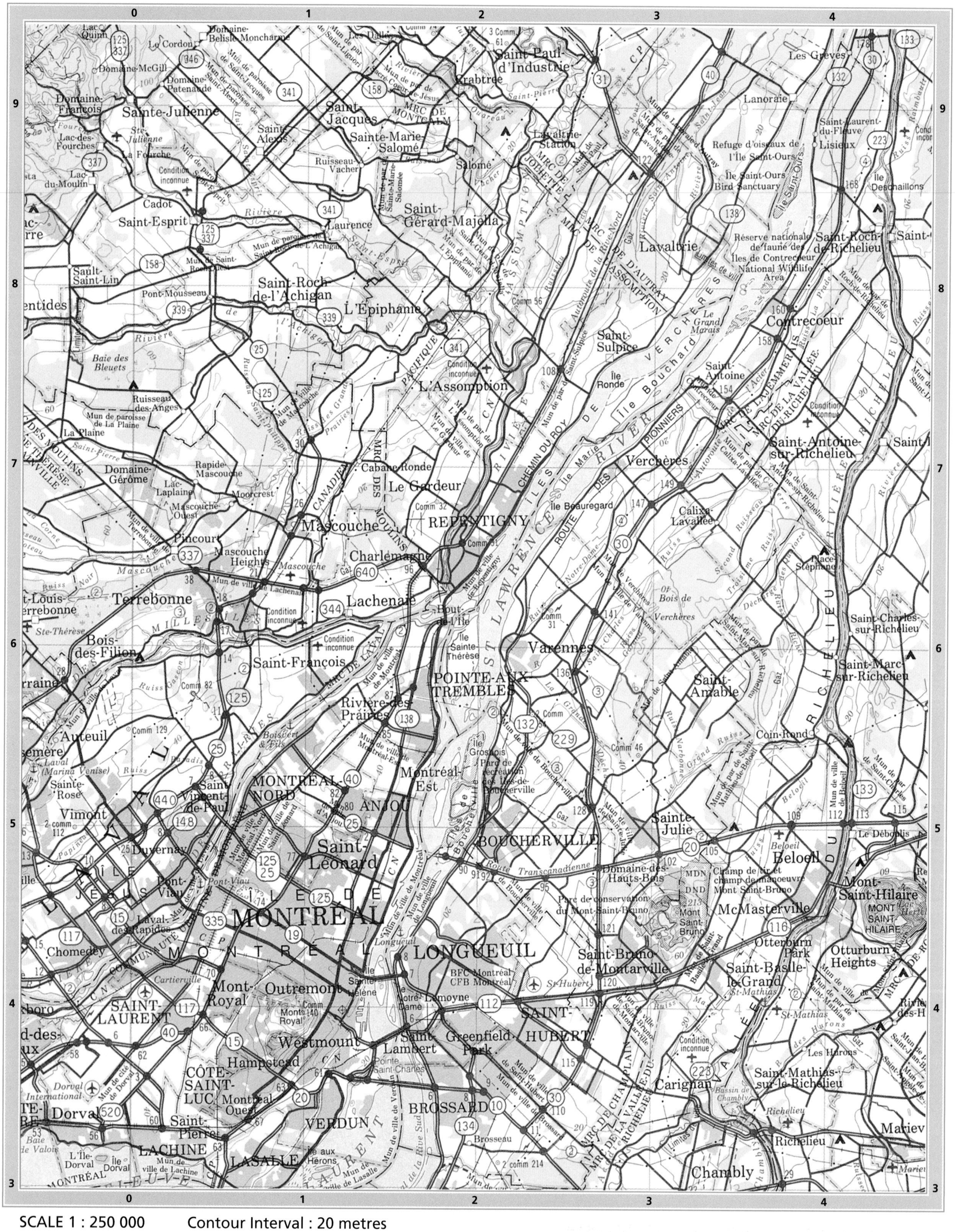
Sainte-Julienne
Saint-Alexis
Saint-Jacques
Sainte-Marie-Salomé
Saint-Paul-d'Industrie
Crabtree
Lavaltrie
Lanoraie
Les Grèves
Saint-Laurent-du-Fleuve
Lisieux
Refuge d'oiseaux de l'Île Saint-Ours
Île Saint-Ours Bird Sanctuary
Île Deschaillons
Saint-Esprit
Cadot
Saint-Gérard-Majella
Saint-Roch-de-l'Achigan
L'Épiphanie
Sault-Saint-Lin
Pont-Mousseau
Saint-Roch-de-Richelieu
Réserve nationale de faune des Îles de Contrecoeur
National Wildlife Area
Contrecoeur
Saint-Sulpice
Saint-Antoine
L'Assomption
Baie des Bleuets
Ruisseau-des-Anges
La Plaine
Saint-Antoine-sur-Richelieu
Domaine-Gérôme
Rapide-Mascouche
Lac-Laplaine
Moorcrest
Cabane-Ronde
Le Gardeur
Verchères
Calixa-Lavallée
Île Beauregard
Mascouche
Mascouche Heights
Pincourt
Charlemagne
REPENTIGNY
Terrebonne
Lachenaie
Bout-de-l'Île
Bois-des-Filion
Saint-François
Varennes
Saint-Charles-sur-Richelieu
Saint-Marc-sur-Richelieu
Saint-Amable
POINTE-AUX-TREMBLES
Rivière-des-Prairies
Auteuil
Sainte-Rose
Vimont
Duvernay
Saint-Vincent-de-Paul
MONTRÉAL-NORD
ANJOU
Montréal-Est
BOUCHERVILLE
Sainte-Julie
Beloeil
Mont-Saint-Hilaire
Saint-Léonard
Domaine-des-Hauts-Bois
Pont-Viau
Laval-des-Rapides
McMasterville
Otterburn Park
Otturburn Heights
MONTRÉAL
Chomedey
LONGUEUIL
Saint-Bruno-de-Montarville
Saint-Basile-le-Grand
Mont-Royal
Outremont
SAINT-LAURENT
SAINT-HUBERT
Westmount
Saint-Lambert
Greenfield Park
Hampstead
CÔTE-SAINT-LUC
Montréal-Ouest
Carignan
Saint-Mathias-sur-le-Richelieu
Dorval
Dorval International
VERDUN
BROSSARD
Saint-Pierre
LACHINE
LASALLE
Brosseau
Richelieu
Chambly
Marieville
ST LAWRENCE
RIVIÈRE RICHELIEU

SCALE 1 : 250 000   Contour Interval : 20 metres

Glenmont
Middle Pereaux
Community centre
Peraux
Woodside
Norths Corner
Pereaux
Barkhouse Bk
Bass Creek
Intervale Brook
Dill Brook
Bradleys Meadow
Hollow Brook
North
Arena
Community centre
Canning
Kingsport
Sheffield Mills Marsh
Community Centre
Sheffield Mills
Sewage
Habitant
Tanks
River
GLOOSCAP TRAIL
Hillaton
Habitant
ANNAPOLIS VALLEY
Porter Point
Lower Canard
Dewey Creek Wildlife Management Area
Canard
Upper Canard
Starrs Point
Upper Dyke Village
Beau Dyke
River
Canard
Starrs Point
Sewage
Grand Dyke
Museum
Church Street
Chipmans Corner
Water
Port Williams
Hillcrest Brook
Belcher Street
Sewage
Senior Citizens Home
Water
Kentville
CORNWALLIS RIVER
Greenwich
Community Centre
EVANGELINE TRAIL
Hospital
Wolfville
Town Limits
Motel

Relief and physical features
Relief metres
5000
3000
2000
1000
500
200
sea level
0
200
4000
6000
below sea level
1606 ▲ Mountain height (in metres)
Historic site
Water features
River
Lake / Reservoir
Marsh
Urban population
100 000 - 500 000
25 000 - 100 000
10 000 - 25 000
under 10 000
Square symbols denote provincial capital cities.
Communications
Major highway
Other highway
Railway
Ferry route
Airport
Administration
Boundaries
International
Internal
National park
Labrador
QUÉBEC
Lac Fonteneau
Petit Mécatina
St-Augustin
Lac Robertson
La Tabatière
Île du Petit Mécatina
Harrington Harbour
Musquaro
Lac Musquaro
Natashquan
Pointe du Vieux Poste
Havre-St-Pierre
Longue-Pointe
Îles de Mingan
RÉSERVE DU PARC NATIONAL DE L'ARCHIPÉLAGO DE MINGAN
Manitou
Moisie
Sept-Îles
Clarke City
Port-Cartier
Réservoir Outardes
Lac Ste Anne
Manicouagan
Réservoir Manicouagan
Détroit de Jacques-Cartier
Pointe de l'Ouest
Port-Menier
Île d'Anticosti
Pointe de l'Est
Détroit d'Honguedo
Baie-Trinite
Pointe des Monts
Godbout
Baie-Comeau
Hauterive
Pointe Lebel
Ragueneau
Pointe Manicouagan
Pointe-aux-Outardes
Betsiamites
Forestville
Ste-Anne-de-Portneuf
St Lawrence
Cap-Chat
Ste-Anne-des-Monts
Gros-Morne
Grande-Vallée
Mont Jacques Cartier ▲ 1268
Cloridorme
Murdochville
Rivière-au-Renard
PARC NATIONAL DE FORILLON
Fontenelle
Gaspé
Cap-des-Rosiers
Cap Gaspé
Baie de Gaspé
Barachois
Percé
Grande-Rivière
Chandler
Port-Daniel
New Richmond
Bonaventure
Carleton
Monts Chic-Chocs
Péninsule de Gaspé
Monts Notre Dame
Matane
St-Ulric
Grosses Roches
Mont-Joli
Rimouski
Price
Sayabec
Lac Matapédia
St-Gabriel-de-Rimouski
Amqui
Lac-au-Saumon
Causapscal
St-Léon-le-Grand
Routhierville
Matapédia
St-Fabien
Ste-Blandine
Trois-Pistoles
St-Michel-du-Squatec
St-Honoré
Cabano
Notre-Dame-du-Lac
Dégelis
Lac Témiscouata
Rivière-Bleue
St-Jacques
Edmundston
Lac Baker
Dalhousie
Campbellton
New Carlisle
Chaleur Bay
Miscou Island
Caraquet
Caraquet Bay
Nipisiguit Bay
Île Lamèque
Shippegan
Shippegan Island
Jacquet River
Beresford
Bathurst
Allardville
Tracadie-Sheila
Kedgwick
St Quentin
Mount Carleton 820
St-Anne-de-Madawaska
St-Léonard
Grand Falls
Nictau
Fort Kent
Van Buren
Wayerton
Point Escuminac
Miramichi
KOUCHIBOUGUAC NATIONAL PARK
St-Louis-de-Kent
Richibucto
Limestone
Caribou
New Denmark
Plaster Rock
Washburn
Presque Isle
Mars Hill
Perth-Andover
NEW BRUNSWICK
Todd Mountain 503 ▲
Upper Blackville
Doaktown
Harcourt
Bouctouche
St-Antoine
Shediac
Cap-Pelé
Moncton
Bristol
Napadogan
Hartland
Stanley
McGivney
Gaspereau Forks
Woodstock
Minto
Chipman
Houlton
Patten
Mount Katahdin ▲1606
U.S.A.
MAINE
Nackawic
Fredericton
Marysville
Oromocto
Canterbury
Harvey
Youngs Cove
Petitcodiac
Salisbury
Hillsborough
Dorchester
Sackville
Amherst
Sussex
McAdam
Tracy
Hampstead
FUNDY NATIONAL PARK
Alma
Riverside-Albert
Hampton
Norton
Mount Pleasant 358
Welsford
Lawrence Station
Quispamsis
St Stephen
Grand Bay
Saint John
St Martins
Chignecto Bay
Advocate Harbour
Calais
Woodland
St Andrews
Pennfield
Blacks Harbour
Eastport
Campobello Island
Grand Manan Island
Machias
Milo
Lincoln
Howland
Millinocket
East Millinocket
Milford
Orono
Bangor
Winterport
Bucksport
Ellsworth
Mount Desert Island
Bar Harbor
Jonesport
ACADIA NATIONAL PARK
Bay of Fundy
Long Island
Freeport
Brier Island
St Mary's Bay
Digby
Annapolis Royal
Bridgetown
Middleton
Kingston-Greenwood
Berwick
Kentville
Wolfville
Windsor
Minas Channel
Minas Basin
Parrsboro
Cobequid Bay
Noel
Shubenacadie
Stewiacke
Truro
Brookfield
Enfield
Fall River
Lower Sackville
Dartmouth
Halifax
Lake Echo
Musquodoboit Harbour
Upper Musquodoboit
Sheet Harbour
Sherbrooke
Melrose
Guysborough
Canso
Cape Canso
Chedabucto Bay
NOVA SCOTIA
Weymouth
KEJIMKUJIK NATIONAL PARK
Caledonia
Bridgewater
New Germany
Mahone Bay
Chester
Lunenburg
Peggy's Cove
Pennant Point
New Ross
Milton
Liverpool
Brooklyn
Salmon River
Yarmouth
Argyle
Sable River
Shelburne
Lockeport
Barrington
Clarks Harbour
Cape Sable Island
Springhill
Great Village
Debert
Oxford
Pugwash
Tatamagouche
Cobequid Mountains
Pictou
Pictou Island
Trenton
New Glasgow
Stellarton
Antigonish
Cape George
St George's Bay
Mulgrave
Port Hawkesbury
Arichat
Isle Madame
Cape Tormentine
Northumberland Strait
North Cape
Tignish
Alberton
O'Leary
Egmont Bay
Wellington
Summerside
Borden
Kensington
Darnley
PRINCE EDWARD ISLAND
PRINCE EDWARD ISLAND NATIONAL PARK
Cornwall
Charlottetown
Montague
Georgetown
Murray Harbour
Souris
East Point
Îles de la Madeleine
Fatima
L'Etang-du-Nord
Havre-aux-Maisons
Cap-aux-Meules
GULF OF ST LAWRENCE
Cabot Strait
Cape St Lawrence
Cape North
Dingwall
CAPE BRETON HIGHLANDS NATIONAL PARK
White Hill 532▲
Ingonish
Chéticamp
Cape Breton Island
Margaree Forks
Inverness
North River Bridge
Sydney Mines
New Waterford
Glace Bay
North Sydney
Sydney
Baddeck
Whycocomagh
Judique
Bras d'Or Lake
Eskasoni
St Peter's
Fourchu
Louisbourg
Sable Island
Bay of Islands
Lark Harbour
Lewis Hills 815
Port-au-Port Peninsula
Cape St George
Stephenville Crossing
St George's
St George's Bay
Robinsons
Cape Anguille
Doyles
Long Range
Cape Ray
Channel-Port-aux-Basques
Rose Blanche

SCALE 1 : 3 750 000

0 40 80 120 160 km

Conic Equidistant projection

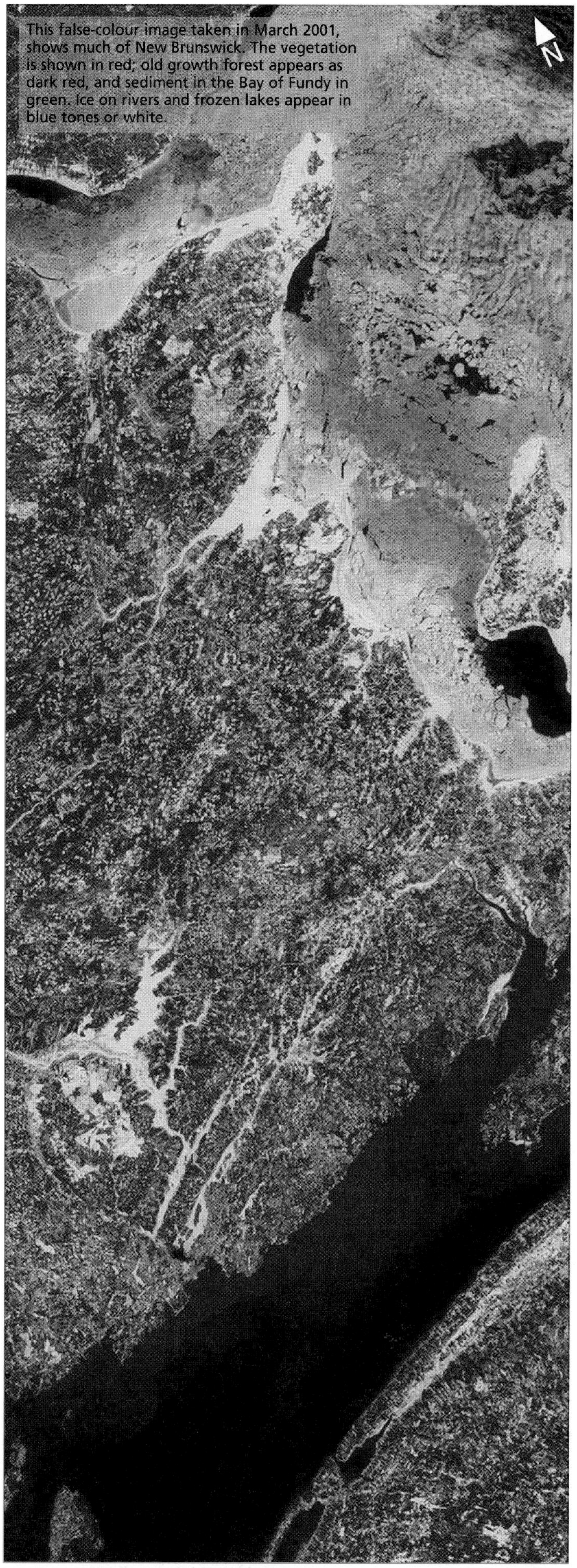

This false-colour image taken in March 2001, shows much of New Brunswick. The vegetation is shown in red; old growth forest appears as dark red, and sediment in the Bay of Fundy in green. Ice on rivers and frozen lakes appear in blue tones or white.

ARCTIC OCEAN
BEAUFORT SEA
Chukchi Sea
QUEEN ELIZABETH ISLANDS
Parry Islands
U.S.A.
ALASKA
YUKON TERRITORY
NORTHWEST TERRITORIES
NUNAV
BRITISH COLUMBIA
ALBERTA
SASKATCHEWAN
MANITOBA
ROCKY MOUNTAINS
Brooks Range
Mackenzie Mountains
Selwyn Mountains
Ogilvie Mountains
Cassiar Mountains
Franklin Mountains
Wrangell Mountains
Chugach Mountains
St Elias Mts
Skeena Mts
De Long Mountains
Baird Mountains
Endicott Mountains
British Empire Range
Mount McKinley 6194
Mt Logan 5959
Mount Fairweather 4670
Mount Lloyd George 2972
Mount Tom White 3240
Point Hope
Wainwright
Point Barrow
Barrow
Prudhoe Bay
Kaktovik
Fairbanks
Fort Yukon
Circle
Stevens Village
Hughes
Kotzebue
Arctic Circle
Glennallen
Valdez
Cordova
Tok
Yakutat
Juneau
Sitka
Petersburg
Wrangell
Ketchikan
Haines
Skagway
Whitehorse
Carcross
Teslin
Atlin
Dawson
Beaver Creek
Burwash Landing
Carmacks
Haines Junction
Faro
Ross River
Mayo
Elsa
Old Crow
Inuvik
Aklavik
Tuktoyaktuk
Fort McPherson
Tsiigehtchic
Paulatuk
Fort Good Hope
Colville Lake
Norman Wells
Tulita
Déline
Echo Bay
Wrigley
Tungsten
Fort Simpson
Nahanni Butte
Fort Liard
Fort Providence
Hay River
Enterprise
Fort Resolution
Pine Point
Fort Smith
Rae Lakes
Wekweti
Rae-Edzo
Yellowknife
Reliance
Lutselk'e
Kugluktuk
Cambridge Bay
Gjoa Haven
Taloyoak
Pelly Bay
Umingmaktok
Bathurst Inlet
Repulse
Qamanittuaq
Igluligaarjuk
Rankin Inlet
Whale Cove
Arviat
Churchill
Cape Churchill
Resolute Bay
Grise Fiord
Eureka
Isachsen
Ikaahuk
Uluqsaqtuuq
Watson Lake
Upper Liard
Dease Lake
Telegraph Creek
Stewart
Hazelton
Prince Rupert
Masset
Fort Nelson
Prophet River
Toad River
Coal River
Rainbow Lake
High Level
Meander River
Fort Vermilion
La Crete
Keg River
Wonowon
Takla Landing
Fort Chipewyan
Uranium City
Stony Rapids
Wollaston Lake
Brochet
Lynn Lake
Leaf Rapids
Split Lake
Gillam
Thompson
Shamattawa
Flin Flon
Ponton
The Pas
Norway House
St Theresa Point
Hudson Bay
Grand Rapids
Sandy Lake
Berens River
Banks Island
Victoria Island
Melville Island
Prince Patrick Island
Borden Island
Brock Island
Mackenzie King Island
Ellef Ringnes Island
Amund Ringnes Island
Axel Heiberg Island
Sverdrup Islands
Ellesmere Island
Devon Island
Cornwallis Island
Bathurst Island
Somerset Island
Prince of Wales Island
King William Island
Stefansson Island
Boothia Peninsula
Brodeur Peninsula
Prince Albert Peninsula
Wollaston Peninsula
North Magnetic Pole
Cape Columbia
Cape Prince Alfred
Cape Kellett
Cape Bathurst
Cape Parry
Amundsen Gulf
Coronation Gulf
Queen Maud Gulf
Gulf of Boothia
Dease Strait
Dolphin and Union Strait
McClure Strait
Viscount Melville Sound
McClintock Channel
Peary Channel
Hazen Str.
Jones Sound
Lancaster Sound
Barrow Strait
Prince Regent Inlet
Mackenzie Bay
Dixon Entrance
Chesterfield Inlet
Alexander Archipelago
Chichagof Island
Baranof Island
Kupreanof Island
Prince of Wales Island
Graham Island
Great Bear Lake
Great Slave Lake
Lac la Martre
Contwoyto Lake
Aylmer Lake
Dubawnt Lake
Baker Lake
Yathkyed Lake
Kaminak Lake
Wholdaia Lake
Ennadai Lake
Kasba Lake
Nueltin Lake
Lake Athabasca
Tathlina Lake
Reindeer Lake
Southern Indian Lake
Lake Winnipeg
Lake Winnipegosis
Cedar Lake
Island Lake
Gods Lake
Yukon
Colville
Koyukuk
Chandalar
Porcupine
Peel
Arctic Red
Mackenzie
Anderson
Horton
Hart
Stewart
Liard
Keele
South Nahanni
Coppermine
Back
Thelon
Kazan
Ellice
Quoich
Hay
Peace
Slave
Stikine
Nass
Kechika
Seal
Churchill
Nelson
Burntwood
Hayes
Severn
Poplar
NOATAK NATIONAL PRESERVE
KOBUK VALLEY NATIONAL PARK
GATES OF THE ARCTIC NATIONAL PARK AND PRESERVE
DENALI NATIONAL PARK AND PRESERVE
WRANGELL-ST ELIAS NATIONAL PARK AND PRESERVE
GLACIER BAY NATIONAL PARK AND PRESERVE
KLUANE NATIONAL PARK
IVVAVIK NATIONAL PARK
VUNTUT NATIONAL PARK
NAHANNI NATIONAL PARK
TUKTUT NOGAIT NATIONAL PARK
AULAVIK NATIONAL PARK
WOOD BUFFALO NATIONAL PARK
QUTTINIRPAAQ NATIONAL PARK
170° 160° 150° 140° 130° 120° 110° 100° 90°
80° 70° 60°
Relief and physical features
Relief metres
5000
3000
2000
1000
500
200
sea level
below sea level
0
200
4000
6000
6194 Mountain height (in metres)
Permanent ice
Water features
River
Lake / Reservoir
Marsh
Urban Population
25 000 - 100 000
10 000 - 25 000
under 10 000
Square symbols denote provincial, territorial or state capital cities.
Communications
Other highway
Railway
Airport
Administration
Boundaries
International
Internal
National park

SCALE 1 : 13 000 000

0 200 400 600 800 km

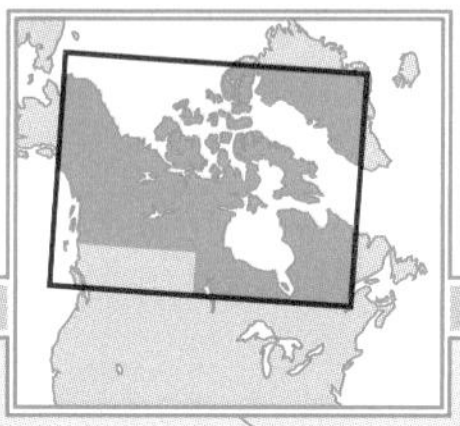

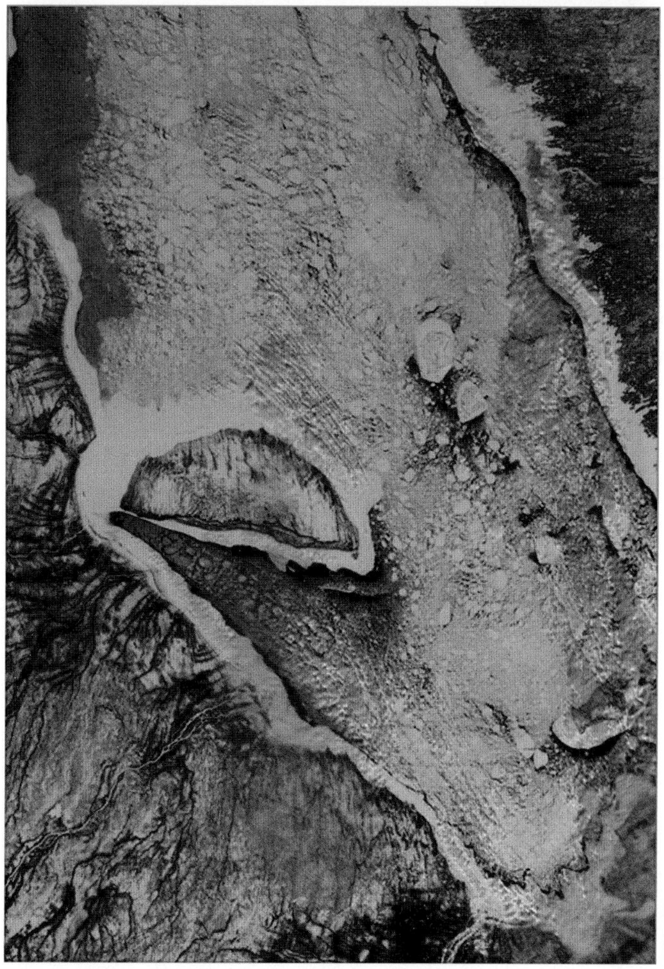

Images taken in August and January (2001) by the Multi-angle Imaging Spectroradiometer (MISR), illustrate the differences in the landscape of James Bay and Akimiski Island. The Harricana, Moose, Albany and Attawapiskat rivers can be seen flowing into James Bay.

Lambert Conformal Conic projection

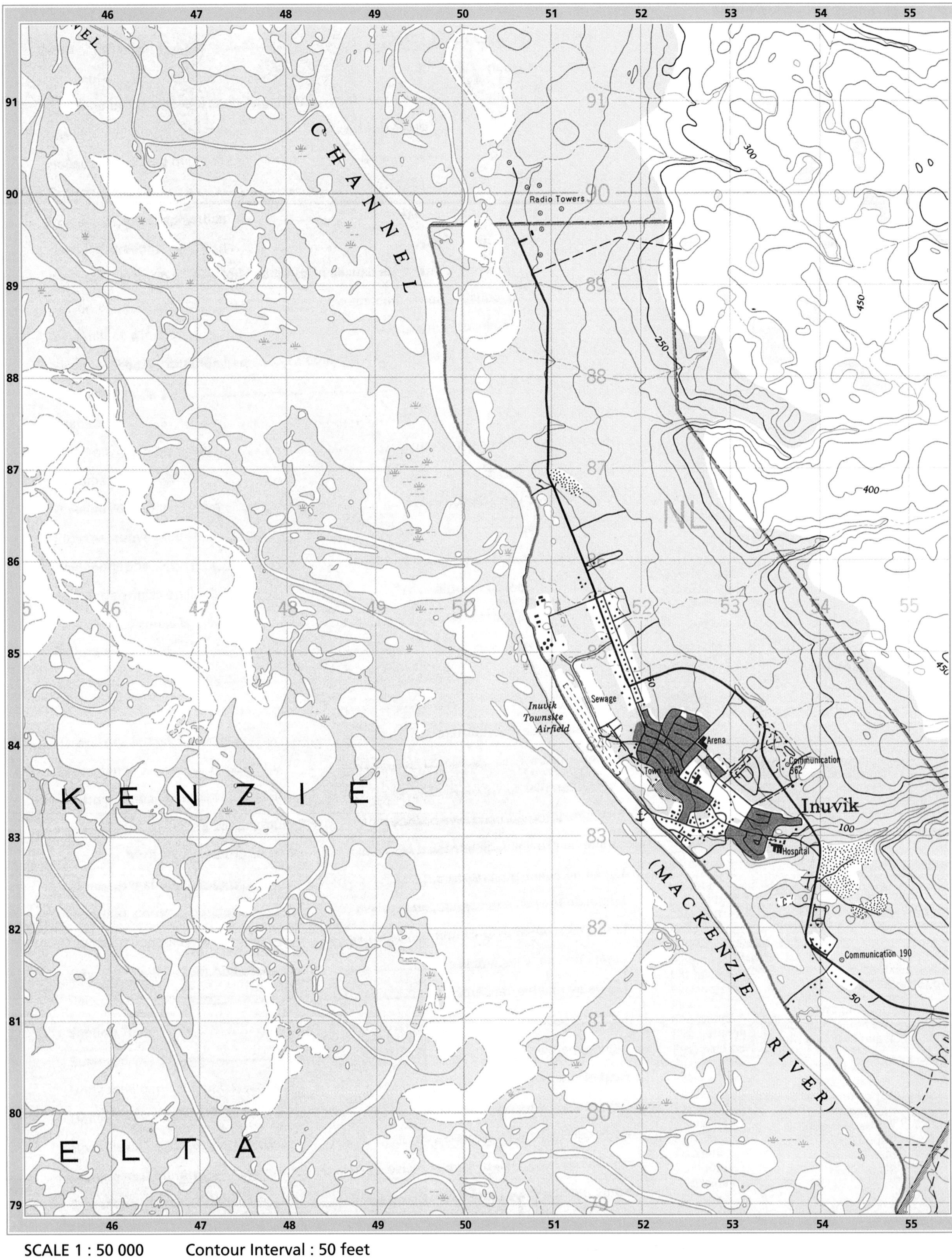
CHANNEL
Radio Towers
NL
Inuvik Townsite Airfield
Sewage
Arena
Town Hall
Communication 362
Inuvik
Hospital
Communication 190
(MACKENZIE RIVER)
KENZIE
ELTA
300
450
250
400
100
50

SCALE 1 : 50 000   Contour Interval : 50 feet

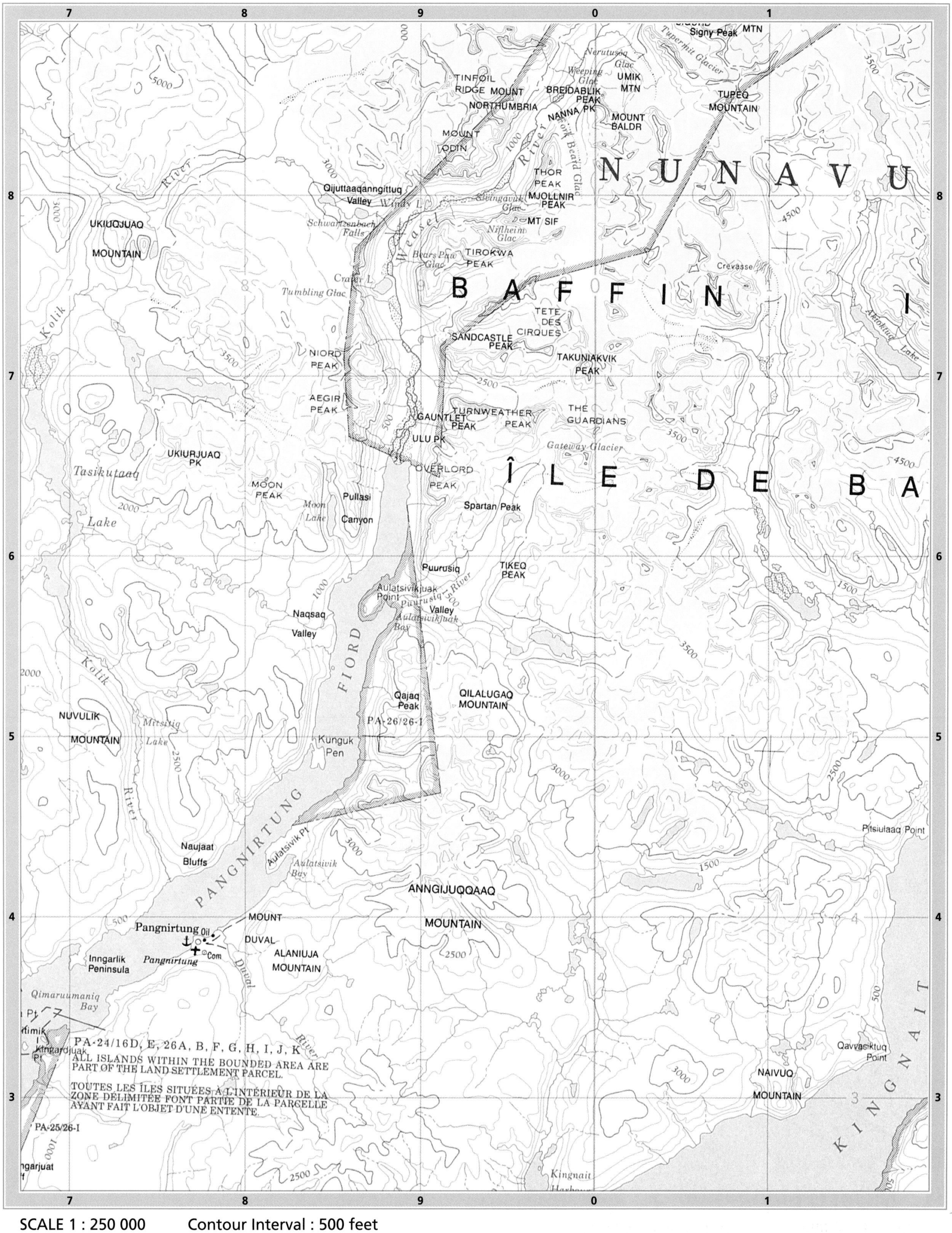
NUNAVUT
BAFFIN I
ÎLE DE BA
Signy Peak
MTN
Tupermit Glacier
Nerutusoq Glac
Weeping Glac
UMIK MTN
TINFOIL RIDGE
MOUNT NORTHUMBRIA
BREIDABLIK PEAK
NANNA PK
MOUNT BALDR
TUPEQ MOUNTAIN
MOUNT ODIN
Weasel River
Fork Beard Glac
THOR PEAK
MJOLLNIR PEAK
MT SIF
Niflheim Glac
Qijuttaaqanngittuq Valley
Windy L
Schwartzenbach Falls
Bears Paw Glac
TIROKWA PEAK
Crater L
Tumbling Glac
Crevasse
UKIUQJUAQ MOUNTAIN
River
Kolik
TETE DES CIRQUES
SANDCASTLE PEAK
NIORD PEAK
TAKUNIAKVIK PEAK
Akuktuq Lake
AEGIR PEAK
TURNWEATHER PEAK
THE GUARDIANS
GAUNTLET PEAK
ULU PK
Gateway Glacier
UKIURJUAQ PK
Tasikutaaq Lake
MOON PEAK
Moon Lake
Pullasi Canyon
OVERLORD PEAK
Spartan Peak
Puurusiq
TIKEQ PEAK
Aulatsivikjuak Point
Puurusiq River
Valley
Aulatsivikjuak Bay
Naqsaq Valley
Kolik
FIORD
Qajaq Peak
QILALUGAQ MOUNTAIN
PA-26/26-I
NUVULIK MOUNTAIN
Mitsitiq Lake
Kunguk Pen
River
PANGNIRTUNG
Pitsiulaaq Point
Naujaat Bluffs
Aulatsivik Pt
Aulatsivik Bay
ANNGIJUQQAAQ MOUNTAIN
Pangnirtung
MOUNT DUVAL
ALANIUJA MOUNTAIN
Oil
Com
Inngarlik Peninsula
Pangnirtung
Duval
Qimaruumaniq Bay
Kingardjuak Pt
River
PA-24/16D, E, 26A, B, F, G, H, I, J, K
ALL ISLANDS WITHIN THE BOUNDED AREA ARE PART OF THE LAND SETTLEMENT PARCEL.
TOUTES LES ÎLES SITUÉES À L'INTÉRIEUR DE LA ZONE DÉLIMITÉE FONT PARTIE DE LA PARCELLE AYANT FAIT L'OBJET D'UNE ENTENTE.
PA-25/26-I
Qavvasiktuq Point
NAIVUQ MOUNTAIN
KINGNAIT
Kingnait Harbour
7
8
9
0
1
6
5
4
3

SCALE 1 : 250 000 Contour Interval : 500 feet

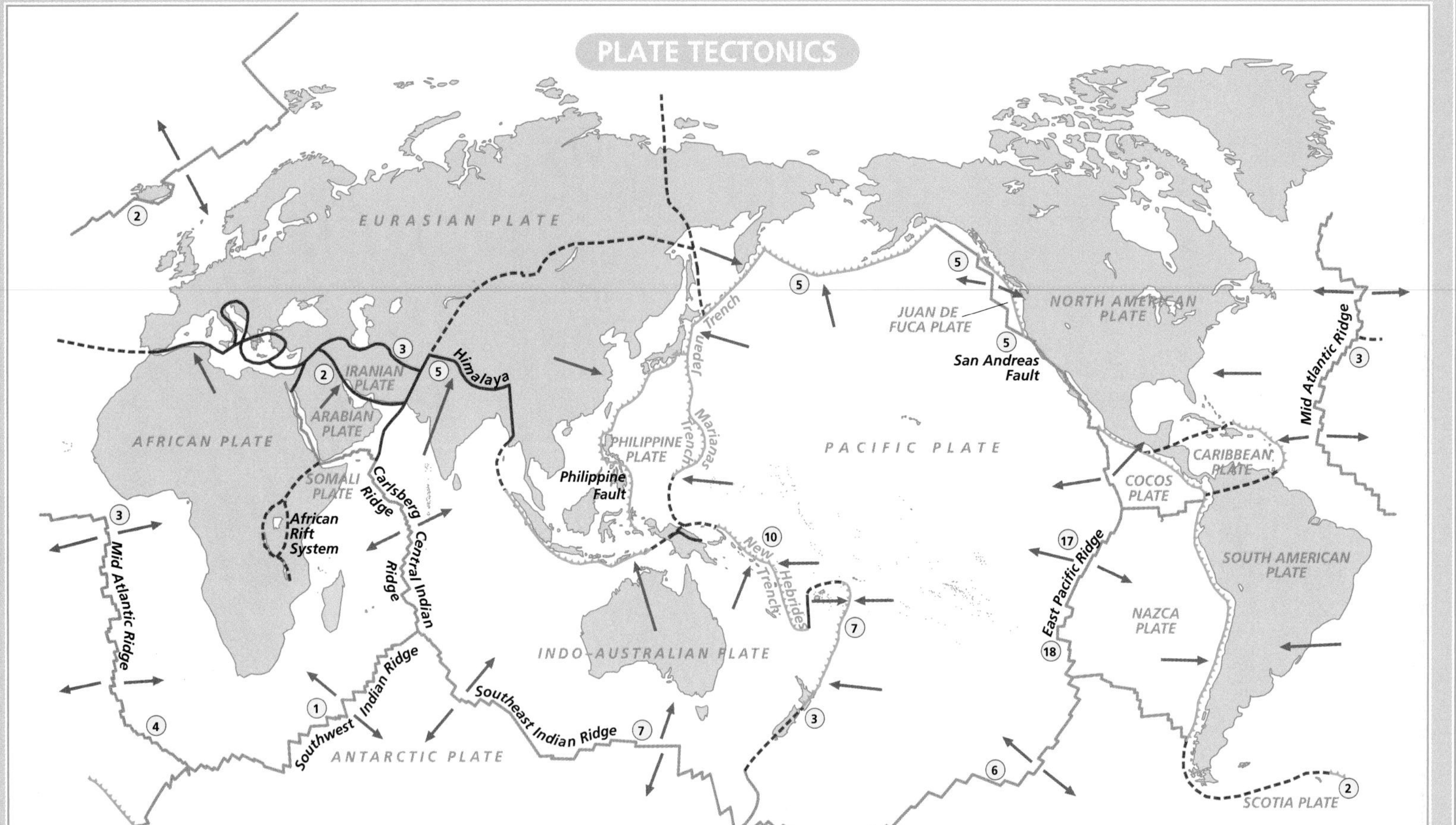

Subduction Zone - the downward movements of an oceanic plate along converging continental or oceanic plate boundaries.

Collision Zone - the upward movement of the earth's crust into fold mountains in response to converging continental plates.

Oceanic Ridges - produced when plates separate, allowing volcanic material to rise and cool.

Line of plate boundary uncertain

6 Rate of plate movement (cm per year)

Direction of plate movement

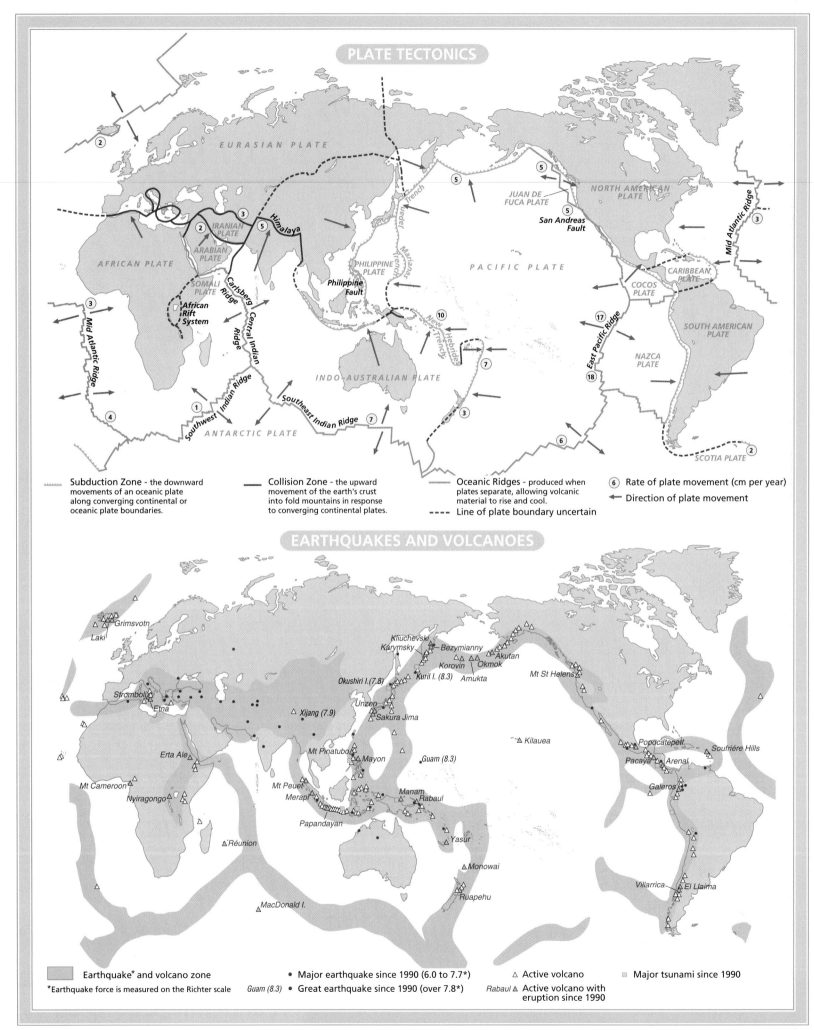

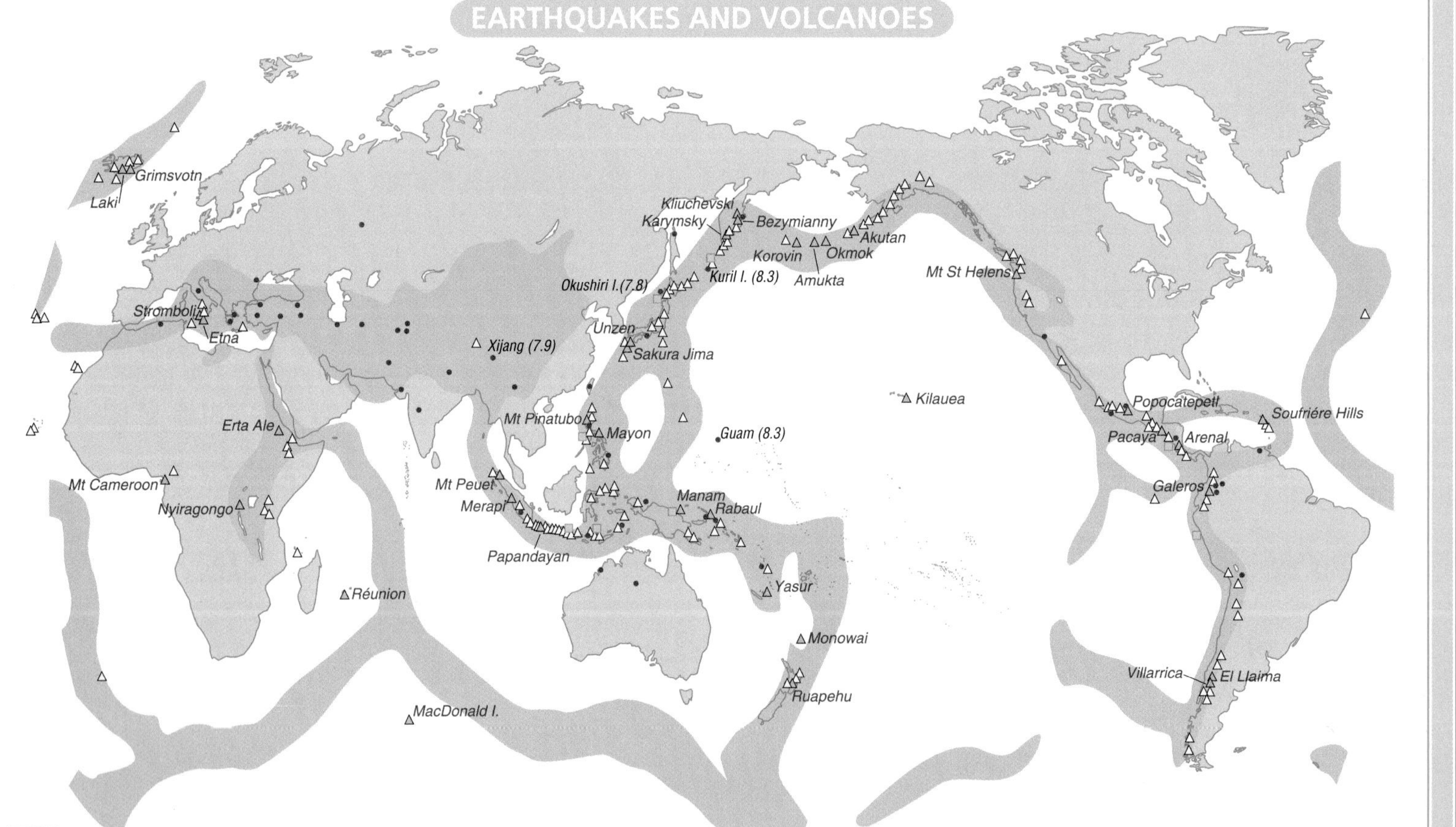

Earthquake* and volcano zone

*Earthquake force is measured on the Richter scale

• Major earthquake since 1990 (6.0 to 7.7*)

Guam (8.3) • Great earthquake since 1990 (over 7.8*)

△ Active volcano

Rabaul ▲ Active volcano with eruption since 1990

Major tsunami since 1990

SCALE 1 : 150 000 000

0 2000 4000 6000 8000 km

Times projection

THE EARTH'S CORE

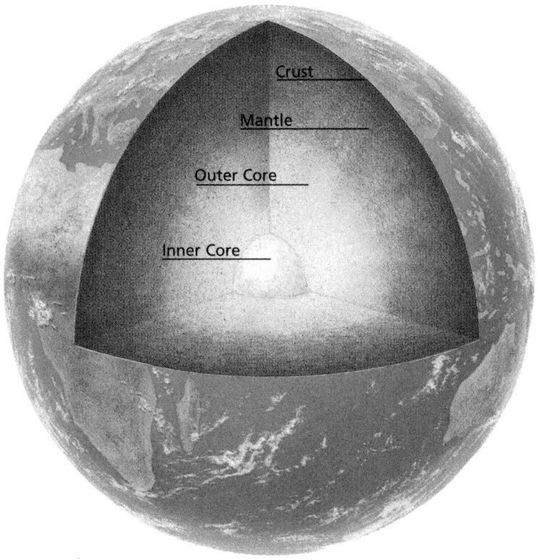
Crust
Mantle
Outer Core
Inner Core

OCEANIC CRUST
Convection currents
LITHOSPHERE OR UPPER MANTLE
ASTHENOSPHERE
LOWER MANTLE
LIQUID CORE
SOLID CORE
Sedimentary layer
TEMPERATURES
6500 °C
4500 °C
3500 °C
2000 °C
600 °C
1200 km
2260 km
2530 km
340 km
10 km

CONTINENTAL DRIFT

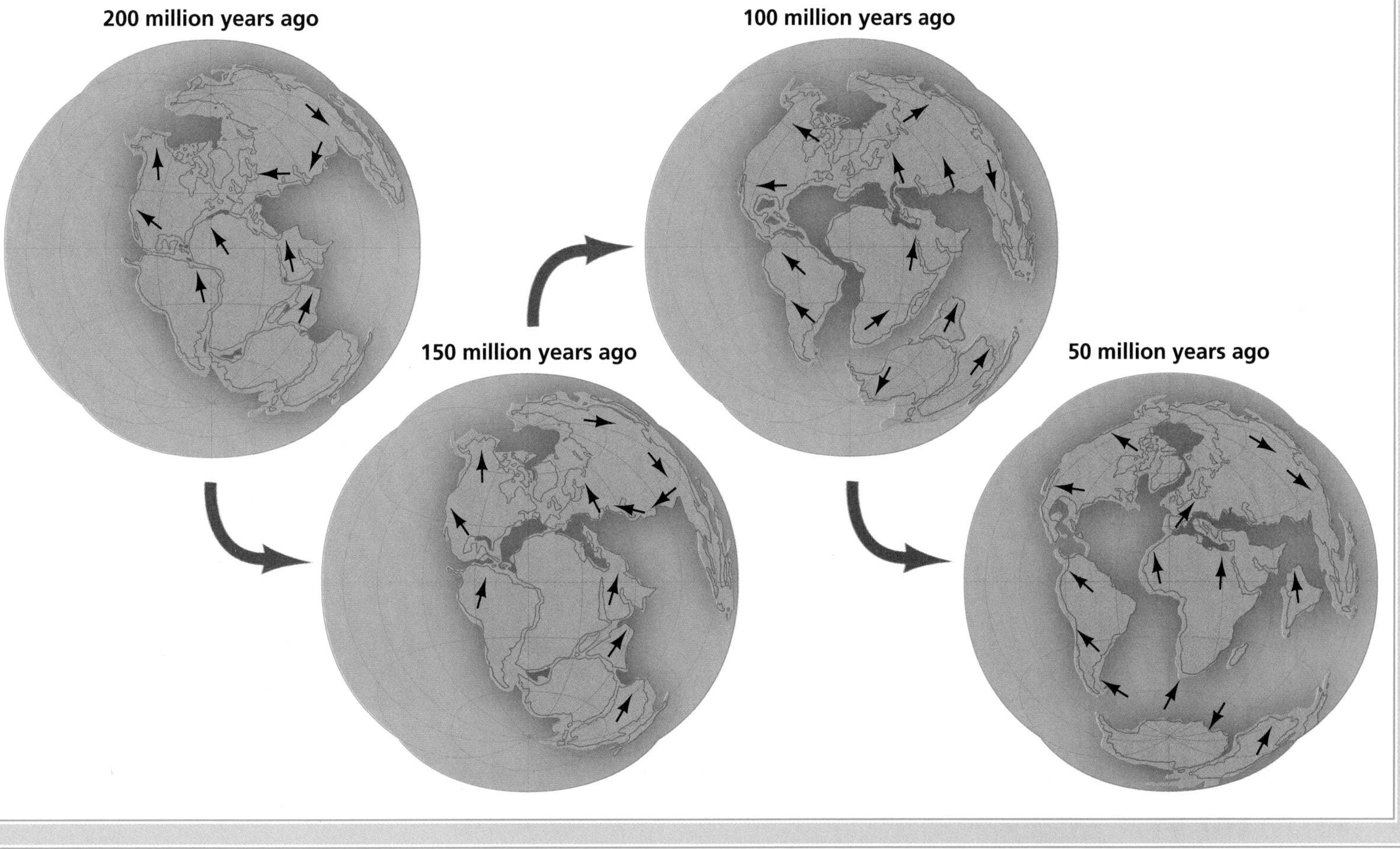
200 million years ago
150 million years ago
100 million years ago
50 million years ago

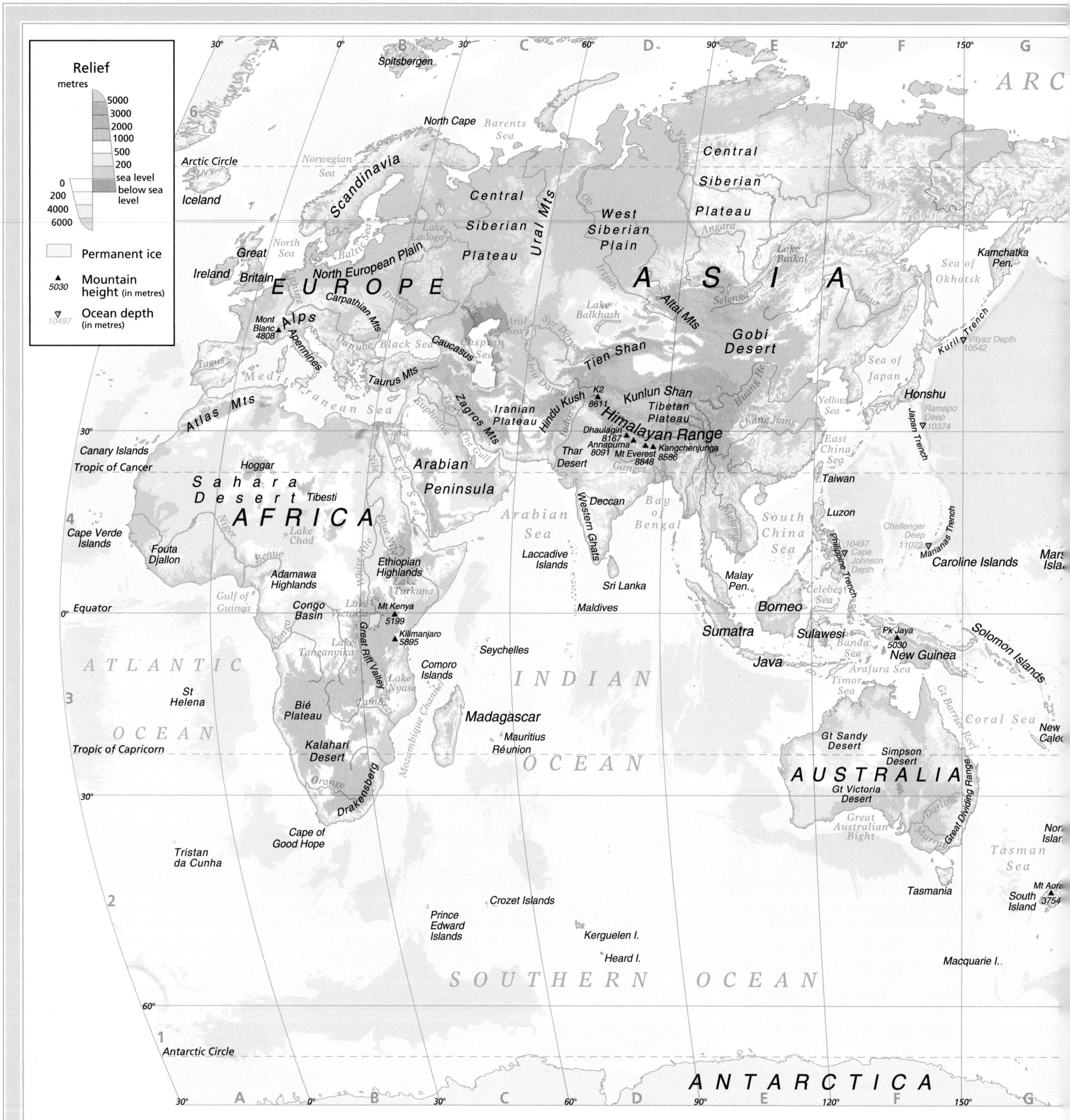
Relief
metres
5000
3000
2000
1000
500
200
sea level
below sea level
0
200
4000
6000
Permanent ice
5030 Mountain height (in metres)
10497 Ocean depth (in metres)
A
B
C
D
E
F
G
30°
0°
30°
60°
90°
120°
150°
Spitsbergen
North Cape
Barents Sea
Arctic Circle
Norwegian Sea
Scandinavia
Iceland
Central Siberian Plateau
Ural Mts
West Siberian Plain
Central Siberian Plateau
Great Britain
North Sea
Baltic Sea
Lake Ladoga
North European Plain
Ireland
EUROPE
Carpathian Mts
ASIA
Lake Baikal
Sea of Okhotsk
Kamchatka Pen.
Mont Blanc 4808
Alps
Apennines
Danube
Black Sea
Caucasus
Caspian Sea
Aral Sea
Lake Balkhash
Altai Mts
Gobi Desert
Kuril Trench
Vityaz Depth 10542
Tagus
Mediterranean Sea
Taurus Mts
Tien Shan
Sea of Japan
Atlas Mts
Zagros Mts
Iranian Plateau
Hindu Kush
K2 8611
Kunlun Shan
Tibetan Plateau
Honshu
Ramapo Deep 10374
Himalayan Range
Dhaulagiri 8167
Annapurna 8091
Mt Everest 8848
Kangchenjunga 8586
Yellow Sea
Japan Trench
Canary Islands
Tropic of Cancer
Hoggar
Arabian Peninsula
Thar Desert
East China Sea
Taiwan
Sahara Desert
Tibesti
AFRICA
Deccan
Western Ghats
Bay of Bengal
Arabian Sea
South China Sea
Luzon
Cape Verde Islands
Fouta Djallon
Lake Chad
Ethiopian Highlands
Lake Turkana
Laccadive Islands
Philippine Trench
10497 Cape Johnson Depth
Challenger Deep 11022
Marianas Trench
Caroline Islands
Adamawa Highlands
Sri Lanka
Malay Pen.
Gulf of Guinea
Congo Basin
Mt Kenya 5199
Maldives
Borneo
Celebes Sea
Equator
Kilimanjaro 5895
Great Rift Valley
Lake Victoria
Sumatra
Sulawesi
Pk Jaya 5030
New Guinea
Solomon Islands
Lake Tanganyika
Seychelles
Banda Sea
Java
ATLANTIC
Comoro Islands
INDIAN
Arafura Sea
Timor Sea
Lake Nyasa
Zambezi
St Helena
Bié Plateau
Madagascar
Coral Sea
Mozambique Channel
Mauritius
Réunion
Gt Sandy Desert
Simpson Desert
OCEAN
Tropic of Capricorn
Kalahari Desert
OCEAN
AUSTRALIA
Great Dividing Range
Gt Barrier Reef
Gt Victoria Desert
Orange
Drakensberg
Darling
Murray
Great Australian Bight
Cape of Good Hope
Tasman Sea
Tristan da Cunha
Tasmania
Mt Aoraki 3754
South Island
Crozet Islands
Prince Edward Islands
Kerguelen I.
Heard I.
Macquarie I.
SOUTHERN OCEAN
60°
Antarctic Circle
ANTARCTICA
6
5
4
3
2
1

CONTINENT CROSS SECTIONS

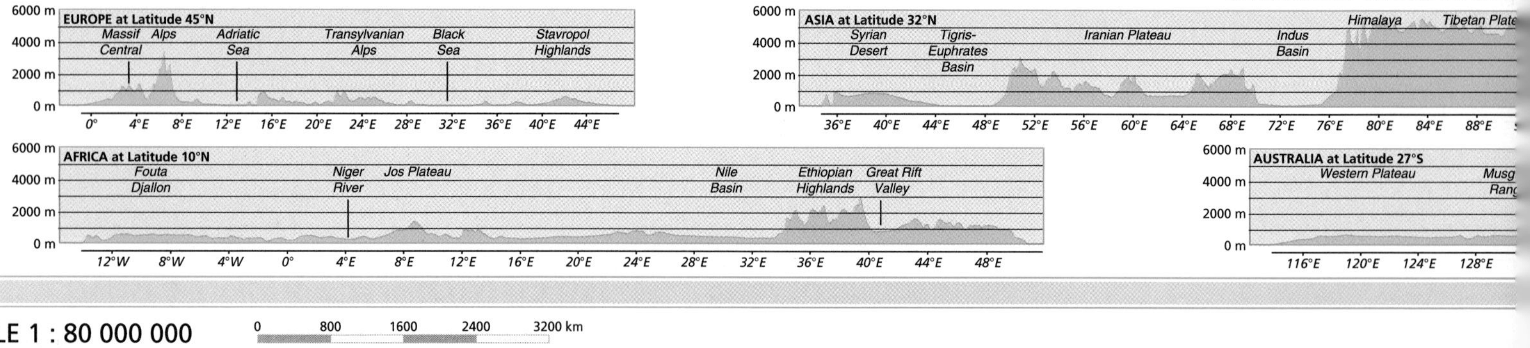
EUROPE at Latitude 45°N
Massif Central
Alps
Adriatic Sea
Transylvanian Alps
Black Sea
Stavropol Highlands
6000 m
4000 m
2000 m
0 m
0°
4°E
8°E
12°E
16°E
20°E
24°E
28°E
32°E
36°E
40°E
44°E
ASIA at Latitude 32°N
Syrian Desert
Tigris-Euphrates Basin
Iranian Plateau
Indus Basin
Himalaya
Tibetan Plate
36°E
40°E
44°E
48°E
52°E
56°E
60°E
64°E
68°E
72°E
76°E
80°E
84°E
88°E
AFRICA at Latitude 10°N
Fouta Djallon
Niger River
Jos Plateau
Nile Basin
Ethiopian Highlands
Great Rift Valley
12°W
8°W
4°W
0°
4°E
8°E
12°E
16°E
20°E
24°E
28°E
32°E
36°E
40°E
44°E
48°E
AUSTRALIA at Latitude 27°S
Western Plateau
116°E
120°E
124°E
128°E

SCALE 1 : 80 000 000

0 800 1600 2400 3200 km

orizontal scale 1 cm to 500 km, Vertical scale in metres, Vertical exaggeration = 105)

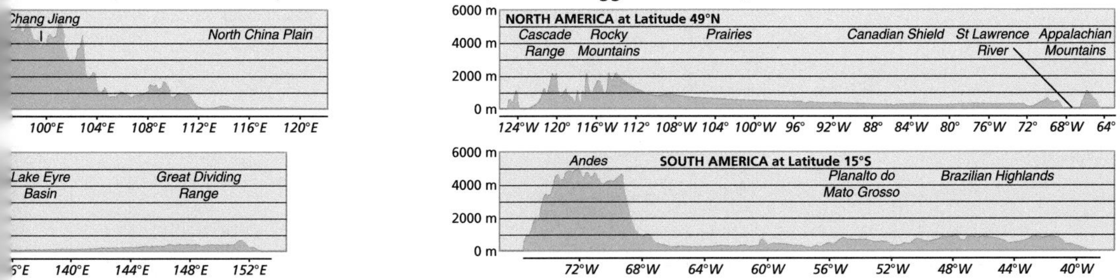

CONTINENTS	km^2
Asia	45 036 492
Africa	30 343 578
North America	24 680 331
South America	17 815 420
Antarctica	12 093 000
Europe	9 908 599
Australia	7 682 300

OCEANS	km^2
Pacific Ocean	166 624 000
Atlantic Ocean	86 557 000
Indian Ocean	73 427 000
Arctic Ocean	9 485 000

ISLANDS	km^2
Greenland	2 175 600
New Guinea	808 510
Borneo	745 561
Madagascar	587 040
Baffin Island	507 451
Sumatra	473 606
Honshu	227 414
Great Britain	218 476
Victoria Island	217 291
Ellesmere Island	196 236

MOUNTAINS	metres
Mt Everest *(Nepal/China)*	8848
K2 *(Jammu & Kashmir/China)*	8611
Kangchenjunga *(Nepal/China)*	8586
Dhaulagiri *(Nepal)*	8167
Annapurna *(Nepal)*	8091
Aconcagua *(Argentina)*	6960
Ojos del Salado *(Argentina/Chile)*	6908
Chimborazo *(Ecuador)*	6310
Mt McKinley *(USA)*	6194
Mt Logan *(Canada)*	5959

RIVERS	km
Nile *(Africa)*	6695
Amazon *(S. America)*	6516
Chang Jiang *(Asia)*	6380
Mississippi-Missouri *(N. America)*	5969
Ob-Irtysh *(Asia)*	5568
Yenisey-Angara-Selenga *(Asia)*	5500
Huang-He *(Asia)*	5464
Congo *(Africa)*	4667
Río de la Plata-Paraná *(S. America)*	4500
Mekong *(Asia)*	4425

LAKES	km^2
Caspian Sea *(Asia)*	371 000
Lake Superior *(Canada/USA)*	82 100
Lake Victoria *(Africa)*	68 800
Lake Huron *(Canada/USA)*	59 600
Lake Michigan *(USA)*	57 800
Lake Tanganyika *(Africa)*	32 900
Great Bear Lake *(Canada)*	31 328
Lake Baikal *(Asia)*	30 500
Lake Nyasa *(Africa)*	30 044

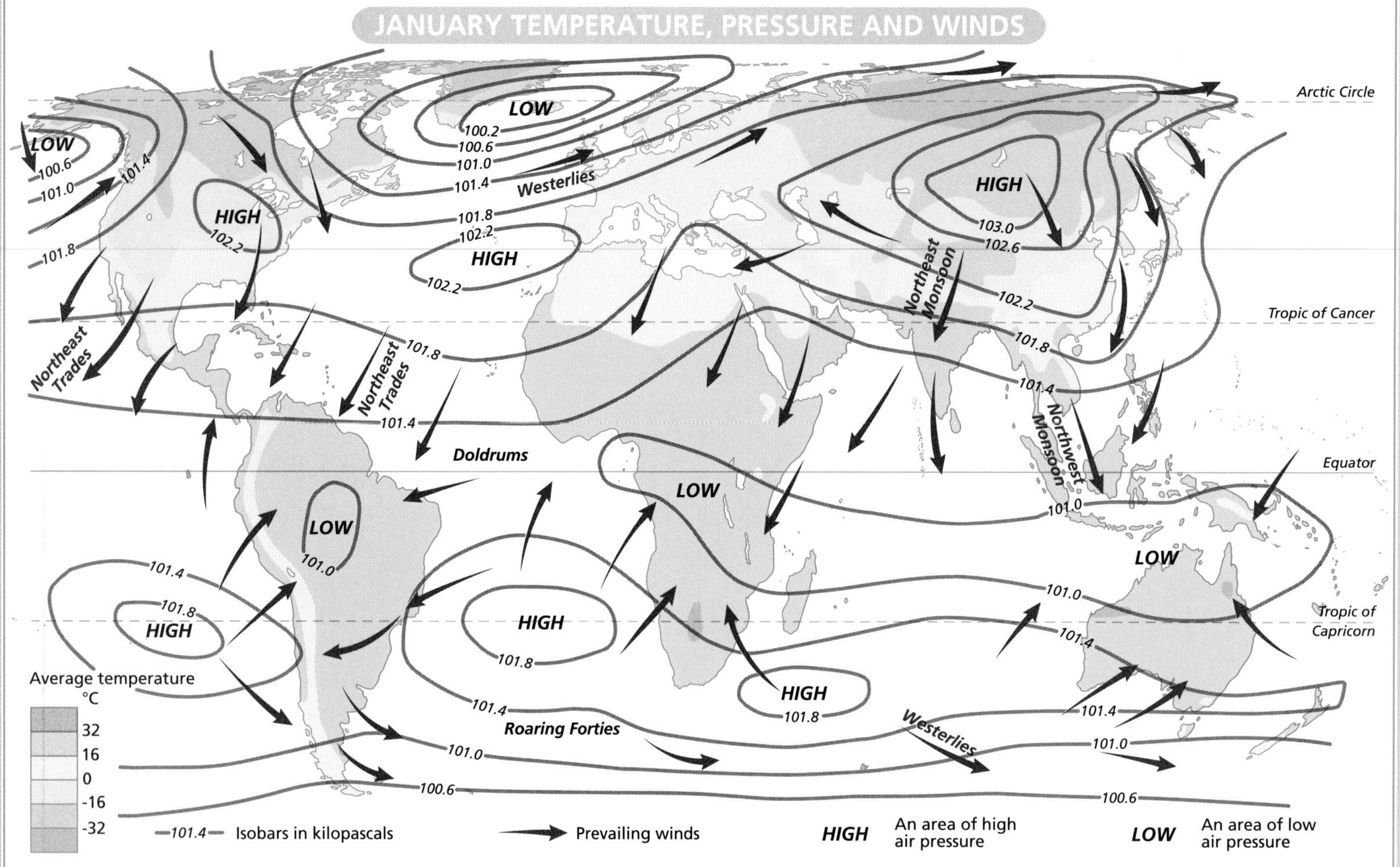

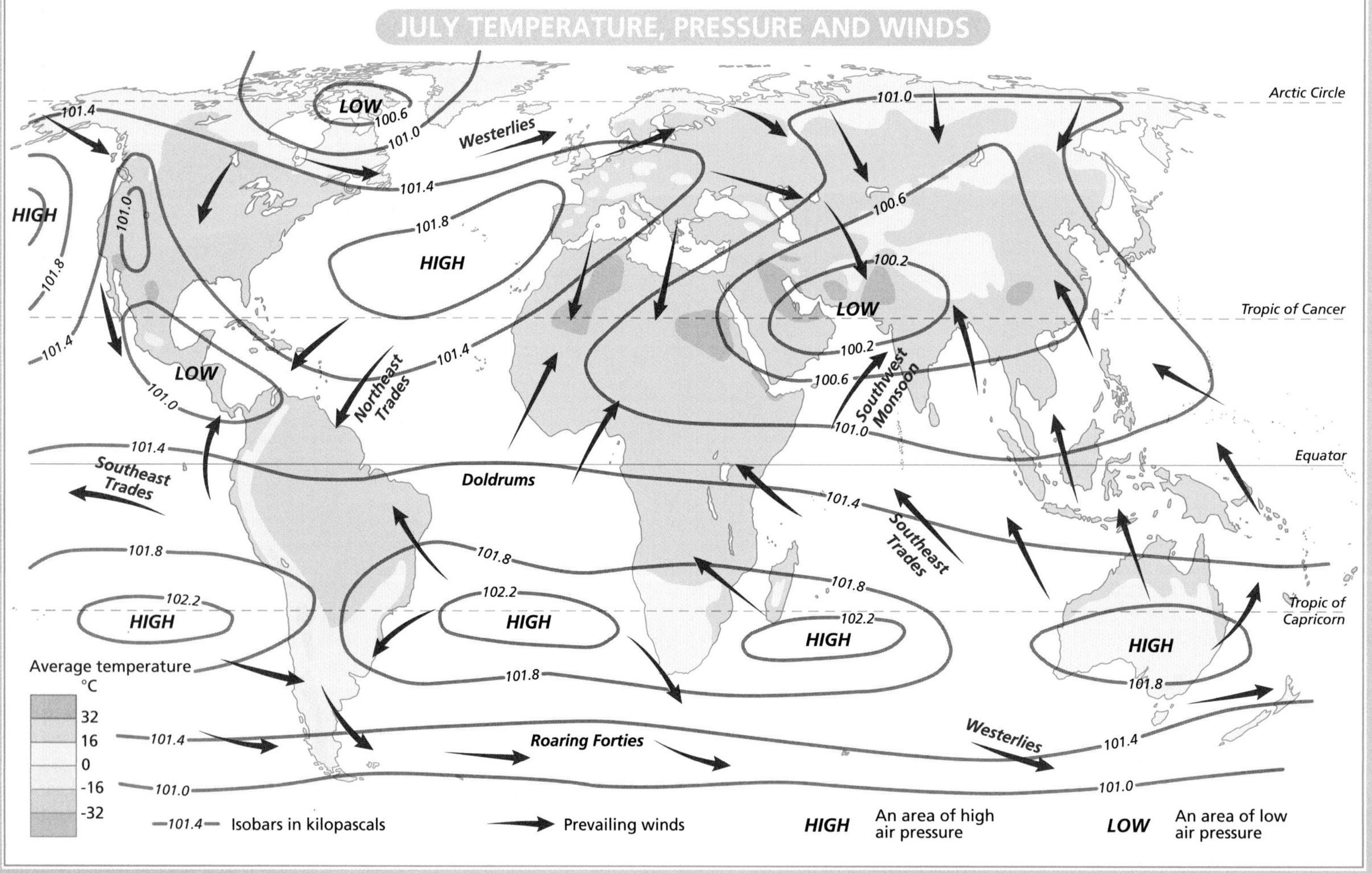

SCALE 1 : 140 000 000

0 2000 4000 6000 8000 km

Eckert IV projection

JANUARY PRECIPITATION AND OCEAN CURRENTS

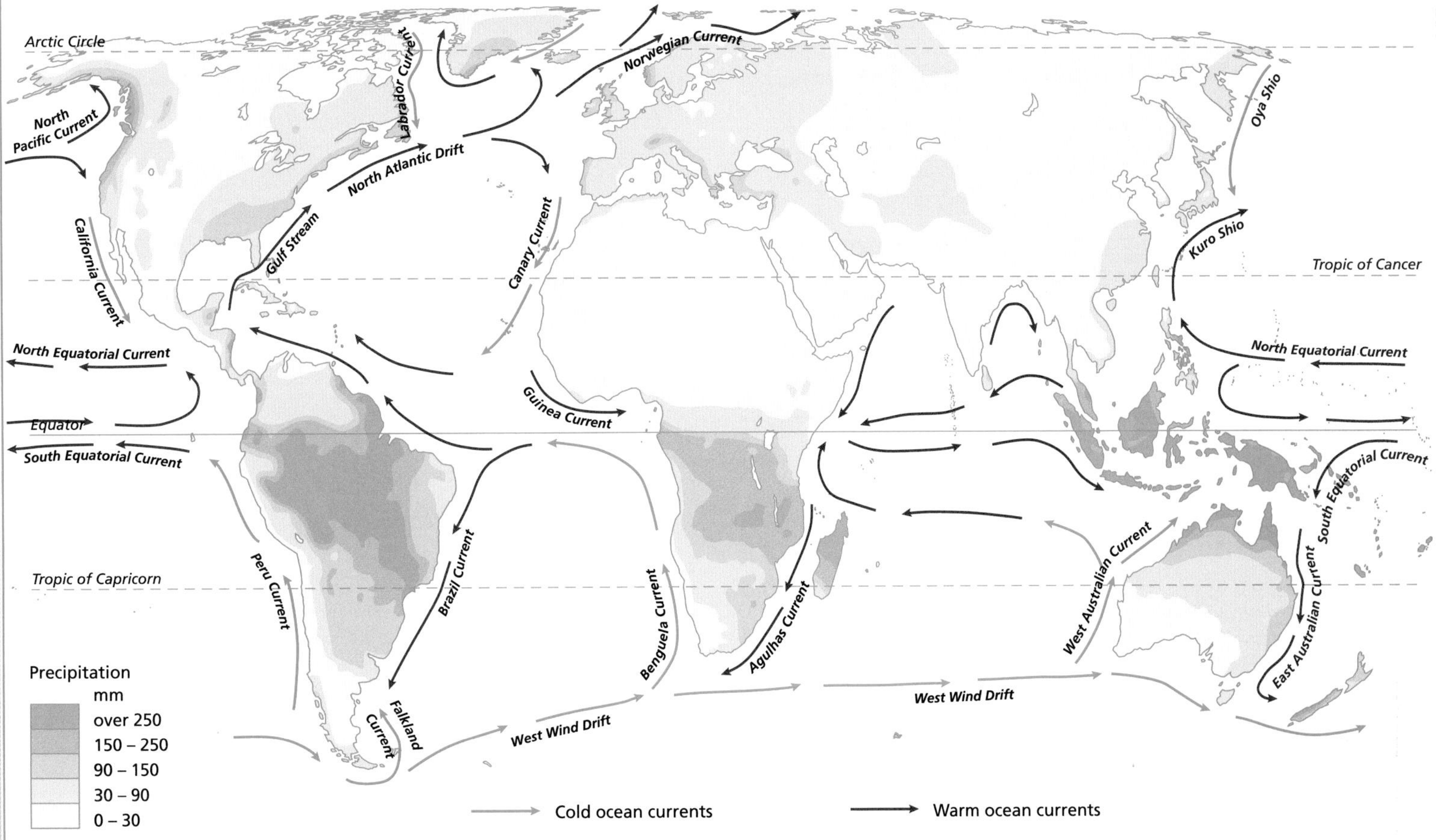

JULY PRECIPITATION AND OCEAN CURRENTS

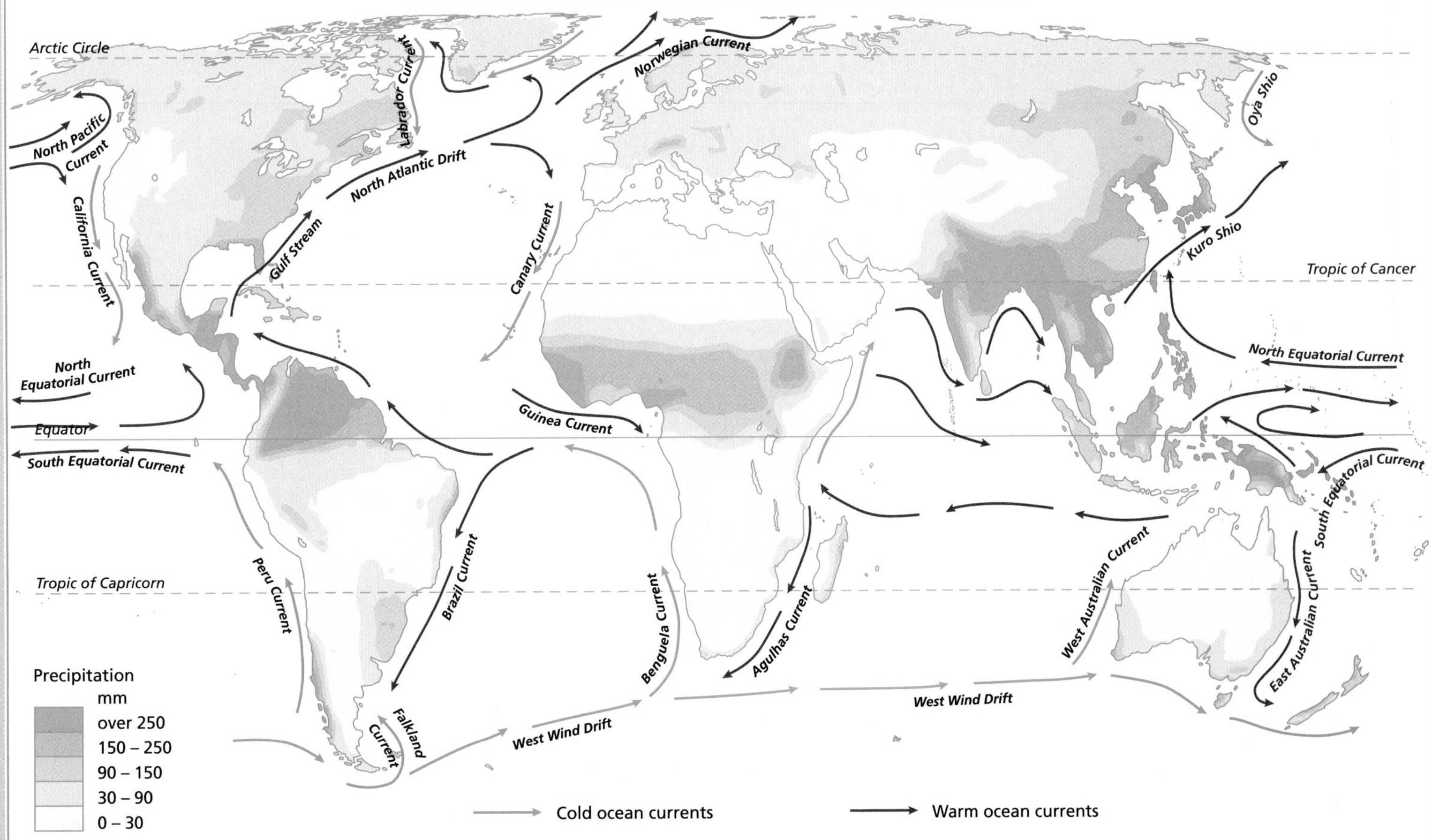

SCALE 1 : 140 000 000

0 2000 4000 6000 8000 km

Eckert IV projection

AIR MASSES

January

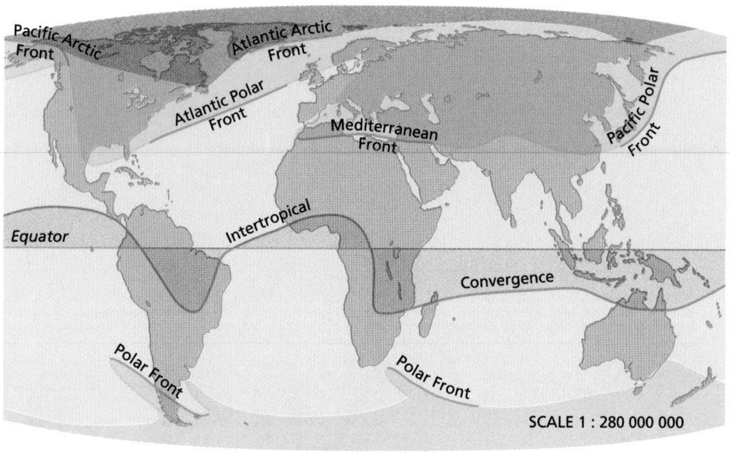

July

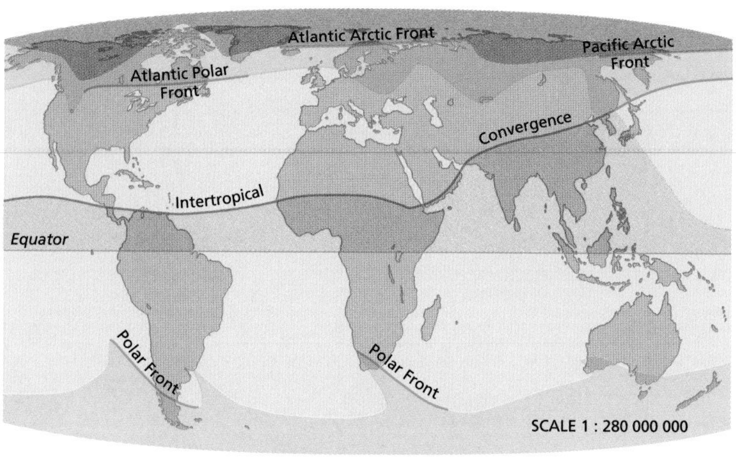

Arctic air | Polar air | Temperate air | Equatorial air | Fronts

Four types of air masses are identified above. The temperature and humidity characteristics of these air masses stay relatively constant over large distances. They remain relatively stationary over an area for a number of days. Fronts separate air masses in the temperate regions. The Intertropical Convergence Zone has low atmospheric pressure and ascending air located at or near the equator.

Air masses and fronts migrate with the apparent movement of the overhead sun (seasons). The movement of the Intertropical Convergence Zone is most obvious. It pushes south of the equator in January, and "fronts" north of the equator in July, moving as far north as central China. Much of Canada is influenced by polar air in January, and temperate air in July.

STORMS

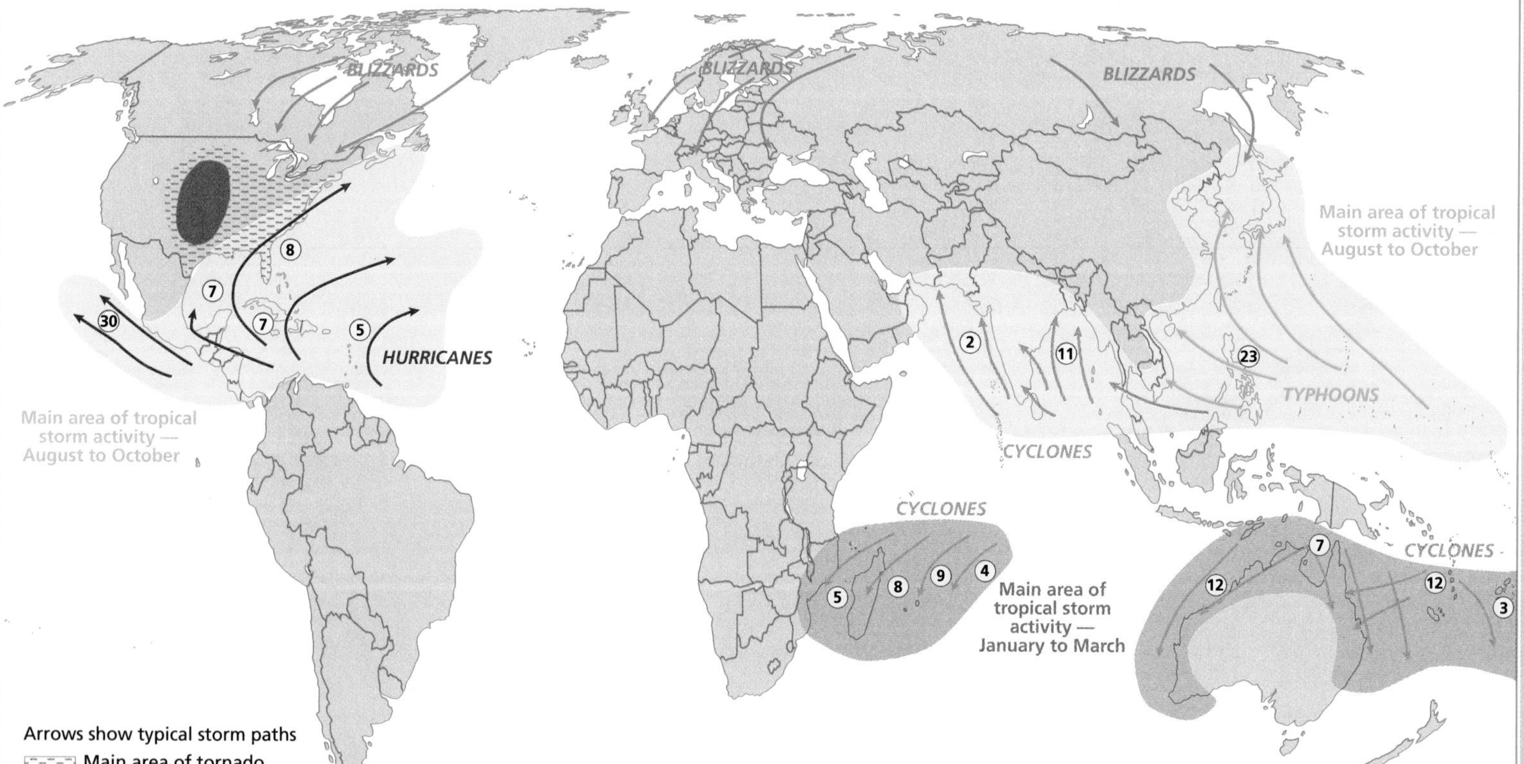

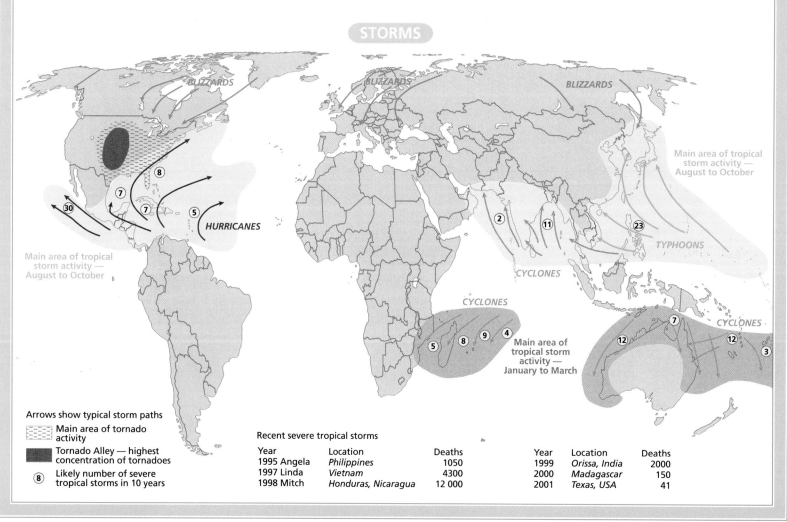

Arrows show typical storm paths

- Main area of tornado activity
- Tornado Alley — highest concentration of tornadoes
- (8) Likely number of severe tropical storms in 10 years

Recent severe tropical storms

Year	Location	Deaths
1995 Angela	*Philippines*	1050
1997 Linda	*Vietnam*	4300
1998 Mitch	*Honduras, Nicaragua*	12 000
1999	*Orissa, India*	2000
2000	*Madagascar*	150
2001	*Texas, USA*	41

SCALE 1 : 140 000 000 — 0, 2000, 4000, 6000, 8000 km

Eckert IV projection

WATER DEFICIENCY AND SURPLUS

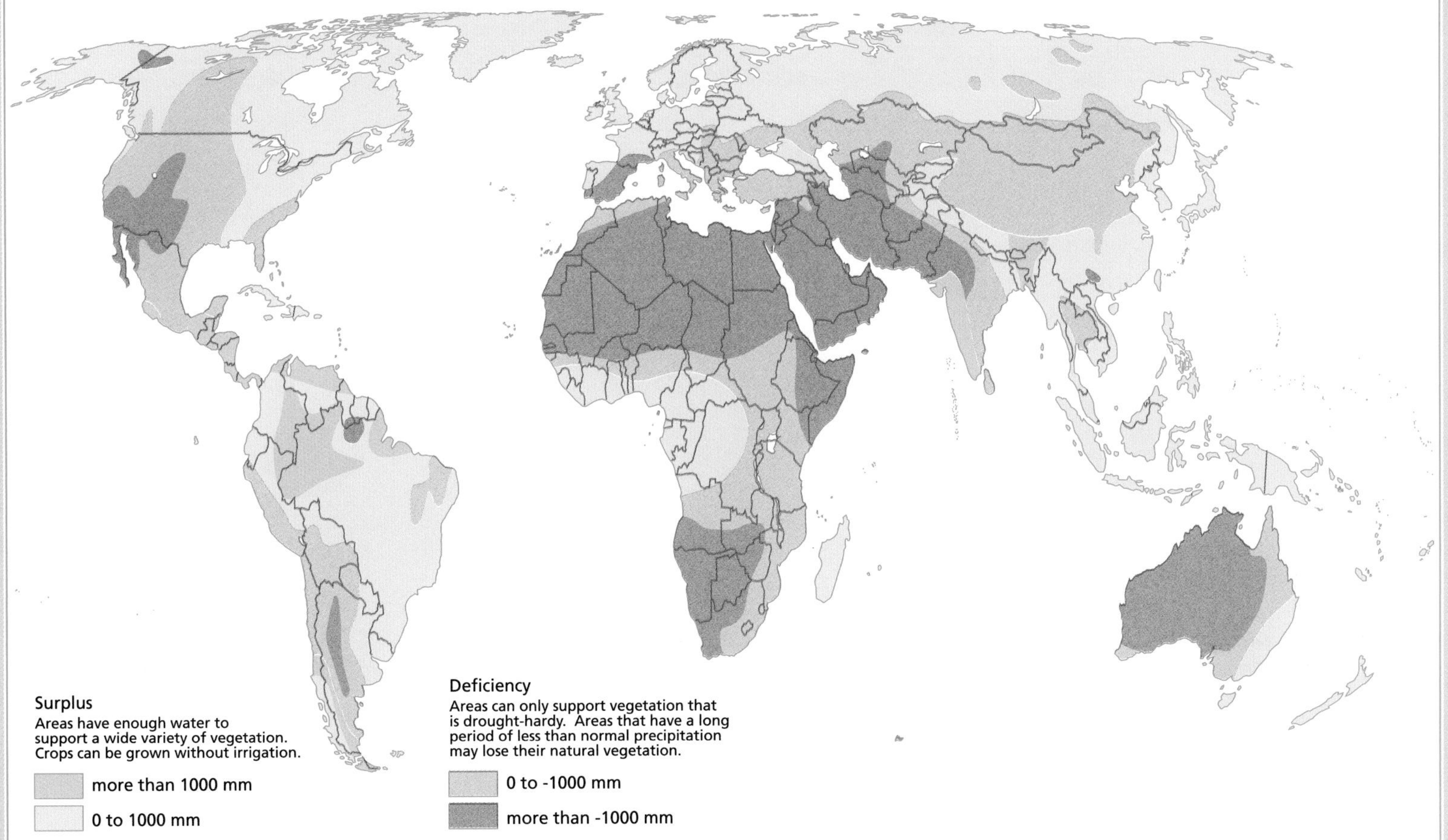

CLIMATE REGIONS

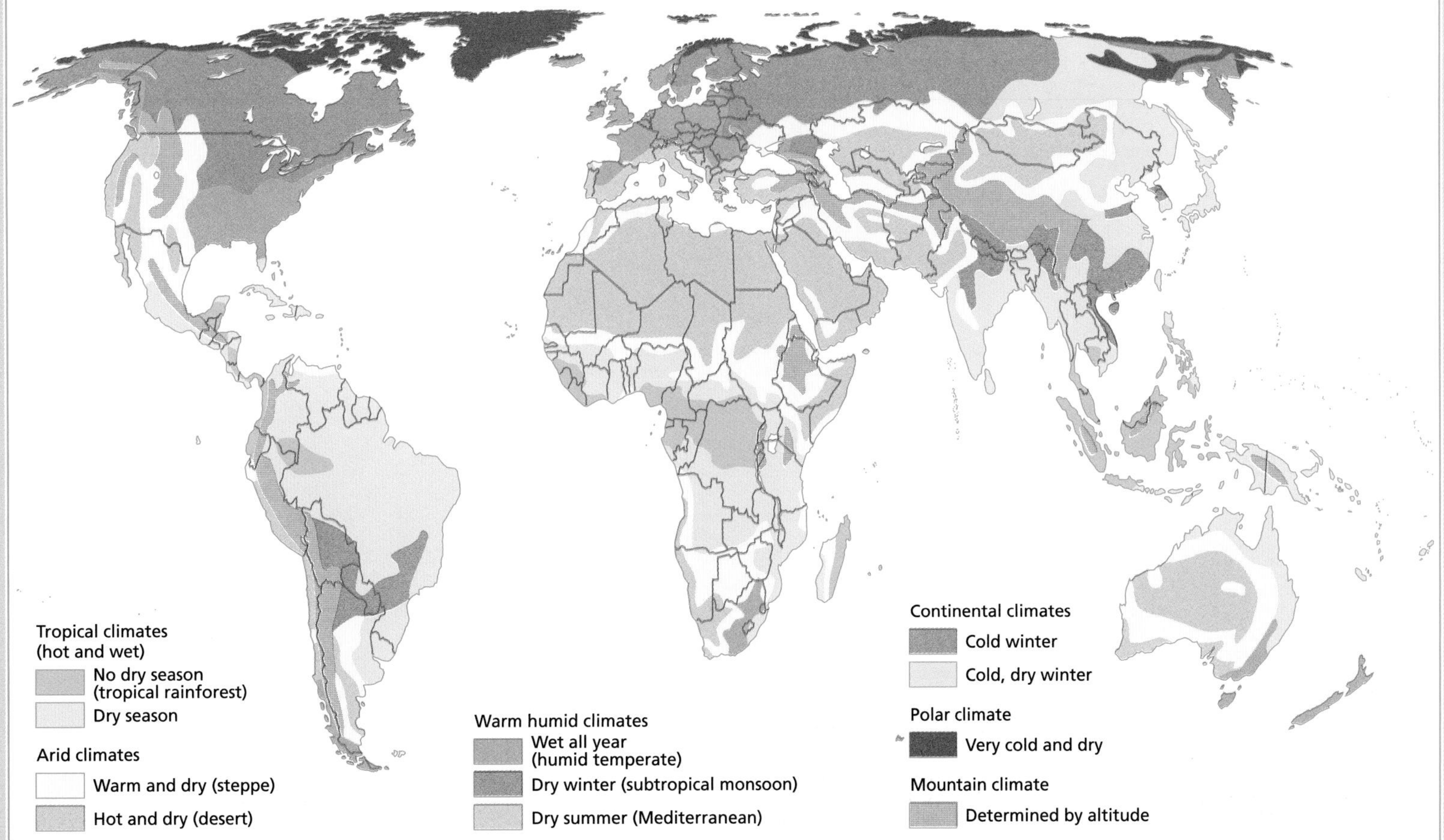

SCALE 1 : 140 000 000

0 2000 4000 6000 8000 km

Eckert IV projection

VEGETATION

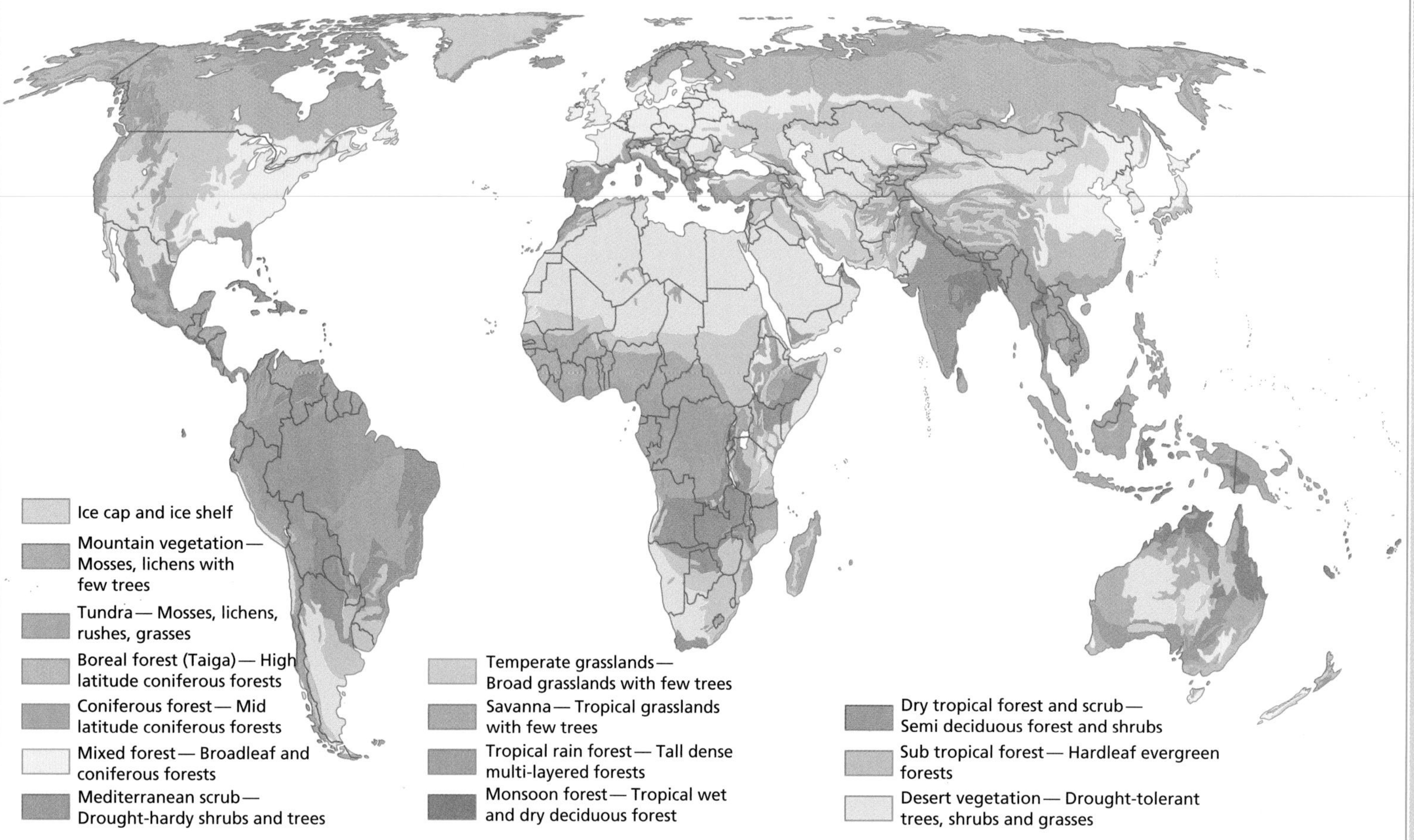
Ice cap and ice shelf
Mountain vegetation— Mosses, lichens with few trees
Tundra— Mosses, lichens, rushes, grasses
Boreal forest (Taiga)— High latitude coniferous forests
Coniferous forest— Mid latitude coniferous forests
Mixed forest— Broadleaf and coniferous forests
Mediterranean scrub— Drought-hardy shrubs and trees
Temperate grasslands— Broad grasslands with few trees
Savanna— Tropical grasslands with few trees
Tropical rain forest— Tall dense multi-layered forests
Monsoon forest— Tropical wet and dry deciduous forest
Dry tropical forest and scrub— Semi deciduous forest and shrubs
Sub tropical forest— Hardleaf evergreen forests
Desert vegetation— Drought-tolerant trees, shrubs and grasses

SOILS

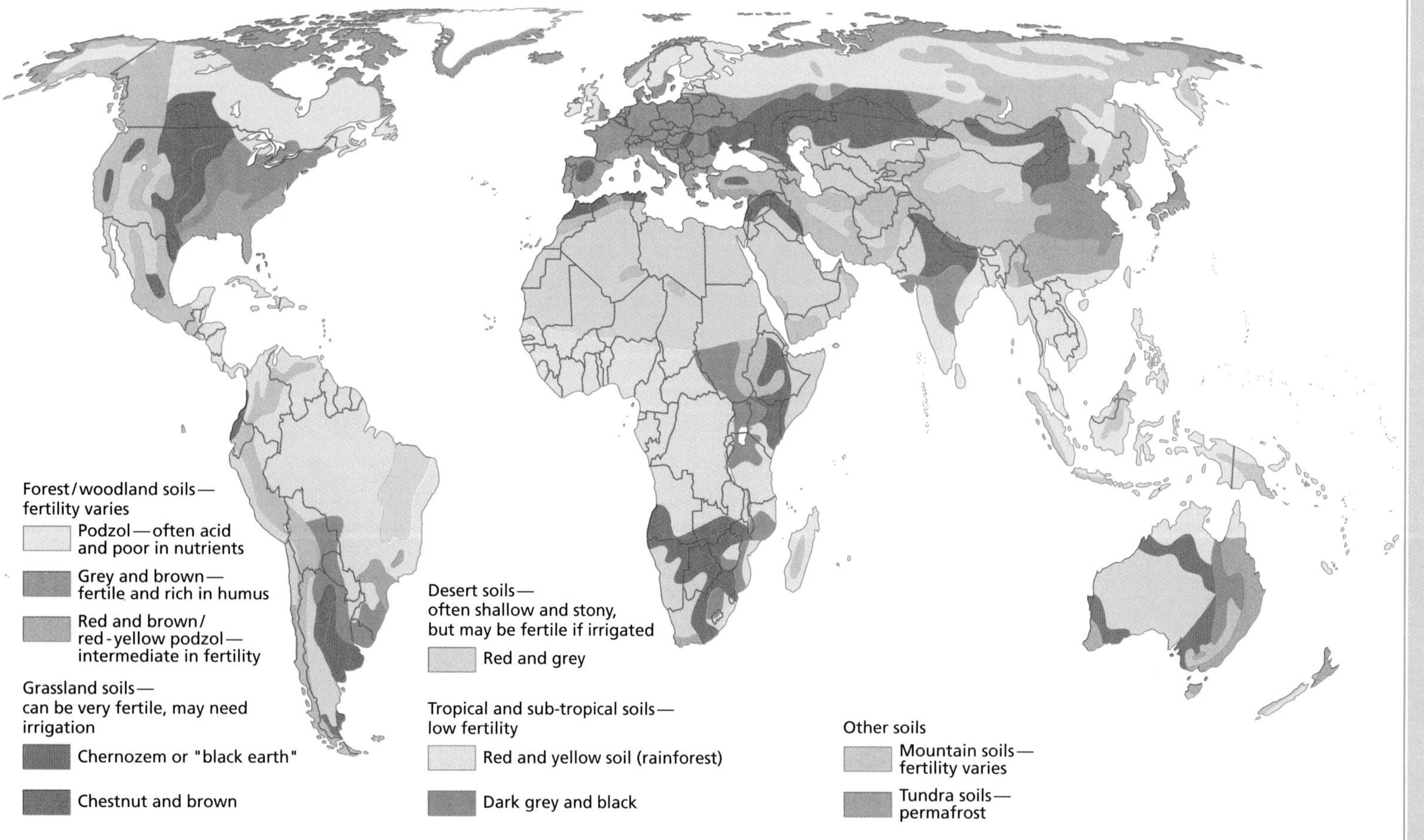
Forest/woodland soils— fertility varies
Podzol—often acid and poor in nutrients
Grey and brown— fertile and rich in humus
Red and brown/ red-yellow podzol— intermediate in fertility
Grassland soils— can be very fertile, may need irrigation
Chernozem or "black earth"
Chestnut and brown
Desert soils— often shallow and stony, but may be fertile if irrigated
Red and grey
Tropical and sub-tropical soils— low fertility
Red and yellow soil (rainforest)
Dark grey and black
Other soils
Mountain soils— fertility varies
Tundra soils— permafrost

SCALE 1 : 140 000 000

0 2000 4000 6000 8000 km

Eckert IV projection

AGRICULTURE

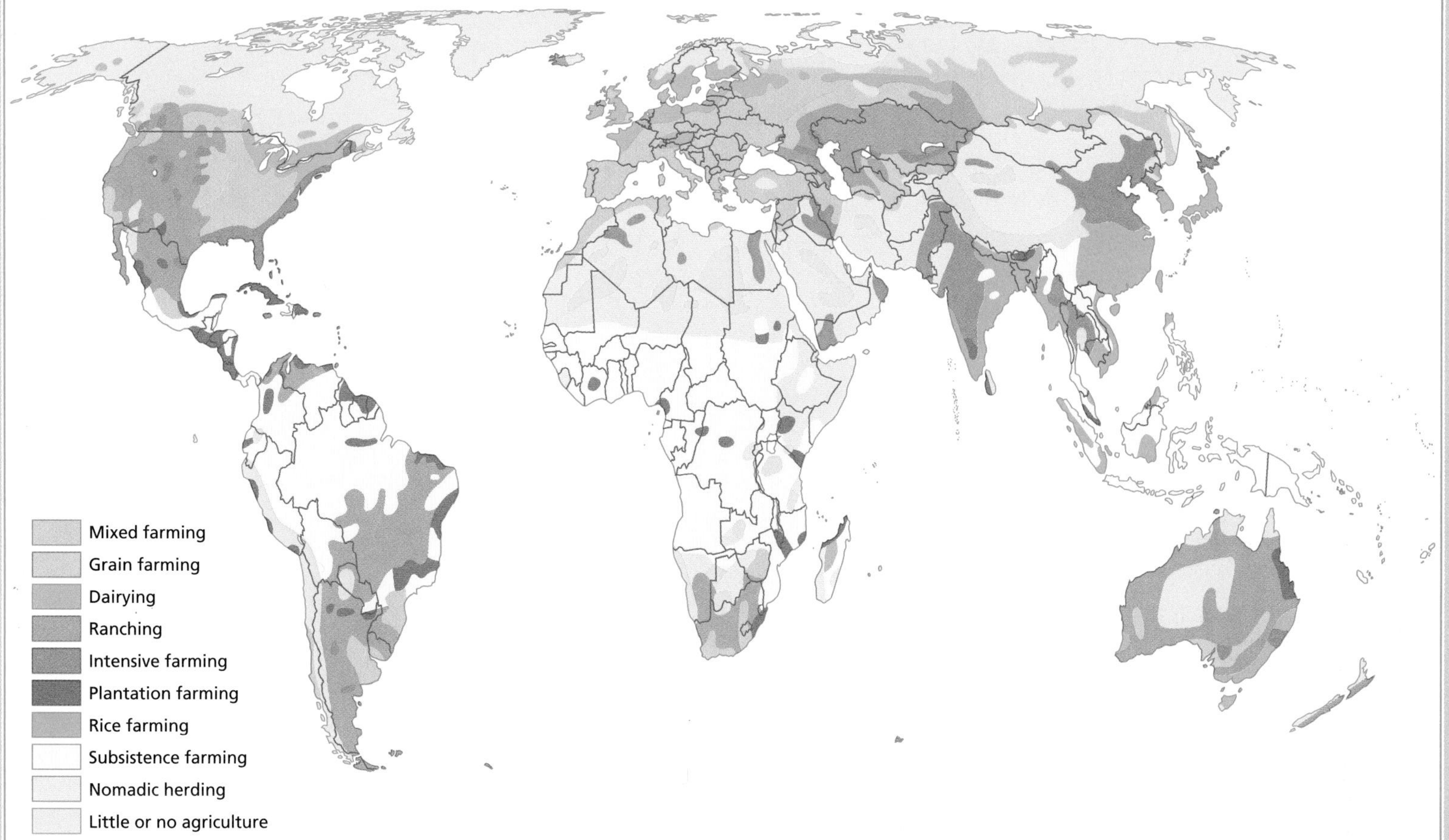

FISHING

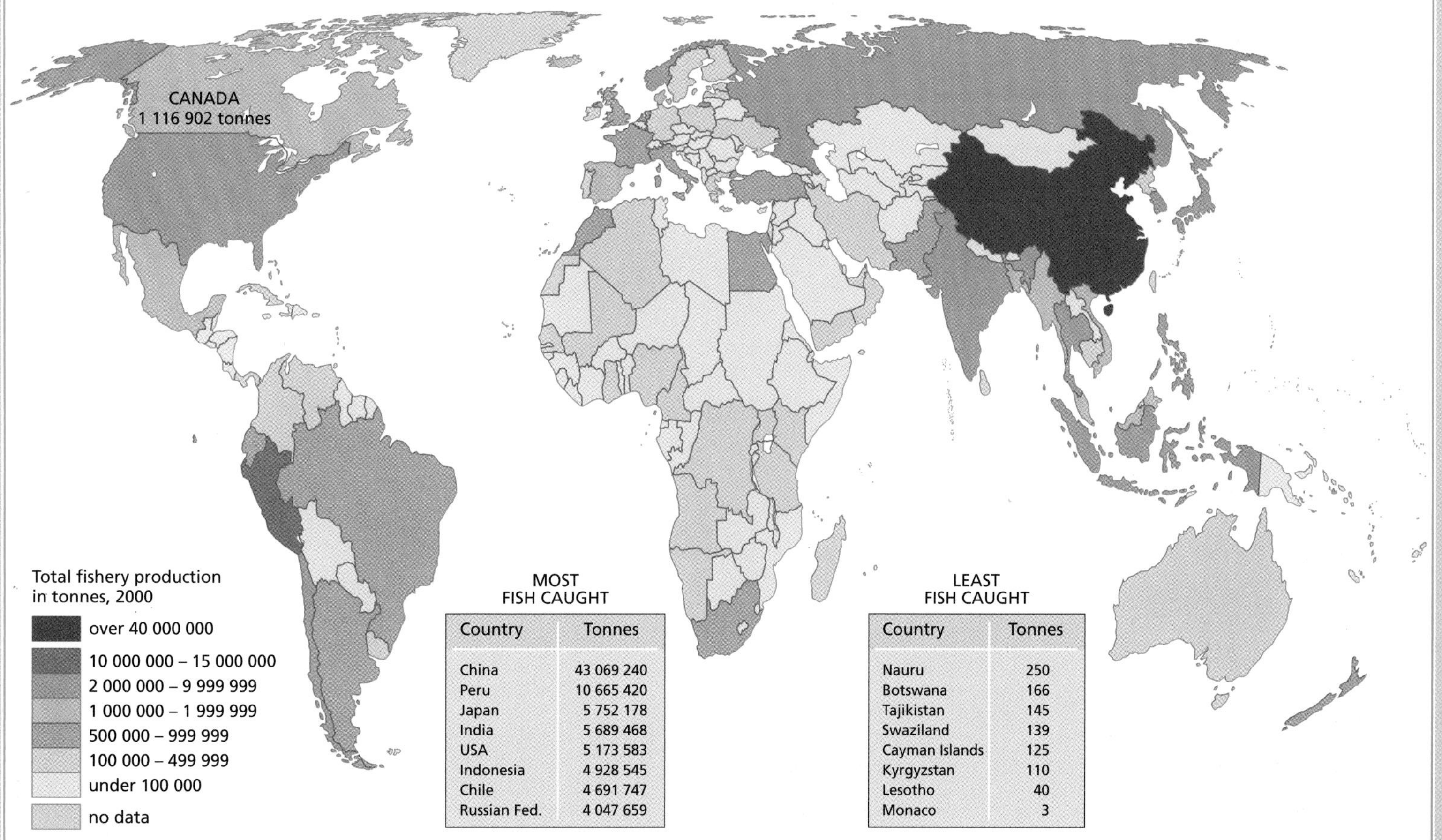

MOST FISH CAUGHT

Country	Tonnes
China	43 069 240
Peru	10 665 420
Japan	5 752 178
India	5 689 468
USA	5 173 583
Indonesia	4 928 545
Chile	4 691 747
Russian Fed.	4 047 659

LEAST FISH CAUGHT

Country	Tonnes
Nauru	250
Botswana	166
Tajikistan	145
Swaziland	139
Cayman Islands	125
Kyrgyzstan	110
Lesotho	40
Monaco	3

SCALE 1 : 140 000 000 (0, 2000, 4000, 6000, 8000 km)

Eckert IV projection

POPULATION DISTRIBUTION

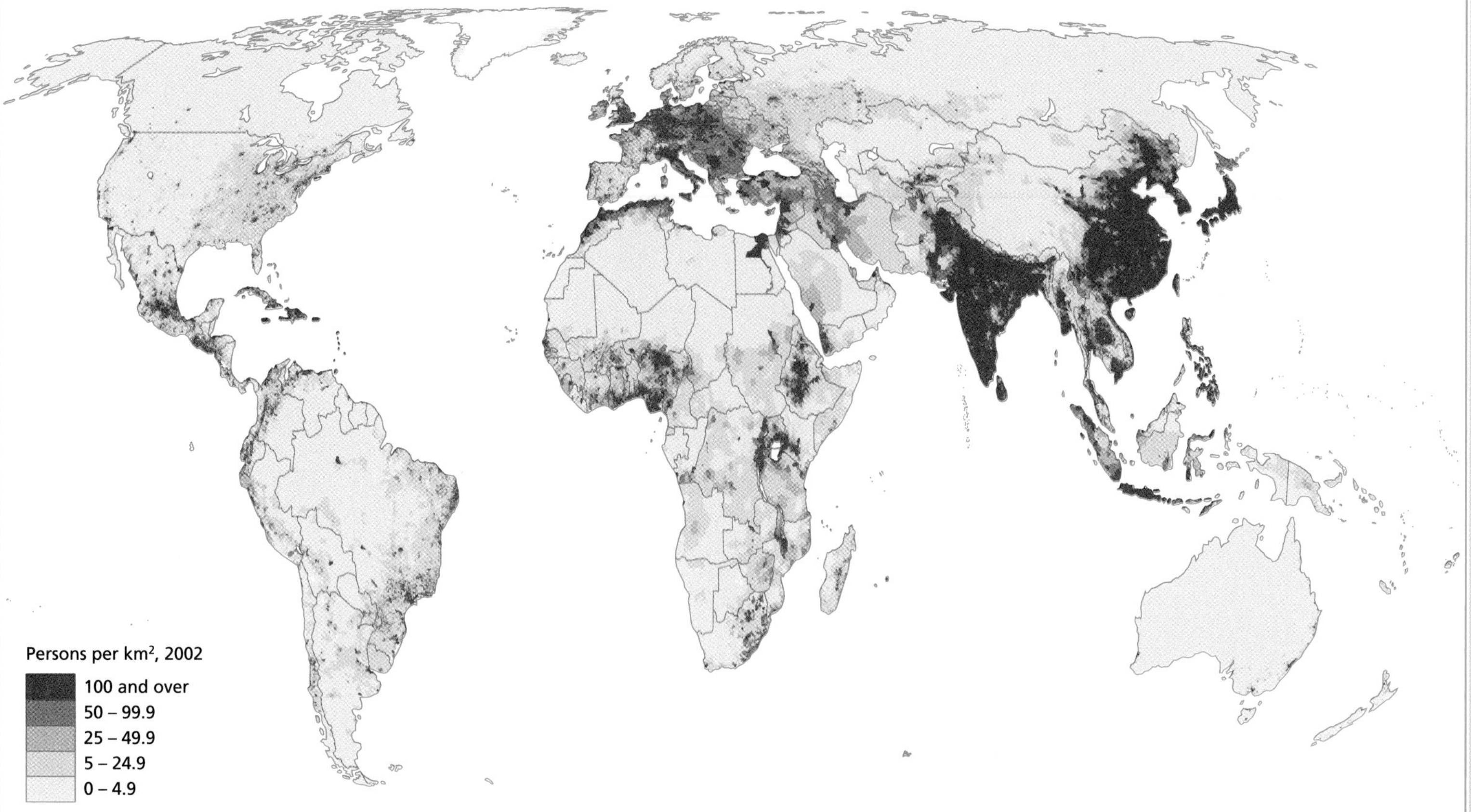

POPULATION DENSITY

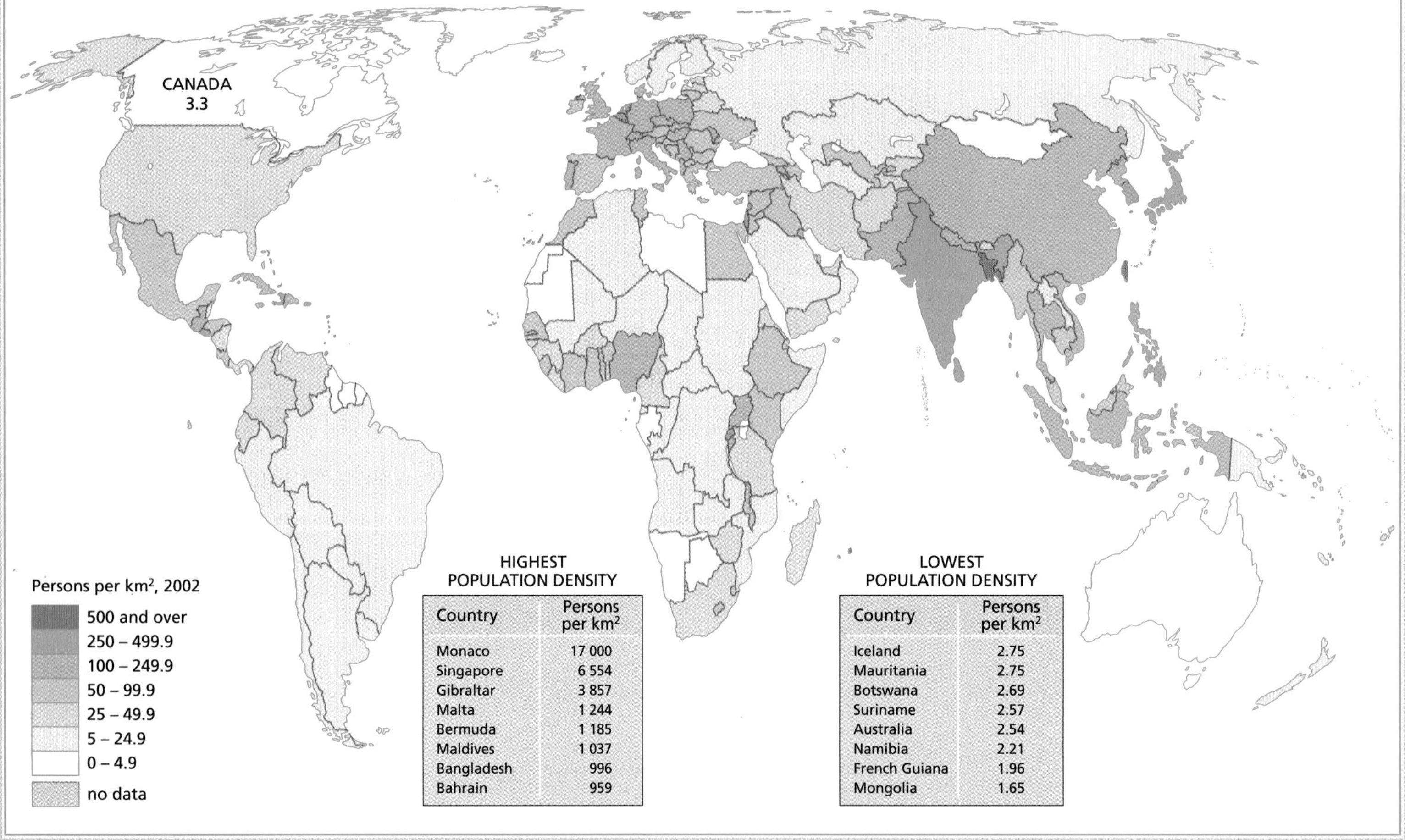

HIGHEST POPULATION DENSITY

Country	Persons per km^2
Monaco	17 000
Singapore	6 554
Gibraltar	3 857
Malta	1 244
Bermuda	1 185
Maldives	1 037
Bangladesh	996
Bahrain	959

LOWEST POPULATION DENSITY

Country	Persons per km^2
Iceland	2.75
Mauritania	2.75
Botswana	2.69
Suriname	2.57
Australia	2.54
Namibia	2.21
French Guiana	1.96
Mongolia	1.65

SCALE 1 : 140 000 000 — 0, 2000, 4000, 6000, 8000 km

Eckert IV projection

LIFE EXPECTANCY

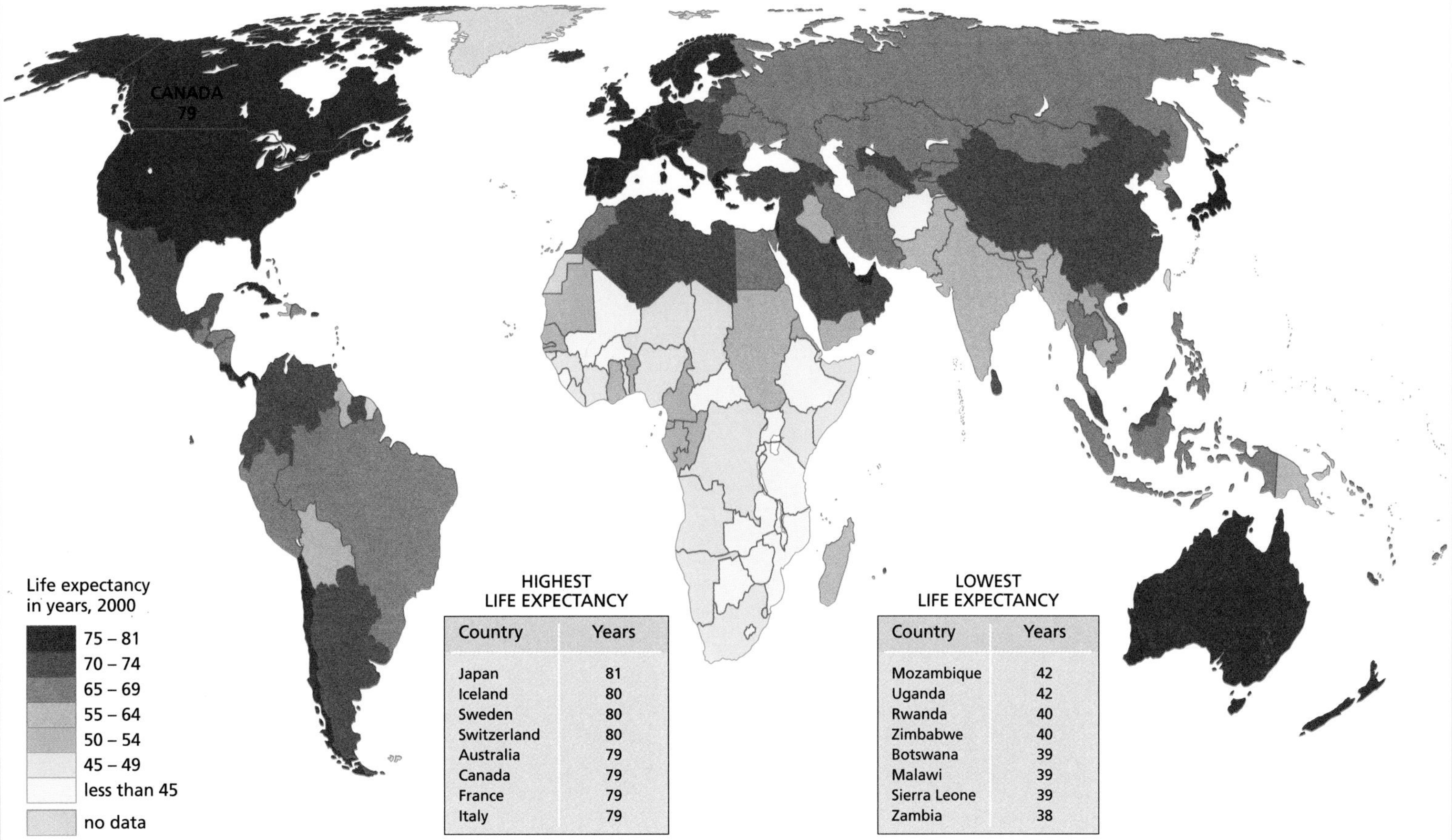

HIGHEST
LIFE EXPECTANCY

Country	Years
Japan	81
Iceland	80
Sweden	80
Switzerland	80
Australia	79
Canada	79
France	79
Italy	79

LOWEST
LIFE EXPECTANCY

Country	Years
Mozambique	42
Uganda	42
Rwanda	40
Zimbabwe	40
Botswana	39
Malawi	39
Sierra Leone	39
Zambia	38

INFANT MORTALITY

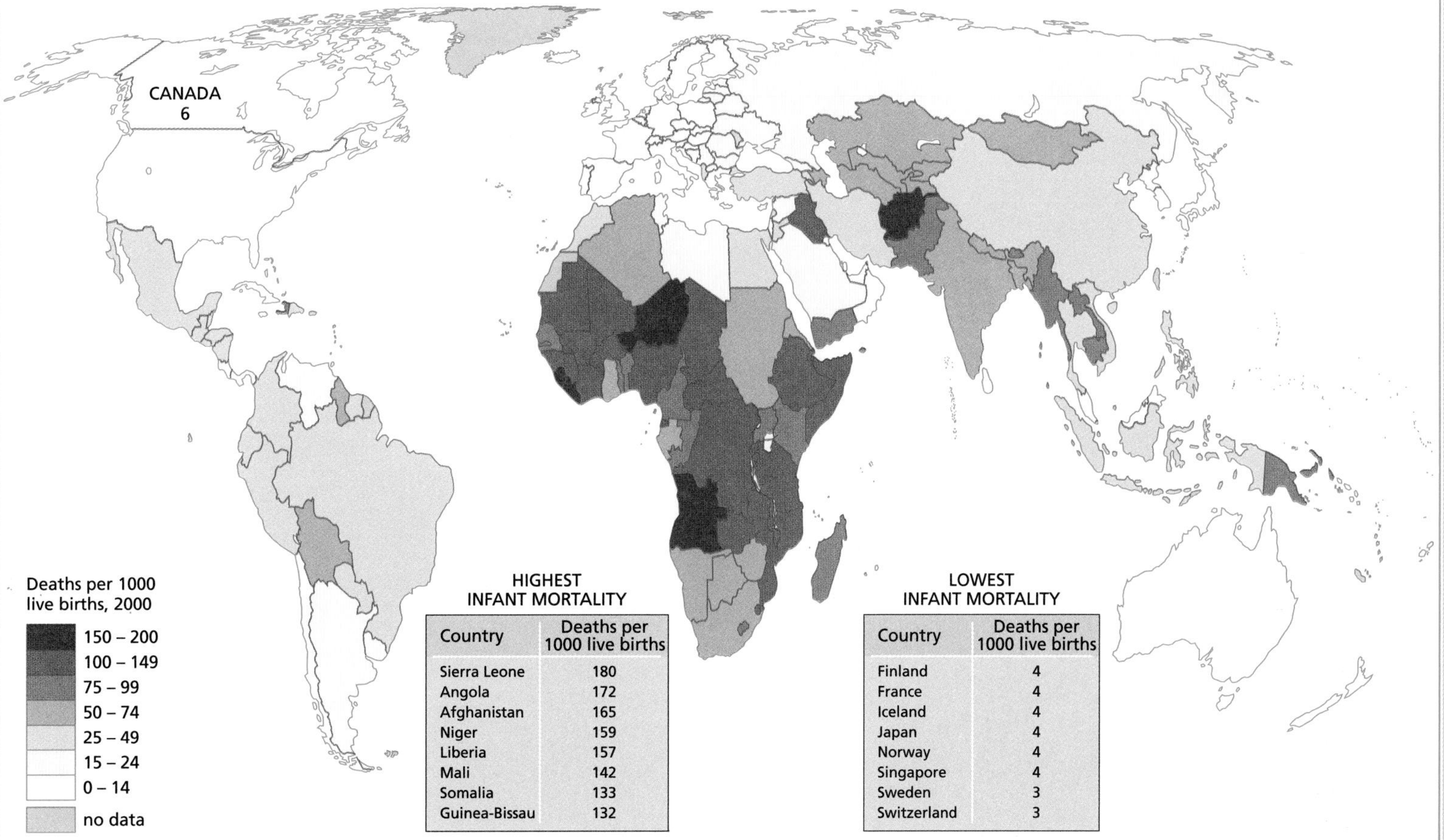

HIGHEST
INFANT MORTALITY

Country	Deaths per 1000 live births
Sierra Leone	180
Angola	172
Afghanistan	165
Niger	159
Liberia	157
Mali	142
Somalia	133
Guinea-Bissau	132

LOWEST
INFANT MORTALITY

Country	Deaths per 1000 live births
Finland	4
France	4
Iceland	4
Japan	4
Norway	4
Singapore	4
Sweden	3
Switzerland	3

SCALE 1 : 140 000 000

0 2000 4000 6000 8000 km

Eckert IV projection

POPULATION CHANGE

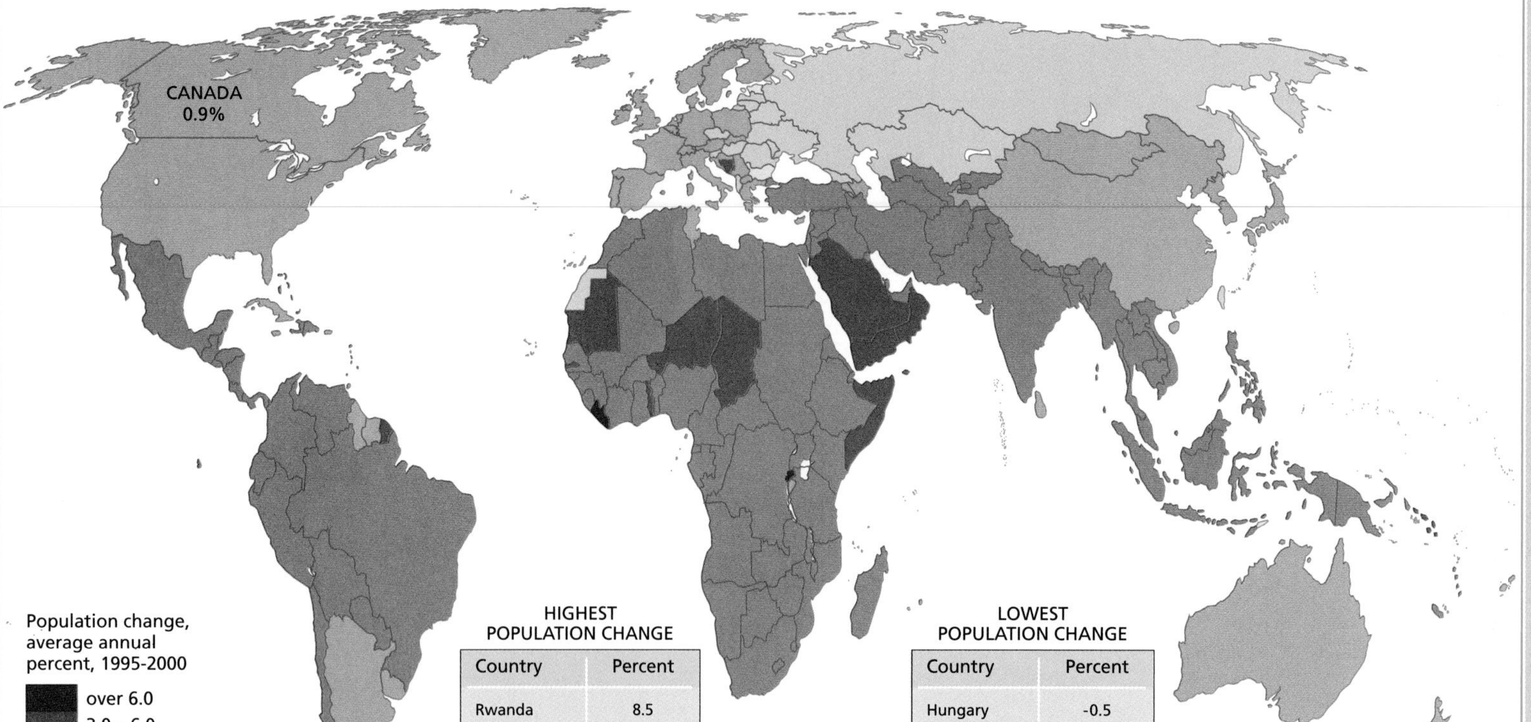

HIGHEST POPULATION CHANGE

Country	Percent
Rwanda	8.5
Liberia	7.1
Yemen	4.2
Somalia	3.6
French Guiana	3.5
Niger	3.5
Saudi Arabia	3.5
Solomon Is.	3.4

LOWEST POPULATION CHANGE

Country	Percent
Hungary	-0.5
Kazakhstan	-0.5
Latvia	-0.7
St Kitts & Nevis	-0.7
Ukraine	-0.7
Bulgaria	-1.1
Estonia	-1.3
East Timor	-2.6

URBAN POPULATION

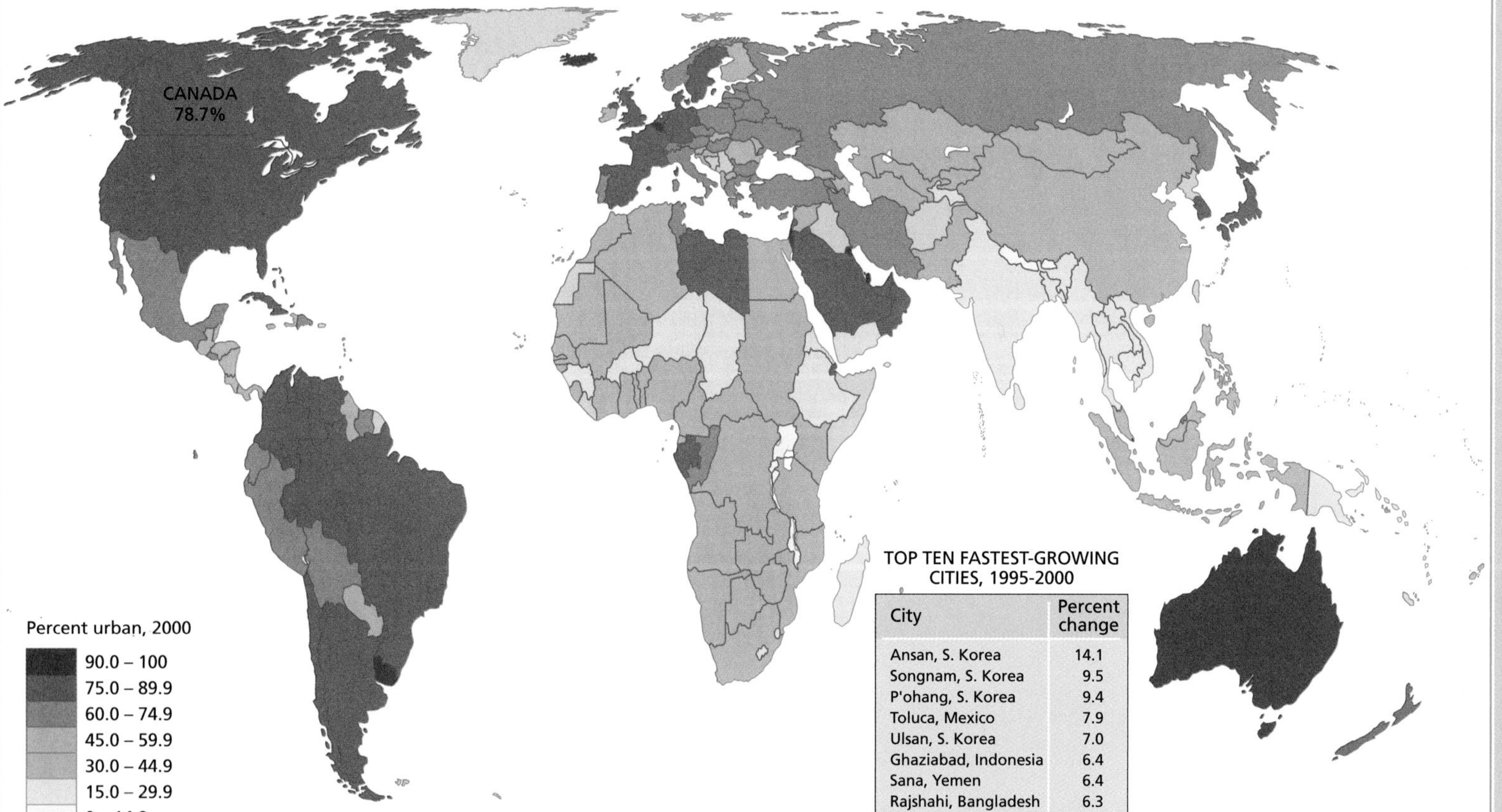

TOP TEN FASTEST-GROWING CITIES, 1995-2000

City	Percent change
Ansan, S. Korea	14.1
Songnam, S. Korea	9.5
P'ohang, S. Korea	9.4
Toluca, Mexico	7.9
Ulsan, S. Korea	7.0
Ghaziabad, Indonesia	6.4
Sana, Yemen	6.4
Rajshahi, Bangladesh	6.3
Dubai, UAE	6.2
Surat, India	6.2

SCALE 1 : 140 000 000 — 0, 2000, 4000, 6000, 8000 km

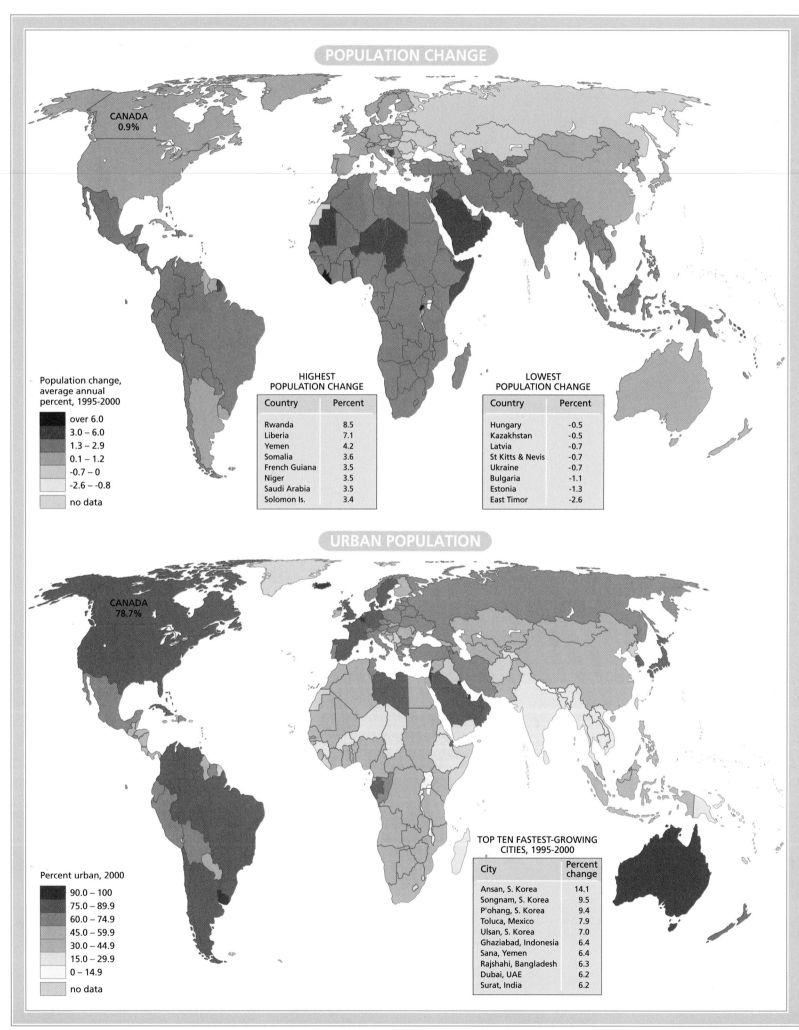

Eckert IV projection

MILLION CITIES

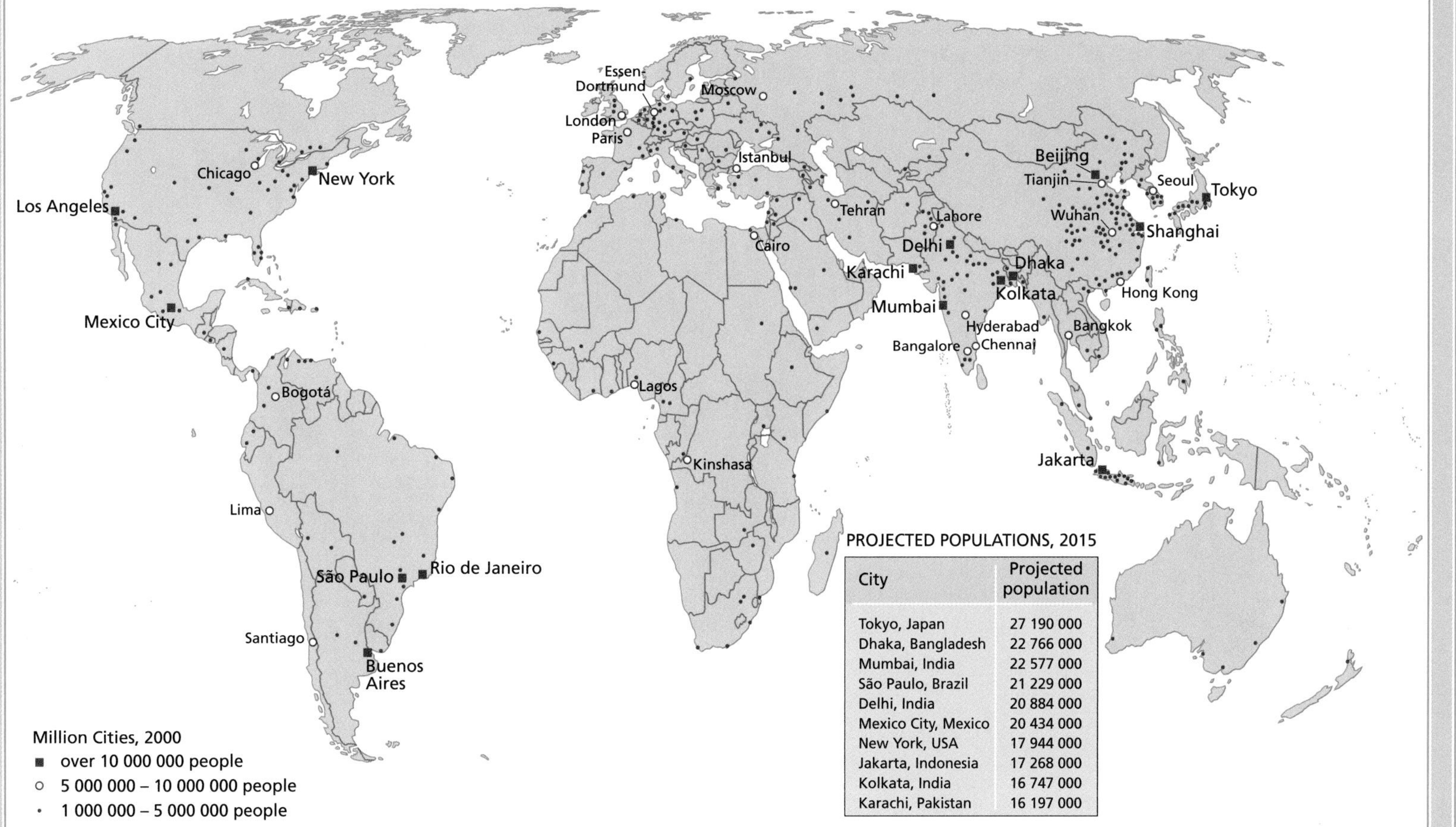

PROJECTED POPULATIONS, 2015

City	Projected population
Tokyo, Japan	27 190 000
Dhaka, Bangladesh	22 766 000
Mumbai, India	22 577 000
São Paulo, Brazil	21 229 000
Delhi, India	20 884 000
Mexico City, Mexico	20 434 000
New York, USA	17 944 000
Jakarta, Indonesia	17 268 000
Kolkata, India	16 747 000
Karachi, Pakistan	16 197 000

URBAN GROWTH

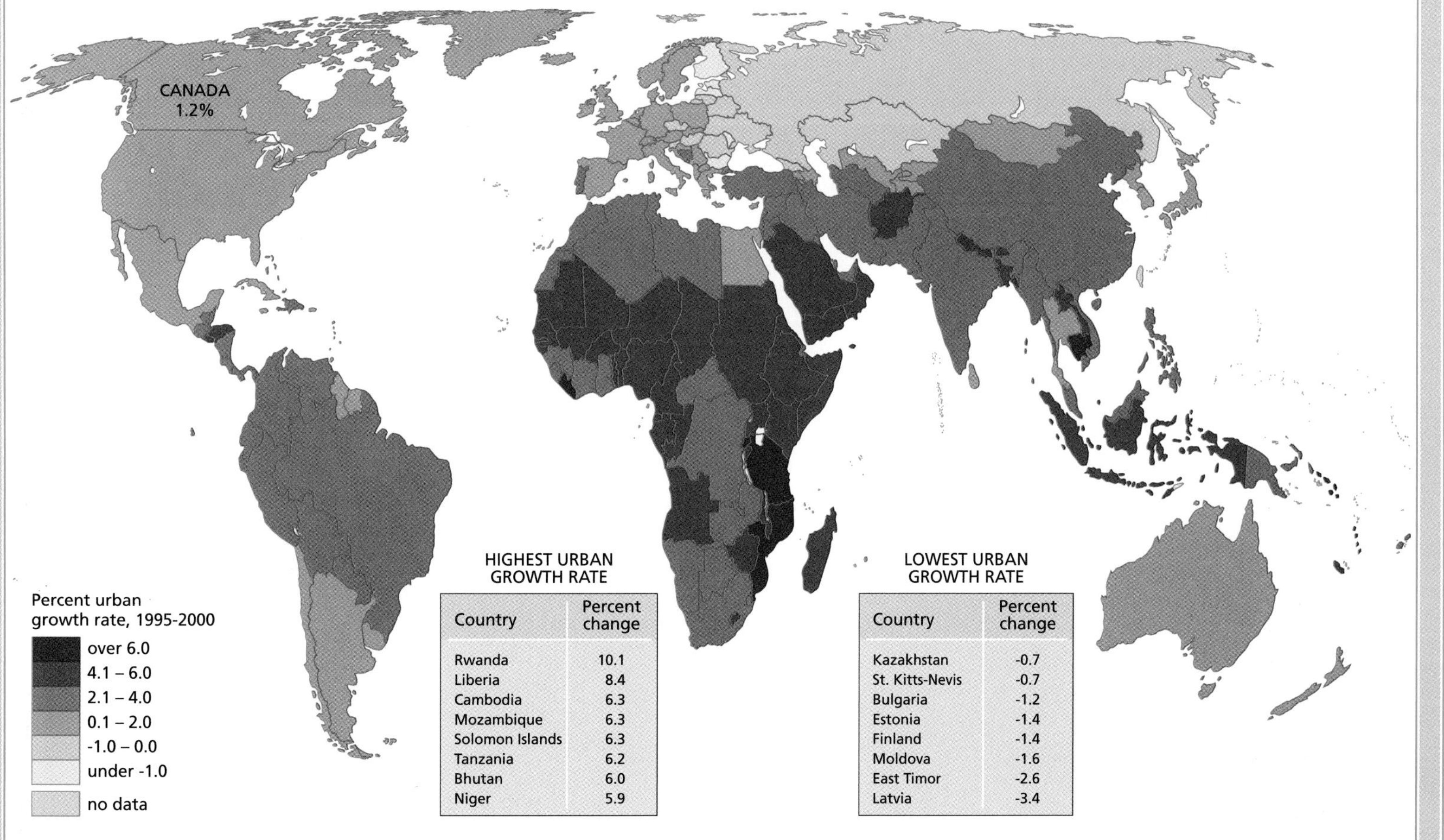

HIGHEST URBAN GROWTH RATE

Country	Percent change
Rwanda	10.1
Liberia	8.4
Cambodia	6.3
Mozambique	6.3
Solomon Islands	6.3
Tanzania	6.2
Bhutan	6.0
Niger	5.9

LOWEST URBAN GROWTH RATE

Country	Percent change
Kazakhstan	-0.7
St. Kitts-Nevis	-0.7
Bulgaria	-1.2
Estonia	-1.4
Finland	-1.4
Moldova	-1.6
East Timor	-2.6
Latvia	-3.4

SCALE 1 : 140 000 000 — 0, 2000, 4000, 6000, 8000 km

Eckert IV projection

GDP PER CAPITA

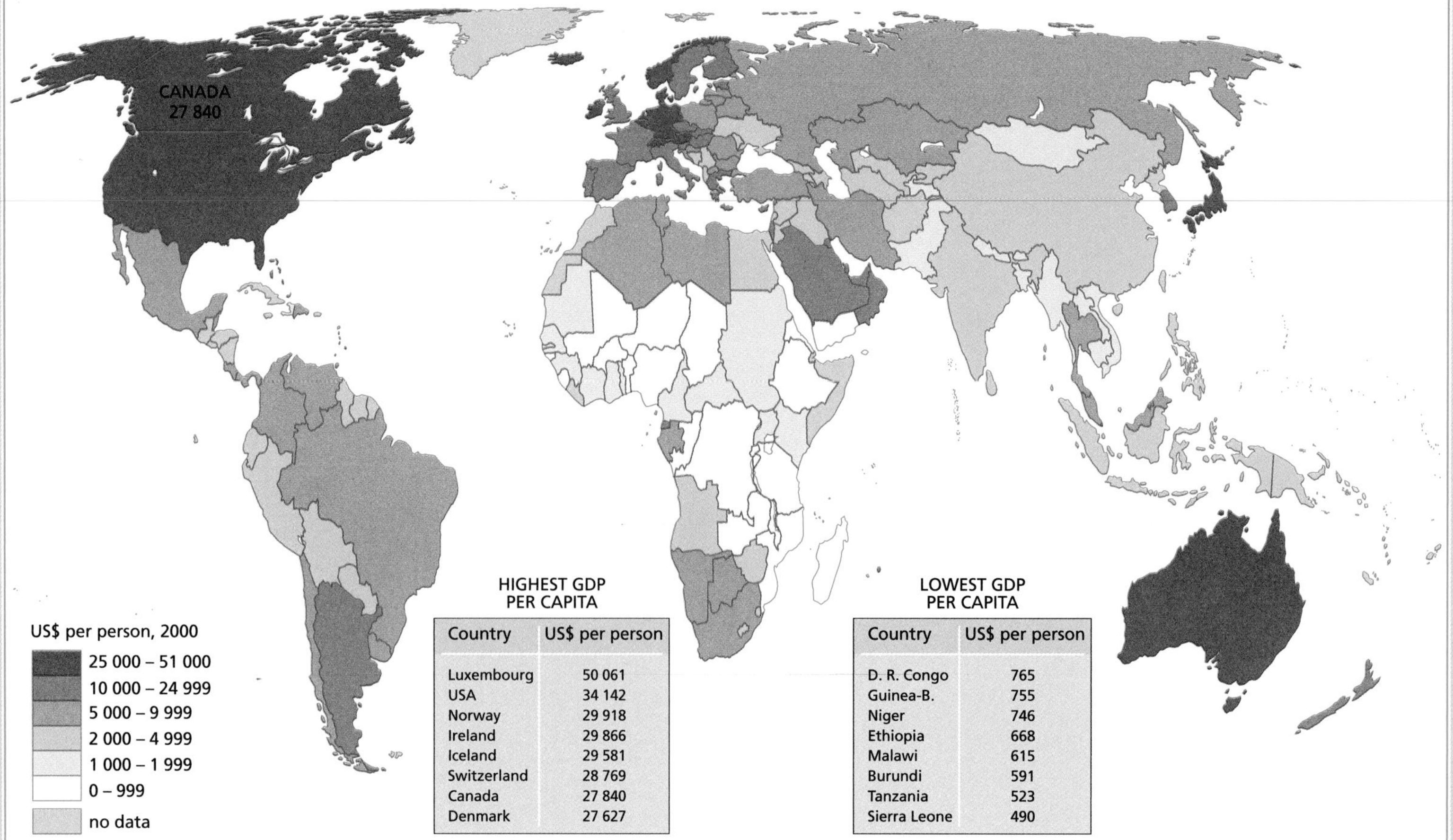

HIGHEST GDP PER CAPITA

Country	US$ per person
Luxembourg	50 061
USA	34 142
Norway	29 918
Ireland	29 866
Iceland	29 581
Switzerland	28 769
Canada	27 840
Denmark	27 627

LOWEST GDP PER CAPITA

Country	US$ per person
D. R. Congo	765
Guinea-B.	755
Niger	746
Ethiopia	668
Malawi	615
Burundi	591
Tanzania	523
Sierra Leone	490

EMPLOYMENT BY SECTOR

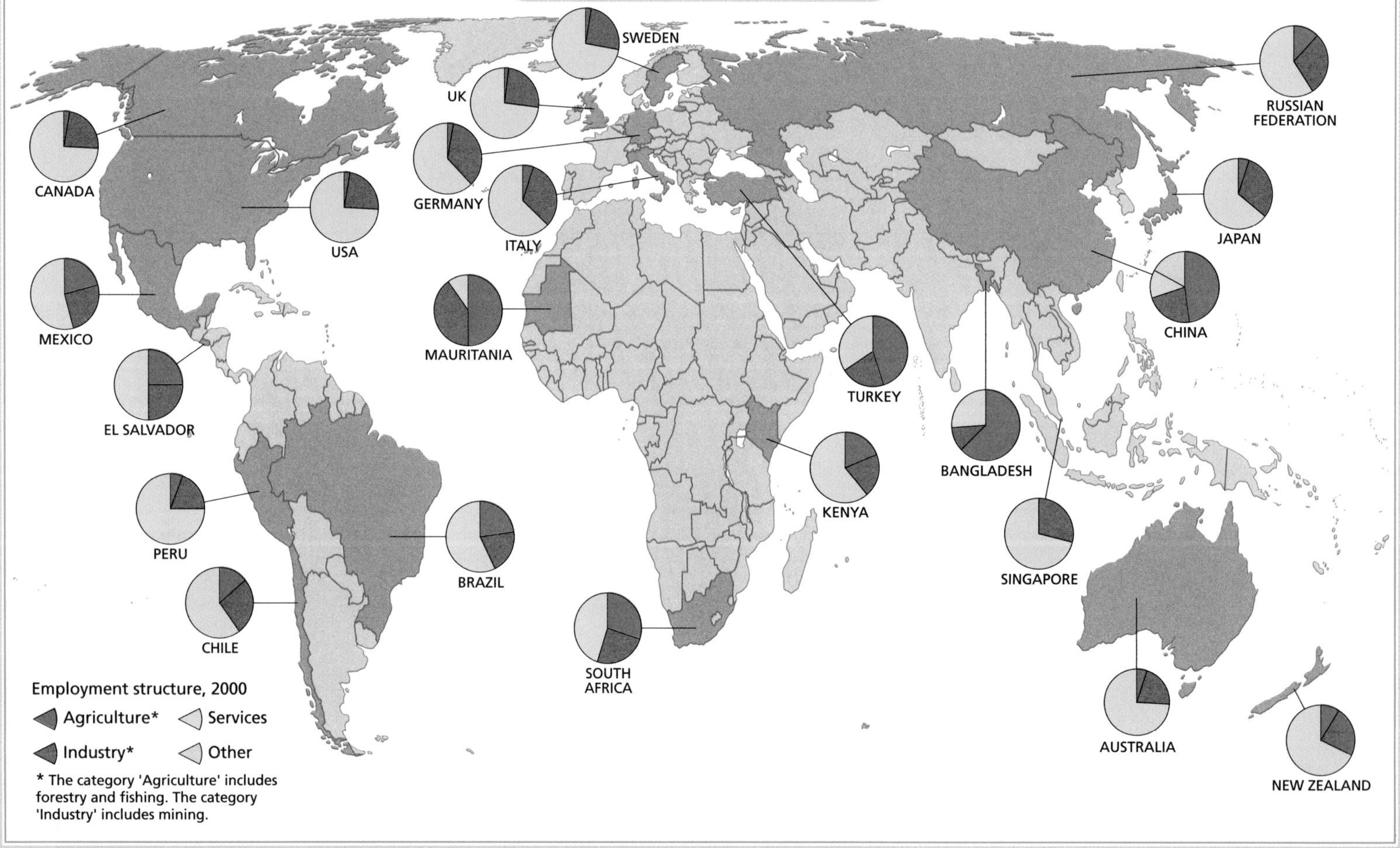

SCALE 1 : 140 000 000

0 2000 4000 6000 8000 km

Eckert IV projection

TRADE : IMPORTS

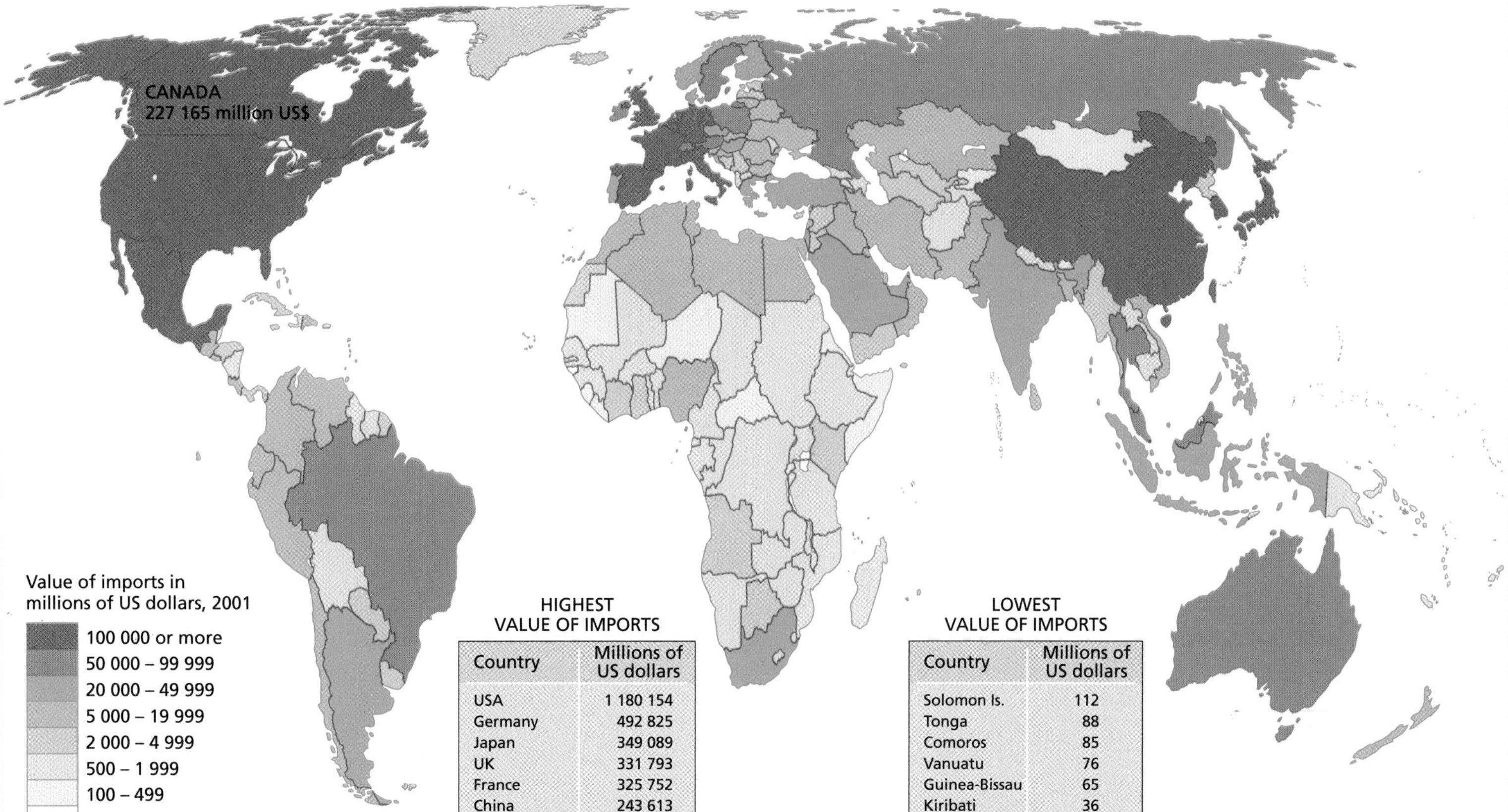

HIGHEST VALUE OF IMPORTS

Country	Millions of US dollars
USA	1 180 154
Germany	492 825
Japan	349 089
UK	331 793
France	325 752
China	243 613
Italy	232 910
Canada	227 165

LOWEST VALUE OF IMPORTS

Country	Millions of US dollars
Solomon Is.	112
Tonga	88
Comoros	85
Vanuatu	76
Guinea-Bissau	65
Kiribati	36
São Tomé & P.	23
Tuvalu	6

TRADE : EXPORTS

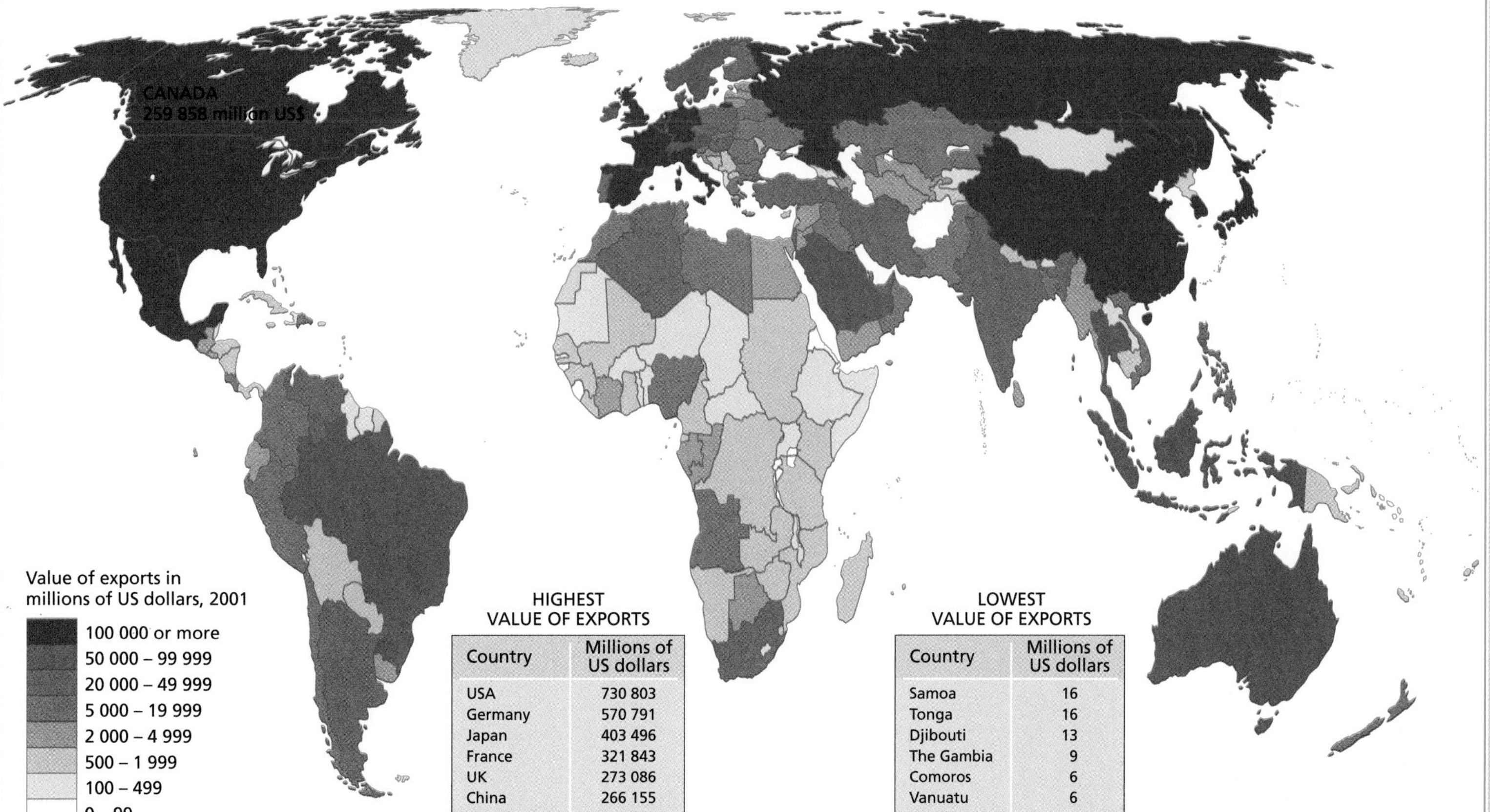

HIGHEST VALUE OF EXPORTS

Country	Millions of US dollars
USA	730 803
Germany	570 791
Japan	403 496
France	321 843
UK	273 086
China	266 155
Canada	259 858
Italy	241 134

LOWEST VALUE OF EXPORTS

Country	Millions of US dollars
Samoa	16
Tonga	16
Djibouti	13
The Gambia	9
Comoros	6
Vanuatu	6
São Tomé & P.	4
Tuvalu	0

SCALE 1 : 140 000 000 — 0 2000 4000 6000 8000 km

Eckert IV projection

ENERGY PRODUCTION

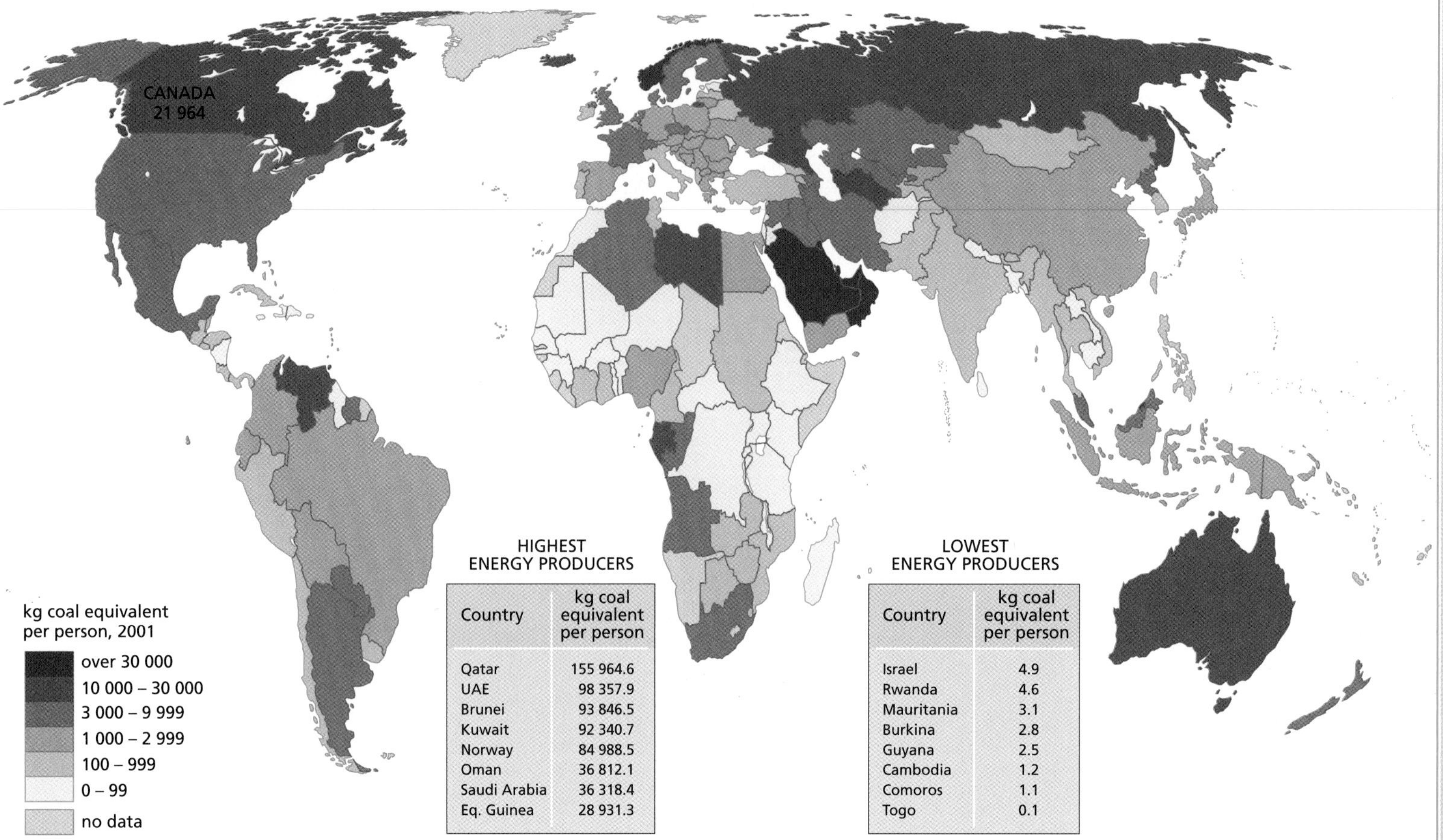

HIGHEST ENERGY PRODUCERS

Country	kg coal equivalent per person
Qatar	155 964.6
UAE	98 357.9
Brunei	93 846.5
Kuwait	92 340.7
Norway	84 988.5
Oman	36 812.1
Saudi Arabia	36 318.4
Eq. Guinea	28 931.3

LOWEST ENERGY PRODUCERS

Country	kg coal equivalent per person
Israel	4.9
Rwanda	4.6
Mauritania	3.1
Burkina	2.8
Guyana	2.5
Cambodia	1.2
Comoros	1.1
Togo	0.1

ENERGY PRODUCTION AND CONSUMPTION

Percent of World Energy Production, 2000

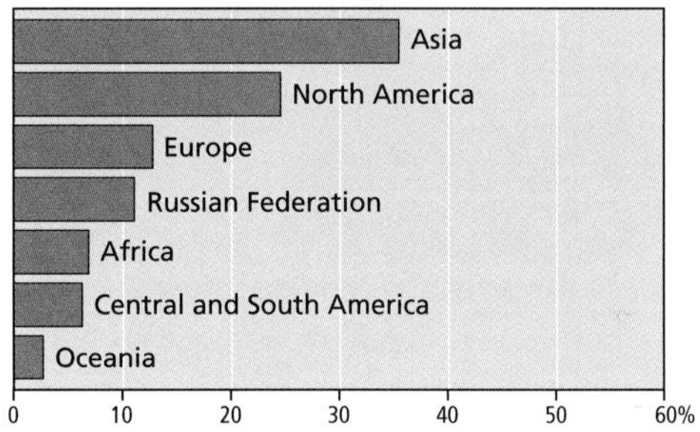

Percent of World Energy Consumption, 2000

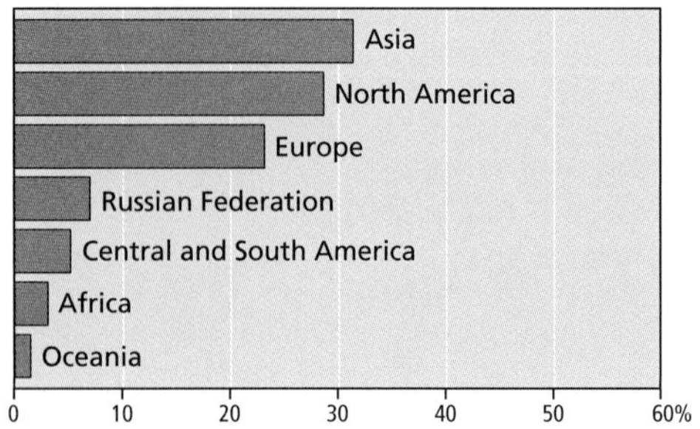

OTHER ENERGY SOURCES

Top Hydro Electric Power Producers, 2000

Country	Percent of world total
Canada	13.2
Brazil	11.3
USA	10.2
China	8.2
Russian Federation	6.1
Norway	5.2
Japan	3.6
Sweden	2.9
India	2.7
France	2.7

Top Nuclear Power Producers, 2000

Country	Percent of world total
USA	30.9
France	16.0
Japan	12.4
Germany	6.6
Russian Federation	5.1
South Korea	4.2
United Kingdom	3.3
Ukraine	3.0
Canada	2.8
Spain	2.4

Top Fuelwood Producers, 2001

Country	Percent of world total
India	15.5
China	10.7
Brazil	7.5
Ethiopia	5.0
Indonesia	4.8
USA	4.1
D.R. Congo	3.7
Nigeria	3.3
Russian Federation	2.5
Philippines	2.3

Top Alternative* Energy Producers, 2001

Country	Percent of world total
USA	34.0
Germany	9.0
Japan	7.6
Brazil	5.8
Philippines	4.8
Spain	3.6
Italy	3.1
Canada	2.8

* Geothermal, solar, wind, wood, and waste

SCALE 1 : 140 000 000 — 0 2000 4000 6000 8000 km

Eckert IV projection

ENERGY CONSUMPTION

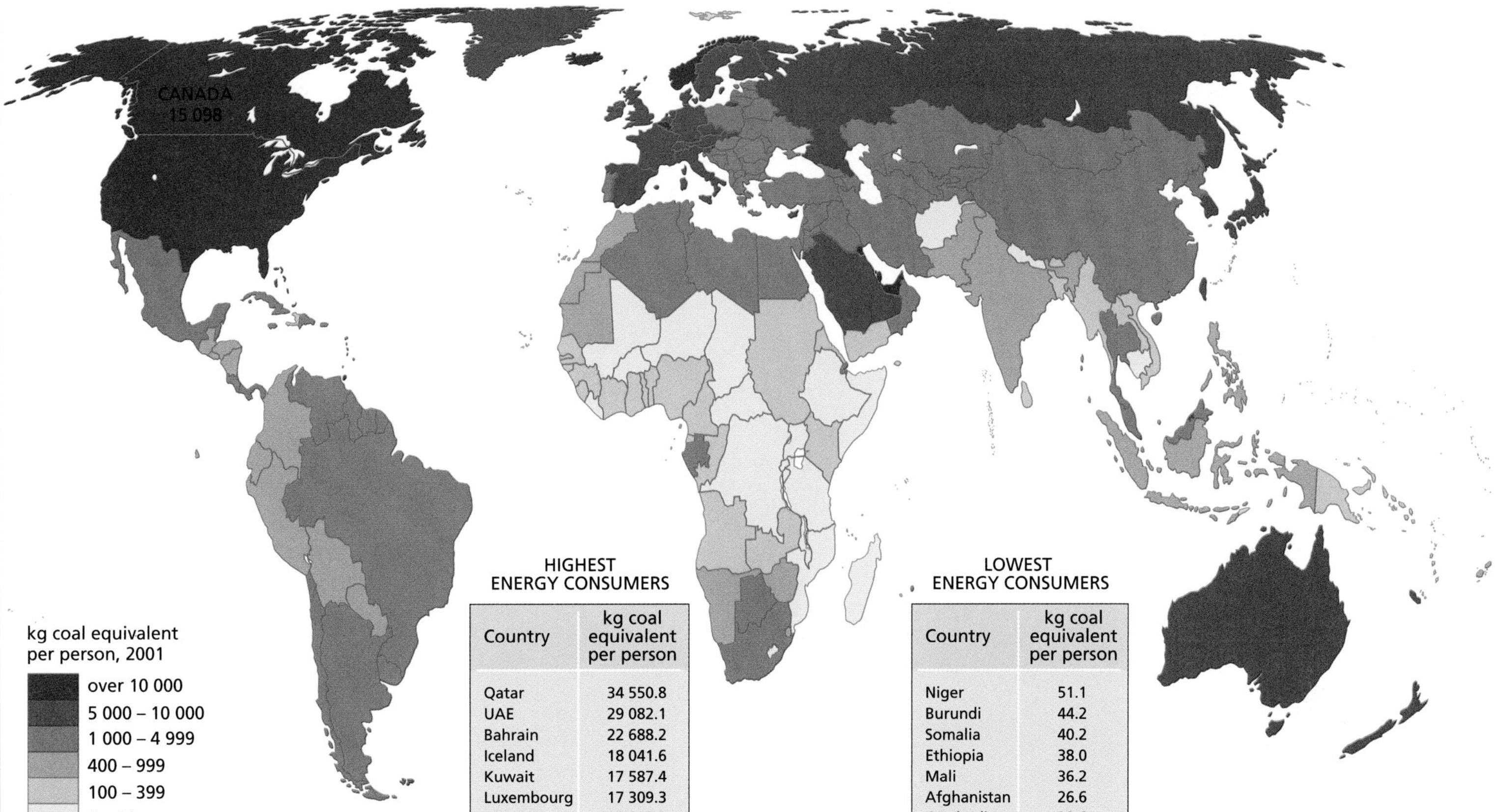

HIGHEST ENERGY CONSUMERS

Country	kg coal equivalent per person
Qatar	34 550.8
UAE	29 082.1
Bahrain	22 688.2
Iceland	18 041.6
Kuwait	17 587.4
Luxembourg	17 309.3
Norway	15 848.9
Canada	15 097.8

LOWEST ENERGY CONSUMERS

Country	kg coal equivalent per person
Niger	51.1
Burundi	44.2
Somalia	40.2
Ethiopia	38.0
Mali	36.2
Afghanistan	26.6
Cambodia	22.6
Chad	14.3

OIL

Reserves, 2001

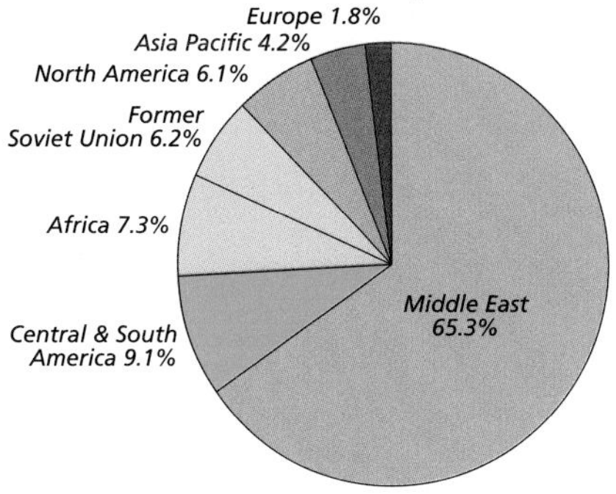

Total Reserves : 1 050 thousand million barrels

GAS

Reserves, 2001

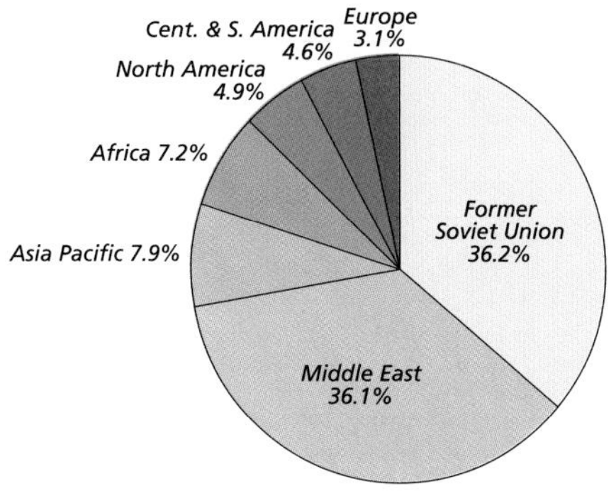

Total Reserves : 155 trillion cubic metres

COAL

Reserves, 2001

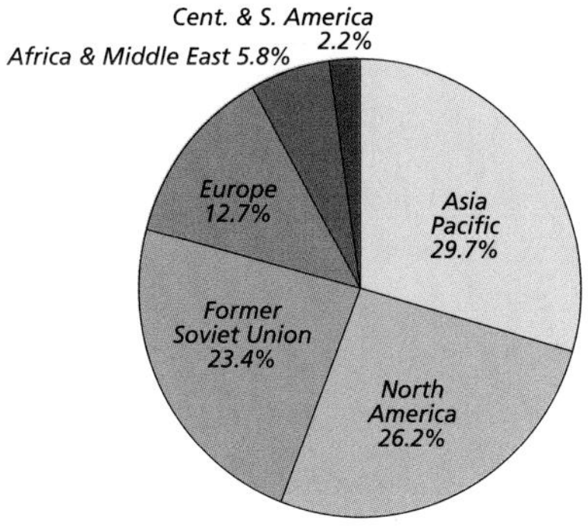

Total Reserves : 984 453 million tonnes

Top Oil Producers, 2001

Country	Percent of world total
Saudi Arabia	11.8
USA	9.8
Russian Federation	9.7
Iran	5.1
Mexico	4.9
Venezuela	4.9
China	4.6
Norway	4.5
Canada	3.6
Iraq	3.3

Top Gas Producers, 2001

Country	Percent of world total
USA	22.5
Russian Federation	22.0
Canada	7.0
United Kingdom	4.3
Algeria	3.2
Indonesia	2.6
Netherlands	2.5
Iran	2.5
Norway	2.3
Saudi Arabia	2.2

Top Coal Producers, 2001

Country	Percent of world total
USA	26.3
China	24.4
Australia	7.5
India	7.2
South Africa	5.6
Russian Federation	5.4
Poland	3.2
Indonesia	2.5
Germany	2.4
Ukraine	1.9

SCALE 1 : 140 000 000 — 0 2000 4000 6000 8000 km

Eckert IV projection

GLOBAL WARMING

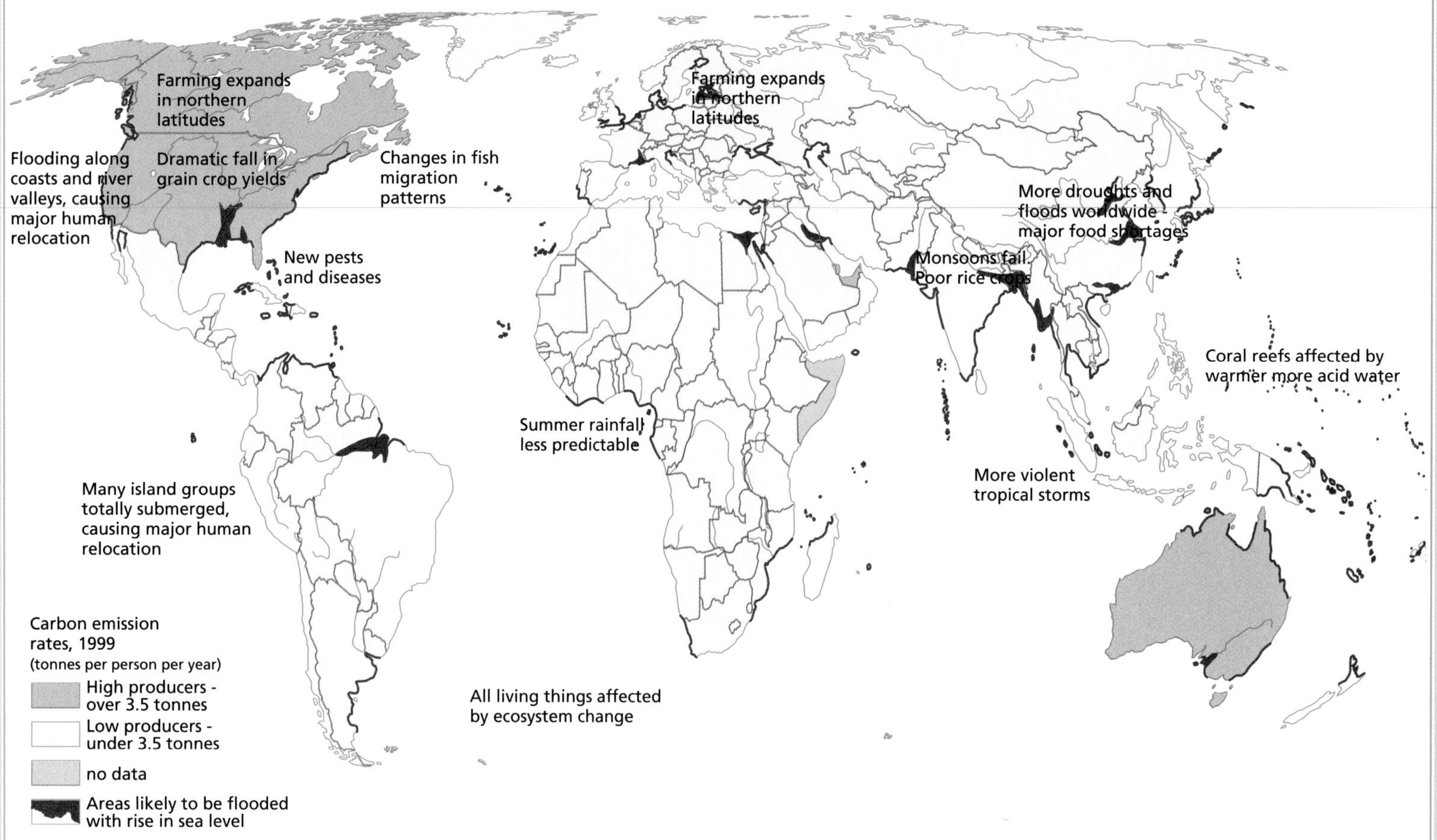
Farming expands in northern latitudes
Flooding along coasts and river valleys, causing major human relocation
Dramatic fall in grain crop yields
Changes in fish migration patterns
New pests and diseases
Farming expands in northern latitudes
More droughts and floods worldwide - major food shortages
Monsoons fail. Poor rice crops
Coral reefs affected by warmer more acid water
Summer rainfall less predictable
More violent tropical storms
Many island groups totally submerged, causing major human relocation
All living things affected by ecosystem change
Carbon emission rates, 1999 (tonnes per person per year)
High producers - over 3.5 tonnes
Low producers - under 3.5 tonnes
no data
Areas likely to be flooded with rise in sea level

HABITAT DESTRUCTION

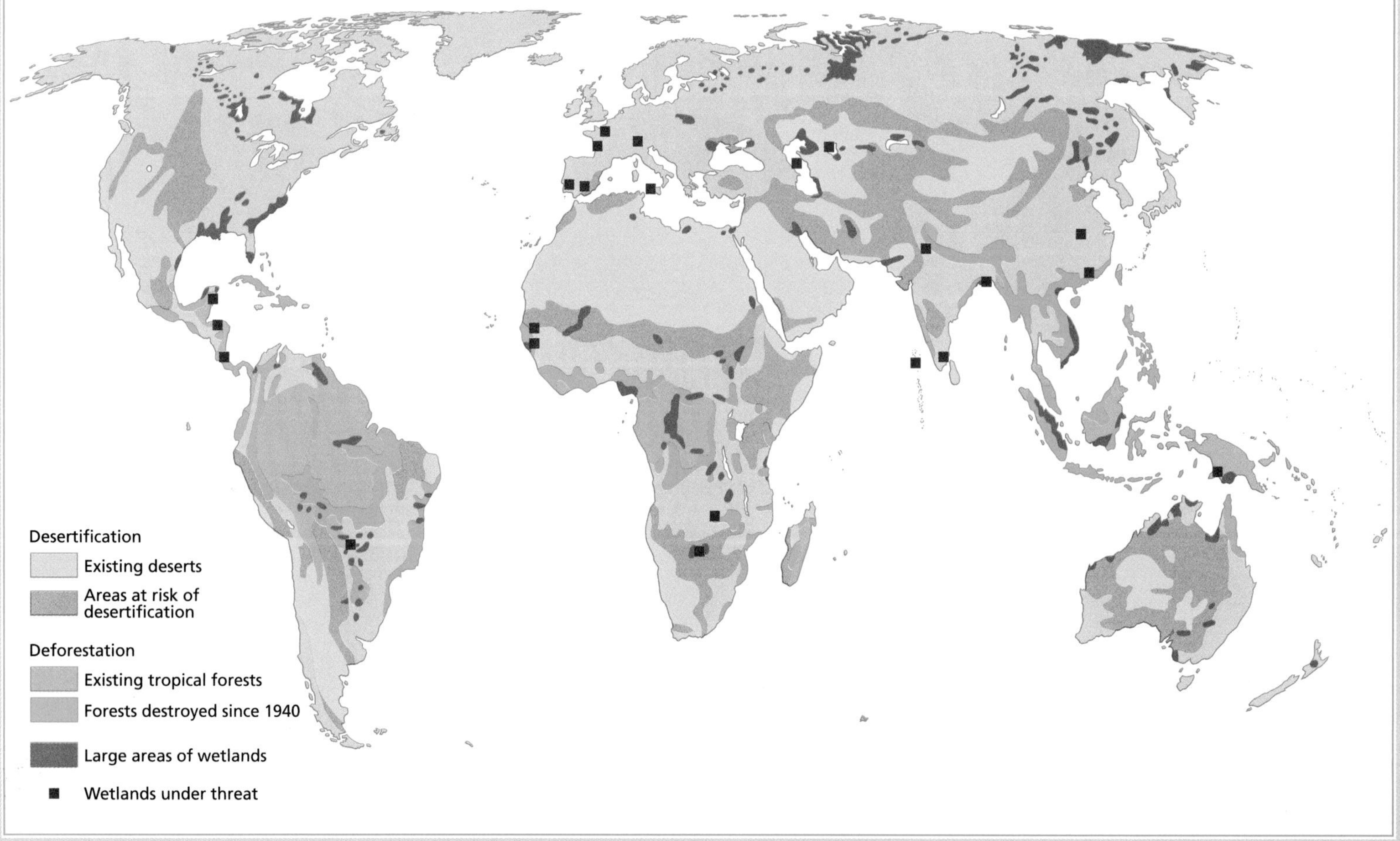
Desertification
Existing deserts
Areas at risk of desertification
Deforestation
Existing tropical forests
Forests destroyed since 1940
Large areas of wetlands
Wetlands under threat

SCALE 1 : 140 000 000

0 2000 4000 6000 8000 km

Eckert IV projection

PROTECTED AREAS

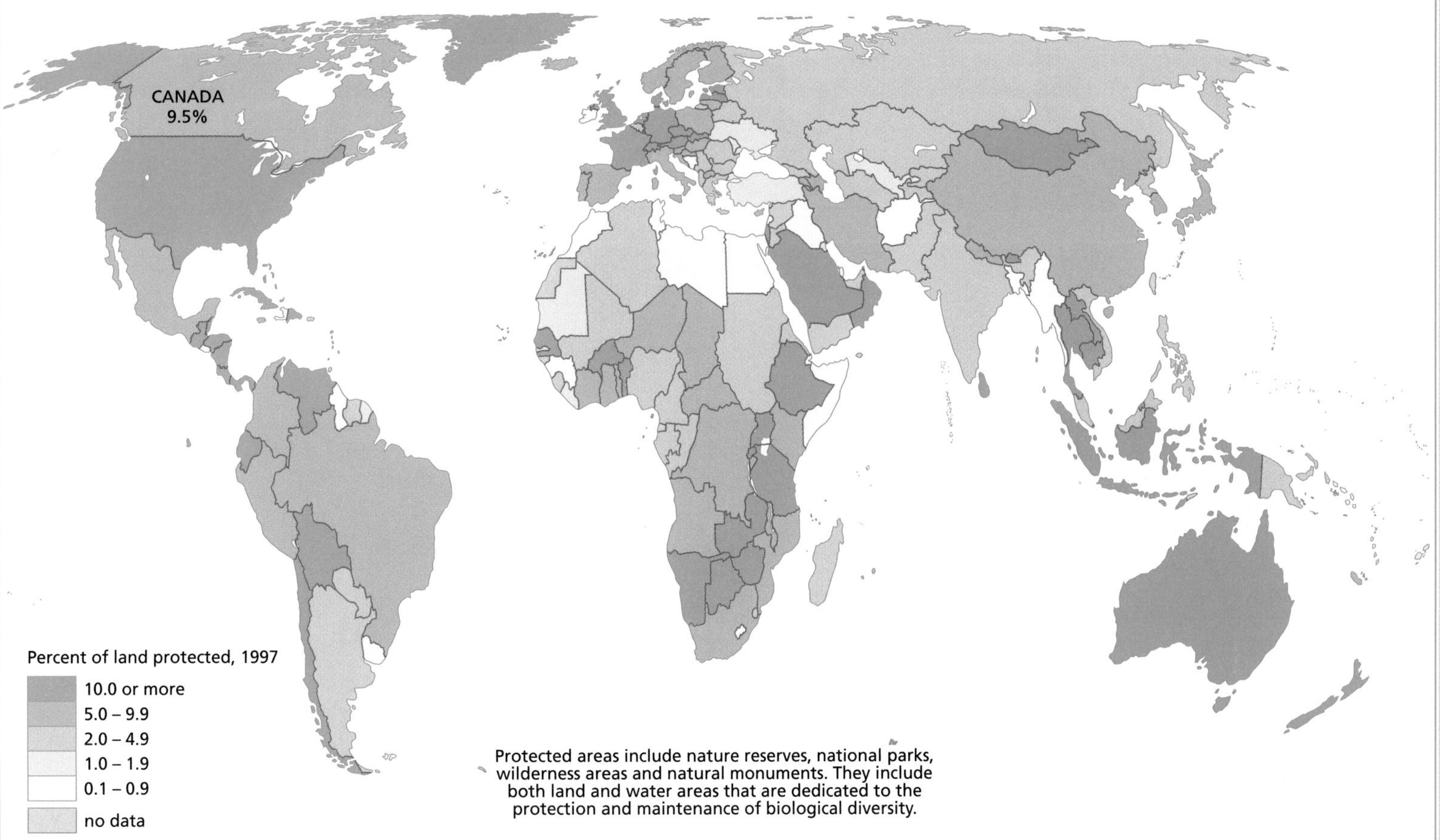

Protected areas include nature reserves, national parks, wilderness areas and natural monuments. They include both land and water areas that are dedicated to the protection and maintenance of biological diversity.

POLLUTION

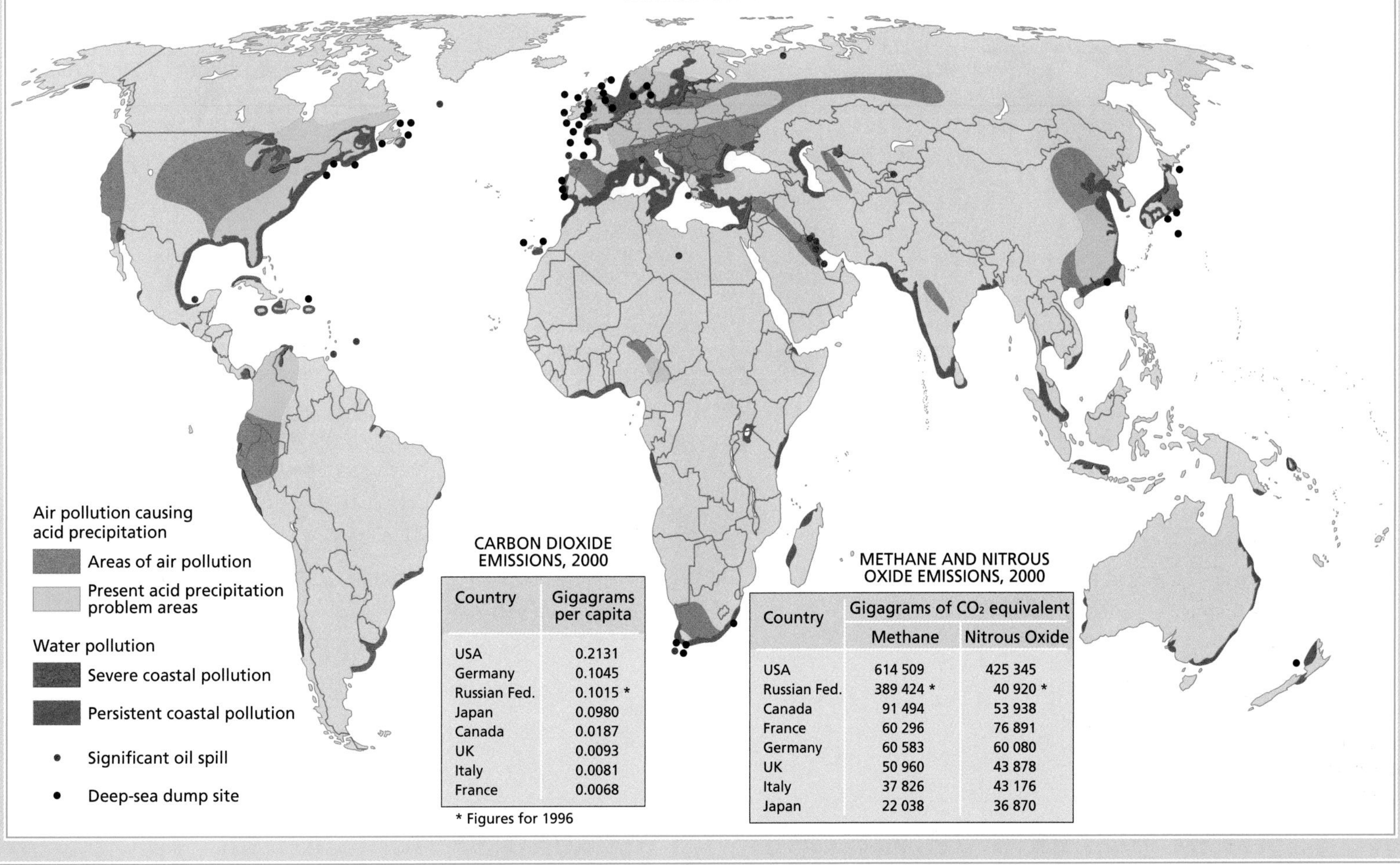

CARBON DIOXIDE EMISSIONS, 2000

Country	Gigagrams per capita
USA	0.2131
Germany	0.1045
Russian Fed.	0.1015 *
Japan	0.0980
Canada	0.0187
UK	0.0093
Italy	0.0081
France	0.0068

* Figures for 1996

METHANE AND NITROUS OXIDE EMISSIONS, 2000

Country	Gigagrams of CO_2 equivalent	
	Methane	Nitrous Oxide
USA	614 509	425 345
Russian Fed.	389 424 *	40 920 *
Canada	91 494	53 938
France	60 296	76 891
Germany	60 583	60 080
UK	50 960	43 878
Italy	37 826	43 176
Japan	22 038	36 870

SCALE 1 : 140 000 000

0 2000 4000 6000 8000 km

Eckert IV projection

NUMBER OF PHYSICIANS

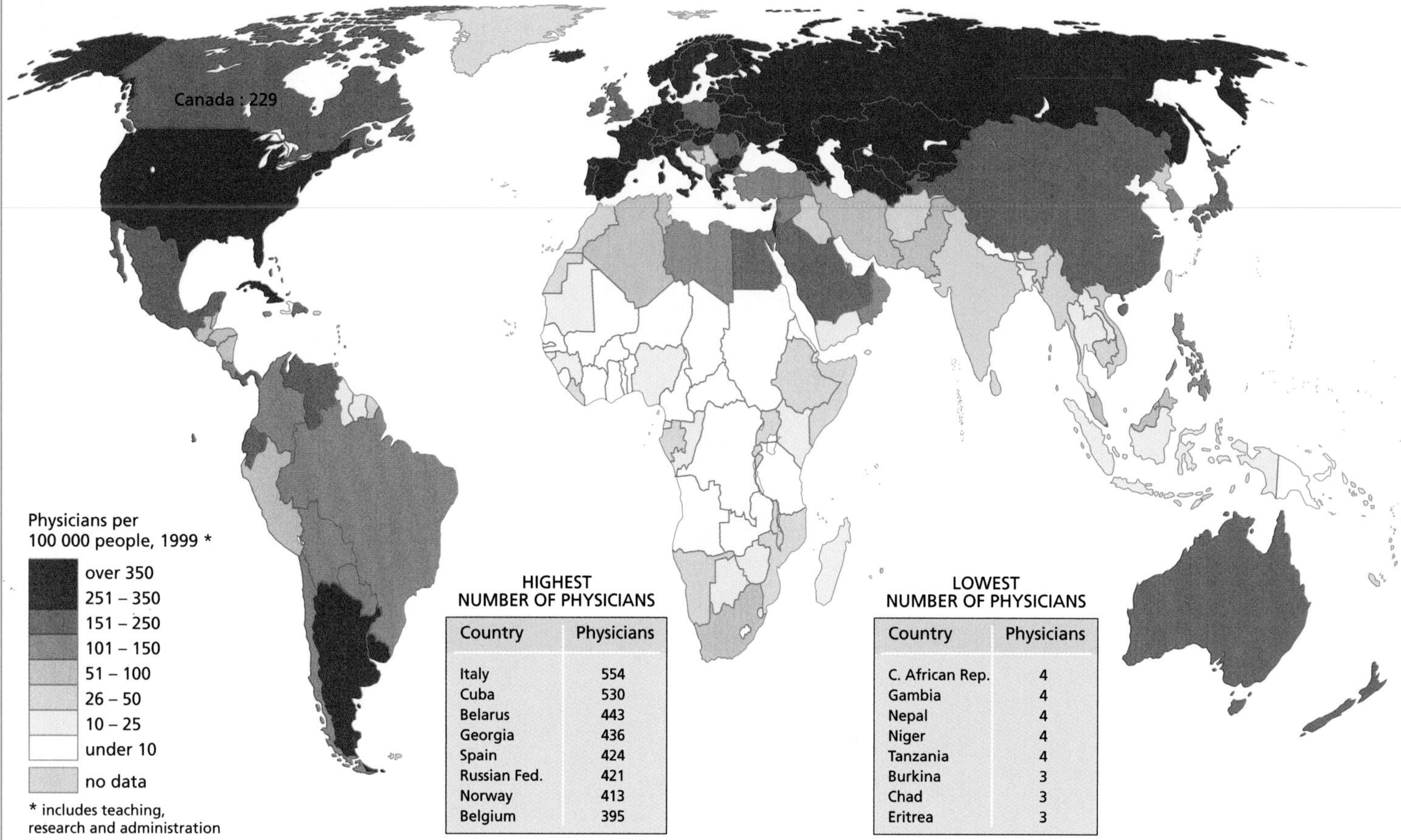

HIGHEST NUMBER OF PHYSICIANS

Country	Physicians
Italy	554
Cuba	530
Belarus	443
Georgia	436
Spain	424
Russian Fed.	421
Norway	413
Belgium	395

LOWEST NUMBER OF PHYSICIANS

Country	Physicians
C. African Rep.	4
Gambia	4
Nepal	4
Niger	4
Tanzania	4
Burkina	3
Chad	3
Eritrea	3

ACCESS TO SAFE WATER

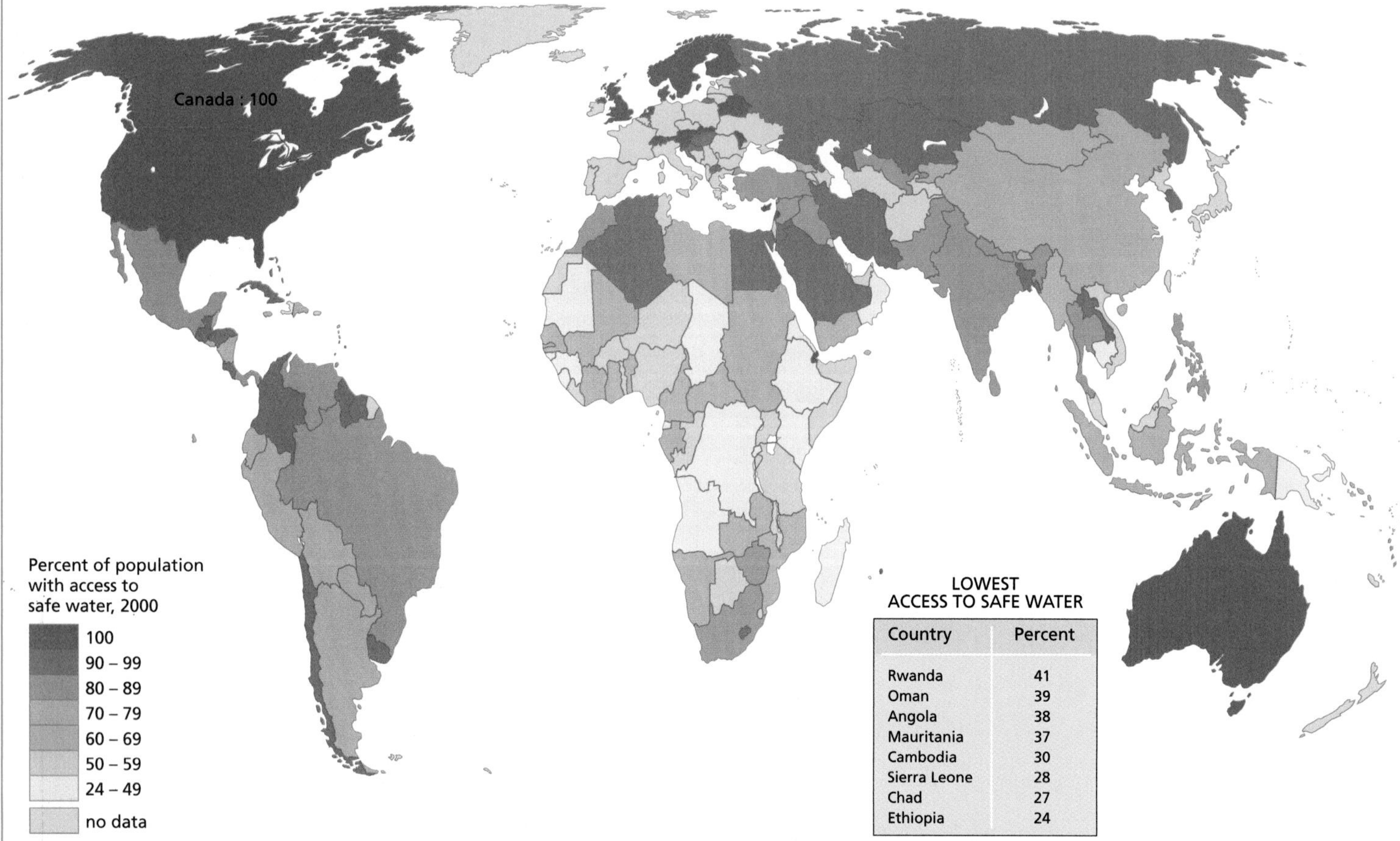

LOWEST ACCESS TO SAFE WATER

Country	Percent
Rwanda	41
Oman	39
Angola	38
Mauritania	37
Cambodia	30
Sierra Leone	28
Chad	27
Ethiopia	24

SCALE 1 : 140 000 000

0 2000 4000 6000 8000 km

Eckert IV projection

NUTRITION

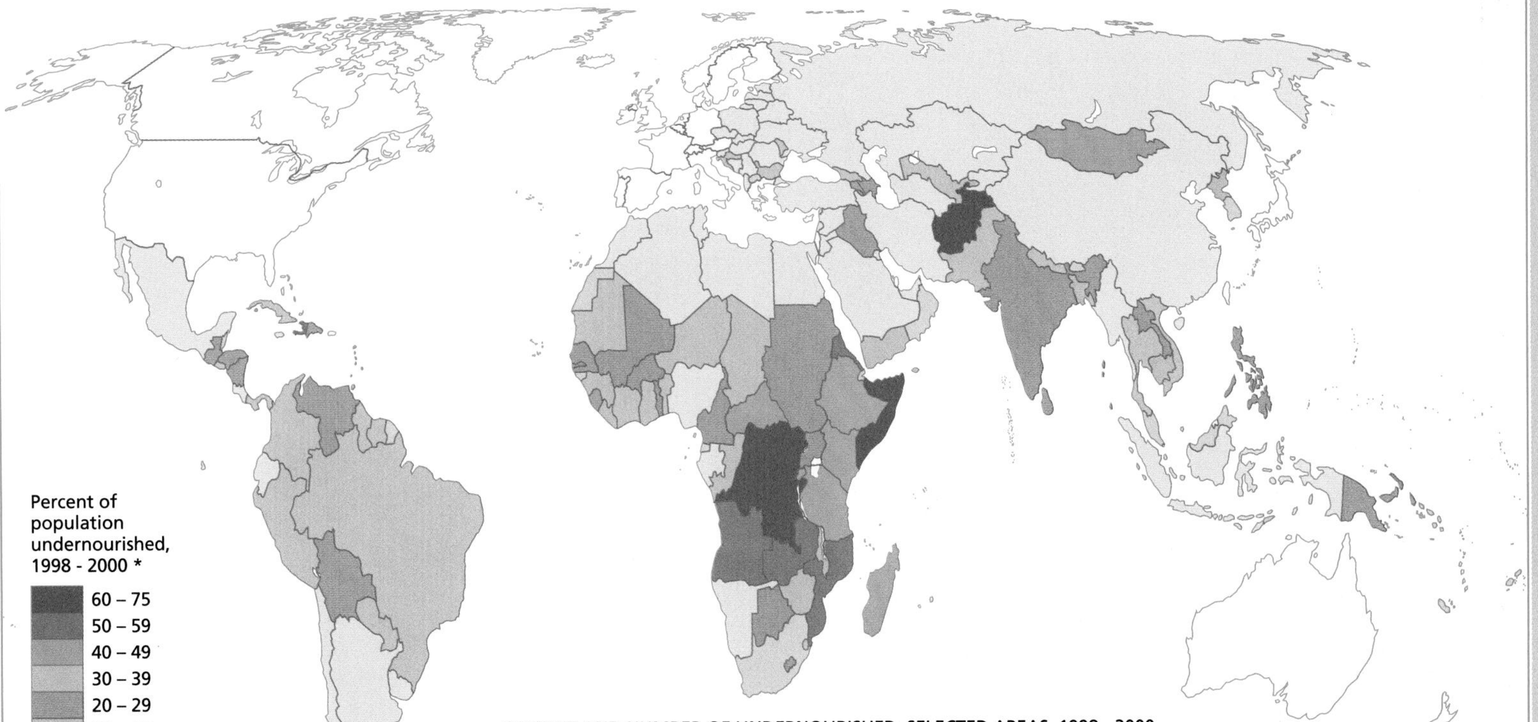

PERCENT AND NUMBER OF UNDERNOURISHED, SELECTED AREAS, 1998 - 2000

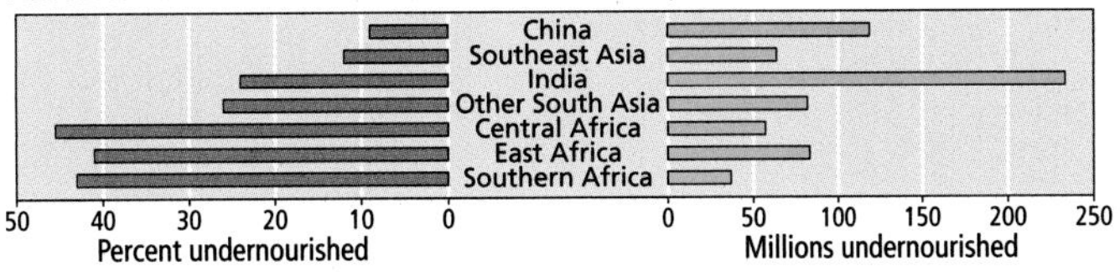

HIV/AIDS

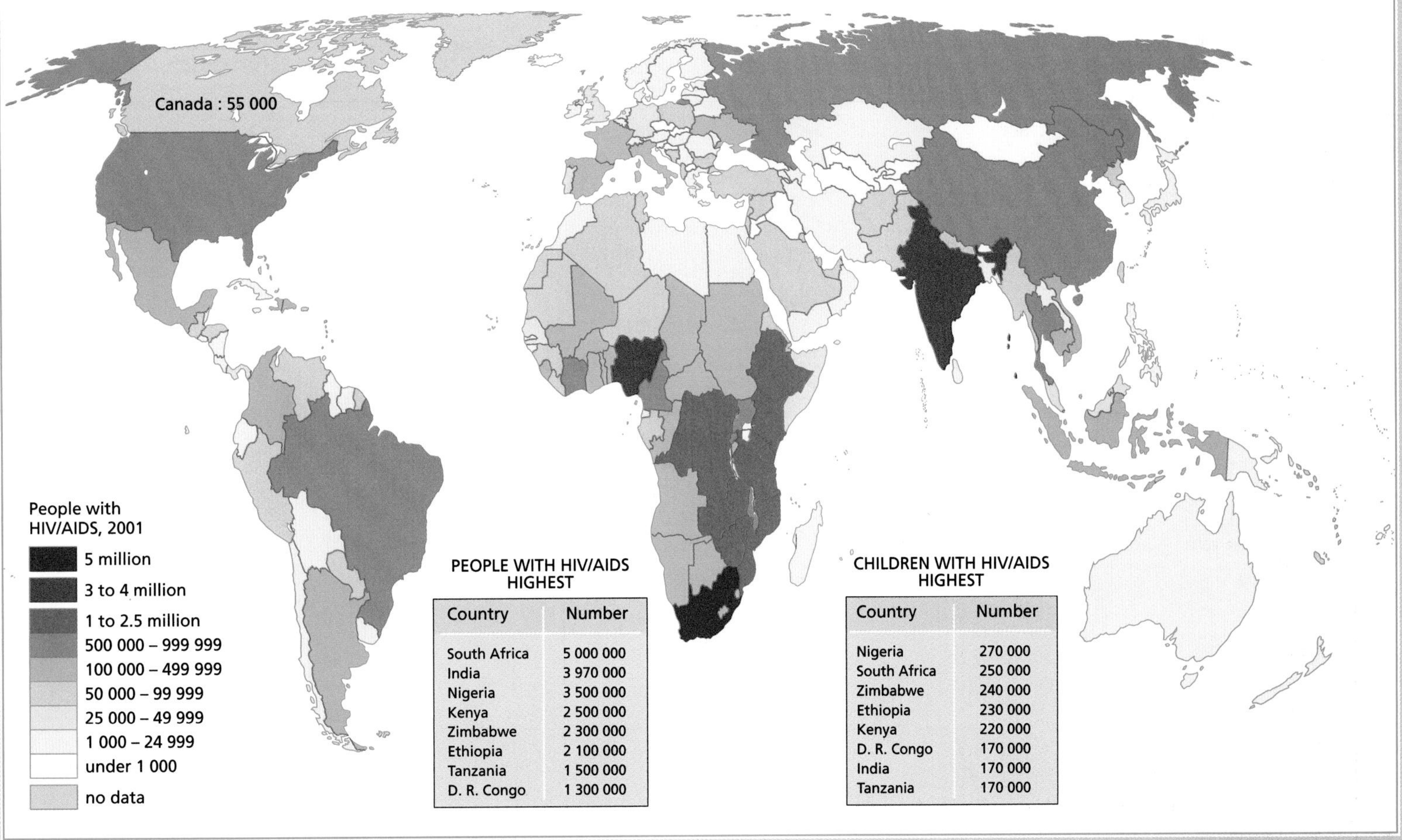

PEOPLE WITH HIV/AIDS HIGHEST

Country	Number
South Africa	5 000 000
India	3 970 000
Nigeria	3 500 000
Kenya	2 500 000
Zimbabwe	2 300 000
Ethiopia	2 100 000
Tanzania	1 500 000
D. R. Congo	1 300 000

CHILDREN WITH HIV/AIDS HIGHEST

Country	Number
Nigeria	270 000
South Africa	250 000
Zimbabwe	240 000
Ethiopia	230 000
Kenya	220 000
D. R. Congo	170 000
India	170 000
Tanzania	170 000

SCALE 1 : 140 000 000

0 2000 4000 6000 8000 km

Eckert IV projection

HUMAN DEVELOPMENT INDEX

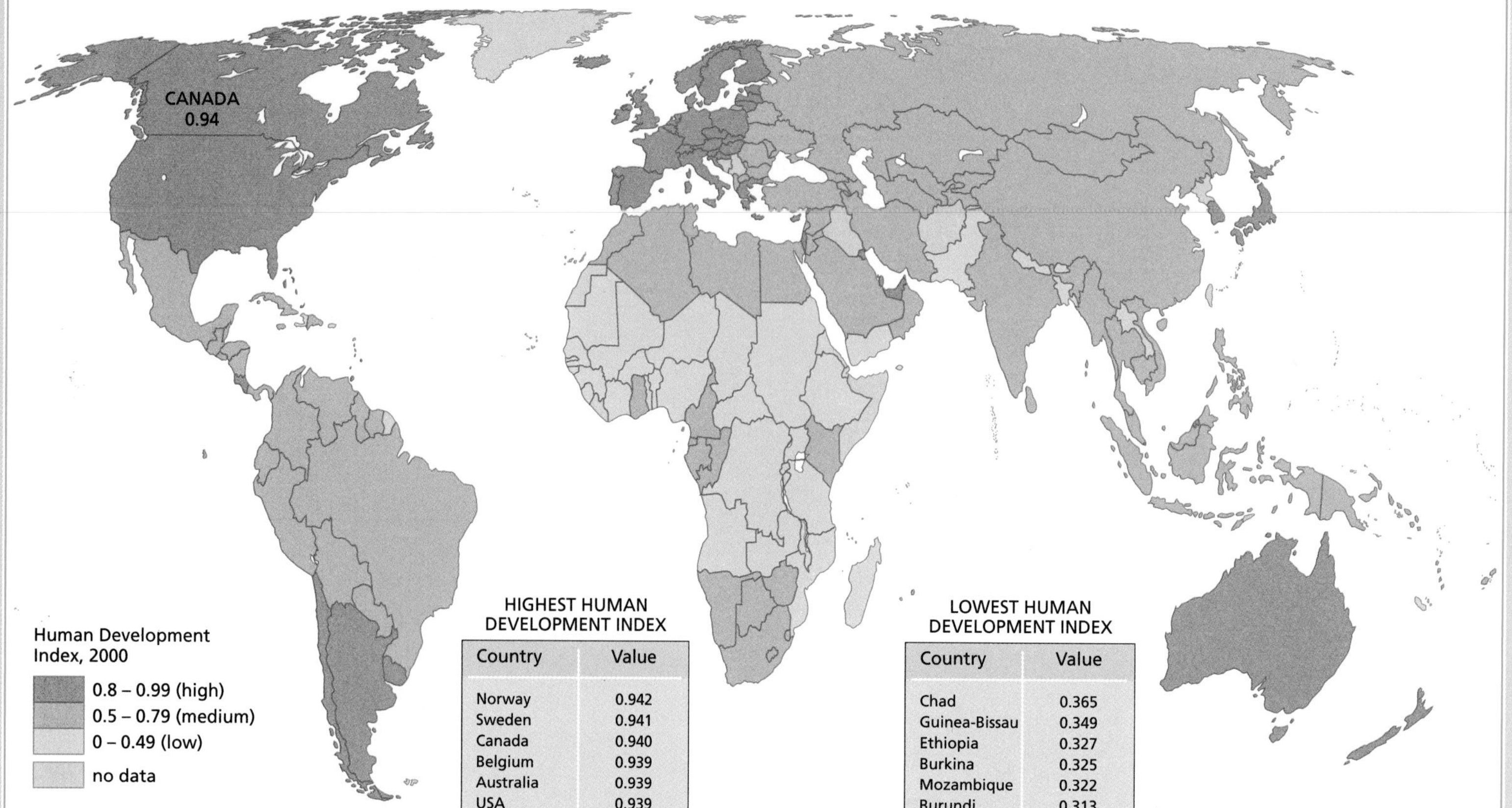

Human Development Index, 2000

- 0.8 – 0.99 (high)
- 0.5 – 0.79 (medium)
- 0 – 0.49 (low)
- no data

HIGHEST HUMAN DEVELOPMENT INDEX

Country	Value
Norway	0.942
Sweden	0.941
Canada	0.940
Belgium	0.939
Australia	0.939
USA	0.939
Iceland	0.936
Netherlands	0.935

LOWEST HUMAN DEVELOPMENT INDEX

Country	Value
Chad	0.365
Guinea-Bissau	0.349
Ethiopia	0.327
Burkina	0.325
Mozambique	0.322
Burundi	0.313
Niger	0.277
Sierra Leone	0.275

WOMEN IN THE LABOUR FORCE

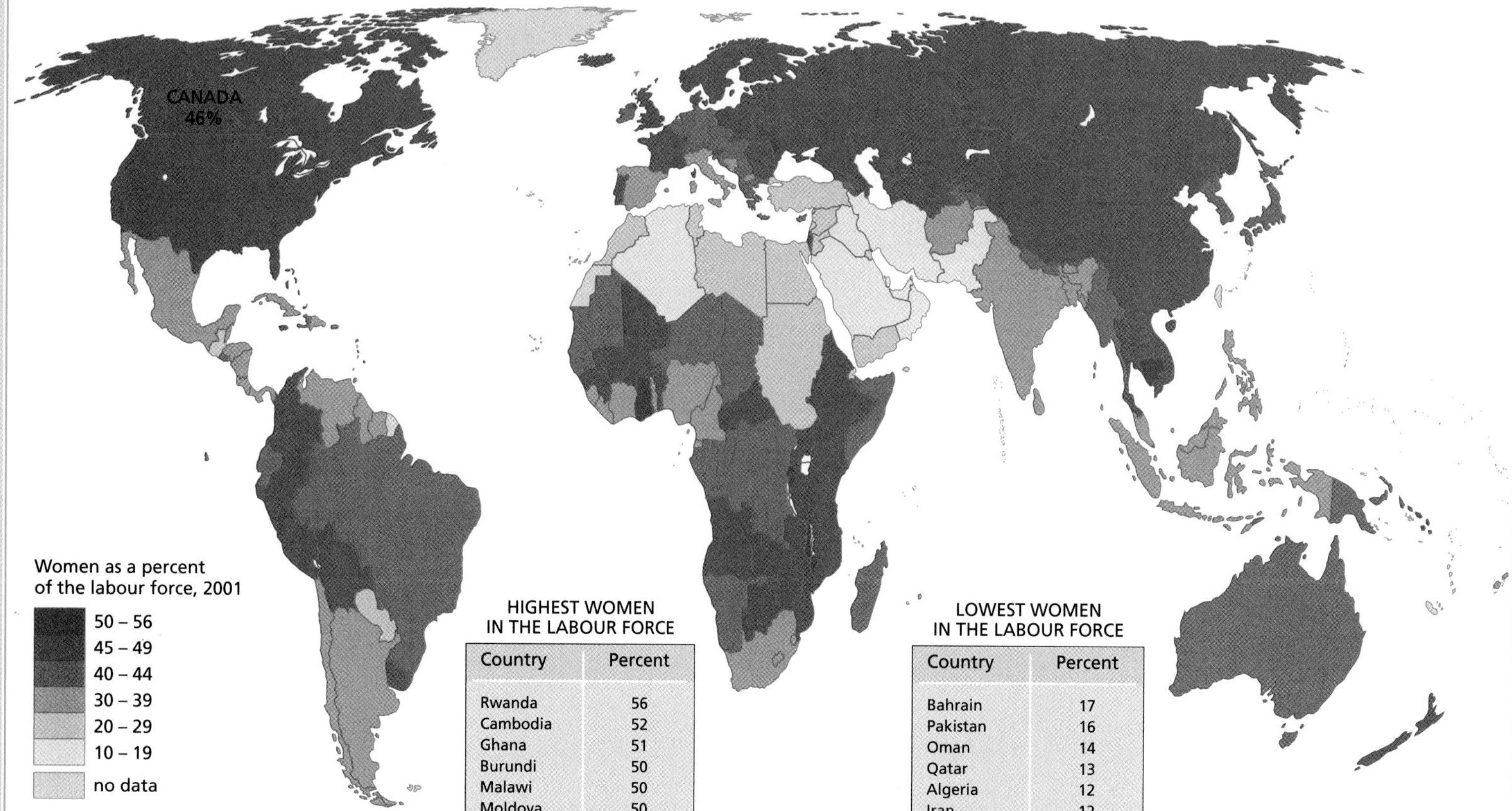

Women as a percent of the labour force, 2001

- 50 – 56
- 45 – 49
- 40 – 44
- 30 – 39
- 20 – 29
- 10 – 19
- no data

HIGHEST WOMEN IN THE LABOUR FORCE

Country	Percent
Rwanda	56
Cambodia	52
Ghana	51
Burundi	50
Malawi	50
Moldova	50
Barbados	49
Belarus	49

LOWEST WOMEN IN THE LABOUR FORCE

Country	Percent
Bahrain	17
Pakistan	16
Oman	14
Qatar	13
Algeria	12
Iran	12
UAE	12
Saudi Arabia	11

SCALE 1 : 140 000 000 — 0, 2000, 4000, 6000, 8000 km

Eckert IV projection

REFUGEES

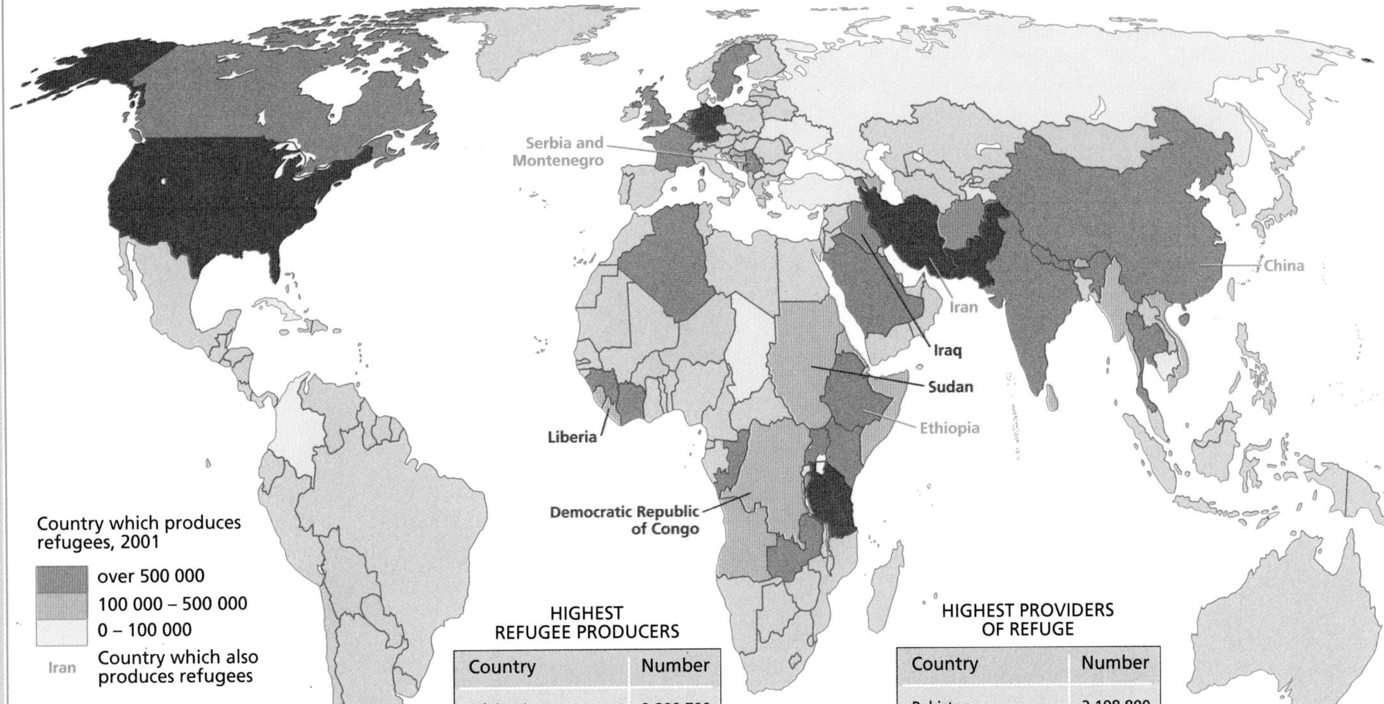

Country which produces refugees, 2001

- over 500 000
- 100 000 – 500 000
- 0 – 100 000
- Iran — Country which also produces refugees

Country which provides refuge, 2001

- over 500 000
- 100 000 – 500 000
- 0 – 100 000
- **Sudan** — Country which also provides refuge

HIGHEST REFUGEE PRODUCERS

Country	Number
Afghanistan	3 809 700
Burundi	554 000
Iraq	530 100
Sudan	489 500
Angola	470 600
Bosnia-Herzegovina	450 000
Somalia	439 900
D. R. Congo	392 100

HIGHEST PROVIDERS OF REFUGE

Country	Number
Pakistan	2 198 800
Iran	1 868 000
Germany	903 000
Tanzania	646 900
USA	515 900
Serbia & Montenegro	400 300
D. R. Congo	362 000
Sudan	349 200

CONFLICT

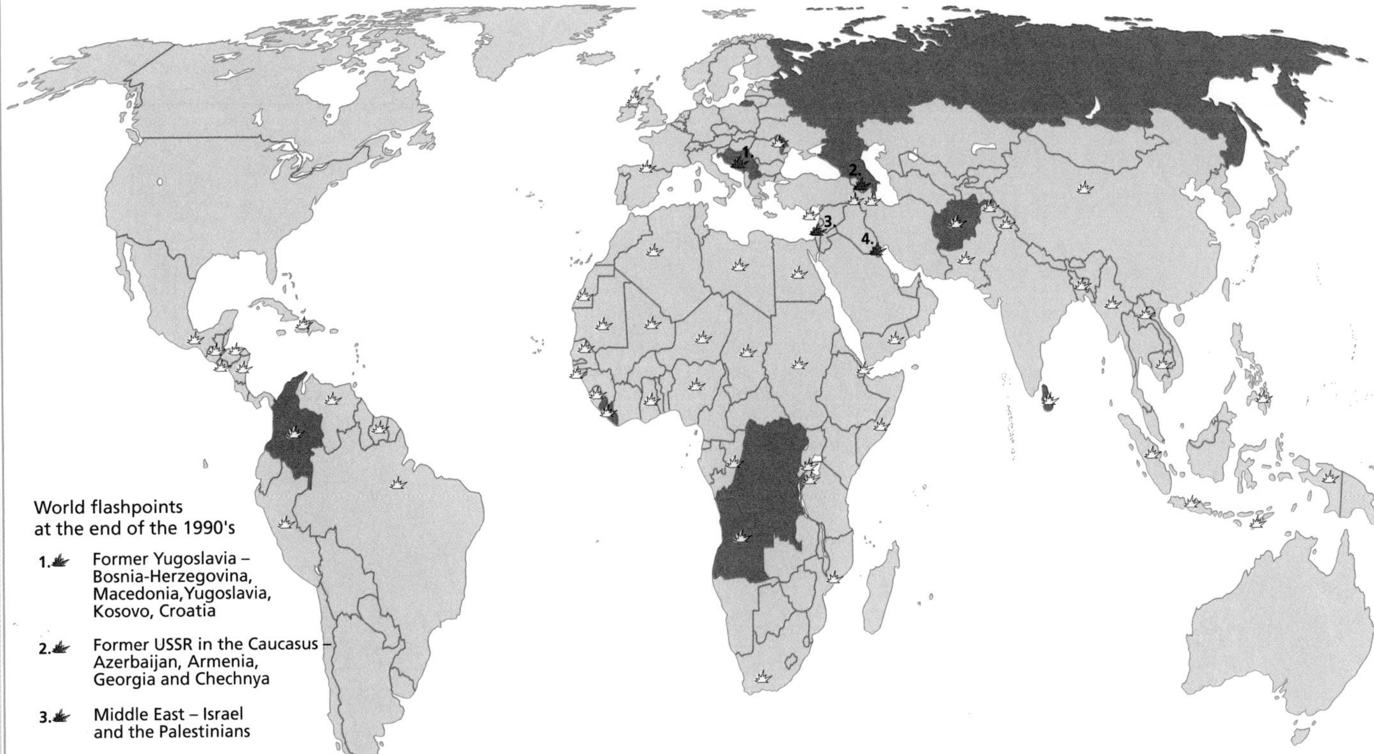

World flashpoints at the end of the 1990's

1. Former Yugoslavia – Bosnia-Herzegovina, Macedonia, Yugoslavia, Kosovo, Croatia
2. Former USSR in the Caucasus – Azerbaijan, Armenia, Georgia and Chechnya
3. Middle East – Israel and the Palestinians
4. Gulf – Iraq, Kuwait and their neighbours

- Internal conflict in the 1990's
- Countries with refugees in their own lands

News reports often involve conflict, with a focus on conflict between nations. Most conflict however, is domestic and lasts for many years. These internal conflicts cause disruption of human lives, the movement of people within and out of their own country, and have resulted in many deaths.

SCALE 1 : 140 000 000 — 0 2000 4000 6000 8000 km

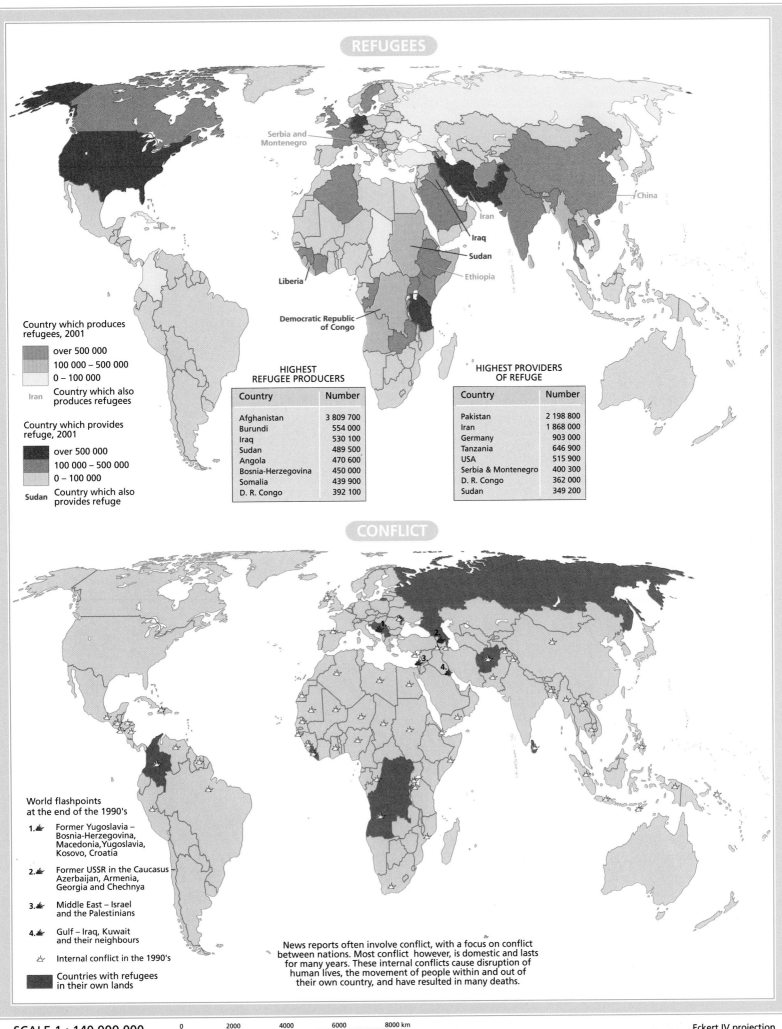

Eckert IV projection

TOURISM

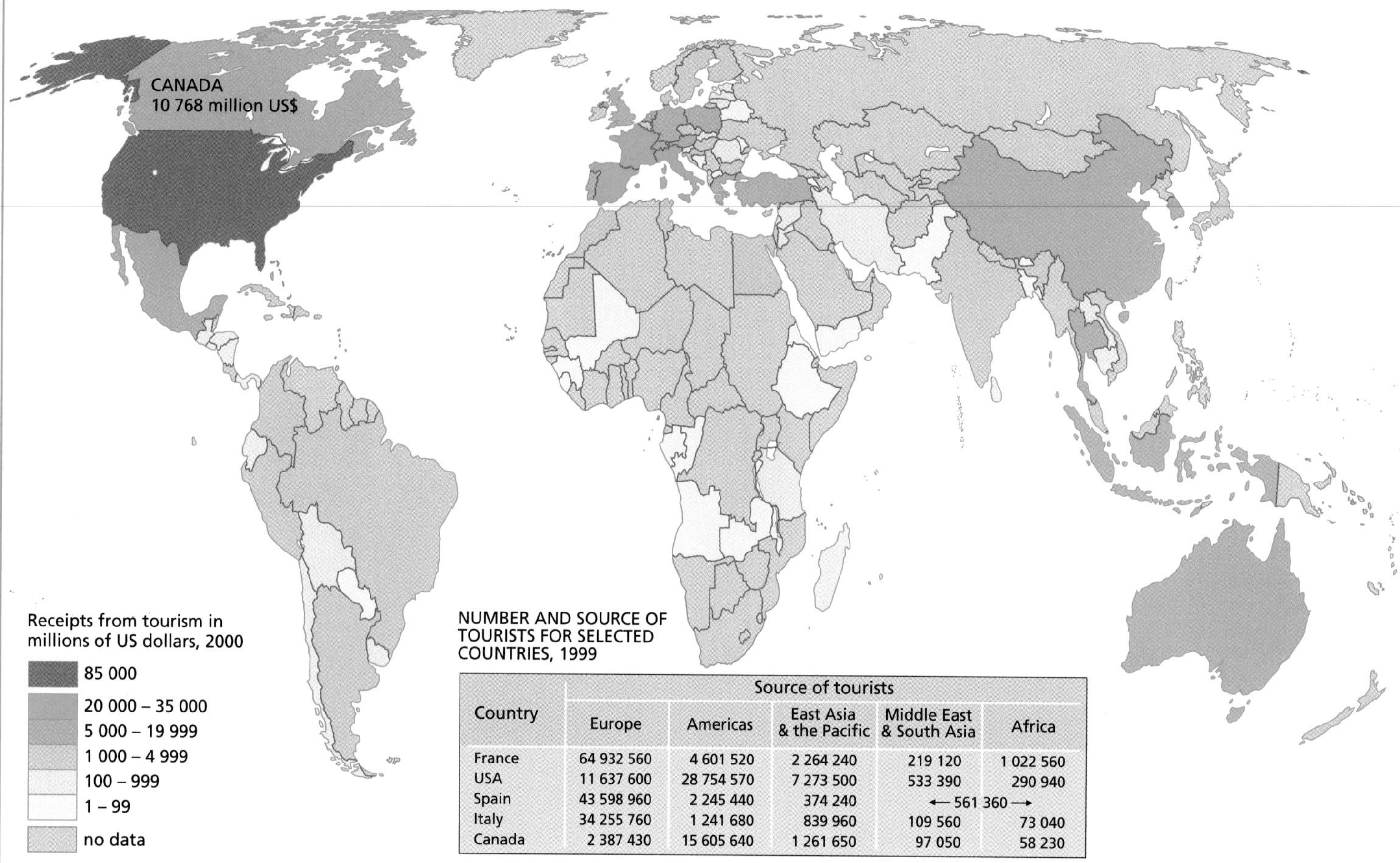

NUMBER AND SOURCE OF TOURISTS FOR SELECTED COUNTRIES, 1999

Country	Source of tourists				
	Europe	Americas	East Asia & the Pacific	Middle East & South Asia	Africa
France	64 932 560	4 601 520	2 264 240	219 120	1 022 560
USA	11 637 600	28 754 570	7 273 500	533 390	290 940
Spain	43 598 960	2 245 440	374 240	← 561 360 →	
Italy	34 255 760	1 241 680	839 960	109 560	73 040
Canada	2 387 430	15 605 640	1 261 650	97 050	58 230

LANGUAGE

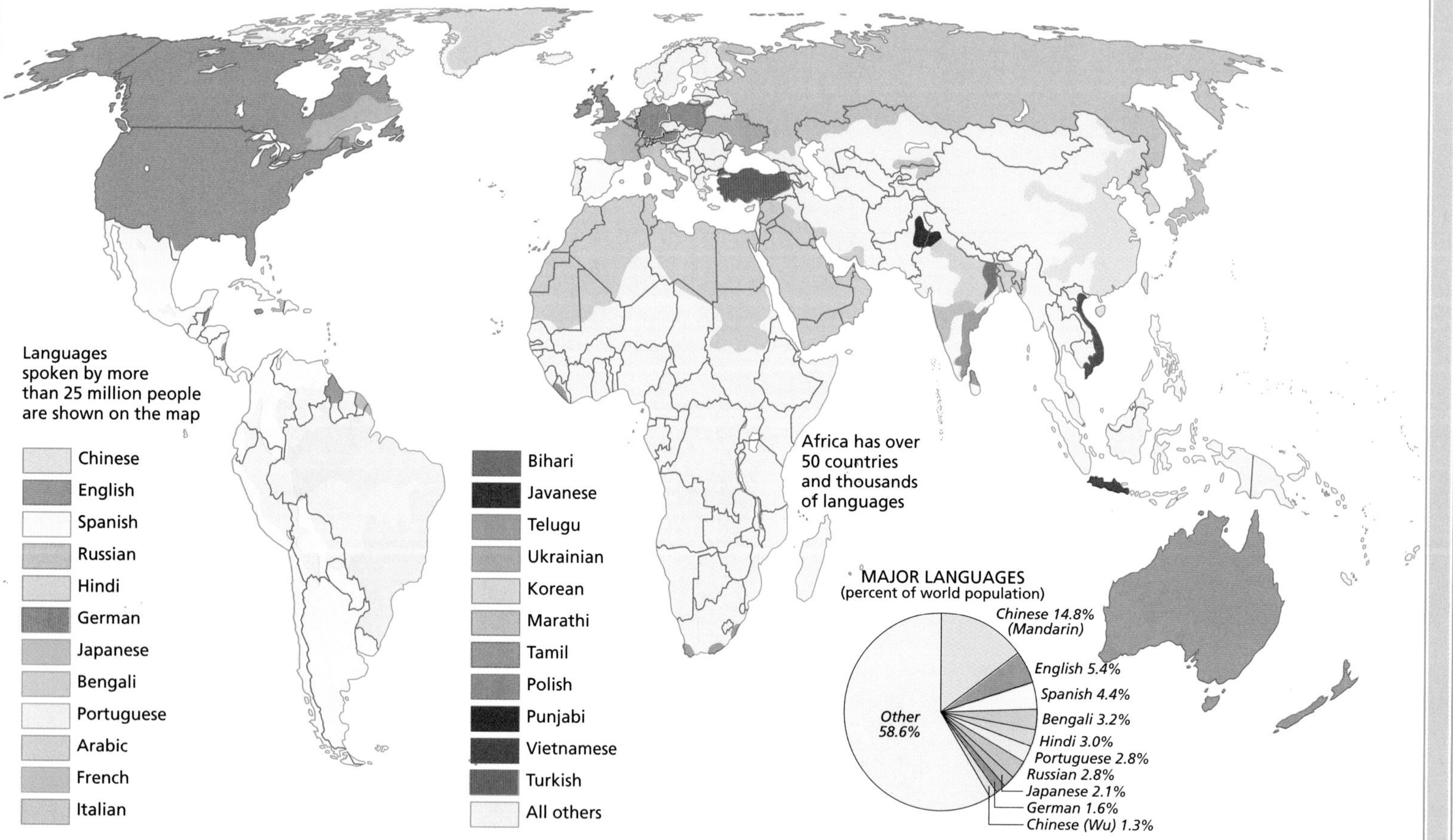

RELIGION

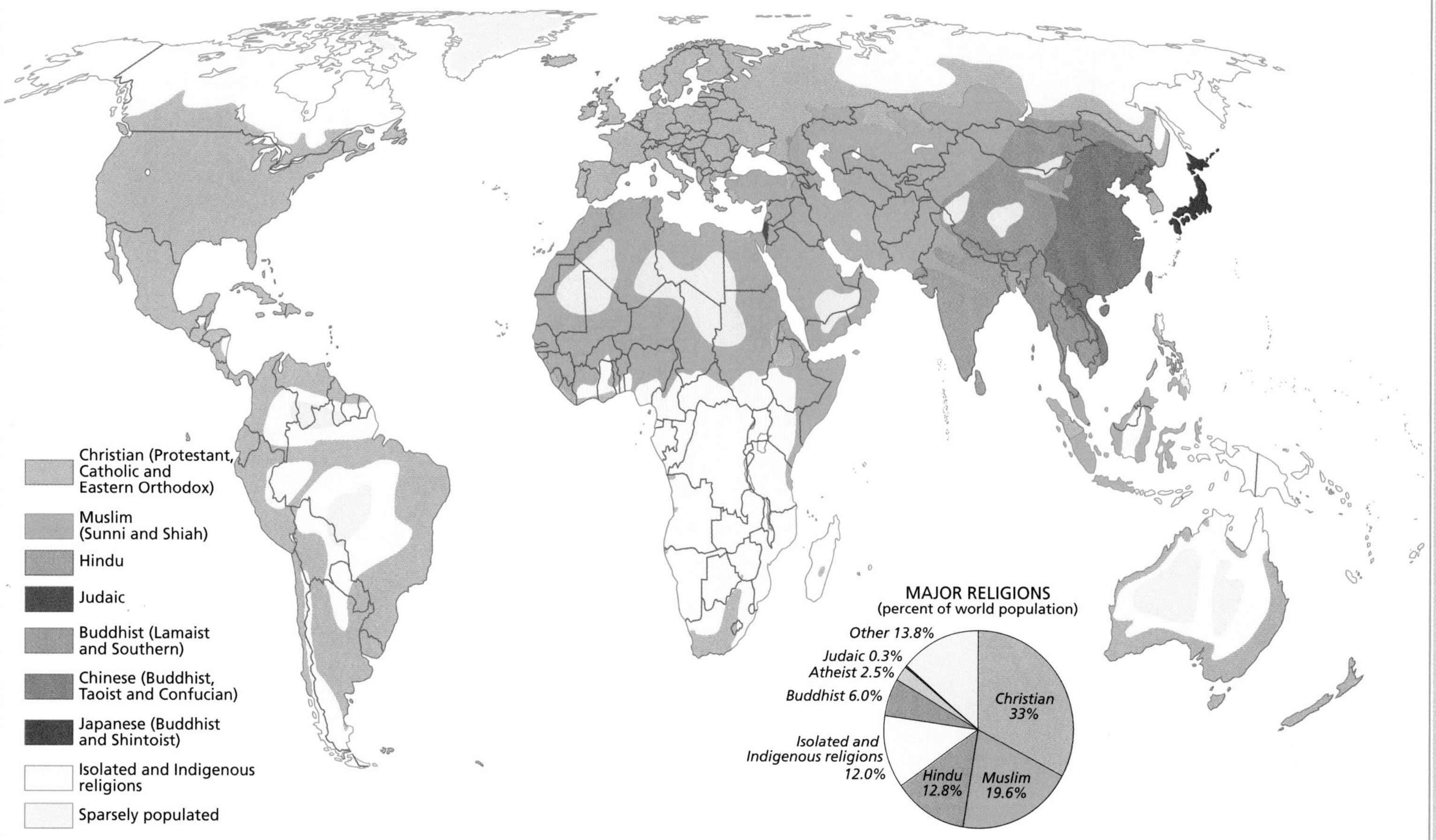

LITERACY

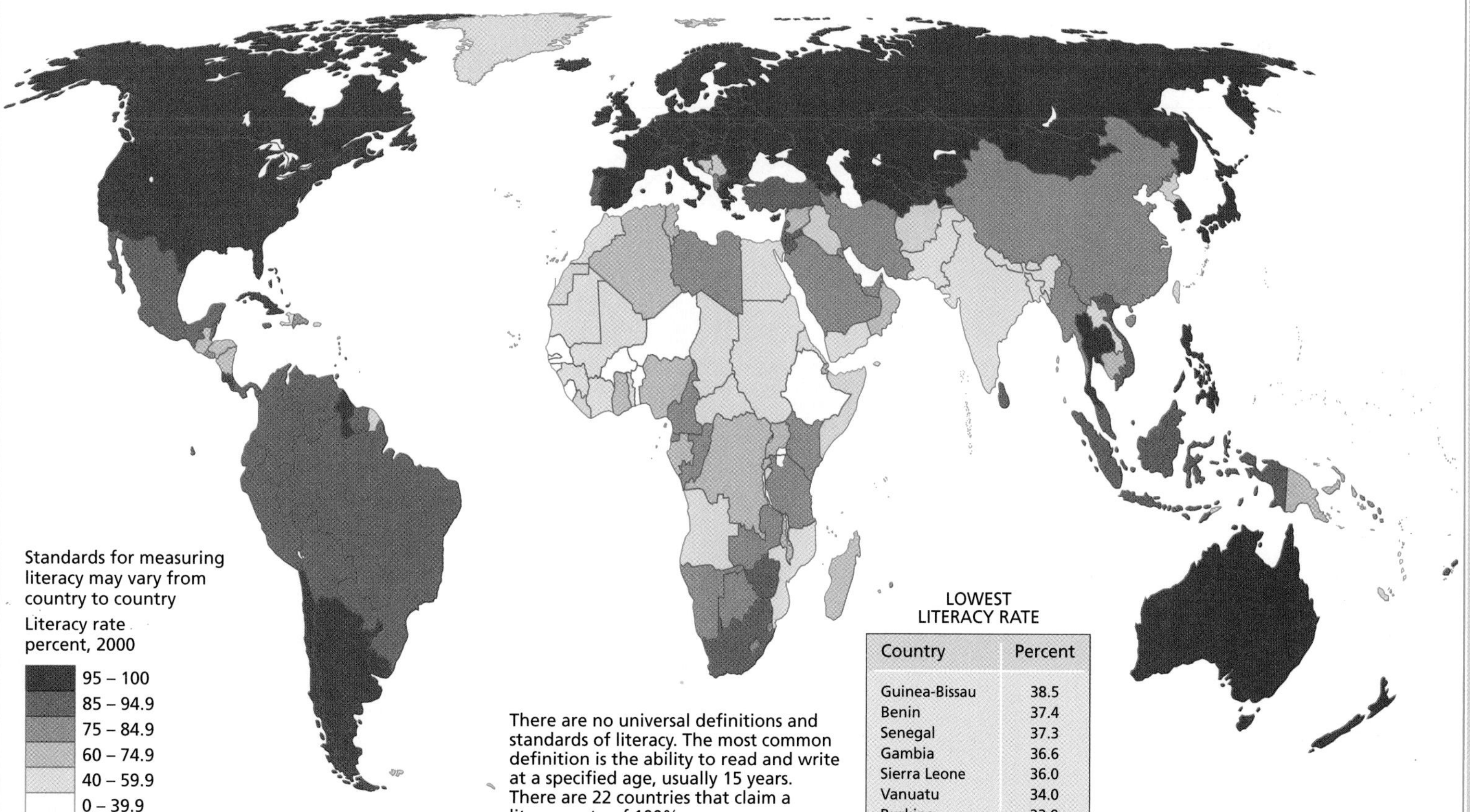

There are no universal definitions and standards of literacy. The most common definition is the ability to read and write at a specified age, usually 15 years. There are 22 countries that claim a literacy rate of 100%.

LOWEST LITERACY RATE

Country	Percent
Guinea-Bissau	38.5
Benin	37.4
Senegal	37.3
Gambia	36.6
Sierra Leone	36.0
Vanuatu	34.0
Burkina	23.9
Niger	15.9

SCALE 1 : 140 000 000

0 2000 4000 6000 8000 km

Eckert IV projection

ABORIGINAL PEOPLES

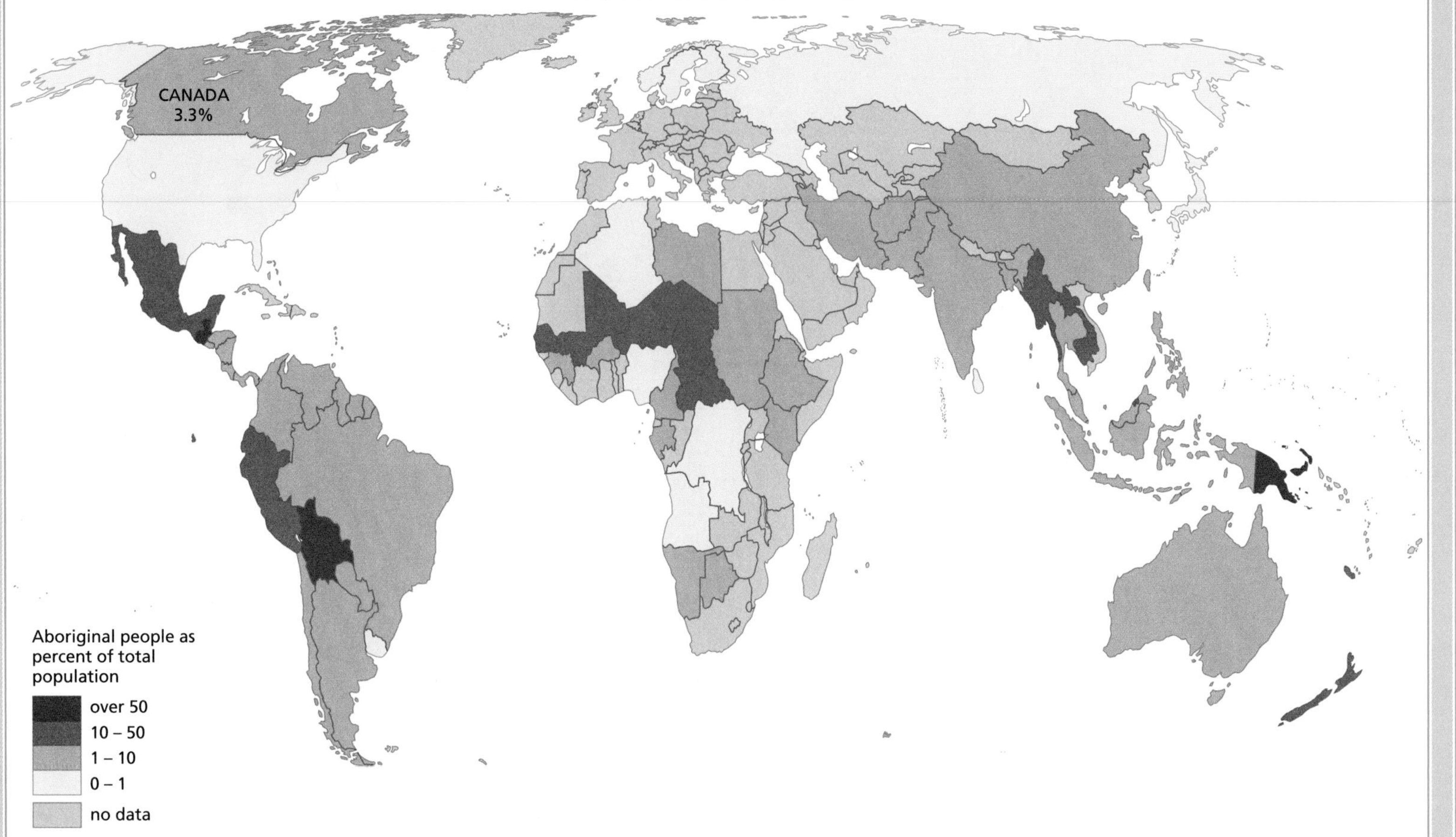

DATE OF INDEPENDENCE

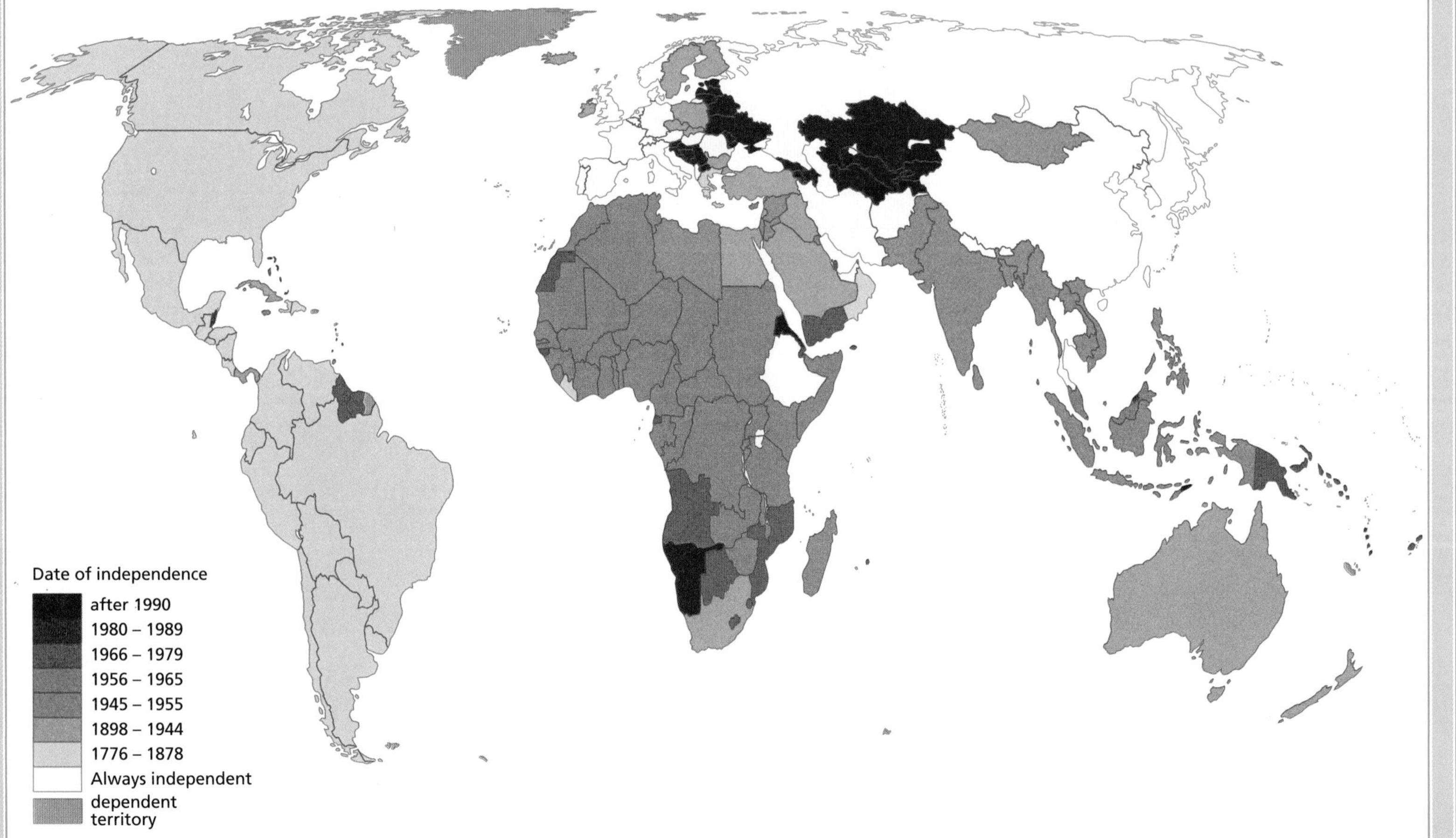

SCALE 1 : 140 000 000

0 2000 4000 6000 8000 km

Eckert IV projection

TYPES OF GOVERNMENT

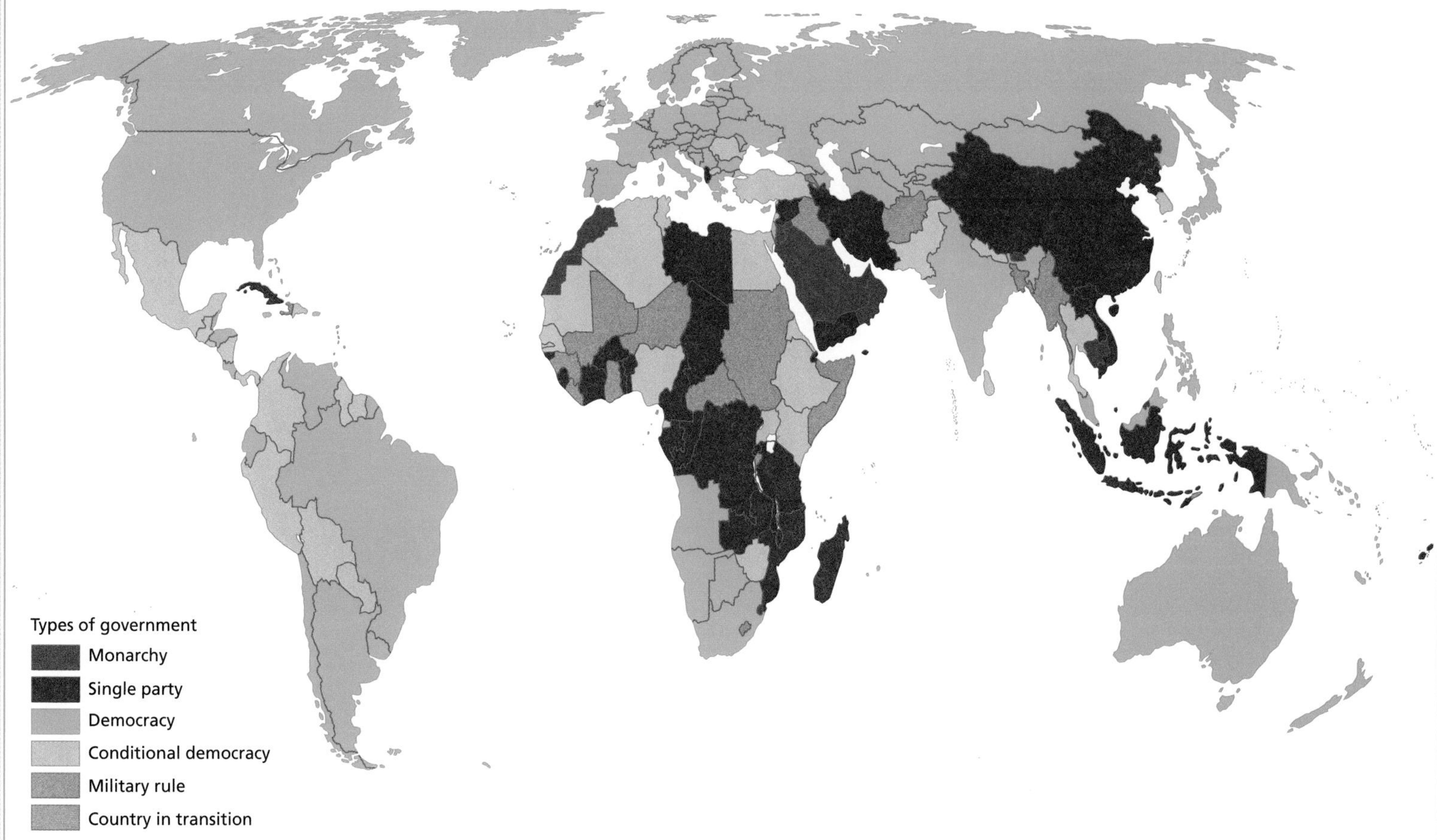
Types of government
Monarchy
Single party
Democracy
Conditional democracy
Military rule
Country in transition

TIME ZONES

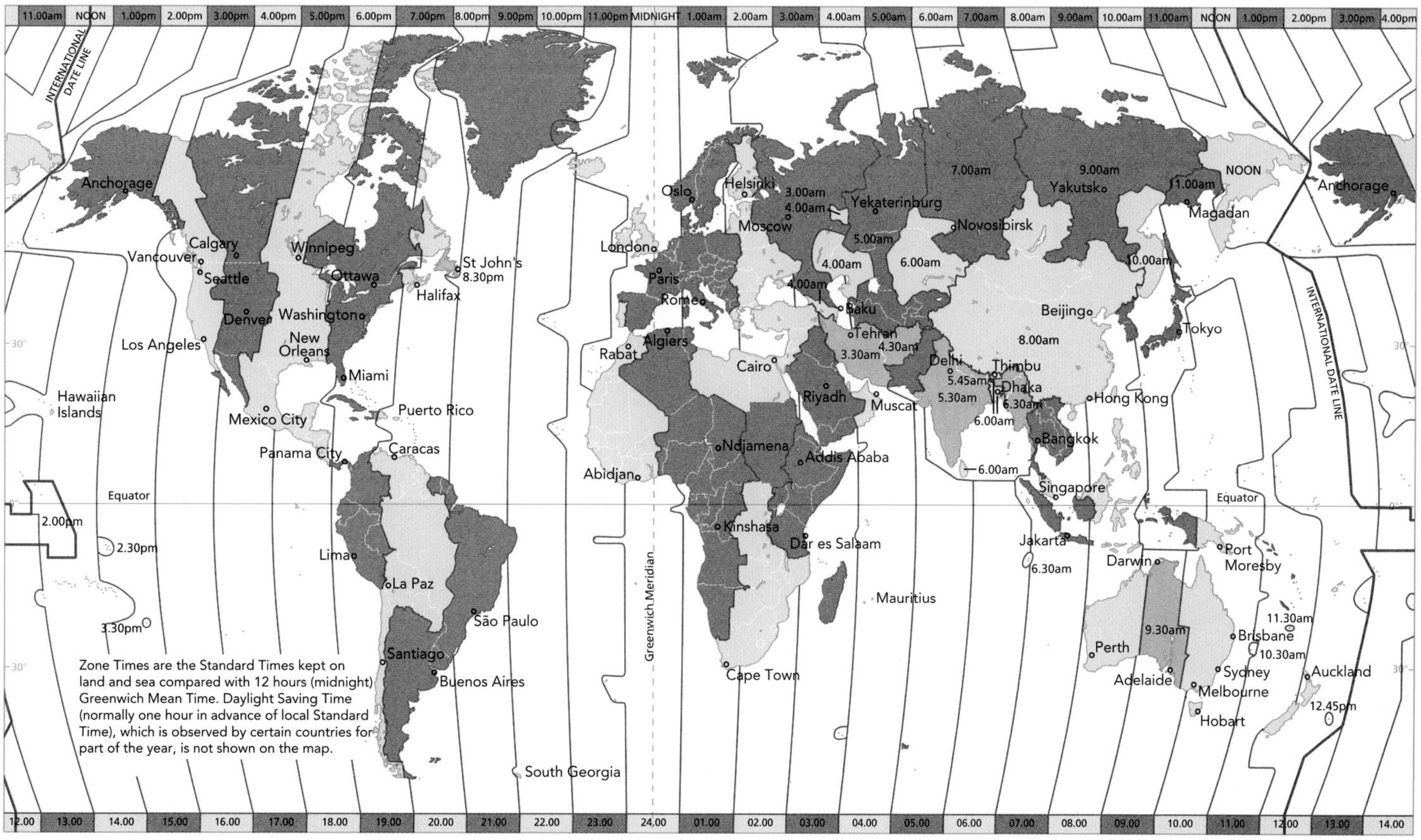
11.00am
NOON
1.00pm
2.00pm
3.00pm
4.00pm
5.00pm
6.00pm
7.00pm
8.00pm
9.00pm
10.00pm
11.00pm
MIDNIGHT
1.00am
2.00am
3.00am
4.00am
5.00am
6.00am
7.00am
8.00am
9.00am
10.00am
11.00am
NOON
1.00pm
2.00pm
3.00pm
4.00pm
INTERNATIONAL DATE LINE
Anchorage
Vancouver
Calgary
Seattle
Winnipeg
Ottawa
St John's
8.30pm
Halifax
Washington
Denver
Los Angeles
New Orleans
Miami
Hawaiian Islands
Mexico City
Puerto Rico
Panama City
Caracas
Equator
2.00pm
2.30pm
Lima
La Paz
São Paulo
3.30pm
Santiago
Buenos Aires
South Georgia
Zone Times are the Standard Times kept on land and sea compared with 12 hours (midnight) Greenwich Mean Time. Daylight Saving Time (normally one hour in advance of local Standard Time), which is observed by certain countries for part of the year, is not shown on the map.
Greenwich Meridian
London
Oslo
Helsinki
3.00am
4.00am
Moscow
Paris
Rome
Algiers
Rabat
Cairo
Abidjan
Ndjamena
Addis Ababa
Kinshasa
Dar es Salaam
Cape Town
Mauritius
Yekaterinburg
Novosibirsk
5.00am
4.00am
6.00am
4.00am
Baku
Tehran
3.30am
4.30am
Riyadh
Muscat
Delhi
5.45am
5.30am
Thimbu
Dhaka
6.30am
6.00am
6.00am
7.00am
8.00am
Beijing
Bangkok
Hong Kong
Singapore
Jakarta
6.30am
9.00am
Yakutsk
11.00am
NOON
Magadan
10.00am
Tokyo
Darwin
Port Moresby
9.30am
Perth
Adelaide
Melbourne
Hobart
11.30am
Brisbane
10.30am
Sydney
Auckland
12.45pm
12.00
13.00
14.00
15.00
16.00
17.00
18.00
19.00
20.00
21.00
22.00
23.00
24.00
01.00
02.00
03.00
04.00
05.00
06.00
07.00
08.00
09.00
10.00
11.00
12.00
13.00
14.00

SCALE 1 : 140 000 000 — 0 2000 4000 6000 8000 km

Eckert IV projection

AID PROVIDERS AND RECEIVERS

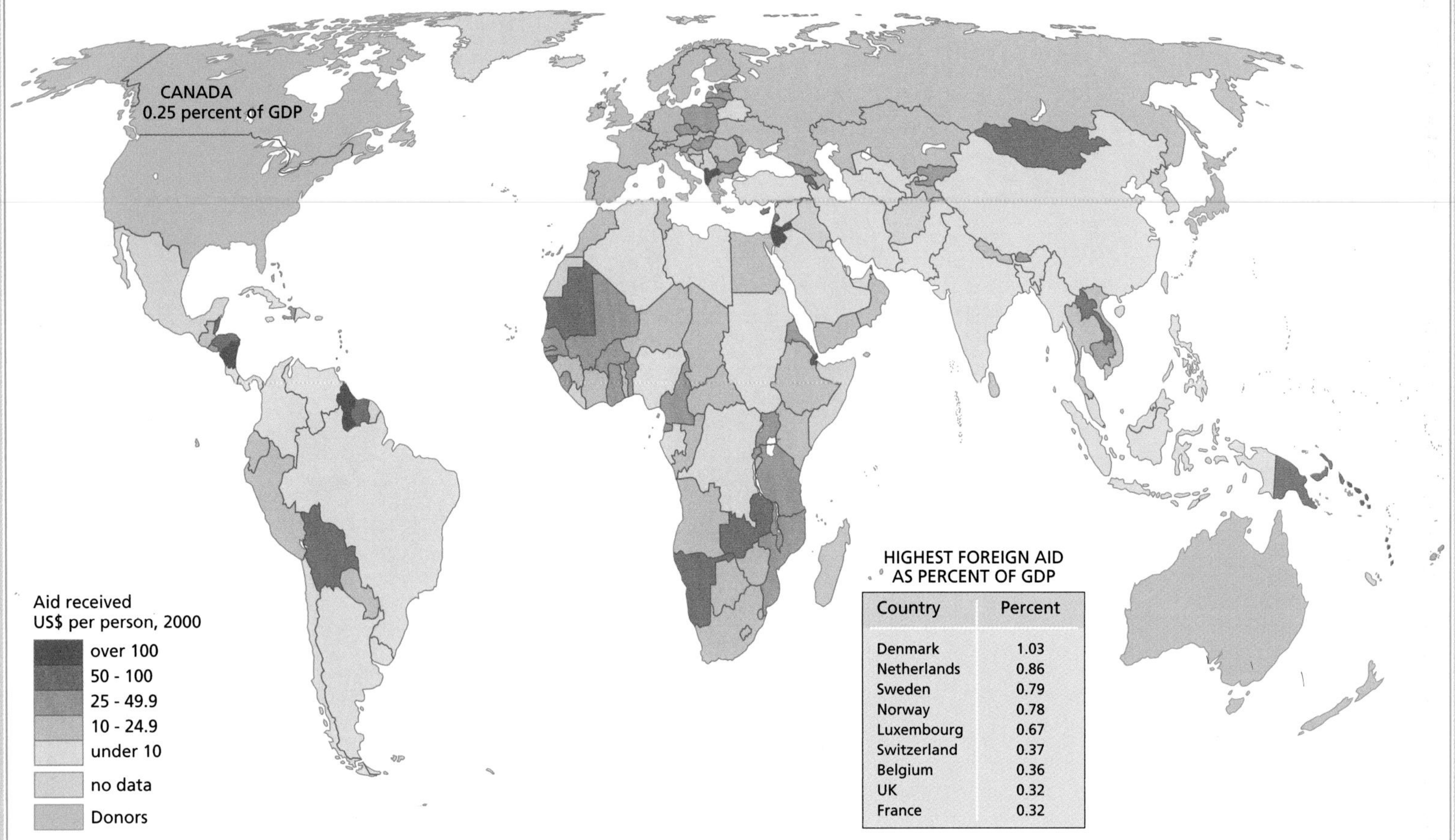

HIGHEST FOREIGN AID AS PERCENT OF GDP

Country	Percent
Denmark	1.03
Netherlands	0.86
Sweden	0.79
Norway	0.78
Luxembourg	0.67
Switzerland	0.37
Belgium	0.36
UK	0.32
France	0.32

MILITARY EXPENDITURES

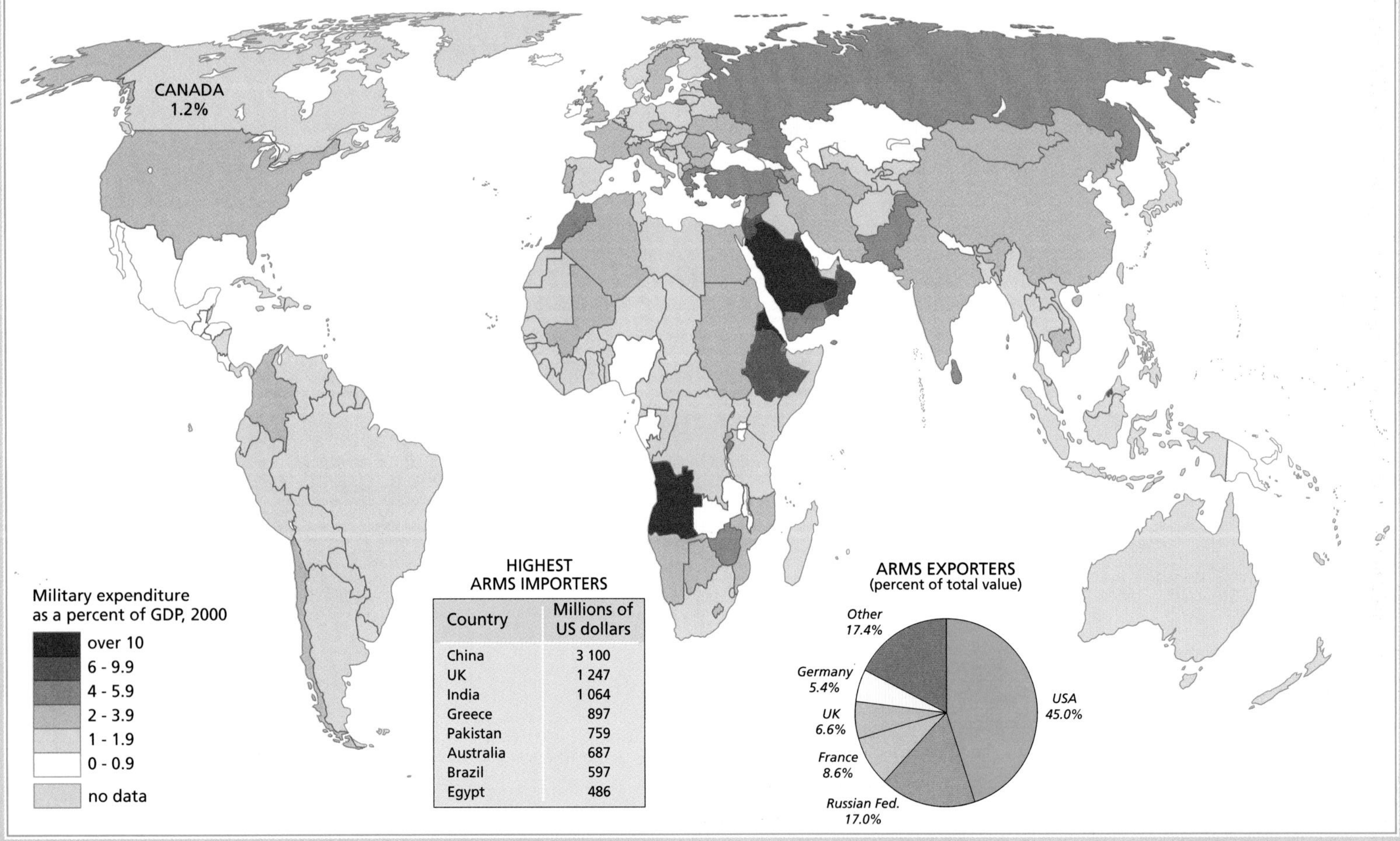

HIGHEST ARMS IMPORTERS

Country	Millions of US dollars
China	3 100
UK	1 247
India	1 064
Greece	897
Pakistan	759
Australia	687
Brazil	597
Egypt	486

ARMS EXPORTERS
(percent of total value)

INTERNATIONAL ORGANIZATIONS: POLITICAL

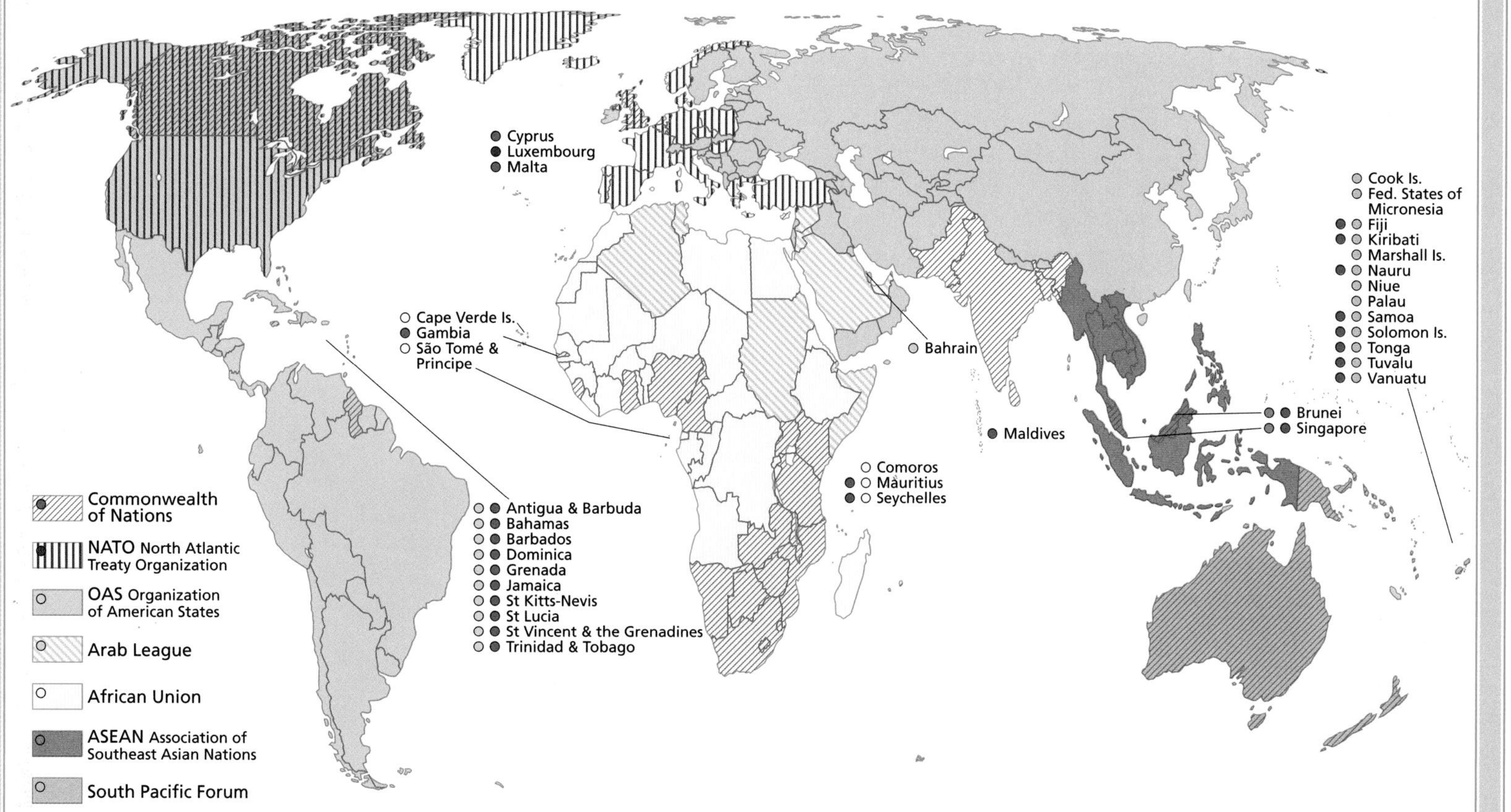

INTERNATIONAL ORGANIZATIONS: ECONOMIC

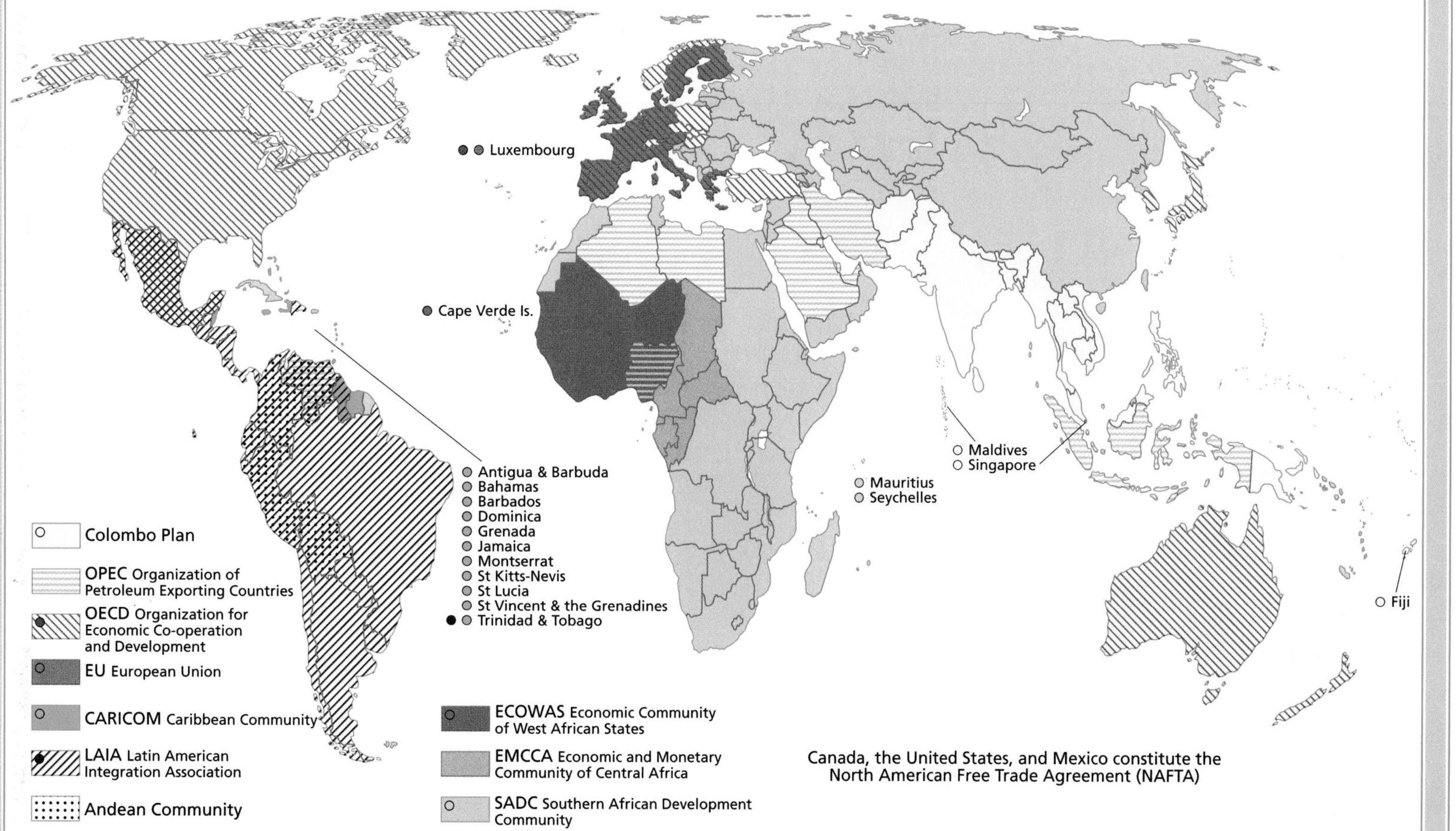

SCALE 1 : 140 000 000 — 0, 2000, 4000, 6000, 8000 km

Eckert IV projection

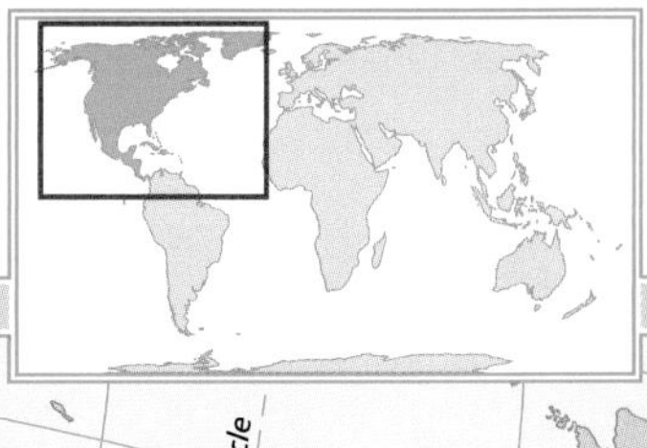

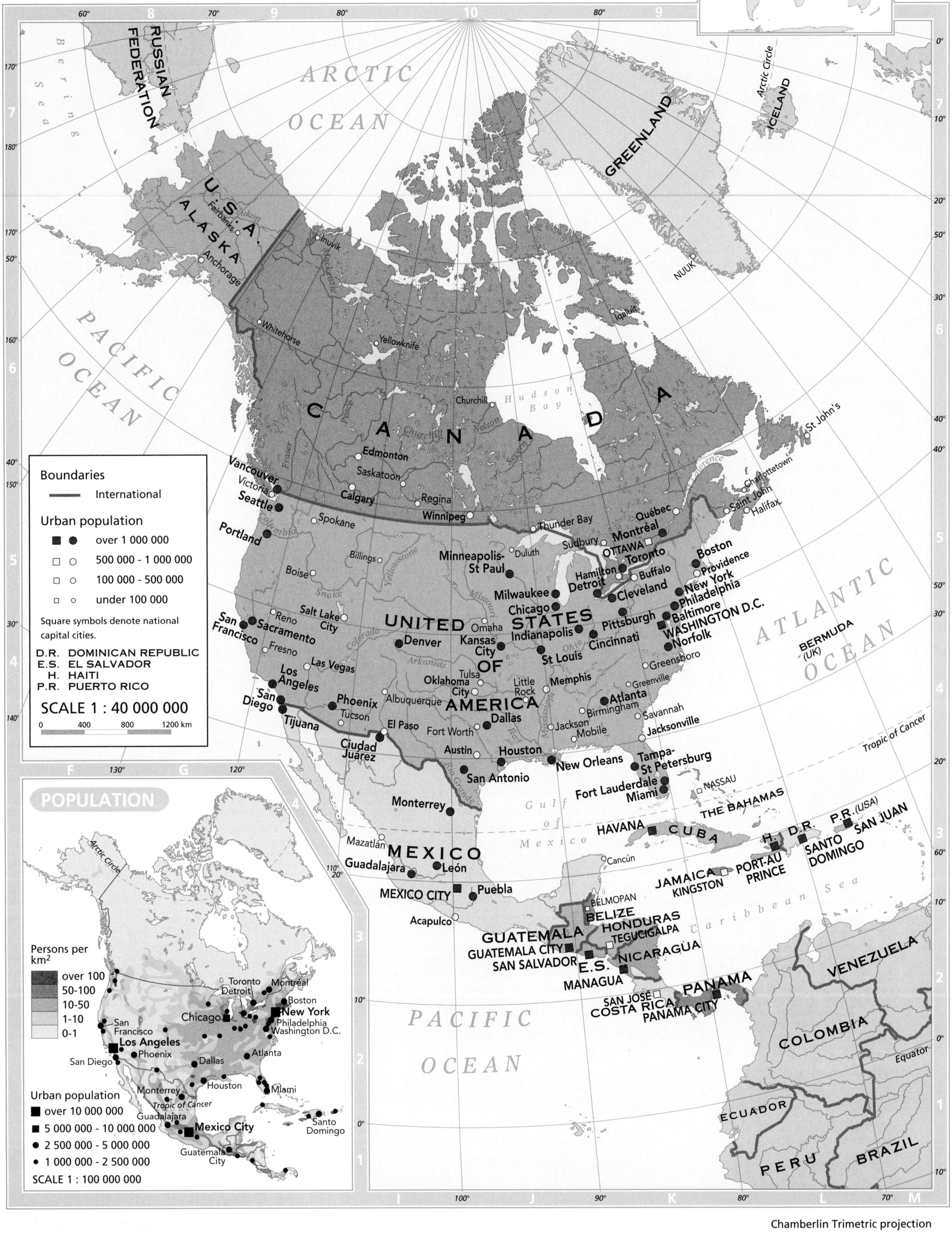
ARCTIC OCEAN
PACIFIC OCEAN
ATLANTIC OCEAN
Bering Sea
Hudson Bay
Gulf of Mexico
Caribbean Sea
RUSSIAN FEDERATION
U.S.A.
ALASKA
GREENLAND
ICELAND
CANADA
UNITED STATES OF AMERICA
MEXICO
CUBA
THE BAHAMAS
BERMUDA (UK)
JAMAICA
H.
D.R.
P.R. (USA)
BELIZE
GUATEMALA
HONDURAS
E.S.
NICARAGUA
COSTA RICA
PANAMA
VENEZUELA
COLOMBIA
ECUADOR
PERU
BRAZIL
Arctic Circle
Tropic of Cancer
Equator
Fairbanks
Anchorage
Inuvik
Whitehorse
Yellowknife
Iqaluit
NUUK
Churchill
Edmonton
Saskatoon
Calgary
Regina
Winnipeg
Vancouver
Victoria
Seattle
Spokane
Portland
Thunder Bay
Sudbury
Québec
Montréal
OTTAWA
Toronto
Hamilton
Buffalo
Detroit
Cleveland
Charlottetown
Saint John
Halifax
St John's
Boston
Providence
New York
Philadelphia
Baltimore
WASHINGTON D.C.
Norfolk
Greensboro
Greenville
Pittsburgh
Cincinnati
Indianapolis
Chicago
Milwaukee
Minneapolis-St Paul
Duluth
Billings
Boise
Salt Lake City
Reno
San Francisco
Sacramento
Fresno
Las Vegas
Los Angeles
San Diego
Tijuana
Phoenix
Tucson
Albuquerque
El Paso
Ciudad Juárez
Denver
Omaha
Kansas City
St Louis
Tulsa
Oklahoma City
Little Rock
Memphis
Atlanta
Birmingham
Savannah
Jacksonville
Dallas
Fort Worth
Jackson
Mobile
Austin
Houston
San Antonio
New Orleans
Tampa-St Petersburg
Fort Lauderdale
Miami
NASSAU
HAVANA
PORT-AU PRINCE
SANTO DOMINGO
SAN JUAN
KINGSTON
Cancún
Monterrey
Mazatlán
Guadalajara
León
MEXICO CITY
Puebla
Acapulco
BELMOPAN
TEGUCIGALPA
GUATEMALA CITY
SAN SALVADOR
MANAGUA
SAN JOSÉ
PANAMA CITY
Mackenzie
Yukon
Peace
Churchill
Nelson
Severn
Fraser
Columbia
Snake
Yellowstone
Missouri
Colorado
Arkansas
Red
Mississippi
Ohio
Rio Grande
St Lawrence
Boundaries
International
Urban population
over 1 000 000
500 000 - 1 000 000
100 000 - 500 000
under 100 000
Square symbols denote national capital cities.
D.R. DOMINICAN REPUBLIC
E.S. EL SALVADOR
H. HAITI
P.R. PUERTO RICO
SCALE 1 : 40 000 000
0 400 800 1200 km
POPULATION
Persons per km²
over 100
50-100
10-50
1-10
0-1
Urban population
over 10 000 000
5 000 000 - 10 000 000
2 500 000 - 5 000 000
1 000 000 - 2 500 000
SCALE 1 : 100 000 000
Toronto
Detroit
Montréal
Boston
New York
Philadelphia
Washington D.C.
Chicago
San Francisco
Los Angeles
Phoenix
San Diego
Dallas
Atlanta
Houston
Miami
Monterrey
Guadalajara
Mexico City
Guatemala City
Santo Domingo

Chamberlin Trimetric projection

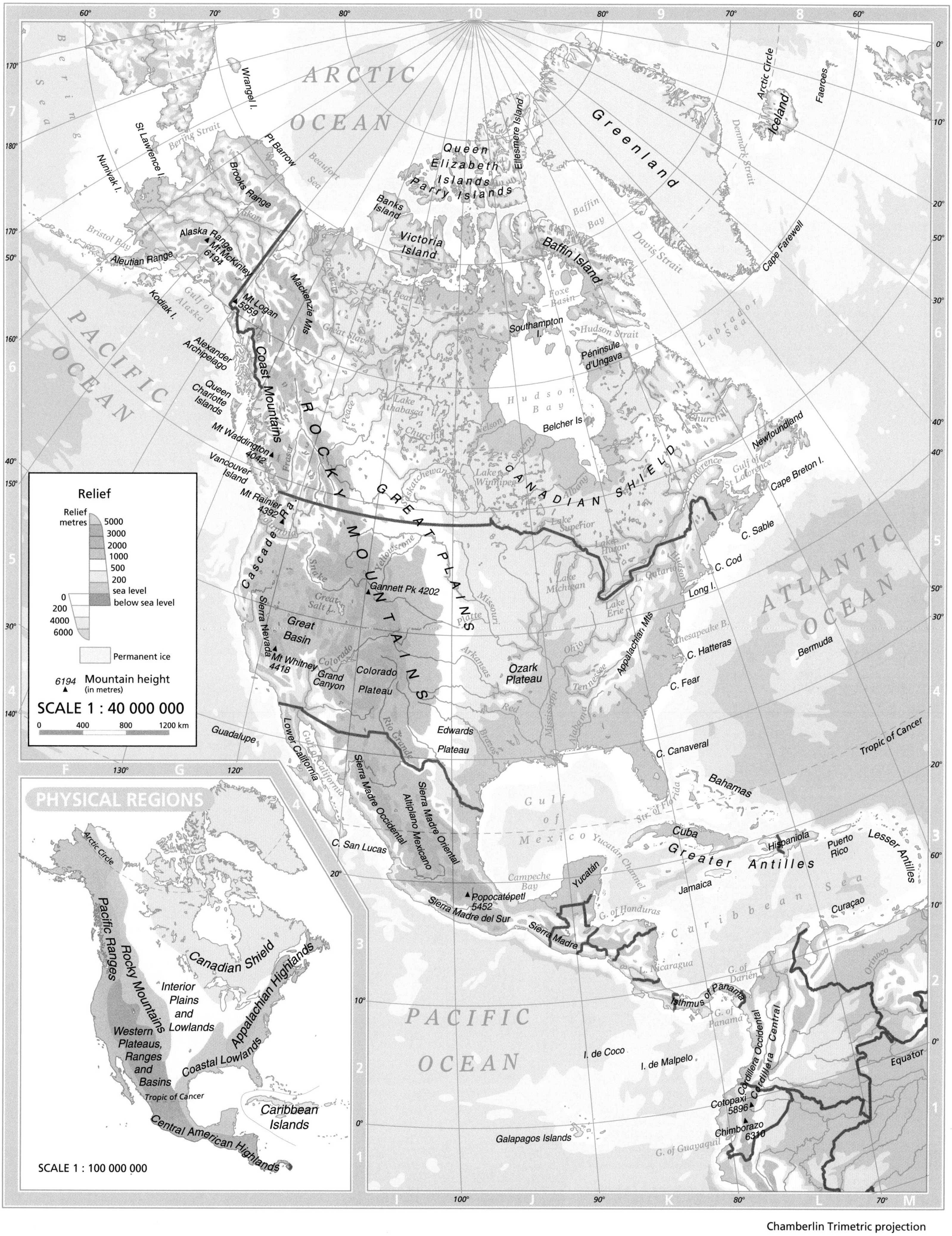
ARCTIC OCEAN
PACIFIC OCEAN
ATLANTIC OCEAN
Bering Sea
Wrangel I.
St Lawrence I.
Bering Strait
Nunivak I.
Pt Barrow
Beaufort Sea
Brooks Range
Yukon
Bristol Bay
Alaska Range
Mt McKinley 6194
Aleutian Range
Kodiak I.
Gulf of Alaska
Mt Logan 5959
Mackenzie Mts
Mackenzie
Alexander Archipelago
Queen Charlotte Islands
Coast Mountains
Mt Waddington 4042
Vancouver Island
Fraser
Mt Rainier 4392
Columbia
Cascade Ra.
Snake
Great Salt L.
Sierra Nevada
Great Basin
Mt Whitney 4418
Grand Canyon
Colorado
Colorado Plateau
Yellowstone
Gannett Pk 4202
ROCKY MOUNTAINS
GREAT PLAINS
Platte
Missouri
Arkansas
Red
Brazos
Rio Grande
Edwards Plateau
Ozark Plateau
Mississippi
Ohio
Tennessee
Alabama
Appalachian Mts
Lake Michigan
Lake Superior
Lake Huron
Lake Erie
L. Ontario
Hudson
Chesapeake B.
C. Hatteras
C. Fear
C. Canaveral
Long I.
C. Cod
C. Sable
Cape Breton I.
Gulf of St Lawrence
St Lawrence
Newfoundland
Bermuda
Tropic of Cancer
Bahamas
Str. of Florida
Gulf of Mexico
Cuba
Hispaniola
Puerto Rico
Greater Antilles
Lesser Antilles
Jamaica
Caribbean Sea
Curaçao
Yucatán
Yucatán Channel
Campeche Bay
Popocatépetl 5452
Sierra Madre del Sur
Sierra Madre
G. of Honduras
L. Nicaragua
G. of Darién
Isthmus of Panama
G. of Panamá
Guadalupe
Lower California
Gulf of California
C. San Lucas
Sierra Madre Occidental
Sierra Madre Oriental
Altiplano Mexicano
I. de Coco
I. de Malpelo
Galapagos Islands
G. of Guayaquil
Cordillera Occidental
Cordillera Central
Cotopaxi 5896
Chimborazo 6310
Orinoco
Equator
Queen Elizabeth Islands
Parry Islands
Ellesmere Island
Banks Island
Victoria Island
Great Bear L.
Great Slave L.
Lake Athabasca
Peace
Churchill
Nelson
Saskatchewan
Lake Winnipeg
Severn
Albany
CANADIAN SHIELD
Hudson Bay
Belcher Is
Southampton I.
Foxe Basin
Hudson Strait
Péninsule d'Ungava
Baffin Island
Baffin Bay
Davis Strait
Labrador Sea
Greenland
Cape Farewell
Denmark Strait
Arctic Circle
Iceland
Faeroes
Relief
Relief metres
5000
3000
2000
1000
500
200
sea level
below sea level
0
200
4000
6000
Permanent ice
6194 Mountain height (in metres)
SCALE 1 : 40 000 000
0 400 800 1200 km
PHYSICAL REGIONS
Arctic Circle
Pacific Ranges
Rocky Mountains
Canadian Shield
Interior Plains and Lowlands
Appalachian Highlands
Western Plateaus, Ranges and Basins
Coastal Lowlands
Tropic of Cancer
Caribbean Islands
Central American Highlands
SCALE 1 : 100 000 000

Chamberlin Trimetric projection

1600 – 1690

British
French
Disputed claim
Spanish
Approximate extent of settlement 1690

1690 – 1713

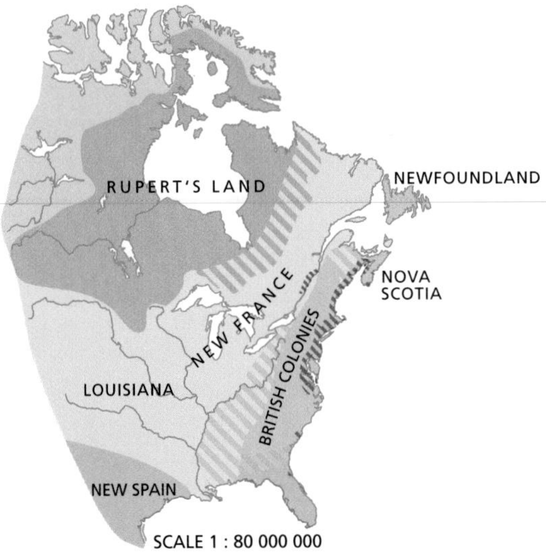

British
French
Disputed claim
Spanish
Disputed claim
Approximate extent of settlement 1713

1713 – 1763

British
Spanish
Approximate extent of settlement 1763

1763 – 1784

British
American
Disputed claim
Spanish
Approximate extent of settlement 1784

1784 – 1825

British
American
Joint occupation
Spanish
Russian
Approximate extent of settlement 1825

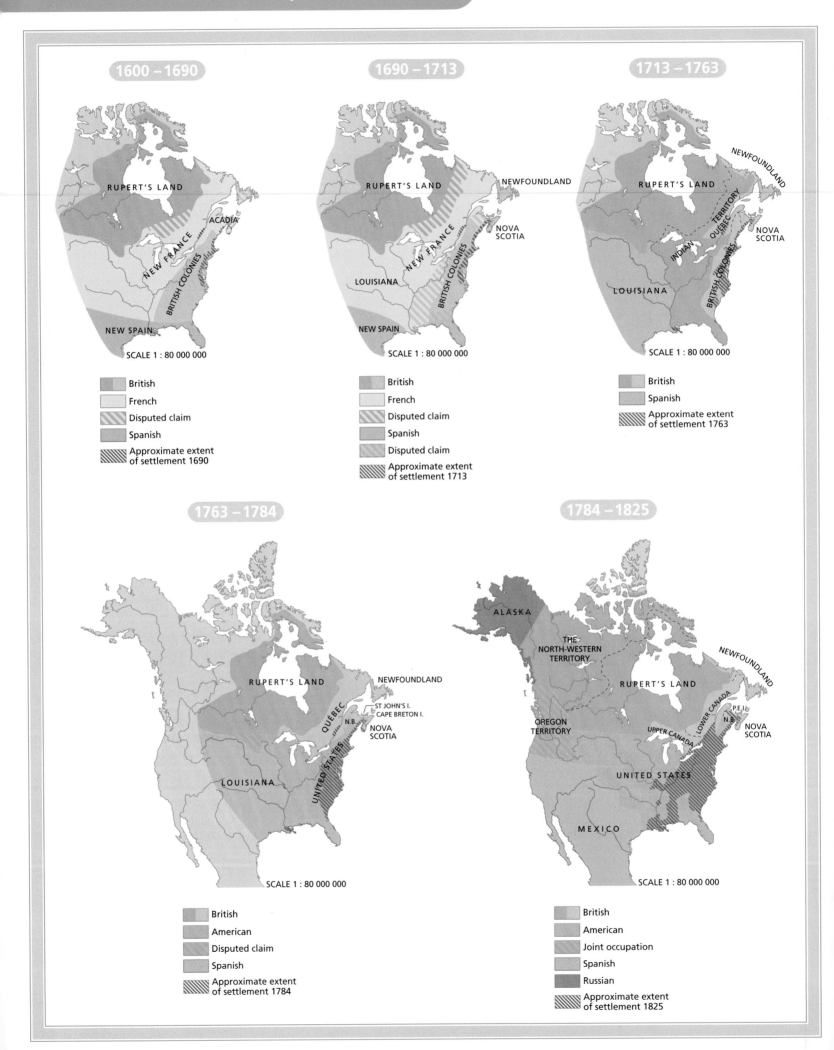

TOURISM

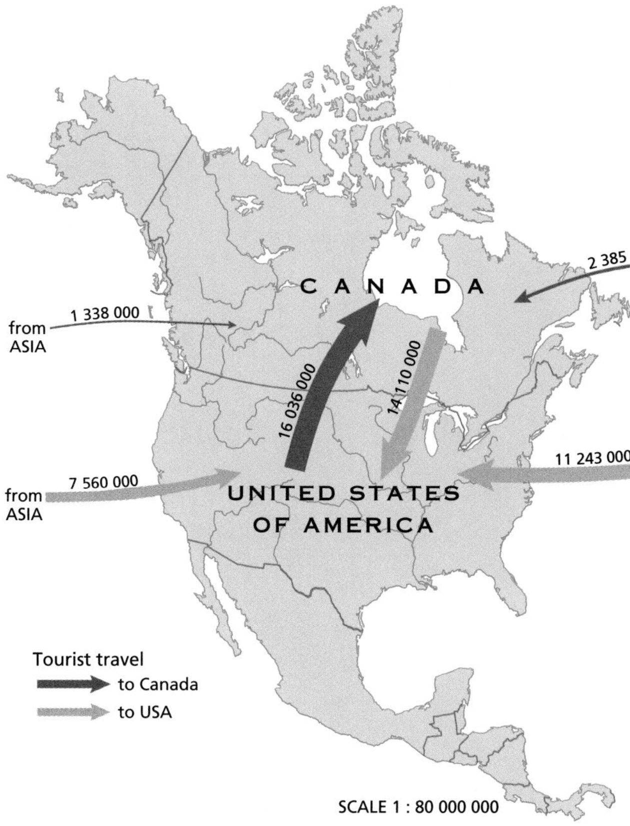
CANADA
UNITED STATES OF AMERICA
from ASIA
1 338 000
from EUROPE
2 385 000
16 036 000
14 110 000
from ASIA
7 560 000
from EUROPE
11 243 000
Tourist travel
to Canada
to USA
SCALE 1 : 80 000 000

ENERGY FLOW

CANADA
UNITED STATES OF AMERICA
88 million
4.87 billion
109.02 billion
40.76 million
17.90 million
Oil (tonnes)
Natural gas (cubic metres)
Electricity (MWh)
SCALE 1 : 80 000 000

TRADE

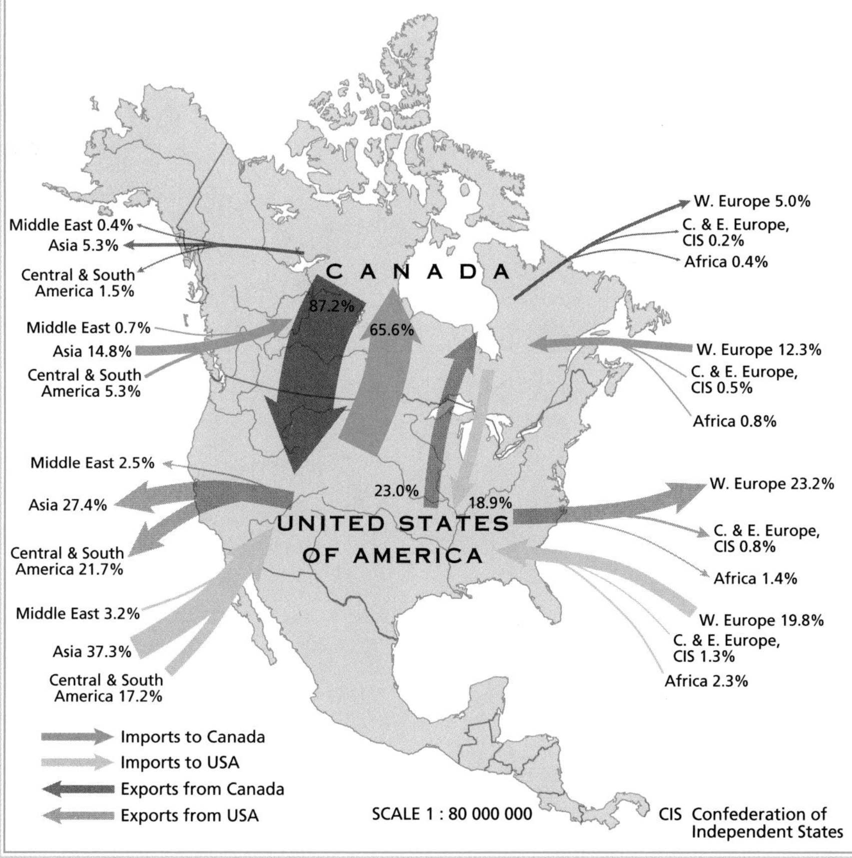
CANADA
UNITED STATES OF AMERICA
Middle East 0.4%
Asia 5.3%
Central & South America 1.5%
W. Europe 5.0%
C. & E. Europe, CIS 0.2%
Africa 0.4%
87.2%
65.6%
Middle East 0.7%
Asia 14.8%
Central & South America 5.3%
W. Europe 12.3%
C. & E. Europe, CIS 0.5%
Africa 0.8%
Middle East 2.5%
Asia 27.4%
Central & South America 21.7%
23.0%
18.9%
W. Europe 23.2%
C. & E. Europe, CIS 0.8%
Africa 1.4%
Middle East 3.2%
Asia 37.3%
Central & South America 17.2%
W. Europe 19.8%
C. & E. Europe, CIS 1.3%
Africa 2.3%
Imports to Canada
Imports to USA
Exports from Canada
Exports from USA
SCALE 1 : 80 000 000
CIS Confederation of Independent States

ECOSYSTEM SENSITIVITY TO ACID PRECIPITATION

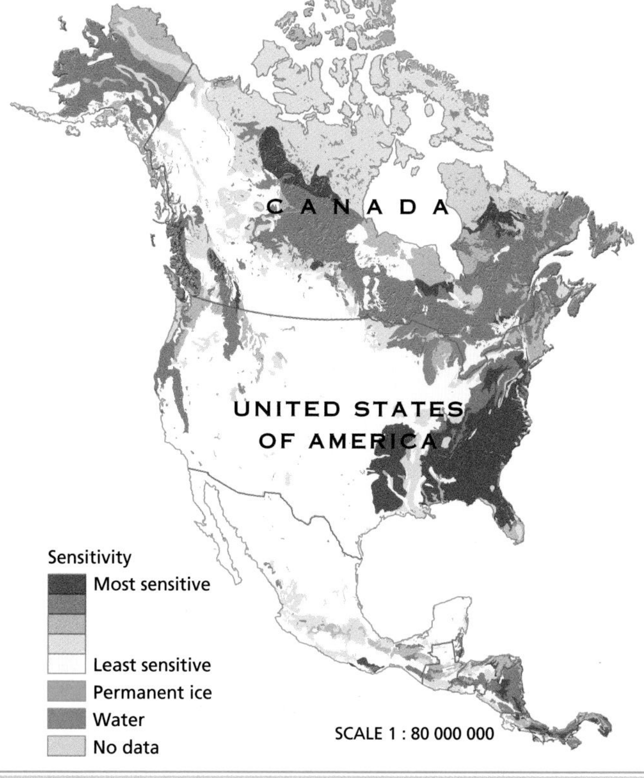
CANADA
UNITED STATES OF AMERICA
Sensitivity
Most sensitive
Least sensitive
Permanent ice
Water
No data
SCALE 1 : 80 000 000

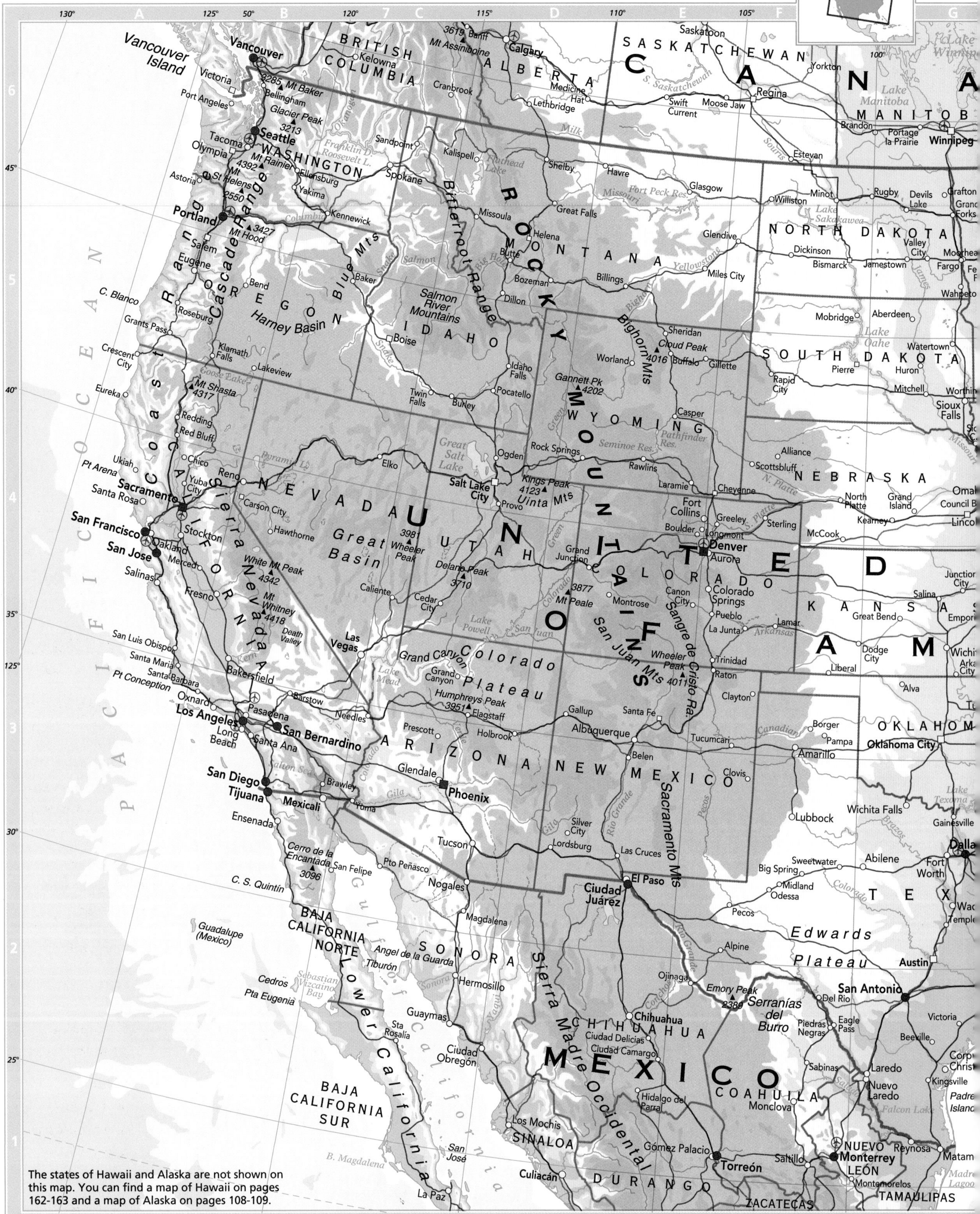

Vancouver Island

BRITISH COLUMBIA

Vancouver
Victoria
Port Angeles
3285 ▲Mt Baker
Bellingham
Glacier Peak 3213
Tacoma ● Seattle
WASHINGTON
Olympia
Mt Rainier 4392
Ellensburg
Yakima
Astoria
St Helens
2550
Portland ●
Mt Hood 3427
Salem
Eugene
Bend
Roseburg
Grants Pass
Crescent City
Klamath Falls
Lakeview

C. Blanco
OREGON
Harney Basin

ALBERTA
3619 Banff
Mt Assiniboine
Calgary
Cranbrook
Lethbridge
Medicine Hat
Sandpoint
Kalispell
Shelby
Havre
Glasgow
Great Falls
Missoula
Helena
Butte
Bozeman
Billings
Miles City
Dillon

SASKATCHEWAN
Saskatoon
Yorkton
Regina
Swift Current
Moose Jaw
Williston
Minot
NORTH DAKOTA
Dickinson
Bismarck
Jamestown
Valley City

CANADA
Lake Manitoba
MANITOBA
Brandon
Portage la Prairie
Winnipeg
Lake Winnipeg

Blue Mts
IDAHO
Bitterroot Range
Salmon River Mountains
Boise
Twin Falls
Burley
Oldaho Falls
Pocatello

MONTANA
ROCKY
Sheridan
Cloud Peak 4016
Worland
Gannett Pk 4202
WYOMING
Bighorn Mts

SOUTH DAKOTA
Pierre
Rapid City
Mobridge
Lake Oahe
Aberdeen
Watertown
Huron
Mitchell

Eureka
Redding
Red Bluff
Ukiah
Pt Arena
Santa Rosa
Chico
Yuba City
CALIFORNIA
Sacramento ●
Stockton
Mt Shasta 4317
Reno
Carson City
Hawthorne
NEVADA
Pyramid L.
Great Salt Lake
Ogden
Salt Lake City
Provo
Kings Peak 4123
Uinta Mts

Rock Springs
Rawlins
Laramie
Seminoe Res.
Pathfinder Res.
MOUNTAINS
UNITED
Casper
Cheyenne
Fort Collins
Greeley
Boulder
Longmont

NEBRASKA
Scottsbluff
Alliance
North Platte
Grand Island
Kearney
McCook
Sioux Falls
Omaha
Council Bluffs
Lincoln

San Francisco ●
Oakland ●
San Jose ●
Salinas
Fresno
Merced
Sierra Nevada
White Mt Peak 4342
Mt Whitney 4418
Death Valley
Great Basin
Wheeler Peak 3981
3981
Caliente
Cedar City
Delano Peak 3710
UTAH
Grand Junction
Denver ●
Aurora
COLORADO
Colorado Springs
Pueblo
La Junta
Lamar

KANSAS
Salina
Great Bend
Dodge City
Liberal
Wichita

San Luis Obispo
Santa Maria
Pt Conception
Bakersfield
Barstow
Las Vegas
Lake Mead
Grand Canyon
Grand Canyon
Humphreys Peak 3951
Flagstaff
Mt Peale 3877
Colorado Plateau
Sangre de Cristo Ra.
Wheeler Peak 4011
Montrose
Canon City
Trinidad
Raton
Clayton

OKLAHOMA
Borger
Pampa
Amarillo
Oklahoma City
Wichita

Santa Barbara
Oxnard
Los Angeles ●
Pasadena
Long Beach
Santa Ana
San Bernardino ●
San Diego ●
Tijuana
Mexicali
Ensenada
Needles
Prescott
Holbrook
ARIZONA
Glendale
Phoenix ■
Yuma
Brawley
Salton Sea
Tucson
Gallup
Albuquerque
Belen
NEW MEXICO
Silver City
Lordsburg
Las Cruces
Socorro
Santa Fe
Tucumcari
Clovis

Lubbock
Wichita Falls
Gainesville
Dallas ●
Fort Worth

Cerro de la Encantada 3096
San Felipe
C. S. Quintín
Nogales
Pto Peñasco
El Paso
Ciudad Juárez
Sacramento Mts
Rio Grande
Pecos
TEXAS
Big Spring
Sweetwater
Abilene
Midland
Odessa
Pecos

BAJA CALIFORNIA NORTE
Guadalupe (Mexico)
Cedros
Pta Eugenia
Sebastián Vizcaíno Bay
Angel de la Guarda
Tiburón
SONORA
Hermosillo
Magdalena
Edwards Plateau
Alpine
Austin
San Antonio ●
Del Rio

Guaymas
Sta Rosalía
Ciudad Obregón
Los Mochis
Sierra Madre Occidental
Emory Peak 2386
Serranías del Burro
Ojinaga
Chihuahua
Ciudad Delicias
Ciudad Camargo
Piedras Negras
Eagle Pass
CHIHUAHUA
COAHUILA
Sabinas
Laredo
Nuevo Laredo
Victoria
Beeville
Corpus Christi

BAJA CALIFORNIA SUR
B. Magdalena
San José
La Paz
Culiacán
SINALOA
Gómez Palacio
Torreón ●
DURANGO
Hidalgo del Parral
Monclova
Saltillo
Monterrey ●
NUEVO LEÓN
Montemorelos
ZACATECAS
TAMAULIPAS
Reynosa
Falcon Lake
Padre Island

PACIFIC OCEAN

Gulf of California

MEXICO

The states of Hawaii and Alaska are not shown on this map. You can find a map of Hawaii on pages 162-163 and a map of Alaska on pages 108-109.

SCALE 1 : 12 000 000

0 150 300 450 600 km

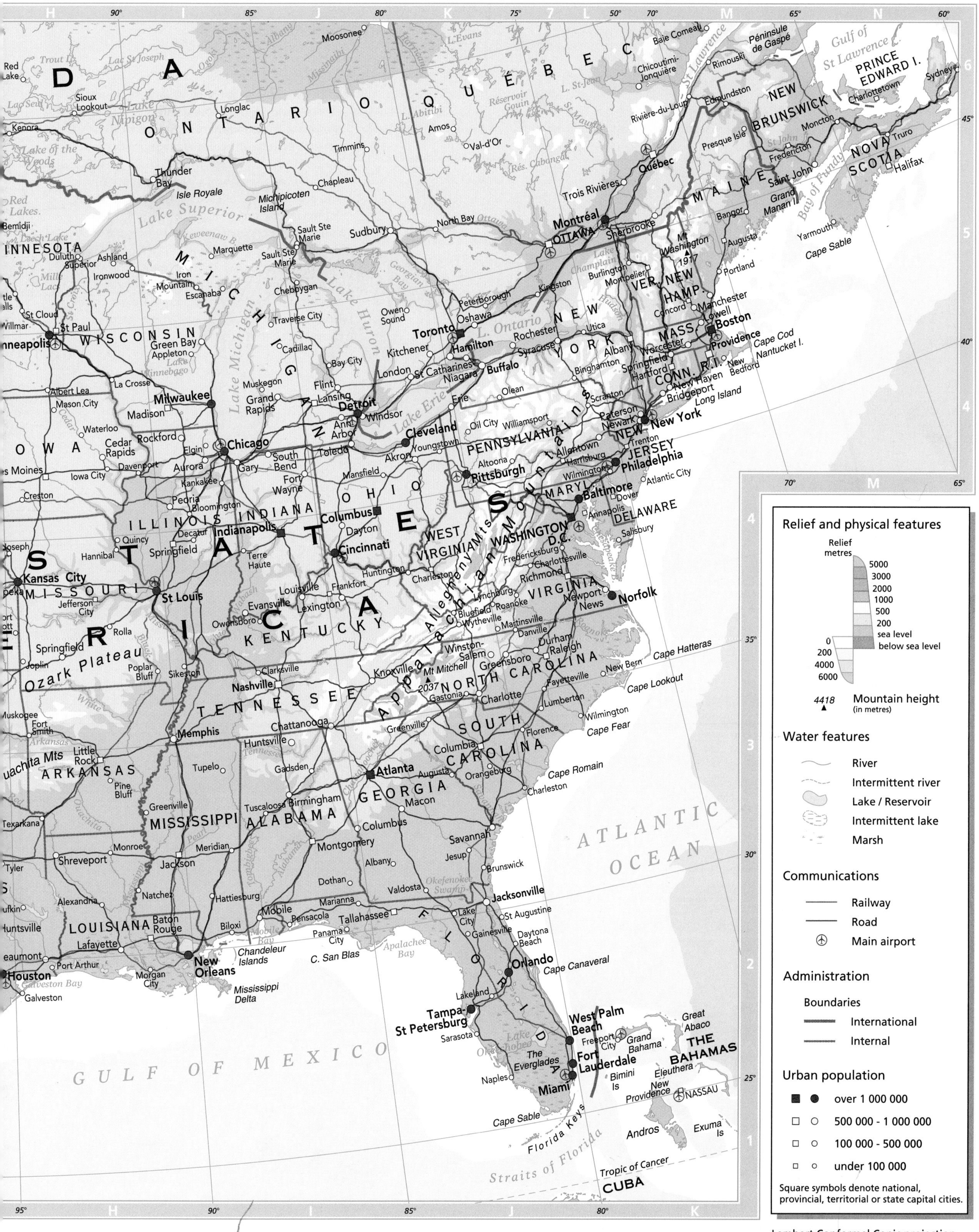

C A N A D A
O N T A R I O
Q U É B E C
U N I T E D S T A T E S
A M E R I C A
Moosonee
Red Lake
Trout L.
Lac St Joseph
Lac Seul
Sioux Lookout
Lake Nipigon
Longlac
Kenora
Lake of the Woods
Thunder Bay
Isle Royale
Lake Superior
Michipicoten Island
Red Lakes
Bemidji
Leech Lake
MINNESOTA
Duluth
Superior
Ashland
Ironwood
Mille Lacs L.
St Cloud
St Paul
Minneapolis
Marquette
Keweenaw B.
Iron Mountain
Escanaba
Sault Ste Marie
Chapleau
Timmins
Amos
Val-d'Or
L. Abitibi
L. Evans
Réservoir Gouin
Rés. Cabonga
L. St-Jean
Baie Comeau
Chicoutimi-Jonquière
Rimouski
Péninsule de Gaspé
Gulf of St Lawrence
PRINCE EDWARD I.
Charlottetown
Sydney
Rivière-du-Loup
Edmundston
NEW BRUNSWICK
Moncton
Truro
NOVA SCOTIA
Halifax
Presque Isle
Fredericton
Saint John
Bay of Fundy
Grand Manan I.
Yarmouth
Cape Sable
Québec
Trois Rivières
Montréal
OTTAWA
Sherbrooke
MAINE
Bangor
Augusta
Portland
Mt Washington 1917
NEW HAMP.
Concord
Manchester
Lowell
Boston
MASS.
Worcester
Providence
R.I.
Cape Cod
Nantucket I.
New Bedford
VER.
Montpelier
Burlington
Lake Champlain
Sudbury
North Bay
Georgian Bay
Lake Huron
Cheboygan
Traverse City
Owen Sound
Kingston
Peterborough
Oshawa
Toronto
L. Ontario
Hamilton
Kitchener
London
St Catharines
Niagara
Buffalo
Rochester
Syracuse
Utica
Albany
NEW YORK
Binghamton
Springfield
Hartford
CONN.
New Haven
Bridgeport
Long Island
New York
Newark
Paterson
Scranton
NEW JERSEY
Trenton
Philadelphia
Atlantic City
Allentown
Harrisburg
Wilmington
Williamsport
PENNSYLVANIA
Oil City
Olean
Erie
Altoona
Pittsburgh
Baltimore
Dover
Annapolis
DELAWARE
MARYLAND
Salisbury
WASHINGTON D.C.
WISCONSIN
Green Bay
Appleton
Lake Winnebago
La Crosse
Albert Lea
Mason City
Madison
Milwaukee
Lake Michigan
MICHIGAN
Muskegon
Grand Rapids
Cadillac
Bay City
Flint
Lansing
Detroit
Windsor
Ann Arbor
Lake Erie
Toledo
Cleveland
Youngstown
Akron
Mansfield
OHIO
Columbus
Dayton
Cincinnati
IOWA
Waterloo
Cedar Rapids
Rockford
Chicago
Elgin
Aurora
Gary
South Bend
Davenport
Des Moines
Iowa City
Kankakee
Fort Wayne
Peoria
Bloomington
ILLINOIS
INDIANA
Indianapolis
Decatur
Springfield
Quincy
Hannibal
Creston
Terre Haute
Kansas City
MISSOURI
Jefferson City
St Louis
Rolla
Springfield
Joplin
Ozark Plateau
Poplar Bluff
Sikeston
Evansville
Owensboro
Louisville
Frankfort
Lexington
KENTUCKY
Huntington
Charleston
WEST VIRGINIA
Allegheny Mts
Appalachian Mountains
Fredericksburg
Charlottesville
Richmond
VIRGINIA
Lynchburg
Roanoke
Bluefield
Wytheville
Martinsville
Danville
Newport News
Norfolk
Chesapeake B.
Winston-Salem
Greensboro
Durham
Raleigh
NORTH CAROLINA
Cape Hatteras
New Bern
Cape Lookout
Fayetteville
Mt Mitchell 2037
Knoxville
Clarksville
Nashville
TENNESSEE
Gastonia
Charlotte
Lumberton
Wilmington
Cape Fear
Florence
SOUTH CAROLINA
Columbia
Greenville
Chattanooga
Memphis
Huntsville
Muskogee
Fort Smith
Arkansas
Ouachita Mts
Little Rock
ARKANSAS
Pine Bluff
Tupelo
Gadsden
Atlanta
Augusta
Orangeburg
Cape Romain
Charleston
GEORGIA
Macon
Birmingham
Tuscaloosa
ALABAMA
Greenville
MISSISSIPPI
Texarkana
Columbus
Montgomery
Savannah
Jesup
Brunswick
Monroe
Shreveport
Meridian
Jackson
Tyler
Albany
Dothan
Valdosta
Okefenokee Swamp
Jacksonville
Natchez
Hattiesburg
Alexandria
Mobile
Marianna
Tallahassee
Pensacola
Lake City
St Augustine
Gainesville
Daytona Beach
LOUISIANA
Baton Rouge
Biloxi
Mobile Bay
Panama City
Apalachee Bay
Lafayette
Beaumont
Port Arthur
New Orleans
Chandeleur Islands
C. San Blas
Orlando
Cape Canaveral
Houston
Galveston Bay
Galveston
Morgan City
Mississippi Delta
Lakeland
FLORIDA
Tampa-St Petersburg
Sarasota
West Palm Beach
Lake Okeechobee
Fort Lauderdale
The Everglades
Naples
Miami
Freeport
Grand Bahama
Great Abaco
THE BAHAMAS
Eleuthera
Bimini Is
New Providence
NASSAU
Cape Sable
Florida Keys
Andros
Exuma Is
Straits of Florida
Tropic of Cancer
CUBA
GULF OF MEXICO
ATLANTIC OCEAN
90° 85° 80° 75° 70° 65° 60° 50° 45° 40° 35° 30° 25° 95°
Relief and physical features
Relief metres
5000
3000
2000
1000
500
200
sea level
below sea level
0
200
4000
6000
4418 Mountain height (in metres)
Water features
River
Intermittent river
Lake / Reservoir
Intermittent lake
Marsh
Communications
Railway
Road
Main airport
Administration
Boundaries
International
Internal
Urban population
over 1 000 000
500 000 - 1 000 000
100 000 - 500 000
under 100 000
Square symbols denote national, provincial, territorial or state capital cities.

Lambert Conformal Conic projection

LAND USE

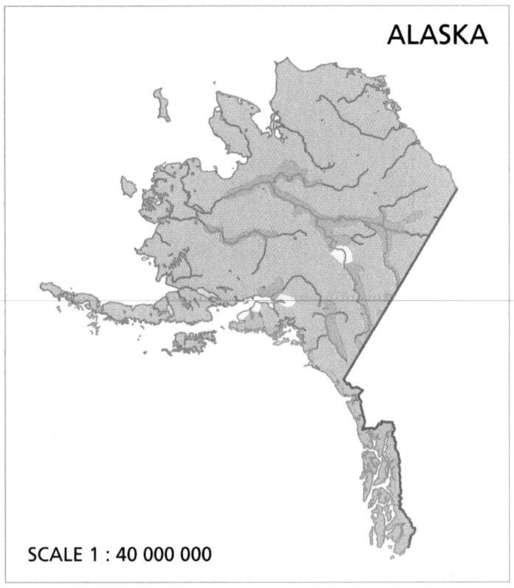

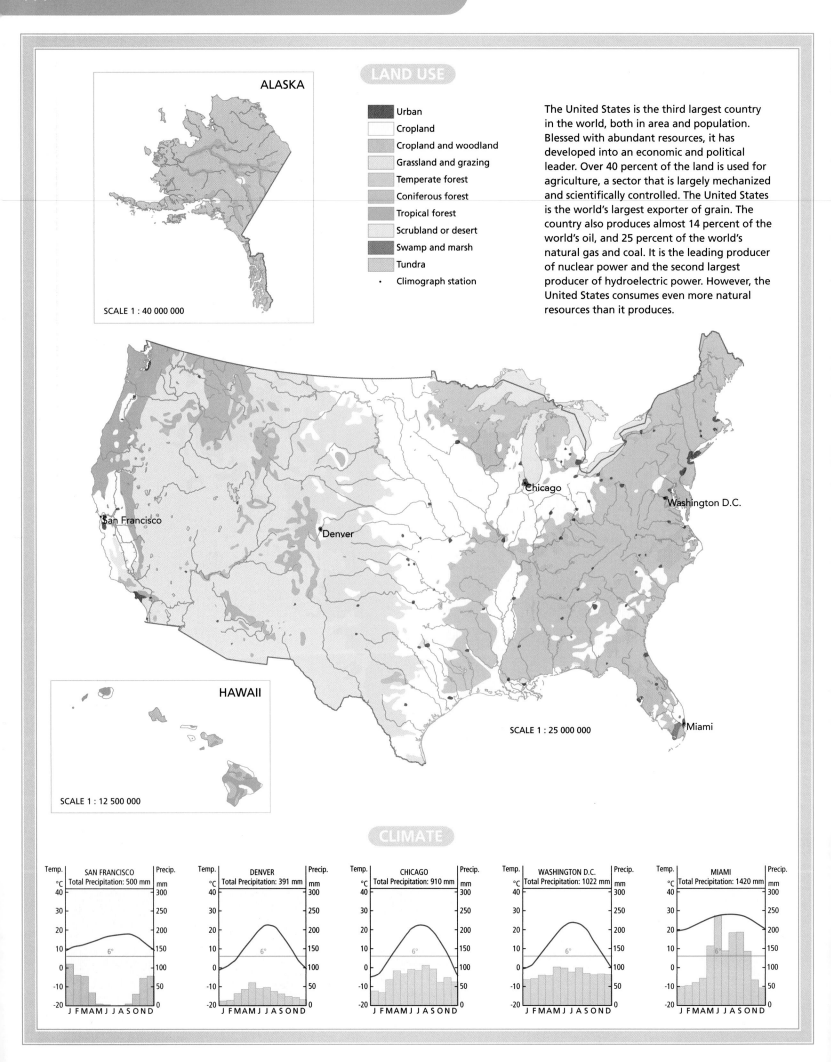

- Urban
- Cropland
- Cropland and woodland
- Grassland and grazing
- Temperate forest
- Coniferous forest
- Tropical forest
- Scrubland or desert
- Swamp and marsh
- Tundra
- • Climograph station

The United States is the third largest country in the world, both in area and population. Blessed with abundant resources, it has developed into an economic and political leader. Over 40 percent of the land is used for agriculture, a sector that is largely mechanized and scientifically controlled. The United States is the world's largest exporter of grain. The country also produces almost 14 percent of the world's oil, and 25 percent of the world's natural gas and coal. It is the leading producer of nuclear power and the second largest producer of hydroelectric power. However, the United States consumes even more natural resources than it produces.

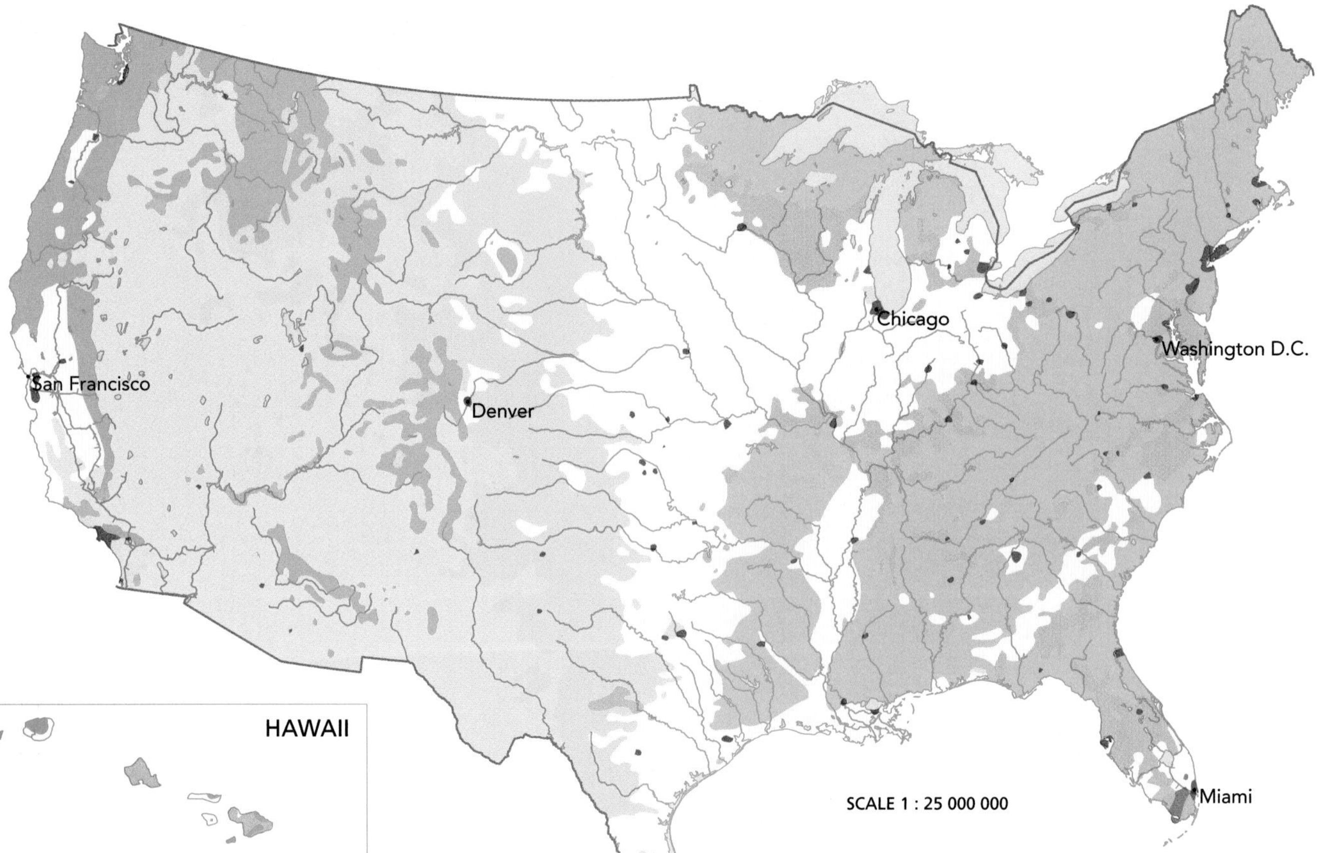

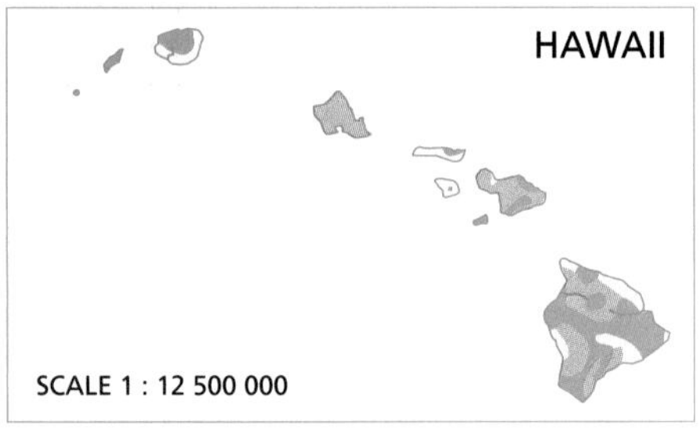

CLIMATE

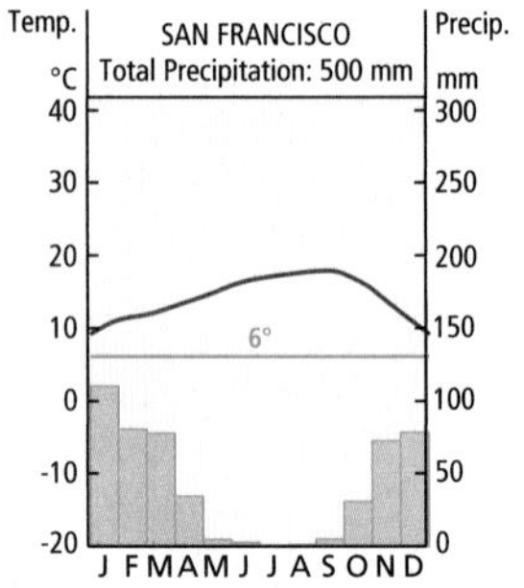

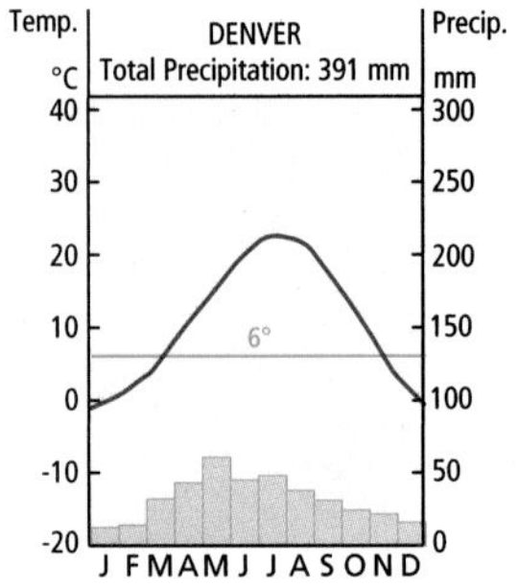

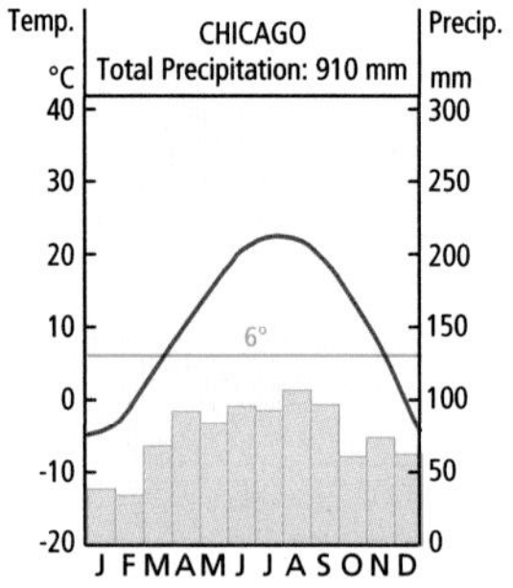

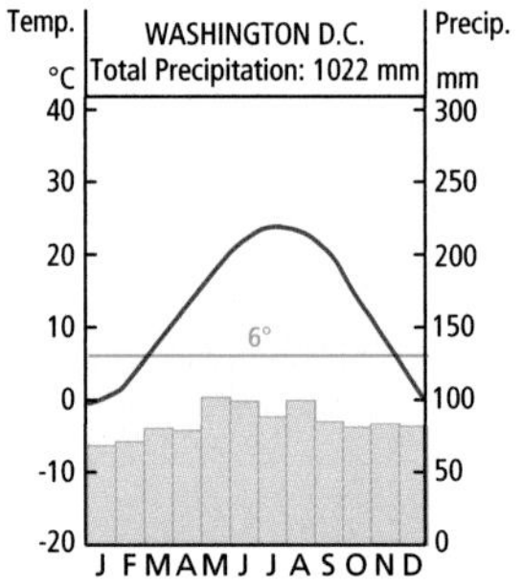

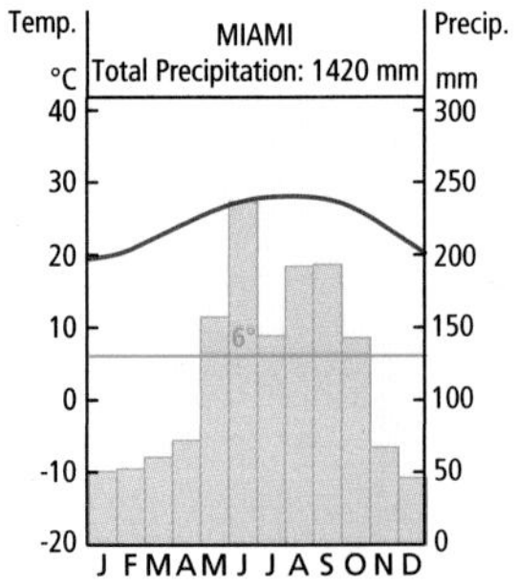

POPULATION CHANGE

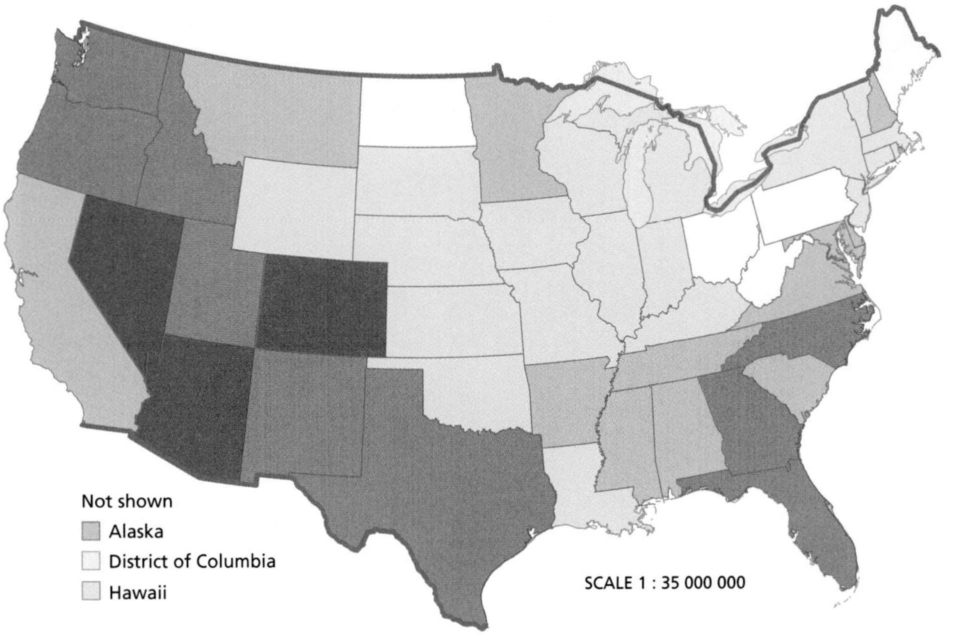

Population change is often linked to economic change. People pursuing jobs move to areas where the economy is strong. However, retirees can also stimulate an area's economy, as they have in Florida and the Southwest. Generally, the American population continues to move west and southwest. California and Texas are becoming the centers for the fast-growing high-tech industry. The Northeast still features heavy industry.

TOURISM

Top Destinations, 1999

State	Income from tourism	
	Millions, US$	Percent of GDP
Hawaii	7 092	17.5
Florida	16 648	3.8
Nevada	2 661	3.8
D.C.	1 613	2.9
New York	9 448	1.3
Arizona	1 620	1.1
California	13 828	1.1
Alaska	215	0.8
Vermont	130	0.8
Maine	246	0.7
Massachusetts	1 939	0.7
Utah	359	0.6
Colorado	731	0.5
Texas	3 242	0.5
Illinois	1 647	0.4
Louisiana	459	0.4
Montana	91	0.4
Oregon	389	0.4
Rhode Island	113	0.4
South Carolina	448	0.4
Washington	931	0.4

ECONOMY

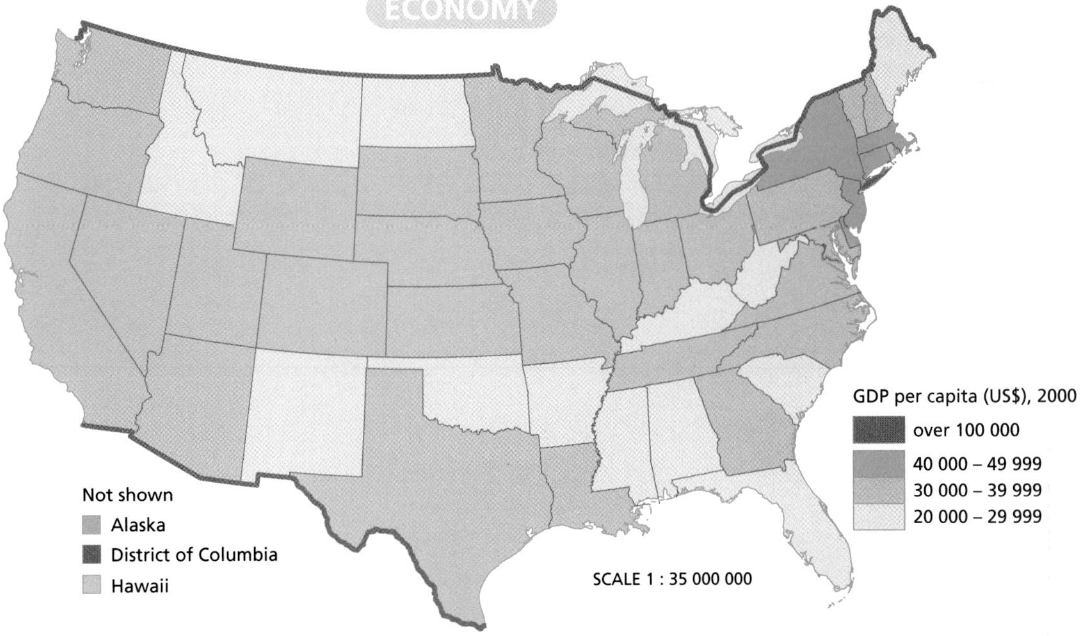

Imports, 2001

Exports, 2001

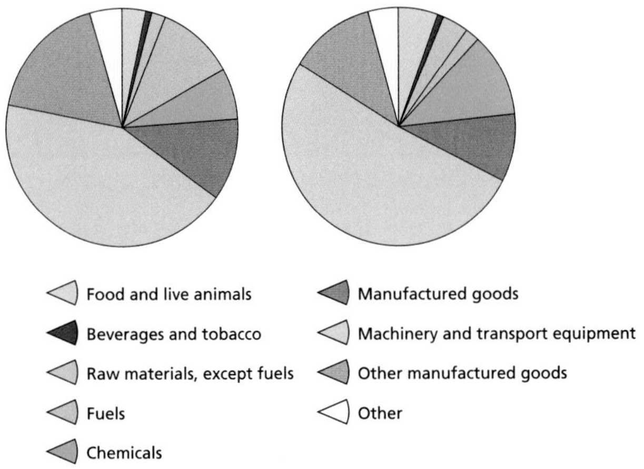

GDP by sector, 2000

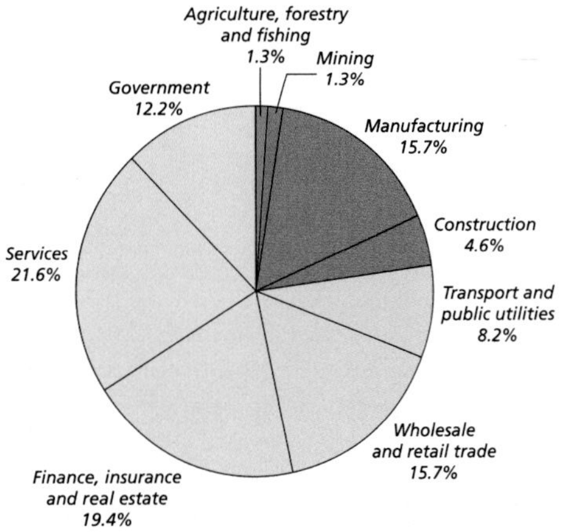

Trade, 2001

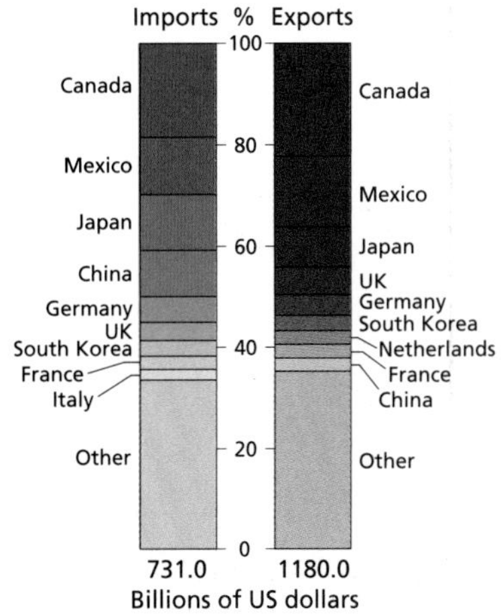

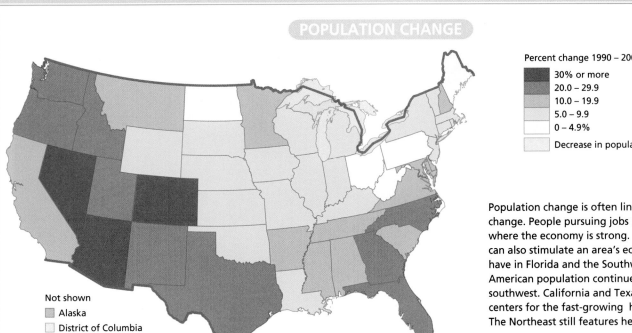

UNITED STATES OF AMERICA
MEXICO
GUATEMALA
BELIZE
EL SALVADOR
HOND
ARIZONA
NEW MEXICO
OKLAHOMA
ARKANSAS
TEXAS
LOUISIANA
MISSISSIPPI
TENNESSEE
ALABAMA
San Diego
Tijuana
Mexicali
Glendale
Phoenix
Tucson
Ensenada
Cerro. de la Encantada 3096
San Felipe
Pto Peñasco
Nogales
Magdalena
Hermosillo
Guaymas
Ciudad Obregón
Los Mochis
Culiacán
La Paz
Mazatlán
Durango
Silver City
Lordsburg
Las Cruces
Sacramento Mts
El Paso
Ciudad Juárez
Clovis
Lubbock
Big Spring
Midland
Odessa
Pecos
Sweetwater
Abilene
Wichita Falls
Oklahoma City
Fort Smith
Ouachita Mts
Little Rock
Pine Bluff
Memphis
Tupelo
Huntsville
Birmingham
Tuscaloosa
Greenville
Meridian
Montgomery
Jackson
Hattiesburg
Mobile
Pensacola
Biloxi
Baton Rouge
New Orleans
Chandeleur Islands
Mississippi Delta
Morgan City
Lafayette
Alexandria
Shreveport
Monroe
Texarkana
Tyler
Lufkin
Huntsville
Beaumont
Port Arthur
Houston
Galveston
Galveston Bay
Gainesville
Fort Worth
Dallas
Lake Texoma
Waco
Temple
Austin
San Antonio
Edwards Plateau
Alpine
Ojinaga
Emory Peak 2386
Serranías del Burro
Del Rio
Eagle Pass
Piedras Negras
Sabinas
Chihuahua
Ciudad Delicias
Ciudad Camargo
Hidalgo del Parral
Monclova
Laredo
Nuevo Laredo
Falcon Lake
Victoria
Beeville
Corpus Christi
Kingsville
Padre I.
Reynosa
Matamoros
Monterrey
Saltillo
Torreón
Gómez Palacio
Montemorelos
Madre Lagoon
C. Peña Nevada 3644
Ciudad Victoria
Zacatecas
Sierra Madre Occidental
Sierra Madre Oriental
Sierra Madre del Sur
San Luis Potosí
Aguascalientes
Ciudad Madero
Tampico
Cd de Valles
Tamiahua Lagoon
Tepic
I. Marías
Banderas Bay
C. Corrientes
Guadalajara
León
Guanajuato
Irapuato
Celaya
Querétaro
Poza Rica
Pachuca
Colima 4339
Colima
Morelia
Uruapán
Toluca
MEXICO CITY
Tlaxcala
Cuernavaca
Popocatepetl 5452
Puebla
Jalapa
Veracruz
Córdoba
Orizaba
Campeche Bay
Términos Lagoon
Coatzacoalcos
Minatitlán
Villahermosa
Chilpancingo
Acapulco
Oaxaca
Cd Ixtepec
Juchitán
Tuxtla Gutiérrez
Gulf of Tehuantepec
Tapachula
4210
Quezaltenango
GUATEMALA CITY
Sipacate
Santa Ana
SAN SALVADOR
San Miguel
TEGUCIGALPA
G. of Fonseca
L. Managua
MANAGUA
C. Sta Elena
San Pedro Sula
L. Izabal
Maya Mts
BELMOPAN
Belize
Ambergris Cay
Turneffe Is
Gulf of Honduras
Banco Chinchorro
Cozumel
Campeche
Mérida
Cancún
C. Catoche
Yucatán Peninsula
GULF OF MEXICO
PACIFIC OCEAN
Gulf of California
Lower California
Sebastián Vizcaíno B.
Pta Eugenia
Sa Vizcaíno
Sta Rosalía
Tiburón
Angel de la Guarda
B. Magdalena
San José
Espíritu Santo
Cerralvo
C. San Lucas
Tropic of Cancer
I. San Benedicto
I. Socorro
Revillagigedo Is (Mexico)
Relief and physical features
Relief metres
5000
3000
2000
1000
500
200
sea level
below sea level
0
200
4000
6000
5775 Mountain height (in metres)
Water features
River
Intermittent river
Lake / Reservoir
Intermittent lake
Marsh
Communications
Railway
Road
Main airport
Administration
Boundaries
International
Internal
Urban population
over 1 000 000
500 000 - 1 000 000
100 000 - 500 000
under 100 000
Square symbols denote national capital cities.

SCALE 1 : 13 000 000

0 200 400 600 800 km

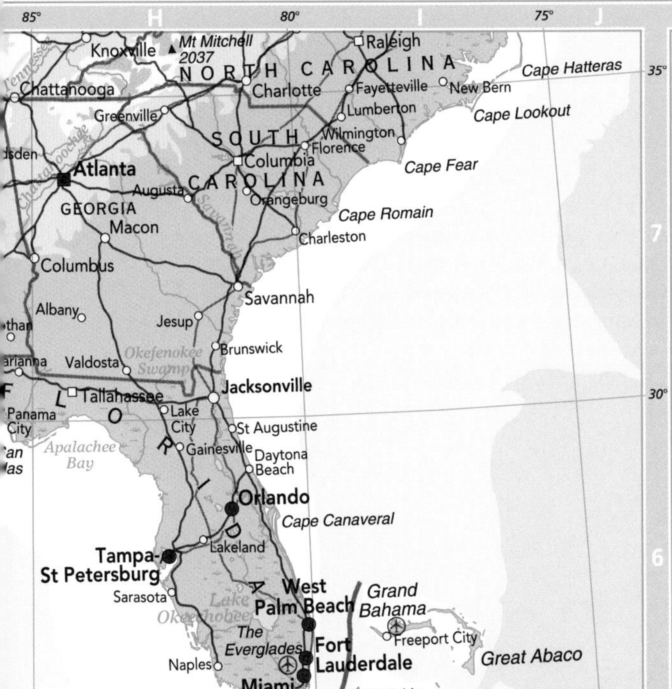
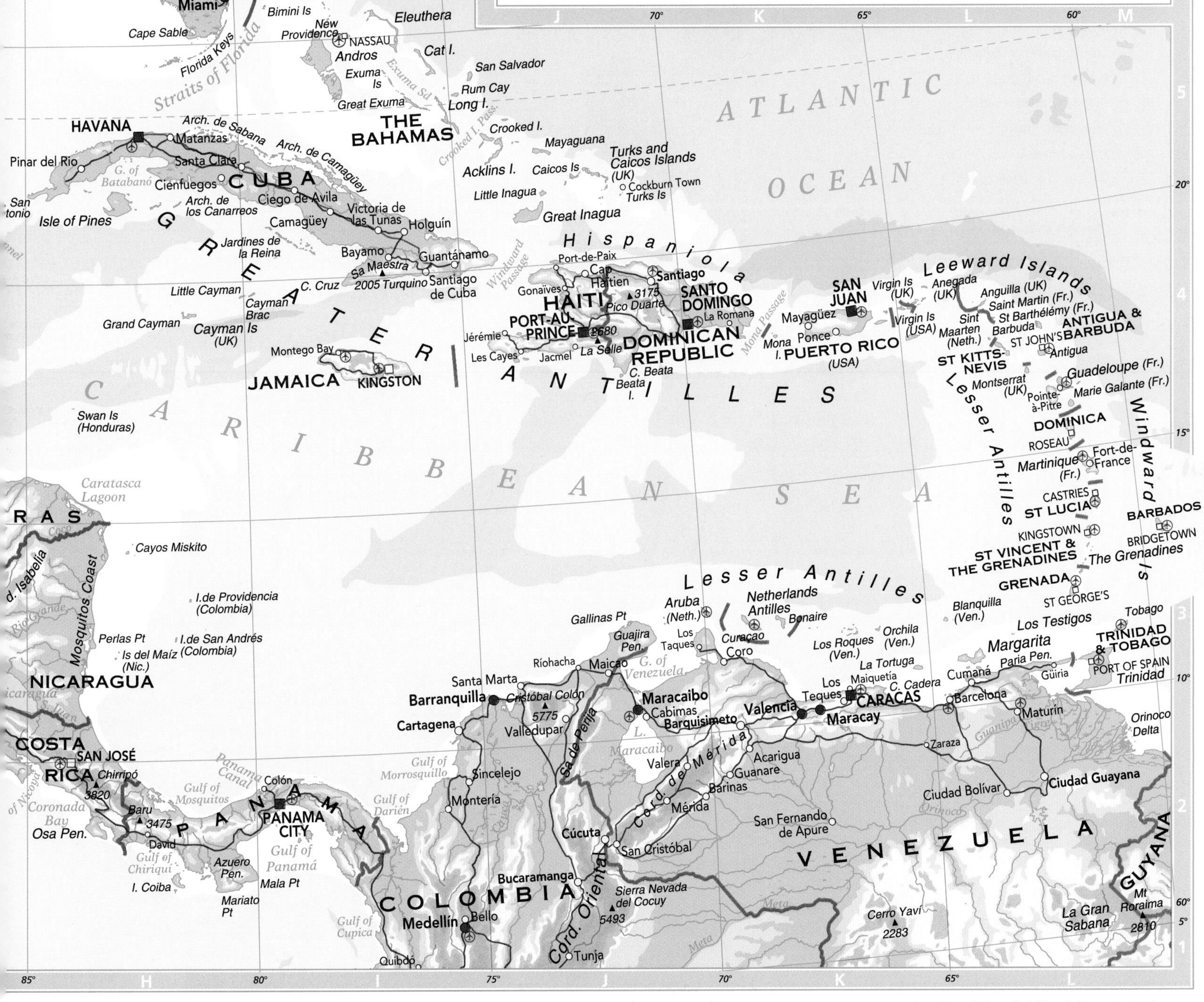

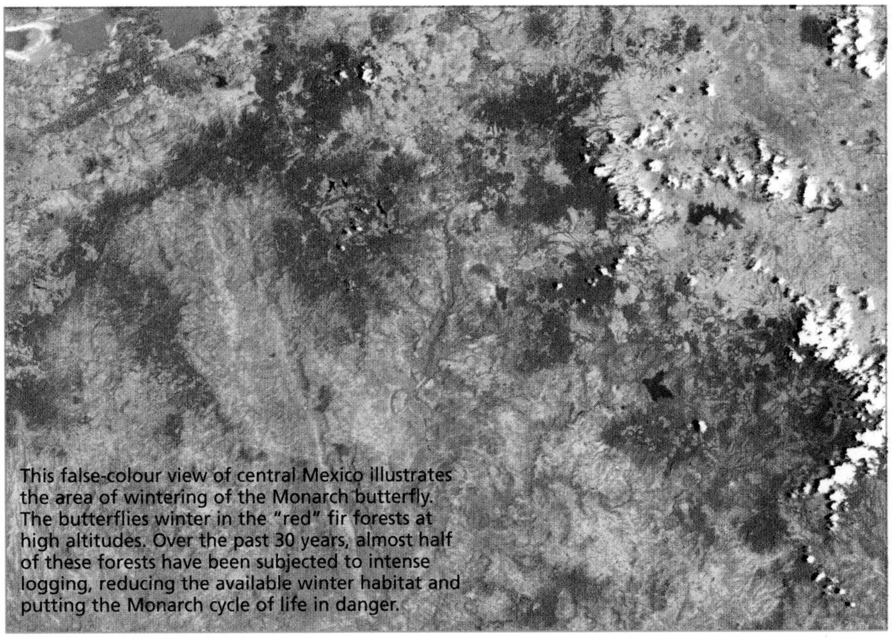

This false-colour view of central Mexico illustrates the area of wintering of the Monarch butterfly. The butterflies winter in the "red" fir forests at high altitudes. Over the past 30 years, almost half of these forests have been subjected to intense logging, reducing the available winter habitat and putting the Monarch cycle of life in danger.

LAND USE

Although small in size and population, this region is physically and culturally diverse. Dominated by fold and volcanic mountains, there are more than 30 active volcanoes in the region. Land use reflects the variety of climate, which ranges from the deserts of the Baja peninsula to the tropical forests of Nicaragua, Costa Rica, and Honduras. Culturally, the region reflects the influence of the Mayans and Toltecs, who developed highly advanced agriculture and urban development long before the incursion of the Spanish into the region.

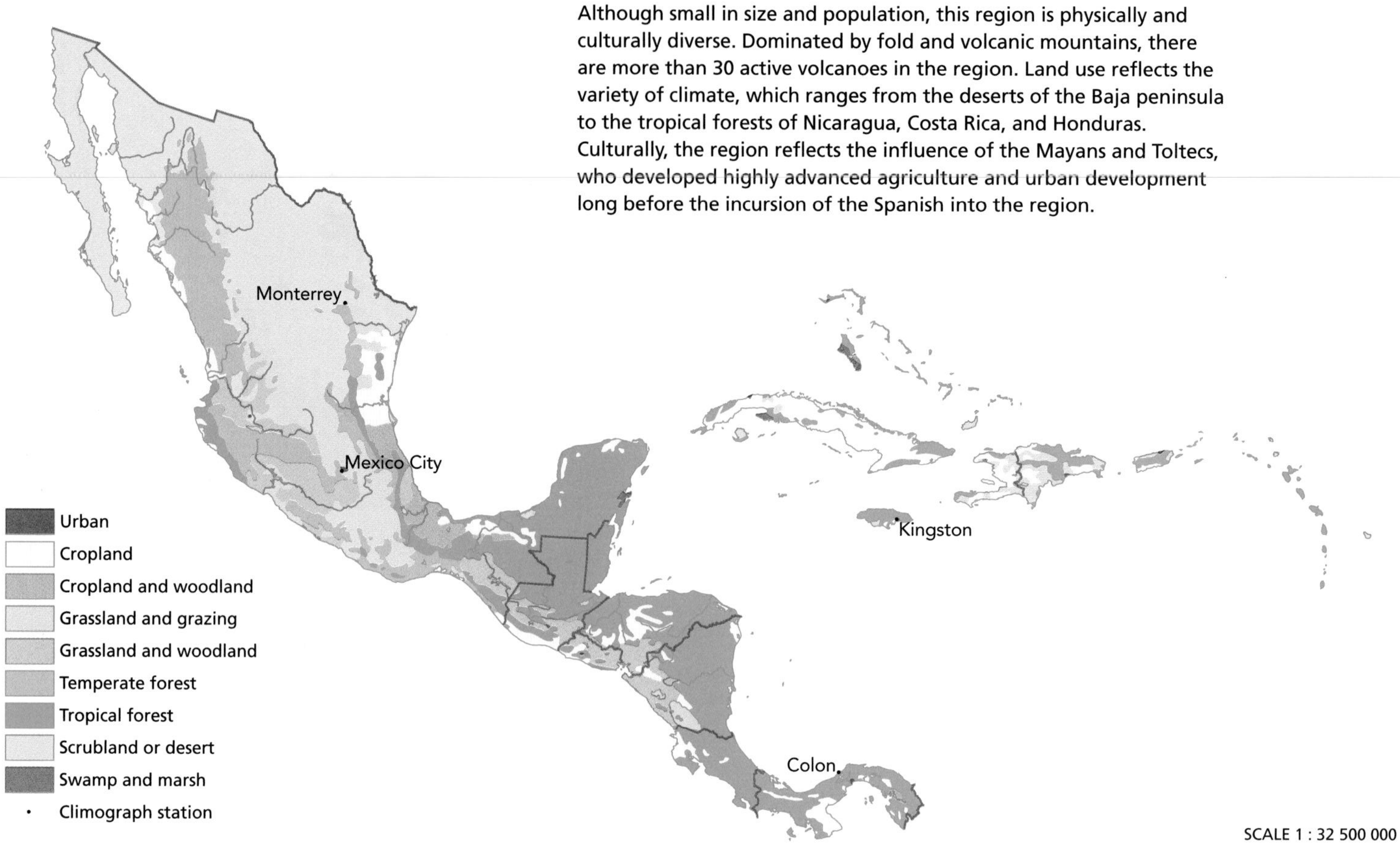

CLIMATE

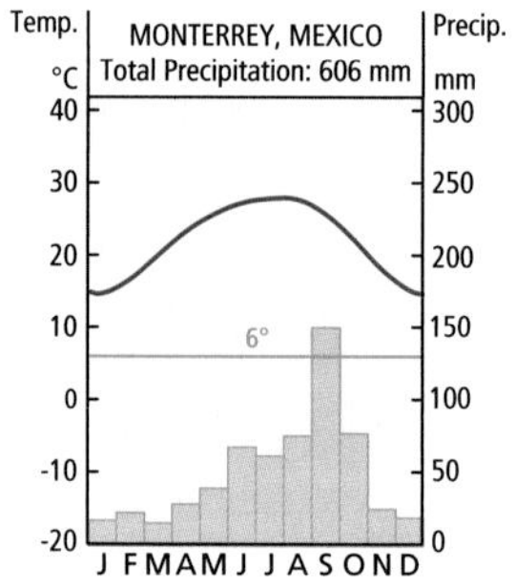

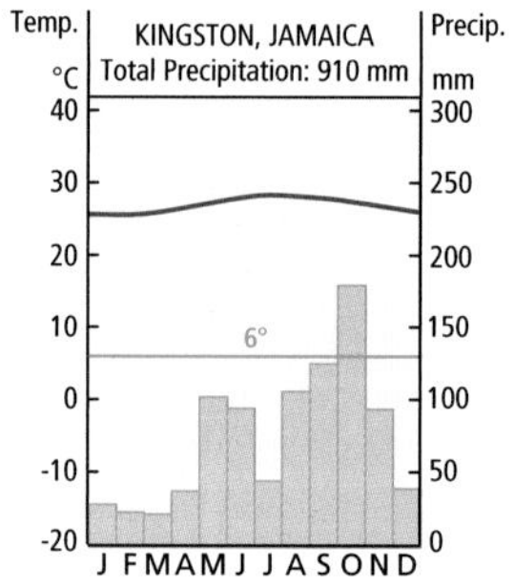

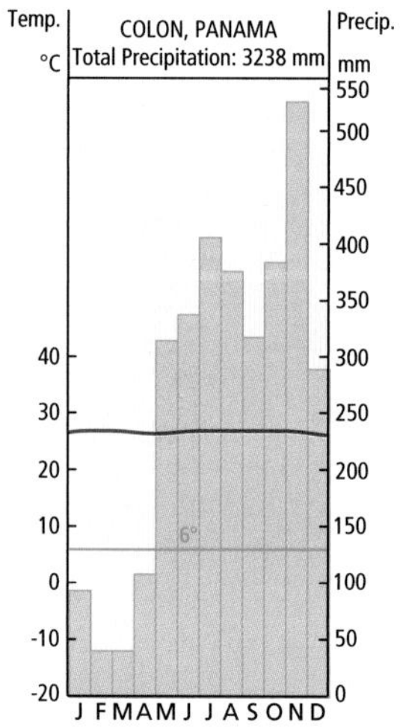

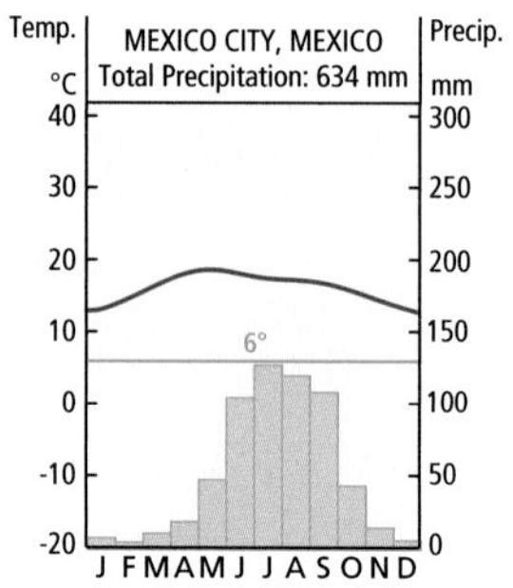

HURRICANES

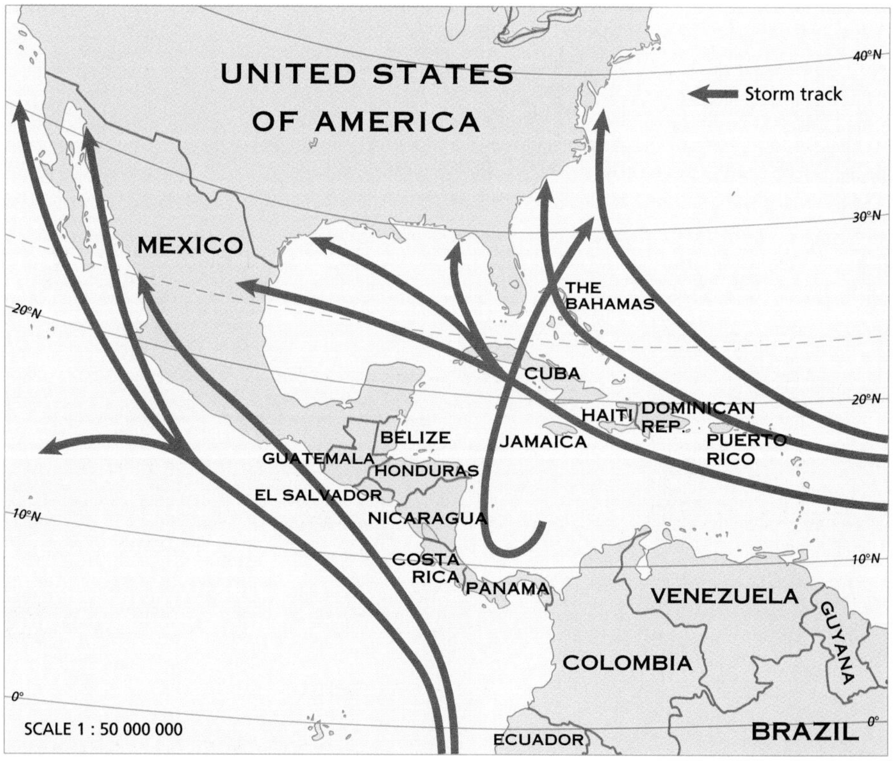

PANAMA CANAL

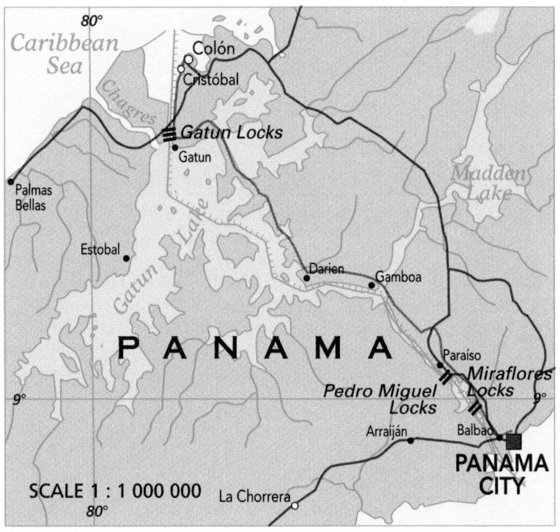

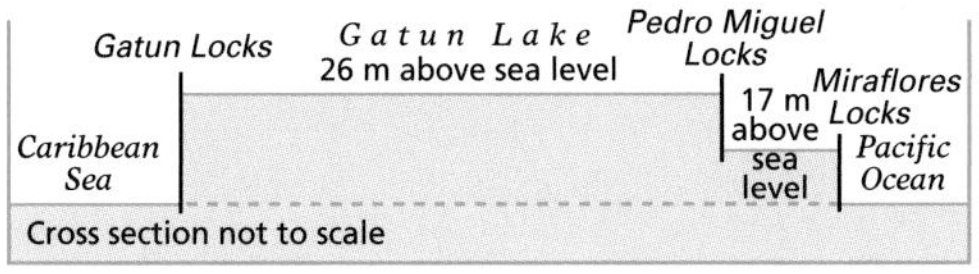

PANAMA CANAL
Opened *1914*
Length *64 km*
Minimum depth *12 m*
Minimum width *152 m*

POLITICAL CONFLICT

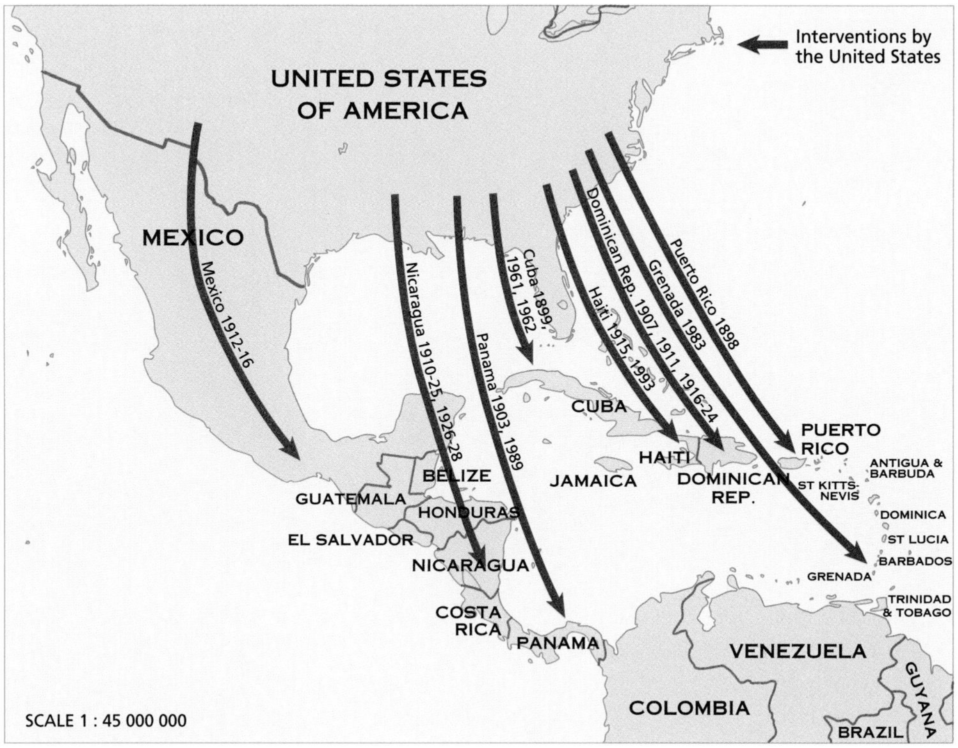

TOURISM

Top Destinations, 2000

Country	Income from tourism: Millions, US$	Income from tourism: Percent of GDP
Virgin Islands (USA)	965	53.6
St Lucia	311	46.7
Antigua and Barbuda	291	44.5
Cayman Islands	439	37.2
The Bahamas	1 503	33.2
Barbados	745	28.7
St Vincent and the Grenadines	77	23.4
St Kitts and Nevis	70	23.3
Bermuda	431	19.5
Dominica	49	18.5
Jamaica	1 333	18.0
Grenada	63	16.7
Belize	112	15.4
Dominican Republic	2 918	14.8
Costa Rica	1 102	7.0
Cuba	1 756	6.9
Panama	576	5.8
Puerto Rico	2 541	5.8
Nicaragua	116	4.8
Honduras	240	4.0
Trinidad and Tobago	210	3.1
Guatemala	518	2.7
El Salvador	254	1.9
Mexico	8 295	1.4
Haiti	55	1.3

ECONOMY

CUBA

Trade, 1999

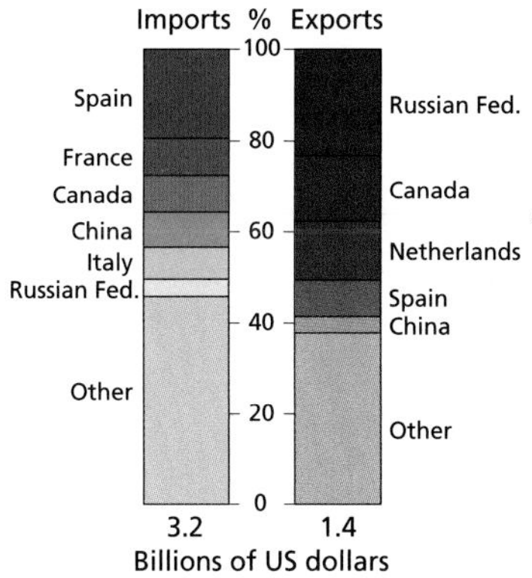

GDP by sector, 2000

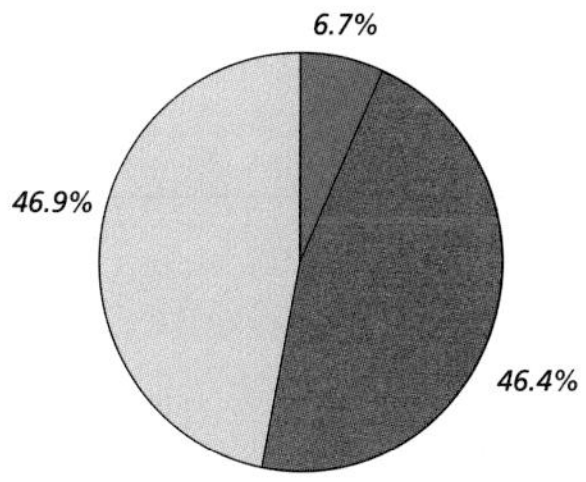

Total : US$ 18.6 billion

MEXICO

Trade, 2000

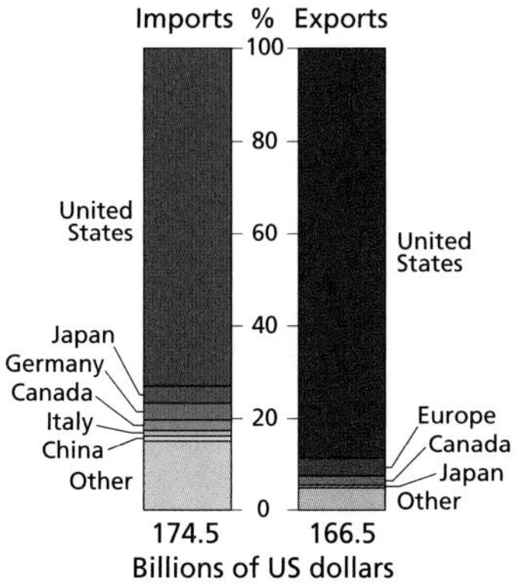

GDP by sector, 2000

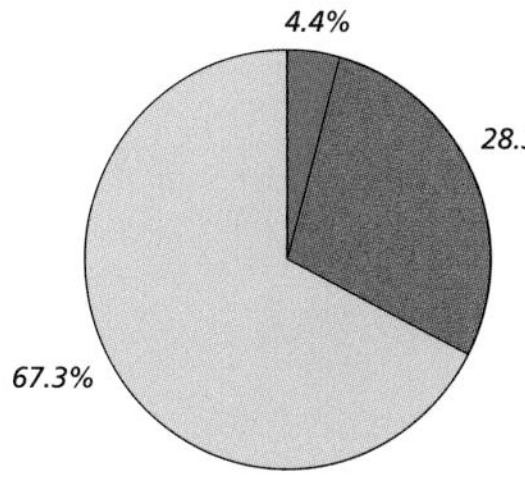

Total : US$ 574.5 billion

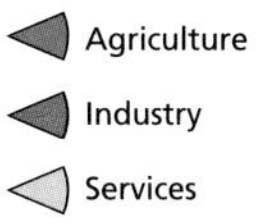

COSTA RICA

Trade, 2001

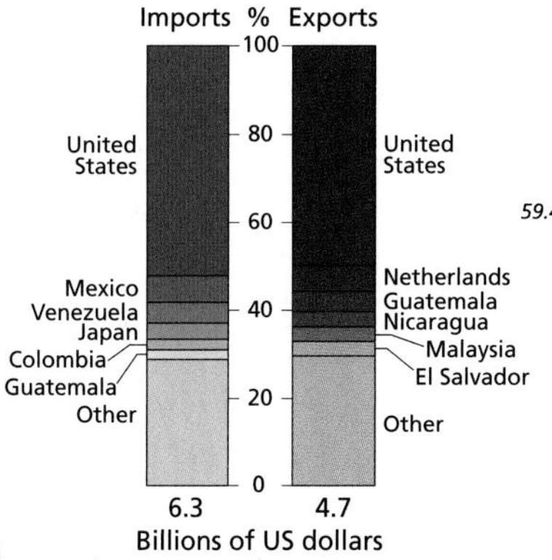

GDP by sector, 2000

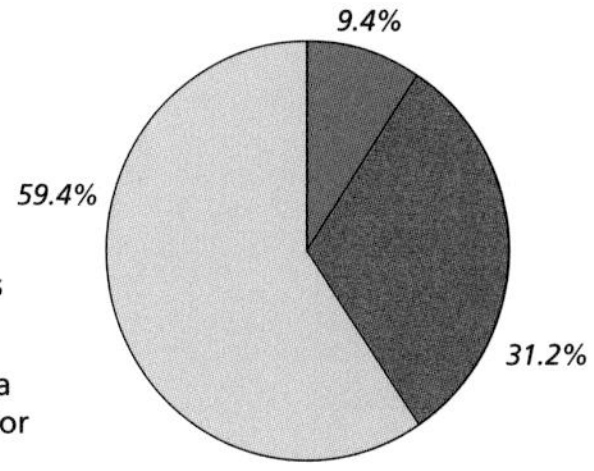

Total : US$ 15.9 billion

*The category 'Agriculture' includes forestry and fishing, the category 'Industry' includes mining.

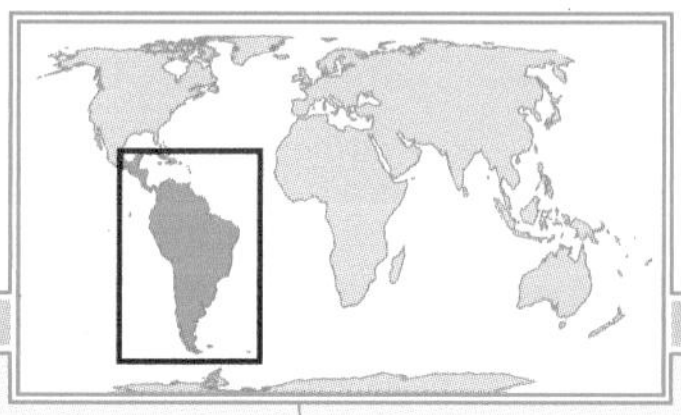

THE BAHAMAS
CUBA
HAITI
DOMINICAN REP.
PUERTO RICO (USA)
JAMAICA
MEXICO
BELIZE
G. of Honduras
GUATEMALA
HONDURAS
EL SALVADOR
NICARAGUA
COSTA RICA
PANAMA
CARIBBEAN SEA
ATLANTIC OCEAN
TRINIDAD AND TOBAGO
Barranquilla
Cartagena
Maracaibo
Valencia
Cabimas
CARACAS
Maracay
Cúcuta
San Cristóbal
Ciudad Bolívar
Ciudad Guayana
Orinoco
Bucaramanga
VENEZUELA
GUYANA
GEORGETOWN
PARAMARIBO
CAYENNE
SURINAME
FRENCH GUIANA
Essequibo
Medellín
Manizales
Buenaventura
BOGOTÁ
Meta
COLOMBIA
Cali
I. de Coco (Costa Rica)
I. de Malpelo (Colombia)
QUITO
ECUADOR
Guayaquil
G. of Guayaquil
Galapagos Islands (Ecuador)
Equator
Negro
Japurá
Amazon
Manaus
Belém
São Luís
Fortaleza
Fernando de Noronha (Brazil)
Teresina
Natal
Campina Grande
João Pessoa
Recife
Maceió
Aracaju
Salvador
Iquitos
Marañón
PERU
Chiclayo
Trujillo
LIMA
Callao
Huancayo
Cuzco
Juruá
Purus
Madeira
Tapajós
Xingu
Araguaia
Tocantins
Parnaíba
São Francisco
Rio Branco
BRAZIL
BRASÍLIA
Goiânia
Cuiabá
L. Titicaca
BOLIVIA
LA PAZ
Santa Cruz
Cochabamba
L. Poopó
SUCRE
Arequipa
Arica
Iquique
Corumbá
Belo Horizonte
Ribeirão Prêto
Vitória
Campos
Nova Iguaçu
Rio de Janeiro
Campinas
São Paulo
Santos
Trindade (Brazil)
Martin Vaz Is
Tropic of Capricorn
PACIFIC OCEAN
Antofagasta
PARAGUAY
ASUNCIÓN
Paraná
Salta
San Miguel de Tucumán
Corrientes
Curitiba
Florianopolis
Uruguay
Porto Alegre
CHILE
Córdoba
Santa Fé
Paraná
Rosario
Valparaíso
Mendoza
SANTIAGO
URUGUAY
Pelotas
BUENOS AIRES
MONTEVIDEO
Río de la Plata
La Plata
Talcahuano
Concepción
Mar del Plata
ARGENTINA
Bahía Blanca
Puerto Montt
Golfo San Matías
Comodoro Rivadavia
Bahía Grande
Str. of Magellan
Punta Arenas
Stanley
Falkland Islands (UK)
South Georgia (UK)
South Sandwich Is (UK)
POPULATION
Persons per km²
over 100
50-100
10-50
1-10
0-1
Caracas
Medellín
Bogotá
Equator
Fortaleza
Recife
Lima
Salvador
Belo Horizonte
Rio de Janeiro
Tropic of Capricorn
São Paulo
Curitiba
Porto Alegre
Santiago
Buenos Aires
Urban population
over 10 000 000
5 000 000 - 10 000 000
2 500 000 - 5 000 000
1 000 000 - 2 500 000
SCALE 1 : 80 000 000
Boundaries
International
Urban population
over 1 000 000
500 000 - 1 000 000
100 000 - 500 000
under 100 000
Square symbols denote national capital cities.
SCALE 1 : 35 000 000
0
400
800
1200 km

Lambert Azimuthal Equal Area projection

Bahamas
Cuba
Yucatan Channel
Yucatán
Greater Antilles
Hispaniola
Puerto Rico
Jamaica
Leeward Is
Lesser Antilles
G. of Honduras
Sierra Madre
CARIBBEAN SEA
ATLANTIC OCEAN
Windward Is
Gallinas Pt
Curaçao
L. Nicaragua
Trinidad
G. of Darien
L. Maracaibo
Orinoco Delta
Cordillera Central
Llanos
Orinoco
2810 Mt Roraima
Meta
Essequibo
Guiana Highlands
I. de Coco
I. de Malpelo
Amazon Delta
5897 Cotopaxi
6310 Chimborazo
Equator
Japurá
Amazon
Negro
Galapagos Islands
G. of Guayaquil
Fernando de Noronha
Marañón
Juruá
Purus
Madeira
Tapajós
Xingu
C. de São Roque
Pta Negra
Parnaíba
Tocantins
Araguaia
Selvas
6768 Huascarán
Mato Grosso Plateau
Brazilian Highlands
ANDES
L. Titicaca
São Francisco
Atacama Desert
Altiplano
L. Poopó
PACIFIC OCEAN
Gran Chaco
Paraguay
Paraná
2797 Agulhas Negras
Trindade
Martin Vaz Is
Tropic of Capricorn
6908 Ojos del Salado
Uruguay
6960 Aconcagua
Pampas
Río de la Plata
ATLANTIC OCEAN
Golfo San Matías
Isla de Chiloé
Patagonia
Bahía Grande
Str. of Magellan
Falkland Islands
Tierra del Fuego
Cape Horn
South Georgia
South Sandwich Is
PHYSICAL REGIONS
Guiana Highlands
Equator
Central Plains and Lowlands
Brazilian Plateau
Andes Mountains
Tropic of Capricorn
SCALE 1 : 80 000 000
Relief
Relief metres
5000
3000
2000
1000
500
200
sea level
below sea level
0
200
3000
5000
6960 Mountain height (in metres)
SCALE 1 : 35 000 000
0
400
800
1200 km

Lambert Azimuthal Equal Area projection

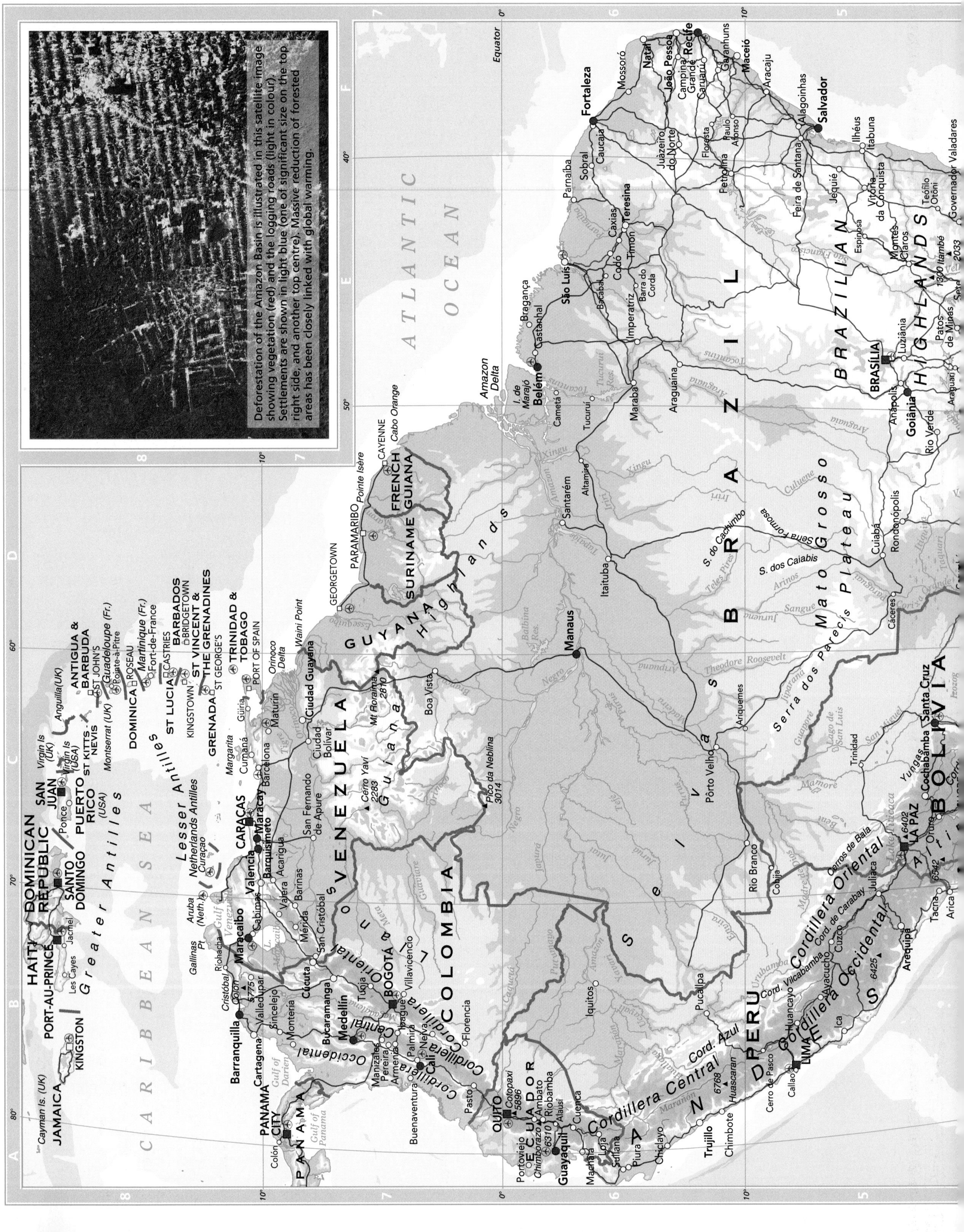

Deforestation of the Amazon Basin is illustrated in this satellite image showing vegetation (red) and the logging roads (light in colour). Settlements are shown in light blue (one of significant size on the top right side, and another top centre). Massive reduction of forested areas has been closely linked with global warming.

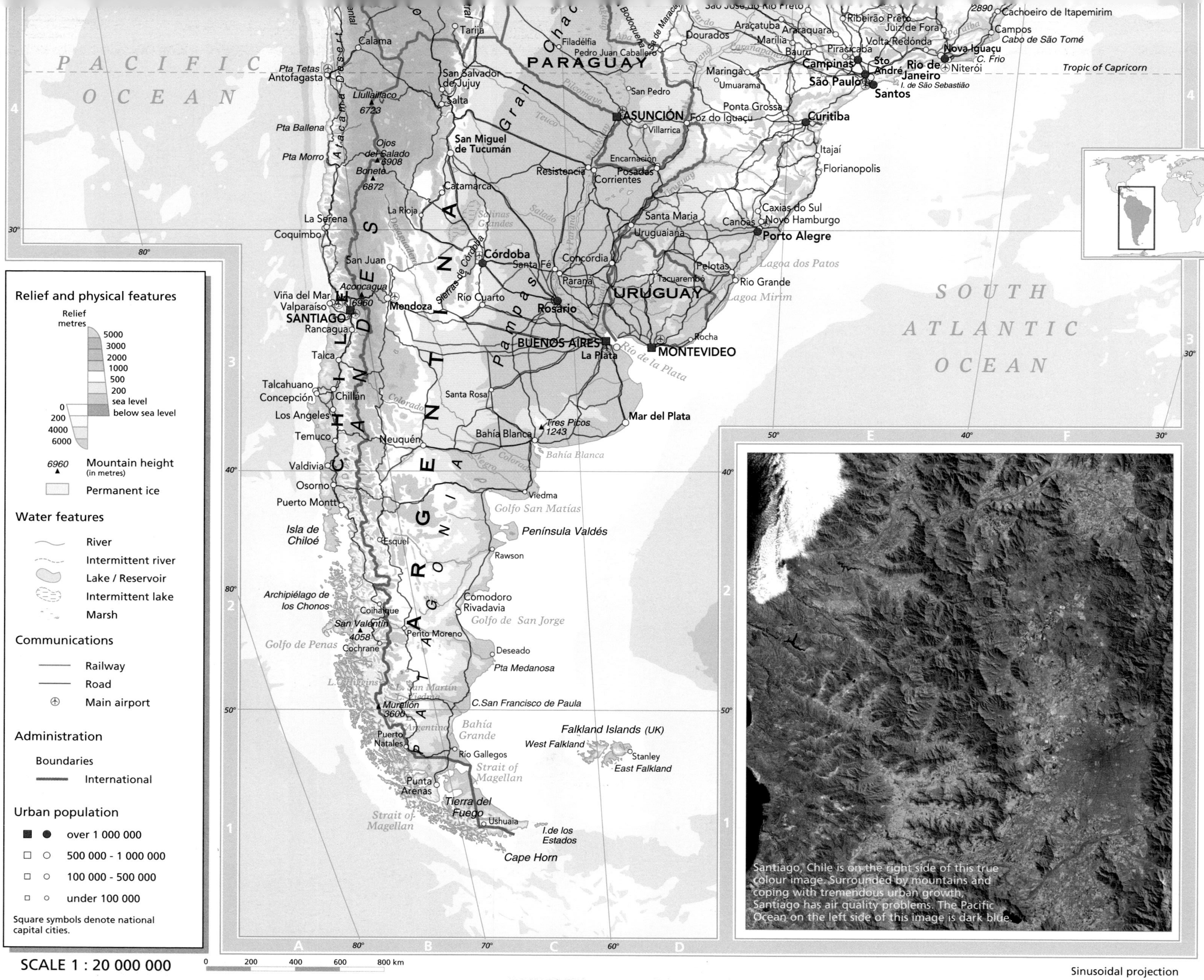

Santiago, Chile is on the right side of this true colour image. Surrounded by mountains and coping with tremendous urban growth, Santiago has air quality problems. The Pacific Ocean on the left side of this image is dark blue.

LAND USE

A continent as vast as South America differs greatly in land use, resources, economic development and culture. The vast tropical rain forests of Amazonia are in sharp contrast to the Atacama Desert, which is one of the driest areas in the world. Although dominated by tropical conditions, the extreme south and the high altitude areas along the plateaus and mountains of the Andes are very cold. Land use in southern Chile is similar to that in Mediterranean areas. Extremes of wealth and poverty have led to political and economic instability in many South American countries. However, most countries are currently moving towards increased democracy and greater social justice.

CLIMATE

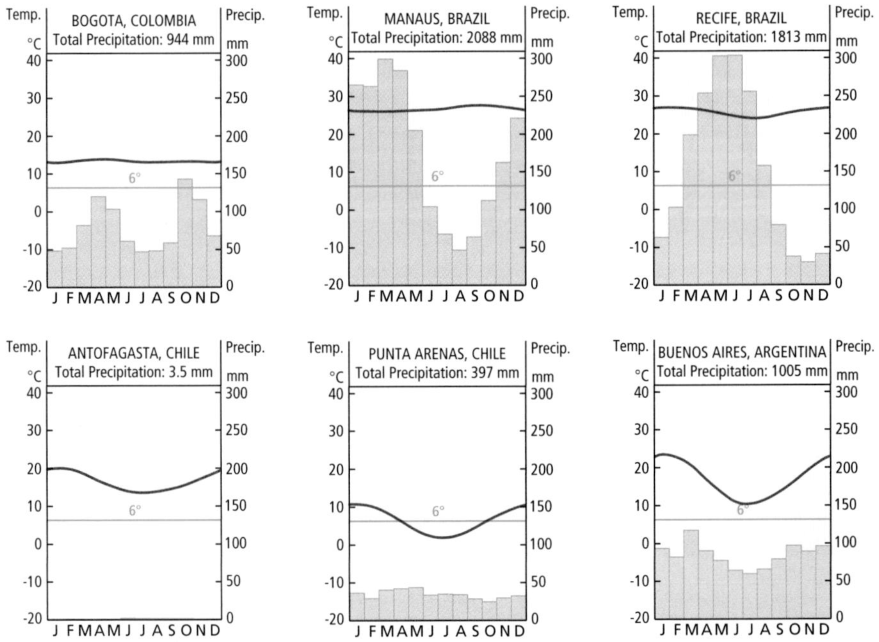

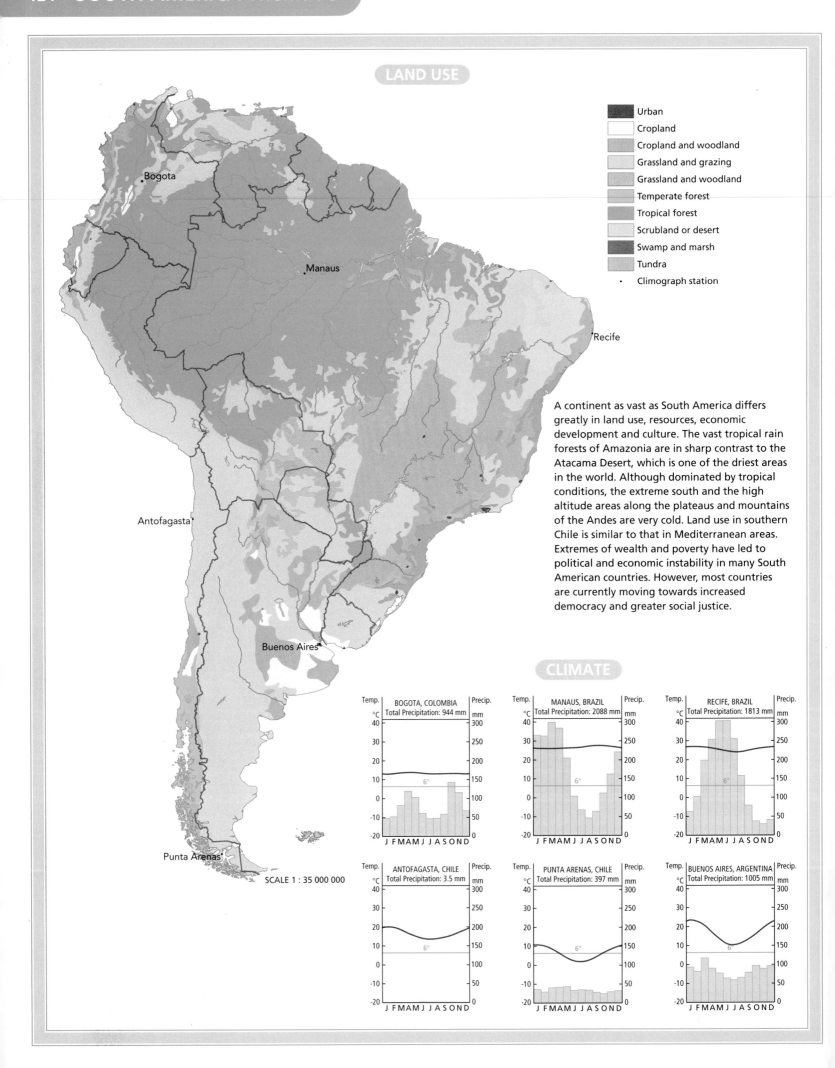

TOURISM

Top Destinations, 2000

Country	Income from tourism	
	Millions, US$	Percent of GDP
Guyana	59	8.7
Suriname	53	6.1
Uruguay	652	3.3
Trinidad and Tobago	210	3.1
Ecuador	402	3.0
Bolivia	160	1.9
Peru	1 001	1.9
Colombia	1 028	1.3
Chile	827	1.2
Argentina	2 903	1.0
Paraguay	66	0.9
Brazil	4 228	0.7
Venezuela	656	0.6

COLONIZATION

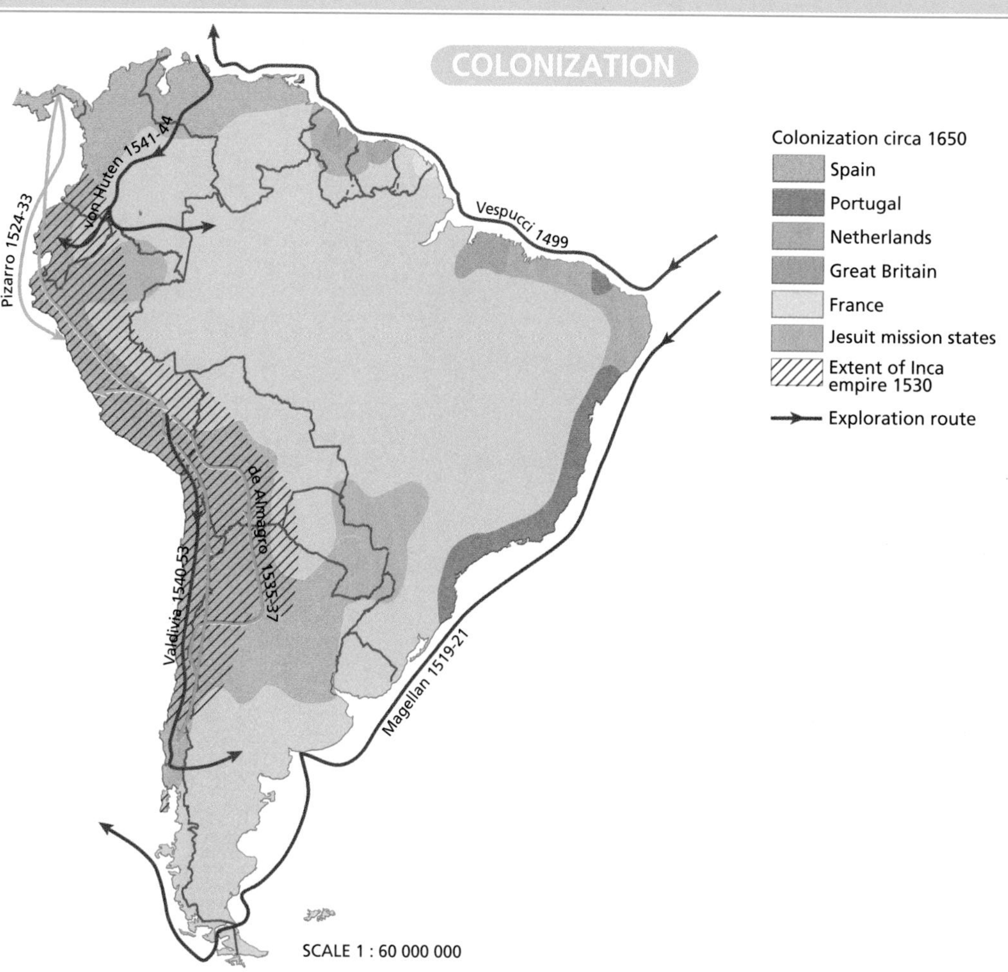

ECONOMY

VENEZUELA

Trade, 2001

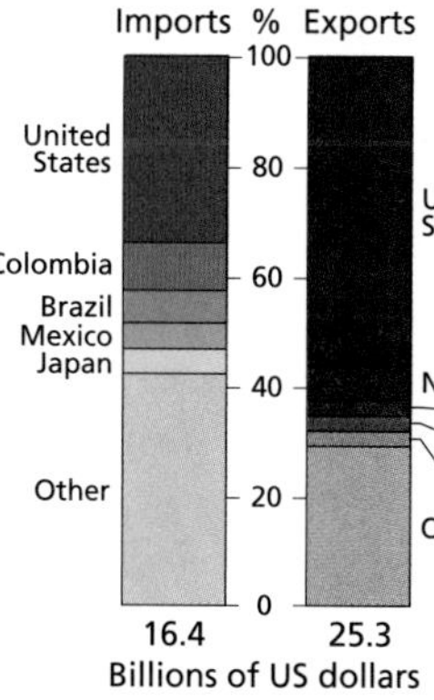

GDP by sector, 2000

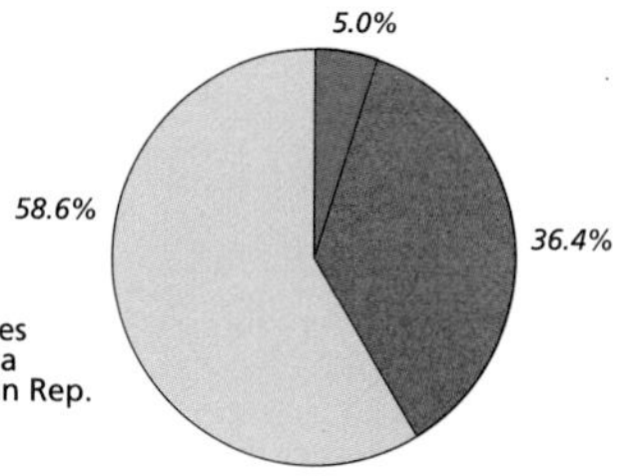

Total : US$ 120.5 billion

BRAZIL

Trade, 2001

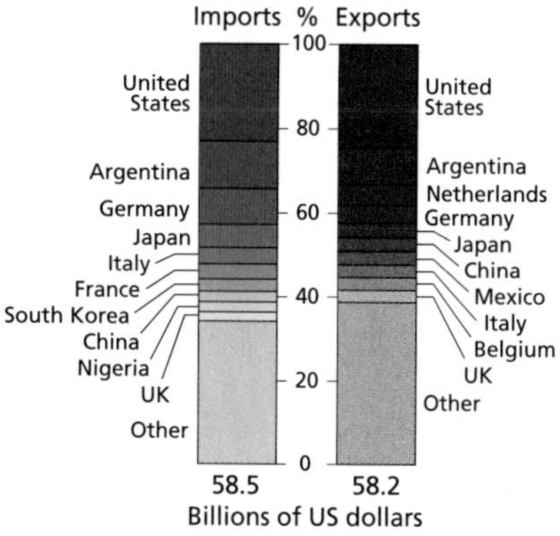

GDP by sector, 2000

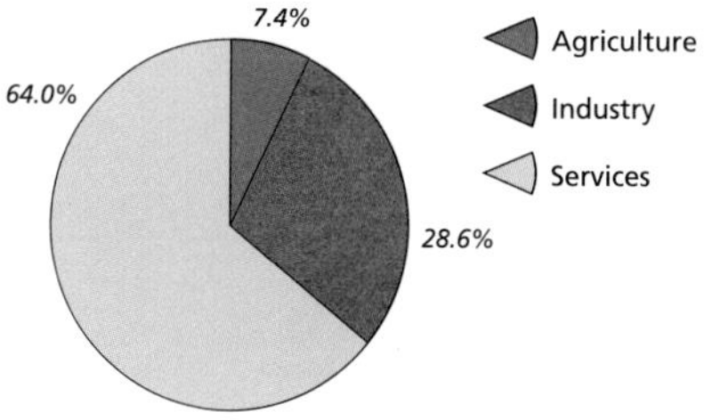

Total : US$ 595.5 billion

CHILE

Trade, 2001

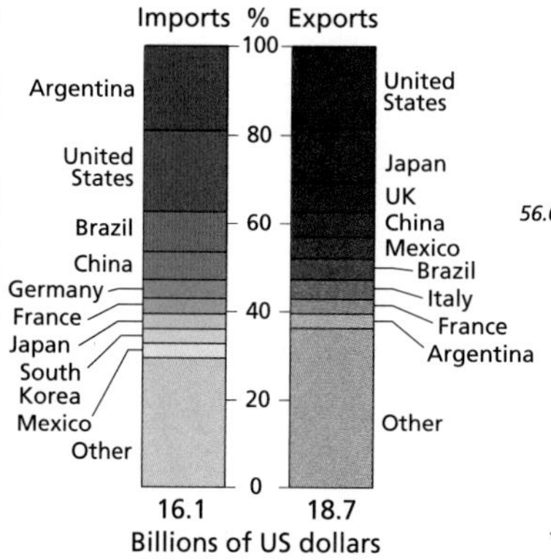

GDP by sector, 2000

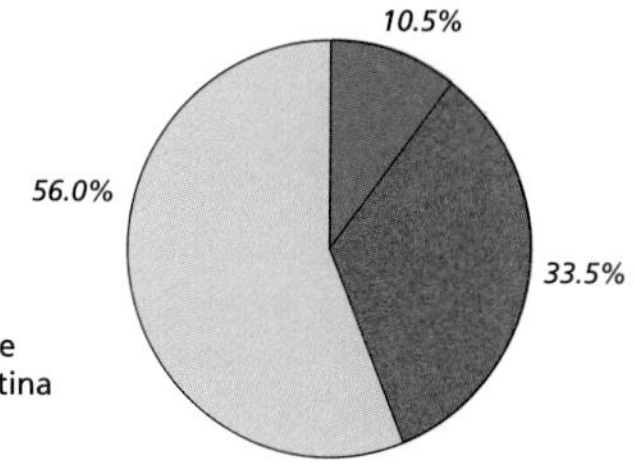

Total : US$ 70.5 billion

*The category 'Agriculture' includes forestry and fishing, the category 'Industry' includes mining.

EXTERNAL DEBT, 2000

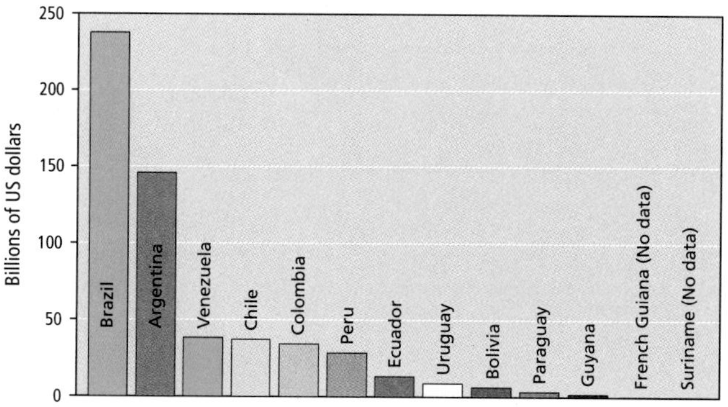

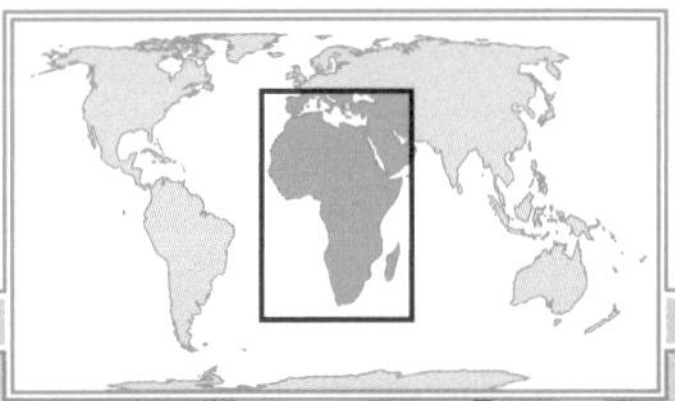

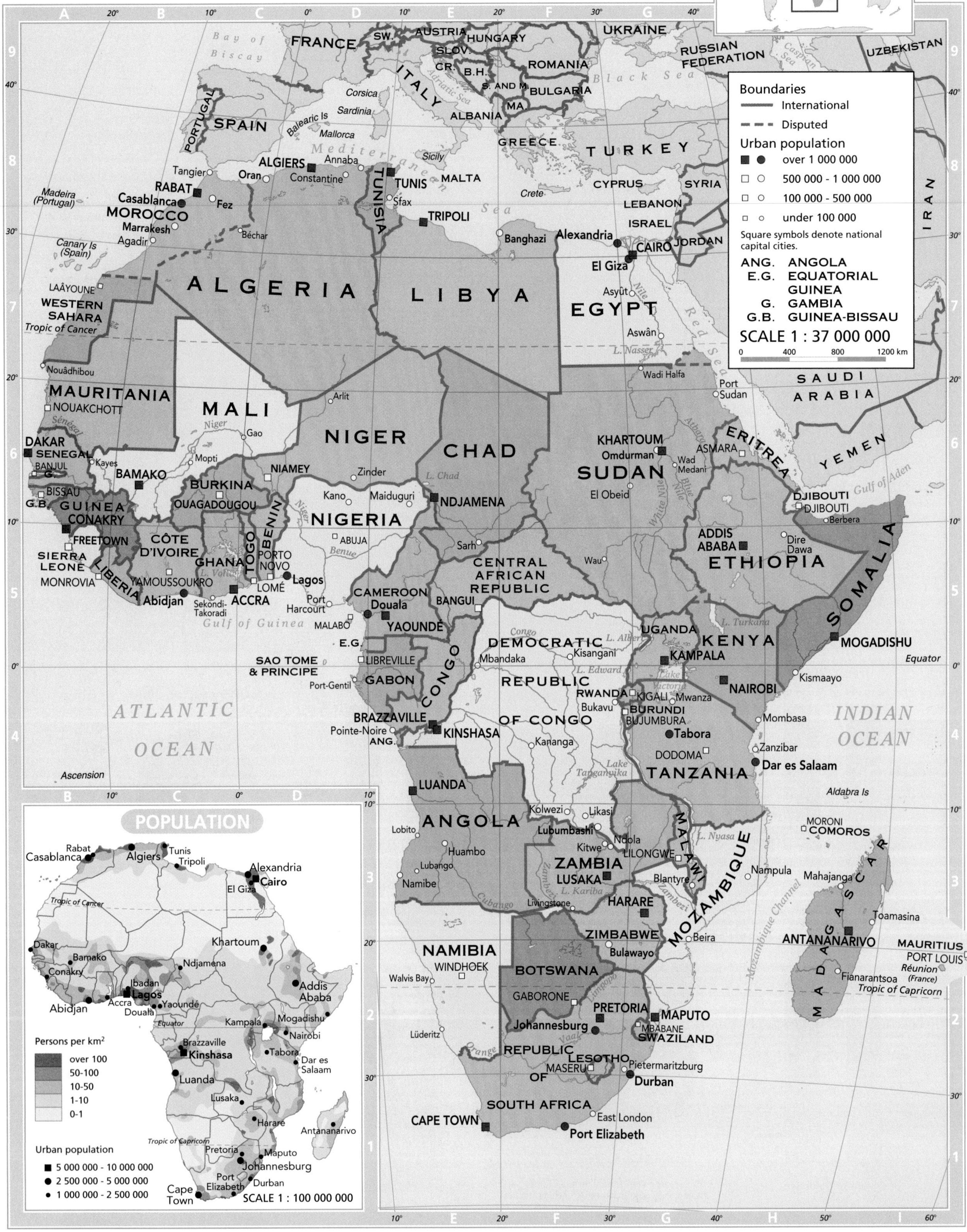
Boundaries
International
Disputed
Urban population
over 1 000 000
500 000 - 1 000 000
100 000 - 500 000
under 100 000
Square symbols denote national capital cities.
ANG. ANGOLA
E.G. EQUATORIAL GUINEA
G. GAMBIA
G.B. GUINEA-BISSAU
SCALE 1 : 37 000 000
0 400 800 1200 km
FRANCE
SW.
AUSTRIA
HUNGARY
SLOV.
CR.
B.H.
S. AND M.
MA
ROMANIA
BULGARIA
UKRAINE
RUSSIAN FEDERATION
UZBEKISTAN
PORTUGAL
SPAIN
ITALY
ALBANIA
GREECE
TURKEY
CYPRUS
SYRIA
LEBANON
ISRAEL
JORDAN
IRAN
Bay of Biscay
Black Sea
Caspian Sea
Adriatic Sea
Mediterranean Sea
Red Sea
Gulf of Aden
Gulf of Guinea
ATLANTIC OCEAN
INDIAN OCEAN
Corsica
Sardinia
Balearic Is
Mallorca
Sicily
MALTA
Crete
Madeira (Portugal)
Canary Is (Spain)
Tropic of Cancer
Equator
Tropic of Capricorn
MOROCCO
RABAT
Casablanca
Marrakesh
Agadir
Tangier
Fez
ALGERIA
ALGIERS
Oran
Annaba
Constantine
Béchar
TUNISIA
TUNIS
Sfax
LIBYA
TRIPOLI
Banghazi
EGYPT
CAIRO
Alexandria
El Giza
Asyût
Aswân
L. Nasser
Nile
WESTERN SAHARA
LAÂYOUNE
MAURITANIA
NOUAKCHOTT
Nouâdhibou
MALI
BAMAKO
Gao
Mopti
Kayes
NIGER
NIAMEY
Arlit
Zinder
CHAD
NDJAMENA
L. Chad
Sarh
SUDAN
KHARTOUM
Omdurman
Wad Medani
El Obeid
Wau
Wadi Halfa
Port Sudan
ERITREA
ASMARA
DJIBOUTI
SAUDI ARABIA
YEMEN
SENEGAL
DAKAR
BANJUL
G.
BISSAU
G.B.
GUINEA
CONAKRY
SIERRA LEONE
FREETOWN
LIBERIA
MONROVIA
CÔTE D'IVOIRE
YAMOUSSOUKRO
Abidjan
BURKINA
OUAGADOUGOU
GHANA
ACCRA
Sekondi-Takoradi
L. Volta
TOGO
LOMÉ
BENIN
PORTO NOVO
NIGERIA
ABUJA
Lagos
Kano
Maiduguri
Port Harcourt
Benue
Niger
CAMEROON
YAOUNDÉ
Douala
MALABO
E.G.
SAO TOME & PRINCIPE
GABON
LIBREVILLE
Port-Gentil
CONGO
BRAZZAVILLE
Pointe-Noire
ANG.
CENTRAL AFRICAN REPUBLIC
BANGUI
DEMOCRATIC REPUBLIC OF CONGO
KINSHASA
Mbandaka
Kisangani
Kananga
Lubumbashi
Kolwezi
Likasi
Bukavu
Congo
ETHIOPIA
ADDIS ABABA
Dire Dawa
Berbera
SOMALIA
MOGADISHU
Kismaayo
UGANDA
KAMPALA
L. Albert
L. Edward
L. Turkana
KENYA
NAIROBI
Mombasa
RWANDA
KIGALI
BURUNDI
BUJUMBURA
Mwanza
TANZANIA
DODOMA
Dar es Salaam
Tabora
Zanzibar
Lake Tanganyika
Aldabra Is
ANGOLA
LUANDA
Lobito
Huambo
Lubango
Namibe
Cubango
ZAMBIA
LUSAKA
Kitwe
Ndola
Livingstone
L. Kariba
Zambezi
MALAWI
LILONGWE
Blantyre
L. Nyasa
MOZAMBIQUE
MAPUTO
Beira
Nampula
Mozambique Channel
COMOROS
MORONI
MADAGASCAR
ANTANANARIVO
Mahajanga
Toamasina
Fianarantsoa
MAURITIUS
PORT LOUIS
Réunion (France)
ZIMBABWE
HARARE
Bulawayo
Limpopo
NAMIBIA
WINDHOEK
Walvis Bay
Lüderitz
Orange
BOTSWANA
GABORONE
REPUBLIC OF SOUTH AFRICA
PRETORIA
Johannesburg
Durban
Pietermaritzburg
East London
Port Elizabeth
CAPE TOWN
Vaal
SWAZILAND
MBABANE
LESOTHO
MASERU
Ascension
POPULATION
Persons per km²
over 100
50-100
10-50
1-10
0-1
Urban population
5 000 000 - 10 000 000
2 500 000 - 5 000 000
1 000 000 - 2 500 000
SCALE 1 : 100 000 000

Lambert Azimuthal Equal Area projection

Relief
Relief metres
5000
3000
2000
1000
500
200
sea level
below sea level
0
200
3000
5000
5895 Mountain height (in metres)
SCALE 1 : 37 000 000
0 400 800 1200 km
Bay of Biscay
C. Finisterre
Pyrenees
Alps
Apennines
Adriatic Sea
Danube
Black Sea
Caspian Sea
Corsica
Sardinia
Balearic Is
Mallorca
Sierra Nevada
C. St Vincent
Mediterranean Sea
Sicily
Taurus Mts
Crete
Cyprus
Madeira
Atlas Mountains
4167 Jbel Toubkal
G. of Gabès
Gulf of Sirte
Canary Is
Tenerife
Suez Canal
Sinai
Qattara Depression
Libyan Desert
Nile
Red Sea
Hijaz
SAHARA DESERT
2918 Mt Tahat
Hoggar
El Djouf
Djado Plateau
Tibesti
3415 Emi Koussi
1800 Mt Gréboun
Aïr
L. Nasser
Nubian Desert
Asir
Rub 'al Khali
Tropic of Cancer
Sénégal
Niger
Gambia
Bani
White Volta
Black Volta
Lake Volta
Fouta Djallon
L. Chad
Chari
Darfur
3070 J. Gimbala
Atbara
Blue Nile
White Nile
Gezira
4620 Ras Dashen
L. Tana
Danakil
Gulf of Aden
Ethiopian Highlands
Jos Plateau
Benue
Logone
Adamawa Highlands
4100 Mt Cameroun
Sudd
Akobo
Shabeelle
C. Palmas
Bight of Benin
Gulf of Guinea
Bioco
Príncipe
São Tomé
Uele
Congo
Ubangi
Sangha
Aruwimi
L. Albert
L. Turkana
Jubba
5110 Mt Stanley
L. Edward
Lake Victoria
5199 Mt Kenya
Equator
ATLANTIC OCEAN
Congo Basin
Kasai
Kwilu
5895 Kilimanjaro
Masai Steppe
Great Rift Valley
Lake Tanganyika
INDIAN OCEAN
Pemba I.
Zanzibar I.
Mafia I.
Rufiji
Ascension
Chaîne des Mitumba
L. Mweru
Aldabra Is
Cuanza
Comoro Islands
Bié Plateau
Muchinga Mts
Luangwa
L. Nyasa
Cunene
Cubango
Zambezi
L. Kariba
Etosha Pan
Victoria Falls
Matabele Upland
Mozambique Channel
Madagascar
Mauritius
Réunion
Makgadikgadi
Namib Desert
Kalahari Desert
Limpopo
Save
Tropic of Capricorn
Vaal
Orange
3482 Thabana Ntlenyana
Drakensberg
Great Karoo
Cape of Good Hope
C. Agulhas
PHYSICAL REGIONS
Northern Highlands
Tropic of Cancer
Western Plateau
Nile Basin
Coastal Lowlands
Equator
Congo Basin
Eastern Highlands
Great Rift Valley
Great Rift Valley
Coastal Lowlands
Southern Plateau
Tropic of Capricorn
Central Highlands
SCALE 1 : 100 000 000

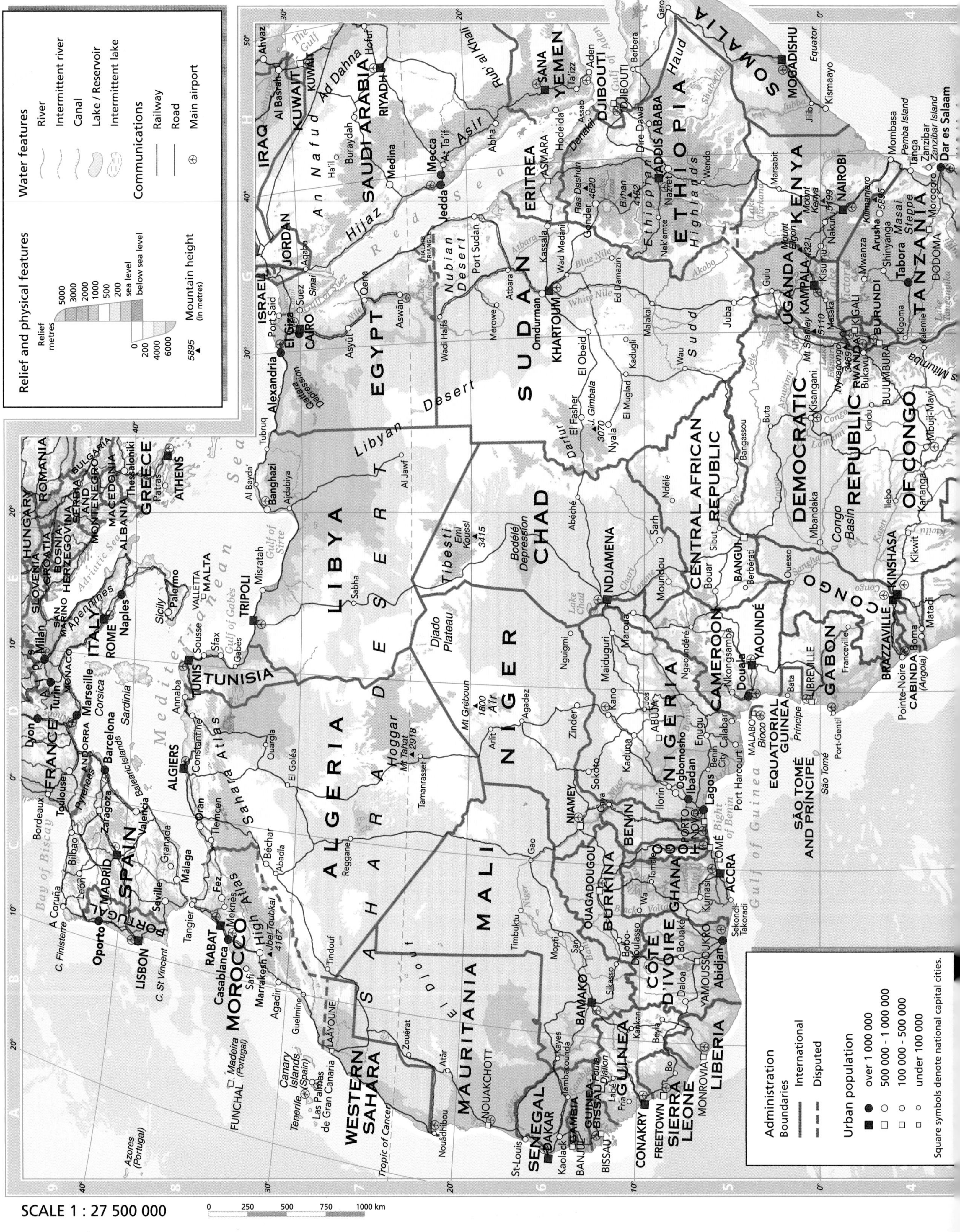
Relief and physical features
Relief metres
5000
3000
2000
1000
500
200
sea level
below sea level
0
200
4000
6000
5895
Mountain height (in metres)
Water features
River
Intermittent river
Canal
Lake / Reservoir
Intermittent lake
Communications
Railway
Road
Main airport
Administration
Boundaries
International
Disputed
Urban population
over 1 000 000
500 000 - 1 000 000
100 000 - 500 000
under 100 000
Square symbols denote national capital cities.
MOROCCO
ALGERIA
TUNISIA
LIBYA
EGYPT
SUDAN
CHAD
NIGER
MALI
MAURITANIA
WESTERN SAHARA
SENEGAL
GAMBIA
GUINEA-BISSAU
GUINEA
SIERRA LEONE
LIBERIA
CÔTE D'IVOIRE
BURKINA
GHANA
TOGO
BENIN
NIGERIA
CAMEROON
CENTRAL AFRICAN REPUBLIC
EQUATORIAL GUINEA
SÃO TOMÉ AND PRÍNCIPE
GABON
CONGO
DEMOCRATIC REPUBLIC OF CONGO
UGANDA
KENYA
RWANDA
BURUNDI
TANZANIA
ETHIOPIA
ERITREA
DJIBOUTI
SOMALIA
YEMEN
SAUDI ARABIA
KUWAIT
IRAQ
JORDAN
ISRAEL
SPAIN
PORTUGAL
FRANCE
ITALY
GREECE
MALTA
S A H A R A   D E S E R T
Libyan Desert
Mediterranean Sea
Red Sea
Gulf of Guinea
Tropic of Cancer
Equator

SCALE 1 : 27 500 000

0 250 500 750 1000 km

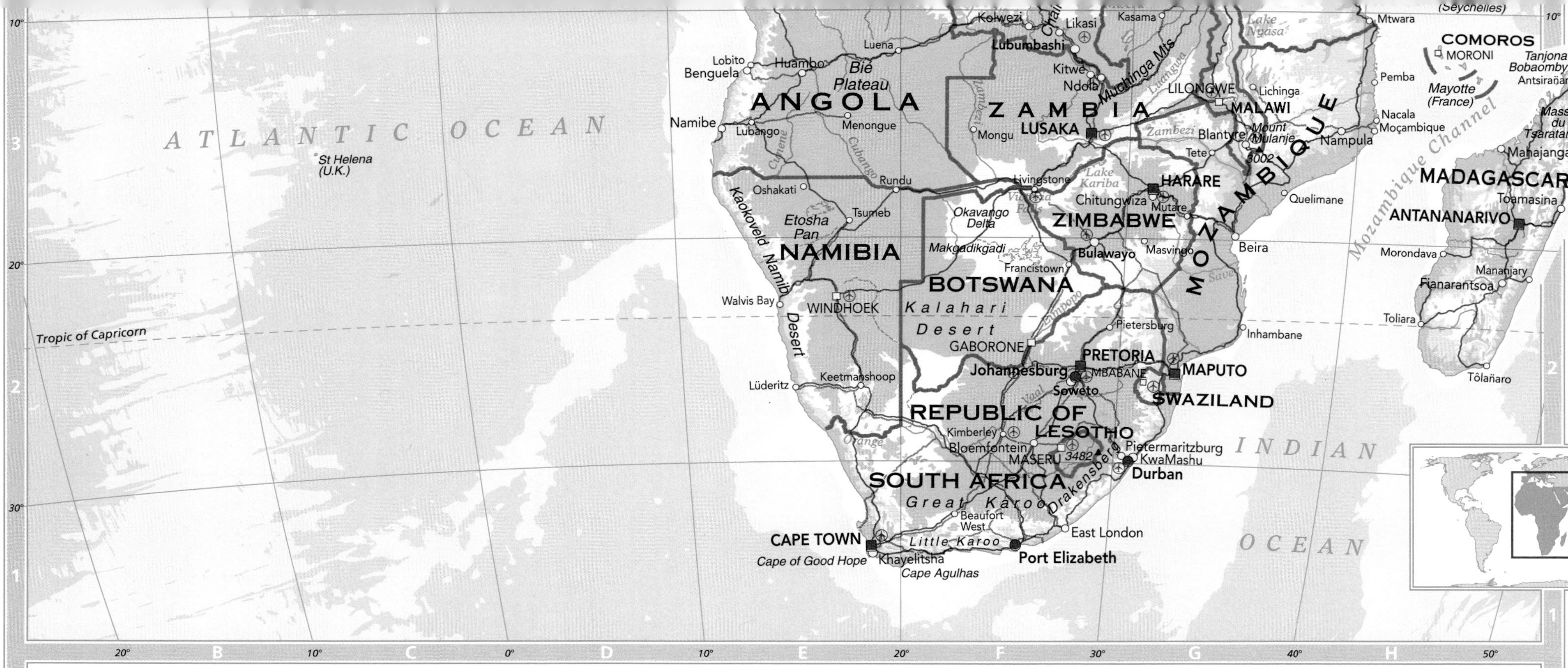

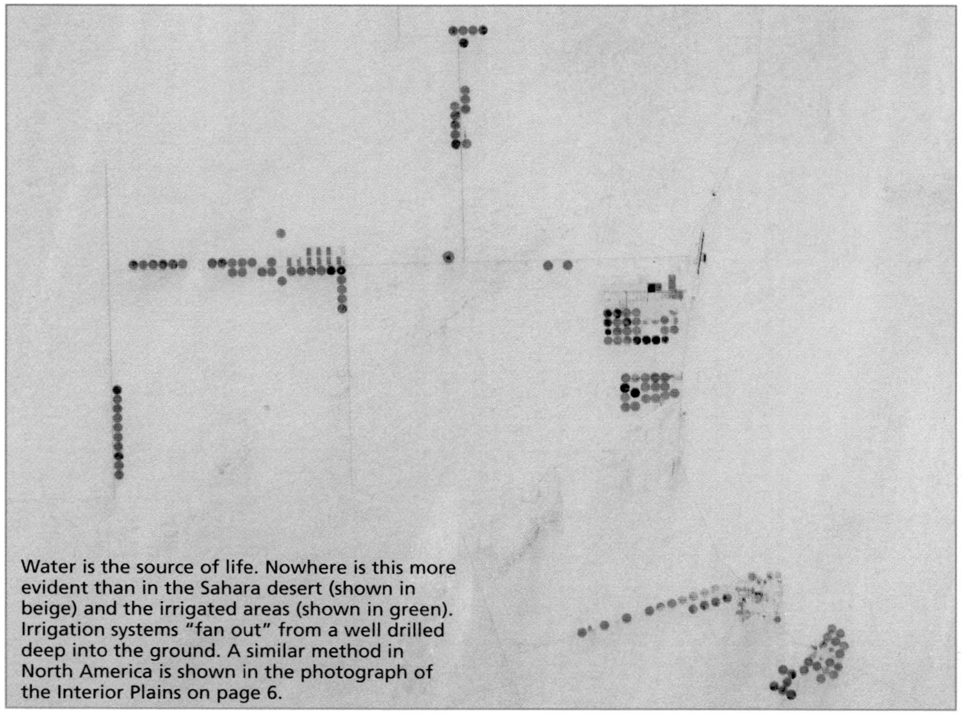

Water is the source of life. Nowhere is this more evident than in the Sahara desert (shown in beige) and the irrigated areas (shown in green). Irrigation systems "fan out" from a well drilled deep into the ground. A similar method in North America is shown in the photograph of the Interior Plains on page 6.

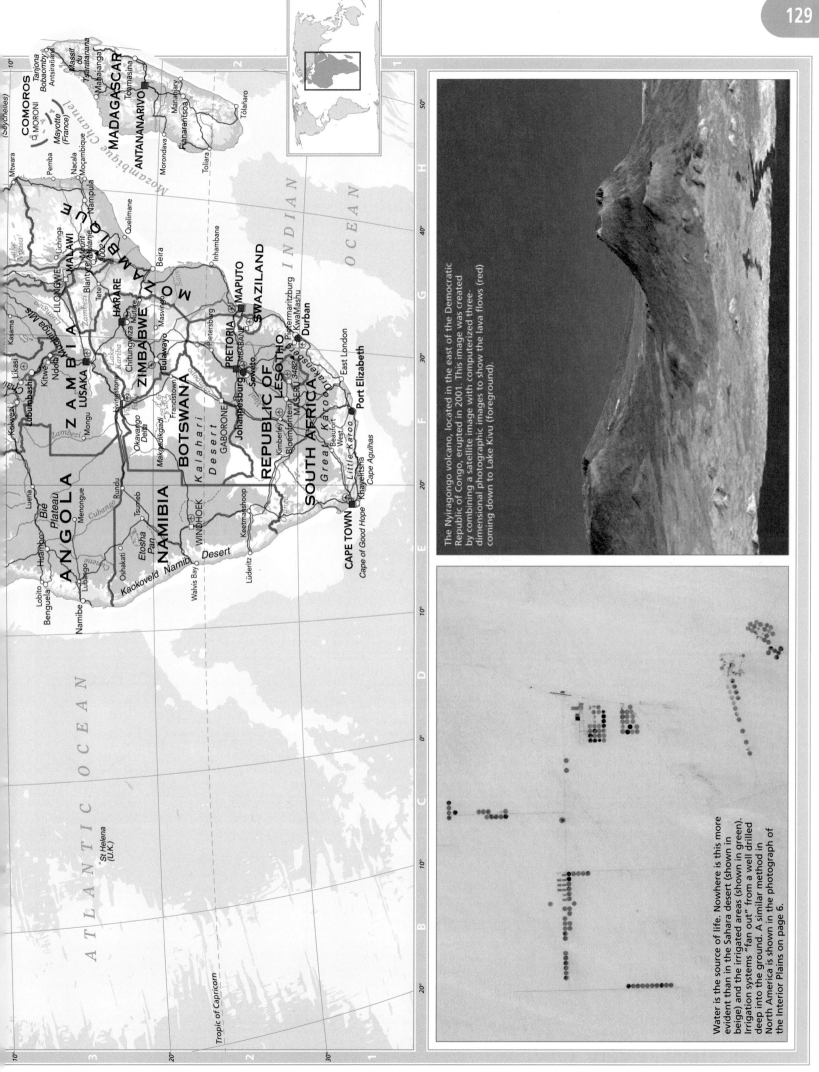

The Nyiragongo volcano, located in the east of the Democratic Republic of Congo, erupted in 2001. This image was created by combining a satellite image with computerized three-dimensional photographic images to show the lava flows (red) coming down to Lake Kivu (foreground).

Lambert Azimuthal Equal Area projection

LAND USE

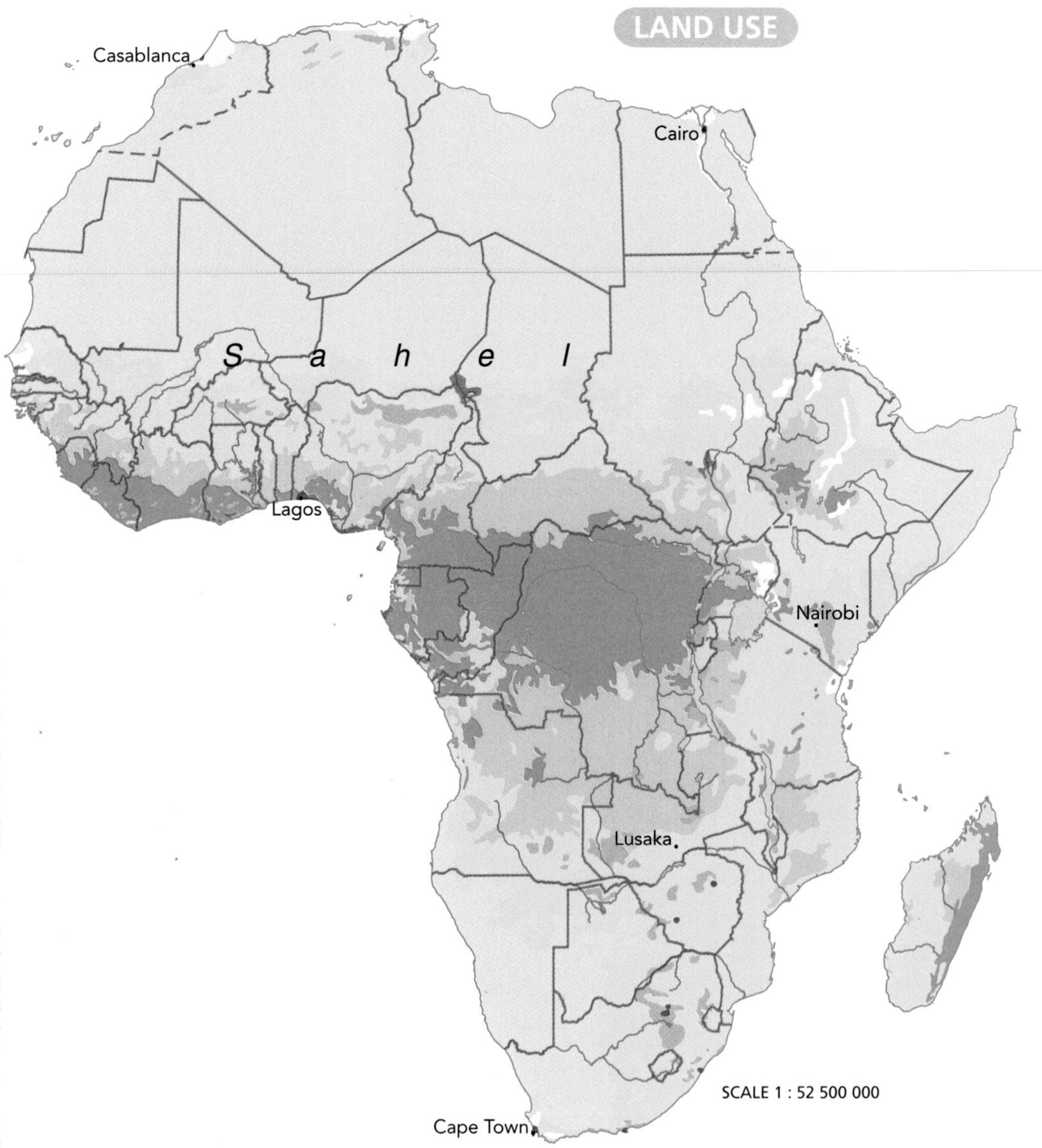

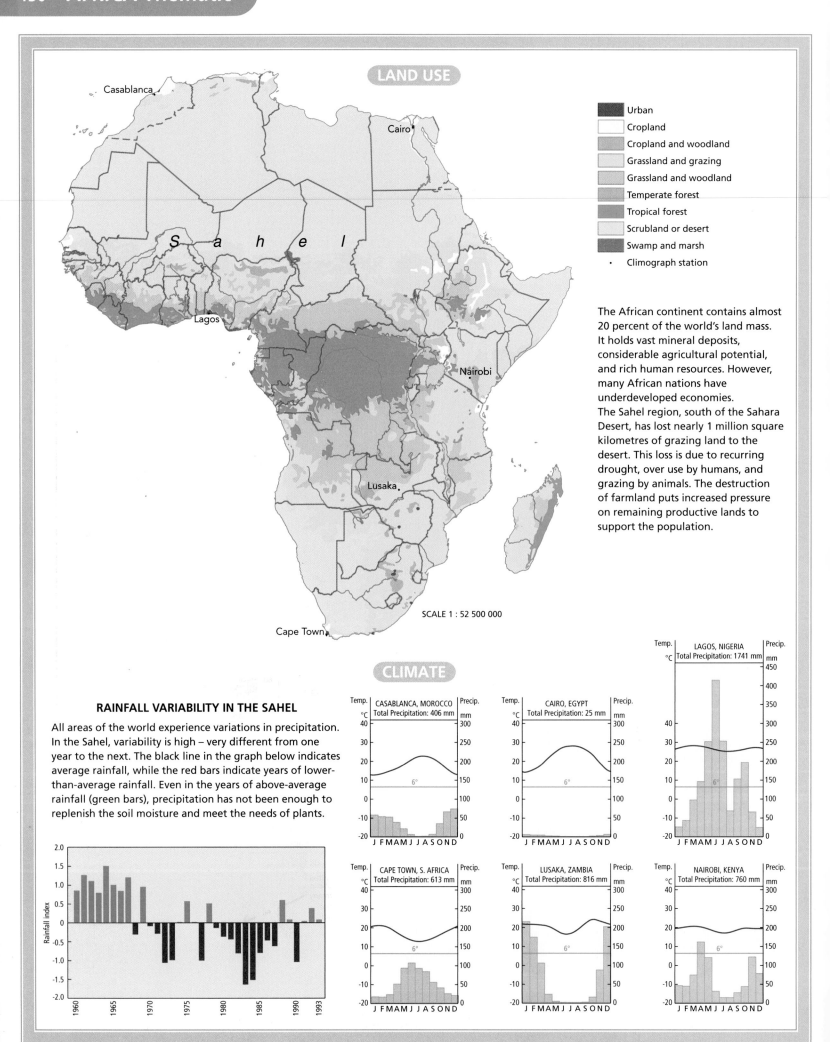

- Urban
- Cropland
- Cropland and woodland
- Grassland and grazing
- Grassland and woodland
- Temperate forest
- Tropical forest
- Scrubland or desert
- Swamp and marsh
- Climograph station

The African continent contains almost 20 percent of the world's land mass. It holds vast mineral deposits, considerable agricultural potential, and rich human resources. However, many African nations have underdeveloped economies.

The Sahel region, south of the Sahara Desert, has lost nearly 1 million square kilometres of grazing land to the desert. This loss is due to recurring drought, over use by humans, and grazing by animals. The destruction of farmland puts increased pressure on remaining productive lands to support the population.

CLIMATE

RAINFALL VARIABILITY IN THE SAHEL

All areas of the world experience variations in precipitation. In the Sahel, variability is high – very different from one year to the next. The black line in the graph below indicates average rainfall, while the red bars indicate years of lower-than-average rainfall. Even in the years of above-average rainfall (green bars), precipitation has not been enough to replenish the soil moisture and meet the needs of plants.

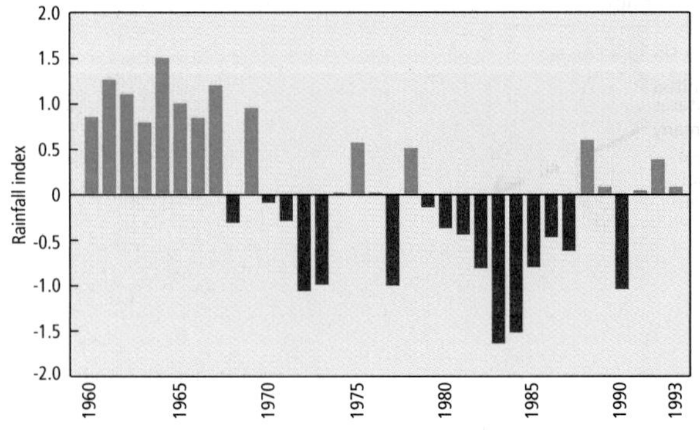

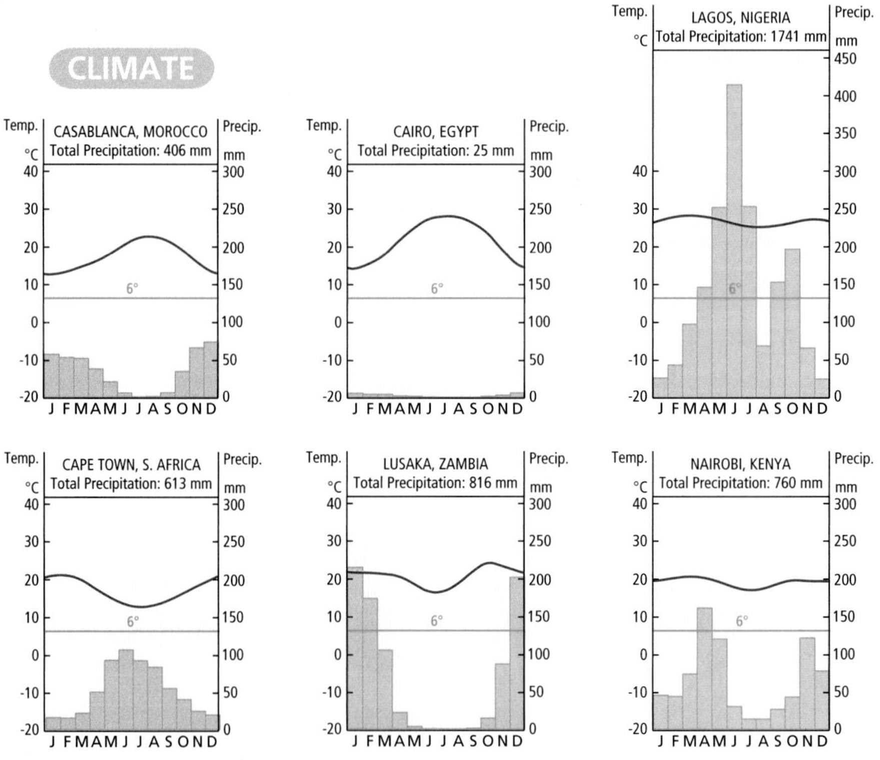

TOURISM

Top Destinations, 2000

Country	Income from tourism	
	Millions, US$	Percent of GDP
Seychelles	110	17.9
Mauritius	585	13.4
Comoros	19	8.5
Tanzania	739	8.2
Tunisia	1 496	7.7
Morocco	2 040	6.1
Eritrea	36	5.9
Botswana	234	4.6
Egypt	4 345	4.4
Cape Verde	23	3.9
Ghana	304	3.9
Zimbabwe	202	3.7
Senegal	166	3.5
Zambia	91	3.1
Madagascar	116	3.0
Kenya	304	2.9
Mauritania	28	2.9
Swaziland	35	2.6
Uganda	149	2.3
Mali	50	2.2
Lesotho	19	2.1
Sierra Leone	12	1.9
South Africa	2 526	1.9
Malawi	27	1.6
Niger	24	1.2
Rwanda	17	0.9
Libya	28	0.7
Ethiopia	24	0.4
Guinea	12	0.4
Togo	6	0.4

COLONIZATION AND INDEPENDENCE

ECONOMY

EGYPT

Trade, 2001

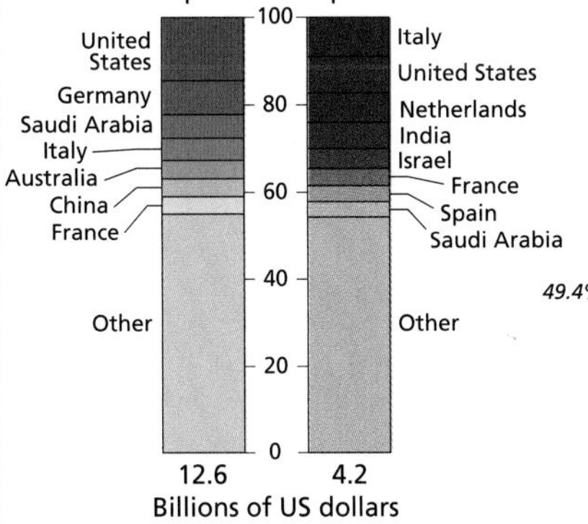

Billions of US dollars

GDP by sector, 2000

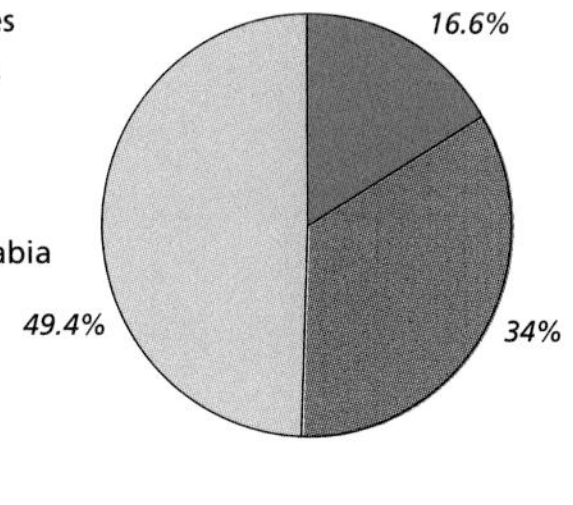

Total : US$ 98.7 billion

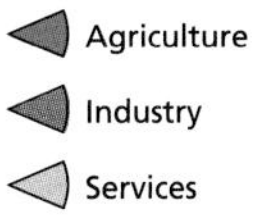

MALI

Trade, 1999

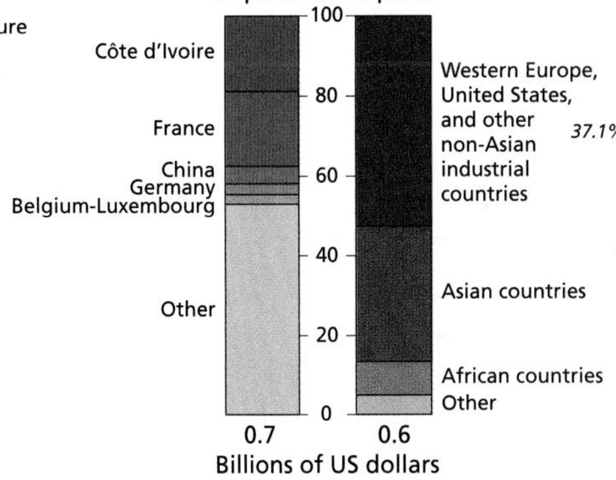

Billions of US dollars

GDP by sector, 2000

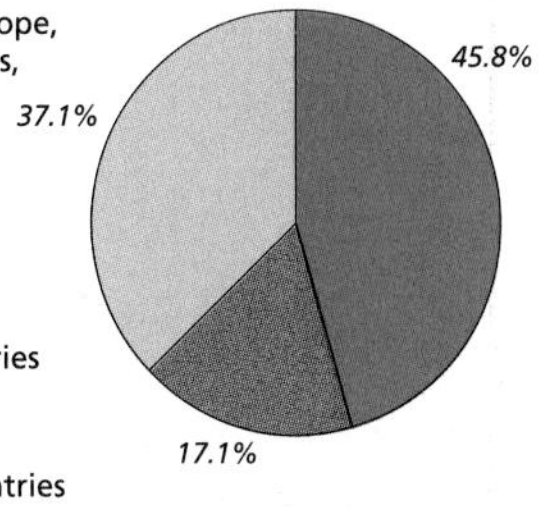

Total : US$ 2.3 billion

SOUTH AFRICA

Trade, 2001

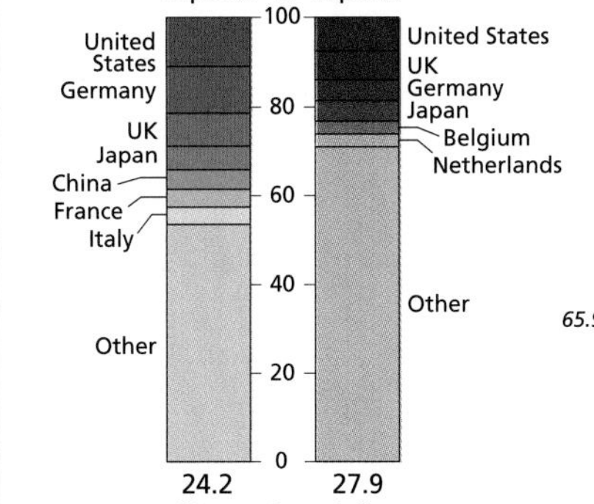

Billions of US dollars

GDP by sector, 2000

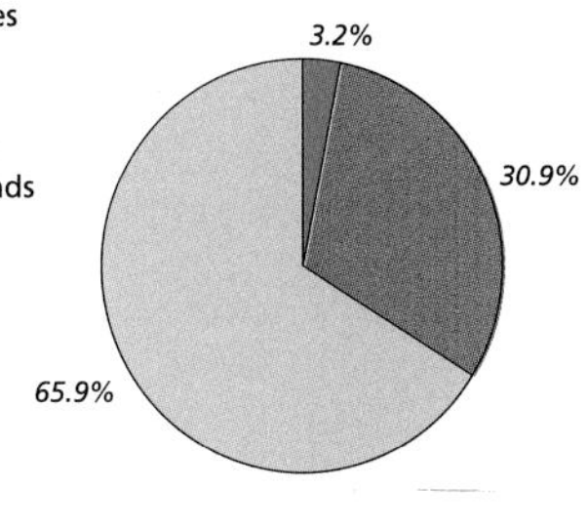

Total : US$ 125.9 billion

*The category 'Agriculture' includes forestry and fishing, the category 'Industry' includes mining.

NIGERIA

Trade, 2000

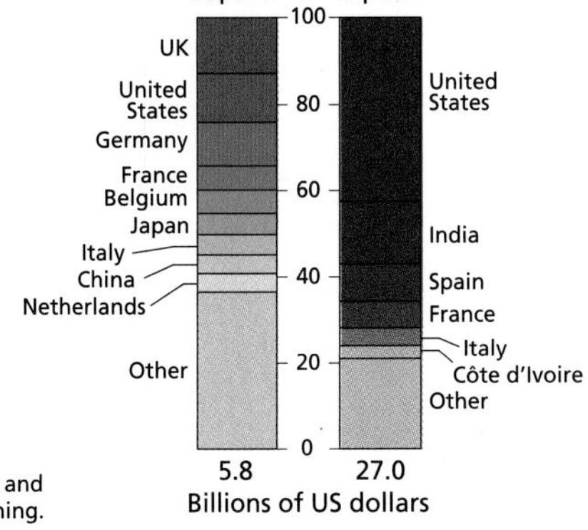

Billions of US dollars

GDP by sector, 2000

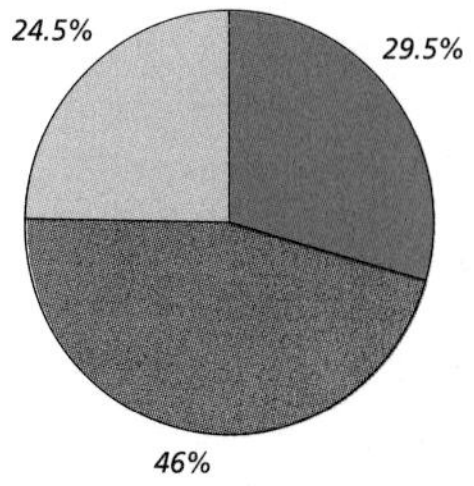

Total : US$ 41.1 billion

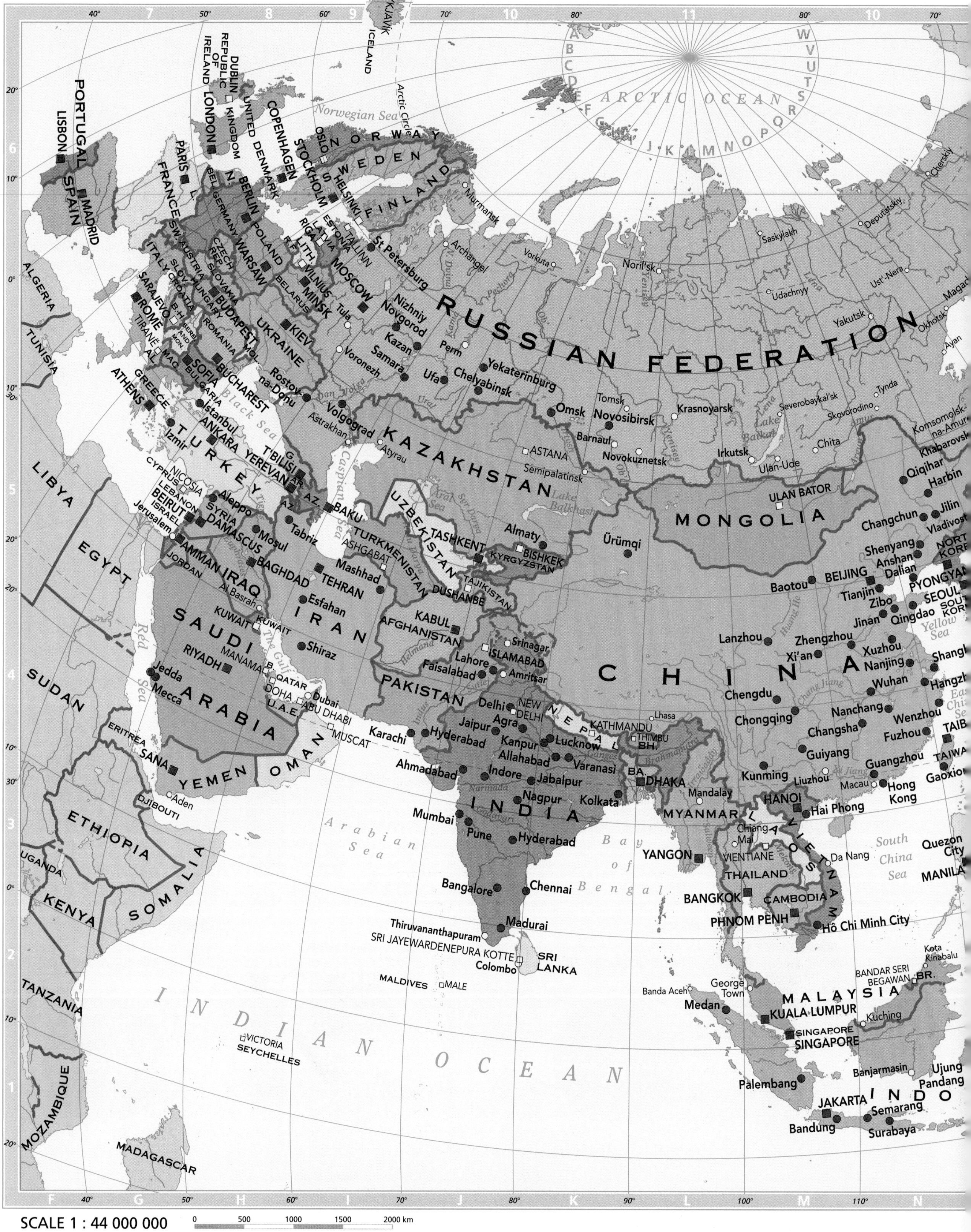
ARCTIC OCEAN
Norwegian Sea
Arctic Circle
REYKJAVIK
ICELAND
DUBLIN
REPUBLIC OF IRELAND
UNITED KINGDOM
LONDON
PORTUGAL
LISBON
SPAIN
MADRID
PARIS
FRANCE
COPENHAGEN
DENMARK
OSLO
NORWAY
SWEDEN
STOCKHOLM
HELSINKI
FINLAND
TALLINN
ESTONIA
RIGA
LATVIA
LITH.
VILNIUS
BERLIN
GERMANY
POLAND
WARSAW
CZECH REP.
AUSTRIA
SLOVAKIA
HUNGARY
BUDAPEST
ITALY
ROME
CROATIA
SARAJEVO
SERB.
MON.
TIRANË
AL.
MAC.
SOFIA
BULGARIA
BUCHAREST
ROMANIA
GREECE
ATHENS
BELARUS
MINSK
UKRAINE
KIEV
MOSCOW
St Petersburg
Murmansk
Archangel
Vorkuta
Nizhniy Novgorod
Kazan
Perm
Tula
Voronezh
Samara
Ufa
Yekaterinburg
Chelyabinsk
Rostov-na-Donu
Volgograd
Astrakhan
RUSSIAN FEDERATION
Noril'sk
Saskylakh
Deputatskiy
Cherskiy
Udachnyy
Ust'-Nera
Yakutsk
Okhotsk
Ayan
Omsk
Tomsk
Novosibirsk
Krasnoyarsk
Barnaul
Novokuznetsk
Irkutsk
Ulan-Ude
Chita
Tynda
Skovorodino
Severobaykal'sk
Komsomolsk-na-Amur
Khabarovsk
Lake Baikal
ASTANA
Semipalatinsk
Atyrau
KAZAKHSTAN
Lake Balkhash
Aral Sea
Caspian Sea
Black Sea
Istanbul
ANKARA
Izmir
TURKEY
T'BILISI
YEREVAN
BAKU
AZ.
NICOSIA
CYPRUS
LEBANON
BEIRUT
ISRAEL
Jerusalem
SYRIA
Aleppo
DAMASCUS
AMMAN
JORDAN
Mosul
IRAQ
BAGHDAD
Al Basrah
KUWAIT
Tabriz
TEHRAN
Mashhad
Esfahan
IRAN
Shiraz
UZBEKISTAN
TASHKENT
TURKMENISTAN
ASHGABAT
KYRGYZSTAN
BISHKEK
Almaty
TAJIKISTAN
DUSHANBE
KABUL
AFGHANISTAN
ISLAMABAD
Srinagar
Lahore
Faisalabad
Amritsar
PAKISTAN
Karachi
Hyderabad
SAUDI ARABIA
RIYADH
MANAMA
QATAR
DOHA
U.A.E.
Dubai
ABU DHABI
MUSCAT
OMAN
Jedda
Mecca
SANA
YEMEN
Aden
ERITREA
DJIBOUTI
ETHIOPIA
SOMALIA
KENYA
UGANDA
TANZANIA
MOZAMBIQUE
MADAGASCAR
SUDAN
EGYPT
LIBYA
TUNISIA
ALGERIA
Red Sea
The Gulf
Arabian Sea
INDIAN OCEAN
VICTORIA
SEYCHELLES
MALDIVES
MALE
Delhi
NEW DELHI
Agra
Jaipur
Kanpur
Lucknow
Allahabad
Varanasi
Indore
Jabalpur
Ahmadabad
Nagpur
Kolkata
Mumbai
Pune
Hyderabad
INDIA
Bangalore
Chennai
Madurai
Thiruvananthapuram
SRI JAYEWARDENEPURA KOTTE
Colombo
SRI LANKA
NEPAL
KATHMANDU
THIMBU
BH.
BA.
DHAKA
Bay of Bengal
Lhasa
CHINA
Ürümqi
MONGOLIA
ULAN BATOR
Lanzhou
Baotou
BEIJING
Tianjin
Zibo
Jinan
Qingdao
Zhengzhou
Xi'an
Xuzhou
Nanjing
Shanghai
Wuhan
Hangzhou
Chengdu
Chongqing
Nanchang
Changsha
Wenzhou
Fuzhou
Guiyang
Kunming
Liuzhou
Guangzhou
Macau
Hong Kong
Qiqihar
Harbin
Changchun
Jilin
Vladivostok
Shenyang
Anshan
Dalian
PYONGYANG
SEOUL
Yellow Sea
Mandalay
MYANMAR
YANGON
Chiang Mai
VIENTIANE
LAOS
HANOI
Hai Phong
VIETNAM
Da Nang
THAILAND
BANGKOK
CAMBODIA
PHNOM PENH
Hô Chi Minh City
South China Sea
Quezon City
MANILA
Kota Kinabalu
BANDAR SERI BEGAWAN
BR.
MALAYSIA
KUALA LUMPUR
Kuching
SINGAPORE
Banda Aceh
George Town
Medan
Palembang
Banjarmasin
Ujung Pandang
JAKARTA
INDONESIA
Bandung
Semarang
Surabaya

SCALE 1 : 44 000 000   0 500 1000 1500 2000 km

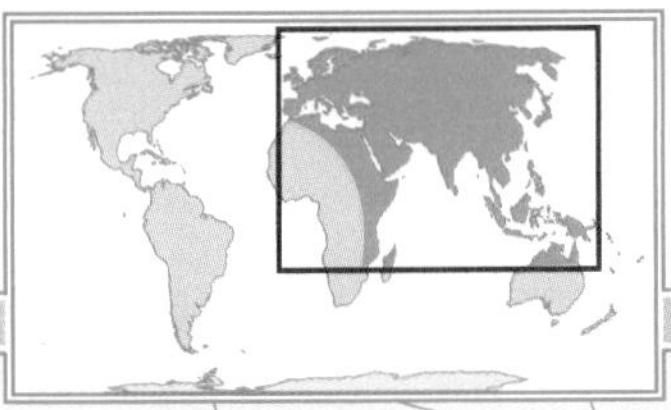

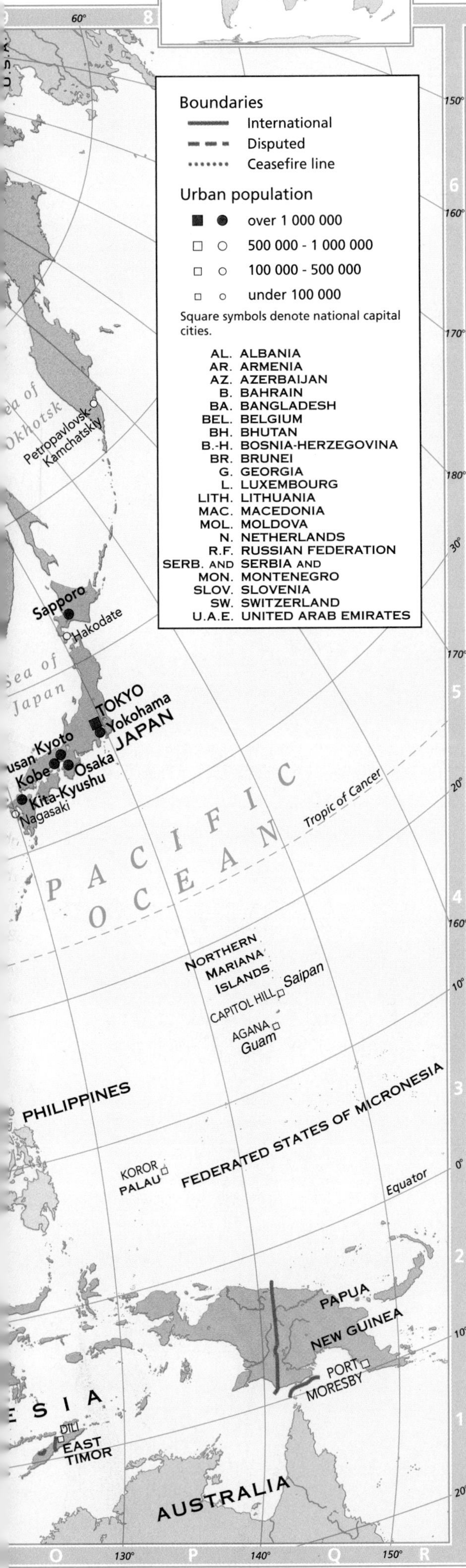

Lambert Azimuthal Equal Area projection

POPULATION

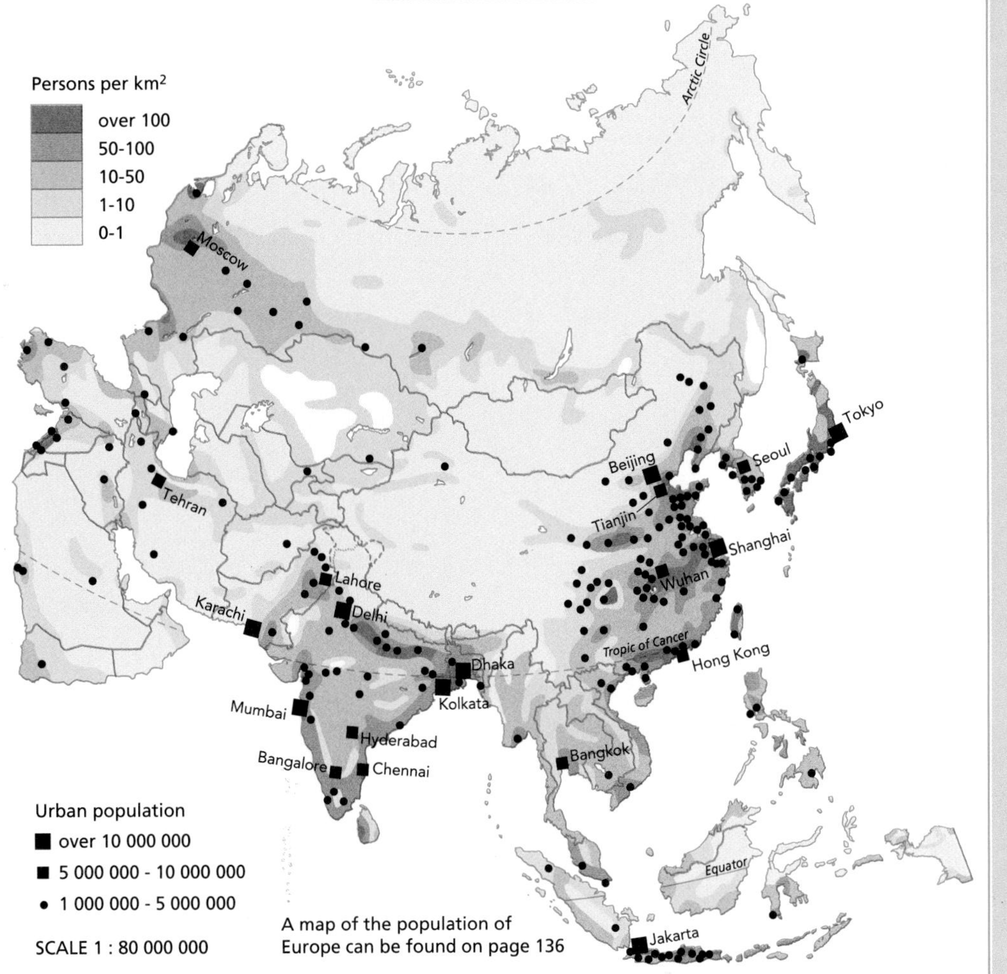

A map of the population of Europe can be found on page 136

POPULATION COMPARISONS

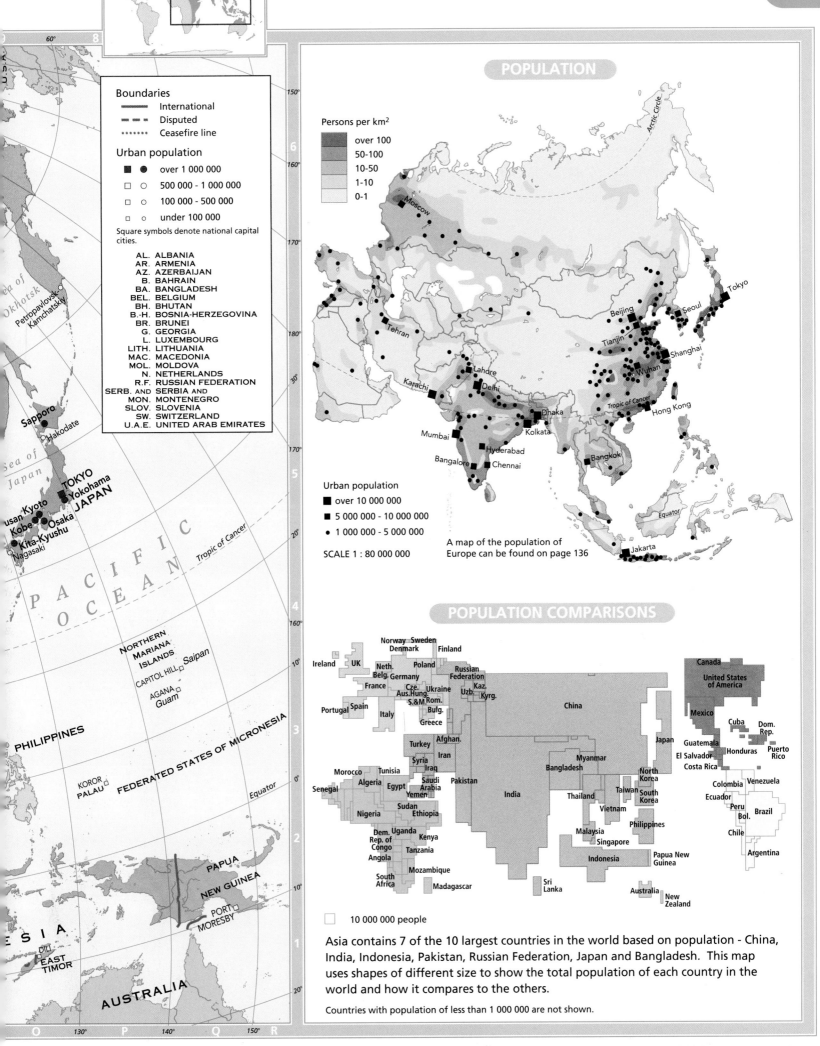

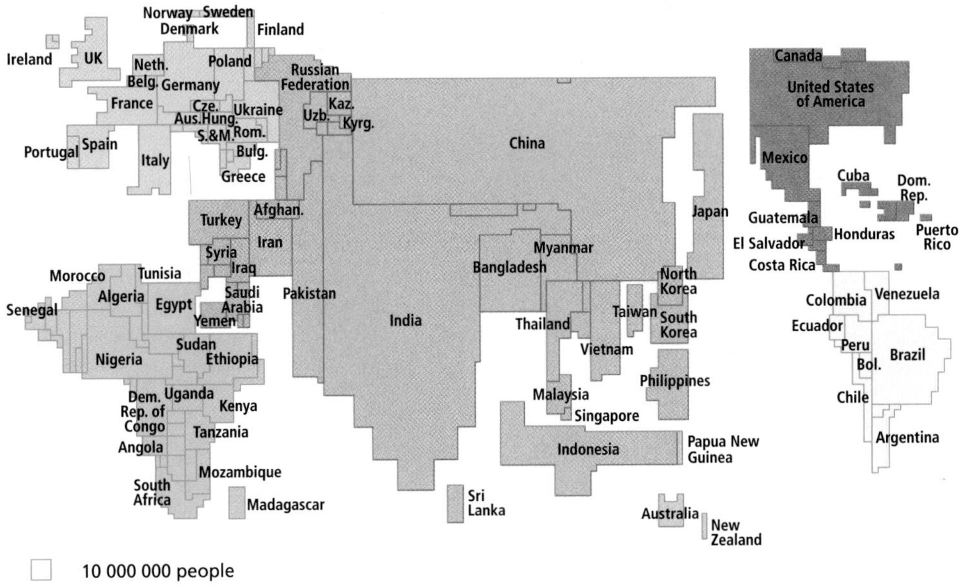

Asia contains 7 of the 10 largest countries in the world based on population - China, India, Indonesia, Pakistan, Russian Federation, Japan and Bangladesh. This map uses shapes of different size to show the total population of each country in the world and how it compares to the others.

Countries with population of less than 1 000 000 are not shown.

ATLANTIC OCEAN
ARCTIC OCEAN
INDIAN OCEAN
Iceland
British Isles
Great Britain
C. Finisterre
C. St Vincent
Bay of Biscay
North Sea
Norwegian Sea
Arctic Circle
Spitsbergen
Barents Sea
Franz Josef Land
Severnaya Zemlya
New Siberia Islands
Wrangel I.
North Cape
Scandinavia
Kola Peninsula
White Sea
Novaya Zemlya
Taymyr Peninsula
C. Chelyuskin
Laptev Sea
Kolyma Range
Verkhoyansk Range
Dzhugdzhur Range
Stanovoy Range
Yablonovyy Range
Baltic Sea
Pyrenees
Alps
Corsica
Sardinia
Apennines
Sicily
Mediterranean Sea
Carpathian Mts
North European Plain
Central Russian Uplands
Ural Mountains
Narodnaya 1894
West Siberian Plain
Central Siberian Plateau
Lower Tunguska
S I B E R I A
Lake Baikal
Amur
Black Sea
Caucasus
Caspian Sea
Kirghiz Steppe
Aral Sea
Syr Darya
Amu Darya
Lake Balkhash
Lake Zaysan
Altai Mts
Gobi Desert
Selenga
Da Hinggan Ling
Manchuria
Taurus Mts
Mt Ararat 5165
Cyprus
Libyan Desert
Tropic of Cancer
Lake Nasser
Nile
Elburz Mts.
Dasht-e Kavir
Iranian Plateau
Zagros Mts.
An Nafud
Hijaz
Arabian Peninsula
Asir
Rub'al Khali
Red Sea
The Gulf
Makran
Gulf of Oman
Masirah
Tien Shan
Lop Nur
Taklimakan Desert
Hindu Kush
K2 8611
Karakoram Ra.
Kunlun Shan
Tibetan Plateau
Sulaiman Range
Helmand
Indus
Sutlej
Thar Desert
Himalayan Range
Dhaulagiri 8167
Annapurna 8091
Mt Everest 8848
Gongga Shan 7514
Huang He
Bo Hai
Yellow Sea
North China Plain
East China Sea
Chang Jiang
Nan Ling
Xi Jiang
Taiwan
Luzon Strait
Hainan
Ganges
Brahmaputra
Ganges Delta
Arakan Yoma
Irrawaddy
Salween
Mekong
Narmada
Godavari
Deccan
Western Ghats
Eastern Ghats
2633
Ethiopian Highlands
White Nile
Blue Nile
Atbara
Gulf of Aden
Socotra
Arabian Sea
Bay of Bengal
Andaman Islands
Andaman Sea
South China Sea
Luzon
Shabeelle
Lake Turkana
Lake Victoria
Kilimanjaro 5895
Equator
Laccadive Is
C. Comorin
Sri Lanka
Maldives
Nicobar Islands
Gulf of Thailand
Strait of Malacca
Malay Peninsula
Palawan
Sumatra
Borneo
Mentawai Islands
Java Sea
Java
Bali
Lombok
Seychelles
Aldabra Is
Comoro Is
Chagos Archipelago
Lake Nyasa
Zambezi
Mozambique Channel
Madagascar

SCALE 1 : 44 000 000

0 500 1000 1500 2000 km

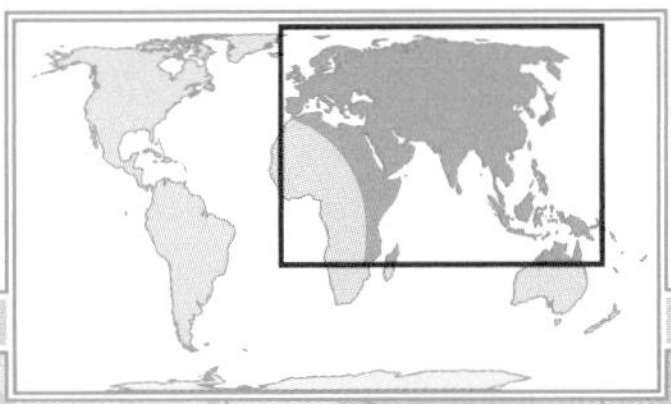

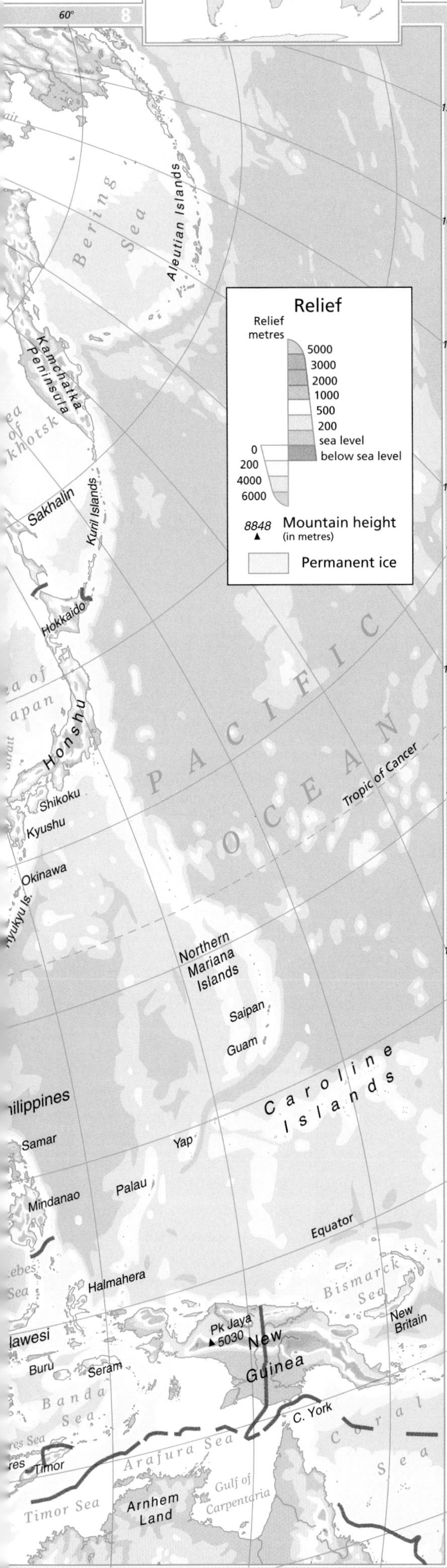

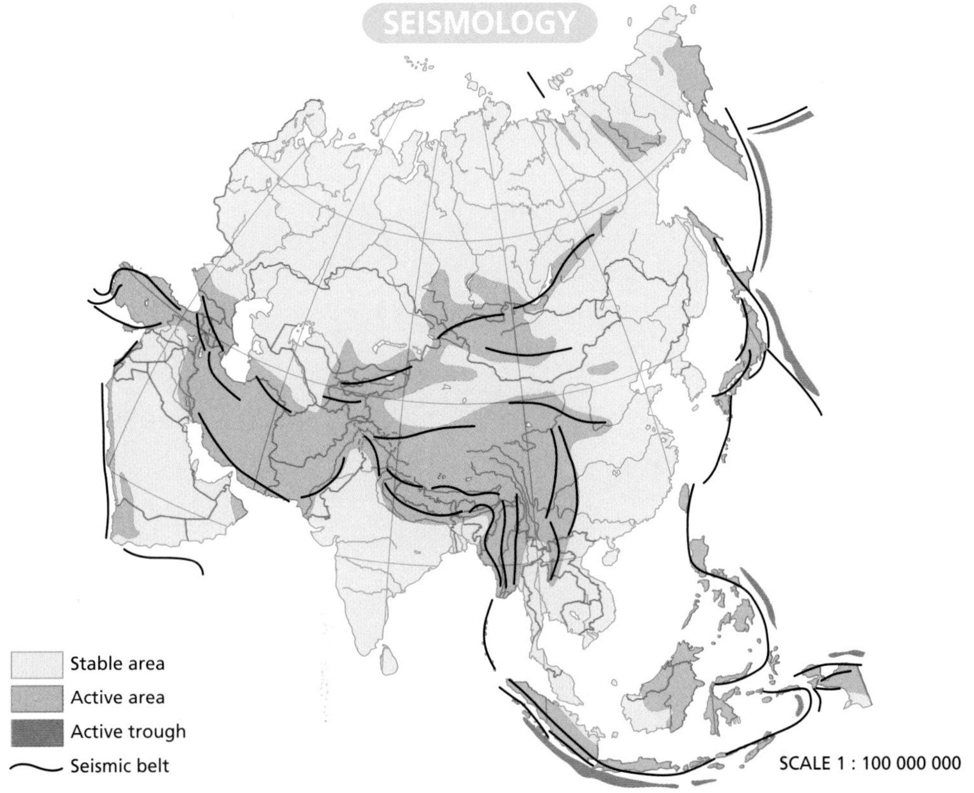

The Ganges River enters this satellite image from the northwest, and is joined by two more rivers from the north. The Ganges Delta has been formed by the deposit of sediment into the Bay of Bengal (dark area to the south). Sediment is indicated by the red tone, both in the rivers and extending out into the bay.

SCALE 1 : 2 500 000

Lambert Azimuthal Equal Area projection

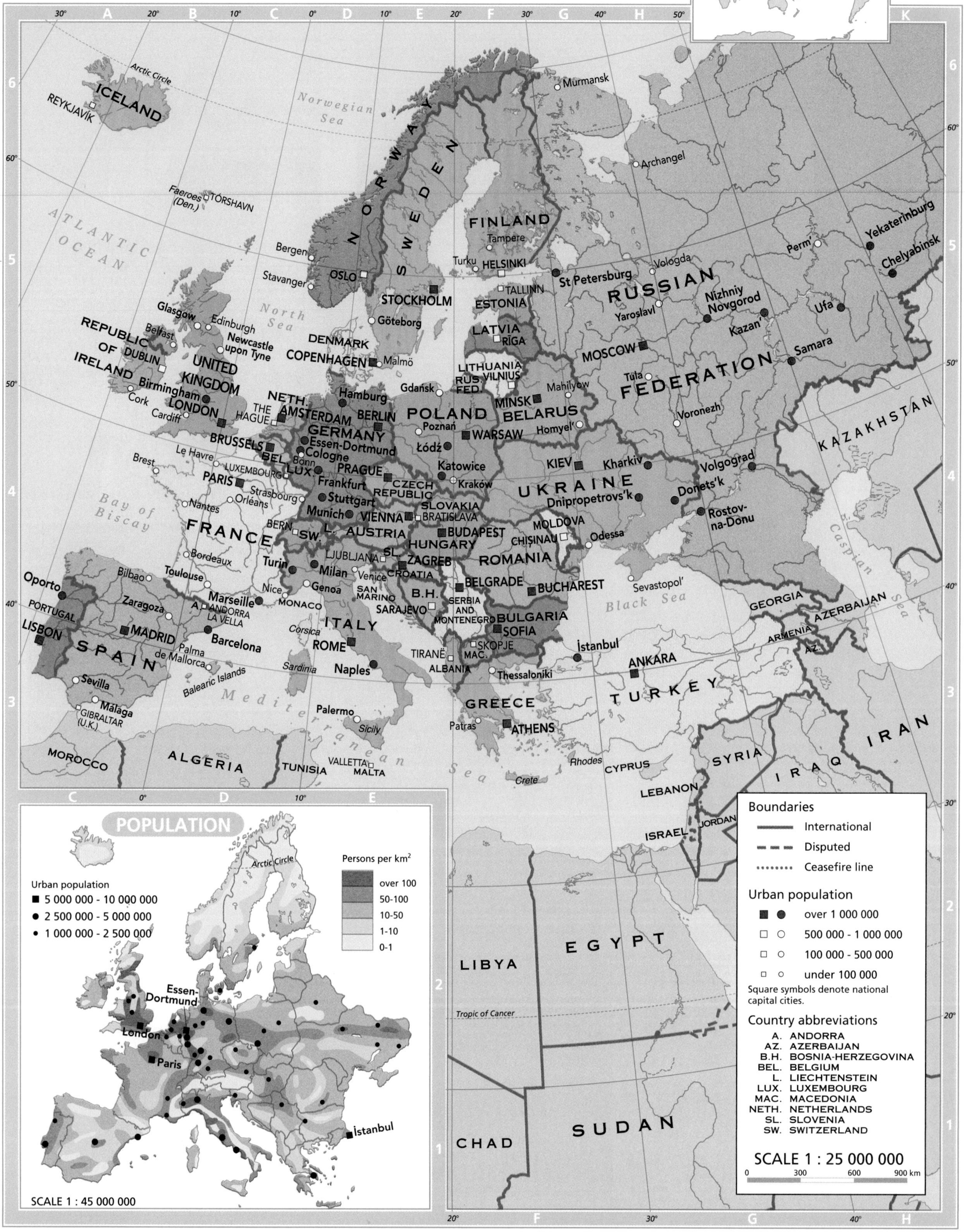

ICELAND
REYKJAVÍK
Arctic Circle
Norwegian Sea
Faeroes (Den.)
TÓRSHAVN
ATLANTIC OCEAN
NORWAY
SWEDEN
FINLAND
Tampere
Turku
HELSINKI
Murmansk
Archangel
Bergen
Stavanger
OSLO
STOCKHOLM
Göteborg
TALLINN
ESTONIA
LATVIA
RĪGA
LITHUANIA
VILNIUS
RUS. FED.
North Sea
DENMARK
COPENHAGEN
Malmö
Glasgow
Edinburgh
Belfast
Newcastle upon Tyne
REPUBLIC OF IRELAND
DUBLIN
UNITED KINGDOM
Birmingham
Cork
Cardiff
LONDON
NETH.
AMSTERDAM
THE HAGUE
BRUSSELS
BEL.
LUX.
LUXEMBOURG
Hamburg
BERLIN
GERMANY
Essen-Dortmund
Cologne
Bonn
Frankfurt
Stuttgart
Munich
PRAGUE
CZECH REPUBLIC
Gdańsk
POLAND
Poznań
WARSAW
Łódź
Katowice
Kraków
MINSK
BELARUS
Mahilyow
Homyel'
St Petersburg
Vologda
Perm'
Yekaterinburg
Chelyabinsk
RUSSIAN FEDERATION
Yaroslavl
Nizhniy Novgorod
Kazan'
Ufa
MOSCOW
Tula
Samara
Voronezh
KAZAKHSTAN
KIEV
Kharkiv
UKRAINE
Dnipropetrovs'k
Donets'k
Volgograd
Rostov-na-Donu
Caspian Sea
Brest
Le Havre
PARIS
Strasbourg
Orléans
Nantes
Bay of Biscay
FRANCE
Bordeaux
Toulouse
Marseille
Nice
MONACO
BERN
SW.
L.
VIENNA
BRATISLAVA
SLOVAKIA
AUSTRIA
BUDAPEST
HUNGARY
MOLDOVA
CHIŞINĂU
Odessa
Sevastopol'
ROMANIA
LJUBLJANA
SL.
ZAGREB
CROATIA
Turin
Milan
Venice
Genoa
SAN MARINO
B.H.
SARAJEVO
BELGRADE
SERBIA AND MONTENEGRO
BUCHAREST
BULGARIA
SOFIA
SKOPJE
MAC.
TIRANË
ALBANIA
Black Sea
Istanbul
ANKARA
TURKEY
Thessaloniki
GREECE
ATHENS
Patras
Rhodes
Crete
CYPRUS
GEORGIA
AZERBAIJAN
ARMENIA
AZ.
IRAN
SYRIA
IRAQ
LEBANON
ISRAEL
JORDAN
Oporto
PORTUGAL
LISBON
Bilbao
Zaragoza
A.
ANDORRA LA VELLA
MADRID
SPAIN
Barcelona
Palma de Mallorca
Balearic Islands
Sevilla
Málaga
GIBRALTAR (U.K.)
Corsica
ITALY
ROME
Sardinia
Naples
Palermo
Sicily
Mediterranean Sea
VALLETTA
MALTA
MOROCCO
ALGERIA
TUNISIA
LIBYA
EGYPT
SUDAN
CHAD
Tropic of Cancer
POPULATION
Urban population
■ 5 000 000 - 10 000 000
● 2 500 000 - 5 000 000
• 1 000 000 - 2 500 000
Persons per km²
over 100
50-100
10-50
1-10
0-1
Arctic Circle
Essen-Dortmund
London
Paris
İstanbul
SCALE 1 : 45 000 000
Boundaries
International
Disputed
Ceasefire line
Urban population
over 1 000 000
500 000 - 1 000 000
100 000 - 500 000
under 100 000
Square symbols denote national capital cities.
Country abbreviations
A. ANDORRA
AZ. AZERBAIJAN
B.H. BOSNIA-HERZEGOVINA
BEL. BELGIUM
L. LIECHTENSTEIN
LUX. LUXEMBOURG
MAC. MACEDONIA
NETH. NETHERLANDS
SL. SLOVENIA
SW. SWITZERLAND
SCALE 1 : 25 000 000
0 300 600 900 km

Lambert Azimuthal Equal Area projection

EUROPE'S CHANGING BOUNDARIES

1914, The Eve of the First World War

1925, The Aftermath of the First World War

1949, Cold War Europe

2003, The European Union

Abbreviations

ALB.	ALBANIA
A.	ANDORRA
B.-H.	BOSNIA-HERZEGOVINA
BEL.	BELGIUM
CZECH REP.	CZECH REPUBLIC
FED. REP. OF GER.	FEDERAL REPUBLIC OF GERMANY
F. S. OF TR.	FREE STATE OF TRIESTE
GER.	GERMANY
GER. DEM. REP.	GERMAN DEMOCRATIC REPUBLIC
L.	LIECHTENSTEIN
LEB.	LEBANON
LITH.	LITHUANIA
LUX.	LUXEMBOURG
M.	MONACO
MAC.	MACEDONIA
MOL.	MOLDOVA
MONT.	MONTENEGRO
NETH.	NETHERLANDS
R. F.	RUSSIAN FEDERATION
SER. AND MON.	SERBIA AND MONTENEGRO
SL.	SLOVENIA
SM.	SAN MARINO
SW.	SWITZERLAND

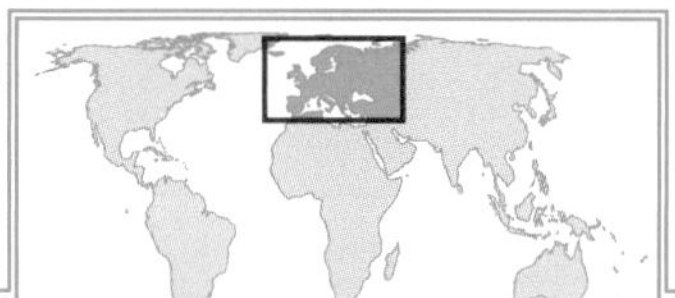

30°
20°
10°
0°
A
B
C
D
E
F
G
1
2
3
4
60°
50°
40°
Arctic Circle
ICELAND
REYKJAVIK
Akureyri
Fontur
Keflavík
Vatnajökull
Snaefell 1833
Norwegian Sea
North Cape
Hammerfest
Kirkenes
Murmansk
Kola Peninsu
Tromsø
Narvik
Lofoten
Vestfjorden
Lappland
Ivalo
Inarijärvi
Oz. Imandra
Bodø
Gällivare
Kemijärvi
NORWAY
SWEDEN
FINLAND
Mosjøen
Arvidsjaur
Tornio
Oulu
Luleå
Kem'
Trondheim
Umeå
Gulf of Bothnia
Iisalmi
Faeroes (Den.)
TÓRSHAVN
ATLANTIC OCEAN
Ålesund
Galdhøpiggen 2470
Östersund
Sundsvall
Vaasa
Joensuu
Jyväskylä
Shetland Islands
Lillehammer
Hamar
Mora
Pori
Tampere
Lahti
Petrozavodsk
Lake Ladoga
Bergen
Voss
Hønefoss
OSLO
Gävle
Åland
Turku
HELSINKI
St Petersburg
Orkney Islands
Thurso
Outer Hebrides
Stavanger
Skien
Västerås
Uppsala
Örebro
STOCKHOLM
Gulf of Finland
TALLINN
ESTONIA
Tartu
Pärnu
Hiiumaa
Saaremaa
Lake Peipus
Novgorod
Inverness
Ben Nevis 1344
Aberdeen
Kristiansand
Skagerrak
Uddevalla
Mariestad
Norrköping
Gotland
Göteborg
Kattegat
Jönköping
Visby
Edinburgh
Glasgow
Londonderry
Ålborg
Holstebro
Århus
Växjö
Ventspils
Gulf of Riga
LATVIA
Pskov
North Sea
DENMARK
Helsingborg
Karlskrona
Öland
Baltic Sea
Liepāja
RIGA
Rēzekne
Velikiye Luki
Valdai Hills
REPUBLIC OF IRELAND
Galway
Galway Bay
DUBLIN
Belfast
Isle of Man
Irish Sea
Pennines
Newcastle upon Tyne
Middlesbrough
UNITED KINGDOM
Manchester
Leeds
Liverpool
Snowdon 1085
Sheffield
Kingston upon Hull
Birmingham
Odense
Fyn
Esbjerg
Sjælland
COPENHAGEN
Malmö
Bornholm
Šiauliai
Daugavpils
Klaipėda
Panevėžys
LITHUANIA
Kaunas
VILNIUS
Vitsyebsk
Orsha
Smolen
Cape Clear
Cork
Waterford
Gloucester
Leicester
Norwich
Swansea
Cardiff
Oxford
Bristol
Ipswich
LONDON
Southampton
Land's End
Plymouth
English Channel
Frisian Islands
NETH.
Groningen
THE HAGUE
AMSTERDAM
Rotterdam
Antwerpen
BRUSSELS
Lille
BELGIUM
Liège
Kiel
Rostock
Lübeck
Hamburg
Bremen
Hannover
BERLIN
Szczecin
Gdańsk
Kaliningrad
RUS. FED.
Olsztyn
Bydgoszcz
Toruń
Białystok
MINSK
Hrodna
BELARUS
Mahilyow
Baranavichy
Homyel
Essen
Düsseldorf
Cologne
Bonn
GERMANY
Leipzig
Dresden
Legnica
POLAND
Poznań
WARSAW
Łódź
Wrocław
Radom
Brest
Pinsk
Pripet Marshes
Mazyr
Chern
North European Plain
Channel Islands
Le Havre
Caen
Amiens
Brest
Brittany
Rennes
PARIS
Reims
LUXEMBOURG
LUX.
Frankfurt
Chemnitz
Liberec
PRAGUE
Plzeň
Opole
Katowice
Ostrava
Kraków
Lublin
Rzeszów
Rivne
Zhytomyr
KIEV
Ternopil'
Lviv
Cherkasy
Metz
Nancy
Mainz
Mannheim
Stuttgart
Nürnberg
CZECH REP.
Brno
SLOVAKIA
Carpathian Mountains
Vinnytsya
UKR
Angers
Orléans
Troyes
Vosges
Strasbourg
Augsburg
Munich
Linz
Danube
VIENNA
BRATISLAVA
Košice
Uzhhorod
Miskolc
Chernivtsi
Kirovohra
Bay of Biscay
Nantes
Tours
Mulhouse
Basel
Salzburg
AUSTRIA
Győr
Debrecen
Baia Mare
Bălţi
MOLDOVA
La Rochelle
FRANCE
Dijon
BERN
Zürich
LIECH.
Innsbruck
BUDAPEST
HUNGARY
Oradea
Suceava
CHIȘINAU
Mykolay
Poitiers
Limoges
Clermont-Ferrand
Lyon
Geneva
Mt Blanc 4808
SWITZERLAND
Graz
Maribor
Kecskemét
Cluj-Napoca
Târgu Mureș
Odes
Cape Finisterre
A Coruña
Gulf of Gascogne
Dordogne
Mt Dore 1885
St-Etienne
Trento
SLOVENIA
LJUBLJANA
Pécs
Szeged
ROMANIA
Iași
Oviedo
Gijón
San Sebastián
Donostia-
Bilbao
Bordeaux
Massif Central
Milan
Verona
Venice
Trieste
ZAGREB
Osijek
Timișoara
Brașov
Galați
Vigo
Cantabrian Mts
Vitoria-Gasteiz
León
Bayonne
Toulouse
Montpellier
Nîmes
Turin
Genoa
Parma
Rijeka
CROATIA
Banja Luka
Novi Sad
Transylvanian Alps
Pitești
Bragança
Burgos
Pamplona
Pyrenees
Logroño
Nice
MONACO
Bologna
Florence
SAN MARINO
Zadar
Dinaric Alps
BOSNIA-HERZ.
BELGRADE
Drobeta-Turnu Severin
BUCHAREST
Constanta
Oporto
Douro
Valladolid
Ebro
ANDORRA
Marseille
Golfe du Lion
Ligurian Sea
Livorno
Apennines
Adriatic Sea
SERBIA
AND
MONTENEGRO
Ruse
Varna
Coimbra
PORTUGAL
Salamanca
Zaragoza
Perpignan
Toulon
Perugia
Split
SARAJEVO
Mostar
Niš
Pleven
BULGARIA
Guarda
MADRID
SPAIN
Lleida
Barcelona
Corsica (France)
Bastia
Ajaccio
Elba
Terni
Pristina
Balkan Mountains
Burgas
LISBON
Tagus
Alcalá de Henares
ROME
Pescara
Podgorica
SKOPJE
SOFIA
Stara Zagora
Plovdiv
Mérida
Badajoz
Beja
Sierra Morena
Albacete
Bonifacio
Olbia
ITALY
Foggia
MACEDONIA
Bitola
Rhodope Mts
Xanthi
Istanbul
Sea of Marmara
Bursa
Córdoba
Sevilla
Valencia
Balearic Islands
Menorca
Palma de Mallorca
Mallorca
Ibiza
Sassari
Sardinia (Italy)
Oristano
Naples
Vesuvius 1281
Bari
TIRANË
ALBANIA
Vlorë
Lecce
Gulf of Taranto
Thessaloniki
Murcia
Alicante
Granada
Sierra Nevada
Cape St Vincent
Faro
Cádiz
Tyrrhenian Sea
Corfu
Pindus Mts
Larisa
Volos
Aegean Sea
Igoumenitsa
Evvoia
Balikesir
Eskişehir
Málaga
GIBRALTAR (U.K.)
Strait of Gibraltar
Almería
Cartagena
Mediterranean Sea
Cagliari
Catanzaro
Ionian Sea
GREECE
ATHENS
Usak
İzmir
Tanger
Ceuta (Spain)
Melilla (Spain)
Oran
ALGIERS
Palermo
Messina
Mt Etna 3323
Reggio di Calabria
Patras
Corinth
Zakynthos
Kyparissia
RABAT
MOROCCO
Fez
Tlemcen
Ech Chélif
Constantine
Sétif
Annaba
TUNIS
TUNISIA
Sicily
Siracusa
Dodecanese
Casablanca
Meknès
Hauts Plateaux
ALGERIA
Sousse
MALTA
VALLETTA
Crete
Iraklion
Rhodes

SCALE 1 : 15 000 000

0 200 400 600 800 km

Lambert Azimuthal Equal Area projection

PHYSICAL REGIONS

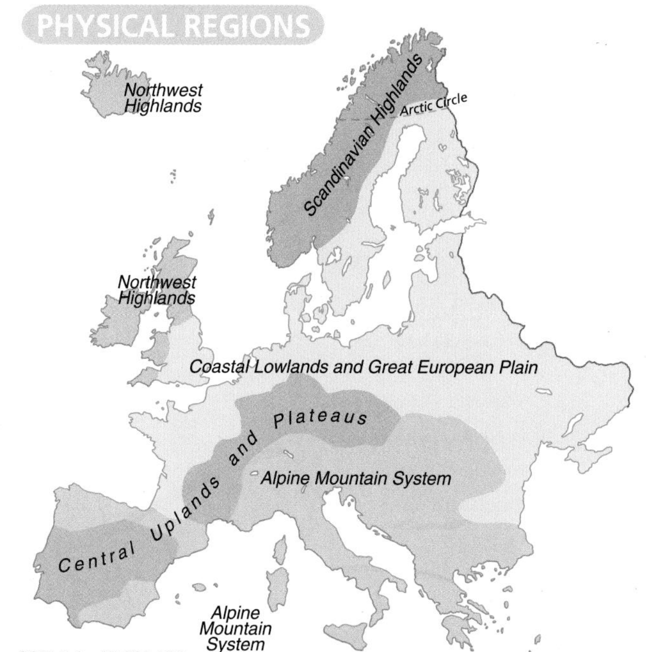

SCALE 1 : 45 000 000

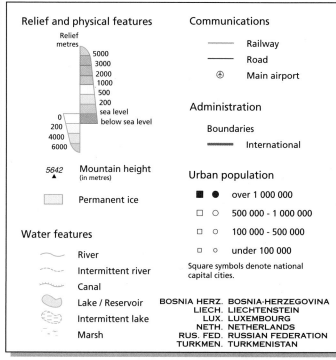

Northern Europe is shown in this true-colour satellite image showing Denmark, Germany, the Baltic Sea, and clouds coming in from the Atlantic Ocean (left side). Forested areas appear as a darker shade of green. The North European plain has intense agricultural activity and industry.

Relief and physical features

Relief metres: 5000, 3000, 2000, 1000, 500, 200, sea level, below sea level; 0, 200, 4000, 6000

5642 ▲ Mountain height (in metres)

Permanent ice

Water features

- River
- Intermittent river
- Canal
- Lake / Reservoir
- Intermittent lake
- Marsh

Communications

- Railway
- Road
- Main airport

Administration

Boundaries

- International

Urban population

- ■ ● over 1 000 000
- □ ○ 500 000 - 1 000 000
- □ ○ 100 000 - 500 000
- □ ○ under 100 000

Square symbols denote national capital cities.

BOSNIA HERZ.	BOSNIA-HERZEGOVINA
LIECH.	LIECHTENSTEIN
LUX.	LUXEMBOURG
NETH.	NETHERLANDS
RUS. FED.	RUSSIAN FEDERATION
TURKMEN.	TURKMENISTAN

LAND USE

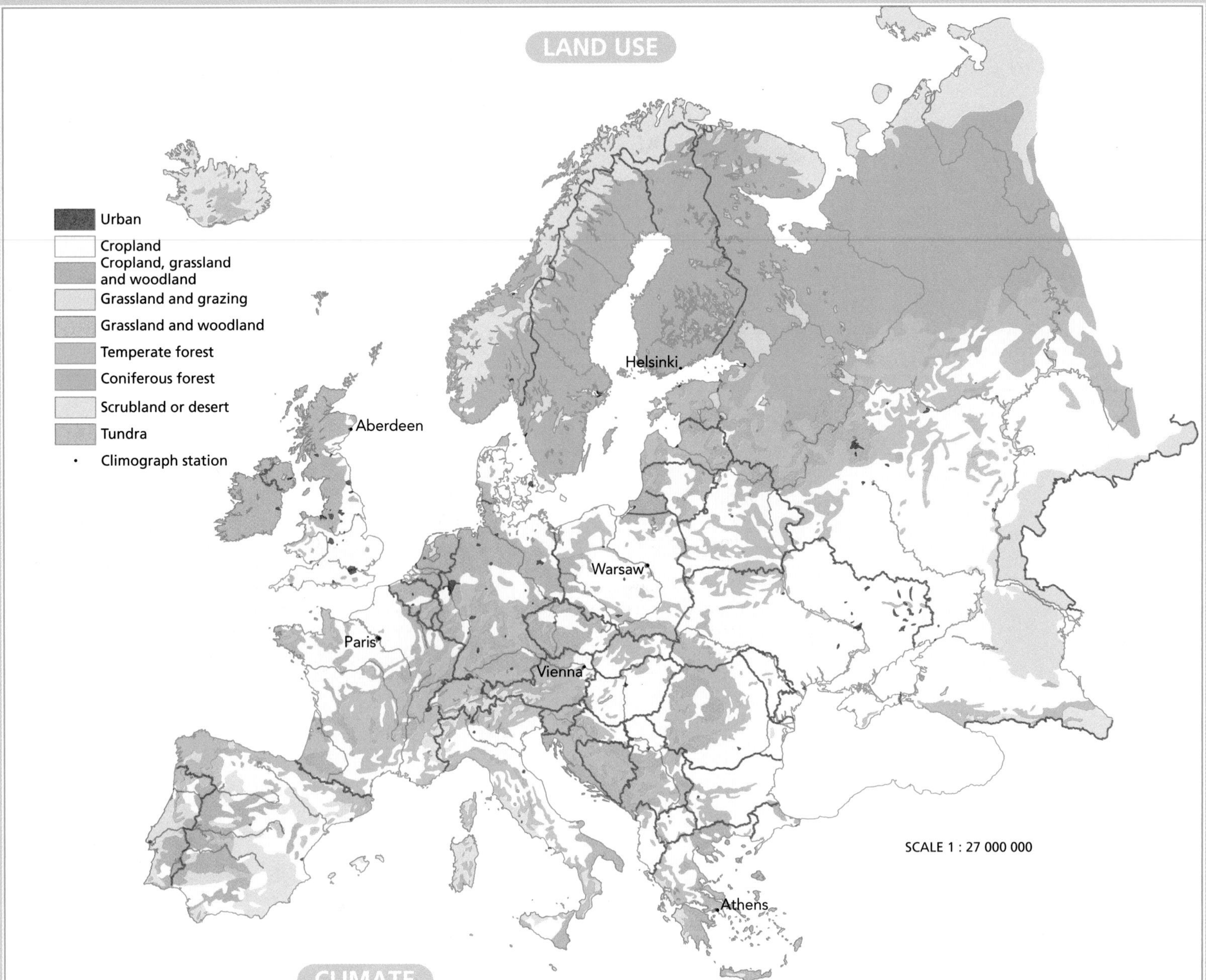

CLIMATE

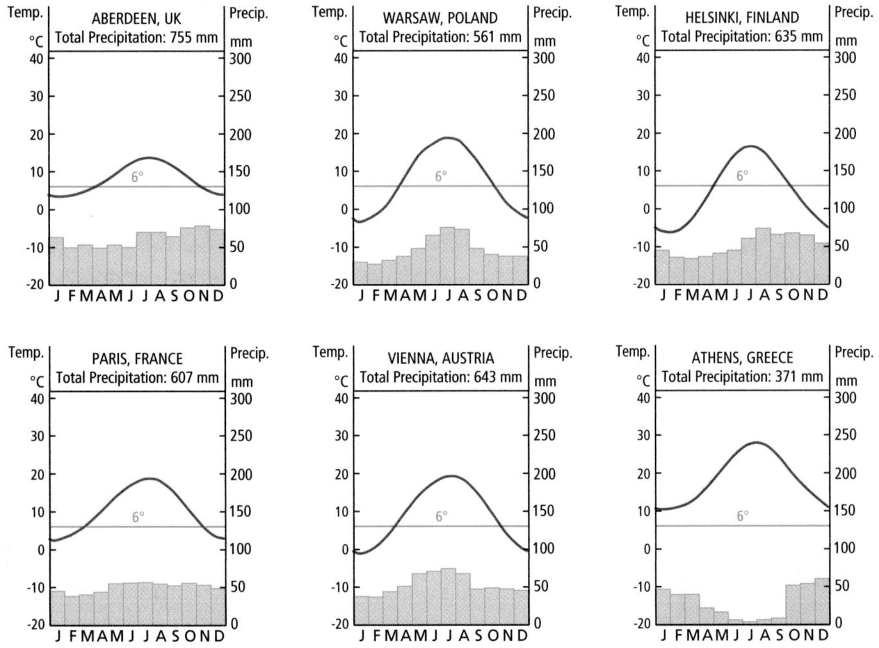

Physically and economically, this region is tied to the water. Europeans are never more than 600 km from a sea or ocean. Major rivers – Rhine, Rhône, Seine – also add to the region's connection to water. The westerly flow of air from the Atlantic and the presence of the Gulf Stream influence the climate of the area. Land use reflects the high density of population. Large areas of cropland extend from the United Kingdom and northern France, east to the Ukraine, and wherever possible, agriculture is highly developed and intense.

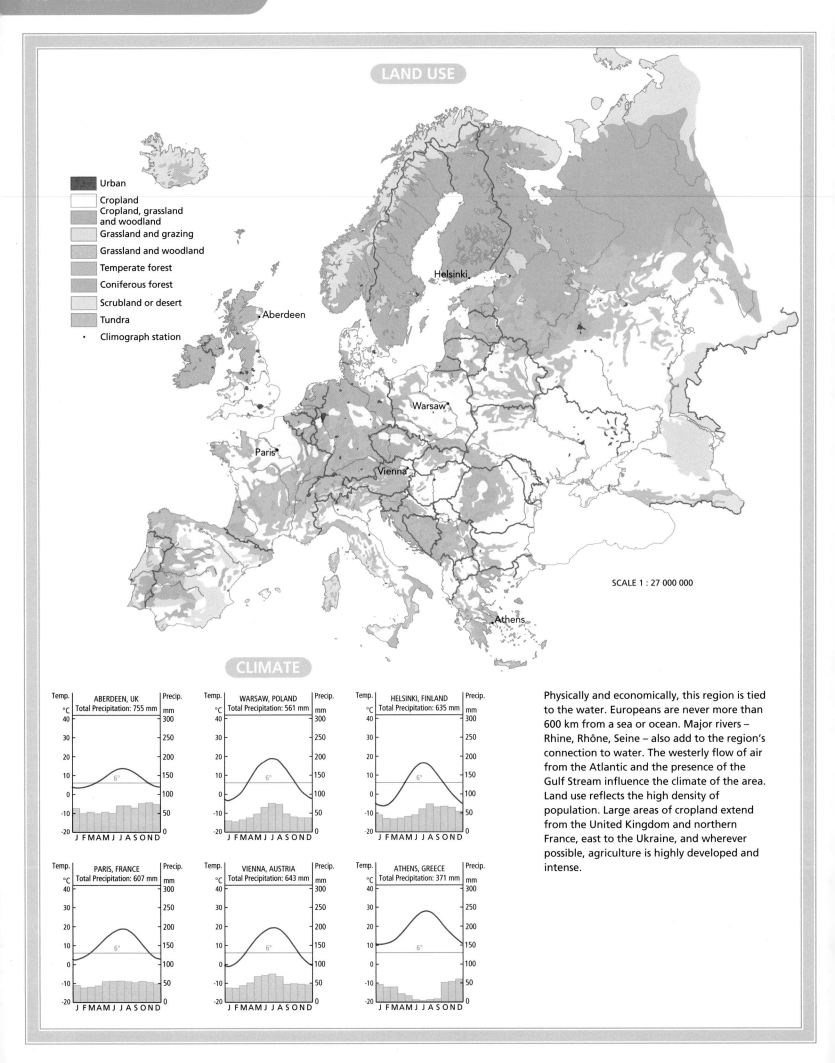

TOURISM

Top Destinations by Expenditure, 2000

Country	Income from tourism: Millions, US$	Income from tourism: Percent of GDP	Country	Income from tourism: Millions, US$	Income from tourism: Percent of GDP
Spain	31 000	5.5	Denmark	4 025	2.5
France	29 900	2.3	Ireland	3 571	3.8
Italy	27 439	2.5	Hungary	3 424	7.5
United Kingdom	19 544	1.4	Czech. Republic	2 869	5.6
Germany	17 812	0.9	Croatia	2 758	14.5
Austria	11 440	6.0	Norway	* 2 229	1.4
Greece	9 221	8.2	Ukraine	* 2 124	6.7
Russian Fed.	* 7 510	3.9	Finland	1 401	1.1
Switzerland	7 303	3.0	Bulgaria	1 074	8.9
Belgium	* 7 039	2.8	Slovenia	957	5.3
Netherlands	6 951	1.9	Malta	650	18.2
Poland	6 100	3.9	Estonia	505	10.2
Portugal	5 206	4.9	Slovakia	432	2.2
Sweden	4 107	1.8	Georgia	* 400	14.2

* 1999 figures

Top Destinations by Visitors, 2000

Country	Visitors (thousands)	Country	Visitors (thousands)
France	75 500	Croatia	5 831
Spain	48 201	Czech. Republic	5 700
Italy	41 182	Norway	* 4 481
United Kingdom	25 191	Ukraine	* 4 232
Russian Fed.	21 169	Romania	3 274
Germany	18 983	Andorra	2 949
Austria	17 982	Bulgaria	2 785
Poland	17 400	Sweden	2 746
Greece	12 500	Finland	2 700
Portugal	12 037	Cyprus	2 686
Switzerland	11 400	Denmark	2 088
Netherlands	10 200	Lithuania	1 226
Ireland	6 728	Malta	1 216
Belgium	6 457	Estonia	1 100

* 1999 figures

ECONOMY

WORLD GDP, 2000

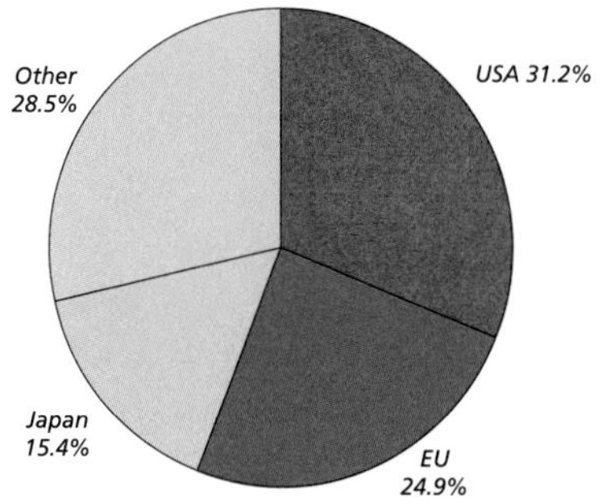

Total World GDP : US$ 31.5 trillion

Europe was the first major world region to construct a modern economy, consisting of a strong base in commercial agriculture and advanced industrial development. During the latter half of the twentieth century, two organizations – the European Economic Community (EEC) and the European Free Trade Association (EFTA) – started the process of economic integration that allowed the region to develop into an economic powerhouse. Average per capita incomes are among the world's highest. The European Union (EU) allows the free flow of people, goods, and services across its members' borders, and continues to incorporate more partner countries. The Council of Ministers, which meets in Brussels, is the EU's decision-making body. The European Court of Justice, located in Luxembourg, rules on disputes among member nations. A common currency, the Euro, has been adopted to replace the local currency in most of the Union nations.

UNITED KINGDOM

Trade, 2001

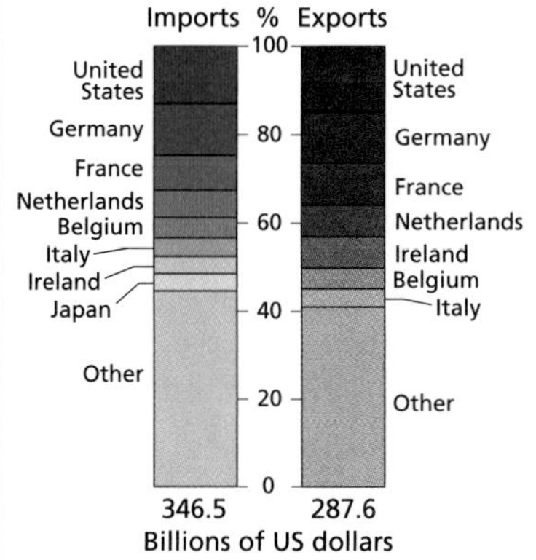

GDP by sector, 2000

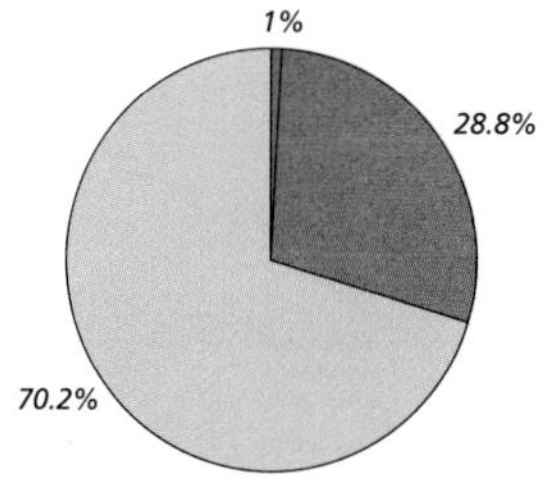

Total : US$ 1 414.6 billion

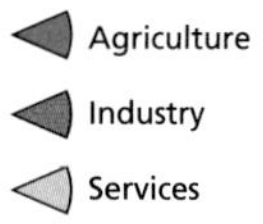

POLAND

Trade, 2001

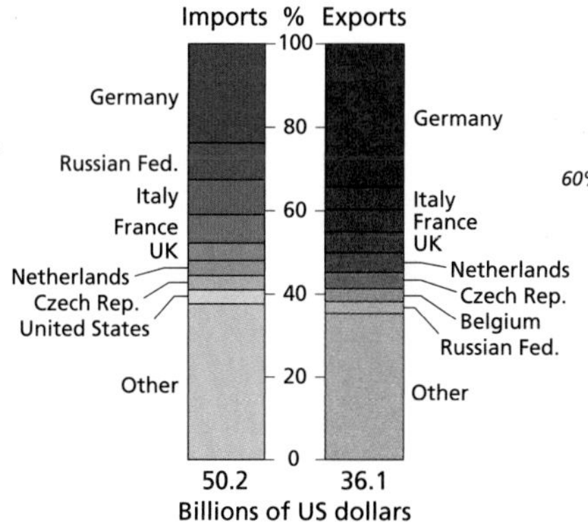

GDP by sector, 2000

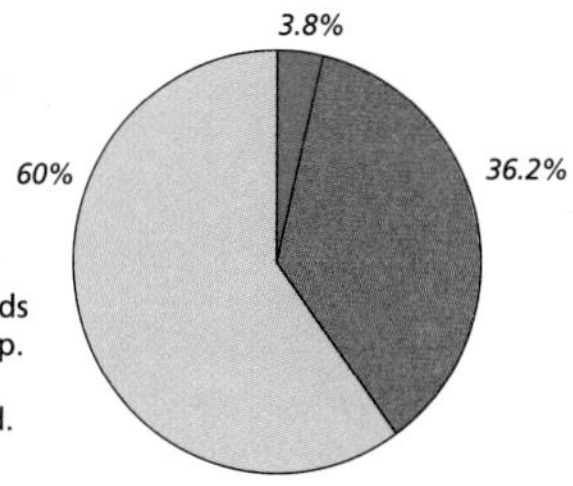

Total : US$ 157.7 billion

SPAIN

Trade, 2001

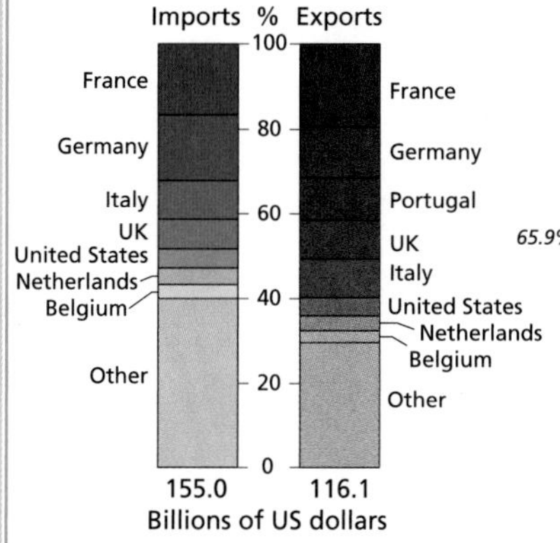

GDP by sector, 2000

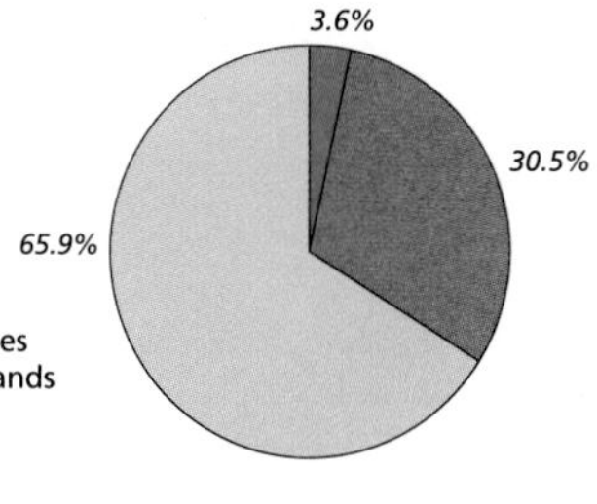

Total : US$ 558.6 billion

GERMANY

Trade, 2001

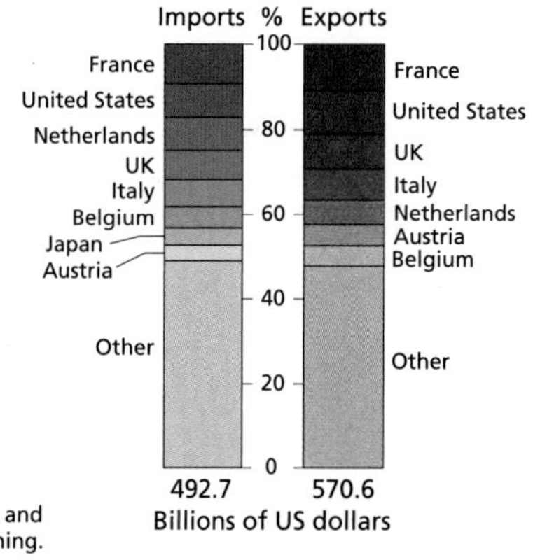

GDP by sector, 2000

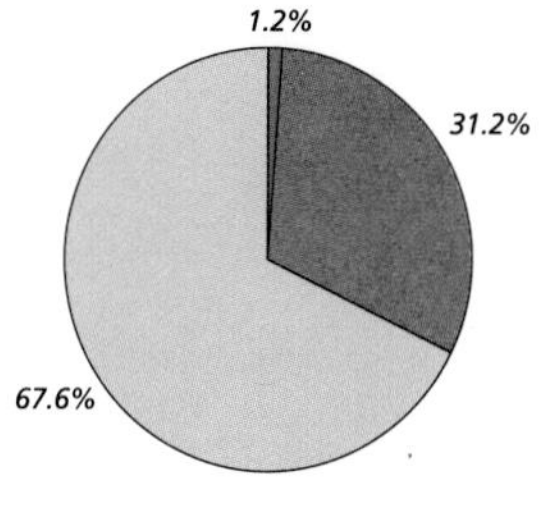

Total : US$ 1 873 billion

*The category 'Agriculture' includes forestry and fishing, the category 'Industry' includes mining.

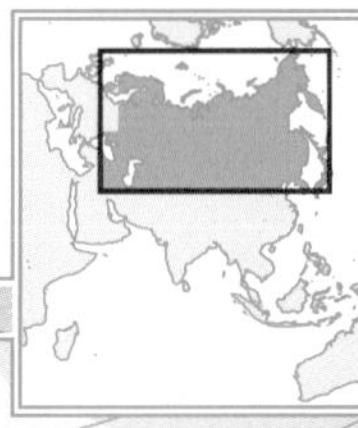

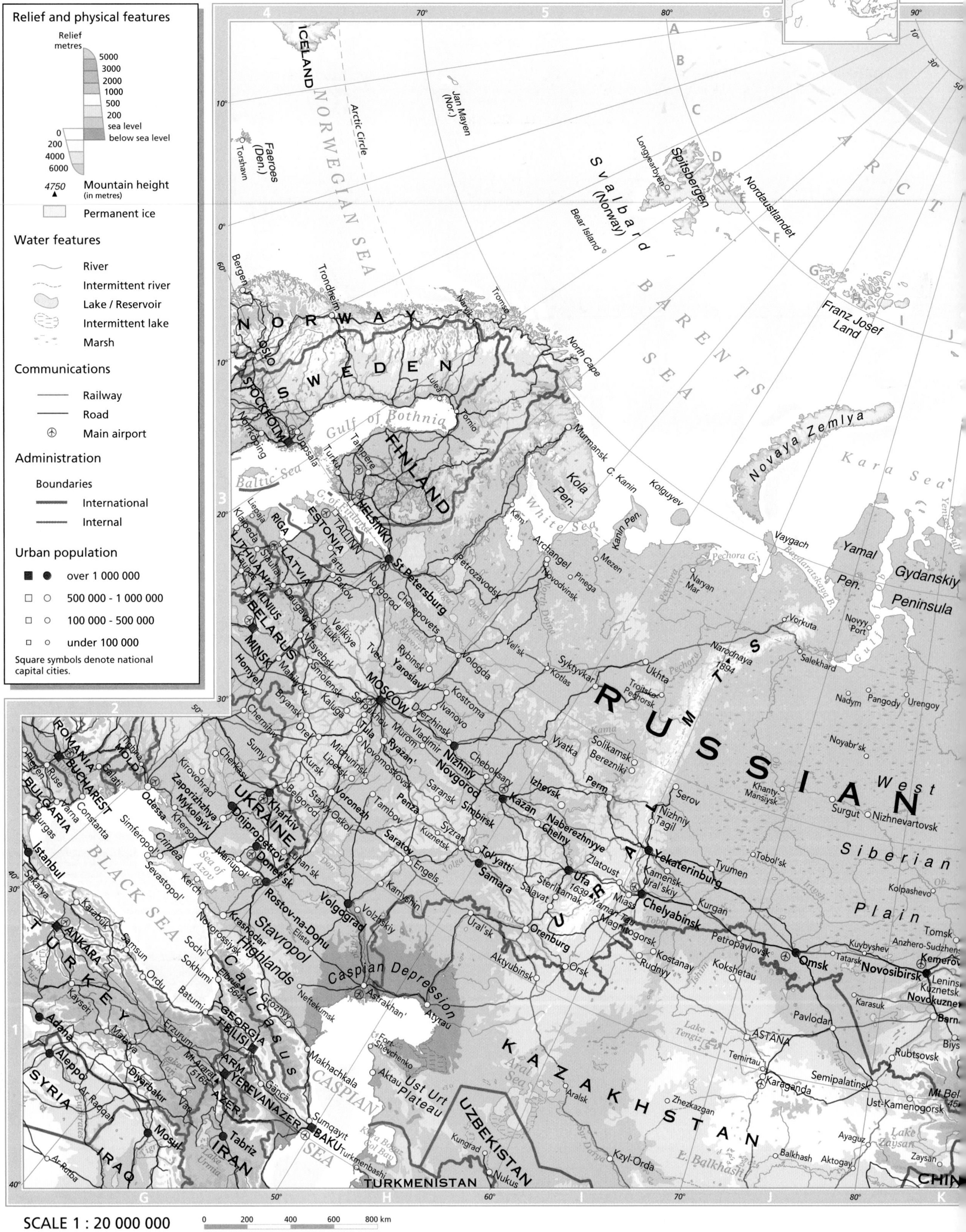
Relief and physical features
Relief metres
5000
3000
2000
1000
500
200
sea level
below sea level
0
200
4000
6000
4750 Mountain height (in metres)
Permanent ice
Water features
River
Intermittent river
Lake / Reservoir
Intermittent lake
Marsh
Communications
Railway
Road
Main airport
Administration
Boundaries
International
Internal
Urban population
over 1 000 000
500 000 - 1 000 000
100 000 - 500 000
under 100 000
Square symbols denote national capital cities.
ICELAND
NORWEGIAN SEA
Arctic Circle
Jan Mayen (Nor.)
Faeroes (Den.)
Torshavn
Svalbard (Norway)
Spitsbergen
Longyearbyen
Nordaustlandet
Bear Island
BARENTS SEA
ARCTIC
Franz Josef Land
North Cape
Tromsø
Narvik
Trondheim
Bergen
NORWAY
Oslo
SWEDEN
STOCKHOLM
Uppsala
Norrköping
Luleå
Tornio
Gulf of Bothnia
Baltic Sea
FINLAND
Turku
Tampere
HELSINKI
G. of Finland
TALLINN
ESTONIA
Tartu
RIGA
LATVIA
Liepaja
Klaipeda
Šiauliai
Kaunas
LITHUANIA
VILNIUS
Daugavpils
BELARUS
MINSK
Homyel'
Mahilyow
Vitsyebsk
Murmansk
Kola Pen.
White Sea
Kem'
C. Kanin
Kanin Pen.
Kolguyev
Novaya Zemlya
Kara Sea
Vaygach
Pechora G.
Yamal Pen.
Gydanskiy Peninsula
Baydaratskaya B.
Novyy Port
Archangel
Mezen
Pinega
Novodvinsk
Naryan Mar
Petrozavodsk
St Petersburg
Pskov
Novgorod
Cherepovets
Velikiye Luki
Smolensk
Tver'
Rybinsk
Yaroslavl'
Vologda
Vel'sk
Kotlas
Syktyvkar
Ukhta
Vorkuta
Salekhard
Narodnaya 1894
Troitsko-Pechorsk
URAL MTS
RUSSIAN
MOSCOW
Kaluga
Bryansk
Orel
Tula
Serpukhov
Dzerzhinsk
Ivanovo
Kostroma
Vladimir
Murom
Ryazan'
Novomoskovsk
Nizhniy Novgorod
Cheboksary
Kazan
Izhevsk
Vyatka
Solikamsk
Berezniki
Perm
Serov
Nizhniy Tagil
Yekaterinburg
Tyumen
Tobol'sk
Kamensk-Ural'skiy
Chelyabinsk
Miass
Zlatoust
Ufa
Yamantau 1639
Sterlitamak
Salavat
Magnitogorsk
Orenburg
Orsk
Naberezhnyye Chelny
Simbirsk
Syzran'
Tol'yatti
Samara
Saransk
Penza
Kuznetsk
Saratov
Engels
Kamyshin
Volzhskiy
Volgograd
Tambov
Michurinsk
Lipetsk
Voronezh
Staryy Oskol
Kursk
Belgorod
Kharkiv
Sumy
Chernihiv
Cherkasy
Kirovohrad
UKRAINE
Dnipropetrovs'k
Donets'k
Luhans'k
Zaporizhzhya
Mykolayiv
Kherson
Odessa
Mariupol'
Rostov-na-Donu
Sea of Azov
Kerch
Crimea
Simferopol'
Sevastopol'
MOLD.
ROMANIA
BUCHAREST
Galati
Constanta
Ruse
Pleven
BULGARIA
Varna
Burgas
İstanbul
Sakarya
Karabük
ANKARA
TURKEY
Samsun
Ordu
Kayseri
Malatya
Erzurum
Diyarbakır
Adana
Aleppo
SYRIA
Ar Raqqah
Mosul
IRAQ
Ar Rutba
Van
Mt Ararat 5165
ARM.
YEREVAN
AZER.
Gäncä
Tabriz
IRAN
Lake Urmia
GEORGIA
TBILISI
Batumi
Sokhumi
Sochi
Novorossiysk
Krasnodar
Stavropol
Stavropol Highlands
Elbrus 5642
Caucasus
Groznyy
Elista
Neftekumsk
Makhachkala
Sumqayit
BAKU
CASPIAN SEA
Caspian Depression
Astrakhan'
Atyrau
Fort Shevchenko
Aktau
Ust Urt Plateau
Kara Bogaz Gol Bay
Turkmenbashi
TURKMENISTAN
UZBEKISTAN
Kungrad
Nukus
Aral Sea
Aralsk
KAZAKHSTAN
Ural'sk
Aktyubinsk
Kostanay
Rudnyy
Kokshetau
Petropavlovsk
Omsk
ASTANA
Lake Tengiz
Temirtau
Karaganda
Zhezkazgan
Kzyl-Orda
Syr Darya
L. Balkhash
Balkhash
Aktogay
Ayaguz
Lake Zaysan
Zaysan
Ust-Kamenogorsk
Semipalatinsk
Rubtsovsk
Pavlodar
Mt Belukha 4506
Barnaul
Biysk
Novokuznetsk
Leninsk-Kuznetskiy
Kemerovo
Novosibirsk
Tatarsk
Kuybyshev
Karasuk
Anzhero-Sudzhensk
Tomsk
Kolpashevo
West Siberian Plain
Surgut
Nizhnevartovsk
Khanty-Mansiysk
Noyabr'sk
Nadym
Pangody
Urengoy
BLACK SEA
CHINA
Volga
Don
Ural
Ob
Irtysh
Ishim
Tobol
Kama
Pechora
Dvina
Onega
Ladoga
Rybinsk Reservoir
Amu Darya
Euphrates
Tigris
10°
20°
30°
40°
50°
60°
70°
80°
90°
0°
A
B
C
D
E
F
G
H
I
J
K
1
2
3
4
5
6

SCALE 1 : 20 000 000

0 200 400 600 800 km

ARCTIC OCEAN
Wrangel I.
Chukchi Sea
Point Hope
Bering Strait
Seward Pen.
U.S.A.
St Lawrence I.
Nunivak
Uelen
Chuckchi Pen.
Iul'tin
Uel'kal'
Gulf of Anadyr
Ugol'nyye Kopi
Anadyr
St Matthew I.
BERING SEA
De Longa Str.
East Siberian Sea
Pevek
New Siberia Islands
Novaya Sibir'
Kotel'nyy
Bolshoi Lyakhovskiy
Komsomolets
October Revolution
Bolshevik
Severnaya Zemlya
C. Chelyuskin
Laptev Sea
Taymyr Peninsula
Byrranga Mts
Lake Taymyr
Nordvik
Sagastyr
G. of Tona
Nizhneyansk
Kazachye
Deputatskiy
Ambarchik
Cherskiy
Bilibino
Omolon
Srednekolymsk
Dzhigudzhak
Koryak Range
Kamenskoye
Gizhiga
Gizhiga Gulf
Kolyma Range
Kolyma
Mt Pobeda 3147
Cherskogo Range
Ust'-Nera
Susuman
Yagodnoye
Palatka
Magadan
Palana
Kamchatka Peninsula
Klyuchevskaya Sopka 4750
Ust-Kamchatsk
Petropavlovsk-Kamchatskiy
Tiksi
Bulun
Ust-Olenek
Saskylakh
Khatanga
Verkhoyansk
Verkhoyansk Range
Olenek
Noril'sk
Udachnyy
Vilyuy
Vilyuysk
Yakutsk
Churapcha
Ust-Maya
Okhotsk
SEA OF OKHOTSK
Severo-Kurilsk
Kuril Islands
Dzhugdzhur Range
Ayan
Nelkan
Shantar Islands
Okha
Sakhalin
Nikolayevsk-na-Amure
Aleksandrovsk-Sakhalinskiy
Poronaysk
Uglegorsk
Yuzhno-Sakhalinsk
Kholmsk
Tatar Strait
Administered by Rus. Fed. Claimed by Japan
CENTRAL SIBERIAN PLATEAU
FEDERATION
Nyurba
Tura
Lower Tunguska
Mirnyy
Lensk
Olekminsk
Lena
Aldan
Stanovoy Range
Bodaybo
Khani
Neryungri
Tynda
Stony Tunguska
Ust-Ilimsk
Yeniseysk
Lesosibirsk
Angara
Ust-Kut
Bratsk
Severobaykal'sk
Skovorodino
Amur
Svobodnyy
Blagoveshchensk
Komsomolsk-na-Amure
Amursk
Vanino
Birobidzhan
Khabarovsk
Sikhote-Alin Range
Wakkanai
Asahikawa
Asahi-dake 2290
Hokkaido
Sapporo
Hakodate
Aomori
Hachinohe
Akita
Sendai
Niigata
Honshu
JAPAN
Nagoya
Kobe
Osaka
Kansk
Krasnoyarsk
Nizhneudinsk
Lake Baikal
Yablonovyy Range
Chita
Karymskoye
Krasnokamensk
Abakan
Western Sayan
Eastern Sayan
Usol'ye-Sibirskoye
Angarsk
Irkutsk
Ulan-Ude
Kyzyl
Yenisey
Hövsgöl Nuur
Selenga
Uvs Nuur
Altai Mts
ULAN BATOR
MONGOLIA
Bayanhongor
Hulun Nur
Da Hinggan Ling
Bei'an
Yichun
Qiqihar
Harbin
Mudanjiang
Jilin
Changchun
CHINA
Lesozavodsk
Ussuriysk
Vladivostok
Nakhodka
Chongjin
NORTH KOREA
Fushun
Shenyang
Anshan
Sea of Japan

Conic Equidistant projection

LAND USE

Because of its size, no region can match the range of land uses and climatic conditions found in Northern Eurasia, from the polar ice and cold deserts of Siberia to the hot deserts of Turkmenistan. The vast nature of the region is also emphasized in its longitudinal extent: from 20°E to 170°W – almost half the circumference of the earth.

The Russian Federation continues to dominate the region, although the former Soviet Union collapsed in the late 1980s. In recent years, the former Soviet states have had difficulty reaching an appropriate balance in achieving economic development, political stability, human rights and environmental goals.

CLIMATE

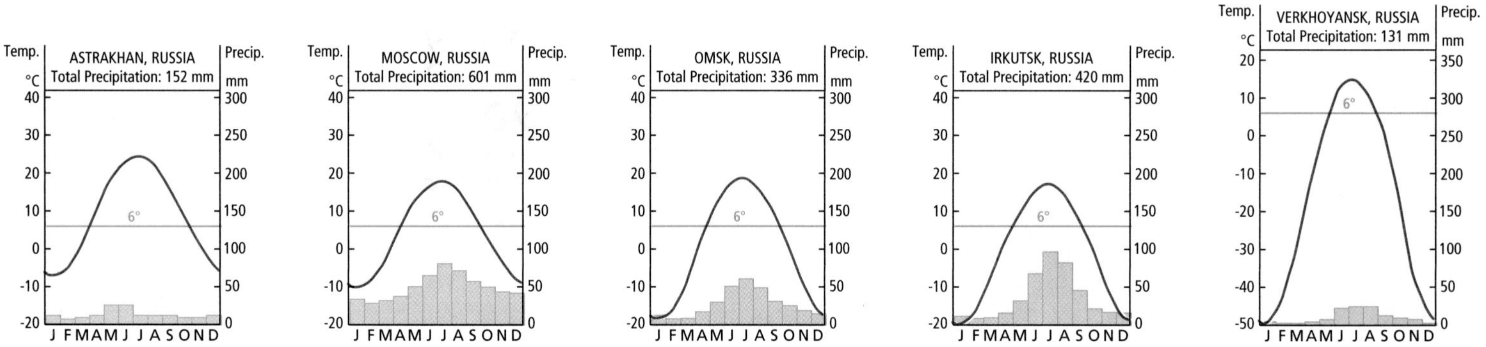

LANGUAGE

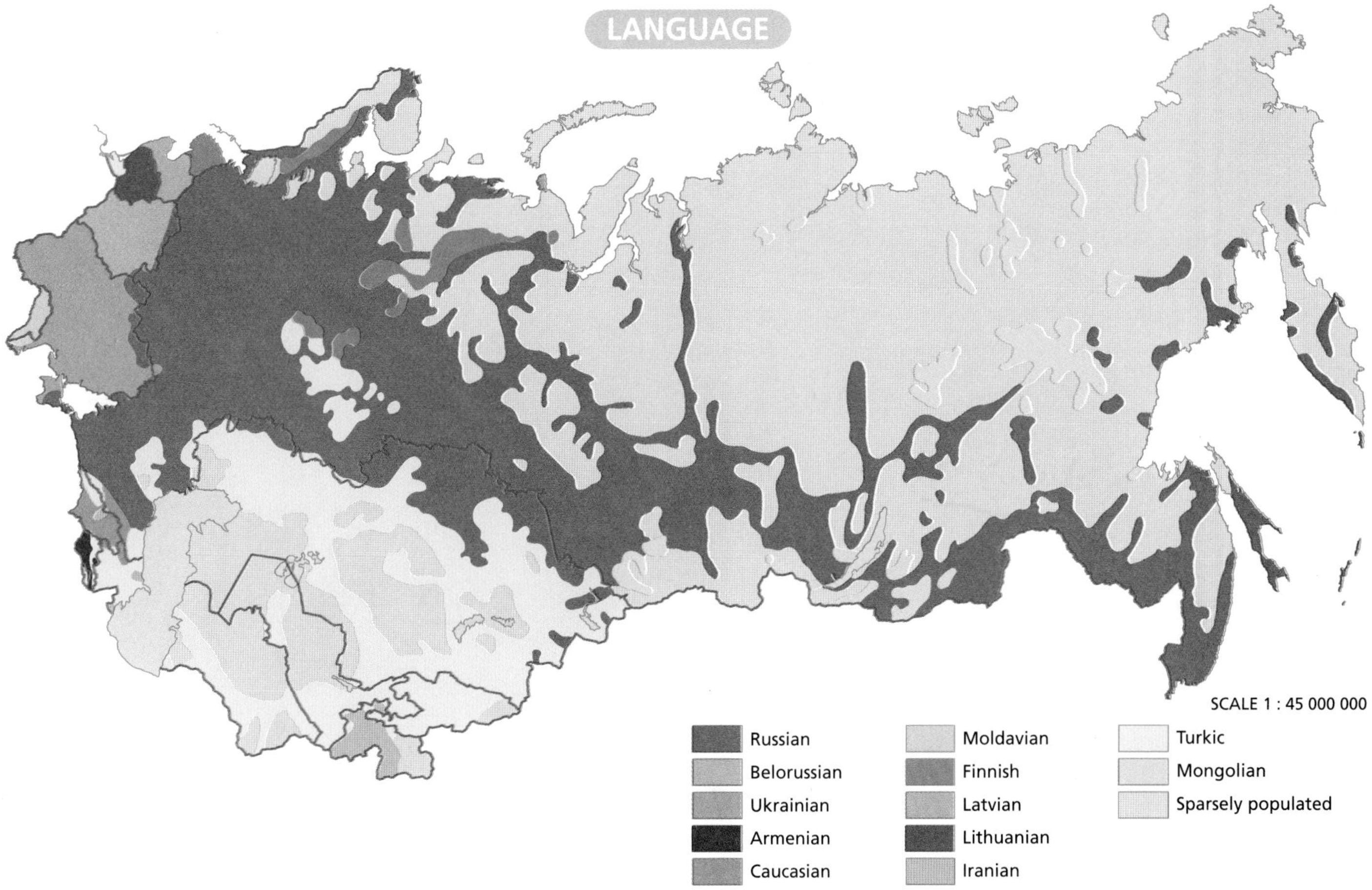

ECONOMY

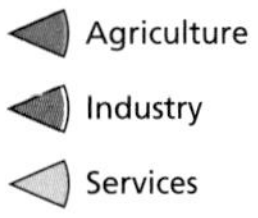

LATVIA

Trade, 2001

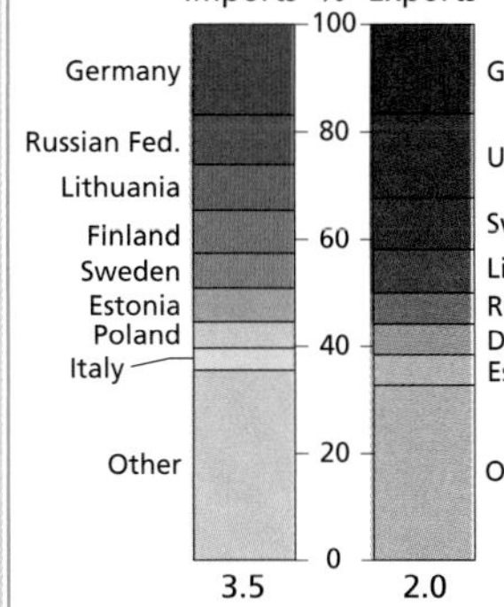

GDP by sector, 2000

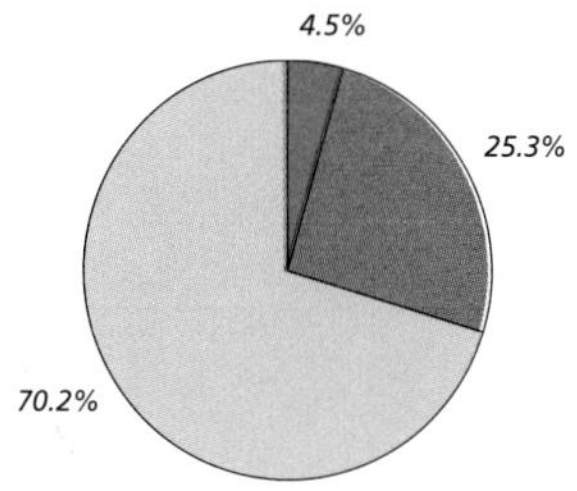

Total : US$ 7.2 billion

UKRAINE

Trade, 2000

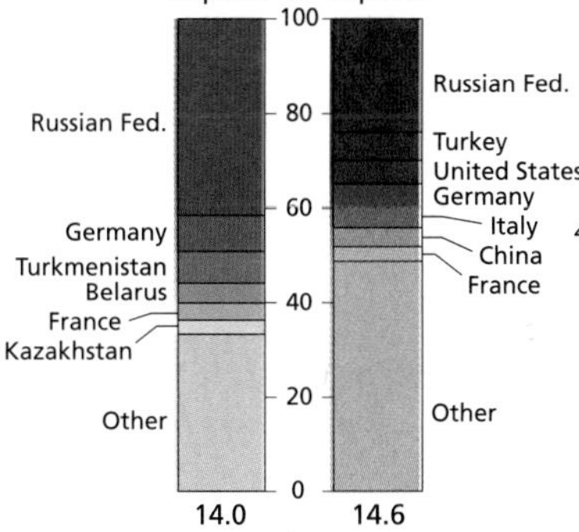

GDP by sector, 2000

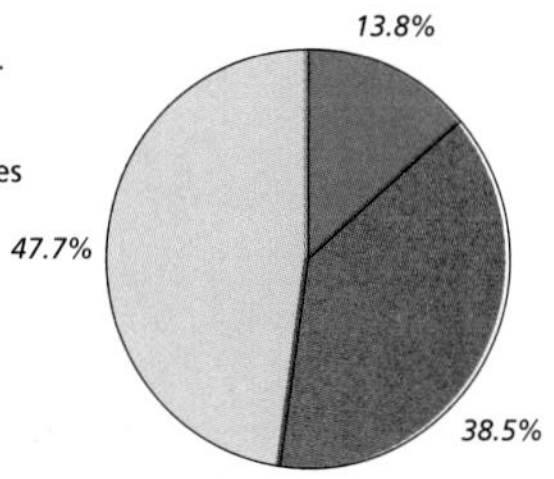

Total : US$ 31.8 billion

RUSSIAN FEDERATION

Trade, 2001

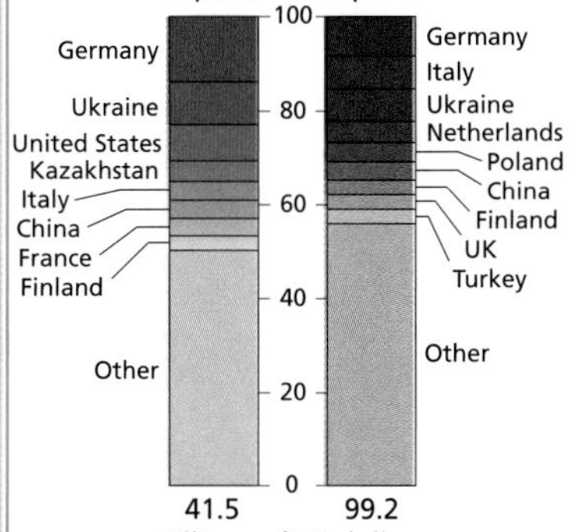

GDP by sector, 2000

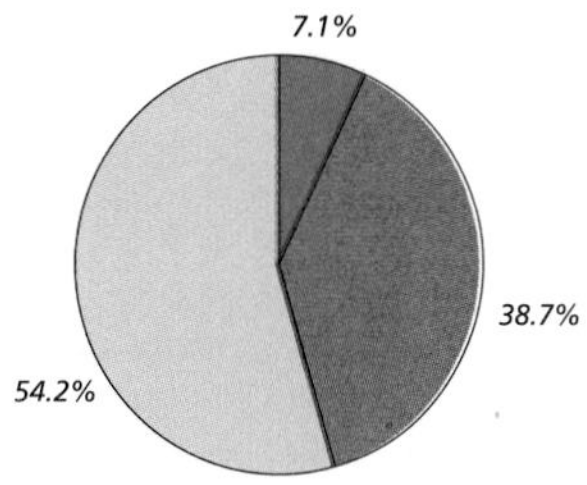

Total : US$ 251.1 billion

KAZAKHSTAN

Trade, 2000

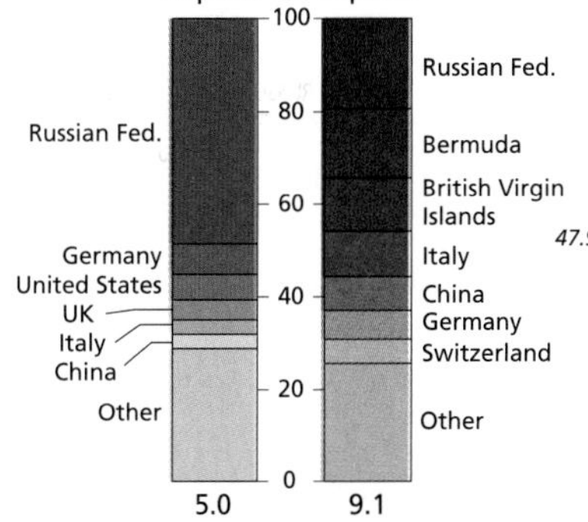

GDP by sector, 2000

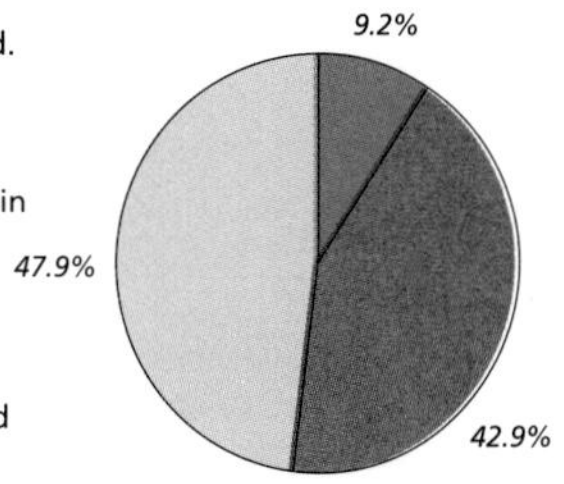

Total : US$ 18.2 billion

*The category 'Agriculture' includes forestry and fishing, the category 'Industry' includes mining.

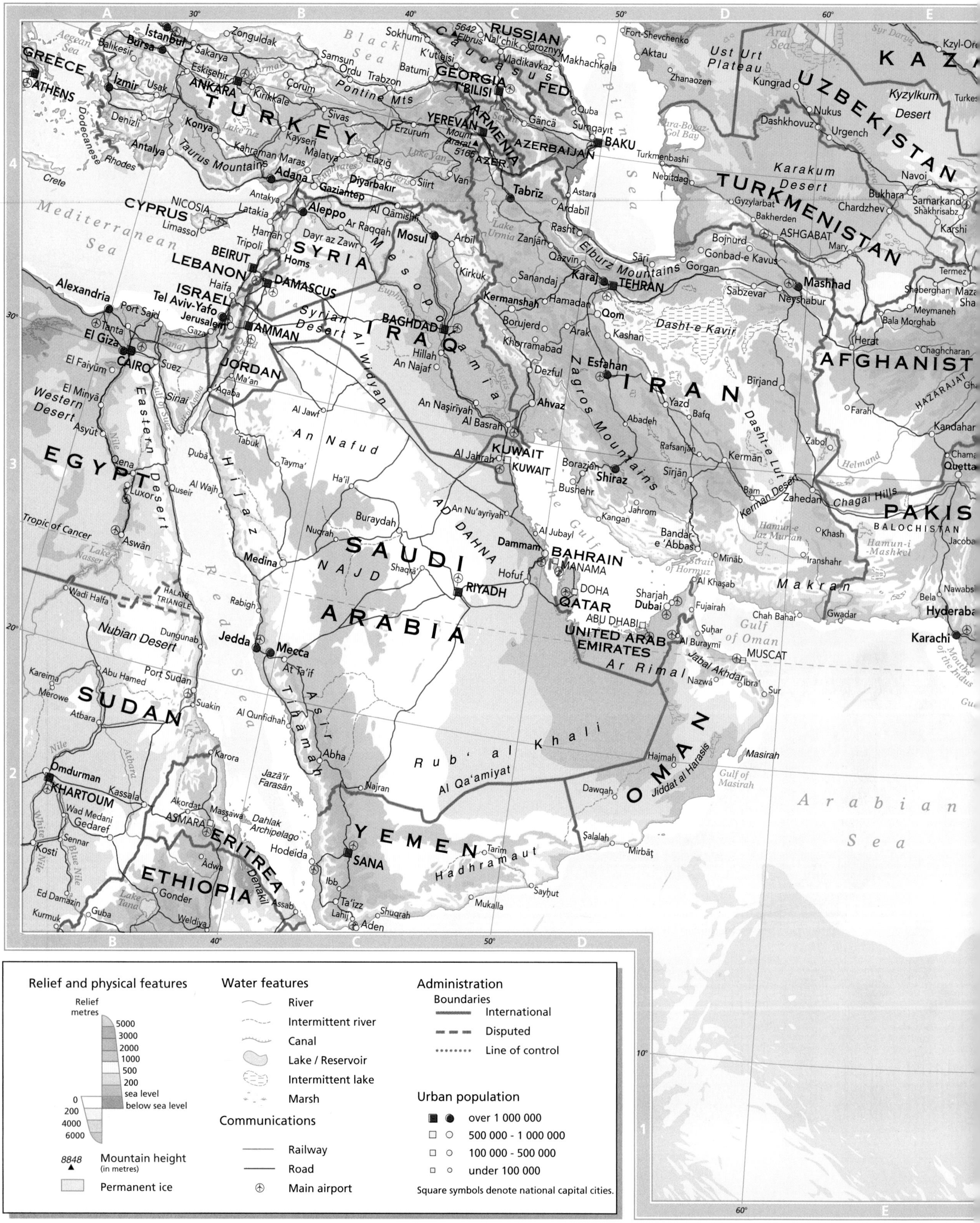

TURKEY
SYRIA
LEBANON
ISRAEL
JORDAN
IRAQ
IRAN
KUWAIT
SAUDI ARABIA
BAHRAIN
QATAR
UNITED ARAB EMIRATES
OMAN
YEMEN
EGYPT
SUDAN
ERITREA
ETHIOPIA
CYPRUS
GREECE
GEORGIA
ARMENIA
AZERBAIJAN
AZER.
RUSSIAN FED.
TURKMENISTAN
UZBEKISTAN
AFGHANISTAN
PAKIS
KAZ
HALAIB TRIANGLE
BALOCHISTAN
HAZARAJAT
ATHENS
ANKARA
NICOSIA
BEIRUT
DAMASCUS
AMMAN
Jerusalem
BAGHDAD
TEHRAN
KUWAIT
RIYADH
MANAMA
DOHA
ABU DHABI
MUSCAT
SANA
ASMARA
KHARTOUM
CAIRO
T'BILISI
YEREVAN
BAKU
ASHGABAT
İstanbul
Bursa
İzmir
Balikesir
Sakarya
Zonguldak
Eskişehir
Uşak
Kirikkale
Çorum
Samsun
Ordu
Trabzon
Sivas
Konya
Kayseri
Malatya
Erzurum
Elaziğ
Diyarbakir
Siirt
Van
Antalya
Adana
Gaziantep
Antakya
Kahraman Maraş
Denizli
Aleppo
Latakia
Hamah
Homs
Tripoli
Ar Raqqah
Dayr az Zawr
Al Qāmishli
Mosul
Arbīl
Kirkuk
Haifa
Tel Aviv-Yafo
Gaza
Limassol
Alexandria
Port Said
Tanta
El Giza
Suez
El Faiyûm
El Minyâ
Asyût
Qena
Luxor
Aswân
Quseir
Sinai
Aqaba
Ma'an
Tabuk
Al Jawf
Tayma'
Ḑubā
Al Wajh
Medina
Ha'il
Buraydah
Nuqrah
Shaqrā'
Al Jahrah
An Nu'ayrīyah
Al Jubayl
Dammam
Hofuf
Rabigh
Jedda
Mecca
At Ta'if
Al Qunfidhah
Abha
Najran
Jazā'ir Farasān
Hodeida
Ibb
Ta'izz
Lahij
Aden
Shuqrah
Mukalla
Sayḩut
Tarīm
Şalalah
Mirbāţ
Dawqah
Hajmah
Masirah
Sur
Ibra'
Nazwá
Al Buraymī
Şuḩar
Fujairah
Sharjah
Dubai
Al Khaşab
Bandar-e 'Abbās
Minab
Kangan
Jahrom
Bushehr
Borazjān
Shiraz
Sīrjān
Kermān
Rafsanjān
Abadeh
Yazd
Bafq
Esfahan
Kashan
Qom
Arak
Hamadan
Kermanshah
Borujerd
Khorramabad
Dezful
Ahvaz
Al Basrah
An Naşirīyah
An Najaf
Hillah
Sanandaj
Zanjān
Qazvīn
Karaj
Rasht
Ardabīl
Tabriz
Astara
Sārī
Gorgan
Bojnurd
Gonbad-e Kavus
Mashhad
Neyshabur
Sabzevar
Bīrjand
Zabol
Zahedan
Khash
Iranshahr
Chah Bahar
Gwadar
Karachi
Hyderabad
Nawabshah
Bela
Jacobabad
Quetta
Chaman
Kandahar
Farah
Herat
Chaghcharan
Bala Morghab
Meymaneh
Sheberghan
Mazar
Termez
Karshi
Shakhrisabz
Samarkand
Bukhara
Navoi
Chardzhev
Mary
Bakherden
Gyzylarbat
Nebitdag
Turkmenbashi
Urgench
Nukus
Dashkhovuz
Kungrad
Zhanaozen
Aktau
Fort-Shevchenko
Kzyl-Orda
Makhachkala
Quba
Sumqayıt
Gäncä
Vladikavkaz
Groznyy
Nal'chik
Sokhumi
K'ut'aisi
Batumi
Elbrus
5642
Mount Ararat
5165
Wadi Halfa
Dungunab
Port Sudan
Suakin
Abu Hamed
Kareima
Merowe
Atbara
Omdurman
Kassala
Wad Medani
Gedaref
Sennar
Kosti
Ed Damazin
Kurmuk
Karora
Akordat
Massawa
Adwa
Gonder
Guba
Weldiya
Assab
Denakil
Dahlak Archipelago
Black Sea
Caspian Sea
Aral Sea
Kara-Bogaz-Gol Bay
Aegean Sea
Mediterranean Sea
Red Sea
The Gulf
Gulf of Oman
Arabian Sea
Gulf of Masirah
Strait of Hormuz
Gulf of Suez
Gulf of Aqaba
Lake Tuz
Lake Van
Lake Urmia
Lake Nasser
Lake Tana
Dead Sea
Suez Canal
Euphrates
Tigris
Nile
Atbara
Blue Nile
White Nile
Helmand
Amu Darya
Syr Darya
Hamun-e Jaz Murian
Hamun-i-Mashkel
Mouths of the Indus
Caucasus
Pontine Mts
Taurus Mountains
Elburz Mountains
Zagros Mountains
Chagai Hills
Jabal Akhdar
Jiddat al Harasis
Ust Urt Plateau
Karakum Desert
Kyzylkum Desert
Dasht-e Kavir
Dasht-e Lut
Kerman Desert
Makran
Mesopotamia
Syrian Desert
Al Widyan
An Nafud
Ad Dahna
Najd
Hijaz
Asir
Tihāmah
Rub' al Khali
Ar Rimal
Al Qa'amiyat
Hadhramaut
Eastern Desert
Western Desert
Nubian Desert
Tropic of Cancer
Crete
Rhodes
Dodecanese
A
B
C
D
E
1
2
3
4
30°
40°
50°
60°
20°
10°
Relief and physical features
Relief metres
5000
3000
2000
1000
500
200
sea level
below sea level
0
200
4000
6000
8848
Mountain height (in metres)
Permanent ice
Water features
River
Intermittent river
Canal
Lake / Reservoir
Intermittent lake
Marsh
Communications
Railway
Road
Main airport
Administration
Boundaries
International
Disputed
Line of control
Urban population
over 1 000 000
500 000 - 1 000 000
100 000 - 500 000
under 100 000
Square symbols denote national capital cities.

SCALE 1 : 17 500 000

0 200 400 600 800 km

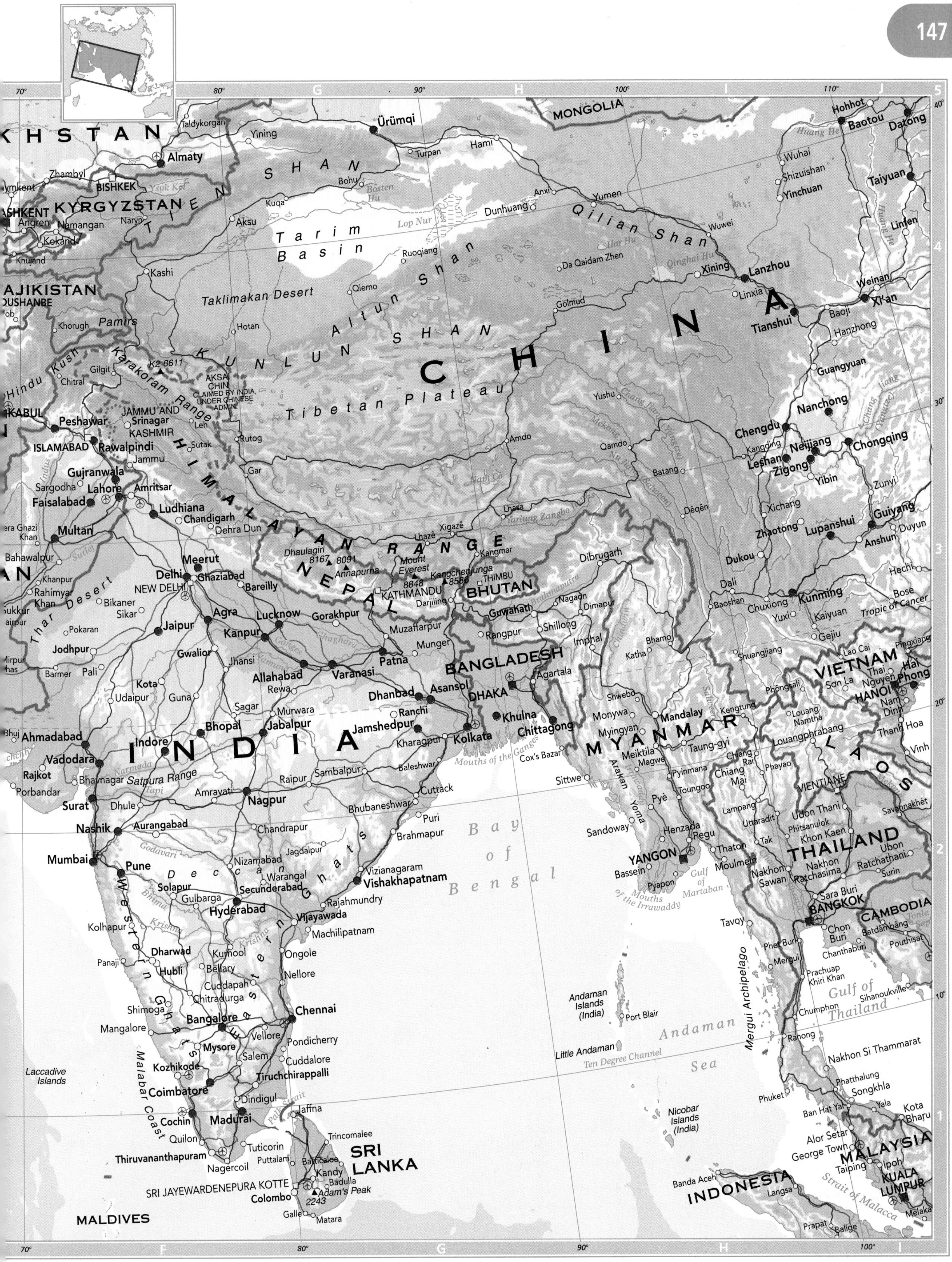
MONGOLIA
KAZAKHSTAN
KYRGYZSTAN
TAJIKISTAN
DUSHANBE
BISHKEK
TASHKENT
KABUL
ISLAMABAD
CHINA
INDIA
NEPAL
KATHMANDU
BHUTAN
THIMBU
BANGLADESH
DHAKA
MYANMAR
YANGON
THAILAND
BANGKOK
LAOS
VIENTIANE
VIETNAM
HANOI
CAMBODIA
MALAYSIA
KUALA LUMPUR
INDONESIA
SRI LANKA
SRI JAYEWARDENEPURA KOTTE
MALDIVES
NEW DELHI
T I E N   S H A N
Tarim Basin
Taklimakan Desert
Lop Nur
Bosten Hu
Ysyk Kol
Pamirs
Hindu Kush
Karakoram Range
K2 8611
AKSAI CHIN CLAIMED BY INDIA, UNDER CHINESE ADMIN.
JAMMU AND KASHMIR
K U N L U N   S H A N
Altun Shan
Qilian Shan
Tibetan Plateau
Qinghai Hu
Har Hu
Nam Co
Yarlung Zangbo Jiang
H I M A L A Y A N   R A N G E
Dhaulagiri 8167
8091
Annapurna
Mount Everest 8848
Kangchenjunga 8586
Thar Desert
Satpura Range
Deccan
Western Ghats
Eastern Ghats
Malabar Coast
Laccadive Islands
Palk Strait
Adam's Peak 2243
Bay of Bengal
Mouths of the Ganges
Mouths of the Irrawaddy
Gulf of Martaban
Andaman Islands (India)
Little Andaman
Ten Degree Channel
Nicobar Islands (India)
Andaman Sea
Mergui Archipelago
Gulf of Thailand
Strait of Malacca
Arakan Yoma
Tropic of Cancer
Indus
Sutlej
Ganges
Yamuna
Ghaghara
Narmada
Tapi
Godavari
Krishna
Bhima
Brahmaputra
Chindwin
Irrawaddy
Salween
Mekong
Nu Jiang (Salween)
Chang Jiang (Yangtze)
Huang He
Tonle Sap
Ürümqi
Yining
Almaty
Taldykorgan
Zhambyl
Shymkent
Angren
Namangan
Kokand
Khujand
Naryn
Turpan
Hami
Bohu
Kuqa
Aksu
Kashi
Khorugh
Ruoqiang
Qiemo
Hotan
Gilgit
Chitral
Peshawar
Srinagar
Leh
Rawalpindi
Sutak
Rutog
Jammu
Gujranwala
Sargodha
Lahore
Amritsar
Faisalabad
Ludhiana
Chandigarh
Dehra Dun
Dera Ghazi Khan
Multan
Bahawalpur
Khanpur
Rahimyar Khan
Sukkur
Meerut
Delhi
Ghaziabad
Bareilly
Bikaner
Sikar
Jaipur
Agra
Lucknow
Gorakhpur
Kanpur
Pokaran
Jodhpur
Gwalior
Jhansi
Barmer
Pali
Allahabad
Varanasi
Patna
Rewa
Kota
Udaipur
Guna
Sagar
Murwara
Jabalpur
Bhopal
Indore
Ahmadabad
Vadodara
Rajkot
Bhavnagar
Porbandar
Surat
Dhule
Amravati
Nagpur
Raipur
Sambalpur
Nashik
Aurangabad
Chandrapur
Mumbai
Pune
Nizamabad
Warangal
Solapur
Gulbarga
Secunderabad
Hyderabad
Kolhapur
Vijayawada
Machilipatnam
Rajahmundry
Visakhapatnam
Vizianagaram
Jagdalpur
Brahmapur
Puri
Bhubaneshwar
Cuttack
Baleshwar
Dharwad
Hubli
Panaji
Kurnool
Bellary
Ongole
Nellore
Cuddapah
Chitradurga
Shimoga
Mangalore
Bangalore
Chennai
Vellore
Mysore
Pondicherry
Salem
Cuddalore
Kozhikode
Tiruchchirappalli
Coimbatore
Dindigul
Cochin
Madurai
Quilon
Tuticorin
Thiruvananthapuram
Nagercoil
Jaffna
Trincomalee
Puttalam
Batticaloa
Kandy
Badulla
Colombo
Galle
Matara
Muzaffarpur
Munger
Dhanbad
Asansol
Ranchi
Jamshedpur
Kharagpur
Kolkata
Khulna
Chittagong
Cox's Bazar
Agartala
Darjiling
Guwahati
Shillong
Nagaon
Dimapur
Dibrugarh
Imphal
Rangpur
Lhazê
Xigazê
Lhasa
Kangmar
Gar
Amdo
Qamdo
Batang
Dêqên
Yushu
Golmud
Da Qaidam Zhen
Dunhuang
Anxi
Yumen
Wuwei
Xining
Lanzhou
Linxia
Tianshui
Xi'an
Weinan
Baoji
Hanzhong
Guangyuan
Nanchong
Chengdu
Kangding
Leshan
Neijiang
Zigong
Chongqing
Yibin
Zunyi
Xichang
Zhaotong
Lupanshui
Guiyang
Anshun
Duyun
Dukou
Dali
Baoshan
Chuxiong
Kunming
Yuxi
Kaiyuan
Gejiu
Hechi
Bose
Hohhot
Baotou
Datong
Wuhai
Shizuishan
Yinchuan
Taiyuan
Linfen
Bhamo
Katha
Shwebo
Monywa
Mandalay
Myingyan
Meiktila
Magwe
Taung-gyi
Kengtung
Sittwe
Pyinmana
Toungoo
Pyè
Sandoway
Henzada
Pegu
Bassein
Pyapon
Thaton
Moulmein
Tavoy
Mergui
Shuangjiang
Phongsali
Louangnamtha
Louangphrabang
Lao Cai
Pingxiang
Thai Nguyen
Hai Phong
Son La
Nam Dinh
Thanh Hoa
Vinh
Chiang Rai
Chiang Mai
Phayao
Lampang
Uttaradit
Tak
Udon Thani
Phitsanulok
Khon Kaen
Savannakhét
Nakhon Sawan
Nakhon Ratchasima
Ubon Ratchathani
Surin
Sara Buri
Chon Buri
Batdâmbâng
Chanthaburi
Pouthisat
Phet Buri
Prachuap Khiri Khan
Sihanoukville
Chumphon
Ranong
Nakhon Si Thammarat
Phatthalung
Songkhla
Phuket
Yala
Kota Bharu
Ban Hat Yai
Alor Setar
George Town
Taiping
Ipoh
Melaka
Banda Aceh
Langsa
Prapat
Balige
Port Blair

Lambert Azimuthal Equal Area projection

LAND USE

Lying south of the Himalayas, this region is dominated by the Indian subcontinent in the east, and the Arabian Peninsula in the west. Land use reflects the climate of the area, which ranges from vast deserts in Saudi Arabia to the wettest location in the world in eastern India. In the east, the climate is dominated by the effects of the monsoon. Culturally, the region is also diverse, with many differences in religion, language, and ethnicity.

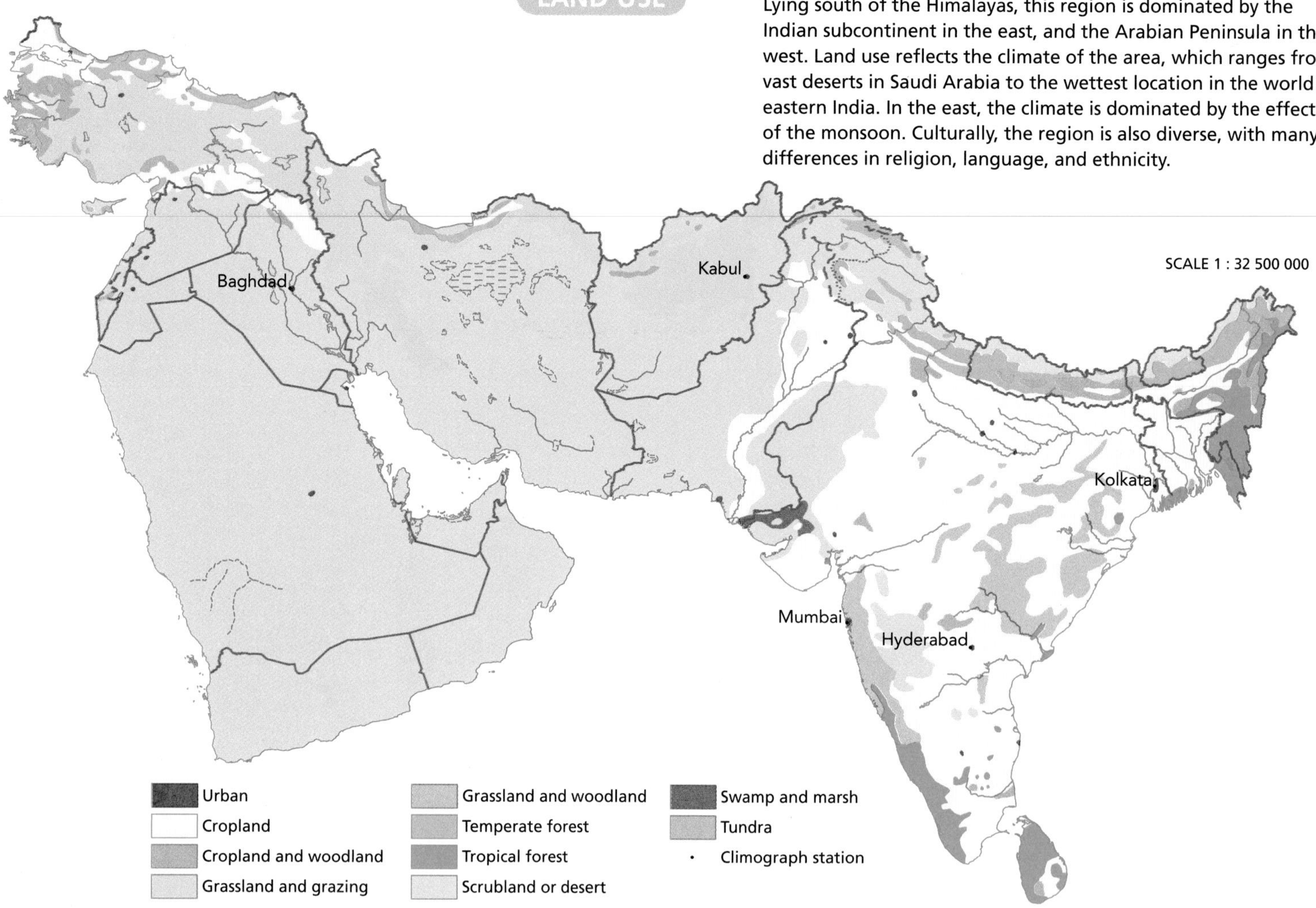

CLIMATE

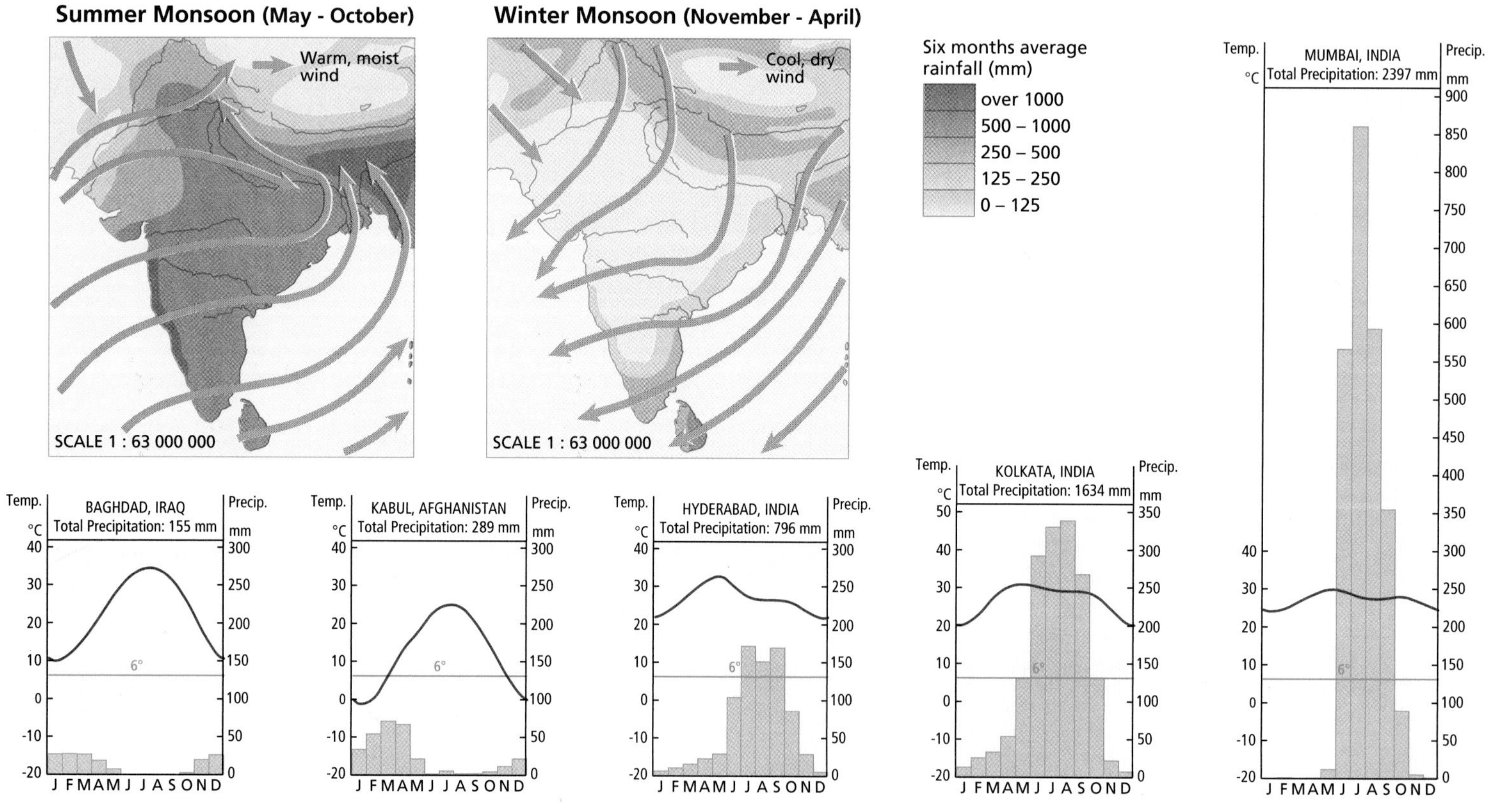

TOURISM

Top Destinations, 2000

Country	Income from tourism	
	Millions, US$	Percent of GDP
Maldives	344	61.8
Cyprus	1 894	21.8
Jordan	722	8.7
Bahrain	408	6.2
Lebanon	742	4.5
Turkey	7 636	3.8
Nepal	168	3.3
Israel	3 100	2.8
Syria	474	2.8
Sri Lanka	253	1.6
UAE	607	1.2
Yemen	76	0.9
Iran	850	0.8
Kuwait	243	0.8
India	3 296	0.7
Oman	104	0.5
Bangladesh	59	0.1
Pakistan	86	0.1

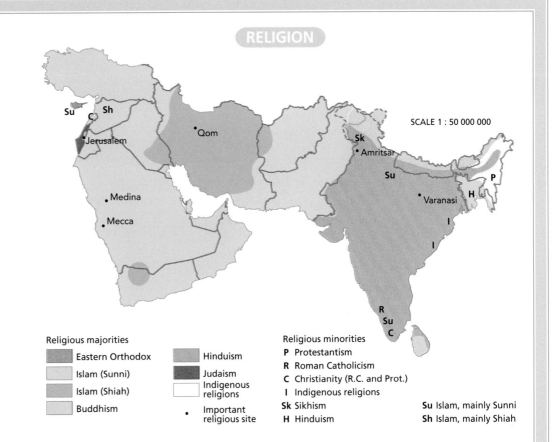

RELIGION

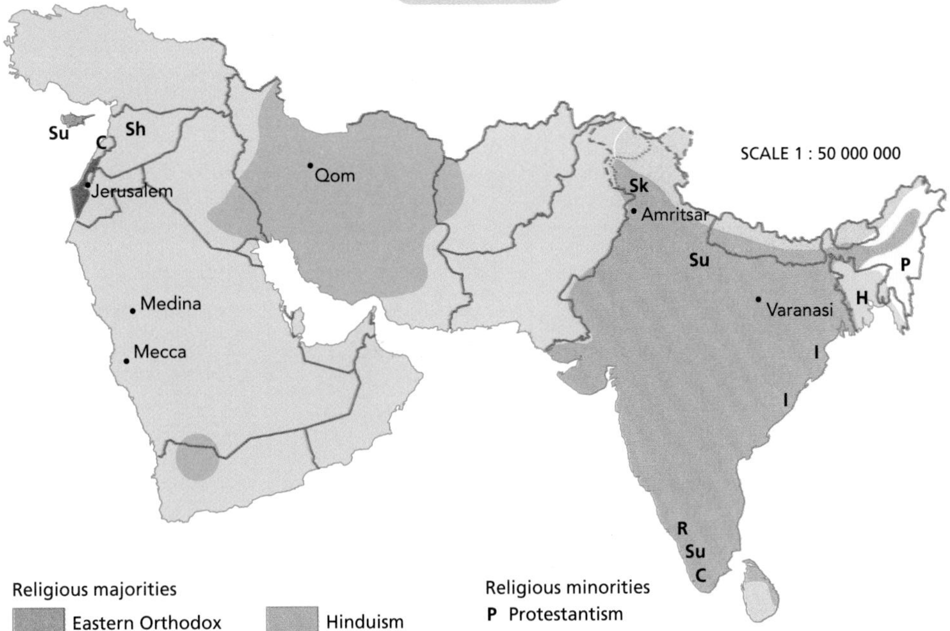

Religious majorities
- Eastern Orthodox
- Islam (Sunni)
- Islam (Shiah)
- Buddhism
- Hinduism
- Judaism
- Indigenous religions
- • Important religious site

Religious minorities
- **P** Protestantism
- **R** Roman Catholicism
- **C** Christianity (R.C. and Prot.)
- **I** Indigenous religions
- **Sk** Sikhism
- **H** Hinduism
- **Su** Islam, mainly Sunni
- **Sh** Islam, mainly Shiah

REFUGEES

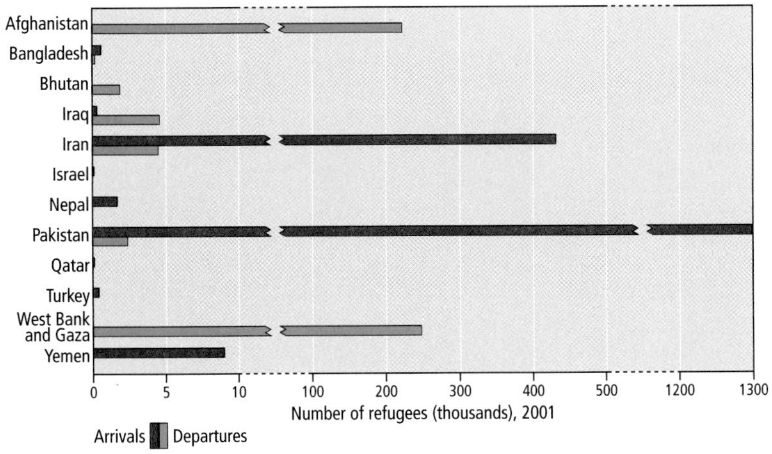

ECONOMY

IRAN

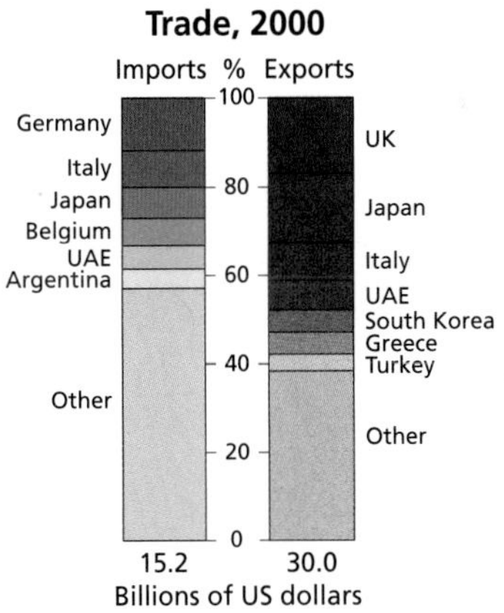

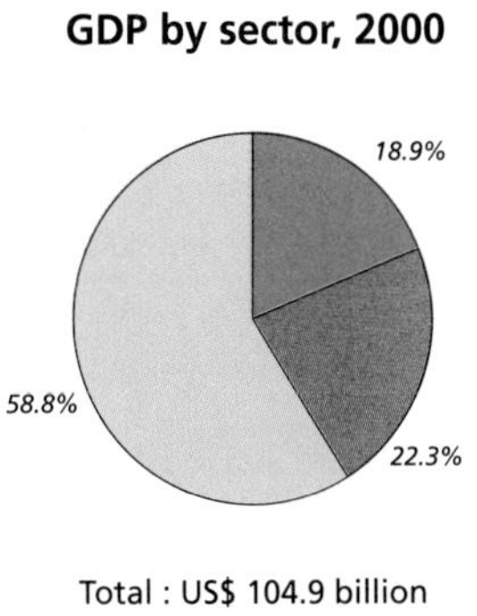

PAKISTAN

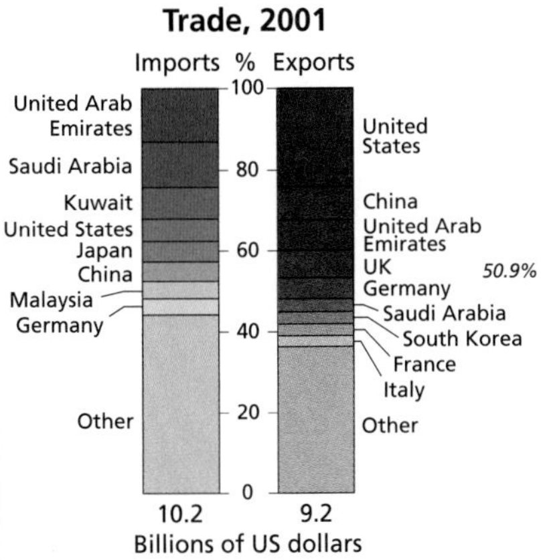

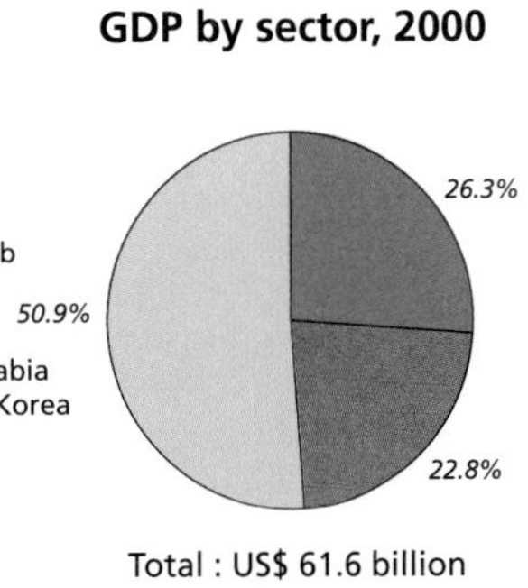

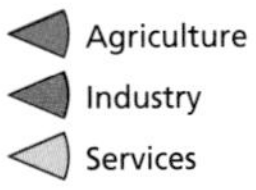

*The category 'Agriculture' includes forestry and fishing, the category 'Industry' includes mining.

INDIA

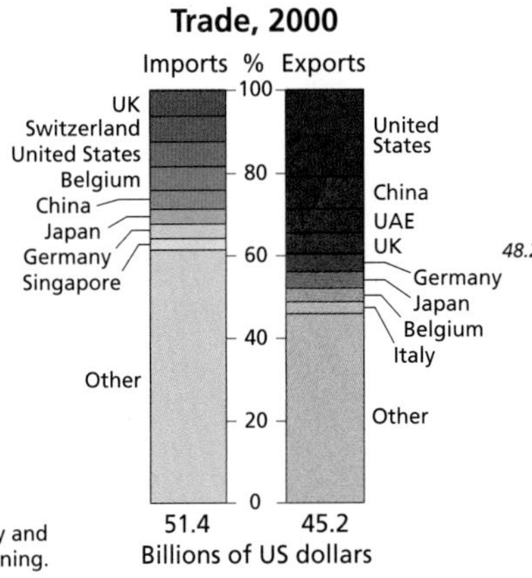

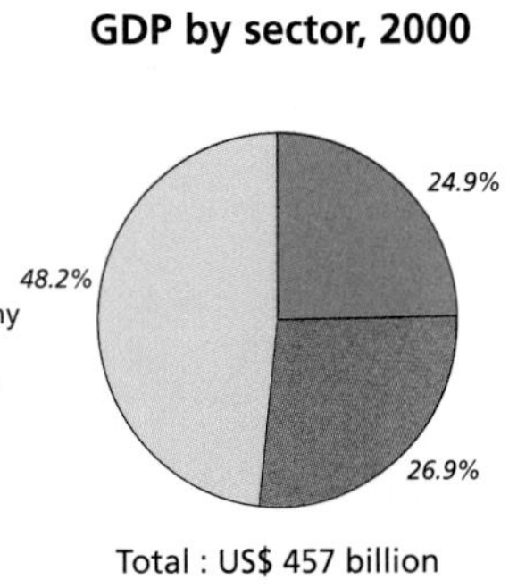

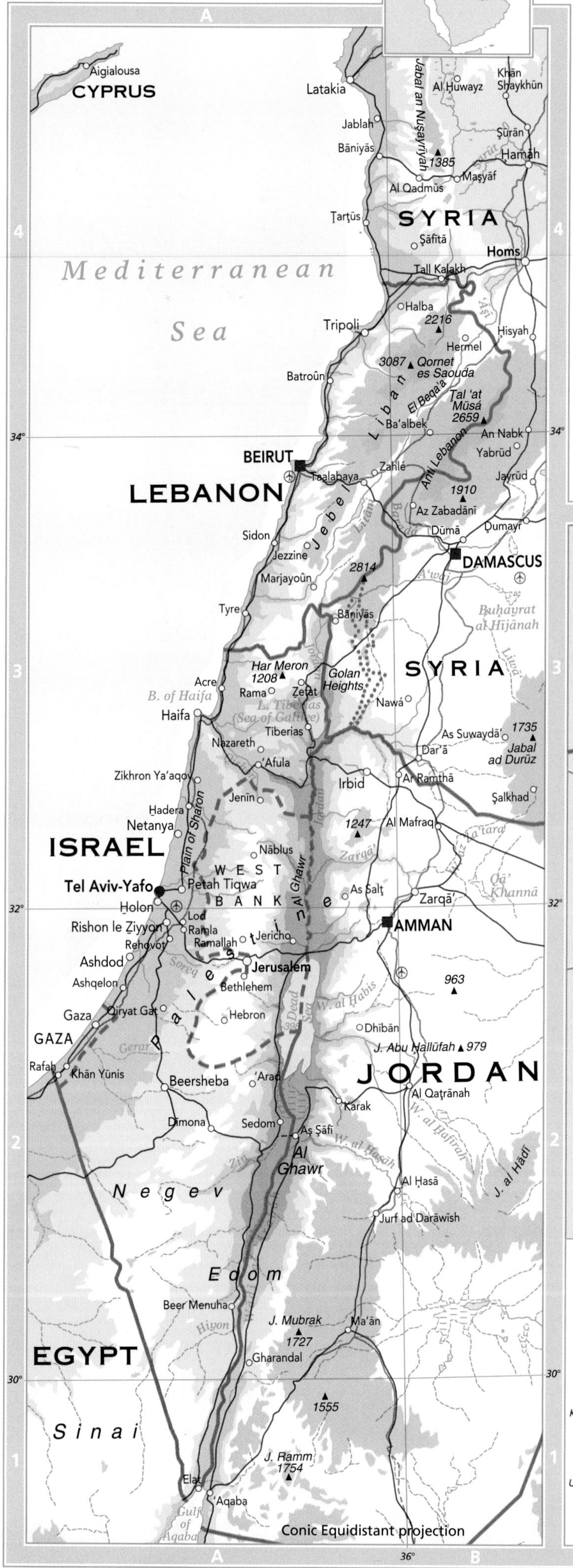

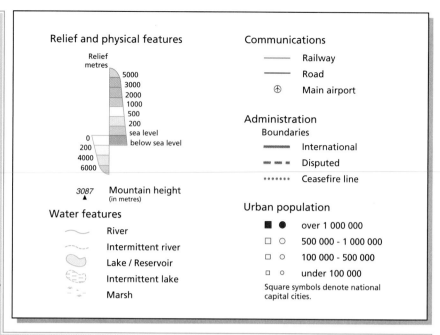

Relief and physical features

Relief metres: 5000, 3000, 2000, 1000, 500, 200, sea level, below sea level, 0, 200, 4000, 6000

3087 ▲ Mountain height (in metres)

Water features

- River
- Intermittent river
- Lake / Reservoir
- Intermittent lake
- Marsh

Communications

- Railway
- Road
- Main airport

Administration

Boundaries

- International
- Disputed
- Ceasefire line

Urban population

- over 1 000 000
- 500 000 - 1 000 000
- 100 000 - 500 000
- under 100 000

Square symbols denote national capital cities.

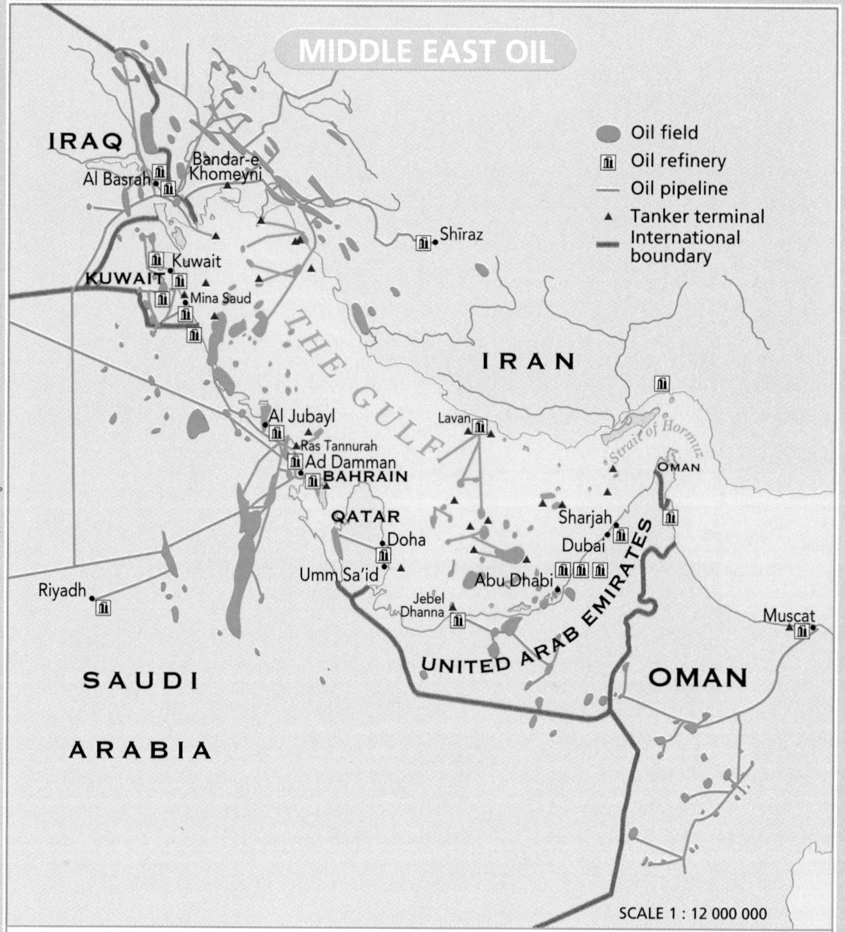

RESERVES, 2001 (65.3% of world reserves)

PRODUCTION, 2001 (30% of world production)

DESTINATIONS OF EXPORTS, 2001

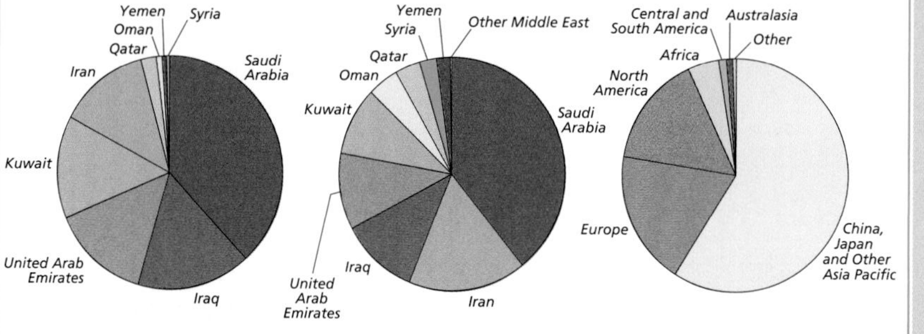

SCALE 1 : 2 750 000

0 30 60 90 120 km

CHANGING BORDERS

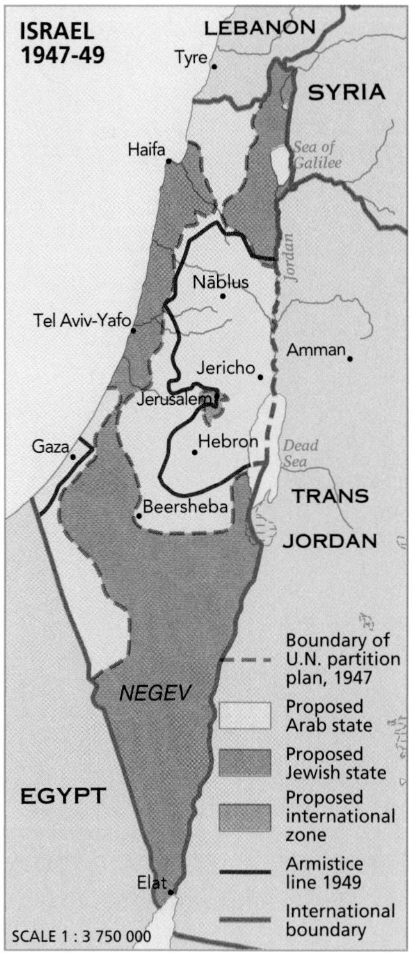

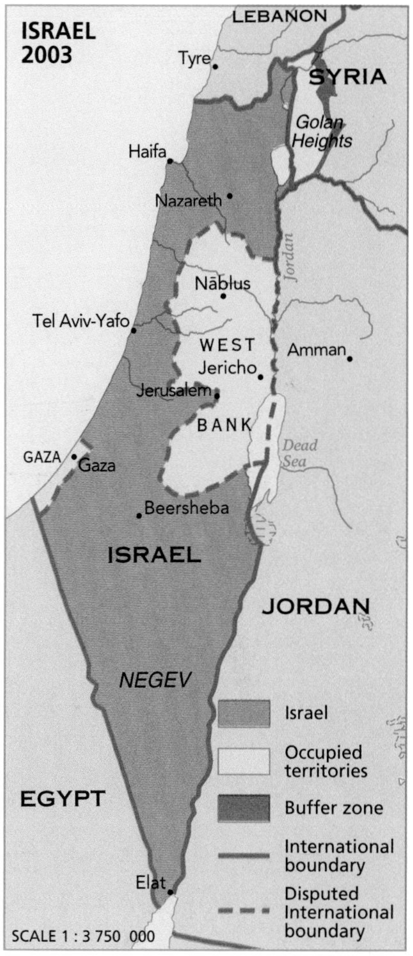

ARAB POPULATION

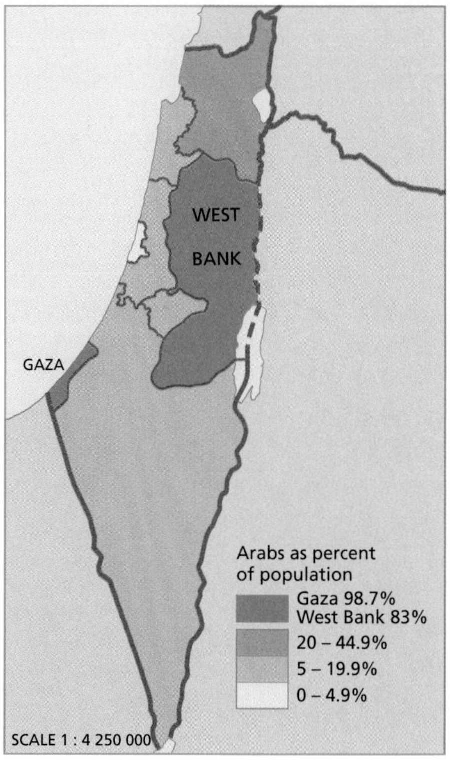

Jerusalem is the holy city for Judaism, Christianity, and Islam. All three faiths have historic interest in this area. From the late 1850s Jewish nationalists advocated a homeland for their people who had been scattered since the time of the Romans. During the 1920s and 1930s, Jews fleeing persecution in Europe came to Palestine. Following World War II, and the genocide of millions of Jews by Nazi Germany, migration to Palestine increased. The Arab majority who lived there did not welcome the Jews' arrival, and there was frequent fighting. In 1948, the United Nations took up the cause of a Jewish homeland and Israel was created out of Palestine. Warfare erupted. Hundreds of thousands of Palestinian Arabs were displaced from their homes and became refugees. Since then, the area has endured almost constant strife between Israel and its Arab neighbours. Wars in 1967 and 1973 resulted in changing borders. Attempts at creating a lasting peace among the peoples of the region have not been successful.

Israel's own population of about 6 million is more than 80% Jewish. The West Bank and Gaza, areas that were occupied by Israel in 1967, are inhabited predominantly by Arabs.

COMPARISON OF SELECTED DATA

	Israel	Gaza	West Bank
Area	20 770 km²	363 km²	5800 km²
Compares in size to...	Half of Nova Scotia	Washington, DC	Prince Edward Island
Resources	Copper, phosphates, potash, manganese, natural gas	Natural gas	Negligible
Arable land	17%	26%	na
Population	6.2 million	1.2 million	2.2 million
Ethnicity	81.4% Jewish 18.6% Arab and Druze	98.7% Palestinian Arab	83% Palestinian Arab
Religion	80.1% Jewish	98.7% Sunni Muslim	75% Sunni Muslim
GDP per capita (US$)	20 000	625	1000

A
B
C
D
E
F
G
H
I
65°
70°
75°
80°
85°
90°
95°
100°
45°
40°
35°
30°
25°
20°
7
6
5
4
3
2
1
KAZAKHSTAN
RUSSIAN
MONGO
KYRGYZSTAN
UZBEKISTAN
TAJIKISTAN
AFGHANISTAN
PAKISTAN
JAMMU AND KASHMIR
INDIA
NEPAL
BHUTAN
CHIN
MYANMAR
LAOS
VIET
Aral'sk
Karaganda
Temirtau
Zhezkazgan
Mikhaylovskiy
Rubtsovsk
Gornyak
Aleysk
Biysk
Gorno-Altaysk
Abaza
Semipalatinsk
Ust'-Kamenogorsk
Georgiyevka
Zyryanovsk
Mt Belukha 4506
Kokpekty
Ayaguz
L. Zaysan
Zaysan
Kzyl-Orda
Balkhash
Aktogay
Kyzylkum Desert
Syr Darya
Turkestan
Taldykorgan
Lake Alakol'
Karamay
Ebinur Hu
Dzungarian Basin
Altay
Altai Mountains
Hovd
Uliastay
Tsetserleg
Altay
Bayanhongor
Bulgan
Mörön
Ulaangom
Uvs Nuur
Hyargas Nuur
Har Nuur
Döröö Nuur
Chadan
Kyzyl
Usol'ye-Sibirskoye
Angarsk
Irkutsk
Slyudyanka
Zima
Hövsgöl Nuur
Zhambyl
Shymkent
TASHKENT
BISHKEK
Almaty
Navoi
Angren
Namangan
Kokand
Khujand
Karshi
Yining
Ysyk Köl
Naryn
TIEN SHAN
Ürümqi
Gobi De
Turpan
Hami
Kuqa
Aksu
Bohu
Bosten Hu
DUSHANBE
Kashi
Khorugh
Pamirs
Mazar-e Sharif
Baghlam
Charikar
KABUL
Chitral
Gilgit
Karakoram Range
K2 8611
Tarim Basin
Taklimakan Desert
Lop Nur
Anxi
Dunhuang
Ruoqiang
Qiemo
Hotan
KUNLUN SHAN
Altun Shan
Yumen
Qilian Shan
Da Qaidam Zhen
Har Hu
Qinghai Hu
Wuwei
Xining
Lanzho
Linxia
Golmud
Gardez
Ghazni
Peshawar
ISLAMABAD
Srinagar
Rawalpindi
Dera Ismail Khan
Faisalabad
Jammu
Sutak
Rutog
Tibetan Plateau
Dera Ghazi Khan
Multan
Amritsar
Lahore
Ludhiana
Jampur
Sutlej
Gar
Chandigarh
Dehra Dun
Khanpur
HIMALAYAN RANGE
Yushu
Amdo
Thar Desert
Bikaner
Pokaran
Delhi
NEW DELHI
Meerut
Sikar
Ghaziabad
Bareilly
Dhaulagiri 8167
Nam Co
Siling Co
Nu Jiang (Salween)
Chang Jiang (Yangtze)
Mekong
Qamdo
Chengdu
Jodhpur
Pali
Jaipur
Mathura
Agra
Fatehgarh
8091 Annapurna
Lhazê
Xigazê
Lhasa
Yarlung Zangbo Jiang
Kangding
Batang
7514 Gongga Shan
Leshan
Neijia
Zigon
Yibin
Gwalior
Lucknow
KATHMANDU
Mt Everest 8848
Kangmar
Kangchenjunga 8586
Udaipur
Kota
Kanpur
Gorakhpur
Ghaghara
THIMBU
Darjiling
Dêqên
Dibrugarh
Xichang
Zhaoton
Tropic of Cancer
Gandhinagar
Ahmadabad
Guna
Jhansi
Allahabad
Ganges
Mirzapur
Varanasi
Darbhanga
Muzaffarpur
Patna
Tezpur
Brahmaputra
Dukou
Liupans
Dali
Imphal
Chindwin
Baoshan
Chuxiong
Kunming
Bhamo
Katha
Yuxi
Kaiyua
Shuangjiang
Shwebo
Gejiu
Mandalay
Yunjinghong
Phongsali
Meiktila
Kengtung
Taung-gyi
Louang Namtha
Magwe
Irrawaddy
Chiang Rai
Louangphrabang
Pyè
Toungoo
Muang Phayao
Relief and physical features
Relief metres
5000
3000
2000
1000
500
200
sea level
below sea level
0
200
4000
6000
8848
Mountain height (in metres)
Water features
River
Intermittent river
Canal
Lake / Reservoir
Intermittent lake
Marsh
Communications
Railway
Road
Main airport
Administration
Boundaries
International
Disputed
Ceasefire line
Urban population
over 1 000 000
500 000 - 1 000 000
100 000 - 500 000
under 100 000
Square symbols denote national capital cities.

SCALE 1 : 15 000 000

0 200 400 600 800 km

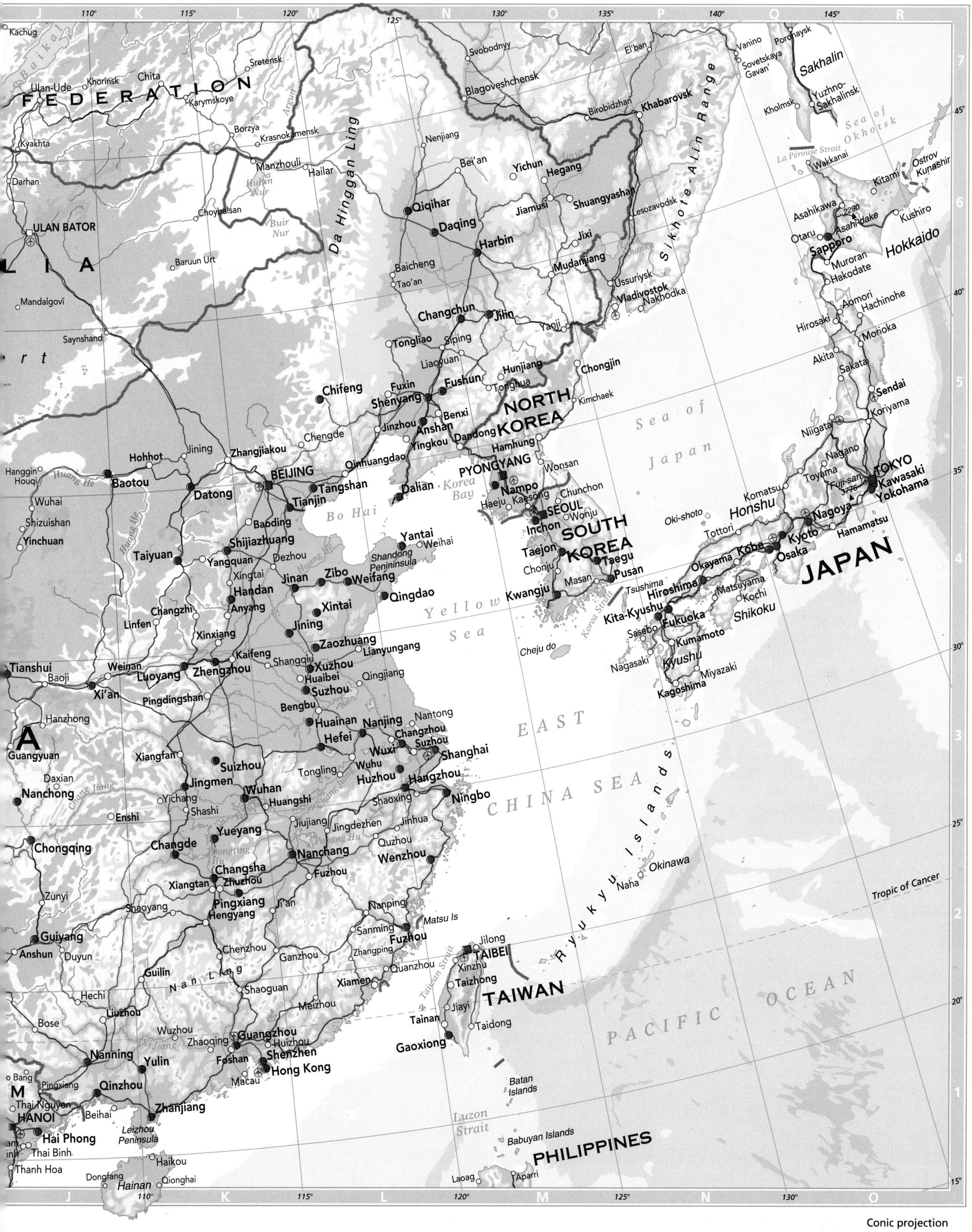
FEDERATION
Ulan-Ude
Khorinsk
Chita
Sretensk
Karymskoye
Kachug
Baikal
Kyakhta
Darhan
Borzya
Krasnokamensk
Manzhouli
Hailar
Hulun Nur
Choybalsan
Buir Nur
ULAN BATOR
L I A
Baruun Urt
Mandalgovĭ
Saynshand
r t
Argun
Da Hinggan Ling
Svobodnyy
Blagoveshchensk
Nenjiang
Bei'an
Amur
Yichun
Hegang
Qiqihar
Daqing
Harbin
Jiamusi
Shuangyashan
Jixi
Mudanjiang
Baicheng
Tao'an
Changchun
Jilin
Tongliao
Siping
Liaoyuan
Yanji
Hunjiang
Tonghua
Fushun
Fuxin
Shenyang
Chifeng
Benxi
Anshan
Jinzhou
Yingkou
Dandong
Chengde
El'ban
Birobidzhan
Khabarovsk
Sikhote-Alin Range
Lesozavodsk
Ussuriysk
Vladivostok
Nakhodka
Chongjin
Kimchaek
NORTH KOREA
Hamhung
PYONGYANG
Nampo
Wonsan
Korea Bay
Haeju
Kaesong
Chunchon
SEOUL
Wonju
Inchon
SOUTH KOREA
Taejon
Taegu
Chonju
Pusan
Masan
Kwangju
Cheju do
Korea Strait
Tsushima
Vanino
Sovetskaya Gavan'
Poronaysk
Sakhalin
Kholmsk
Yuzhno-Sakhalinsk
Sea of Okhotsk
La Pérouse Strait
Wakkanai
Ostrov Kunashir
Kitami
Asahikawa
2290
Asahi-dake
Kushiro
Otaru
Sapporo
Hokkaido
Muroran
Hakodate
Aomori
Hachinohe
Hirosaki
Morioka
Akita
Sakata
Sendai
Koriyama
Niigata
Sea of Japan
Nagano
Toyama
TOKYO
Kawasaki
Yokohama
Fuji-san
3776
Komatsu
Honshu
Oki-shoto
Tottori
Nagoya
Hamamatsu
Kyoto
Osaka
Kobe
Okayama
JAPAN
Hiroshima
Matsuyama
Kochi
Shikoku
Kita-Kyushu
Fukuoka
Sasebo
Kumamoto
Nagasaki
Kyushu
Miyazaki
Kagoshima
Hohhot
Jining
Zhangjiakou
Hanggin Houqi
Huang He
Baotou
Datong
BEIJING
Qinhuangdao
Tangshan
Dalian
Tianjin
Bo Hai
Wuhai
Shizuishan
Yinchuan
Baoding
Shijiazhuang
Taiyuan
Yangquan
Dezhou
Yantai
Weihai
Shandong Peninsula
Xingtai
Jinan
Zibo
Weifang
Handan
Qingdao
Changzhi
Anyang
Xintai
Yellow Sea
Linfen
Jining
Xinxiang
Zaozhuang
Lianyungang
Kaifeng
Tianshui
Weinan
Luoyang
Zhengzhou
Shangqiu
Xuzhou
Baoji
Xi'an
Huaibei
Qingjiang
Pingdingshan
Suzhou
Bengbu
Hanzhong
Huainan
Nanjing
Nantong
Hefei
Changzhou
Wuxi
Suzhou
Shanghai
A
Guangyuan
Xiangfan
Suizhou
Tongling
Wuhu
Huzhou
Hangzhou
Daxian
Nanchong
Jingmen
Chang Jiang
Yichang
Wuhan
Huangshi
Shaoxing
Ningbo
Shashi
Enshi
Jiujiang
Jingdezhen
Jinhua
Poyang Hu
EAST CHINA SEA
Chongqing
Changde
Yueyang
Dongting Hu
Nanchang
Quzhou
Wenzhou
Changsha
Xiangtan
Zhuzhou
Fuzhou
Zunyi
Shaoyang
Pingxiang
Ji'an
Hengyang
Nanping
Matsu Is
Sanming
Fuzhou
Guiyang
Anshun
Duyun
Chenzhou
Ganzhou
Zhangping
Quanzhou
Jilong
TAIBEI
Xinzhu
Taizhong
Taiwan Strait
Guilin
Nan Ling
Shaoguan
Xiamen
Hechi
Liuzhou
Meizhou
Jiayi
TAIWAN
Tainan
Taidong
Gaoxiong
Bose
Wuzhou
Zhaoqing
Guangzhou
Huizhou
Xi Jiang
Nanning
Yulin
Foshan
Shenzhen
Hong Kong
Macau
Bang
M
Pingxiang
Qinzhou
Thai Nguyen
HANOI
Beihai
Zhanjiang
Leizhou Peninsula
Hai Phong
Thai Binh
Thanh Hoa
Haikou
Dongfang
Qionghai
Hainan
Ryukyu Islands
Okinawa
Naha
Tropic of Cancer
PACIFIC OCEAN
Batan Islands
Luzon Strait
Babuyan Islands
PHILIPPINES
Laoag
Aparri
J K L M N O P Q R
110° 115° 120° 125° 130° 135° 140° 145°
45° 40° 35° 30° 25° 20° 15°
1 2 3 4 5 6 7

Conic projection

A
B
C
D
E
F
95°
100°
105°
110°
115°
120°
20°
15°
10°
5°
0°
5°
10°
INDIA
Chittagong
BANGLA-DESH
Monywa
Shwebo
Mandalay
Mt Pakokku
Victoria
3053
Myingyan
MYANMAR
Kengtung
Meiktila
Taung-gyi
Magwe
Sittwe
Arakan Yoma
Pyinmana
Sandoway
Pyè
Toungoo
Shwegyin
Bay of Bengal
Henzada
Pegu
Bassein
Thaton
Martaban
YANGON
Pyapon
Moulmein
Gulf of Martaban
Mouths of the Irrawaddy
Preparis I.
Tavoy
Andaman Islands (India)
Port Blair
Mergui
Tenasserim
Mergui Archipelago
Little Andaman
Andaman Sea
Ten Degree Channel
Car Nicobar
Nicobar Islands (India)
Great Nicobar
CHINA
Yunjinghong
Phôngsali
Louang Namtha
Chiang Rai
Louangphrabang
Phayao
Xiangkhoang
Chiang Mai
Nan
Phrae
Lampang
Uttaradit
VIENTIANE
LAOS
Tak
Phitsanulok
Udon Thani
Khon Kaen
Nakhon Sawan
THAILAND
Ubon Ratchathani
Pakxé
Sara Buri
Nakhon Ratchasima
Surin
Ayutthaya
Nonthaburi
Rat Buri
BANGKOK
Sisophon
Chon Buri
Phet Buri
Batdâmbâng
Tônlé Sap
CAMBODIA
Chanthaburi
Pouthisat
Prachuap Khiri Khan
Krâcheh
Kâmpóng Cham
PHNOM PENH
Gulf of Thailand
Sihanoukville
Kâmpôt
Chumphon
Ranong
Lao Cai
Cao Bang
Pingxiang
Thai Nguyên
Son La
HANOI
Hai Phong
Nam Dinh
Thai Binh
Gulf of Tongking
Thanh Hoa
Vinh
Ha Tinh
VIETNAM
Dong Hoi
Savannakhét
Quang Tri
Huê
Da Nang
Quang Ngai
Qui Nhon
Buôn Ma Thuôt
Nha Trang
Cam Ranh
Da Lat
Tây Ninh
Phan Thiêt
Hô Chi Minh City
My Tho
Long Xuyên
Rach Gia
Vung Tau
Cân Tho
Mouths of the Mekong
Bac Liêu
Con Son
Mui Ca Mau
Mekong
Nanning
Yulin
Qinzhou
Beihai
Macau
Hong Kong
Zhanjiang
Leizhou Pen.
Haikou
Hainan
Qionghai
Dongfang
Gaoxiong
TAIWAN
Paracel Is
SOUTH CHINA SEA
Spratly Is
Laoag
San Fernando
Baguio
Dagupan
Cabanatuan
Mt Pinatubo
1600
Quezon City
Olongapo
MANILA
Pasig
Batangas
Calapan
Mindoro
Mindoro Str.
Calamian Group
Taytay
Palawan
Puerto Princesa
Brooke's Point
Sulu Sea
Balabac Strait
Nakhon Si Thammarat
Krabi
Phuket
Phatthalung
Songkhla
Ban Hat Yai
Yala
Kota Bharu
Alor Setar
George Town
Pinang
Butterworth
Kuala Terengganu
Taiping
Ipoh
Dungun
MALAYA
Kuantan
MALAYSIA
Banda Aceh
Lhokseumawe
Langsa
G. Leuser
3145
Medan
Tebingtinggi
Simeuluë
Lake Toba
Prapat
Balige
Sibolga
Rantauprapat
Nias
KUALA LUMPUR
Putrajaya
Seremban
Melaka
Keluang
Strait of Malacca
Muar
Johor Bahru
SINGAPORE
Riau Is
Pakanbaru
SUMATRA
Batu Is
Bukittinggi
Padangpanjang
Padang
Siberut
Sipura
Utara I.
Mentawai Is
3805
G. Kerinci
Sungaipenuh
Barisan Range
Muarabungo
Jambi
Palembang
Lubuklinggau
Selatan I.
Bengkulu
Dempo
3159
Lahat
Prabumulih
Martapura
Kotabumi
Tanjungkarang Telukbetung
Enggano
INDIAN OCEAN
Natuna Besar
Anambas Is
Natuna Is
Bangka
Mentok
Pangkalpinang
Tanjungpandan
Toboali
Belitung
Karimata Strait
Tambelan Is
Java Sea
Kota Kinabalu
G. Kinabalu
4094
Sandakan
SABAH
Lahad Datu
Jolo
Tawitawi
BRUNEI
BANDAR SERI BEGAWAN
Miri
Seria
Tawau
Tarakan
Bintulu
Igan
Sibu
SARAWAK
Iran Ra.
2988
Kuching
Sambas
Debak
Simanggang
Singkawang
BORNEO
Kalimantan
Tanjungredeb
Sangkulirang
Pontianak
Samarinda
Balikpapan
Schwaner Mts
Sukadana
Ketapang
Kendawangan
Palangkaraya
Sampit
Amuntai
Pangkalanbuun
Tg Puting
Banjarmasin
Laut
Tg Selatan
Makassar Strait
Sidoa
Tomini Gulf
Palu
Poso
Sulawesi
Mamuju
3074
Palopo
Bt Gandadiwata
Majene
Makale
Gulf of Bone
Parepare
Watampone
Ujung Pandang
2871
Bontosunggu
Bulukumba
Salayar
Flores Sea
Bawean
INDONESIA
Madura
Kangean Is
JAKARTA
Sunda Str.
Serang
Bogor
Bandung
Cirebon
Pekalongan
Tuban
Semarang
Surabaya
Sukabumi
Tasikmalaya
3428
Slamet
Surakarta
Probolinggo
Cilacap
Yogyakarta
Malang
3676
Singaraja
Jember
Bali
Bali Sea
Denpasar
Lombok
3726
Mataram
Raba
Ruteng
Sumbawa
Waingapu
Sumba
JAVA
Christmas I. (Aust.)
8
7
6
5
4
3
2
1

SCALE 1 : 15 000 000

0 200 400 600 800 km

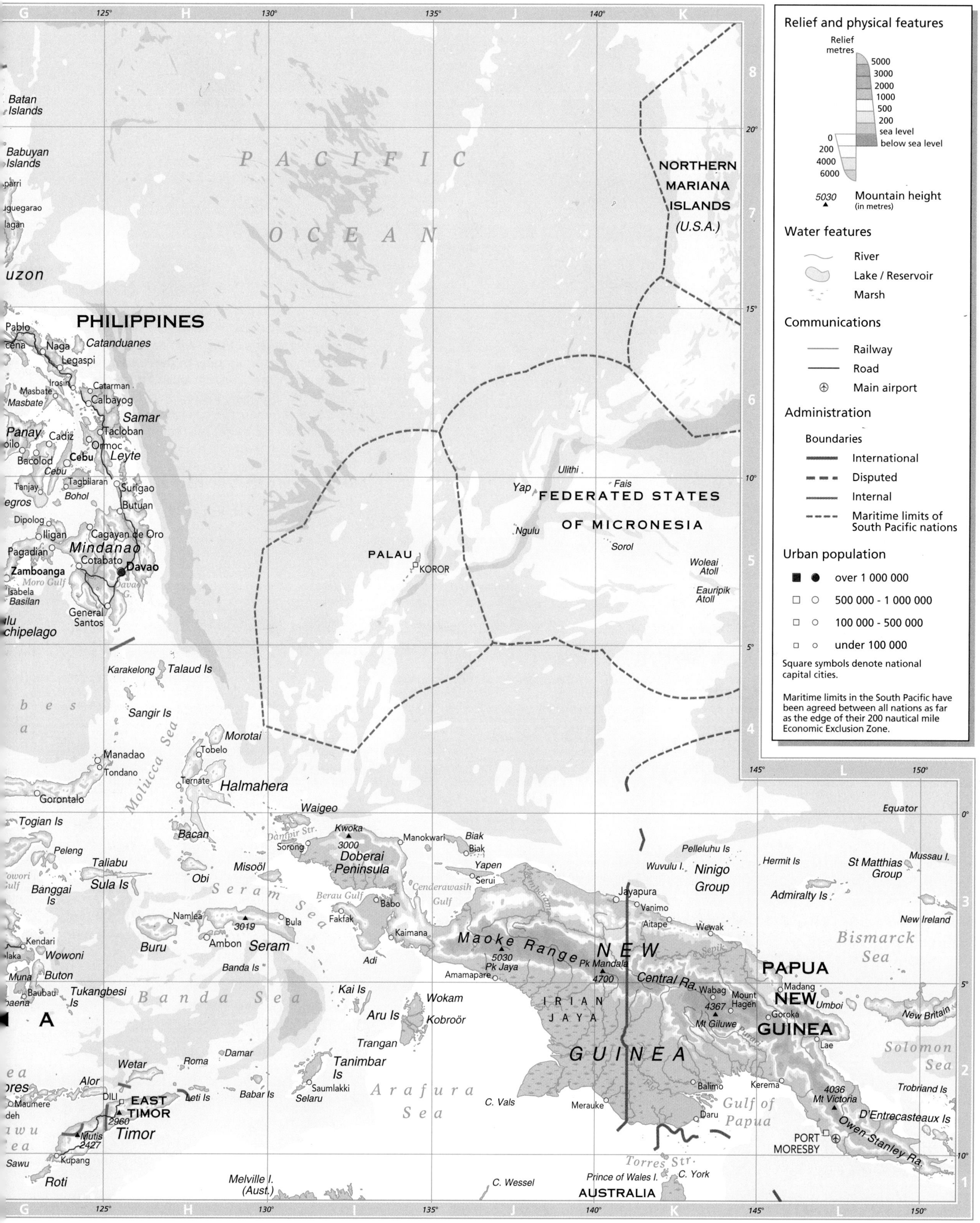

Relief and physical features
Relief metres
5000
3000
2000
1000
500
200
sea level
below sea level
0
200
4000
6000
5030
Mountain height (in metres)
Water features
River
Lake / Reservoir
Marsh
Communications
Railway
Road
Main airport
Administration
Boundaries
International
Disputed
Internal
Maritime limits of South Pacific nations
Urban population
over 1 000 000
500 000 - 1 000 000
100 000 - 500 000
under 100 000
Square symbols denote national capital cities.
Maritime limits in the South Pacific have been agreed between all nations as far as the edge of their 200 nautical mile Economic Exclusion Zone.
PACIFIC OCEAN
NORTHERN MARIANA ISLANDS (U.S.A.)
PHILIPPINES
FEDERATED STATES OF MICRONESIA
PALAU
KOROR
Batan Islands
Babuyan Islands
Luzon
Catanduanes
Naga
Legaspi
Masbate
Catarman
Calbayog
Samar
Panay
Cadiz
Tacloban
Ormoc
Cebu
Leyte
Bacolod
Tagbilaran
Bohol
Surigao
Butuan
Dipolog
Iligan
Cagayan de Oro
Pagadian
Mindanao
Cotabato
Zamboanga
Davao
Moro Gulf
Isabela
Basilan
General Santos
Ulithi
Yap
Fais
Ngulu
Sorol
Woleai Atoll
Eauripik Atoll
Karakelong
Talaud Is
Sangir Is
Molucca Sea
Morotai
Tobelo
Manadao
Tondano
Ternate
Halmahera
Gorontalo
Togian Is
Waigeo
Dampir Str.
Kwoka
3000
Sorong
Manokwari
Biak
Doberai Peninsula
Bacan
Peleng
Taliabu
Sula Is
Obi
Misoöl
Yapen
Serui
Banggai Is
Seram Sea
Berau Gulf
Cenderawasih Gulf
Babo
Fakfak
Namlea
3019
Bula
Kaimana
Kendari
Wowoni
Buru
Ambon
Seram
Adi
Banda Is
Muna
Buton
Baubau
Tukangbesi Is
Banda Sea
Kai Is
Aru Is
Wokam
Kobroör
Trangan
Tanimbar Is
Saumlakki
Selaru
Arafura Sea
Damar
Wetar
Roma
Alor
Babar Is
Leti Is
Flores
Maumere
DILI
EAST TIMOR
2960
Timor
Mutis 2427
Kupang
Sawu
Roti
Melville I. (Aust.)
C. Wessel
C. Vals
Maoke Range
5030 Pk Jaya
Amamapare
Pk Mandala 4700
IRIAN JAYA
NEW GUINEA
Central Ra.
Jayapura
Vanimo
Aitape
Wewak
Sepik
Wabag
4367
Mt Giluwe
Mount Hagen
Madang
Goroka
Umboi
PAPUA NEW GUINEA
Lae
Balimo
Kerema
Merauke
Daru
Gulf of Papua
Torres Str.
Prince of Wales I.
C. York
AUSTRALIA
PORT MORESBY
4036 Mt Victoria
Owen Stanley Ra.
D'Entrecasteaux Is
Trobriand Is
Solomon Sea
New Britain
Bismarck Sea
New Ireland
Admiralty Is
Hermit Is
St Matthias Group
Mussau I.
Pelleluhu Is
Wuvulu I.
Ninigo Group
Equator

Mercator projection

LAND USE

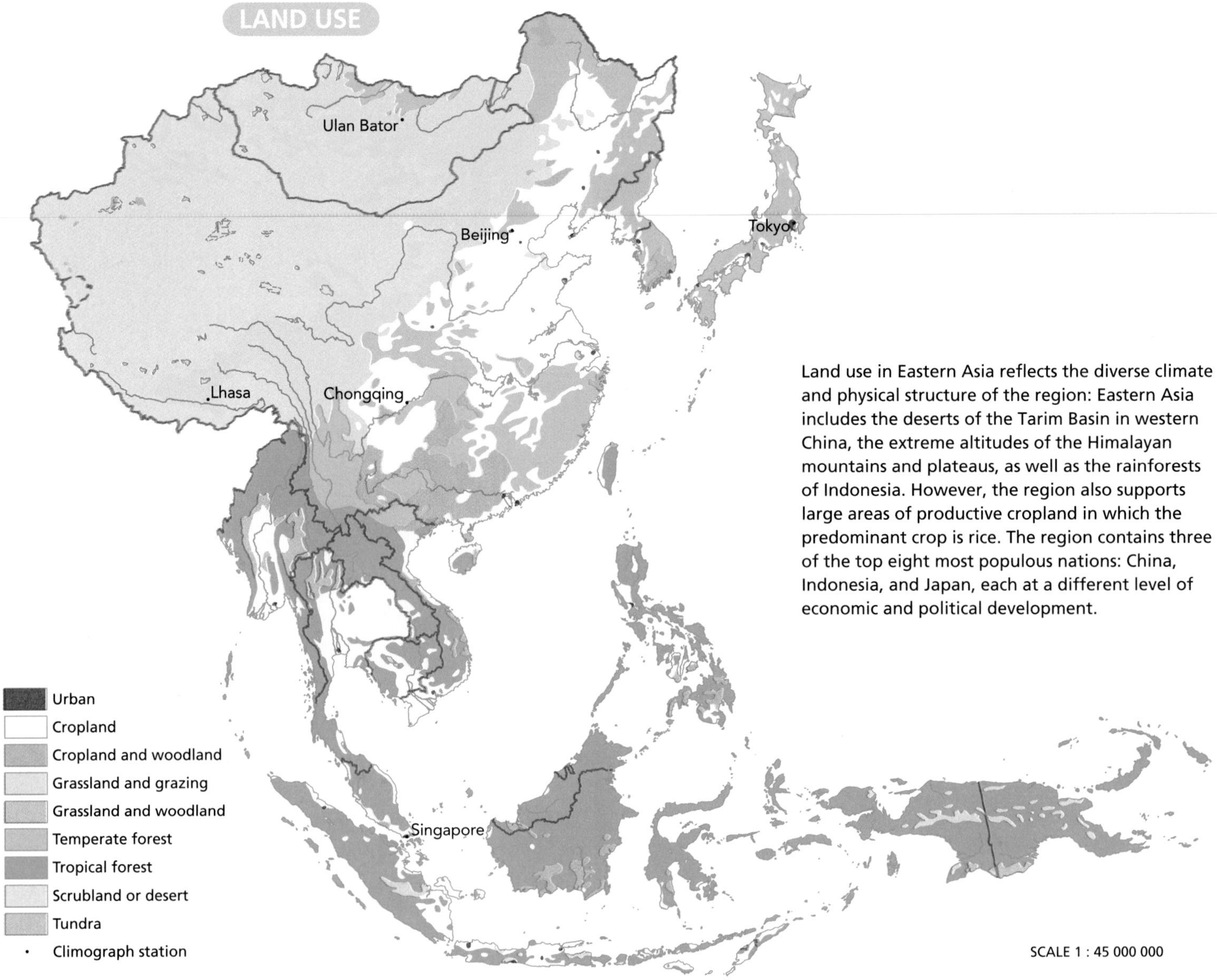

Land use in Eastern Asia reflects the diverse climate and physical structure of the region: Eastern Asia includes the deserts of the Tarim Basin in western China, the extreme altitudes of the Himalayan mountains and plateaus, as well as the rainforests of Indonesia. However, the region also supports large areas of productive cropland in which the predominant crop is rice. The region contains three of the top eight most populous nations: China, Indonesia, and Japan, each at a different level of economic and political development.

CLIMATE

TYPHOONS

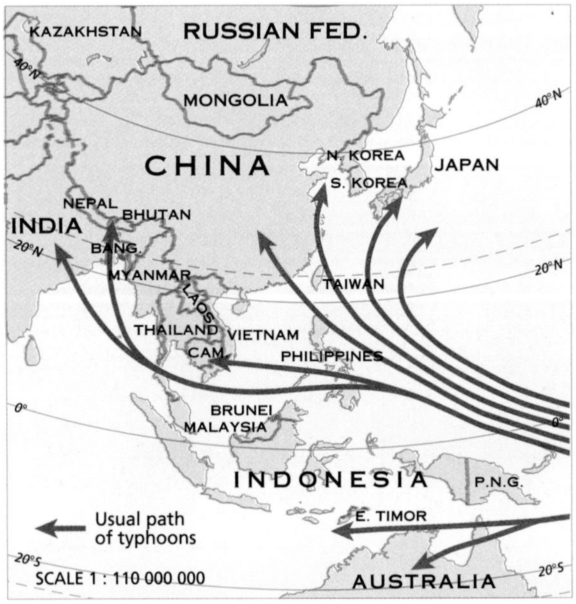

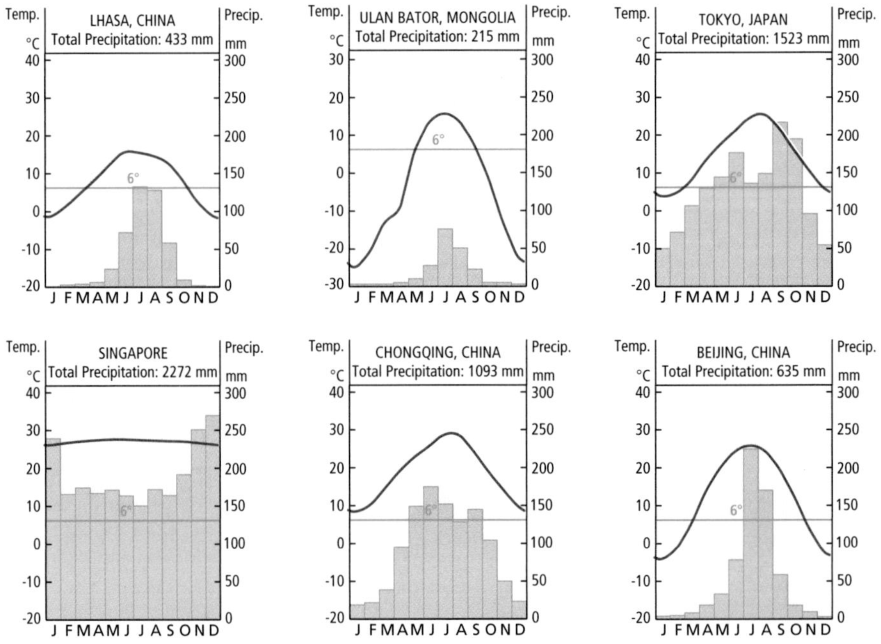

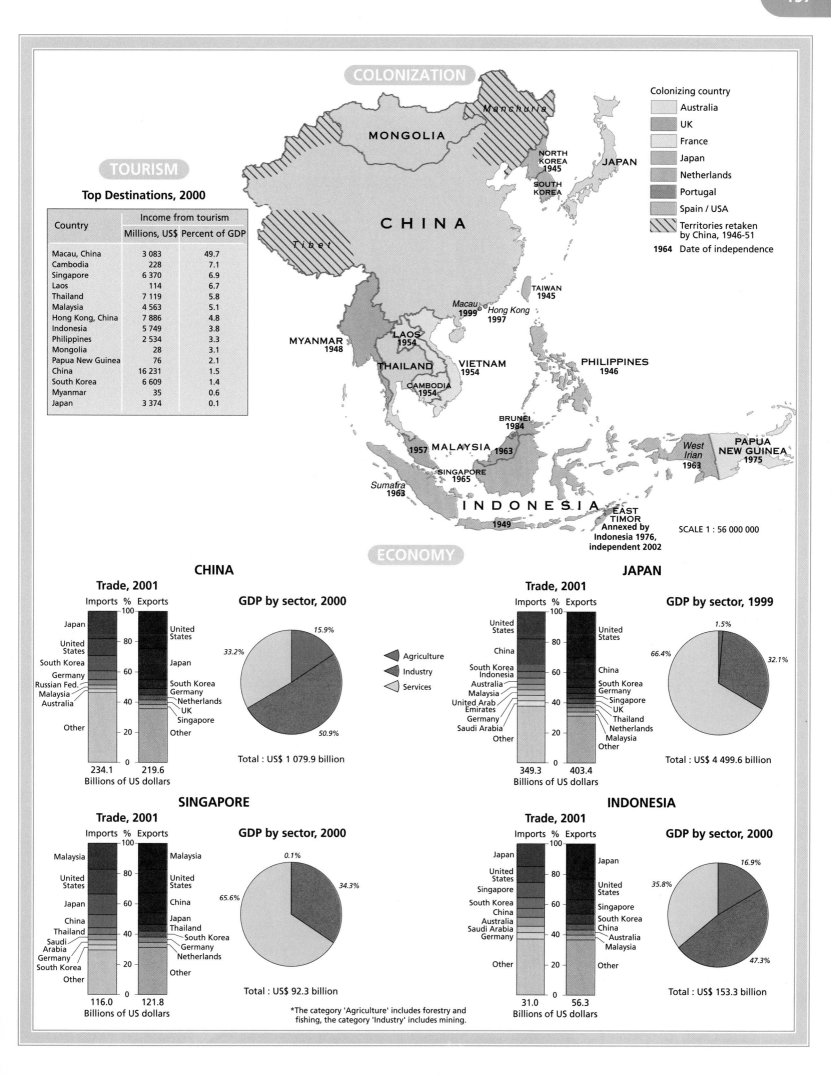

COLONIZATION

TOURISM

Top Destinations, 2000

Country	Income from tourism: Millions, US$	Income from tourism: Percent of GDP
Macau, China	3 083	49.7
Cambodia	228	7.1
Singapore	6 370	6.9
Laos	114	6.7
Thailand	7 119	5.8
Malaysia	4 563	5.1
Hong Kong, China	7 886	4.8
Indonesia	5 749	3.8
Philippines	2 534	3.3
Mongolia	28	3.1
Papua New Guinea	76	2.1
China	16 231	1.5
South Korea	6 609	1.4
Myanmar	35	0.6
Japan	3 374	0.1

ECONOMY

CHINA

Trade, 2001

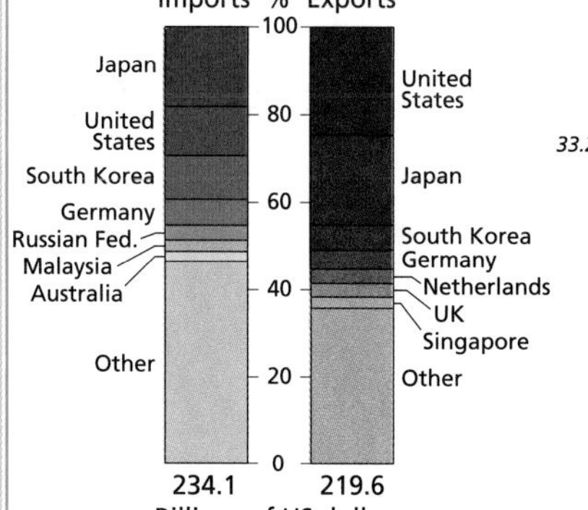

GDP by sector, 2000

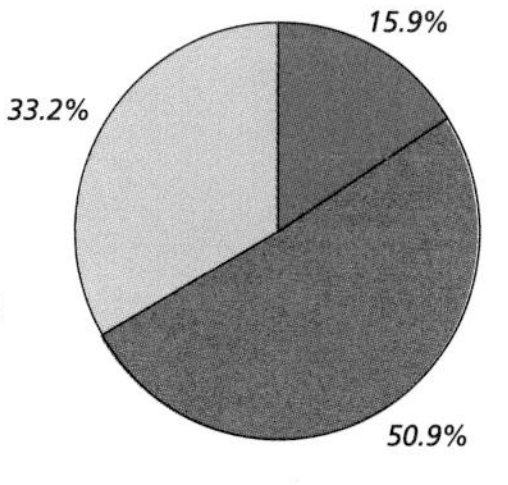

Total : US$ 1 079.9 billion

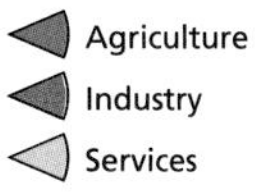

JAPAN

Trade, 2001

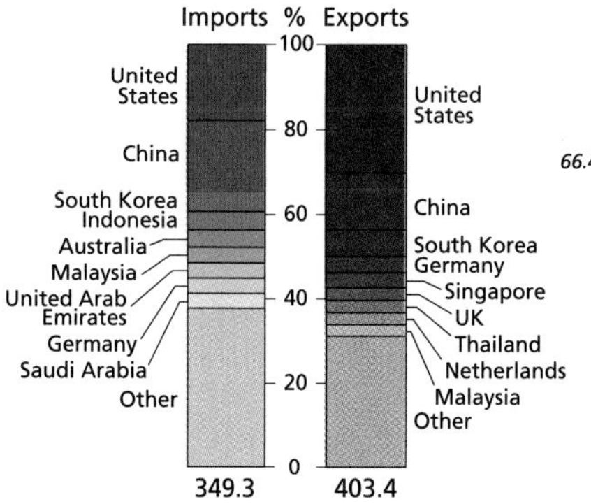

GDP by sector, 1999

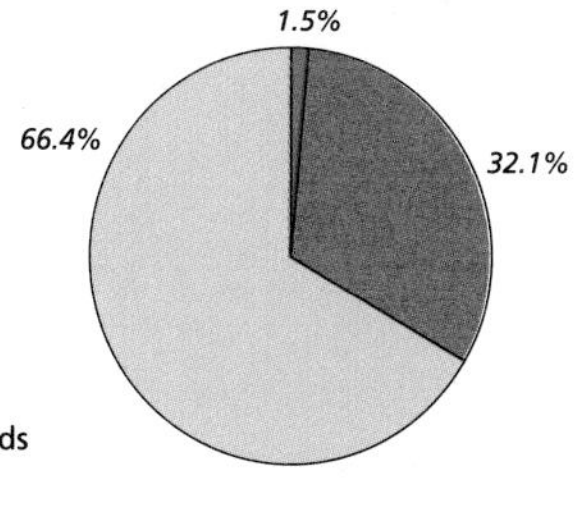

Total : US$ 4 499.6 billion

SINGAPORE

Trade, 2001

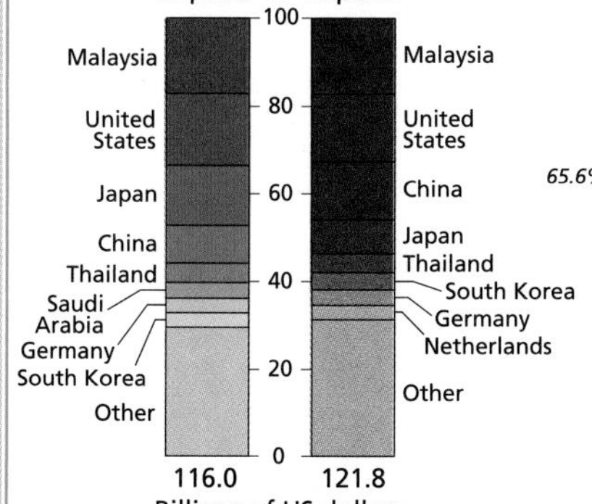

GDP by sector, 2000

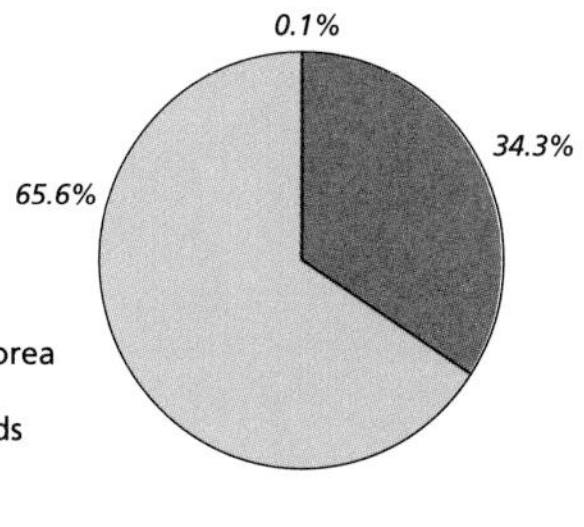

Total : US$ 92.3 billion

INDONESIA

Trade, 2001

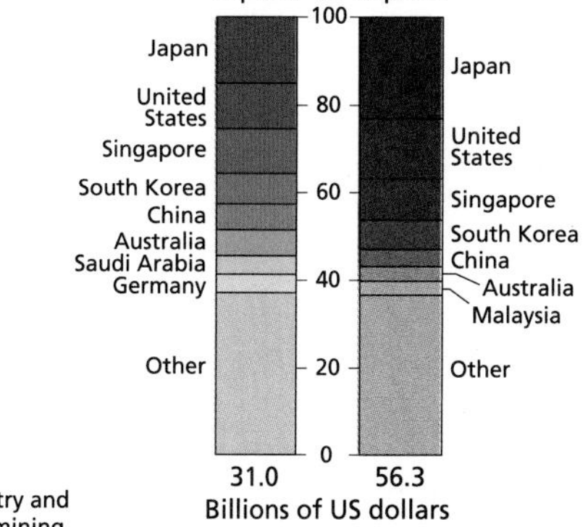

GDP by sector, 2000

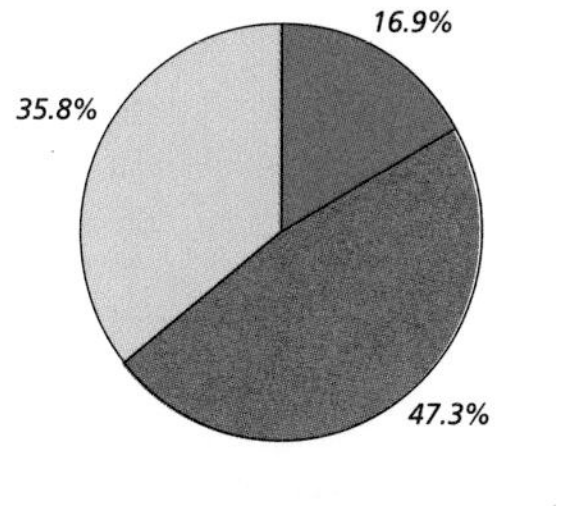

Total : US$ 153.3 billion

*The category 'Agriculture' includes forestry and fishing, the category 'Industry' includes mining.

AUSTRALIA

INDONESIA

EAST TIMOR

NORTHERN TERRITORY

WESTERN AUSTRALIA

SOUTH AUSTRALIA

QUEENSLAND

NEW SOUTH WALES

VICTORIA

TASMANIA

INDIAN OCEAN

Flores Sea

Sawu Sea

Timor Sea

Arafura Sea

Gulf of Carpentaria

Torres Strait

Great Australian Bight

Spencer Gulf

Bass Strait

Lombok, Mataram, Sumbawa, Raba, Endeh, Flores, Waingapu, Sumba, Dili, 2960, Timor, Kupang, Roti

Melville I., Bathurst I., Darwin, Wessel Is, C. Wessel, C. Arnhem, Arnhem Land, Groote Eylandt, Katherine, Roper, Daly, Victoria, Joseph Bonaparte Gulf, C. Londonderry

Prince of Wales I., C. York, Cape York Peninsula, Cooktown, Mitchell, Cairns, Mt Bartle Frere 1612, Gilbert, Normanton, Wellesley Is, Great Barrier, Townsville, Charters Towers, Mt Dalrymple 1277, Great Dividing Range

Wyndham, Kununurra, Lake Argyle, Drysdale, Collier Bay, Kimberley Plateau, Mt Ord 947, Mt Wells 983, Hall's Creek, Derby, C. Lévêque, Broome, Roebuck Bay, Fitzroy, Sturt Plain, Barkly Tableland, McArthur, Tanami Desert, Tennant Creek, Leichhardt, Norman, Flinders, Mount Isa, Selwyn Range, Georgina

Eighty Mile Beach, Port Hedland, De Grey, Great Sandy Desert, L. White, L. Mackay, Barrow I., Dampier, Karratha, North West Cape, Fortescue, L. Disappointment, Hamersley Range, Mt Meharry 1251, Newman, Ashburton, 1531 Mt Zeil, Macdonnell Ranges, Alice Springs, Longreach, Barcaldine, Diamantina, Consuelo Peak 1174, Simpson Desert, Uluru (Ayers Rock) 868, L. Amadeus, Gibson Desert, Musgrave Ranges, Mt Woodroffe 1440, Cooper Creek, Warrego, Charleville, Warburton

Macleod, Gascoyne, Carnarvon, Shark Bay, L. Carnegie, L. Wells, Murchison, L. Eyre (North), L. Eyre (South), Sturt Stony Desert, Grey Range, Dirranbandi, Bourke, Barwon, L. Blanche, Great Victoria Desert, L. Carey, L. Torrens, Flinders Ranges, St Mary Peak 1170, L. Frome, Darling, Broken Hill, Cobar, Dubbo, Parkes

L. Barlee, Geraldton, L. Moore, Kalgoorlie, L. Cowan, Nullarbor Plain, L. Gairdner, Port Augusta, Whyalla, Port Pirie, Eyre Pen., Port Lincoln, Murray, Lachlan, Murrumbidgee, Griffith, Hay, Mildura, Wagga Wagga, Albury, Canberra, Mt Kosciuszko 2230

Perth, Fremantle, Rockingham, Mandurah, Swan, Norseman, Ravensthorpe, Esperance, Point Malcolm, Bunbury, Hood Pt, C. Leeuwin, Albany, Adelaide, Murray Bridge, Kangaroo I., Cape Jaffa, Echuca, Shepparton, Wangaratta, Bendigo, Horsham, Mt William 1167, Ballarat, Mount Gambier, Hamilton, Melbourne, Traralgon, Sale, Bairnsdale, Moe, Portland, Warrnambool, Geelong, Cape Otway, Wilson's Promontory, King I., Flinders I., Furneaux Group, Burnie, Devonport, Mt Ossa 1617, Launceston, Hobart, South West Cape, South East Cape

Relief and physical features

Relief metres

5000, 3000, 2000, 1000, 500, 200, sea level, below sea level, 0, 200, 3000, 5000

3754 Mountain height (in metres)

Water features

River

Intermittent river

Lake / Reservoir

Intermittent lake

Marsh

Coral reef

Communications

Railway

Road

Main airport

Administration

Boundaries

International

Internal

Urban population

over 1 000 000

500 000 - 1 000 000

100 000 - 500 000

under 100 000

Square symbols denote national capital cities.

SCALE 1 : 16 500 000

0 200 400 600 800 km

Just off the east coast of Australia, the Great Barrier Reef is shown as light blue in this true-colour image. Global warming and increased tourist traffic have put many of the areas of the reef in ecological danger.

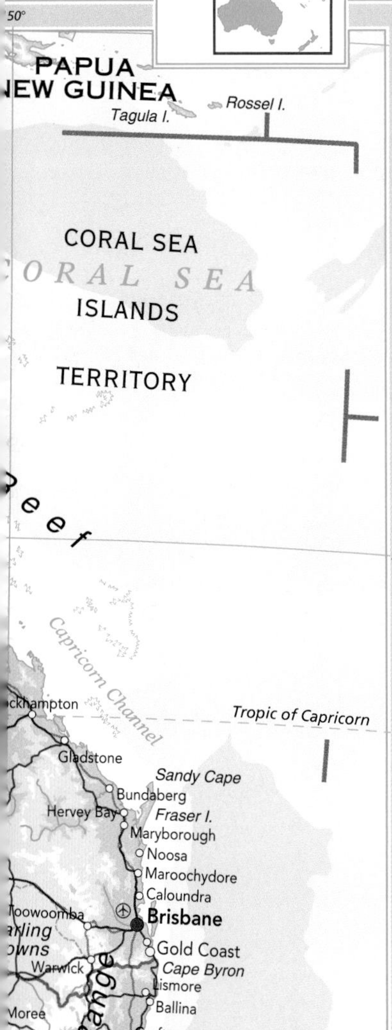

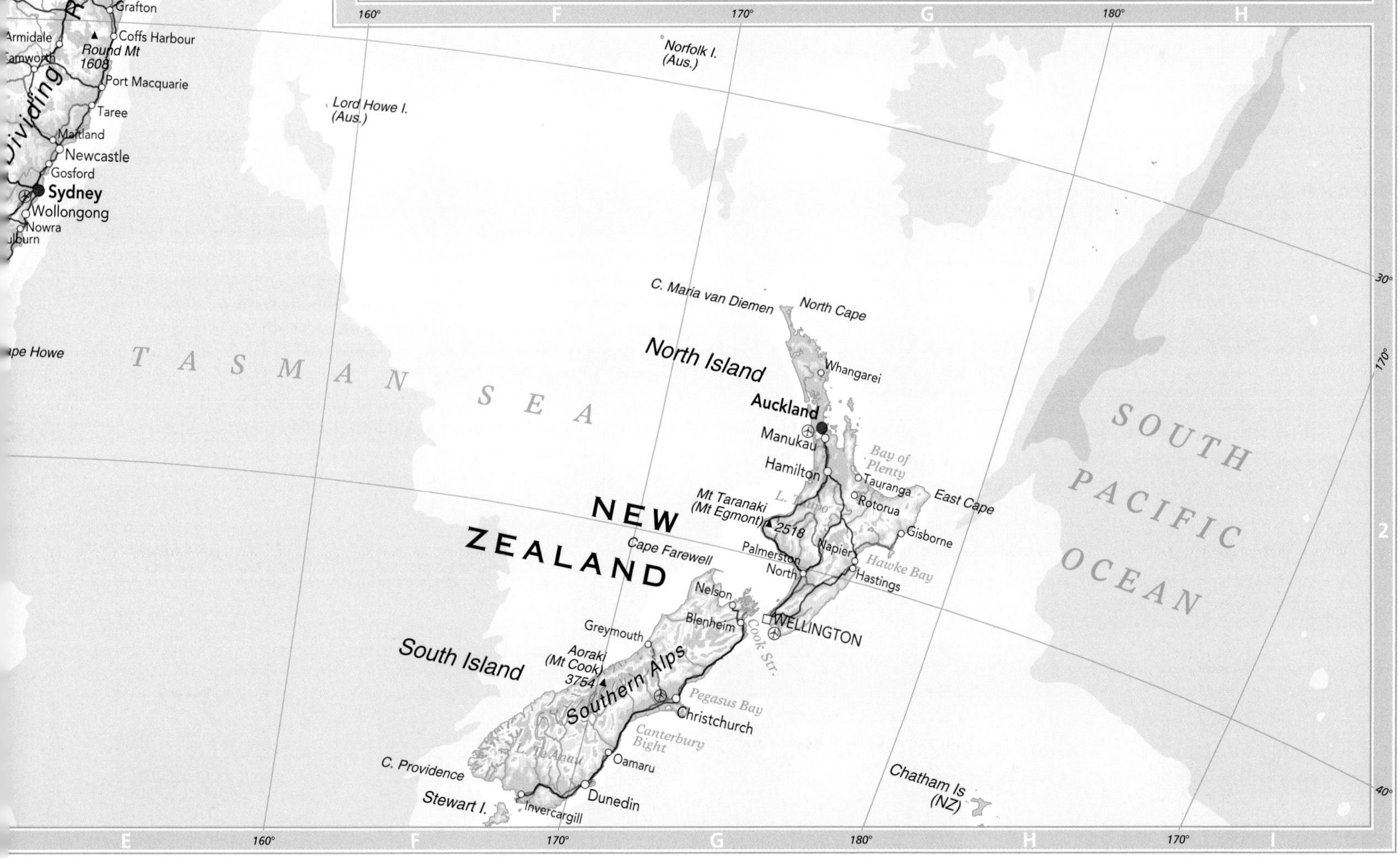

Lambert Azimuthal Equal Area projection

LAND USE

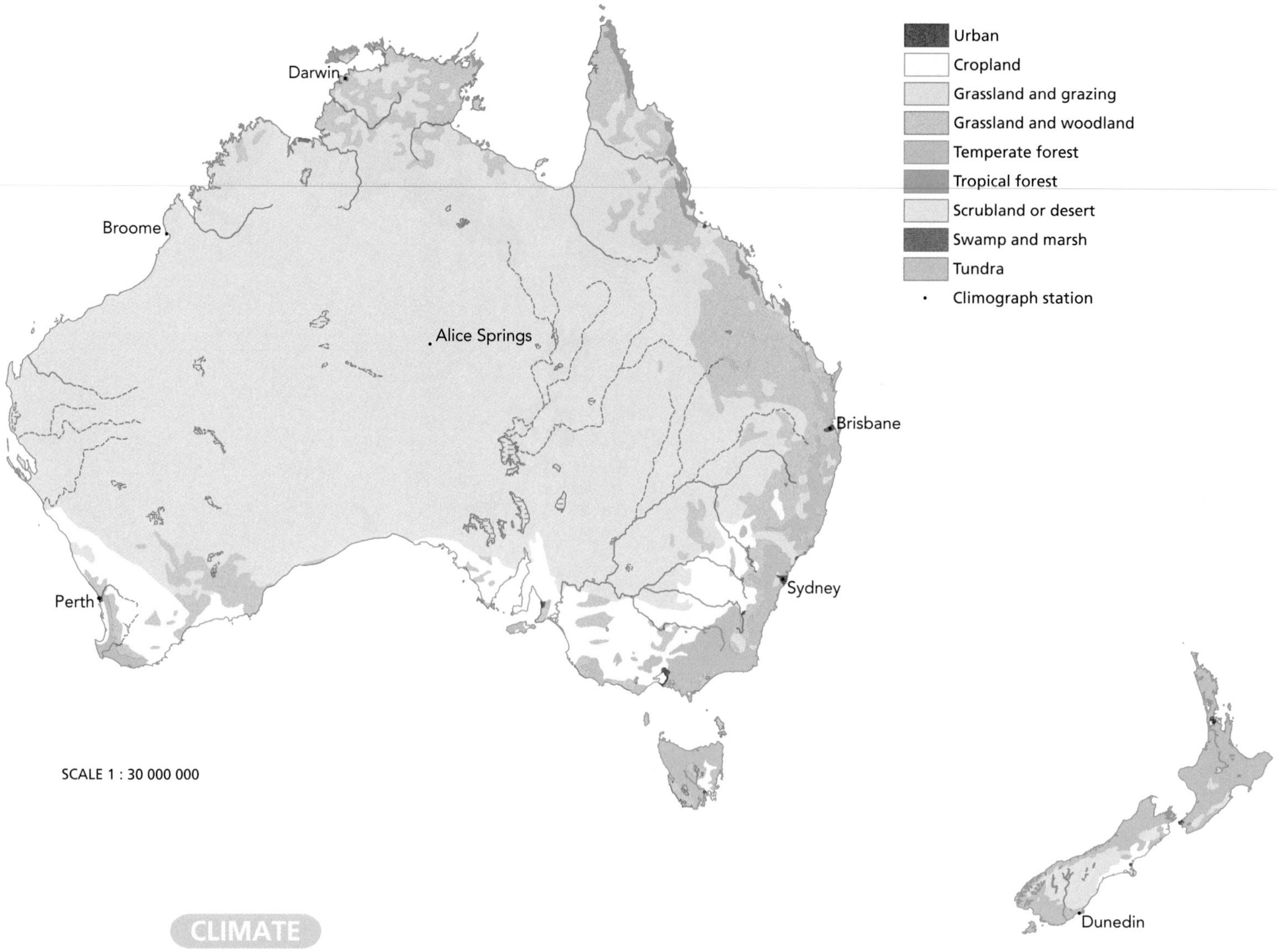

CLIMATE

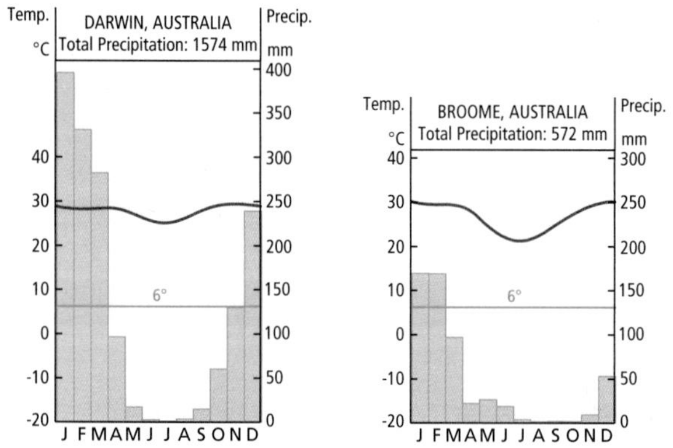

Australia is the sixth largest country in the world. Although the central "outback" is arid, the coastal areas range from Mediterranean in land use and climate (the area near Perth and Adelaide), to subtropical (the Gold Coast near Brisbane), to tropical (Darwin area). New Zealand's land use is dominated by the grazing lands of South Island and the forests of North Island.

The region is home to unique plants and animals not found in other areas – the kiwi, kangaroo, koala, and duck-billed platypus. The presence of unique wildlife has contributed to establishing environmental conservation and protection as priorities.

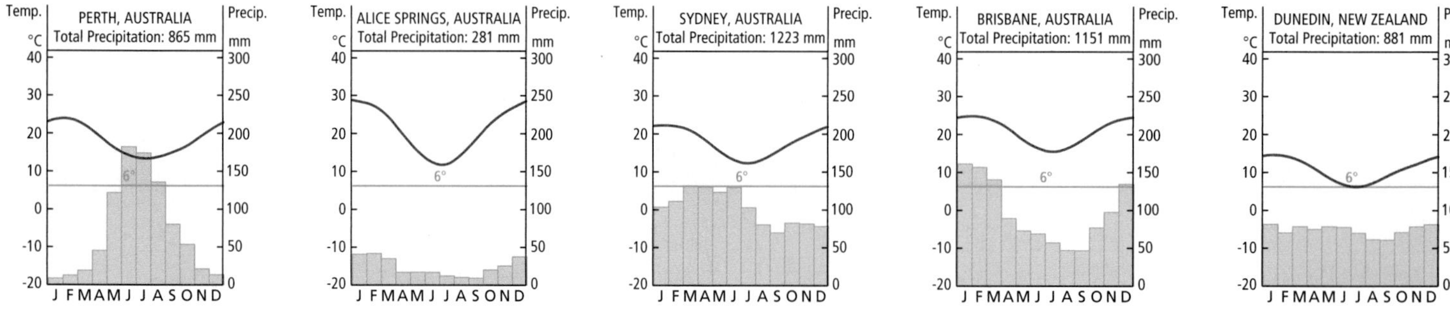

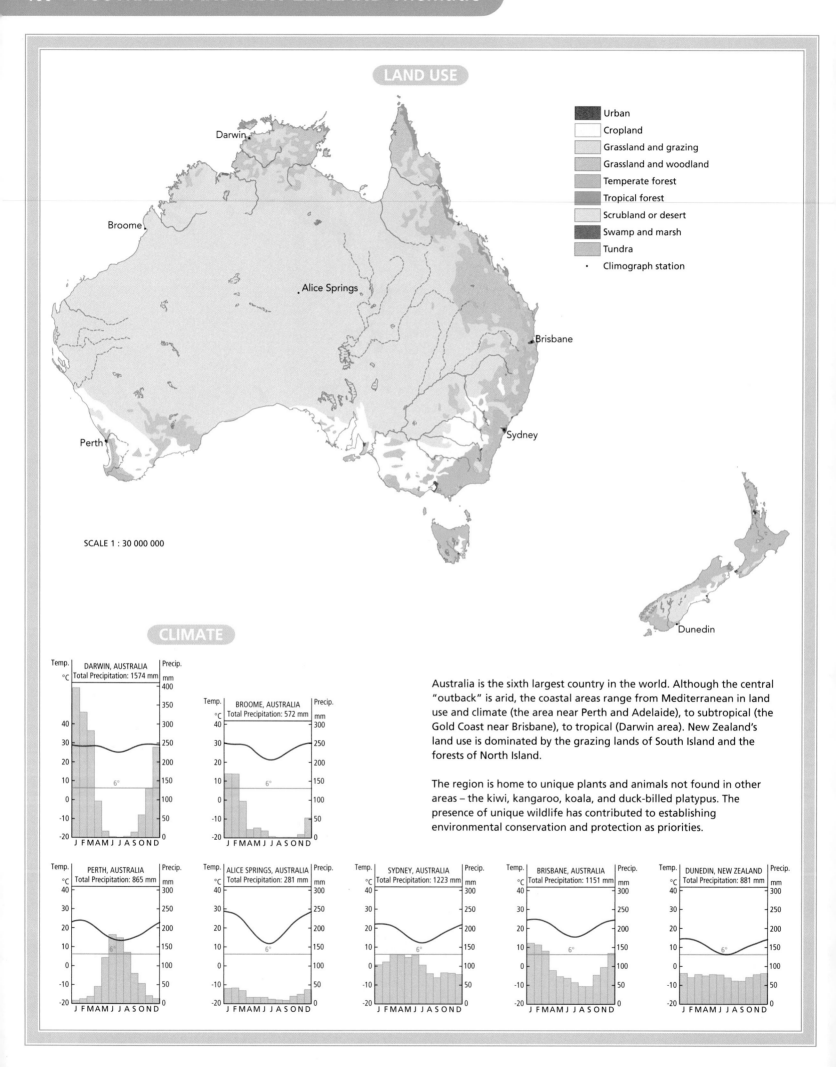

TOURISM

Top Destinations, 2000

Country	Income from tourism	
	Millions, US$	Percent of GDP
New Zealand	2 068	4.1
Australia	8 442	2.2

SETTLEMENT

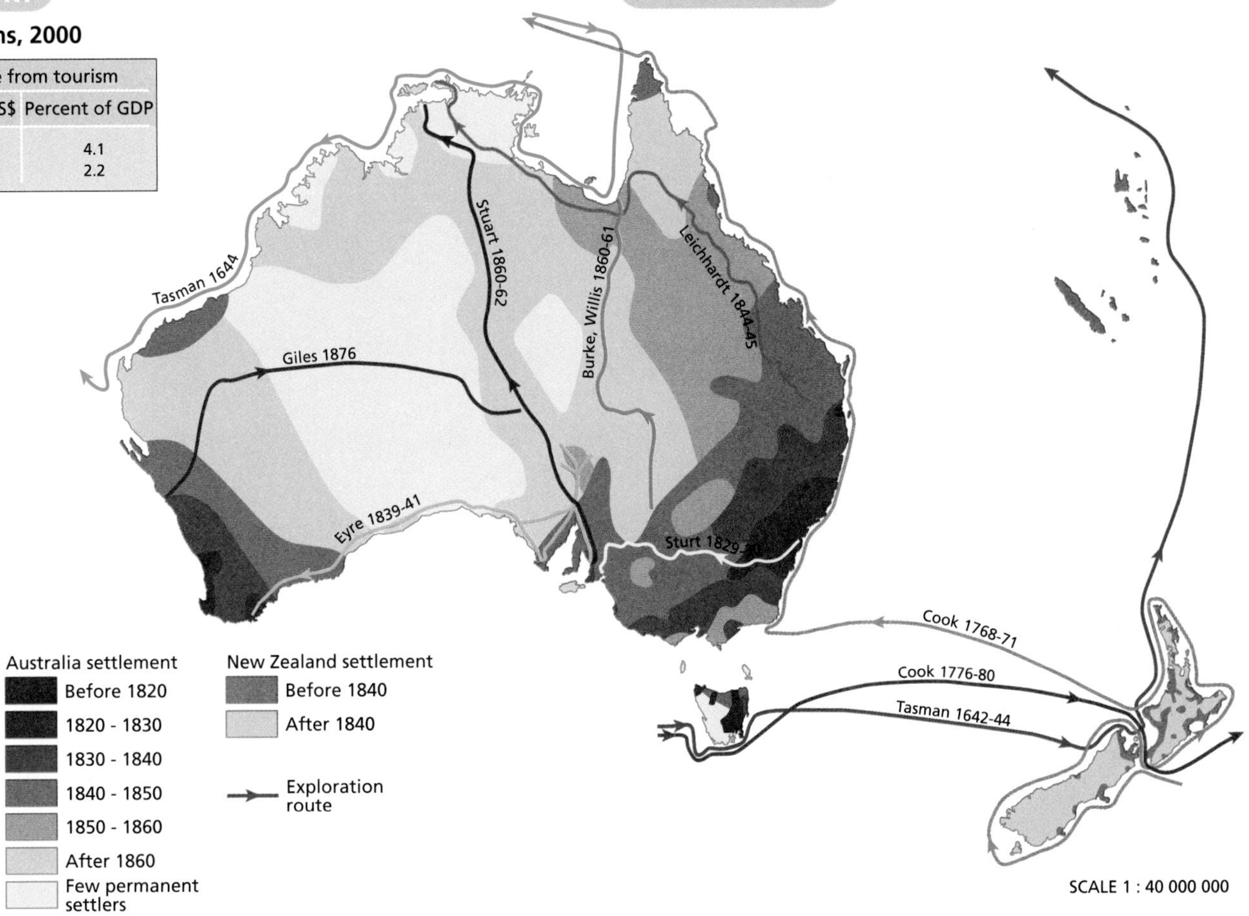

MIGRATION

NET MIGRATION TO AUSTRALIA

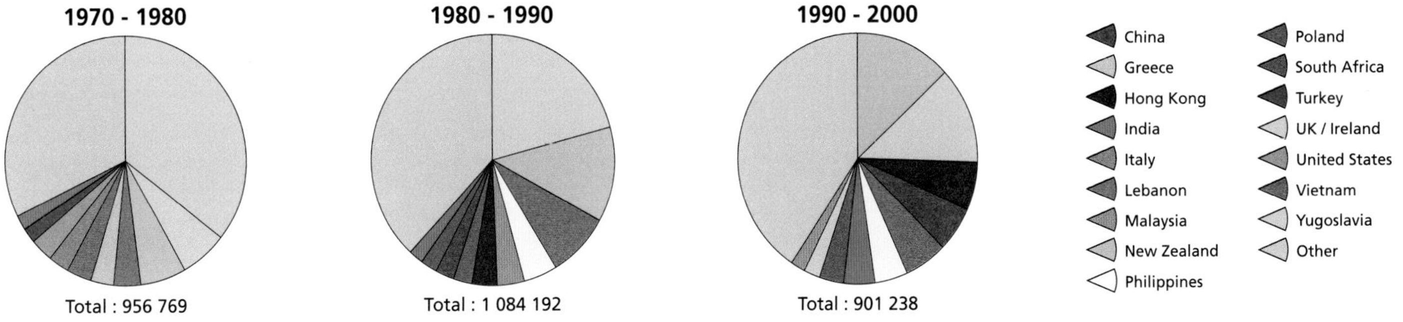

ECONOMY

AUSTRALIA

Trade, 2001

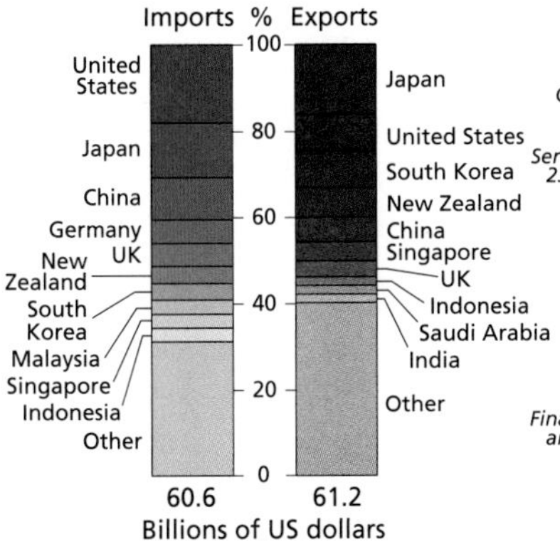

GDP by sector, 2001

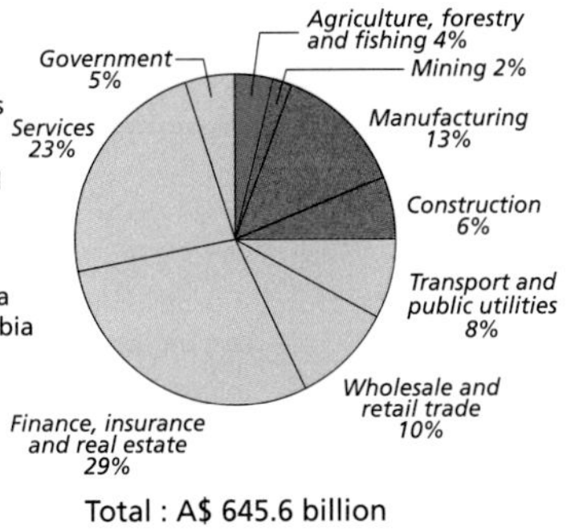

NEW ZEALAND

Trade, 2001

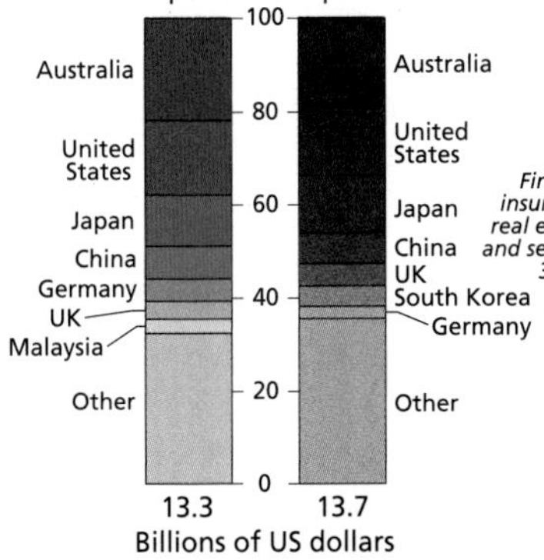

GDP by sector, 2001

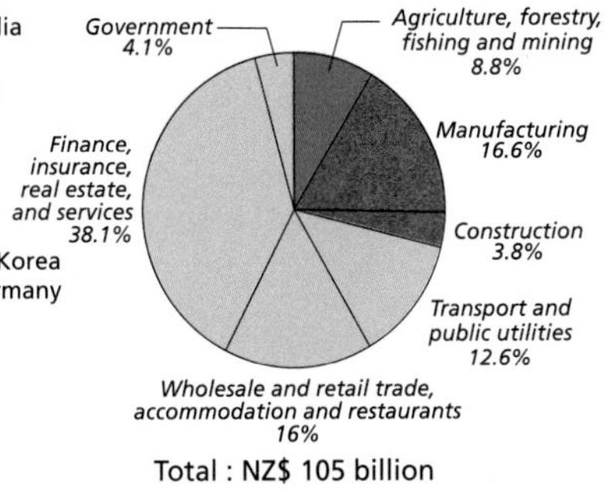

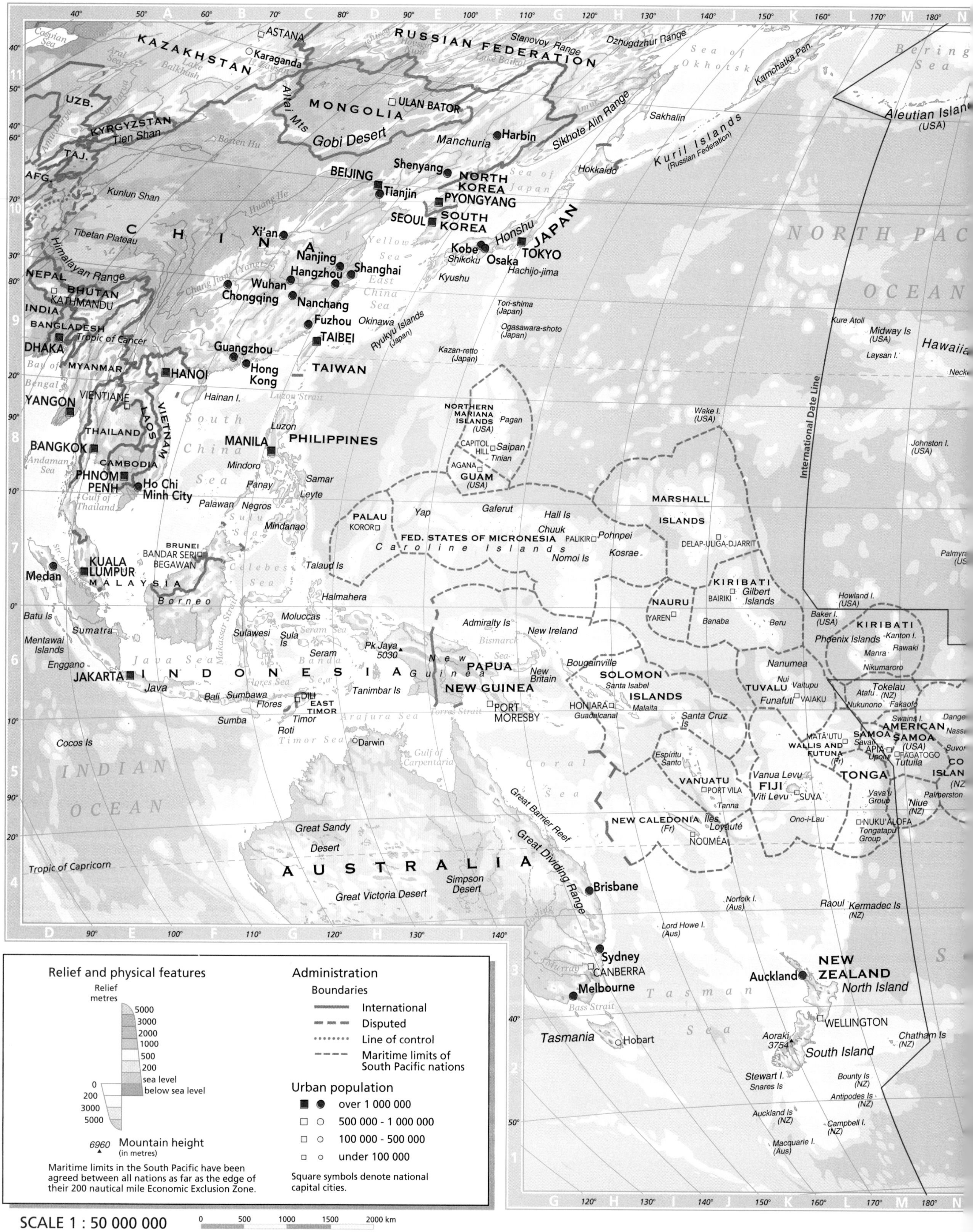
Caspian Sea
KAZAKHSTAN
ASTANA
Karaganda
Aral Sea
Lake Balkhash
RUSSIAN FEDERATION
Stanovoy Range
Dzhugdzhur Range
Sea of Okhotsk
Kamchatka Pen.
Bering Sea
Lake Baikal
UZB.
KYRGYZSTAN
Tien Shan
TAJ.
AFG.
MONGOLIA
ULAN BATOR
Altai Mts
Gobi Desert
Bosten Hu
Manchuria
Harbin
Sikhote Alin Range
Sakhalin
Kuril Islands (Russian Federation)
Aleutian Islands (USA)
Hokkaido
Shenyang
NORTH KOREA
PYONGYANG
Sea of Japan
BEIJING
Tianjin
SEOUL
SOUTH KOREA
Kunlun Shan
Huang He
CHINA
Tibetan Plateau
Himalayan Range
Xi'an
Nanjing
Shanghai
Hangzhou
Wuhan
Chongqing
Nanchang
Chang Jiang (Yangtze)
Yellow Sea
East China Sea
Honshu
JAPAN
Kobe
Osaka
TOKYO
Shikoku
Kyushu
Hachijo-jima
NORTH PACIFIC OCEAN
NEPAL
BHUTAN
KATHMANDU
INDIA
BANGLADESH
DHAKA
Tropic of Cancer
Fuzhou
Okinawa
Ryukyu Islands (Japan)
TAIBEI
TAIWAN
Tori-shima (Japan)
Ogasawara-shoto (Japan)
Kazan-retto (Japan)
Guangzhou
Hong Kong
Bay of Bengal
MYANMAR
HANOI
Hainan I.
Luzon Strait
YANGON
VIENTIANE
LAOS
VIETNAM
THAILAND
BANGKOK
Andaman Sea
CAMBODIA
PHNOM PENH
Ho Chi Minh City
Gulf of Thailand
South China Sea
Luzon
MANILA
PHILIPPINES
Mindoro
Panay
Samar
Leyte
Palawan
Negros
Mindanao
Sulu Sea
NORTHERN MARIANA ISLANDS (USA)
Pagan
CAPITOL HILL
Saipan
Tinian
AGANA
GUAM (USA)
Kure Atoll
Midway Is (USA)
Laysan I.
Hawaiian
Necker
Wake I. (USA)
International Date Line
Johnston I. (USA)
PALAU
KOROR
Yap
Gaferut
Hall Is
Chuuk
FED. STATES OF MICRONESIA
PALIKIR
Pohnpei
Kosrae
Caroline Islands
Nomoi Is
MARSHALL ISLANDS
DELAP-ULIGA-DJARRIT
Palmyra (US)
BRUNEI
BANDAR SERI BEGAWAN
KUALA LUMPUR
MALAYSIA
Medan
Str. of Malacca
Celebes Sea
Talaud Is
Borneo
Halmahera
KIRIBATI
BAIRIKI
Gilbert Islands
NAURU
YAREN
Banaba
Beru
Howland I. (USA)
Baker I. (USA)
KIRIBATI
Phoenix Islands
Kanton I.
Rawaki
Manra
Nikumaroro
Batu Is
Sumatra
Mentawai Islands
Enggano
Moluccas
Seram Sea
Sulawesi
Sula Is
Seram
Makassar Strait
Banda Sea
Admiralty Is
Bismarck Sea
New Ireland
Pk Jaya 5030
Java Sea
JAKARTA
INDONESIA
Java
New Guinea
PAPUA NEW GUINEA
New Britain
Bougainville
SOLOMON ISLANDS
Santa Isabel
Malaita
HONIARA
Guadalcanal
Nanumea
Nui
Vaitupu
TUVALU
Funafuti
VAIAKU
Tokelau (NZ)
Atafu
Nukunonu
Fakaofo
Flores Sea
Bali
Sumbawa
Flores
DILI
EAST TIMOR
Tanimbar Is
Sumba
Timor
Roti
Timor Sea
Arafura Sea
Torres Strait
PORT MORESBY
Santa Cruz Is
Swains I.
AMERICAN SAMOA (USA)
SAMOA
Savai'i
APIA
Upolu
FAGATOGO
Tutuila
MATĀ'UTU
WALLIS AND FUTUNA (Fr)
Darwin
Cocos Is
Gulf of Carpentaria
Coral Sea
Espiritu Santo
VANUATU
PORT VILA
Tanna
Vanua Levu
FIJI
Viti Levu
SUVA
TONGA
Vava'u Group
Niue (NZ)
Palmerston
INDIAN OCEAN
Great Barrier Reef
NEW CALEDONIA (Fr)
Îles Loyauté
NOUMÉA
Ono-i-Lau
NUKU'ALOFA
Tongatapu Group
Great Sandy Desert
Great Dividing Range
AUSTRALIA
Tropic of Capricorn
Simpson Desert
Great Victoria Desert
Brisbane
Norfolk I. (Aus)
Raoul
Kermadec Is (NZ)
Lord Howe I. (Aus)
Darling
Murray
Sydney
CANBERRA
Melbourne
Bass Strait
Tasman Sea
NEW ZEALAND
Auckland
North Island
WELLINGTON
Tasmania
Hobart
Aoraki 3754
South Island
Chatham Is (NZ)
Stewart I.
Snares Is
Bounty Is (NZ)
Antipodes Is (NZ)
Auckland Is (NZ)
Campbell I. (NZ)
Macquarie I. (Aus)
Relief and physical features
Relief metres
5000
3000
2000
1000
500
200
sea level
below sea level
0
200
3000
5000
6960 Mountain height (in metres)
Maritime limits in the South Pacific have been agreed between all nations as far as the edge of their 200 nautical mile Economic Exclusion Zone.
Administration
Boundaries
International
Disputed
Line of control
Maritime limits of South Pacific nations
Urban population
over 1 000 000
500 000 - 1 000 000
100 000 - 500 000
under 100 000
Square symbols denote national capital cities.

SCALE 1 : 50 000 000

0 500 1000 1500 2000 km

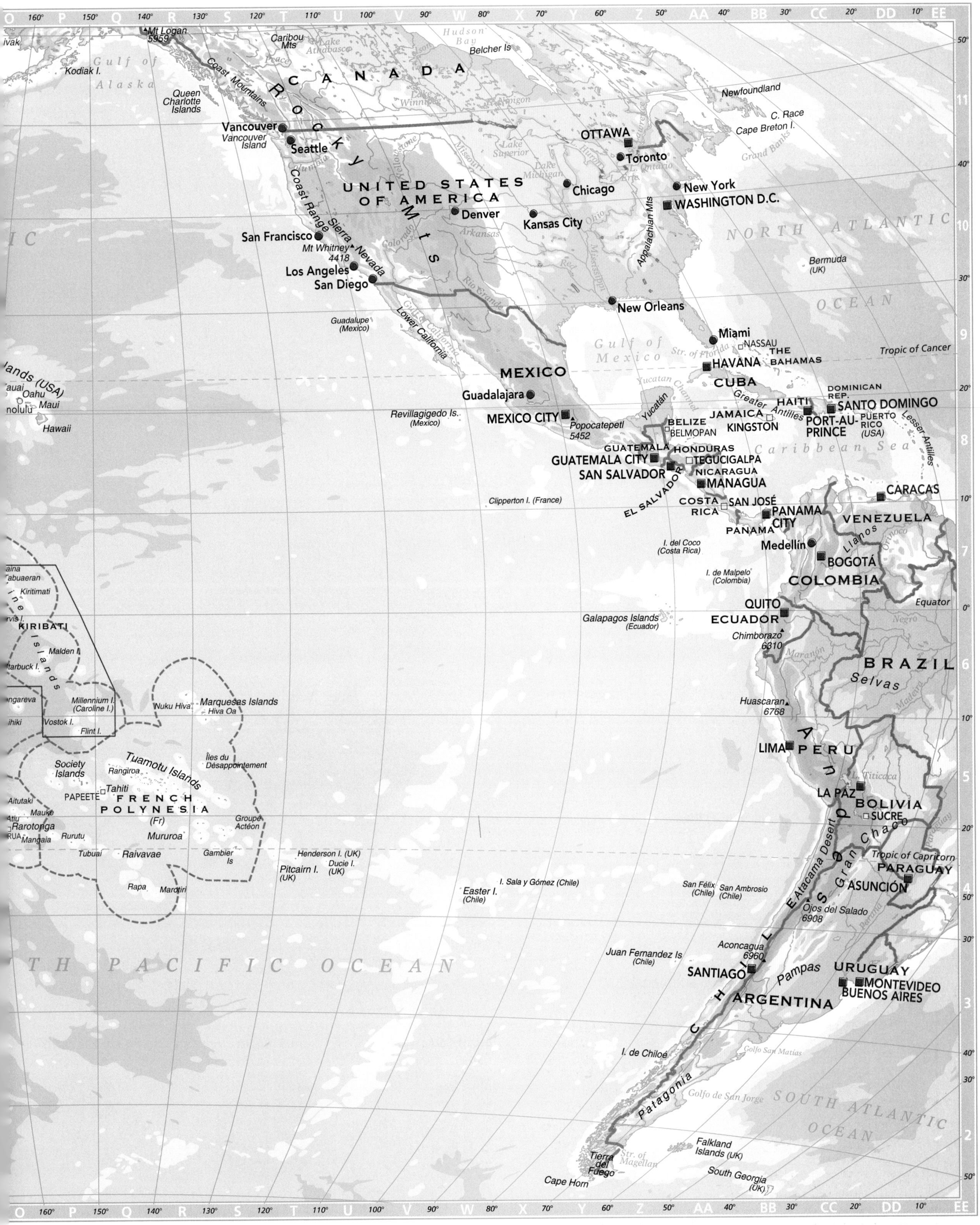

Mt Logan 5959
Caribou Mts
Lake Athabasca
Hudson Bay
Belcher Is
Kodiak I.
Gulf of Alaska
Queen Charlotte Islands
Coast Mountains
CANADA
ROCKY Mts
Lake Winnipeg
Nipigon
Newfoundland
C. Race
Cape Breton I.
Grand Banks
Vancouver
Vancouver Island
Seattle
OTTAWA
Toronto
L. Ontario
Lake Superior
Lake Michigan
Huron
Erie
UNITED STATES OF AMERICA
Chicago
New York
WASHINGTON D.C.
Denver
Kansas City
Coast Range
Sierra Nevada
San Francisco
Mt Whitney 4418
Los Angeles
San Diego
Colorado
Arkansas
Ohio
Mississippi
Missouri
Appalachian Mts
Rio Grande
Red
NORTH ATLANTIC OCEAN
Bermuda (UK)
New Orleans
Guadalupe (Mexico)
Lower California
Gulf of California
Gulf of Mexico
Miami
Str. of Florida
NASSAU
THE BAHAMAS
Tropic of Cancer
MEXICO
HAVANA
CUBA
Yucatan Channel
Yucatán
Guadalajara
Revillagigedo Is. (Mexico)
MEXICO CITY
Popocatepetl 5452
Greater Antilles
DOMINICAN REP.
HAITI
SANTO DOMINGO
PORT-AU-PRINCE
PUERTO RICO (USA)
Lesser Antilles
JAMAICA
KINGSTON
BELIZE
BELMOPAN
GUATEMALA
GUATEMALA CITY
HONDURAS
TEGUCIGALPA
Caribbean Sea
SAN SALVADOR
EL SALVADOR
NICARAGUA
MANAGUA
COSTA RICA
SAN JOSÉ
PANAMA CITY
PANAMA
CARACAS
VENEZUELA
Clipperton I. (France)
Llanos
Orinoco
I. del Coco (Costa Rica)
Medellín
BOGOTÁ
COLOMBIA
I. de Malpelo (Colombia)
QUITO
ECUADOR
Equator
Galapagos Islands (Ecuador)
Chimborazo 6310
Negro
Marañón
BRAZIL
Selvas
Madeira
Huascaran 6768
LIMA
PERU
ANDES
L. Titicaca
LA PAZ
BOLIVIA
SUCRE
Gran Chaco
Atacama Desert
Paraguay
Tropic of Capricorn
PARAGUAY
ASUNCIÓN
Paraná
San Félix (Chile)
San Ambrosio (Chile)
Ojos del Salado 6908
Aconcagua 6960
Juan Fernandez Is (Chile)
SANTIAGO
CHILE
Pampas
URUGUAY
MONTEVIDEO
BUENOS AIRES
ARGENTINA
I. de Chiloé
Golfo San Matías
Golfo de San Jorge
Patagonia
SOUTH ATLANTIC OCEAN
Falkland Islands (UK)
Tierra del Fuego
Str. of Magellan
South Georgia (UK)
Cape Horn
Hawaiian Islands (USA)
Oahu
Maui
Hawaii
Kiritimati
KIRIBATI
Line Islands
Malden I.
Starbuck I.
Millennium I. (Caroline I.)
Vostok I.
Flint I.
Nuku Hiva
Marquesas Islands
Hiva Oa
Îles du Désappointement
Tuamotu Islands
Rangiroa
Society Islands
Tahiti
PAPEETE
FRENCH POLYNESIA (Fr)
Mururoa
Groupe Actéon
Rarotonga
Mangaia
Rurutu
Tubuai
Raivavae
Gambier Is
Rapa
Marotiri
Henderson I. (UK)
Ducie I. (UK)
Pitcairn I. (UK)
Easter I. (Chile)
I. Sala y Gómez (Chile)
PACIFIC OCEAN

Hammer - Aitoff projection

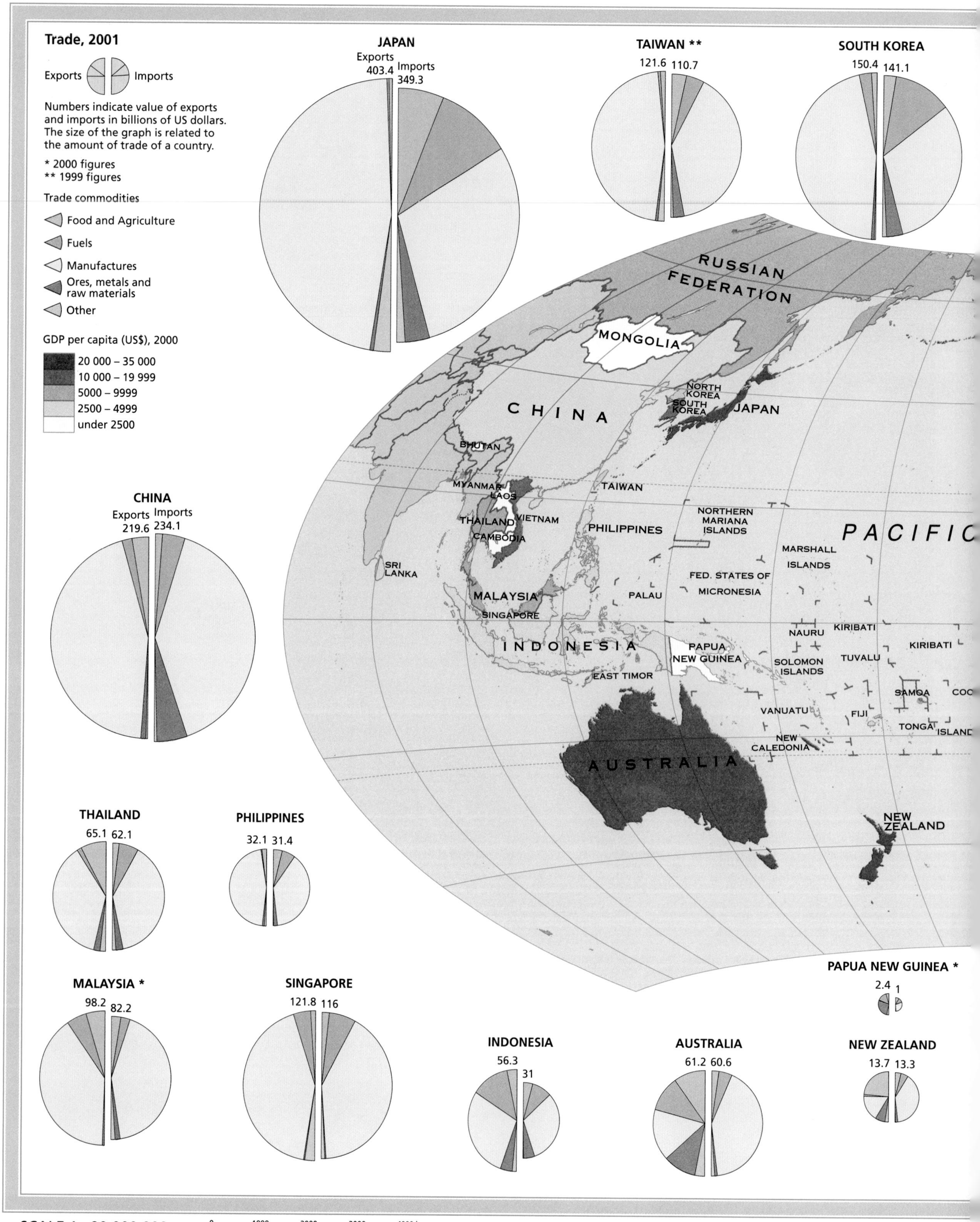
Trade, 2001
Exports
Imports
Numbers indicate value of exports and imports in billions of US dollars. The size of the graph is related to the amount of trade of a country.
* 2000 figures
** 1999 figures
Trade commodities
Food and Agriculture
Fuels
Manufactures
Ores, metals and raw materials
Other
GDP per capita (US$), 2000
20 000 – 35 000
10 000 – 19 999
5000 – 9999
2500 – 4999
under 2500
JAPAN
Exports 403.4
Imports 349.3
TAIWAN **
121.6 110.7
SOUTH KOREA
150.4 141.1
CHINA
Exports 219.6
Imports 234.1
THAILAND
65.1 62.1
PHILIPPINES
32.1 31.4
MALAYSIA *
98.2 82.2
SINGAPORE
121.8 116
INDONESIA
56.3 31
AUSTRALIA
61.2 60.6
PAPUA NEW GUINEA *
2.4 1
NEW ZEALAND
13.7 13.3
RUSSIAN FEDERATION
MONGOLIA
CHINA
NORTH KOREA
SOUTH KOREA
JAPAN
BHUTAN
MYANMAR
LAOS
TAIWAN
THAILAND
VIETNAM
CAMBODIA
PHILIPPINES
SRI LANKA
NORTHERN MARIANA ISLANDS
MARSHALL ISLANDS
PACIFIC
FED. STATES OF MICRONESIA
PALAU
MALAYSIA
SINGAPORE
INDONESIA
PAPUA NEW GUINEA
EAST TIMOR
NAURU
KIRIBATI
KIRIBATI
TUVALU
SOLOMON ISLANDS
SAMOA
VANUATU
FIJI
TONGA
NEW CALEDONIA
AUSTRALIA
NEW ZEALAND

SCALE 1 : 90 000 000

0 1000 2000 3000 4000 km

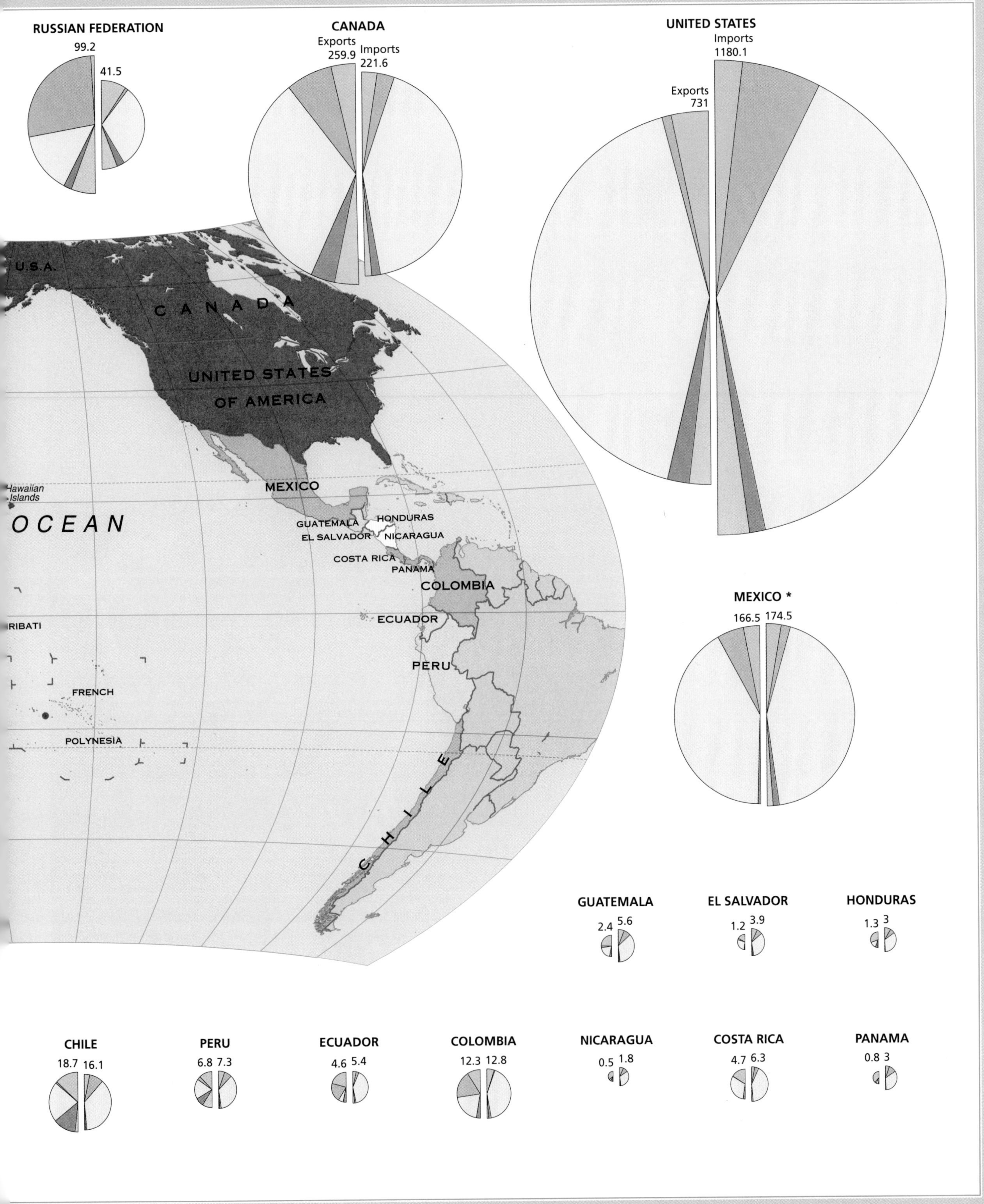
RUSSIAN FEDERATION
99.2
41.5
CANADA
Exports
259.9
Imports
221.6
UNITED STATES
Imports
1180.1
Exports
731
U.S.A.
CANADA
UNITED STATES OF AMERICA
MEXICO
Hawaiian Islands
OCEAN
GUATEMALA
HONDURAS
EL SALVADOR
NICARAGUA
COSTA RICA
PANAMA
COLOMBIA
ECUADOR
PERU
CHILE
KIRIBATI
FRENCH
POLYNESIA
MEXICO *
166.5 174.5
GUATEMALA
2.4 5.6
EL SALVADOR
1.2 3.9
HONDURAS
1.3 3
CHILE
18.7 16.1
PERU
6.8 7.3
ECUADOR
4.6 5.4
COLOMBIA
12.3 12.8
NICARAGUA
0.5 1.8
COSTA RICA
4.7 6.3
PANAMA
0.8 3

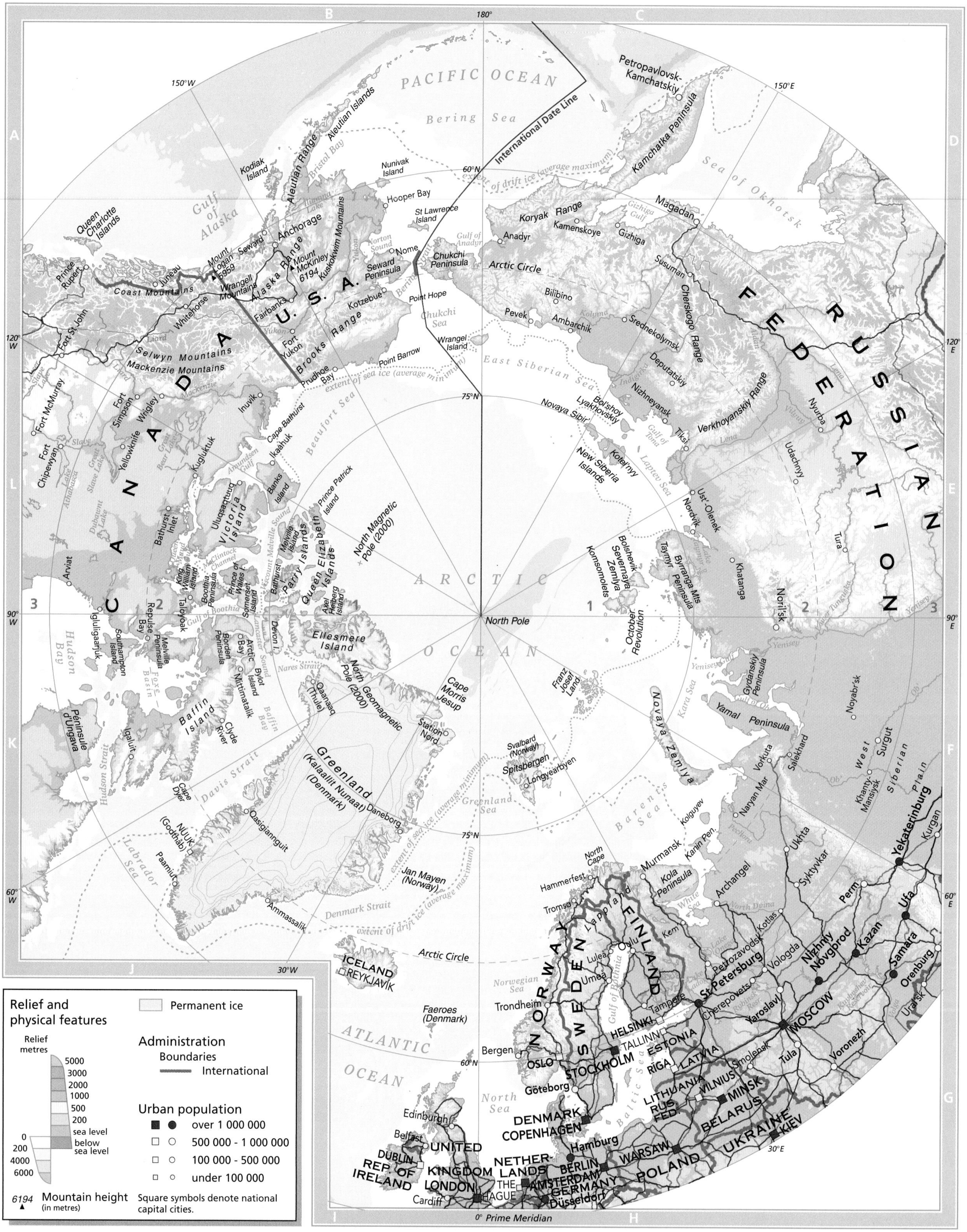

SCALE 1 : 35 000 000 — 0, 500, 1000, 1500, 2000 km — Polar Stereographic projection

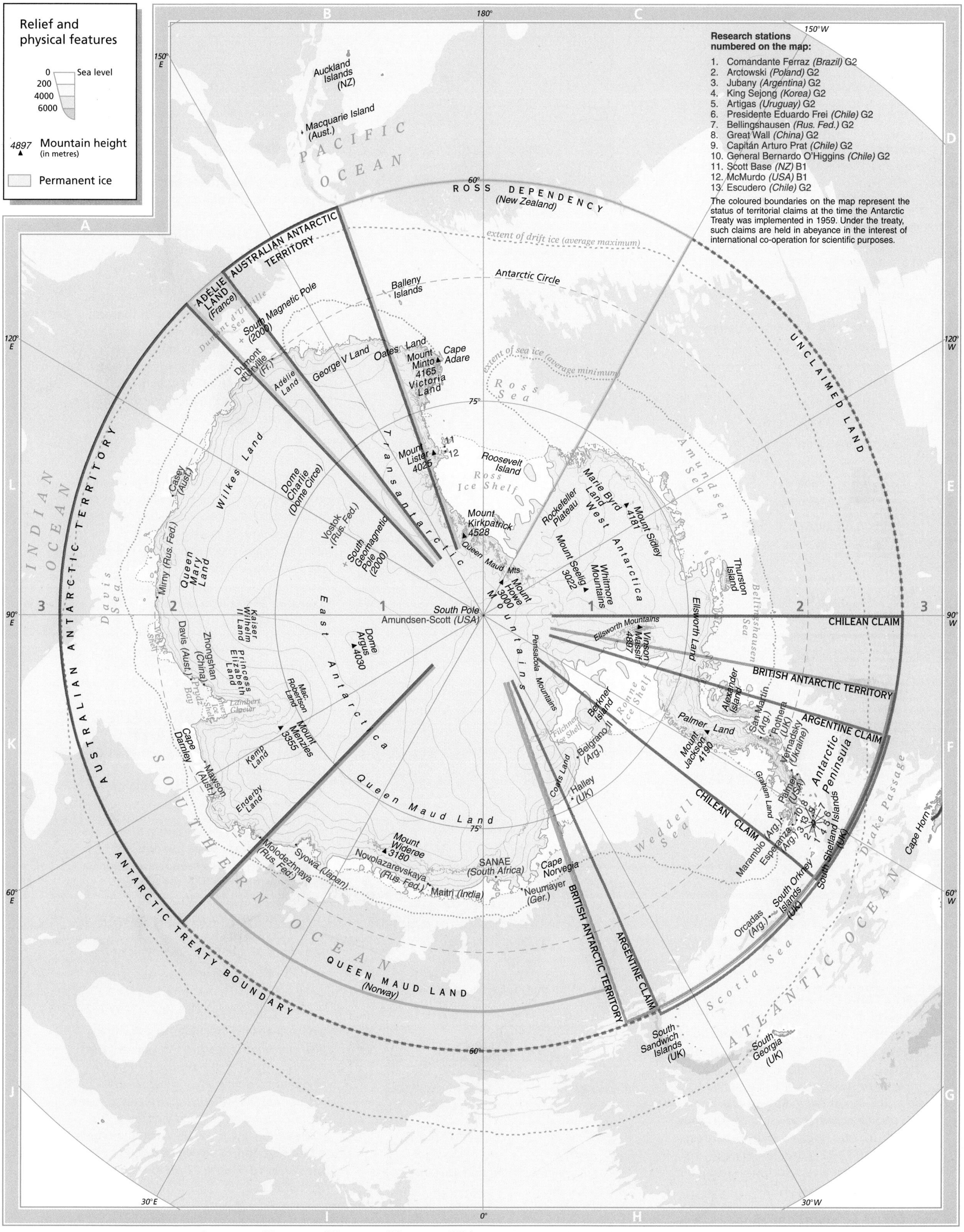

SCALE 1 : 35 000 000

Polar Stereographic Projection

Relief and physical features

Sea level
0
200
4000
6000

4897 ▲ Mountain height
(in metres)

Permanent ice

Research stations numbered on the map:
1. Comandante Ferraz (Brazil) G2
2. Arctowski (Poland) G2
3. Jubany (Argentina) G2
4. King Sejong (Korea) G2
5. Artigas (Uruguay) G2
6. Presidente Eduardo Frei (Chile) G2
7. Bellingshausen (Rus. Fed.) G2
8. Great Wall (China) G2
9. Capitán Arturo Prat (Chile) G2
10. General Bernardo O'Higgins (Chile) G2
11. Scott Base (NZ) B1
12. McMurdo (USA) B1
13. Escudero (Chile) G2

The coloured boundaries on the map represent the status of territorial claims at the time the Antarctic Treaty was implemented in 1959. Under the treaty, such claims are held in abeyance in the interest of international co-operation for scientific purposes.

1 MAP SYMBOLS

Symbols are used on a map to show the location of features such as roads, rivers and towns. The meaning of each symbol used on a map is explained in the legend.

Map symbols often look like the features they represent. The colour of the symbol also provides a clue to its meaning (e.g. water is usually blue). The importance of a feature might be shown by the size of the symbol (e.g. larger cities are usually represented by larger circles).

Some examples of the symbols used in this atlas are shown below :

Water features
- River
- Lake / Reservoir

Communications
- Railway
- Road
- Main airport

Urban population
- over 1 000 000
- 500 000 - 1 000 000
- 100 000 - 500 000
- under 100 000

Square symbols denote national capital cities

2 DIRECTION

Determining direction on a map is important because it indicates where one place is in relation to other places. The points of the compass are used to show the difference in direction between one place and another.

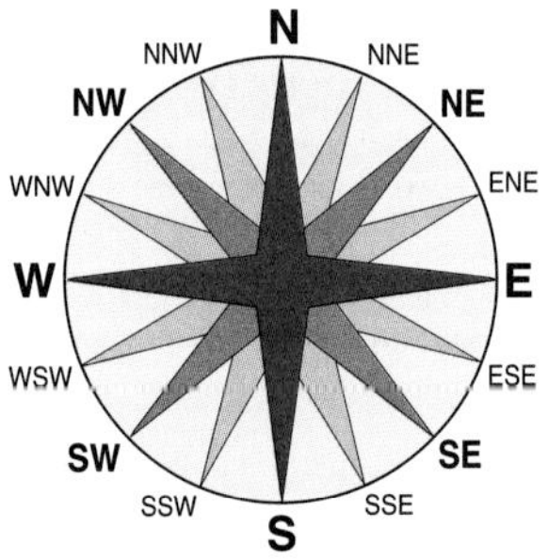

North, south, east and west are called the cardinal points of the compass. The other points are called intermediate points. Many maps have an arrow to indicate the direction toward north. If a map does not have a north arrow, north is assumed to be at the top of the map. Accurate direction can also be determined using the degrees of a circle. Zero degrees and 360 degrees are north (like 12 o'clock on a clock), and the numbers proceed clockwise. East is 90°, south is 180° and west is 270°.

3 MAP TYPES

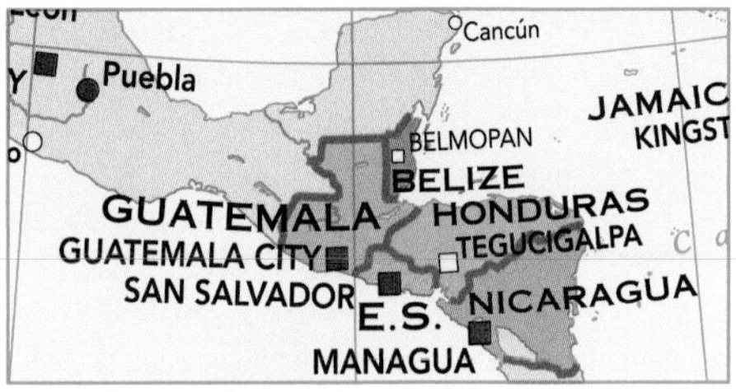

Part of Central America

Political maps provide an overview of the size and location of countries in a specific area, such as a continent. Coloured squares indicate capital cities. Coloured circles represent other cities, with the size of the circle indicating the approximate size of the city.
See pages 108 and 126 for examples of this type of map.

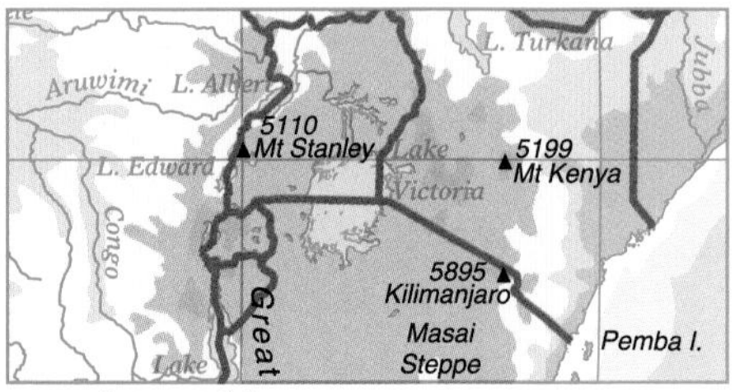

Part of East Africa

Physical maps use colour to show oceans, seas, rivers, lakes, and height of the land. The names and heights of major landforms are also indicated. More information about land height, relief, and colour layers can be found on pages 172 and 175.
See pages 109 and 127 for examples of this type of map.

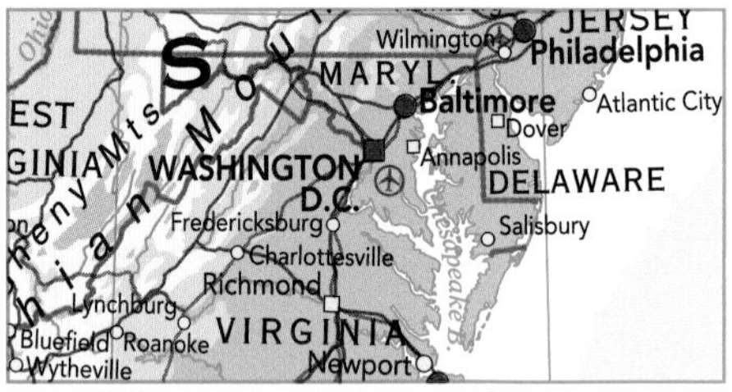

Part of the eastern seaboard of the United States

Physical/political maps bring together the information provided in the two types of map described above. They show relief and physical features as well as country borders, major cities and towns, roads, railways, and airports.
See pages 112–113 and 122–123 for examples of this type of map.

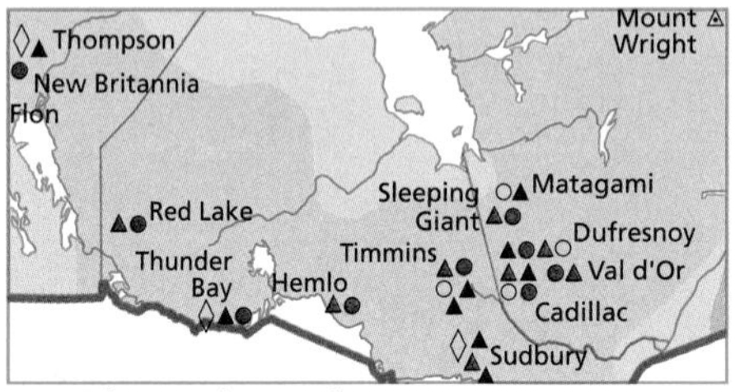

Part of central Canada

Distribution maps use different colours, symbols, or shading to show the location and distribution of natural or human-made features. In this map, different symbols have been used to show the location of iron ore, zinc, copper, nickel, silver and gold.
See pages 20 and 86 for examples of this type of map.

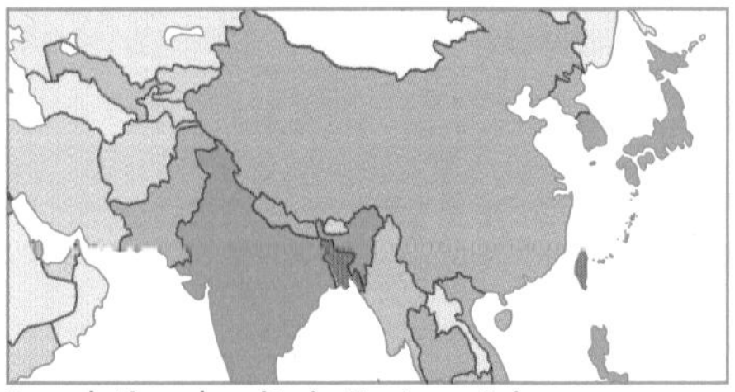

Population density in Eastern Asia

Graduated colour maps use dots, colours, or shading to show a feature's location and intensity. Generally, the highest numbers are shaded with the darkest colours. In this map, colours are used to show population density.
See pages 88 and 92 for examples of this type of map.

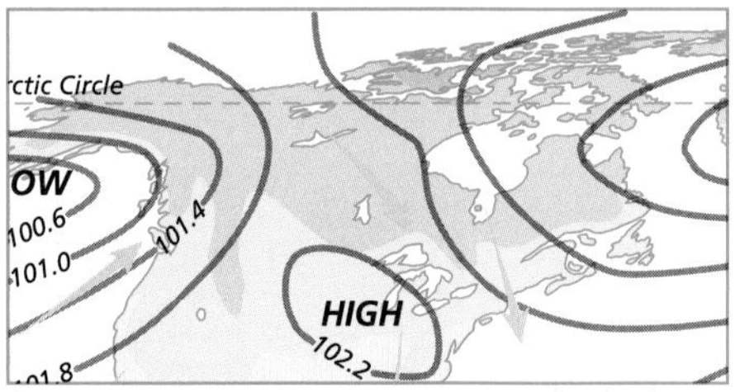

January temperature, pressure, and winds over Canada

Isoline maps use thin lines to show the distribution of a feature. An isoline passes through places that have the same value or quantity. Isolines may show features such as temperature (isotherm), air pressure (isobar), or height of land (contour). The value of the line is usually written on it; on either side, the value will be higher or lower.
See pages 10–11 and 82 for examples of this type of map.

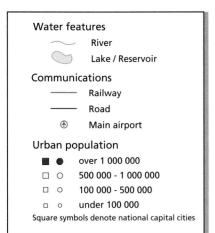

1 SCALE

To draw a map of any part of the world, the area must be reduced, or "scaled down," to the size of a page in this atlas, a foldable road map, or a topographic map. The scale of the map indicates the amount by which an area has been reduced.

The scale of a map can also be used to determine the actual distance between two or more places or the actual size of an area on a map. The scale indicates the relationship between distances on the map and distances on the ground.

Scale can be shown

- **using words:** for example, "one centimetre to one kilometre" (one centimetre on the map represents one kilometre on the ground), or "one centimetre to 100 kilometres" (one centimetre on the map represents 100 kilometres on the ground).
- **using numbers:** for example, "1: 100 000 or 1/100 000" (one centimetre on the map represents 100 000 centimetres on the ground), or "1: 40 000 000 or 1/40 000 000" (one centimetre on the map represents 40 million centimetres on the ground). Normally, the large numbers with centimetres would be converted to metres or kilometres.
- **as a line scale:** for example,

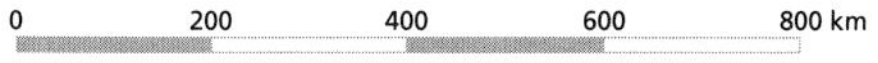

2 USING MAPS OF DIFFERENT SCALE

The scale of the map will determine how much and what type of information can be shown. As the area shown on the map becomes larger and larger, the amount of detail and accuracy of the map becomes less and less.

Excerpt from the topographic map of Montréal at a scale of 1: 250 000. At this scale, the islands and bridges across the St Lawrence River are visible and urban areas (pink) can be seen.

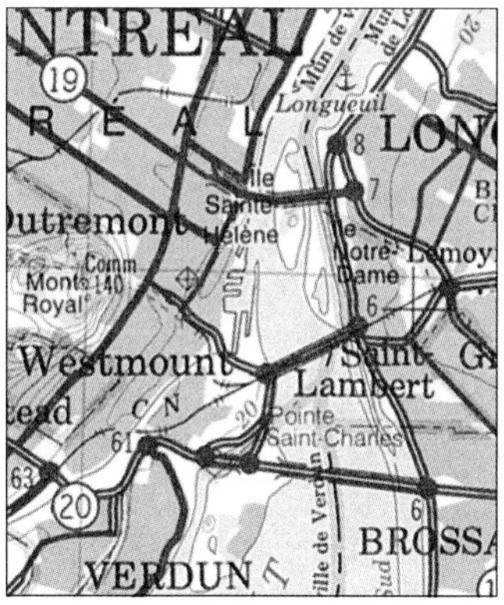

Excerpt from the map of Québec at a scale of 1: 7 500 000. At this scale, the general location of Montréal is indicated at the junction of the Ottawa and St Lawrence rivers, along with many of the surrounding towns and cities.

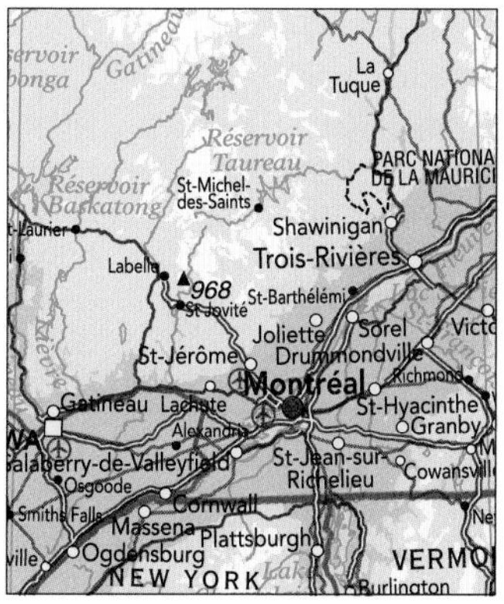

3 USING THE SCALE TO MEASURE DISTANCE

The instructions below show you how to determine how far apart places are on the map, then using the line scale, to determine the actual distance on the ground.

To use the line scale to measure the straight-line distance between two places on a map:

1. place the edge of a sheet of paper on the two places on a map,
2. on the paper, place a mark at each of the two places,
3. place the paper on the line scale,
4. measure the distance on the ground using the scale.

To find the distance between Calgary and Regina, line up the edge of a piece of paper between the two places and mark off the distance.

Compare this distance with the marks on the line scale. The straight-line distance between Calgary and Regina is about 650 kilometres.

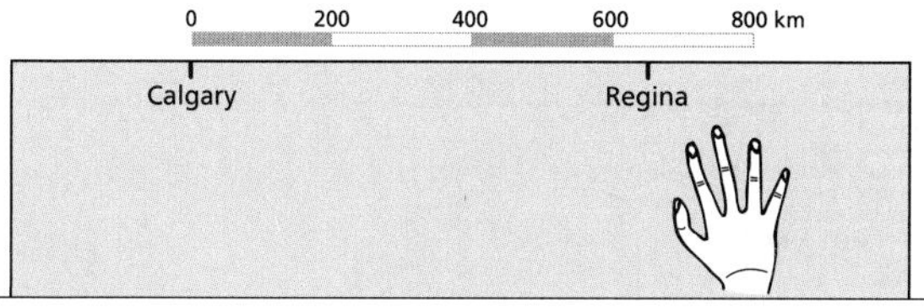

Often, the road or rail distance between two places is greater than the straight-line distance. To measure this distance:

1. place the edge of a sheet of paper on the map and mark off the start point on the paper,
2. move the paper so that its edge follows the bends and curves on the map (Hint: use the tip of your pencil to pin the edge of the paper to the curve as you pivot the paper around each curve),
3. mark off the end point on the sheet of paper,
4. place the paper on the line scale and read the actual distance following a road or railroad.

To find the distance by road between Calgary and Regina, mark off the start point, then twist the paper to follow the curve of the road through Medicine Hat, Swift Current, Moose Jaw, and then into Regina. The actual distance is about 750 kilometres.

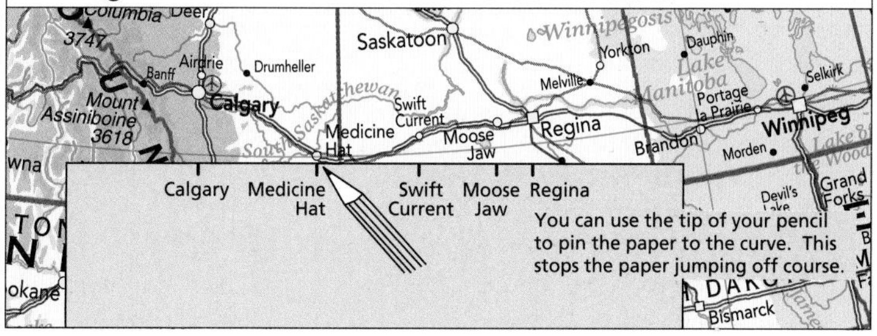

There are several ways of finding places on a map. This atlas uses three different methods:

- letters and numbers around the edge of the map
- lines of latitude and longitude drawn on the map
- the military grid system (see page 175) for Canadian topographic maps

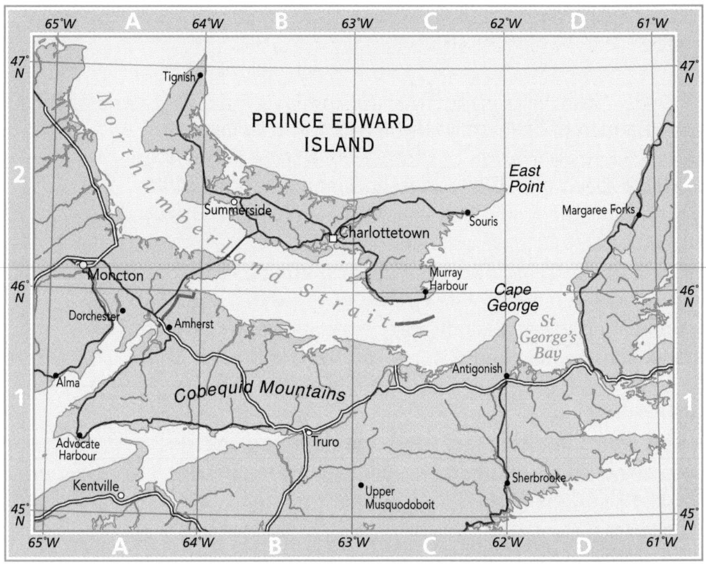

1 LETTERS AND NUMBERS

1. Find the name of the place in the gazetteer.
2. Find the page number and area reference (e.g., page 2, F2).
3. Go to the correct page in the atlas.
4. Find F in the border below the map, and find 2 on the side of the map.
5. Follow the letter up and follow the number across to find the correct square (F2).
6. Locate the place by searching the square.

Look at the map of Atlantic Canada. Charlottetown is located at B2, Truro is located at B1, and Moncton is located at A2.

2 LATITUDE

Latitude is distance, measured in degrees, north and south of the equator. Lines of latitude circle the globe in an east-west direction. The distance between lines of latitude is always the same; therefore, they are also known as parallels of latitude. Because the circumference of Earth gets smaller toward the poles, the lines of latitude are shorter nearer the poles.

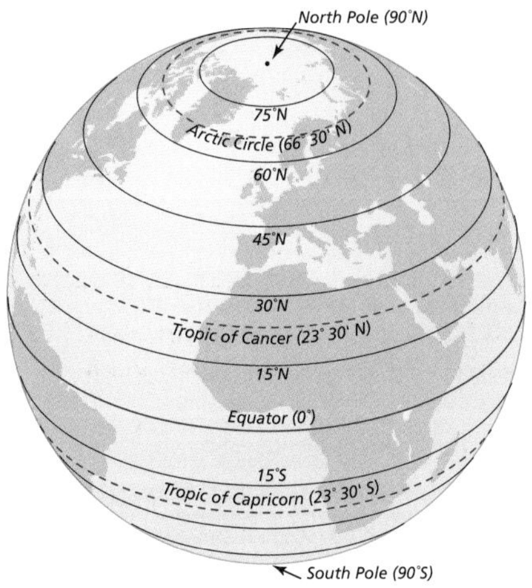

All lines of latitude have numbers between 0° and 90° and a direction, either north or south of the equator. The equator is at 0° latitude. It divides Earth into two halves: the Northern and Southern Hemispheres. The North Pole is at 90° north and the South Pole is at 90° south. The "tilt" of Earth has given particular importance to some lines of latitude . They include:

- the Arctic Circle at 66° 30' north
- the Antarctic Circle at 66° 30' south
- the Tropic of Cancer at 23° 30' north
- the Tropic of Capricorn at 23° 30' south

3 LONGITUDE

Longitude is distance, measured in degrees, east and west of the prime meridian. Lines of longitude join the poles in a north-south direction. Because the lines join the poles, they are always the same length, but are farthest apart at the equator and closest together at the poles. These lines are also called meridians of longitude.

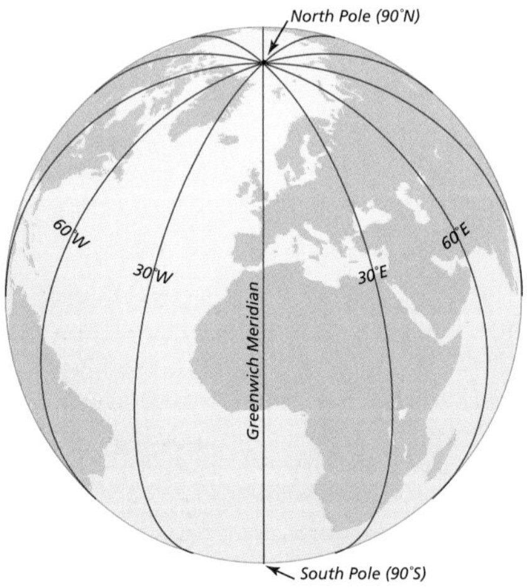

Longitude begins along the Prime Meridian, or Greenwich Meridian, at 0°, in London, England. On the opposite side of Earth is the 180° meridian, which is the International Date Line. These two lines can be used to divide Earth into two halves: the Western Hemisphere and the Eastern Hemisphere. To the west of the Prime Meridian are Canada, the United States, and Brazil; to the east of the Prime Meridian are Germany, India, and China. All lines of longitude have numbers between 0° and 180° and a direction, either east or west of the prime meridian.

4 FINDING PLACES

When lines of latitude and longitude are drawn on a map, they form a grid, which looks like a pattern of squares. This pattern is used to find places on a map. Latitude is always stated before longitude (e.g., 42°N, 78°W).

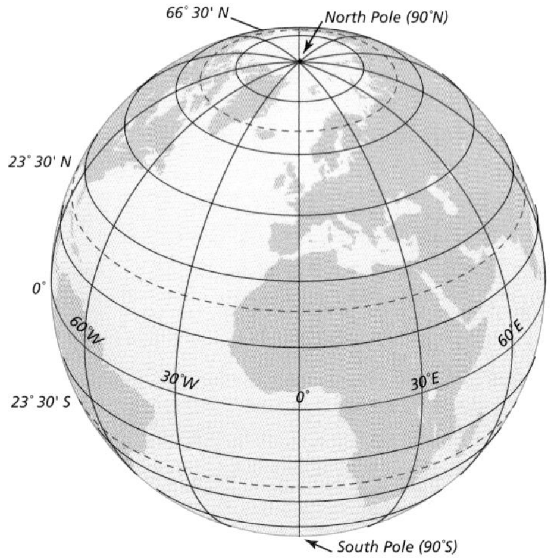

On the map of Atlantic Canada (above), Murray Harbour is directly on a line of **latitude** – representing 46°N. Similarly, Antigonish is directly on a line of **longitude** – representing 62°W. Other places, not exactly on lines, use subdivisions of degrees called minutes. There are 60 minutes in a degree. Truro is located almost halfway between 45°N and 46°N and about one quarter of the distance between the lines 63°W and 64°W longitude. Its latitude and longitude would be 45° 25'N, and 63° 15'W.

Since Earth is a sphere and maps are flat, map makers (cartographers) have invented different ways of drawing the round surface of Earth on a flat piece of paper. These methods are called map projections.

There are many different types of map projections, but none of them can perfectly match the sphere of Earth. Every map projection must "stretch" or "squash" the round surface to make it fit onto a flat piece of paper. As a result, no map projection can correctly show all four aspects of a map – shape, area, direction, and distance – at the same time. In drawing any ONE of these four aspects accurately, the other three become distorted or inaccurate. Each map projection has advantages and disadvantages.

1 CYLINDRICAL PROJECTIONS

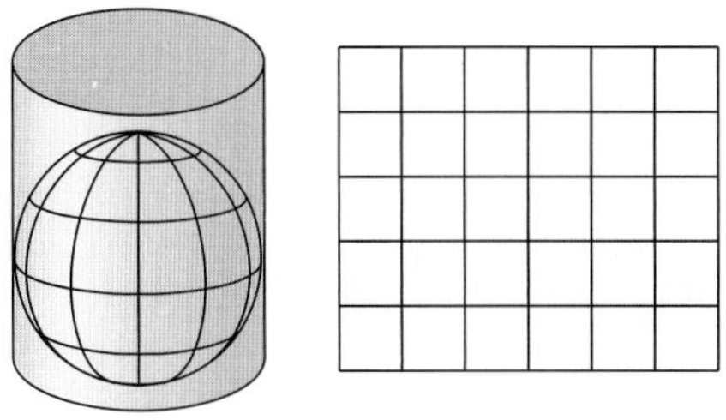

Cylindrical projections are constructed by projecting the surface of the globe or sphere (Earth) onto a cylinder that just touches the outside edges of that globe. Two examples of cylindrical projections are Mercator and Times.

Mercator (see pages 154-155 for an example of this projection)

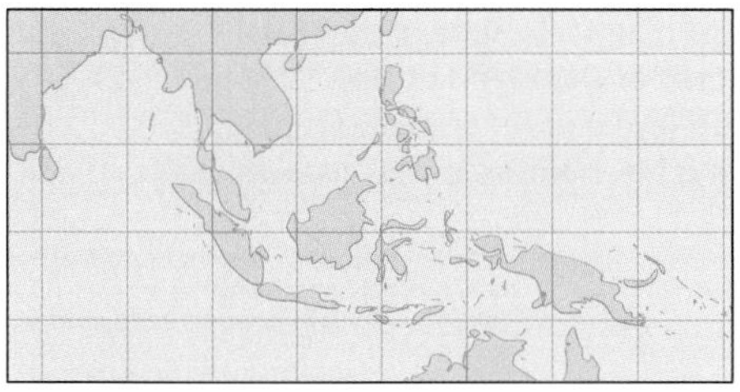

The Mercator cylindrical projection is a useful projection for areas near the equator and to about 15 degrees north or south of the equator, where distortion of shape is minimal. The projection is useful for navigation, since directions are plotted as straight lines.

Times (see pages 80-81 for an example of this projection)

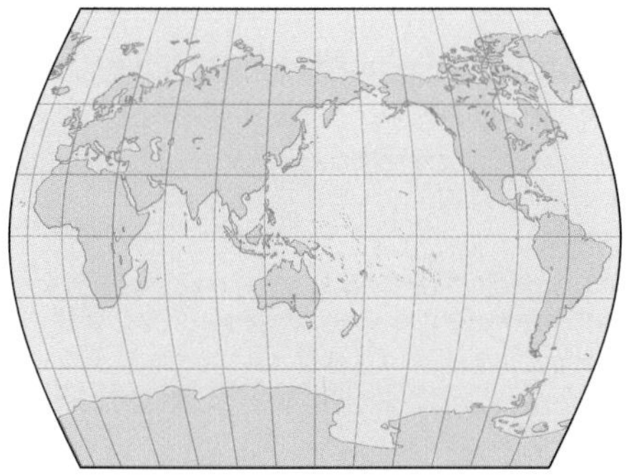

The Times projection is similar to the Mercator projection, but the meridians of longitude are slightly curved. The Times projection is most accurate halfway between the poles at 45°N and 45°S.

2 CONIC PROJECTIONS

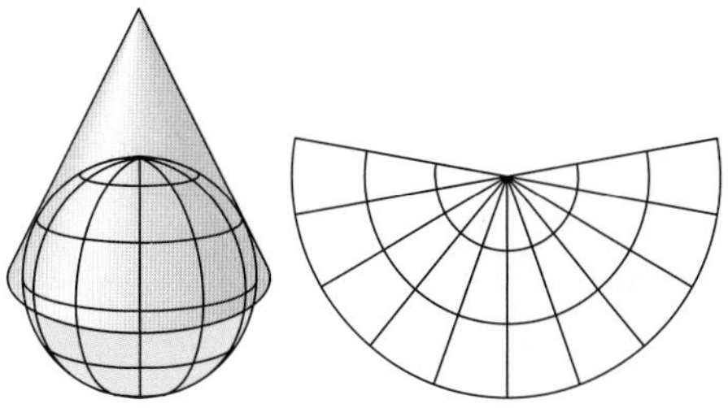

Conic projections are constructed by projecting the surface of a globe or sphere (Earth) onto a cone that just touches the outside edges of that globe. Examples of conic projections are Albers Equal Area Conic and Chamberlin Trimetric.

Conic Equidistant (see pages 142-143 for an example of this projection)

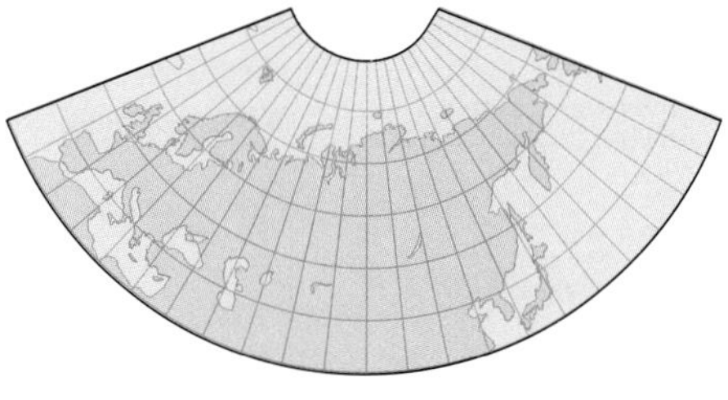

Conic projections are best suited for areas between 30° and 60° north and south of the equator when the east-west distance is greater than the north-south distance (such as Northern Eurasia). The meridians are straight and spaced at equal intervals.

Chamberlin Trimetric (see page 108 for an example of this projection)

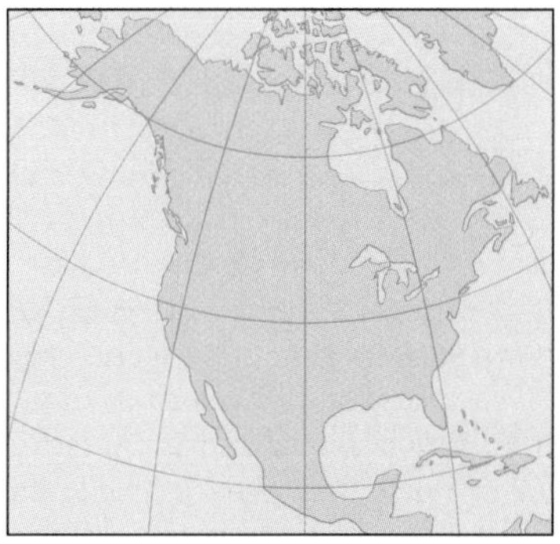

Chamberlin Trimetric is an equidistant projection. It is used to show areas with greater north-south extent than east-west extent (such as North America).

3 AZIMUTHAL PROJECTIONS

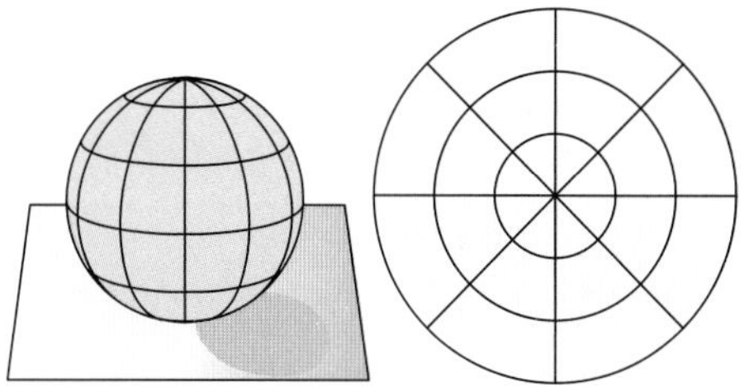

Azimuthal projections are constructed by projecting the surface of the globe or sphere (Earth) onto a flat surface that touches the globe at one point only. Some examples of azimuthal projections are Lambert Azimuthal Equal Area and Polar Stereographic.

Lambert Azimuthal Equal Area (see pages 158-159 for an example of this projection)

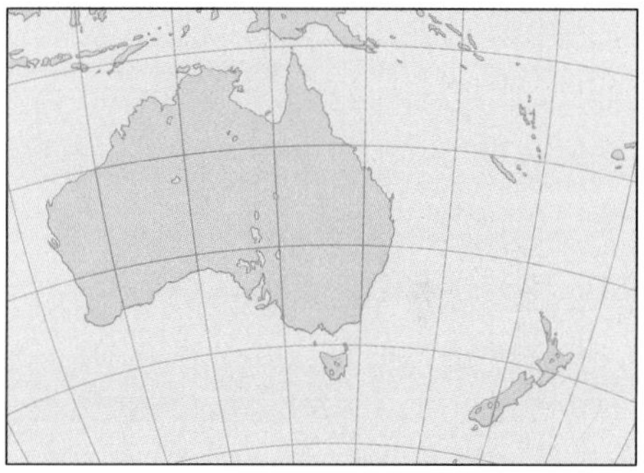

Lambert's projection is useful for areas that have similar east-west and north-south dimensions such as Australia.

Polar Stereographic (see page 167 for an example of this projection)

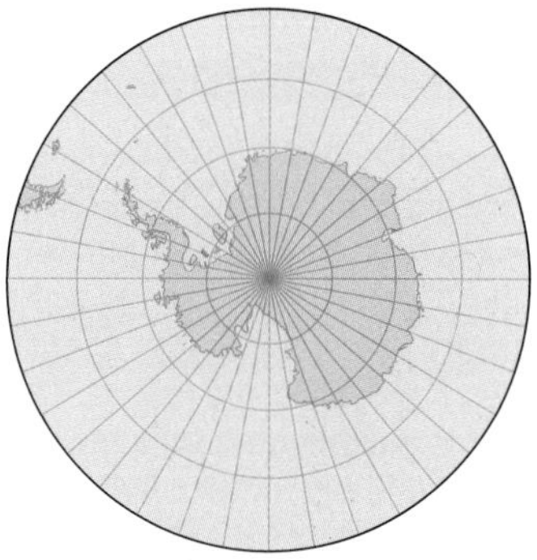

This projection is a good choice for showing travel routes from a central point because points on the map are in constant relative position and distance from the centre.

1 CLIMATE STATISTICS AND TABLES

Climate statistics (temperatures and precipitation) can be found in a number of locations, including textbooks, reference texts in the library, and Web sites dealing with weather and climate. In this atlas, the climate statistics have been transformed into climate graphs (see below). The statistics are usually shown in three rows: the station name (and altitude) and months of the year in the first row; the average temperature for each month in the second row; and the average precipitation for each month in the third row. This information can be used to develop a climate graph similar to the one below.

Saskatoon (515 metres)	Jan	Feb	Mar	Apr	May	Jun	Jul	Aug	Sep	Oct	Nov	Dec
Temperature - (°C)	-17.0	-13.0	-5.8	4.4	11.5	16.0	18.2	17.3	11.2	4.5	-6.2	-14.3
Precipitation - (mm)	15.2	10.3	14.7	23.9	49.4	61.1	60.1	38.8	30.7	16.7	13.3	15.9

2 CLIMATE GRAPHS

A climate graph is a combination of a line graph and a bar graph. The line is used to indicate temperature and is related to the scale at the left side of the graph. The precipitation is shown as a series of 12 bars, each one representing a month, and is related to the scale on the right side. The total annual precipitation is shown at the top of the graph.

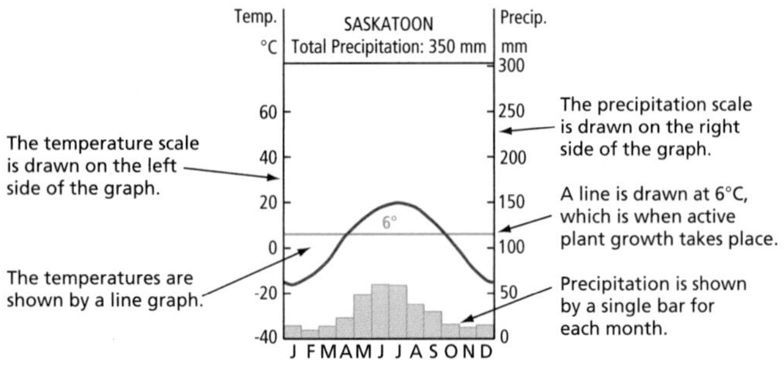

3 UNDERSTANDING CLIMATE GRAPHS

- A temperature line that is almost flat indicates a location close to the equator that has even temperatures all year round.
- A temperature line that has a large bump (∩) or dip (∪) indicates a location that has a definite winter and summer season. If the period from May to September is shown by a bump (∩), indicating higher temperatures in that period, then the location is in the northern hemisphere. If the same time period shows a dip (∪), indicating lower temperatures, then the location is in the southern hemisphere.
- When a number of high precipitation bars are grouped together, this is an indication of a distinctive wet season. If there are few or no bars for a series of months, then this indicates a distinctive dry season. If all the precipitation bars are high throughout the year, the location is wet all year round. If the precipitation bars are quite low or non-existent for most of the year, the location is very dry.

The climate graph for Saskatoon indicates a location that has low winter temperatures, high summer temperatures, and a concentration of precipitation during the summer months.

4 UNDERSTANDING RELIEF

Relief refers to differences in the height of land. In this atlas, the height of land is shown in three ways: colour layers, spot heights, and contours. Contours are dealt with on pages 174 and 175.

- Colour layers: different colours are used to show different heights.
- Spot heights: dots or triangles (with an associated number) show the location and height of significant places on the map.

5 COLOUR LAYERS

A relief scale is placed in the legend or at the side of the page to show the colour layers that have been used to illustrate ranges of elevation. To make comparisons easy, this atlas uses the same colours to represent the same range of elevations on all maps of this type.

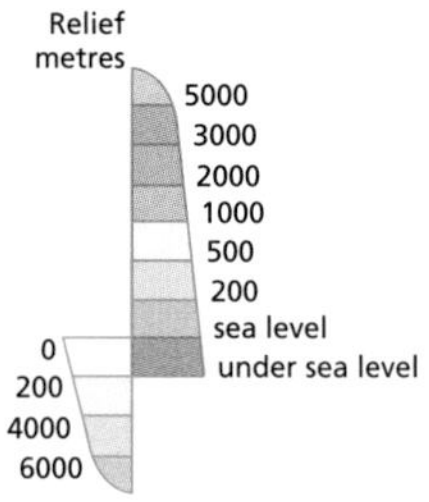

Light purple indicates land that is more than 5000 metres above sea level.

Light yellow indicates land that is between 500 and 1000 metres above sea level.

Light green indicates land that is between 200 and 500 metres above sea level.

Greenish-brown indicates land that is below sea level.

Dark blue indicates water that is more than 6000 metres deep.

6 SPOT HEIGHTS

Physical maps often use spot heights to show the highest mountain in an area. The map of the island of New Guinea illustrates both the coloured layers of relief and spot heights. From this map, the following information can be determined:

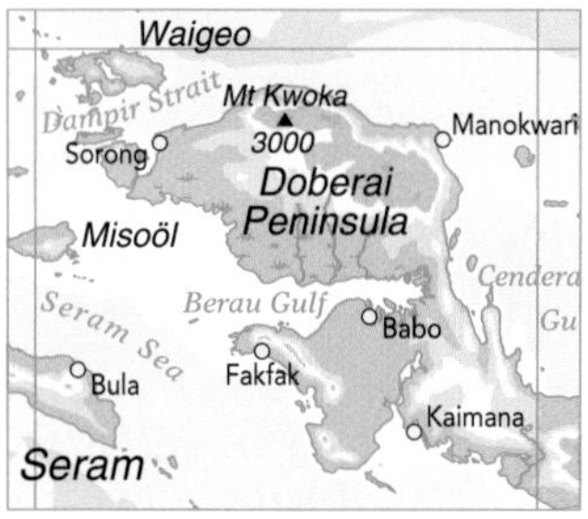

Doberai Peninsula, New Guinea

3000 ▲ Mountain height (in metres)

- The area in the north-eastern portion of the Doberai Peninsula is high.
- The mountainous area covers nearly half of the peninsula.
- Mount Kwoka is 3000 metres in elevation and is located at the northern end of the mountain range.

7 BUT, WHAT DOES IT LOOK LIKE?

The next step is to imagine what the area would look like if we could fly over the area at the bottom edge of the map and look north toward the Doberai Peninsula on a very clear day.

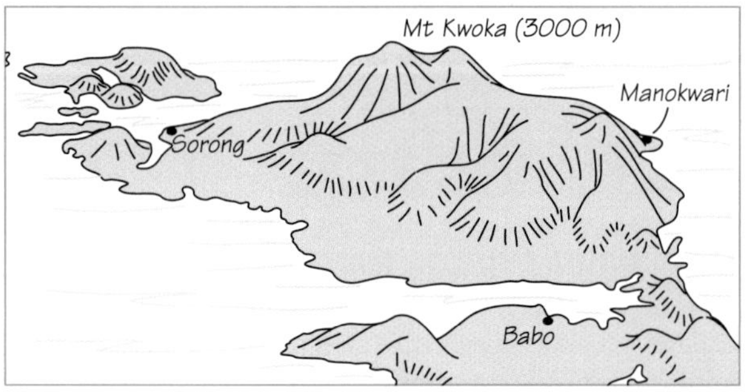

Field sketch of Doberai Peninsula

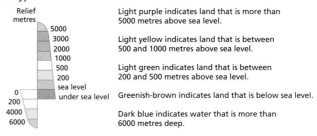

A false-colour image of Calgary, Alberta.

A true-colour image of Calgary, Alberta.

1 REMOTE SENSING

Maps, aerial photographs, and satellite images provide unique views of the Earth – views from above Earth. Geographers use photographs and electronic images taken from aircraft and satellites to determine patterns, trends, and basic characteristics of Earth. Aerial photographs can be used to produce three-dimensional images, which can then be converted into maps.

Since the 1960s, satellites fitted with cameras, scanners, and sensors have been programmed to collect useful information about Earth's lands and waters. The information is gathered using types of electromagnetic radiation – X - ray, ultraviolet, visible, and microwave. It is recorded in digital form, sent back to Earth, and processed into images. Satellites collect information on soil moisture conditions, vegetation coverage, land use, marine resources, ozone levels, geology, air and water pollution, and weather patterns.

2 LANDSAT AND RADARSAT

The United States has a series of satellites, including Landsat, that use different wavelengths to record characteristics of Earth's surface. When the data is sent back to Earth, colours are artificially added to make it easier to interpret the images. In recent years, Landsat imagery has changed from the "false-colour" images to more natural colours. This trend is reflected in the images shown to the left.

Canada has had extensive involvement with remote sensing and has been effective in gathering information from areas that may not be easily accessible. Radarsat is an orbiting satellite that uses radar signals to provide complete coverage of Canada's land area every three days. Since these images are not light sensitive, Radarsat can provide 24-hour coverage in all weather conditions. Radarsat was launched with the assistance of United States facilities in exchange for the sharing of data. The main purposes for Radarsat include monitoring environmental changes and providing resource development data.

3 SATELLITE IMAGES IN THIS ATLAS

The Pearson School Atlas includes a variety of images and maps derived from satellite data. Three of the numerous examples included are:

- a false-colour image of the Amazon Basin (page 122)
- a satellite image of the Great Barrier Reef (page 159)
- a computer-generated, three-dimensional image of Nyirangongo volcano in the Democratic Republic of Congo, which combines both Landsat imagery and radar-topography techniques (page 129)

In a false-colour satellite image, colours are used to signify the following characteristics:

White	bare ground, sand, salt, clouds, ice and snow
Yellow	little vegetation cover, heavily grazed areas
Pink/red	early growth in crops and grasslands
Red	healthy green vegetation, rainforest (deep red), mangroves (red-brown)
Brown	woodland, bare rock
Light green	moist ploughed fields, poor grazing lands
Dark green	forests or scrub, clear shallow water
Blue/light blue	arid scrubland, very shallow water
Blue/grey	urban areas, concrete, houses
Dark blue/black	ocean, deep water, cloud shadows

Topographic maps illustrate the characteristics of an area in great detail. Both natural features (e.g. rivers, wooded areas) and human-made features (e.g. roads, buildings, cemeteries) are identified. This is possible because the scale is usually large.

Most countries have topographic maps in a range of scales from 1: 50 000 to 1: 250 000. Topographic maps are used for a variety of purposes including camping, hiking, biking, urban planning and surveying.

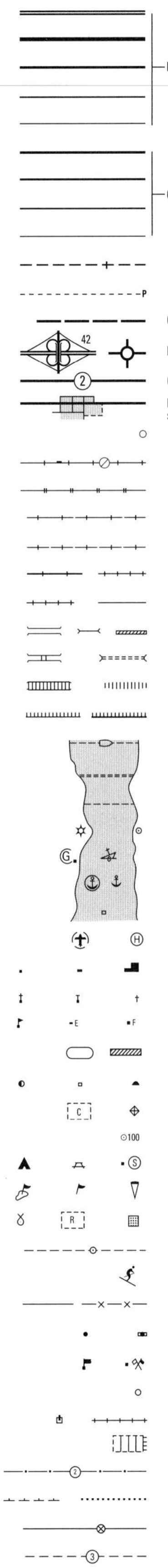

Dual highway, hard surface

Road, hard surface, more than 2 lanes

Road, hard surface, 2 lanes — Red

Road, hard surface, less than 2 lanes

Street

Road, loose or stabilized surface, all season, 2 lanes or more

Road, loose or stabilized surface, all season, less than 2 lanes — Orange

Road, loose surface, dry weather

Unclassified road, street

Vehicle track or winter road; gate

Trail, cut line or portage; portage, short or position uncertain

Road, under construction — Orange or red

Highway interchange with number; traffic circle — Red

Highway route number — Orange or red

Built-up area; street; park/sports field — Red screen; black screen

Indian reserve; small

Railway, single track; railway station; turntable

Railway, multiple tracks

Railway, under construction

Railway, abandoned

Railway on road; special track railway

Rapid transit route: rail; road

Bridge; footbridge; snowshed

Bridge: swing, draw, lift; tunnel

Cut; embankment, causeway

Dyke or levee; with road

Ferry

Ford

Submarine cable

Navigation light; navigation beacon

Coast Guard station; exposed shipwreck

Seaplane base; seaplane anchorage

Crib or abandoned bridge pier

Airfield, position approximate; heliport

Building(s)

Church; non-Christian place of worship; shrine

School; elevator; fire station

Sports track; stadium

Silo; kiln; dome

Cemetery; historic site or point of interest

Landmark object (with height): tower, chimney, etc.

Campground; picnic site; service centre

Golf course; golf driving range; drive-in theatre

Wind-operated device; ruins; greenhouse

Aerial cableway, ski lift, conveyor

Ski area, ski jump

Wall; fence

Tank(s): vertical; horizontal

Warden, ranger station; Customs

Well: oil, gas

Crane: vertical; horizontal

Rifle range with butts

Power transmission line; multiple lines

Telephone line; firebreak

Pipeline with control valve

Pipeline underground; multiple pipelines underground

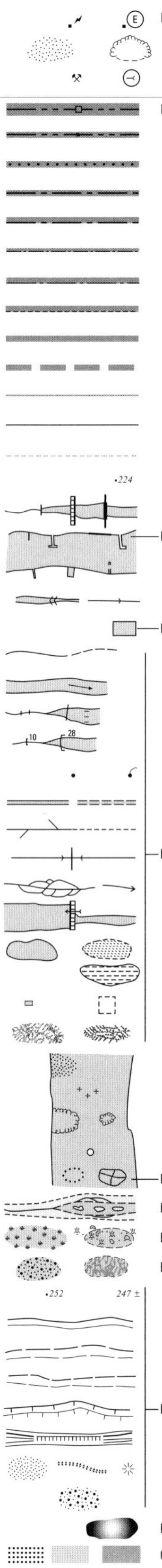

Electric facility; oil or natural gas facility — Red

Pit: sand, gravel, clay; quarry

Mine; cave

International boundary with monument — Red screen

Boundary, first class with mile post

Boundary, first class unsurveyed

Boundary, second class

Boundary, second class in Dominion Land Survey

Boundary, third class

Boundary, fourth class

Boundary, fifth class

Boundary, sixth class

Boundary, sixth class unsurveyed

Boundary, seventh class

Boundary, eighth class

Boundary, ninth class

Precise elevation

Dam: small; large; carrying road

Wharf; pier or dock; seawall; breakwater — Blue

Slip; drydock; boat ramp

Lock; sluice gate

Sewage disposal pond, settling pond — Blue & black

Watercourse or shoreline: definite; indefinite

Watercourse; direction of flow arrow

Rapids

Falls (with height in black)

Well: water, brine; spring

Navigable canal; canal, abandoned

Ditch, conduit; conduit underground

Conduit bridge — Blue

Braided stream; disappearing stream

Fish ladder

Lake or pond; slough, intermittent lake or pond

Flooded area

Reservoir, dugout, swimming pool; underground reservoir

Tundra: ponds; polygons

Foreshore flats or sand in water

Rocks in water or small islands

Rocky ledge; rocky reef

Artificial island, small

Kelp area; fish pond — Blue

Dry river bed — Blue & brown

Marsh, swamp, muskeg; string bog — Blue & green

Debris-covered ice; palsa bog — Blue & brown

Spot elevation, non-precise; water elevation

Contours: index; intermediate

Approximate contours

Auxiliary contours

Depression contours — Brown

Cliff or escarpment

Sand; esker; pingo

Moraine, scree

Glacier, ice cap, snowfield — Blue vignette

Orchard; vineyard, hopfield; wooded area — Green

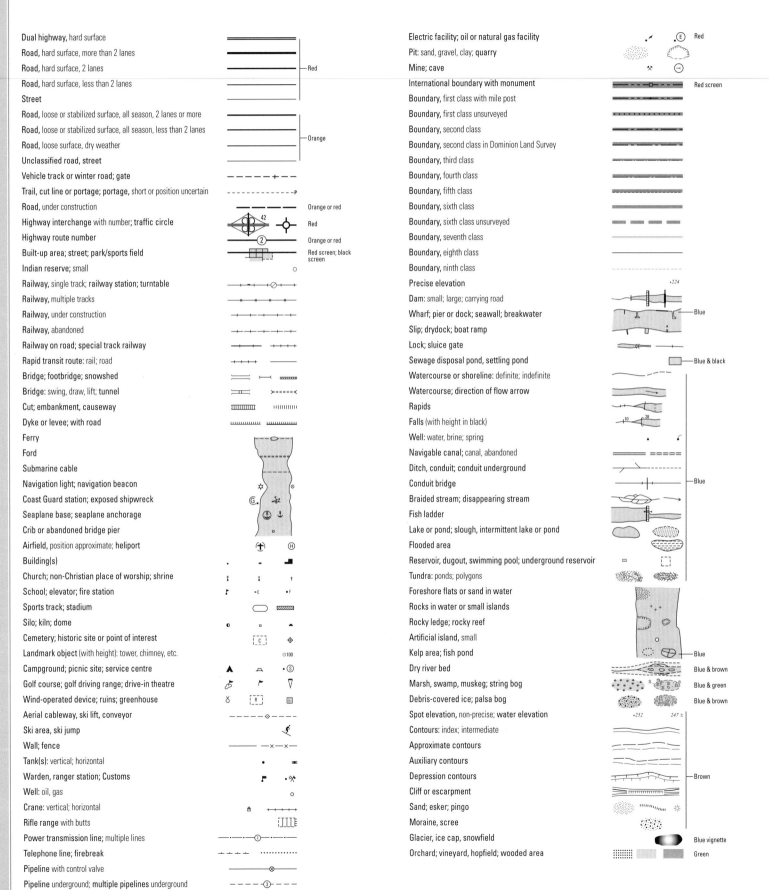

1 SYMBOLS

There are four different kinds of symbols on topographic maps. These are illustrated on page 174. *Point* symbols show locations of features such as schools, cemeteries, or historic sites. *Line* symbols are used for such things as roads, power lines, rivers and political boundaries. *Contours* are special line symbols representing places at the same elevation. *Area* symbols cover a specific area on a map, such as marshes, forests, sand pits and urban areas.

2 ELEVATION AND RELIEF

Contours indicate the height of land above sea level or the depth of water. When contours are close together, they indicate a steep slope (a large change in elevation over a short distance). When contours are far apart, the landscape varies little over large areas. The distance between contours may change from one map to another and may be expressed in metres or in feet. Eventually, all Canadian topographic maps will be in metric figures. Contours can be helpful in determining the direction of water flow, since they form a V-pattern pointing upstream.
On topographic maps, individual elevations – for example, the top of a mountain – are shown by a spot height or a benchmark to indicate a permanent marker set in concrete or in the bedrock.

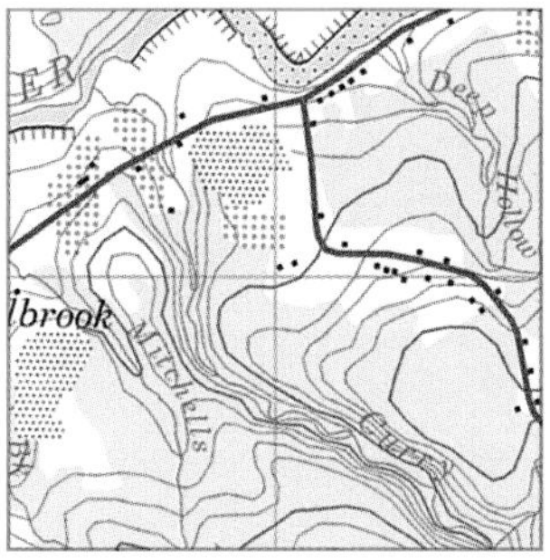

The example above shows part of the Wolfville, Nova Scotia topographic sheet. The contours are 10 metres apart. There are relatively flat areas on the left and right sides and steep slopes along the stream. The contours point in a V upstream indicating that the three streams all flow from south to north.

3 GRIDS AND CO-ORDINATES

Topographic maps use grid lines that are numbered from the bottom to the top of the map and from the left to the right side (or, from south to north and from west to east). In this atlas, the grid lines are numbered around the edges of the map, similar to topographic maps.

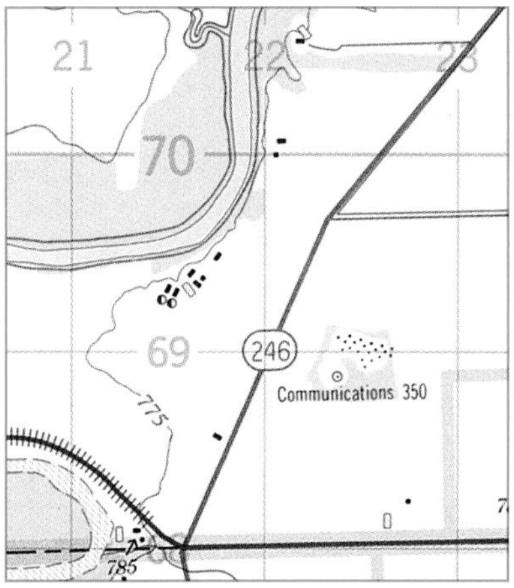

In the sample (at the bottom of the previous column) from the Morris, Manitoba topographic sheet, the communications tower is at grid point 224689. This means that it is 4/10ths of the way between lines 22 and 23 (224), and 9/10ths of the way between lines 68 and 69 (689). Similarly the house at the very top of the example is located at 2/10ths to the east of line 22 (222) and 6/10ths north of line 70 (706). Putting these three digit numbers together provides the co-ordinates 222706 for the location of the house.

4 CROSS-SECTIONAL DIAGRAMS

Cross-sectional diagrams (or profiles) help you to visualize the landscape. However, the vertical scale is different from the horizontal scale and therefore the slope becomes exaggerated.

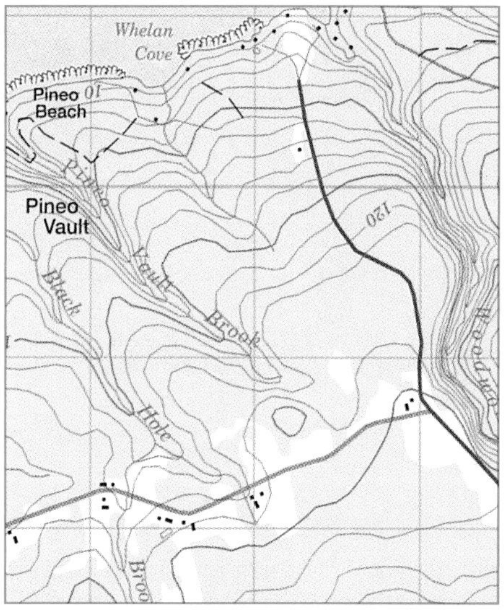

To draw a profile from Whelan Cove to the road junction in the bottom right-hand corner, follow these instructions.

- Determine the contour interval, for example, 10 metres.
- Draw a line on the map joining the two locations.
- Lay a piece of paper along the line, and indicate the elevation at each end of the line.
- Put a mark on the piece of paper where each contour crosses the line.
- Label each mark with the elevation (e.g. edge of the water, 10 m, 20 m, etc.)
- On a second piece of paper, draw a graph scale using the contour interval as the vertical scale, for example 10 metres.
- Place the first piece of paper along the horizontal part of the graph and transfer each mark up to the corresponding value on the vertical scale.
- Join the dots with a smoothly flowing line to create a profile of the landscape.

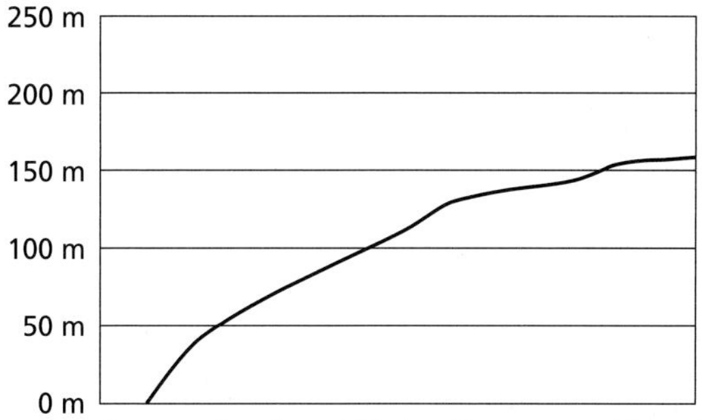

Cross section from Whelan Cove to road junction

THE BASICS

1 Land and Fresh Water Areas

	NL	PE	NS	NB	QC	ON	MB	SK	AB	BC	YT	NWT	NU	CANADA
Total Land and Fresh Water Area	405 212	5 660	55 284	72 908	1 542 056	1 076 395	647 797	651 036	661 848	944 735	482 443	1 346 106	2 093 190	9 984 670
Percent of Canada's Total Area (land and fresh water)	4.1	0.1	0.6	0.7	15.4	10.8	6.5	6.5	6.6	9.5	4.8	13.5	21.0	100
Percent of Canada's Fresh Water Area	3.5	0	0.2	0.2	19.8	17.8	10.6	6.7	2.2	2.2	0.9	18.3	17.6	100

SOURCE: Natural Resources Canada

2 Land Cover

Type	Description	Area (000 km²)	Percentage of Total Land and Fresh Water Area
Forest and Taiga	Forests, some wetlands, barren lands	4 456	45
Tundra	Barrens in arctic or high altitude environments	2 302	23
Wetlands	Swamps, bogs, marshes (including coastal marshes), some with trees	1 244	12
Fresh Water	Lakes, rivers, streams, reservoirs	755	8
Cropland	Farms (including orchards and vineyards), fenced pasture land	658	6
Rangeland	Grazing land (non-fenced)	203	2
Ice and Snow	Permanent glaciers, snow, ice caps	272	3
Human Use	Urban, transportatation, industrial uses	79	1
TOTAL		**9 970**	**100**

Based on a variety of sources; some data has been recently adjusted to reflect the results of new satellite imaging techniques

POPULATION

3 Population Growth in Canada, 1851 to 2001

	Population (000)	Change From Last Major Census Year		Annual Rate of Growth (percent)
		(000)	Percent	
1851	2 436.3	na	na	na
1861	3 229.6	793.3	32.6	2.9
1871	3 689.3	459.6	14.2	1.3
1881	4 324.8	635.6	17.2	1.6
1891	4 833.2	508.4	11.8	1.1
1901	5 371.3	538.1	11.1	1.1
1911	7 206.6	1 835.3	34.2	3.0
1921	8 787.9	1 581.3	21.9	2.0
1931	10 376.8	1 588.8	18.1	1.7
1941	11 506.7	1 129.9	10.9	1.0
1951[a]	14 009.4	2 502.8	21.8	1.7
1961	18 238.2	2 157.5	13.4	2.5
1971	21 568.3	3 330.1	18.3	1.8
1981	24 343.2	2 774.9	12.9	1.3
1991	27 297.0	2 953.8	12.1	1.2
2001	30 007.1	2 710.1	9.9	1.0

[a] Newfoundland included for the first time. Excluding Newfoundland, the increase would have been 2 141 358 or 18.6%.
SOURCE: Census of Canada

4 Population Growth by Province and Territory, 1867 to 2001

	NL (000)	PE (000)	NS (000)	NB (000)	QC (000)	ON (000)	MB (000)	SK (000)	AB (000)	BC (000)	YT (000)	NWT (000)	NU[a] (000)	CANADA (000)
1867	na	88	364	271	1 123	1 525	15	na	na	32	na	45	na	3 463
1871	na	94	388	286	1 191	1 621	25	na	na	36	na	48	na	3 689
1881	na	109	441	321	1 360	1 927	62	na	na	49	na	56	na	4 325
1891	na	109	450	321	1 489	2 114	153	na	na	98	na	99	na	4 833
1901	na	103	460	331	1 649	2 183	255	91	73	179	27	20	na	5 371
1911	na	94	492	352	2 006	2 527	461	492	374	393	9	7	na	7 207
1921	na	88.6	523.8	387.9	2 360.5	2 933.7	610.1	757.5	588.5	524.6	4.1	8.1	na	8 787.4
1931	na	88.0	512.8	408.2	2 874.7	3 431.7	700.1	921.8	731.6	694.3	4.2	9.3	na	10 376.7
1941	na	95.0	578.0	457.4	3 331.9	3 787.7	729.7	896.0	796.2	817.8	5.0	12.0	na	11 506.7
1951	361.4	98.4	642.6	515.7	4 055.7	4 597.6	776.5	831.7	939.5	1 165.2	9.1	16.0	na	14 009.4
1961	457.9	104.6	737.0	597.9	5 259.2	6 236.1	921.7	925.2	1 332.0	1 629.1	14.6	23.0	na	18 238.3
1971	522.1	111.6	789.0	634.6	6 027.8	7 703.1	988.2	926.2	1 627.9	2 184.6	18.4	34.8	na	21 568.3
1981	567.7	122.5	847.4	696.4	6 438.4	8 625.1	1 026.2	968.3	2 237.7	2 744.5	23.2	45.7	na	24 343.2
1991	568.0	130.0	900.0	724.0	6 896.0	10 085.0	1 092.0	989.0	2 546.0	3 282.0	26.9	54.8	na	27 297.0
2001	512.9	135.3	908.0	729.5	7 237.5	11 410.0	1 119.6	978.9	2 974.8	3 907.7	28.7	37.4	26.7	30 007.1

[a] Part of Northwest Territories until 1999
SOURCE: Census of Canada

5 Demographics of Canada, 1851 to 2001

	Total Population Growth[a] (000)	Births (000)	Deaths (000)	Natural Increase (000)	Immigration (000)	Emigration (000)	Net Migration (000)	Population at End of Period (000)
1851–1861	793	1 281	670	611	352	170	182	3 230
1861–1871	460	1 370	760	610	260	410	-150	3 689
1871-1881	636	1 480	790	690	350	404	-54	4 325
1881–1891	508	1 524	870	654	680	826	-146	4 833
1891–1901	538	1 548	880	668	250	380	-130	5 371
1901–1911	1 835	1 925	900	1 025	1 550	740	810	7 207
1911–1921	1 581	2 340	1 070	1 270	1 400	1 089	311	8 788
1921–1931	1 589	2 420	1 060	1 360	1 200	970	230	10 377
1931–1941	1 130	2 294	1 072	1 222	149	241	-92	11 507
1941–1951	2 503	3 212	1 220	1 992	548	382	166	14 009
1951–1961	4 229	4 468	1 320	3 148	1 543	563	980	18 238
1961–1971	3 330	4 105	1 497	2 608	1 429	707	722	21 568
1971–1981	2 775	3 575	1 667	1 908	1 824	636	1 188	24 343
1981–1991	2 954	3 805	1 831	1 974	1 876	491	1 385	27 297
1991–2001	2 710	3 640	2 119	1 521	2 229	410	1 819	30 007

[a]Total population growth is the difference in the census population count at the end of the period
SOURCE: Statistics Canada

6 Demographics by Province and Territory, 2002

		NL	PE	NS	NB	QC	ON	MB	SK	AB	BC	YT	NWT	NU	CANADA
Birth Rate/1000		8.8	10.2	9.4	9.5	9.7	10.6	12.1	11.8	12.0	9.7	11.7	15.6	26.5	10.4
Death Rate/1000		8.3	8.5	8.6	8.5	7.3	7.4	9.0	9.3	6.1	6.9	4.9	4.2	4.9	7.4
Natural Increase Rate/1000		0.5	1.7	0.8	1.0	2.4	3.2	3.1	2.5	5.9	2.8	6.8	11.4	21.6	3.0
International Migration															
Immigration Rate/1000		0.8	1.0	1.7	1.0	5.2	12.7	4.2	1.8	5.3	9.1	2.3	2.2	0.6	8.1
Emigration Rate/1000		0.8	0.3	0.8	0.5	1.7	2.9	1.7	1.2	2.7	2.3	3.6	2.4	2.3	2.3
Net Migration Rate/1000		0.0	0.7	0.9	0.5	3.5	9.8	2.5	0.6	2.6	6.8	-1.3	-0.2	-1.7	5.8
Interprovincial Migration															
Net Migration Rate/1000		-4.7	4.9	-1.3	-1.1	-1.1	0.6	-4.6	-8.5	8.6	-1.7	-13.2	-7.5	0.8	–
Total Net Migration Rate/1000		-4.7	5.6	-0.4	-0.6	2.4	10.4	-2.1	-7.9	11.2	5.1	-14.5	-7.7	-0.9	–
Total Growth Rate/1000		-4.2	7.3	0.4	0.4	4.8	13.6	1.0	-5.4	17.1	7.9	-7.7	3.7	20.7	8.8
Infant Mortality Rate/1000[a]		5.2	4.4	4.4	5.7	5.6	5.5	7.5	8.9	4.8	4.7	8.4	10.9	na	5.5
Life Expectancy at Birth (years)[b]	M	75.0	73.9	74.9	75.2	75.2	76.1	75.5	75.5	76.0	76.1	72.3	69.9	na	75.7
	F	80.5	80.7	80.7	81.2	81.5	81.4	80.8	81.4	81.3	81.9	84.7	75.8	na	81.4

[a]1997 figures
[b]1996 figures
SOURCE: Statistics Canada

7 Population of Census Metropolitan Areas, 1951 to 2001

Census Metropolitan Area	1951 (000)	1961 (000)	1971 (000)	1981 (000)	1991 (000)	2001 (000)	Percent Change 1991–2001	Rank 2001 (1951)
Toronto	1 261.9	1 919.4	2 628.0	2 998.9	3 893.0	4 682.9	20.3	1 (2)
Montréal	1 539.3	2 215.6	2 743.2	2 828.4	3 127.2	3 426.4	9.6	2 (1)
Vancouver	586.2	826.8	1 082.4	1 268.2	1 602.5	1 987.0	24.0	3 (3)
Ottawa-Hull	311.6	457.0	602.5	718.0	920.9	1 063.7	15.5	4 (5)
Calgary	142.3	279.1	403.3	592.7	754.0	951.4	26.2	5 (12)
Edmonton	193.6	359.8	495.7	657.1	839.9	937.8	11.7	6 (8)
Québec	289.3	379.1	480.5	576.1	645.6	682.8	5.8	7 (6)
Winnipeg	357.2	476.5	540.3	548.8	652.4	671.3	2.9	8 (4)
Hamilton	281.9	401.1	498.5	542.1	599.8	662.4	10.4	9 (7)
London	167.7	226.7	286.0	283.7	381.5	432.5	13.4	10 (11)
Kitchener	107.5	154.9	226.8	287.8	356.4	414.3	16.2	11 (15)
St Catharines-Niagara	189.0	257.8	303.4	304.4	364.6	377.0	3.4	12 (9)
Halifax	138.4	193.4	222.6	277.7	320.5	359.2	12.1	13 (13)
Victoria	114.9	155.8	195.8	233.5	288.0	311.9	8.3	14 (14)
Windsor	182.6	217.2	258.6	246.1	262.1	307.9	17.5	15 (10)
Oshawa[a]			120.3	154.2	240.1	296.3	23.4	16 (-)
Saskatoon	55.7	95.6	126.4	154.2	210.0	225.9	7.6	17 (22)
Regina	72.7	113.7	140.7	164.3	191.7	192.8	0.6	18 (21)
St John's, Nfld.	80.9	106.7	131.8	154.8	171.9	172.9	0.6	19 (17)
Greater Sudbury	80.5	127.4	155.4	149.9	157.6	155.6	-1.3	20 (19)
Chicoutimi-Jonquière	91.2	127.6	133.7	135.2	160.9	154.9	-3.7	21 (16)
Sherbrooke[a]				74.1	139.2	153.8	10.5	22 (-)
Abbotsford[a]						147.4		23 (-)
Kingston[a]						146.8		24 (-)
Trois-Rivières	46.1	53.5	55.9	111.5	136.3	137.5	0.9	25 (23)
Saint John, N.B.	80.7	98.1	106.7	114.0	125.0	122.7	-1.8	26 (18)
Thunder Bay	73.7	102.1	112.1	121.4	124.4	122.0	-1.9	27 (20)

[a] Although there may have been an urban centre here, it was not a Census Metropolitan Area until the date indicated

SOURCE: Statistics Canada

8 Population by Age Group, 1911 to 2001

	0–4 years (000)	5–9 years (000)	10–14 years (000)	15–24 years (000)	25–34 years (000)	35–44 years (000)	45–54 years (000)	55–64 years (000)	65 years and over (000)	Total Population (000)
1911	890	785	702	1 398	1 219	863	620	393	336	7 207
1921	1 059	1 050	914	1 518	1 343	1 163	799	521	420	8 787
1931	1 074	1 133	1 074	1 952	1 495	1 334	1 075	662	576	10 377
1941	1 052	1 046	1 101	2 152	1 811	1 436	1 227	914	768	11 507
1951	1 722	1 398	1 131	2 147	2 174	1 869	1 407	1 077	1 086	14 009
1961	2 256	2 080	1 856	2 616	2 481	2 390	1 879	1 289	1 391	18 238
1971	1 817	2 254	2 310	4 004	2 890	2 527	2 292	1 731	1 745	21 568
1981	1 783	1 777	1 921	4 659	4 216	2 968	2 499	2 159	2 361	24 343
1991	1 907	1 908	1 878	3 831	4 866	4 372	2 966	2 400	3 170	27 297
2001	1 696	1 976	2 053	4 009	3 995	5 102	4 419	2 868	3 889	30 007

SOURCE: Census of Canada 2001

9 Population by Age and Sex, 2001

Sex and Age	NL (000)	PE (000)	NS (000)	NB (000)	QC (000)	ON (000)	MB (000)	SK (000)	AB (000)	BC (000)	YT (000)	NWT (000)	NU (000)	CANADA (000)
Male														
0–4 years	12.7	3.9	24.3	19.4	192.3	343.3	36.4	31.0	95.3	105.4	0.9	1.5	1.7	868.1
5–9	15.0	4.7	28.4	22.6	232.7	396.4	41.0	35.4	106.9	123.8	1.0	1.8	1.7	1 011.5
10–14	17.9	5.0	31.5	24.8	234.1	405.0	42.3	39.4	114.1	132.7	1.2	1.8	1.7	1 051.5
15–24	36.8	9.5	58.9	49.3	482.0	754.6	77.7	73.5	223.8	261.1	2.0	2.9	2.4	2 034.4
25–34	31.8	8.0	55.3	46.4	460.0	760.7	71.4	56.8	216.4	253.0	1.8	3.0	2.3	1 966.8
35–44	41.2	10.3	74.1	60.1	617.5	963.8	88.2	73.7	259.5	320.4	2.7	3.5	1.8	2 516.7
45–54	41.1	9.9	67.8	56.0	548.1	801.5	77.3	66.0	213.3	297.0	2.6	2.6	1.2	2 184.5
55–64	26.5	6.6	45.5	36.4	371.0	520.6	49.4	41.8	120.8	188.9	1.4	1.2	0.6	1 410.8
65–74	17.1	4.6	31.2	24.1	248.7	383.6	36.8	34.7	83.9	139.5	0.6	0.6	0.3	1 005.6
75–84	8.9	2.5	17.5	14.1	121.0	202.3	22.7	22.4	42.3	77.3	0.2	0.2	0.09	531.5
85 years and over	2.0	0.7	4.6	3.6	25.6	45.3	6.5	7.0	10.4	19.8	0.06	0.05	0.02	125.6
Female														
0–4 years	12.1	3.7	23.1	18.3	183.5	327.9	34.3	29.9	91.2	100.3	0.8	1.5	1.6	828.2
5–9	14.1	4.4	27.5	21.5	224.6	376.3	39.3	33.9	101.6	117.2	1.0	1.8	1.6	964.7
10–14	17.0	5.0	30.3	23.5	224.4	383.9	40.4	37.6	108.6	126.6	1.1	1.7	1.5	1 001.7
15–24	36.5	9.5	59.0	48.1	467.5	733.3	75.6	70.7	214.3	253.2	1.9	2.7	2.3	1 974.7
25–34	34.8	8.5	60.0	48.4	461.8	797.8	71.8	58.3	213.8	265.6	2.1	3.1	2.3	2 028.2
35–44	44.0	11.0	78.3	62.1	626.5	995.7	88.9	75.6	259.0	335.8	3.0	3.3	1.7	2 584.9
45–54	41.8	10.2	70.4	57.1	561.9	833.7	78.5	64.9	207.6	302.7	2.5	2.3	1.1	2 234.8
55–64	26.5	6.6	47.0	36.5	389.9	543.4	50.7	42.8	120.3	190.8	1.1	1.0	0.6	1 457.2
65–74	18.4	5.1	35.5	28.0	298.5	434.5	41.8	37.9	89.3	147.2	0.5	0.5	0.2	1 137.2
75–84	12.4	3.9	26.9	21.0	197.2	301.7	34.2	31.5	60.1	109.0	0.2	0.2	0.06	798.3
85 years and over	4.3	1.7	10.9	8.3	68.9	104.8	14.5	14.1	22.5	40.2	0.08	0.09	0.01	290.3

SOURCE: Statistics Canada

10 Immigrants by Class and Category, 2001

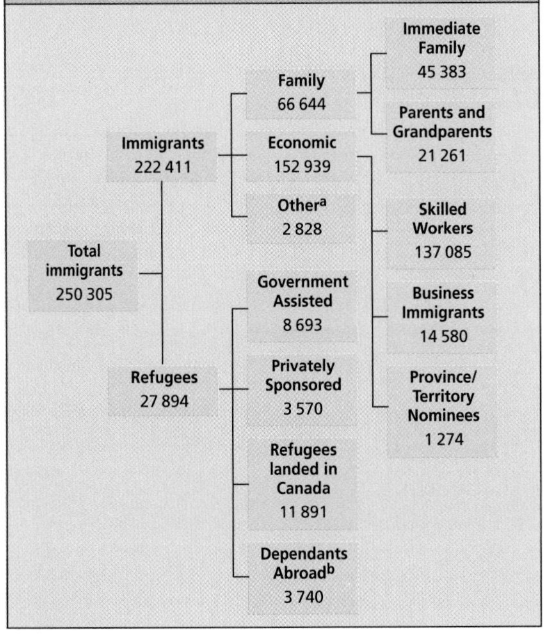

[a] Includes live-in care-givers, post determination refugee claimants, deferred removal orders, retirees
[b] Dependants (of a refugee landed in Canada) who live abroad
SOURCE: Statistics Canada

11 Aboriginal Population, 2001

	First Nations (000)	Métis (000)	Inuit (000)	Total[a] (000)
NL	7.0	5.5	4.6	18.8
PE	1.0	0.2	0.02	1.3
NS	12.9	3.1	0.4	17.0
NB	11.5	4.3	0.2	17.0
QC	51.1	15.9	9.5	79.4
ON	131.6	48.3	1.4	188.3
MB	90.3	56.8	0.3	150.0
SK	83.7	43.7	0.2	130.2
AB	85.0	66.1	1.1	156.2
BC	118.3	44.3	0.8	170.0
YT	5.6	0.5	0.1	6.5
NWT	10.6	3.6	3.9	18.7
NU	0.1	0.06	22.6	22.7
CANADA	608.9	292.3	45.1	976.3

[a] Totals include categories not shown
SOURCE: Statistics Canada

12 Status Indian[a] Population, 2001

	Total Indian[a] Population	On Reserve	Off Reserve
NL	7 040	755	6 285
PE	1 035	370	665
NS	12 920	7 285	5 630
NB	11 490	5 955	5 530
QC	51 125	32 200	18 925
ON	131 560	40 120	91 440
MB	90 345	50 970	39 370
SK	83 745	43 695	40 045
AB	84 990	36 245	48 750
BC	118 295	44 085	74 205
YT	5 600	1 815	3 790
NWT	10 615	8 915	1 700
NU	95	0	95
CANADA	608 850	272 410	336 435

[a] Terms used by Statistics Canada, as defined by the *Indian Act*.
SOURCE: Statistics Canada

13 Population by Ethnic Origin, 2001

	NL	PE	NS	NB	QC	ON	MB	SK	AB	BC	YT	NWT	NU	CANADA
Canadian	208 285	31 985	251 350	242 220	3 414 220	1 598 050	113 060	111 745	387 445	382 135	3 485	3 540	605	6 748 135
British	147 045	26 140	152 820	89 780	125 615	1 259 615	86 350	71 505	267 665	437 535	2 520	2 600	1 190	2 670 360
French	5 005	6 460	27 160	55 985	678 370	190 170	22 710	15 055	42 945	37 670	465	440	260	1 082 700
Chinese	710	150	2 580	1 310	51 640	443 695	10 245	7 015	88 500	329 945	215	185	30	936 210
Italian	215	140	2 150	1 090	161 825	481 735	7 665	1 690	23 105	46 470	60	95	20	726 275
German	845	435	16 350	3 410	20 765	226 220	75 115	84 280	153 185	123 475	925	510	85	705 600
East Indian	670	40	1 920	850	26 680	329 455	9 575	2 365	50 740	159 075	165	120	20	581 665
Aboriginal	11 110	600	9 675	9 140	63 890	89 920	89 045	83 010	82 855	87 355	4 085	14 070	20 290	565 040
Ukrainian	85	50	1 220	300	9 170	90 065	54 925	40 710	88 355	40 785	255	235	50	326 195
Caribbean	60	40	655	320	85 145	219 235	4 175	660	7 875	5 300	40	55	20	323 580
Multiple responses	129 335	64 990	401 495	304 660	1 876 360	4 401 645	500 790	481 920	1 420 680	1 717 615	14 680	13 520	3 795	11 331 490

SOURCE: Statistics Canada

14 Population by First Language, 1991 to 2001

	1991	2001	Percent Change 1991–2001
English[a]	16 169 875	17 352 315	7.3
French[a]	6 502 860	6 703 325	3.1
Chinese	498 845	853 745	71.1
Indo-Iranian	301 335	627 860	108.4
Italian	510 990	469 485	-8.1
German	466 245	438 080	-6.0
Spanish	177 425	245 500	38.4
Portuguese	212 090	213 815	0.8
Polish	189 815	208 375	9.8
Arabic	107 750	199 940	85.6
Aboriginal	172 610	187 675	8.7
Tagalog (Filipino)	99 715	174 060	74.6
Ukrainian	187 010	148 090	-20.8
Dutch	149 870	128 670	-14.1
Vietnamese	78 570	122 055	55.3
Greek	126 205	120 365	-4.6
Russian	35 300	94 555	167.9
Tamil	30 535	92 010	201.3
Korean (Filipino)	36 185	85 070	135.1
Hungarian	79 770	75 555	-5.3
Croatian	39 660	54 880	38.4
Finnish	27 705	22 405	-19.1
Total Single Responses	26 686 850	29 257 885	
Total Multiple Responses	307 190	381 145	
Canada	26 994 045	29 639 035	

[a] Official language
SOURCE: Statistics Canada

15 Refugees to Canada by Country, 1990 to 2001

1990			1995			2001		
Country	Total	Rank	Country	Total	Rank	Country	Total	Rank
Poland	11 902	1	Bosnia-Herzegovina	5 964	1	Afghanistan	2 916	1
Vietnam	5 279	2	Sri Lanka	4 792	2	Sri Lanka	2 504	2
El Salvador	3 750	3	Iraq	1 276	3	Pakistan	2 111	3
Ethiopia	2 174	4	Iran	1 263	4	Yugoslavia	1 745	4
Iran	2 019	5	Afghanistan	1 094	5	Iran	1 474	5
Sri Lanka	1 234	6	Somalia	1 083	6	Colombia	1 281	6
USSR	1 153	7	China	684	7	India	1 153	7
Czechoslovakia	1 151	8	Yugoslavia	579	8	Iraq	1 076	8
Somalia	1 072	9	Ethiopia	415	9	Sudan	1038	9
Romania	1 016	10	Croatia	405	10	Dem. Rep. of Congo	928	10
Others	8 939		Others	7 409		Others	11 673	

SOURCE: Citizenship and Immigration Canada

ECONOMICS

16 Employment by Industry, 1970 to 2001

	1970	1975	1980	1986	1991	1996	2001
Agricultural (000)	–	–	–	513	521	486	
Forestry (000)	–	–	–	113	106	103	568
Fishing (000)	–	–	–	46	48	46	
Mining (000)	–	–	–	193	192	168	170
Manufacturing (000)	1 768	1 871	2 111	2 197	2 084	2 040	2 174
Construction (000)	467	603	624	759	933	822	879
Trans., Comm., Utilities (000)	698	812	906	977	1 061	1 046	893
Trade (000)	1 328	1 637	1 837	2 191	2 446	2 493	2 441
Finance, Insurance, and Real Estate (000)	379	474	611	691	811	788	895
Services (000)	2 040	2 520	3 096	4 090	4 906	5 439	6 651
Public Administration (000)	510	665	744	969	1 111	887	904
Total (000)	–	–	–	12 740	14 220	14 318	15 576

SOURCE: Statistics Canada

17 Employment by Industry by Province and Territory, 2001

	NL (000)	PE (000)	NS (000)	NB (000)	QC (000)	ON (000)	MB (000)	SK (000)	AB (000)	BC (000)	YT (000)	NWT (000)	NU (000)
Agricultural, Forestry and Fishing	15.5	9.5	22.9	20.4	101.6	123.7	37.4	72.7	84.6	78.6	0.3	0.3	0.1
Mining	4.9	0.2	3.4	3.2	16.3	21.1	4.2	14.5	86.0	14.0	0.4	1.4	0.2
Manufacturing	24.0	7.8	44.2	45.9	640.7	984.3	68.0	29.4	134.9	194.4	0.4	0.3	0.2
Construction	15.0	5.3	26.8	23.3	168.4	332.3	28.7	27.2	130.0	118.7	1.4	1.5	0.7
Transportation, Communication, and Other Utilities	13.7	2.6	22.8	23.8	198.3	326.4	41.1	29.0	106.0	125.8	0.9	1.8	0.9
Trade	36.6	10.0	71.1	53.6	581.8	950.7	84.2	73.4	258.7	315.4	2.3	2.2	1.4
Finance, Insurance, and Real Estate	7.1	2.0	20.6	14.8	186.8	401.4	28.8	25.3	84.3	122.2	0.6	0.7	0.4
Services	95.1	28.4	192.9	151.5	1 521.1	2 543.9	244.8	201.3	720.0	932.6	7.7	7.9	4.0
Public Administration	20.4	7.1	37.8	28.5	229.4	309.0	40.2	31.3	77.5	112.8	3.7	4.3	2.6
Total	232.3	72.9	442.4	365.0	3 644.4	5 992.8	577.3	504.0	1 682.0	2 014.5	17.7	20.4	10.7

SOURCE: Statistics Canada

PRIMARY INDUSTRY

18 Agricultural Land Use, 2001

	NL	PE	NS	NB	QC	ON	MB	SK	AB	BC	CANADA
Farmland Area (000 ha)	40.6	261.5	407.0	388.1	3 417.0	5 466.2	7 601.8	26 265.6	21 067.5	2 587.1	67 502.4
Percent Change 1991–2001	-14.3	+1.0	+2.5	+3.3	-0.4	+0.3	-1.6	-2.2	+1.2	+8.1	-0.4
Number of Farms	643	1 845	3 923	3 034	32 139	59 728	21 071	50 598	53 652	20 290	246 923
Average Farm Size (ha)	63.0	142.0	104.0	128.0	106.0	92.0	361.0	519.0	393.0	128.0	273.0
Average Farm Size Percent Change 1991–2001	-3.1	+29.1	+4.0	+10.3	+17.8	+16.5	+19.9	+17.4	+8.0	+3.2	+12.8
Cropland Area (000 ha)	8.4	175.5	119.2	148.9	1 850.0	3 656.7	4 714.8	15 375.9	9 728.2	617.5	36 395.2
Summer Fallow Area (000 ha)	0.1	0.2	0.6	0.6	4.9	14.2	255.7	3 131.6	1 235.6	36.8	4 680.4
Tame or Seeded Pasture (000 ha)	2.5	11.8	22.9	18.2	182.8	313.1	383.5	1 405.7	2 230.9	233.0	4 804.5

SOURCE: Statistics Canada

19 Census Farms by Product, 2001

	NL	PE	NS	NB	QC	ON	MB	SK	AB	BC	CANADA
Total Farms	519	1 739	3 318	2 563	30 539	55 092	19 818	48 990	50 580	17 382	230 540
Cattle Ranching and Farming	119	734	1 123	975	13 390	19 152	7 544	12 294	23 301	5 295	83 927
Hog and Pig Farming	9	95	68	83	2 224	2 491	980	298	868	153	7 269
Poultry and Egg Production	33	22	111	47	759	1 614	286	113	450	977	4 412
Sheep and Goat Farming	27	9	69	28	640	1 017	172	219	626	461	3 268
Other Animal Production	38	124	307	176	1 426	5 428	1 298	2 009	5387	3 305	19 498
Oilseed and Grain Farming	0	57	17	30	3 210	13 371	7 358	30 842	13 133	250	68 268
Vegetable and Melon Farming	90	398	119	304	1 092	1 416	193	119	241	538	4 510
Fruit and Tree Nut Farming	23	91	653	304	1 044	1 739	74	49	75	2 528	6 580
Greenhouse, Nursery and Floriculture Production	102	33	456	251	1 386	2 430	237	242	688	1678	7 503
Other Crop Farming	78	176	395	365	5 368	6 434	1 676	2 805	5 811	2 197	25 305

SOURCE: Statistics Canada

20 Farm Cash Receipts, 1998 to 2002

	1998 ($000 000)	1999 ($000 000)	2000 ($000 000)	2001 ($000 000)	2002 ($000 000)
Total	29 796	30 481	33 027	36 323	35 775
Canadian Wheat Board Payments	949	948	814	1 032	975
Wheat	2 413	2 337	2 352	2 544	2 315
Oats	193	175	196	276	305
Barley	510	421	477	622	500
Deferred Grain Receipts	84	357	45	-248	203
Canola	2 663	1 771	1 560	1 723	1 635
Other Cereals and Oilseeds	1 841	1 639	1 615	1 433	1 760
Other Crops	5 260	5 674	6 114	6 339	6 666
Cattle and Calves	5 720	6 204	6 826	7 824	7 547
Hogs	2 229	2 434	3 388	3 853	3 315
Hens and Chickens	1 352	1 320	1 362	1 519	1 453
Dairy Products	3 846	3 921	4 030	4 142	4 135
Other Livestock Products	1 312	1 314	1 421	1 534	1 556
Payments	1 423	1 965	2 827	3 750	3 409

SOURCE: Statistics Canada

21 Forest Land and Harvest, 2000

	Total Area (000 ha)	Area of Forest (000 ha)	Area of Productive Forest (000 ha)	Total Area Harvested (000 ha) and (Percent Clear-cut)	Total Volume of Wood Cut (000 000m³)
NL	40 600	22 500	11 270	23 (100)	2.7[a]
PE	570	290	280	6 (99.6)	0.7[a]
NS	5 600	3 900	3 770	54 (97.1)	6.2[a]
NB	7 300	6 100	5 950	112 (71.5)	11.3[a]
QC	154 100	83 900	53 990	349 (83.6)	43.3
ON	106 900	58 000	42 200	202 (94.5)	28.1
MB	65 000	26 300	15 240	16 (100)	2.2[a]
SK	65 200	28 800	12 630	21 (100)	4.5
AB	66 100	38 200	25 710	65 (99.5)	21.9
BC	94 800	60 600	51 740	204 (94.5)	75.0
YT	48 300	27 500	7 470	0.01 (100)	0.3[a]
NWT	342 600	61 400	14 320	0.05 (100)	0.1[a]

[a] 1999 figures
SOURCES: The State of Canada's Forests
Statistics Canada

22 Fishing, 2001[a]

	Atlantic Coast			Pacific Coast		
	Quantity (000 metric tonnes)	Percent Change 1991–2001	Value ($000 000)	Quantity (000 metric tonnes)	Percent Change 1991–2001	Value ($000 000)
Total Groundfish	157.6	-74.9	178.7	114.2	-31.1	104.8
Cod	40.3	-87.0	58.4	0.5	-95.8	0.6
Haddock	15.6	-29.0	27.9	0	0	0
Redfish	19.7	-78.7	12.6	21.6	-7.7	29.7
Halibut	1.6	-19.2	12.1	4.5	+4.6	20.6
Flatfish	25.1	-61.0	21.8	5.5	-30.4	6.5
Greenland Turbot	13.8	-31.7	14.8	8.3	+260.9	2.4
Pollock	7.2	-82.4	5.6	1.7	-32.3	0.8
Hake	23.0	-64.1	17.6	61.0	-38.4	12.3
Cusk	1.5	-65.9	1.4	0	0	0
Catfish	0.6	-58.4	0.3	0	0	0
Skate	2.6	+131.3	0.8	1.5	+523.0	0.4
Dogfish	3.8	+1 128.8	1.9	4.3	+38.7	2.7
Other	2.8	-24.3	3.5	5.3	-52.3	28.8
Total Pelagic	250.3	-17.7	81.1	50.4	-60.0	59.8
Herring	199.3	-7.5	42.0	24.2	-39.1	16.8
Mackerel	24.5	-5.4	10.5	0.02	+100.0	0.01
Swordfish	1.1	–	8.5	0	0	0
Tuna	0.9	+73.6	13.4	3.1	+2 040.6	12.0
Alewife	2.8	+63.1	0.7	0	0	0
Eel	0.2	-77.6	0.9	0	0	0
Salmon	0	-100.0	0	22.9	-73.3	30.9
Smelt	0.3	-75.2	0.4	0	0	0
Capelin	19.7	-60.5	3.1	0	0	0
Other	1.5	-33.0	1.6	0.2	+468.3	0.08
Total Shellfish	423.1	+86.3	1 490.2	17.6	-27.7	117.8
Clam/quahaugs	26.9	+111.8	28.5	2.5	-48.8	37.7
Oyster	3.0	+57.9	7.8	0	-100.0	0
Scallop	90.5	+13.8	122.0	0.04	-52.4	0.3
Squid	0.1	-97.5	0.02	0	-100.0	0
Mussel	11.8	+227.8	15.4	0	0	0
Lobster	51.4	+6.0	638.7	0	0	0
Shrimp	125.6	+210.1	261.3	4.2	-0.3	33.8
Crab, Queen	95.3	+171.0	396.3	0	0	0
Crab, Other	12.3	+1 018.2	11.6	5.7	+200.0	36.8
Sea Urchin	2.8	–	6.4	4.3	-	7.8
Other	3.4	+161.5	2.2	0.9	-89.9	1.4
Total All Fisheries	831.0	-28.2	1 750.0	182.2	-42.3	282.4

[a] Statistics do not include Aquaculture production
SOURCE: Fisheries and Oceans Canada

23 Mineral Production, 2001

							$000 000							
	NL	PE	NS	NB	QC	ON	MB	SK	AB	BC	YT	NWT	NU	CANADA
Metals														
Cobalt	0	0	0	0	12.3	53.7	14.9	0	0	0	0	0	0	80.9
Copper	0	0	0	22.6	245.0	455.7	97.1	27.0	0	687.8	0	0	0	1 535.2
Gold	20.2	0	0.6	3.5	456.9	1 073.3	86.3	25.5	0.5	317.4	37.3	54.3	59.4	2 135.2
Iron Ore	7 98.2	0	0	0	na	0	0	0	0	na	0	0	0	1 188.9
Lead	0	0	0	60.0	0	0	0	0	0	25.7	0	0	23.8	109.5
Molybdenum	0	0	0	0	0	0	0	0	0	73.8	0	0	0	73.8
Nickel	0	0	0	0	235.5	1 129.7	412.2	0	0	0	0	0	0	1 777.4
Platinum Group	0	0	0	0	na	na	na	0	0	0	0	0	0	651.9
Silver	0.07	0	0	49.4	52.5	32.1	6.9	0.4	0	132.8	0.2	0.2	3.3	277.9
Zinc	0	0	0	441.1	355.3	109.6	129.3	2.9	0	153.4	0	0	234.4	1 426.0
Uranium	0	0	0	0	0	0	0	605.4	0	0	0	0	0	605.4
Total Metals	818.5	0	0.6	580.2	2 238.8	3 460.5	791.5	661.3	0.5	1 394.5	37.5	54.5	320.9	10 359.3
Non-metals														
Asbestos	0	0	0	0	118.7	0	0	0	0	0	0	0	0	118.7
Peat	0.2	3.2	na	53.8	55.4	0	na	na	24.5	na	0	0	0	186.4
Potash	0	0	0	na	0	0	0	na	0	0	0	0	0	1 617.4
Salt	0	0	na	na	na	270.7	0	35.8	19.2	0	0	0	0	426.1
Sulphur	na	0	na	0	0	na	0	0.2	0.6	na	0	0	0	1.3
Total Structural Minerals (e.g. sand, gravel, cement, stone)	41.8	0.8	73.1	29.8	638.8	1 480.7	50.8	48.1	260.9	448.8	3.6	6.2	0	3367.5
Total Non-Metals	44.7	4.0	241.3	207.1	1 365.1	2 170.8	93.6	1 649.9	600.1	513.0	3.6	724.0	0	7 617.2
Fuels														
Coal	0	0	na	19.9	0	0	0	na	389.4	959.3	0	0	0	1 557.1
Natural Gas	0	0	na	0	0	na	0	1 224.4	26 321.5	4 810.3	98.1	207.3	0	33 677.5
Crude Oil	2 038.2	0	na	0	0	na	138.2	4 040.7	17 721.4	na	0	337.6	0	25 181.4
Total Fuels	2 038.2	0	1 168.7	19.9	0	137.6	138.2	5 422.3	48 707.6	6 715.8	98.1	544.8	0	64 991.3
Total All Minerals	2 901.4	4.0	1 410.6	807.2	3 603.9	5 768.9	1 023.3	7 733.5	49 308.2	8 623.3	139.2	1 323.4	320.9	82 967.8

SOURCE: Natural Resources Canada

MANUFACTURING

24 Manufacturers, 1965 to 1999

	Number of Establishments	Number of Production Employees	Salaries ($000 000)	Cost of Fuel and Electricity ($000 000)	Cost of Materials and Supplies ($000 000)	Value of Shipments of Goods ($000 000)	Value Added ($000 000)
1965	33 310	1 115 892	5 012	676	18 622	33 889	14 927
1970	31 928	1 167 063	7 232	903	25 700	46 380	20 047
1975	30 100	1 271 786	12 699	1 805	51 178	88 427	36 105
1980	35 495	1 346 187	22 162	4 449	99 898	168 058	65 851
1984	36 464	1 240 816	28 294	7 306	136 134	230 070	88 667
1990	39 864	1 393 324	40 406	7 936	168 664	298 918	122 972
1995	31 445	1 276 941	43 400	9 300	226 000	389 800	157 100
1999	29 822	1 494 809	53 300	11 100	277 800	488 600	202 800

SOURCE: Industry Canada

25 Manufacturers by Province and Territory, 1997

	NL	PE	NS	NB	QC	ON	MB	SK	AB	BC	YT/NWT/NU
Number of Establishments	314.0	154.0	727.0	696.0	10 176.0	13 906.0	1 098.0	787.0	2 804.0	4 228.0	45.0
Number of Production Employees	9 071.0	3 823.0	28 330.0	26 637.0	362 788.0	694 624.0	48 114.0	20 376.0	91 878.0	123 722.0	489.0
Salaries ($000 000)	266.1	82.2	845.7	779.9	11 272.3	25 642.1	1 324.5	629.2	3 112.8	4 880.4	12.4
Cost of Fuel and Electricity ($000 000)	82.0	19.7	208.2	374.5	3 265.4	3 968.0	226.8	165.4	813.2	1 050.6	1.1
Cost of Materials and Supplies ($000 000)	780.8	530.9	3 867.1	5 336.8	54 583.9	136 050.5	5 459.8	3 636.7	20 810.0	19 955.0	26.6
Value of Shipments of Goods ($000 000)	1 658.2	802.3	6 464.6	8 434.6	102 825.6	228 505.2	9 969.3	6 114.5	34 675.7	34 582.7	50.4

SOURCE: Statistics Canada

TOURISM

26 Where Canadians Visit, 2000

	Overnight Visits		
Country Visited	Visits (000)	Nights Spent (000)	Spending in Country ($000 000)
USA	14 648	103 024	8 975
United Kingdom	803	9 617	974
Mexico	731	7 451	716
France	442	4 455	561
Germany	277	2 332	234
Cuba	273	2 366	210
Italy	211	2 578	332
Dominican Republic	195	1 737	152
Netherlands	154	1 341	115
Spain	132	1 946	172
Japan	124	1 636	191
Switzerland	124	916	97
Republic of Ireland	97	1 025	115
Belgium	93	549	52
Austria	88	515	65

SOURCE: Statistics Canada

27 Who Visits Canada, 2000

	Overnight Visits		
Country of Origin	Visits (000)	Nights Spent (000)	Spending in Canada ($000 000)
USA	15 225	58 649	7 448
United Kingdom	866	9 324	1 004
Japan	500	3 299	573
France	404	5 198	425
Germany	385	4 732	413
Australia	160	2 055	224
Taiwan	173	2 275	246
Mexico	143	1 372	180
Hong Kong	137	1 327	135
South Korea	134	1 104	175
Netherlands	128	1 658	146
Italy	108	1 048	105
Switzerland	104	1 266	146
Israel	75	707	73
China	74	978	110

SOURCE: Statistics Canada

TRADE

28 Exports from Canada, 1993 to 2002

	1993 ($000 000)	1996 ($000 000)	1999 ($000 000)	2002 ($000 000)
USA	150 657	223 177	308 076	345 427
Japan	8 496	11 210	8 573	8 398
United Kingdom	2 975	4 040	4 828	4 427
China	1 681	3 015	2 664	4 093
Germany	2 568	3 338	2 415	2 950
Mexico	826	1 259	1 613	2 412
South Korea	1 721	2 817	1 989	1 998
France	1 316	1 752	1 890	1 994
Belgium	1 038	1 539	1 881	1 907
Netherlands	1 383	1 668	1 558	1 768
Others	14 855	22 005	19 933	20 747
Total (all countries)	187 515	275 819	355 420	396 121

SOURCE: Statistics Canada

29 Imports to Canada, 1993 to 2002

	1993 ($000 000)	1996 ($000 000)	1999 ($000 000)	2002 ($000 000)
USA	113 846	156 953	215 575	218 308
China	3 098	4 931	8 951	15 978
Japan	10 718	10 439	15 039	15 412
Mexico	3 710	6 035	9 536	12 708
United Kingdom	4 473	5 908	8 107	9 728
Germany	3 522	4 824	6 949	8 290
France	2 275	3 402	5 316	5 843
Re-Imports (Canada)	3 114	4 195	5 538	5 423
South Korea	2 199	2 729	3 572	4 860
Italy	1 936	2 719	3 621	4 438
Others	21 064	30 431	38 204	47 655
Total (all countries)	169 953	232 566	320 409	348 644

SOURCE: Statistics Canada

30 Commodities, 2002

		Imports ($000 000)	Exports ($000 000)			Imports ($000 000)	Exports ($000 000)
1	Transport Equipment	93 381	101583	9	Food	12 627	17 097
2	Mining and Oil and Gas	16 126	47 435	10	Plastics and Rubber Products	10 990	12 643
3	Paper	6 571	23 767	11	Petroleum and Coal Products	2 874	9 971
4	Machinery	32 988	22 328	12	Furniture	3 722	7 487
5	Chemicals	32 837	20 209	13	Electrical Equipment, Appliances and Components	12 550	6 685
6	Primary Metal Products	12 898	19 804		Other	66 440	69 229
7	Computer and Electronic Products	41 855	19 448		**Total**	348 644	396 121
8	Wood Products	2 785	18 435				

SOURCE: Industry Canada

GOVERNMENT

31 National Political Party Representation, 1953 to 2000

	Election Year														
Region	**1953**	**1958**	**1962**	**1963**	**1965**	**1968**	**1972**	**1974**	**1979**	**1980**	**1984**	**1988**	**1993**	**1997**	**2000**
Atlantic Canada – Total Seats	33	33	33	33	32	32	32	31	32	32	32	32	32	32	32
Liberal	27	8	14	20	15	7	10	13	12	19	7	20	31	11	19
Progressive Conservative	5	25	18	13	18	25	22	17	17	13	25	12	1	13	9
New Democratic Party	1	–	1	–	–	–	–	1	2	–	–	–	–	8	4
Québec– Total Seats	70	75	75	75	73	74	73	74	75	75	75	75	75	75	75
Liberal	66	25	35	47	56	56	56	60	67	74	17	12	19	26	36
Progressive Conservative	4	50	14	8	8	4	2	3	2	1	58	63	1	5	1
Bloc Québécois	–	–	–	–	–	–	–	–	–	–	–	–	54	44	38
Others	–	–	–	–	–	–	–	–	–	–	–	–	1	–	–
Ontario – Total Seats	85	85	85	85	85	88	87	88	95	95	95	99	99	103	103
Liberal	51	15	44	52	51	64	36	55	32	52	15	42	98	101	100
Progressive Conservative	33	67	35	27	25	17	40	25	57	38	66	47	–	1	–
New Democratic Party	1	3	6	6	9	6	11	8	6	5	13	10	–	–	1
Reform Party	–	–	–	–	–	–	–	–	–	–	–	–	1	–	2
Others	–	–	–	–	–	–	–	–	–	–	–	–	–	1	–
Western – Total Seats	72	72	72	72	72	70	68	68	80	80	80	89	89	91	91
Liberal	27	1	7	10	9	28	7	13	3	2	2	8	29	17	17
Progressive Conservative	9	66	49	47	46	26	42	49	60	51	61	48	–	1	2
New Democratic Party	21	5	12	11	12	16	19	6	18	27	17	33	9	13	8
Social Credit	15	–	4	4	5	–	–	–	–	–	–	–	–	–	–
Reform Party	–	–	–	–	–	–	–	–	–	–	–	–	51	60	64
Canada – Total Seats in House of Commons	265	265	265	265	265	265	265	282	282	282	282	295	295	301	301
Liberal	171	49	100	129	131	155	109	141	114	147	40	82	177	155	172
Progressive Conservative	51	208	116	95	97	72	107	95	136	103	211	170	2	20	12
New Democratic Party	23	8	19	17	21	22	31	16	26	32	30	43	9	21	13
Social Credit	15	–	30	24	14	14	15	11	6	–	–	–	–	–	–
Bloc Québécois	–	–	–	–	–	–	–	–	–	–	–	–	54	44	38
Reform Party	–	–	–	–	–	–	–	–	–	–	–	–	52	60	66
Others	5	–	–	–	2	2	2	1	–	–	1	–	1	1	–

SOURCE: Elections Canada

FLAG	COUNTRY	CAPITAL CITY	AREA	LAND USE				POPULATION			
			km²	CROP km²	PASTURE km²	FOREST km²	OTHER km²	TOTAL 2002	BIRTH RATE / DEATH RATE per 1000 people 2000	DOUBLING TIME (years) 2000	TOTAL FERTILITY RATE 1995–2000
	AFGHANISTAN	Kabul	652 225	1 440	300 000	17 000	333 785	23 294 000	48/22	28	-
	ALBANIA	Tiranë	28 748	1 210	4 450	10 480	12 608	3 164 000	17/6	55	2.6
	ALGERIA	Algiers	2 381 741	5 200	315 000	39 500	2 022 041	31 403 000	25/5	29	3.2
	ANGOLA	Luanda	1 246 700	3 000	540 000	230 000	473 700	13 936 000	48/19	23	7.2
	ARGENTINA	Buenos Aires	2 766 889	22 000	1 420 000	509 000	815 889	37 944 000	19/8	62	2.6
	ARMENIA	Yerevan	29 800	650	8 340	4 200	16 610	3 790 000	11/6	161	1.4
	AUSTRALIA	Canberra	7 682 300	2 960	4 049 000	1 450 000	2 180 340	19 536 000	13/7	110	1.8
	AUSTRIA	Vienna	83 855	710	19 200	32 400	31 545	8 069 000	10/10	2 310	1.4
	AZERBAIJAN	Baku	86 600	2 630	25 620	9 500	48 850	8 147 000	15/6	77	1.9
	BAHAMAS, THE	Nassau	13 939	40	20	3 240	10 639	312 000	19/6	45	2.4
	BAHRAIN	Manama	691	40	40	-	-	663 000	20/3	37	2.6
	BANGLADESH	Dhaka	143 998	3 450	6 000	18 920	115 628	143 364 000	28/9	38	3.8
	BARBADOS	Bridgetown	430	10	20	50	350	269 000	14/9	130	1.5
	BELARUS	Minsk	207 600	1 240	29 950	72 000	104 410	10 106 000	9/14	-	1.3
	BELGIUM	Brussels	30 520	220	6 850	7 090	16 360	10 276 000	11/10	770	1.5
	BELIZE	Belmopan	22 965	250	500	21 000	1 215	236 000	27/4	26	3.4
	BENIN	Porto Novo	112 620	2 650	5 500	34 000	70 470	6 629 000	39/13	24	6.1
	BERMUDA	Hamilton	54	-	-	10	-	64 000	-	-	-
	BHUTAN	Thimbu	46 620	200	3 000	31 000	12 420	2 198 000	38/9	22	5.5
	BOLIVIA	La Paz	1 098 581	2 620	338 310	580 000	177 651	8 705 000	31/9	34	4.4
	BOSNIA-HERZEGOVINA	Sarajevo	51 130	1 500	12 000	27 100	10 530	4 126 000	12/8	141	-
	BOTSWANA	Gaborone	581 370	30	256 000	265 000	60 340	1 564 000	32/20	45	4.4
	BRAZIL	Brasília	8 511 965	120 000	1 850 000	5 550 000	991 965	174 706 000	20/7	45	2.3
	BRUNEI	Bandar Seri Begawan	5 765	40	60	4 500	1 165	341 000	21/3	32	2.8
	BULGARIA	Sofia	110 994	2 120	16 150	33 480	59 244	7 790 000	9/14	-	1.1
	BURKINA	Ouagadougou	274 200	500	60 000	138 000	75 700	12 207 000	44/19	24	6.9
	BURUNDI	Bujumbura	27 835	3 600	9 350	3 250	11 635	6 688 000	40/20	28	6.8
	CAMBODIA	Phnom Penh	181 000	1 070	15 000	122 000	42 930	13 776 000	30/12	27	5.2
	CAMEROON	Yaoundé	475 442	12 000	20 000	359 000	84 442	15 535 000	37/14	27	5.1
	CANADA	Ottawa	9 984 670	658 000	203 000	4 176 000	4 947 670	30 007 094	11/8	178	1.6
	CENTRAL AFRICAN REPUBLIC	Bangui	622 436	900	31 250	467 000	123 286	3 844 000	36/20	34	5.3
	CHAD	Ndjamena	1 284 000	300	450 000	324 000	509 700	8 390 000	45/16	21	6.6
	CHILE	Santiago	756 945	3 180	129 350	165 000	459 415	15 589 000	17/6	54	2.4
	CHINA	Beijing	9 562 000	114 210	4 000 010	1 305 180	4 142 600	1 279 557 000	15/7	79	1.8
	COLOMBIA	Bogotá	1 141 748	17 270	409 200	530 000	185 278	43 495 000	23/6	34	2.8
	COMOROS	Moroni	1 862	500	150	400	812	749 000	33/8	25	5.4
	CONGO	Brazzaville	342 000	450	100 000	199 000	42 550	3 206 000	43/14	29	6.3
	CONGO, DEM. REP. OF	Kinshasa	2 345 410	11 800	150 000	1 660 000	523 610	54 275 000	46/17	22	6.7
	COSTA RICA	San José	51 100	2 800	23 400	15 700	9 200	4 200 000	20/4	39	2.8
	CÔTE D'IVOIRE	Yamoussoukro	322 463	44 000	130 000	96 000	52 463	16 691 000	37/17	32	5.1
	CROATIA	Zagreb	56 538	1 280	15 700	20 760	18 798	4 657 000	10/12	-	1.7
	CUBA	Havana	110 860	8 350	22 000	26 080	54 430	11 273 000	13/7	103	1.6
	CYPRUS	Nicosia	9 251	420	40	1 230	7 561	797 000	13/8	124	2.0
	CZECH REPUBLIC	Prague	78 864	2 360	9 610	26 290	40 604	10 250 000	9/11	-	1.2
	DENMARK	Copenhagen	43 075	80	3 580	4 170	35 245	5 343 000	12/11	472	1.7
	DJIBOUTI	Djibouti	23 200	-	13 000	220	-	652 000	37/18	30	6.1

LABOUR FORCE			GDP, 2000				COMMUNICATIONS, 2000			
AGRI-CULTURE percent employed	MANU-FACTURING percent employed	SERVICE INDUSTRIES percent employed	PER CAPITA PPP US$	EXTERNAL DEPT repayments percent of GDP	EDUCATION spending percent of GDP	MILITARY spending percent of GDP	INTERNET USERS (000)	TELEPHONES main lines in use (000)	TELEVISIONS per 1000 people	PASSENGER CARS per 1000 people
70	11	19	-	-	-	-	-	29	14	-
24	45	31	3 506	0.7	-	1.2	12	120	123	29
26	31	43	5 308	8.4	6	3.5	180	2 300	110	-
75	8	17	2 187	13.6	3	21.2	60	72	19	-
1	25	74	12 377	9.6	-	1.3	3 880	7 500	-	140
-	-	-	2 559	2.2	2	4.4	30	600	244	-
5	21	74	25 693	-	5	1.7	10 630	10 050	738	-
6	30	63	26 765	-	6	0.8	3 700	4 000	536	495
42	12	46	2 936	3.4	3	2.7	25	865	259	38
4	15	81	17 012	-	3	-	17	96	247	-
1	55	43	15 084	-	4	4.0	140	152	402	250
63	10	25	1 602	1.7	-	1.3	150	500	7	0
4	22	74	15 494	-	5	-	6	108	310	229
21	35	40	7 544	0.8	6	1.3	422	2 313	342	135
2	27	71	27 178	-	-	1.4	3 760	4 769	541	448
28	17	55	5 606	8.1	-	-	18	31	183	44
64	8	28	990	3.5	3	-	25	51	45	-
1	10	82	-	-	-	-	25	52	1 086	-
94	1	5	1 412	1.4	-	-	3	6	20	-
2	29	69	2 424	8.0	-	1.5	78	328	119	-
11	48	41	-	-	-	-	45	303	111	-
3	31	67	7 184	1.3	9	3.7	33	131	25	30
23	20	57	7 625	10.5	5	1.3	13 980	17 039	343	-
2	64	34	16 779	-	4	7.6	35	79	640	293
27	29	44	5 710	9.9	3	3.0	585	3 187	449	233
92	2	6	976	2.5	3	1.6	25	53	12	-
15	22	59	591	3.1	4	5.4	6	20	30	-
75	5	21	1 446	1.0	6	2.4	10	22	8	-
70	9	22	1 703	6.3	3	1.3	45	95	34	-
4	22	74	27 840	-	6	1.2	16 840	20 803	-	459
80	4	16	1 172	1.5	2	-	2	10	6	-
83	4	13	871	1.9	2	1.0	4	10	1	-
14	26	60	9 417	8.7	4	3.3	3 100	2 603	242	88
48	22	13	3 976	2.0	-	2.1	45 800	135 000	293	-
1	24	75	6 248	6.4	-	2.3	1 150	5 434	282	43
77	9	13	1 588	1.3	-	-	3	7	-	-
49	15	37	825	1.3	5	-	0.5	22	-	-
68	13	19	765	0.3	-	-	6	20	-	-
20	23	56	8 650	4.1	6	0.0	384	450	231	88
60	10	31	1 630	10.9	4	-	70	264	60	-
17	31	53	8 091	12.8	-	3.0	480	1 721	293	-
18	30	52	-	-	-	-	120	473	250	-
11	25	63	20 824	-	6	3.2	150	488	179	341
5	40	55	13 991	9.4	4	2.0	2 690	3 869	508	335
4	27	70	27 627	-	8	1.5	3 370	4 785	807	353
-	-	-	-	2.4	-	4.4	3	10	71	-

FLAG	COUNTRY	CAPITAL CITY	AREA	LAND USE				POPULATION			
			km2	CROP km2	PASTURE km2	FOREST km2	OTHER km2	TOTAL 2002	BIRTH RATE / DEATH RATE per 1000 people 2000	DOUBLING TIME (years) 2000	TOTAL FERTILITY RATE 1995–2000
	DOMINICA	Roseau	750	120	20	500	110	70 000	-	83	-
	DOMINICAN REPUBLIC	Santo Domingo	48 442	5 000	21 000	6 000	16 442	8 639 000	23/6	32	2.9
	EAST TIMOR	Dili	14 874	100	1 500	11 000	2 274	779 000	-	39	-
	ECUADOR	Quito	272 045	14 270	51 070	156 000	50 705	13 112 000	24/6	33	3.1
	EGYPT	Cairo	1 000 250	4 660	-	340	995 250	70 278 000	25/6	35	3.4
	EL SALVADOR	San Salvador	21 041	2 500	7 940	1 050	9 551	6 520 000	26/6	29	3.2
	EQUATORIAL GUINEA	Malabo	28 051	1 000	1 040	18 300	7 711	483 000	41/16	28	5.9
	ERITREA	Asmara	117 400	30	69 670	7 360	40 340	3 993 000	39/13	23	5.7
	ESTONIA	Tallinn	45 200	140	2 990	20 170	21 900	1 361 000	9/13	-	1.2
	ETHIOPIA	Addis Ababa	1 133 880	7 280	200 000	133 000	793 600	66 040 000	44/20	29	6.8
	FIJI	Suva	18 330	850	1 750	11 850	3 880	832 000	22/6	46	3.2
	FINLAND	Helsinki	338 145	40	210	231 860	106 035	5 183 000	11/10	433	1.7
	FRANCE	Paris	543 965	11 420	101 240	150 120	281 185	59 670 000	13/9	204	1.7
	FRENCH GUIANA	Cayenne	90 000	40	100	79 900	9 960	176 000	-	29	-
	GABON	Libreville	267 667	1 700	46 650	199 000	20 317	1 293 000	36/16	32	5.4
	GAMBIA, THE	Banjul	11 295	50	4 590	930	5 725	1 371 000	39/13	29	5.2
	GEORGIA	T'bilisi	69 700	2 690	19 380	29 880	17 750	5 213 000	9/9	462	1.6
	GERMANY	Berlin	357 868	2 160	50 480	107 000	198 228	81 990 000	9/11	-	1.3
	GHANA	Accra	238 537	22 000	83 500	92 000	41 037	20 176 000	30/11	29	4.6
	GREECE	Athens	131 957	11 130	46 750	26 200	47 877	10 631 000	12/11	-	1.3
	GRENADA	St George's	378	100	10	30	238	94 000	25/7	30	-
	GUATEMALA	Guatemala City	108 890	5 450	26 020	52 120	25 300	11 995 000	33/7	24	4.9
	GUINEA	Conakry	245 857	6 000	107 000	67 000	65 857	8 381 000	39/17	29	6.3
	GUINEA-BISSAU	Bissau	36 125	500	10 800	10 700	14 125	1 257 000	42/20	31	6.0
	GUYANA	Georgetown	214 969	160	12 300	165 000	37 509	765 000	23/9	40	2.4
	HAITI	Port-au-Prince	27 750	3 500	4 900	1 400	17 950	8 400 000	32/13	40	4.4
	HONDURAS	Tegucigalpa	112 088	3 590	15 080	60 000	33 418	6 732 000	31/6	25	4.3
	HUNGARY	Budapest	93 030	2 010	10 510	17 190	63 320	9 867 000	10/14	-	1.4
	ICELAND	Reykjavík	102 820	-	22 740	1 200	-	283 000	14/7	81	2.0
	INDIA	New Delhi	3 287 263	79 000	109 100	685 000	2 414 163	1 041 144 000	25/9	39	3.3
	INDONESIA	Jakarta	1 919 445	130 460	111 770	1 117 740	559 475	217 534 000	22/7	44	2.6
	IRAN	Tehran	1 648 000	20 020	440 000	114 000	1 073 980	72 376 000	22/6	48	3.2
	IRAQ	Baghdad	438 317	3 400	40 000	1 920	392 997	24 246 000	31/9	25	-
	IRELAND, REPUBLIC OF	Dublin	70 282	30	33 500	5 700	31 052	3 878 000	14/8	116	1.9
	ISRAEL	Jerusalem	20 770	850	1 400	1 260	17 260	6 303 000	21/6	45	2.9
	ITALY	Rome	301 245	28 410	44 460	68 090	160 285	57 449 000	9/10	-	1.2
	JAMAICA	Kingston	10 991	1 000	2 290	1 850	5 851	2 621 000	21/6	45	2.5
	JAPAN	Tokyo	377 727	3 560	4 050	246 210	123 907	127 538 000	9/8	462	1.4
	JORDAN	Amman	89 206	1 570	7 910	700	79 026	5 196 000	29/4	24	4.7
	KAZAKHSTAN	Astana	2 717 300	1 360	1 850 980	96 000	768 960	16 027 000	15/10	161	2.1
	KENYA	Nairobi	582 646	5 200	213 000	168 000	196 446	31 904 000	35/14	33	4.6
	KIRIBATI	Tarawa	717	370	-	20	-	85 000	29/7	28	-
	KUWAIT	Kuwait	17 818	20	1 360	20	16 418	2 023 000	20/2	32	2.9
	KYRGYZSTAN	Bishkek	198 500	670	92 910	7 300	97 620	5 047 000	21/7	47	2.9
	LAOS	Vientiane	236 800	810	8 780	125 500	101 710	5 530 000	37/13	26	5.3
	LATVIA	Riga	63 700	290	6 110	28 700	28 600	2 392 000	9/14	-	1.1

LABOUR FORCE			GDP, 2000				COMMUNICATIONS, 2000			
AGRI-CULTURE percent employed	MANU-FACTURING percent employed	SERVICE INDUSTRIES percent employed	PER CAPITA PPP US$	EXTERNAL DEPT repayments percent of GDP	EDUCATION spending percent of GDP	MILITARY spending percent of GDP	INTERNET USERS (000)	TELEPHONES main lines in use (000)	TELEVISIONS per 1000 people	PASSENGER CARS per 1000 people
24	18	54	5 880	3.8	5	-	2	19	220	-
20	25	55	6 033	2.6	-	-	186	709	-	-
-	-	-	-	-	-	-	-	-	-	-
7	21	71	3 203	9.4	-	-	328	1 115	218	41
30	22	48	3 635	1.8	-	2.3	600	3 972	189	-
25	25	50	4 497	2.8	-	0.7	40	380	201	-
75	5	20	15 073	0.4	2	-	1	6	-	-
81	5	15	837	0.5	5	22.9	10	30	26	-
9	32	59	10 066	8.6	7	1.6	430	502	591	331
98	2	10	668	2.2	4	9.4	20	232	6	1
2	34	64	4 668	2.0	-	1.5	15	81	113	-
6	28	66	24 996	-	-	1.3	2 690	2 848	692	403
1	25	74	24 223	-	6	2.6	16 970	34 860	628	469
-	-	-	-	-	-	-	2	47	-	-
52	16	33	6 237	9.5	3	0.3	18	39	326	-
82	8	11	1 649	4.4	5	1.1	5	32	3	-
49	9	40	2 664	3.9	-	0.9	25	620	474	49
3	35	63	25 103	-	5	1.5	32 100	50 900	586	508
62	10	28	1 964	9.1	4	1.0	200	240	118	-
18	23	59	16 501	-	-	4.9	1 400	5 431	488	254
14	24	59	7 580	2.9	-	-	5	27	-	-
26	22	52	3 821	2.3	2	0.8	200	665	61	52
87	2	11	1 982	4.4	2	1.5	15	37	44	-
85	2	13	755	2.9	0	1.3	4	10	-	-
29	20	48	3 963	16.2	-	-	95	70	81	-
-	-	-	1 467	1.0	-	-	30	60	5	-
35	22	43	2 453	9.7	4	0.6	40	234	96	52
7	35	58	12 416	17.4	5	1.5	1 200	3 095	437	238
9	25	66	29 581	-	7	0.0	220	197	509	546
67	13	-	2 358	2.2	-	2.4	7 000	27 700	78	-
45	16	39	3 043	12.2	1	1.1	4 400	5 588	149	14
23	31	45	5 884	3.3	5	3.8	420	6 313	163	-
16	18	66	-	-	-	-	13	675	83	-
9	29	62	29 866	-	4	0.7	1 310	1 600	399	-
2	25	72	20 131	-	8	8.0	1 940	2 800	335	220
6	33	62	23 626	-	5	2.1	19 250	25 000	494	-
21	19	60	3 639	8.7	6	-	100	353	194	-
5	32	63	26 755	-	3	1.0	56 000	60 381	725	395
6	25	69	3 966	8.0	-	9.5	212	403	84	-
22	18	60	5 871	10.1	-	0.7	100	1 920	241	66
19	20	62	1 022	4.6	7	1.8	500	310	25	-
6	6	87	-	-	-	-	1	4	36	-
-	-	-	15 799	-	6	8.2	200	412	486	-
52	12	36	2 711	13.3	5	1.9	52	351	49	39
78	6	16	1 575	2.5	2	-	10	25	10	-
15	26	59	7 045	7.9	7	1.0	312	735	789	218

FLAG	COUNTRY	CAPITAL CITY	AREA	LAND USE				POPULATION			
			km²	CROP km²	PASTURE km²	FOREST km²	OTHER km²	TOTAL 2002	BIRTH RATE / DEATH RATE per 1000 people 2000	DOUBLING TIME (years) 2000	TOTAL FERTILITY RATE 1995–2000
	LEBANON	Beirut	10 452	1 420	160	800	8 072	3 614 000	20/6	43	2.3
	LESOTHO	Maseru	30 355	-	20 000	-	-	2 076 000	33/17	33	4.8
	LIBERIA	Monrovia	111 369	2 150	20 000	46 000	43 219	3 298 000	44/17	21	-
	LIBYA	Tripoli	1 759 540	3 350	133 000	8 400	1 614 790	5 529 000	27/5	28	3.8
	LITHUANIA	Vilnius	65 200	590	4 970	19 830	39 810	3 682 000	9/11	-	1.4
	LUXEMBOURG	Luxembourg	2 586	-	-	-	-	448 000	13/9	198	1.7
	MACEDONIA	Skopje	25 713	440	6 360	10 200	8 713	2 051 000	13/8	112	1.9
	MADAGASCAR	Antananarivo	587 041	6 000	240 000	232 000	109 041	16 913 000	40/12	24	6.1
	MALAWI	Lilongwe	118 484	1 400	18 500	37 000	61 584	11 828 000	46/24	36	6.8
	MALAYSIA	Kuala Lumpur	332 965	57 850	2 850	222 480	49 785	23 036 000	25/4	34	3.3
	MALDIVES	Male	298	20	10	10	258	309 000	29/5	23	5.8
	MALI	Bamako	1 240 140	440	300 000	116 500	823 200	12 019 000	46/20	22	7.0
	MALTA	Valletta	316	10	-	-	-	393 000	11/8	182	1.9
	MAURITANIA	Nouakchott	1 030 700	120	392 500	44 100	593 980	2 830 000	42/15	25	6.0
	MAURITIUS	Port Louis	2 040	60	70	440	1 470	1 180 000	17/7	66	2.0
	MEXICO	Mexico City	1 972 545	25 000	800 000	487 000	660 545	101 842 000	25/5	36	2.8
	MICRONESIA, FEDERATED STATES OF	Pohnpei	701	320	100	-	-	129 000	26/6	27	-
	MOLDOVA	Chişinău	33 700	3 700	3 780	3 580	22 640	4 273 000	10/11	1 733	1.6
	MONGOLIA	Ulan Bator	1 565 000	10	1 292 940	137 500	134 559	2 587 000	22/6	50	2.7
	MOROCCO	Rabat	446 550	9 670	210 000	89 700	137 180	30 988 000	24/6	41	3.4
	MOZAMBIQUE	Maputo	799 380	2 350	440 000	173 000	184 030	18 986 000	40/20	32	6.3
	MYANMAR	Yangon	676 577	5 950	3 160	324 000	343 467	48 956 000	25/12	35	3.3
	NAMIBIA	Windhoek	824 292	40	380 000	125 000	319 252	1 819 000	36/17	42	5.3
	NEPAL	Kathmandu	147 181	700	17 570	57 500	71 411	24 153 000	33/10	28	4.8
	NETHERLANDS	Amsterdam/The Hague	41 526	350	10 120	3 340	27 716	15 990 000	13/9	193	1.5
	NEW ZEALAND	Wellington	270 534	17 250	133 000	76 670	43 614	3 837 000	15/7	89	2.0
	NICARAGUA	Managua	130 000	2 890	48 150	32 000	46 960	5 347 000	30/5	23	4.3
	NIGER	Niamey	1 267 000	100	120 000	25 000	1 121 900	11 641 000	51/19	23	8.0
	NIGERIA	Abuja	923 768	26 500	392 000	143 000	362 268	120 047 000	40/16	24	5.9
	NORTH KOREA	Pyonyang	120 538	3 000	500	73 700	43 338	22 586 000	18/11	48	-
	NORWAY	Oslo	323 878	-	1 570	83 300	-	4 505 000	13/10	217	1.8
	OMAN	Muscat	309 500	610	10 000	-	-	2 709 000	28/3	18	5.8
	PAKISTAN	Islamabad	803 940	6 580	50 000	34 800	712 560	148 721 000	34/8	25	5.5
	PANAMA	Panama City	77 082	1 550	14 770	32 600	28 162	2 942 000	21/5	41	2.6
	PAPUA NEW GUINEA	Port Moresby	462 840	6 500	1 750	420 000	34 590	5 032 000	32/9	29	4.6
	PARAGUAY	Asunción	406 752	880	217 000	128 500	60 372	5 778 000	30/5	26	4.2
	PERU	Lima	1 285 216	5 100	271 000	848 000	161 116	26 523 000	23/7	32	3.0
	PHILIPPINES	Manila	300 000	45 000	12 800	136 000	106 200	78 611 000	27/5	31	3.6
	POLAND	Warsaw	312 683	3 370	40 830	87 320	181 163	38 542 000	10/10	-	1.5
	PORTUGAL	Lisbon	88 940	7 150	14 370	31 020	36 400	10 049 000	12/11	990	1.5
	PUERTO RICO	San Juan	9 104	460	2 100	1 460	5 084	3 988 000	15/8	75	-
	QATAR	Doha	11 437	30	500	-	-	584 000	14/3	38	3.7
	ROMANIA	Bucharest	237 500	5 000	49 440	66 800	116 260	22 332 000	10/11	-	1.3
	RUSSIAN FEDERATION	Moscow	17 075 400	18 450	899 700	7 659 120	8 498 130	143 752 000	9/15	-	1.2
	RWANDA	Kigali	26 338	2 500	5 450	2 500	15 888	8 148 000	44/22	30	6.2
	ST LUCIA	Castries	616	140	20	80	376	151 000	18/6	56	2.7

LABOUR FORCE			GDP, 2000				COMMUNICATIONS, 2000			
AGRICULTURE percent employed	MANUFACTURING percent employed	SERVICE INDUSTRIES percent employed	PER CAPITA PPP US$	EXTERNAL DEPT repayments percent of GDP	EDUCATION spending percent of GDP	MILITARY spending percent of GDP	INTERNET USERS (000)	TELEPHONES main lines in use (000)	TELEVISIONS per 1000 people	PASSENGER CARS per 1000 people
7	31	62	4 308	11.0	2	3.6	300	700	335	-
40	28	32	2 031	7.3	13	3.1	5	22	16	-
72	6	22	-	-	-	-	0.5	7	25	-
11	23	66	-	-	-	-	20	500	137	-
20	27	53	7 106	8.0	6	1.8	341	1 142	422	294
2	25	73	50 061	-	-	0.7	100	315	589	587
9	49	39	5 086	4.5	-	2.1	100	408	282	-
78	7	15	840	2.4	2	1.2	35	55	24	-
54	22	24	615	3.5	5	0.8	35	38	3	-
18	32	50	9 068	6.7	-	1.9	5 700	4 600	168	170
22	24	50	4 485	3.6	4	-	6	21	40	-
86	2	12	797	4.2	3	2.5	30	45	14	-
3	34	64	17 273	-	5	0.8	59	187	556	455
55	10	34	1 677	10.7	4	-	8	27	-	-
15	40	46	10 017	12.6	4	0.2	158	281	268	73
21	25	53	9 023	10.1	-	0.5	3 500	12 332	283	102
-	-	-	-	-	-	-	2	11	20	-
49	14	38	2 109	10.5	-	0.4	15	627	297	54
49	15	14	1 783	3.0	-	2.5	40	104	65	17
6	33	61	3 546	10.0	-	4.2	400	1 391	166	41
83	8	9	854	2.3	3	2.5	23	90	5	-
63	12	25	-	-	-	1.7	10	250	7	-
53	18	29	6 431	-	8	3.3	45	110	38	-
79	6	21	1 327	1.8	3	0.9	60	237	7	-
3	22	73	25 657	-	5	1.6	9 730	9 132	538	383
10	23	67	20 070	-	7	1.0	2 060	1 920	522	481
42	15	38	2 366	12.5	4	1.1	20	140	69	3
8	48	44	746	1.6	3	1.4	12	20	37	-
3	22	75	896	2.5	-	0.9	100	500	68	-
38	32	30	-	-	-	-	-	1 100	54	-
5	22	73	29 918	-	8	1.8	2 680	2 735	669	407
45	24	32	-	7.7	4	9.7	120	201	563	-
47	17	36	1 928	4.6	-	4.5	1 200	2 861	131	5
17	18	64	6 000	9.4	-	1.2	45	396	194	83
79	7	14	2 280	8.0	-	0.8	135	61	17	-
5	22	73	4 426	4.4	5	1.0	20	290	218	-
6	19	76	4 799	8.1	3	-	3 000	1 800	148	27
39	16	45	3 971	9.0	3	1.2	4 500	3 100	144	10
19	32	49	9 051	6.5	5	1.9	6 400	8 070	400	240
13	35	52	17 290	-	6	2.1	4 400	5 300	630	-
2	22	76	-	-	-	-	600	1 322	330	-
3	32	65	-	-	-	-	75	142	869	-
42	28	31	6 423	6.4	4	2.1	1 000	3 777	381	133
12	29	59	8 377	4.6	-	4.0	18 000	30 000	-	-
92	3	5	943	2.0	-	3.0	20	11	-	-
22	19	59	5 703	5.7	9	-	3	37	365	-

FLAG	COUNTRY	CAPITAL CITY	AREA km²	LAND USE CROP km²	PASTURE km²	FOREST km²	OTHER km²	POPULATION TOTAL 2002	BIRTH / DEATH RATE per 1000 people 2000	DOUBLING TIME (years) 2000	TOTAL FERTILITY RATE 1995–2000
	SAMOA	Apia	2 831	670	10	1 340	811	159 000	30/6	28	4.5
	SÃO TOMÉ AND PRÍNCIPE	São Tomé	964	430	10	-	-	143 000	31/9	20	-
	SAUDI ARABIA	Riyadh	2 200 000	1 910	1 700 000	18 000	480 090	21 701 000	33/4	23	6.2
	SENEGAL	Dakar	196 720	380	56 500	74 500	65 340	9 908 000	37/13	25	5.6
	SERBIA AND MONTENEGRO	Belgrade	102 173	3 300	18 510	17 690	62 673	10 522 000	12/11	866	-
	SEYCHELLES	Victoria	455	60	-	50	-	83 000	19/7	65	-
	SIERRA LEONE	Freetown	71 740	600	22 000	20 400	28 740	4 814 000	44/23	26	6.5
	SINGAPORE	Singapore	639	-	-	30	-	4 188 000	12/4	84	1.6
	SLOVAKIA	Bratislava	49 035	1 260	8 650	19 890	19 235	5 408 000	10/10	866	1.4
	SLOVENIA	Ljubljana	20 251	310	3 140	10 770	6 031	1 983 000	9/10	-	1.2
	SOLOMON ISLANDS	Honiara	28 370	180	400	24 500	3 290	479 000	39/5	23	5.6
	SOMALIA	Mogadishu	637 657	240	430 000	160 000	47 417	9 557 000	51/17	24	-
	SOUTH AFRICA, REPUBLIC OF	Pretoria/Cape Town	1 219 080	9 590	839 280	82 000	288 210	44 203 000	26/16	55	3.1
	SOUTH KOREA	Seoul	99 274	2 000	540	64 560	32 174	47 389 000	13/6	82	1.5
	SPAIN	Madrid	504 782	49 000	114 500	161 370	179 912	39 924 000	10/9	6 931	1.2
	SRI LANKA	Colombo	65 610	10 200	4 400	21 000	30 010	19 287 000	18/6	60	2.1
	SUDAN	Khartoum	2 505 813	2 000	1 171 800	420 000	912 013	32 559 000	34/11	32	4.9
	SURINAME	Paramaribo	163 820	100	210	150 000	13 510	421 000	23/7	37	2.2
	SWAZILAND	Mbabane	17 364	120	12 000	1 000	4 244	948 000	36/15	37	4.8
	SWEDEN	Stockholm	449 964	-	4 470	280 250	-	8 823 000	10/11	-	1.5
	SWITZERLAND	Bern	41 293	240	11 440	11 860	17 753	7 167 000	10/9	315	1.5
	SYRIA	Damascus	185 180	8 100	83 590	4 840	88 650	17 040 000	29/5	25	4.0
	TAIWAN	Taibei	36 179	-	-	-	-	22 548 000	-/-	97	-
	TAJIKISTAN	Dushanbe	143 100	1 300	35 000	5 370	101 430	6 177 000	19/5	43	3.7
	TANZANIA	Dodoma	945 087	9 500	350 000	327 000	258 587	36 820 000	39/17	24	5.5
	THAILAND	Bangkok	513 115	33 000	8 000	145 000	327 115	64 344 000	17/7	70	2.1
	TOGO	Lomé	56 785	1 200	10 000	9 000	36 585	4 779 000	37/15	23	5.8
	TONGA	Nuku'alofa	748	310	40	80	318	100 000	25/7	33	-
	TRINIDAD AND TOBAGO	Port of Spain	5 130	470	110	2 350	2 200	1 306 000	15/7	103	1.6
	TUNISIA	Tunis	164 150	21 050	40 620	6 760	95 720	9 670 000	17/6	44	2.3
	TURKEY	Ankara	779 452	25 340	123 780	201 990	428 342	68 569 000	20/6	46	2.7
	TURKMENISTAN	Ashgabat	488 100	650	307 000	40 000	140 450	4 930 000	21/7	48	3.6
	UGANDA	Kampala	241 038	19 000	18 000	63 000	141 038	24 780 000	45/19	24	7.1
	UKRAINE	Kiev	603 700	9 320	79 100	92 390	422 890	48 652 000	9/15	-	1.3
	UNITED ARAB EMIRATES	Abu Dhabi	83 600	1 870	3 050	30	78 650	2 701 000	17/3	32	3.2
	UNITED KINGDOM	London	244 082	520	110 330	23 900	109 332	59 657 000	11/11	546	1.7
	UNITED STATES OF AMERICA	Washington D.C.	9 809 386	20 500	2 392 500	2 959 900	4 436 486	288 530 000	15/9	120	2.0
	URUGUAY	Montevideo	176 215	400	135 430	9 300	31 085	3 385 000	16/10	107	2.4
	UZBEKISTAN	Tashkent	447 400	3 750	228 000	13 000	202 650	25 618 000	22/6	40	2.8
	VANUATU	Port Vila	12 190	900	420	9 140	1 730	207 000	32/7	25	4.6
	VENEZUELA	Caracas	912 050	9 600	182 400	445 000	275 050	25 093 000	22/4	34	3.0
	VIETNAM	Hanoi	329 565	16 000	6 420	96 500	210 645	80 226 000	19/6	48	2.5
	VIRGIN ISLANDS (USA)	Charlotte Amalie	352	10	50	20	272	124 000	16/5	-	-
	YEMEN	Sana	527 968	1 240	160 650	20 000	346 078	19 912 000	40/11	25	7.6
	ZAMBIA	Lusaka	752 614	190	300 000	320 000	132 424	10 872 000	40/21	35	6.0
	ZIMBABWE	Harare	390 759	1 300	172 000	87 500	129 959	13 076 000	30/18	69	5.0

LABOUR FORCE			GDP, 2000				COMMUNICATIONS, 2000			
AGRI-CULTURE percent employed	MANU-FACTURING percent employed	SERVICE INDUSTRIES percent employed	PER CAPITA PPP US$	EXTERNAL DEPT repayments percent of GDP	EDUCATION spending percent of GDP	MILITARY spending percent of GDP	INTERNET USERS (000)	TELEPHONES main lines in use (000)	TELEVISIONS per 1000 people	PASSENGER CARS per 1000 people
-	-	-	5 041	3.6	-	-	3	8	61	-
-	-	-	-	9.5	4	-	9	5	228	-
19	20	61	11 367	-	-	11.6	570	3 100	264	-
77	8	16	1 510	5.2	3	1.4	100	235	40	-
-	-	-	-	-	4	-	400	2 017	282	176
-	-	-	-	2.8	6	1.8	9	20	203	-
67	15	17	490	6.7	1	1.4	20	25	13	-
0	29	71	23 356	-	-	4.8	2 310	1 950	304	97
7	39	54	11 243	13.5	4	1.8	700	1 935	407	229
11	38	51	17 367	-	6	1.2	600	722	368	418
27	12	38	1 648	3.3	-	-	8	8	23	-
75	8	16	-	-	-	-	0.2	15	14	-
-	-	-	9 401	3.1	6	1.5	3 068	5 000	127	94
12	27	61	17 380	5.1	4	2.8	25 600	24 000	364	167
7	31	62	19 472	-	5	1.3	7 890	17 336	591	-
42	23	33	3 530	4.5	-	4.5	122	495	111	15
70	9	22	1 797	0.5	4	3.0	56	400	273	-
6	25	66	3 799	-	-	-	15	64	253	-
26	27	48	4 492	1.6	6	1.6	14	39	119	34
3	25	72	24 277	-	8	2.1	6 020	6 017	574	437
5	26	69	28 769	-	5	1.1	3 850	4 820	548	486
28	25	47	3 556	2.0	-	5.5	60	1 313	67	9
-	-	-	-	-	-	-	11 600	12 490	-	-
46	17	29	1 152	8.8	-	1.2	5	363	326	-
84	4	12	523	2.4	2	1.3	300	127	20	-
49	18	33	6 402	11.5	5	1.6	1 200	5 600	284	-
66	10	24	1 442	2.4	4	-	50	25	32	-
34	24	43	-	-	-	-	1	8	66	-
8	28	64	8 964	6.8	-	-	120	252	340	-
22	34	43	6 363	9.8	8	1.7	400	654	198	-
47	21	32	6 974	10.6	-	4.9	2 500	19 500	449	63
43	20	11	3 956	10.9	-	3.8	2	363	196	-
90	6	4	1 208	2.6	2	1.8	60	50	27	2
26	26	17	3 816	11.5	4	3.6	750	9 450	456	104
8	27	65	17 935	-	2	-	900	915	292	-
2	26	72	23 509	-	5	2.5	34 300	34 878	653	373
3	23	74	34 142	-	5	3.1	165 700	194 000	854	-
4	25	71	9 035	6.7	3	1.1	400	929	530	-
44	14	10	2 441	11.7	-	1.7	100	1 980	276	-
-	-	-	2 802	1.0	9	-	3	6	12	-
13	25	61	5 794	4.9	-	1.2	1 300	2 600	185	-
69	13	17	1 996	4.2	-	-	400	2 600	185	-
0	14	54	-	-	-	-	12	62	594	-
61	17	22	893	2.6	7	5.2	17	291	283	-
75	8	17	780	6.4	2	0.6	25	130	134	-
26	28	47	2 635	6.4	11	4.8	100	212	30	-

Aboriginal peoples The descendants of the original inhabitants of North America. The Canadian Constitution recognizes three groups of Aboriginal peoples: First Nations (Indians), Métis, and Inuit. These are three separate peoples with unique heritages, languages, cultural practices, and spiritual beliefs.
Aboriginal rights Rights that some Aboriginal peoples of Canada hold as a result of their ancestors' longstanding use and occupancy of the land. The rights of certain Aboriginal peoples to hunt, trap, and fish on ancestral lands are examples of Aboriginal rights. Aboriginal rights will vary from group to group, depending on the customs, practices, and traditions that have formed part of their distinctive cultures.
Acid precipitation Also called acid deposition or acid rain. It is produced by sulphur and nitrogen emissions from the burning of fossil fuels. Coal and oil used in energy production, industrial boilers, and automobile engines all promote acid precipitation. When washed from the atmosphere, the precipitation increases the level of acidity in lakes, streams, and soil, and severely damages vegetation, fish, and wildlife.
Agriculture Farming; this involves the work of cultivating soil, producing field or tree crops and raising animals.
AIDS Acquired immune deficiency syndrome. Caused by HIV (human immunodeficiency virus), transmitted by some body fluids. It breaks down the body's ability to fight off infection. In 2002, 14 000 people were newly infected with AIDS every day, many of them children and heterosexual adults.
Air mass A large body of air with generally the same temperature and moisture conditions throughout. Warm and moist or cool and moist air masses usually develop over large bodies of water. Hot and dry or cold and dry air masses develop over large land areas (continents).
Alluvial soil An azonal soil developed from materials (mud, silt, and sand) deposited by moving water. Alluvial soil is often found in the deltas of rivers. It is usually young, rich in minerals, and valuable for agricultural production.
Alpine Occurring at high altitudes – for example, an alpine climate or alpine vegetation.
Aquaculture Using "farming" methods to cultivate and harvest fish, shellfish, and aquatic plants. This is an increasingly important component of the seafood production sector of both the Canadian and world economies.
Aquifer An underground reservoir in a layer of permeable rock, such as sandstone or limestone that contains water. The water accumulates because its movement is blocked by non-porous rock.
Arable land Land suitable for ploughing and cultivation. Arable land does not include pastureland or forested areas not capable of growing crops.
Arctic The high latitudes in the northern or southern hemispheres with low precipitation, very cold winters, and cold summers.
Assembly of First Nations The Assembly of First Nations (AFN) is the national representative organization of the First Nations in Canada. There are over 630 First Nations communities in Canada. It presents views on areas such as: Aboriginal and treaty rights, economic development, education, languages and literacy, health, housing, social development, justice, taxation, land claims, environment, and other issues as they arise.
Asthenosphere A layer of Earth's interior extending from 80 to 250 kilometres beneath the surface where convection currents exist in its partially molten state.
Atmosphere The vast gaseous envelope of air that surrounds Earth. Its boundaries are not easily defined. The atmosphere contains a complex system of gases and suspended particles. The main components are nitrogen, oxygen and carbon dioxide along with some other gases and water vapour.
Azonal soil One of the three major soil groups, known as orders; these soils are young and have indistinct horizons (layers). Alluvial soil is an example.
Barometric pressure A measurement of the air pressure in the atmosphere, measured in kilopascals.
Barrel A unit of measurement in the imperial system equal to approximately 160 litres.
Bedrock The solid rock that usually lies beneath the soil.
Billion In North America, this number represents one thousand million; elsewhere, the term means one million million.
Biosphere That part of Earth which supports life; it consists of two layers, the atmosphere (above Earth) and the lithosphere (or crust).
Birth rate The number of live births per thousand people in one year.
Boreal The coniferous forest area of Canada, Russia and northern Europe; the term means "of the north". It is also applied to the climate region in the same locations.
Broadleaf trees Trees with wide, flat leaves rather than needle-like leaves. In Canada, broadleaf trees lose their leaves in winter. Examples include oak, maple, birch, and poplar.
Cambrian period The first geological period of the Palaeozoic Era, extending from about 600 000 000 to 500 000 000 years ago. Much of the world was covered by water. Small water animals (invertebrates) flourished.
Canadian Shield An area of Precambrian rock, mostly igneous, that covers almost half of Canada.
Capital Money, property, or goods than can be used to generate income for a person, company, or country.
Census metropolitan area (CMA) In Canada, a city and its nearby area with a population over 100 000.
CFCs Chlorofluorocarbons. Synthetic gases containing chlorine, fluorine, and carbon. When released, they reduce the amount of ozone in the atmosphere. Sources of chlorofluorocarbons include some foam materials (e.g., Styrofoam cups), some refrigerants, aerosol sprays, and cleaning solvents.
Chernozem Fertile black or dark brown soil, rich in humus. Cherozems are found in the grassland environments in the Canadian prairies, Ukraine, Eastern Europe, the United States, South America, and Australia.
Clear-cutting The harvesting of all trees that are large enough for commercial use.
Climatic region An area in which the general conditions of temperature and precipitation are reasonably similar. For example, a "desert climate" describes an area of dry conditions.
Climograph Also called a climate graph. A combination line and bar graph used to illustrate long term average monthly temperature and precipitation for a climatic station. Temperature is shown as a line and precipitation as a series of bars.
Confederation The union of independent political units to form one nation. Canada's confederation took place on July 1, 1867. The British North America Act established the Dominion of Canada by joining Nova Scotia, New Brunswick, Québec, and Ontario. In 1991, the now defunct Confederation of Independent States (CIS), joined many of the former Soviet republics.
Coniferous A type of tree with needle-like leaves, cones and softwood trunks. Examples include Douglas fir, cedar, spruce, and hemlock.
Conservation tillage A method of land conservation whereby residues from a harvesting operation including straw and chaff on sloping land is evenly distributed over the acreage being treated. The land is not "turned over" before the next crop is planted.
Constitution The system of fundamental laws and principles of government, in written form. Canada repatriated its constitution in April, 1982.
Continental climate A type of climate where no large body of water moderates the temperature resulting in cold winters and hot summers; precipitation is generally low and occurs in the summer (e.g., Winnipeg).
Continental crust The solid layer above the lithosphere underlying major continents and thicker than under the oceans.
Continental drift Theory that suggests that Earth's crust is composed of plates that move. First proposed in 1858 and developed by Taylor and Wegener in the early 20th century, it was not until the work of Canadian scientist J. Tuzo Wilson in the 1960s that the theory was widely accepted.
Convection The movement of materials in liquids and gases caused by differences in heat. Warmer and less dense materials tend to rise and cooler, more dense materials fall. In the tropics, convection currents refer to the heating, rising, cooling and condensing of air to produce precipitation.
Core The centre of Earth. The temperature of the innermost part, the solid core, exceeds 4000°C. It contains high concentrations of nickel and iron. The liquid core that surrounds the solid core is not actually liquid, but is more fluid than the solid core.
Cropland Land used to raise crops such as wheat, rice, corn, and sugar cane.
Cross section A side view of a landscape between two specific points to illustrate slope and altitude, and important natural features.
Crude oil Oil in its natural, unrefined form, as it comes from Earth.
Crust The relatively thin outer layer of Earth containing both the ocean basins and the continents. It differs from the mantle beneath in both physical and chemical properties.

Crustacean A class of invertebrates with a hard outer shell and joined appendages (e.g., shrimp, crab, lobster).
Cyclonic storm A low pressure area, often accompanied by warm and cold fronts, bringing precipitation to the middle latitudes.
Death rate The number of deaths per 1000 people in one year.
Deciduous tree A tree that regularly sheds its leaves, usually in the autumn. These trees are dormant in winter (e.g., maple, oak, birch)
Delta A river deposit formed where the river enters a large body of water. Water slows down and fine materials (silt, mud) are deposited. This produces a land feature that is triangular in shape, like the Greek letter "delta."
Deposition The laying down of materials carried by water, wind, or ice. (verb: deposit)
Desertification The process by which deserts extend into surrounding areas. It can be caused by climatic changes or human activities. The process has been significant in the Sahel region of Africa.
Developed country One of two basic classifications of countries (see developing country) determined by examining factors such as economic development, gross domestic product per capita, income per capita, potential for development, energy use, literacy, and quantity and quality of food. Based on their available resources, a developed country is thought to be able to provide a reasonable quality of life for inhabitants.
Developing country One of two basic classifications of countries (see developed country) determined by comparison with developed countries. A developing country is becoming more economically advanced and industrialized, but faces many challenges, particularly in providing a reasonable quality of life for inhabitants.
Devonian period The fourth geological period of the Palaeozoic Era, extending from 400 000 000 to 345 000 000 years ago. This was the period in which fish developed.
Differential erosion The wearing away of different types of rock in the same location. For example, softer sedimentary rocks erode more quickly than harder rock, sometimes forming escarpments (e.g., the Niagara Escarpment).
Domestic trade The movement of goods and services within a country (e.g., the movement of goods among provinces of Canada).
Drainage basin An area drained by a river or series of rivers into a common body of water (e.g., Hudson Bay drainage basin in Canada with an area of nearly 3.8 million square kilometres).
Drumlin A hill, usually oval or tear-shaped, formed by glaciers. Drumlins vary in size, are often found in groups (fields), and are common around Guelph and Peterborough, Ontario.
Ecosystem A living community in the water or on land emphasizing the interactions among the host environment and the plants and animals it contains. Ecosystems can be as small as a pond or as large as a tropical rainforest.
El Niño The occasional development of warm ocean surface waters along the coast of Ecuador and Peru. When this warming occurs the tropical Pacific trade winds weaken and the usual up welling of cold, deep ocean water is reduced. El Niño normally occurs late in the calendar year and lasts for a few weeks to a few months. Sometimes an extremely warm event can develop that lasts for much longer time periods.
Emigration The movement of people (or an organism) out of an area or country.
Endangered species An animal or plant threatened with imminent extinction in all or most of its natural area.
Equator An imaginary circle, indicated by a line, which divides Earth into northern and southern hemispheres. It is equally distant from the north and south poles. The equator is used as the base line for latitude.
Equinox Generally, March 21 and September 21. The approximate dates that the sun is directly overhead at noon at the equator. (plural: equinoxes)
Erosion The wearing down and carrying away of material from Earth's surface by water, wind, and ice. (verb: erode)
Escarpment A steep slope or cliff formed by faulting or differential erosion. For example, the Great Rift Valley in Africa was formed by faulting and the Niagara Escarpment in Ontario was formed by differential erosion.
Esker A long narrow ridge of rounded and sorted materials, usually quite coarse (e.g., sand, gravel). Eskers are formed in or under glaciers, as meltwaters deposit materials.
European Union An alliance of member nations to integrate the economy of countries in Europe and to have a common currency (the Euro). Co-ordinated social development and possible political unity are objectives of the organization. Members are increasing on a regular basis as countries apply and are accepted for membership.
Exports Goods or services sold in other countries.
External aid Assistance provided by one nation for another, usually involving goods, money, or technical expertise.
External debt See foreign debt.
External trade Trade with other countries (as compared to domestic trade that takes place within the country). Trade between Canada and the United States is external trade; trade between Alberta and Ontario is domestic trade.
Extinct species A plant or animal that no longer exists (e.g., the passenger pigeon).
Extirpated species A plant or animal that no longer exists in one location, but is found elsewhere. This official designation has been assigned by COSEWIC (Committee on the Status of Endangered Wildlife in Canada) to a species or sub-species of plant or animal formerly native to Canada and no longer known in Canada but may be found elsewhere in the world.
False colour A method of adding colour to digital satellite images to enhance specific features.
Fault A fracture in Earth's crust along which rock strata have moved vertically or horizontally. Faults may trap oil or natural gas.
First Nations A term, describing one of the groups of Aboriginal people, to replace the word "Indian", which many people found offensive. Although the term First Nation is widely used, no legal definition of it exists.
Flora The plant life of a region.
Folding The bending of rock layers, often resulting in the formation of "fold" mountains.
Foreign debt One nation's debt to another. Also called external debt. Developing nations often owe large amounts of money to other countries, especially developed countries.
Fossil The imprint or preserved remains of a prehistoric plant or animal, usually found in sedimentary rock.
Fossil fuel An energy source originating from prehistoric plants and animals, and associated with sedimentary rock (e.g., coal, peat, natural gas, petroleum). The burning of fossil fuels has been associated with global warming, air pollution, and acid precipitation.
Front The surface or line between masses of air that have different characteristics. A warm front marks the advance of warm air into cooler air. A cold front marks the advance of cold air into warmer areas. An occluded front occurs when a cold front runs underneath a warm front.
Frost-free period The total number of days between the average dates of the last frost in the spring and the first frost in the autumn.
Gauging station A point on a river where information on water flow is gathered. Data is interpreted to predict the implications of variations in stream flow.
Generating station A plant where electricity is produced from falling water (hydro), coal, petroleum, natural gas, nuclear fission, or other source.
Geologic time The division of Earth's history of approximately 4.5 billion years into eras and periods.
Geological province A large area whose rock structure, type and age show common characteristics.
Glacier A slow-moving mass of ice. Glaciers are currently found at high latitudes or high altitudes.
Grassland A region where vegetation consists mainly of grasses; moisture is insufficient to support trees. Grassland areas often have regional names (e.g., Pampas: Argentina; Steppe: Ukraine; Prairie: North America).
Greenhouse effect A warming of the atmosphere created by the retention of energy from Earth's ecosystem. Without the greenhouse effect, Earth's atmosphere would be 30 to 35 Celsius degrees colder than the current world-wide average of 15°C. Human activity has affected the gases that make up the atmosphere and may be causing an acceleration of this natural process.

Greenhouse gases The main greenhouse gases are water vapour (H_20), carbon dioxide (CO_2), methane (CH_4), nitrous oxide (N_2O), ozone (O_3), and halocarbons (CFCs, HFCs, etc.). Fossil fuels for heating and electrical production, gasoline for cars, and manufacturing have added greenhouse gases to the atmosphere. These gases trap the heat and warm the atmosphere.
Gross domestic product The total dollar value of all goods and services produced in a country in a given year. A high gross domestic product (GDP) indicates a high level of development.
Ground water The water in the soil and in the bedrock underlying the soil.
Growing degree days The sum of the number of degrees by which the average temperature of each day in a year exceeds 6°C.
Growing season The season in which the average daily temperature is above 6°C, allowing crops to grow.
Gulf Stream Warm ocean current that originates in and around the Caribbean and flows across the North Atlantic to northwest Europe moderating the climate in that area.
Habitat An environment that supports plant, animal, or human life.
Hardwood Wood produced by most deciduous trees such as oak and maple.
Hazardous waste Discarded materials that pose a risk to humans or the environment.
Hemisphere Any half of a globe or sphere. The Earth has traditionally been divided into hemispheres by the equator (northern and southern hemispheres) and by the prime meridian and international date line (eastern and western hemispheres).
HIV Human immunodeficiency virus (HIV) has been decisively established as the cause of AIDS.
Horizon A distinct layer in a soil profile. Mature soils have three horizons, designated by the letters A, B, and C. There may also be subdivisions of these horizons.
Human development index A measurement of a country's achievements in three areas: longevity, knowledge, and standard of living. Longevity is measured by life expectancy at birth; knowledge is measured by a combination of the adult literacy rate and the combined gross primary, secondary, and tertiary enrolment ratio; and standard of living is measured by GDP per capita (purchasing power).
Humidity The amount of moisture in the air, expressed as a percentage of the total amount of moisture the air could hold. For example, 95% humidity indicates that precipitation will occur shortly since the amount of moisture has almost reached the air's capacity.
Humus The upper layer of the soil consisting of decaying and decayed organic materials.
Hurricane An intense cyclonic storm, which often migrates from its source area in the tropics to temperate areas (e.g., Hurricane Andrew, Hugo, Hazel).
Hydro-electric power Electricity produced by the natural movement of falling water, such as at Niagara Falls in Ontario.
Hydrocarbon A substance containing only compounds of carbon and hydrogen. There are thousands of these compounds (e.g., methane, crude oil).
Ice cap A mass of ice, smaller than an ice sheet, that permanently covers an area of land.
Ice sheet A glacier (thick layer of ice) covering an area greater than 50 000 square kilometres. Greenland and Antarctica are considered ice sheets.
Igneous rock Rock formed by the cooling of molten materials from the interior of Earth.
Immigration The movement of people (or any organism) into an area or country.
Impermeable rock See non-porous rock.
Imports Goods and services purchased from another area, usually another country. Canada's main imports include automobiles, petroleum, and electrical goods.
Improved land Areas of Earth's surface that have been cleared of trees or have been ploughed for the growing of crops.
Indian Act Canadian federal legislation, first passed in 1876, that sets out certain federal government obligations regarding Indian people and regulates the management of Indian reserve lands. The act has been amended several times, most recently in 1985.
Industrial mineral A mineral such as stone, sand, or gravel used in construction.
Industry Extractive processes (mining, forestry, fishing), manufacturing and services such as commerce and insurance. The term does not include agriculture.
Infant mortality rate The number of deaths of children under one year of age, per 1000 live births in a given year. In developed nations, this figure is low (less than 10), but may be as high as 200 in nations where health services are poorly developed.
Inflation A general increase in the price of goods and services over time. In periods of high inflation, the purchasing power of money decreases. High rates of inflation can erode gains made by weak or struggling economies.
Inorganic materials In soil, materials such as rock fragments, liquid, and gases that combine with organic materials to form the soil.
Internal drainage A drainage system with no outlet to the ocean. This occurs when land in the interior is below sea level (e.g., the Dead Sea in Israel, the Caspian Sea in Russia).
International date line An imaginary line that approximately follows 180° longitude. The area of the world just east of the line is one day ahead of the area just west of the line. The line varies slightly from the 180° line to avoid splitting island or countries into separate days.
Intrazonal soil One of the three major soil orders where the influence of soil or drainage supersedes that of climate and vegetation.
Intrusive rock Igneous rock formed within Earth's crust from molten materials called magma (e.g., granite, gabbro, serpentine).
Inuit A group of people who live in the far north of Canada and who have inhabited this area and other polar areas for at least 5000 years.
Intertropical Convergence Zone of low atmospheric pressure and ascending air located at or near the equator. Rising air currents are due to global wind convergence and convection from thermal heating. The zone of convergence "migrates" with the seasons.
Isobar A line on a map joining points with the same atmospheric pressure – this is generally reduced to sea-level equivalents.
Isoline A line on a map joining points with the same numerical value (e.g., isobar, isotherm).
Isotherm A line on a map joining points with the same temperature.
Jet stream A narrow current of high-velocity wind found in the upper atmosphere. The polar jet stream exists in the mid-latitudes at an altitude of approximately 10 kilometres. This jet stream flows from west to east at speeds of 110 to 185 kilometres per hour. The subtropical jet stream occurs above the sub-tropical highs at an altitude of 13 kilometres.
Joule (J) A metric unit of energy defined as the work done by the force of one Newton when it moves its point of application a distance of one metre.
Labour force The number of people working or looking for paid work.
Land claims The cases presented by First Nations for ownership and/or control of lands on which they live or have lived. Some claims have been settled but many more are still in negotiation between First Nations peoples and the federal government, or are before the courts for settlement.
Landsat Series of satellites launched by NASA for the purpose of remotely monitoring resources on Earth. The first Landsat satellite was launched by the United States in 1972.
Land use The type of human activity that a given land area is used for (e.g., agriculture, commercial, residential, industrial).
Landed value The dollar value of fish caught, before marketing and processing.
Landform Any feature of Earth's surface formed by earth movements or by wearing down of the surface of Earth.
Latitude Distance north and south of the equator, measured in degrees. The north pole is at 90°N and the south pole is at 90°S. All lines of latitude are parallel to the equator.
Leaching The natural removal of soluble minerals in soil downward from the A to the B horizon by percolating water.
Life expectancy The average number of years that an individual is expected to live at the time of their birth. Good food and health-care services promote longer life expectancy.

Literacy The ability to read and write. There are no universal definitions and standards of literacy. The most common definition is the ability to read and write at 15 years of age. There are 22 countries that claim a literacy rate of 100%. While not a perfect measure of educational results, literacy is one of the most easily available and valid measures for international comparisons. Low levels of literacy and education in general, can impede the economic development of a country.

Lithosphere The solid outer layer of Earth including the top part of the mantle and Earth's crust.

Longitude Distance east and west of the prime meridian, measured in degrees. Lines of longitude, called meridians, join the north and south poles.

Mantle A concentric layer of Earth's interior, nearly 3000 kilometres thick, between the crust and the core.

Manufacturing Industry that changes raw materials into finished products.

Mass transit The movement of people, usually in an urban area by bus, streetcar, subway, or commuter train.

Meltwater Water produced by the thawing of ice or melting of snow. Meltwaters from the last glacial period covered large areas of Manitoba, southern Ontario and Québec, and the Clay Belts in northern Ontario.

Metallic mineral A mineral that yields a metal when processed (e.g., iron, gold, silver, copper).

Metamorphic rock A type of rock that results from changes – produced by heat and/or pressure – in other rock types (e.g., limestone becomes marble, granite becomes gneiss, and quartz sandstone becomes quartzite).

Métis People of mixed First Nations and European descent. The Métis have a unique culture that draws on their diverse ancestral origins such as Scottish, French, Ojibway, and Cree.

Migration The movement of people, birds, or animals from one location to another.

Mesozoic Geologic era that occurred from 245 to 65 million years ago.

Millibar (mb) A unit of atmospheric pressure. 1000 mb = 1 bar.

Mineral A naturally occurring crystalline substance with specific chemical composition and regular internal structure, composed of two or more elements. Examples of minerals are quartz and feldspar. Most rocks contain a combination of minerals.

Mineral fuel A fuel produced from minerals (e.g., uranium, coal, oil, natural gas).

Mixed farming A type of agriculture which involves the cultivation of crops and the raising of animals.

Moisture deficiency An amount of moisture needed for plant growth that is not produced by precipitation. When high temperatures increase evaporation, a moisture deficiency occurs. Irrigation is often used to reduce the deficiency and promote plant growth.

Monsoon A wind that changes with the seasonal changes in pressure systems resulting in distinctive wet and dry seasons (e.g., the summer monsoon of the Indian sub-continent).

Moraine Materials deposited by a glacier, often in the form of hills. End moraines are found at the farthest point of advance of the glacier.

Natural increase The difference between the number of births and deaths, usually based on 1000 people.

Nautical mile A unit of distance used in navigation, equal to 1.853 kilometres. The distance is one minute of an arc on a Great Circle drawn on a sphere the size of Earth.

Needleleaf A tree with needles rather than flat leaves. The needles fall and are replaced throughout the year (e.g., pine, spruce, fir).

Net migration The difference between immigration and emigration.

Nomadic Without permanent residence. Nomadic peoples may be hunters or herders, who move from place to place in search of food and pastures.

Non-porous rock A dense type of impermeable rock that prevents liquids from passing through its small number of pore spaces (e.g., shale and some forms of limestone).

Northwest Passage A sea route across northern Canada that is difficult to traverse due to ice conditions. Early explorers searched for this route to China (Cathay).

Nuclear power Electricity produced by using the heat from nuclear fission to produce steam to drive a generator.

Offshore fishery The sector of the fishing industry that usually operates more than 80 kilometres from shore using large ships that stay out at sea for several days.

Oil (or gas) field An area in which oil or gas has been discovered. New oil and gas fields have been found off the east coast of Canada and in the Beaufort Sea.

Oil sands Sands saturated with heavy crude oil. Large oil sands have been found near Fort McMurray on the Athabasca River in Alberta.

Organic materials Living materials, such as plants and animals.

Organic soil An incompletely developed soil containing more than 20% dead organic materials. This soil is often called "muck soil" or peat and is found in areas of poor drainage such as marshes and swamps.

Ozone layer A layer of the stratosphere where oxygen (O_2) is converted into ozone (O_3). Ozone absorbs much of the ultraviolet radiation. When the ozone layer is reduced in thickness, these harmful rays increase the likelihood of skin damage that can lead to skin cancer.

Pacific Rim The countries around the Pacific Ocean, from Chile to Alaska on the east side and from New Zealand to Japan and Russia on the west side.

Pack ice Seasonal ice formed by the joining of several ice floes.

Parkland A transitional vegetation zone between grassland and boreal forest containing differing combinations of both grassland and forest.

Percolation The downward movement of water through the soil and through joints in the bedrock.

Permafrost Ground that does not completely thaw in summer. The surface layer may thaw but the ground underneath remains frozen and does not permit meltwater to drain downward. Boggy conditions often result.

Permeable rock A porous type of rock with many pores or spaces that allow liquid to pass through.

Pesticide Chemical used to kill unwanted plants and animals. Some authorities include herbicides, insecticides, algaecides, and fungicides in the definition.

Plantation farming Using the land for a single commercial crop, usually on estates, especially in tropical countries where crops such as tea, rubber, coffee, sugar, and fruit are grown on a large scale.

Plate A section of Earth's crust that "floats" in Earth's mantle in much the same way as an iceberg floats in water. Plate movement (continental drift) can cause earthquakes, volcanoes, and tsunamis.

Plateau An upland area with a fairly flat surface and steep slopes. Rivers often dissect plateau surfaces.

Plate tectonics The theory suggesting that Earth's surface is composed of a number of oceanic and continental plates which move by the forces of convection currents. When these plates meet, one slides over or under the other, often producing earthquakes and volcanic activity.

Podzol A shallow, highly leached and acidic soil usually associated with coniferous forests.

Pollution The release of substances into the environment that harm living organisms and damage resources. A range of problems are created, such as an impairment of the quality of life (e.g., closed beaches) and hazards to human health (e.g., skin cancer).

Population density A figure determined by dividing the total population by the total area for a given region.

Population distribution The pattern of habitation in an area.

Population profile A diagram showing the structure of a population, usually by age and sex. Because of the general shape, the profile is often called a population pyramid.

Porous rock See permeable rock.

Post-glacial lake A body of water formed by the meltwaters of a receding glacier. Where ice blocked the normal drainage routes, ponding occurred. (e.g., Lake Agassiz in Manitoba and Lake Iroquois in Ontario).

Precambrian That period of Earth's prehistory dating from the formation of Earth (approximately 4.5 billion years ago) to approximately 600 million years ago.

Precipitation Moisture that accumulates in clouds and then falls to Earth as rain, snow, hail, sleet, or ice pellets.

Primary industry Industry that works directly with natural resources (e.g., fishing, forestry, mining, agriculture).

Prime meridian An imaginary line at zero degrees longitude, passing through Greenwich, England. All meridians are numbered east and west of this line to a maximum of 180°.
Quaternary The most recent period of the Cenozoic Era, also known as the Age of Humans.
Radarsat Satellites built by the Canadian Space Agency for the purpose of remotely sensing Earth's resources using a system that transmits microwaves.
Rainforest A thick luxuriant evergreen forest in areas of high precipitation, evenly distributed throughout the year. Tropical rainforests are found in such places as the Amazon and Congo basins. Temperate rainforests are found in China, Australia, New Zealand and the United States.
Rangeland Land used for grazing cattle.
Raw material Material that a manufacturing industry processes into a more finished state (e.g., iron to steel, crude oil to gasoline).
Reef A ridge of rock, sand, or coral whose top lies close to the ocean's surface.
Refinery A processing plant for raw materials (e.g., oil, sugar, copper).
Refugee An individual who has been compelled to move to another region or country because of political, economic, or environmental crises.
Relief The general physical variations of the land.
Remote sensing The gathering of information by the use of electronic or other sensing devices in satellites.
Reserve Land belonging to the federal government upon which First Nations peoples (and others) have the right to occupy and use.
Retail Business that sells products or provides services for consumers.
Ridge An area of higher elevation, usually long and narrow, with steep-sloped sides. Ridges are found both on land and in the ocean.
Rift Zone between two diverging tectonic plates. The mid-oceanic ridge is an area where such plate divergence is occurring.
Rift valley Steep-sided valley created by the downward displacement of land between two parallel faults as a result of tectonic movement (e.g., the Great Rift Valley in Africa).
Rock A compact and consolidated mass of mineral matter subdivided into three basic types — igneous, sedimentary and metamorphic.
Run-off Moisture, either from precipitation or from melting snow, that flows over the surface and eventually joins or creates streams and rivers. Excess water occurs often as part of the "spring thaw" and becomes run-off.
Rural Concerning the area outside towns and cities.
Satellite image Similar to a photograph, but recorded on bands of electro-magnetic spectrum, taken from a satellite.
Sea ice A covering of thick ice over a large area of water. Sea ice is common in the Arctic Ocean.
Sedimentary rock A type of rock formed by the compression of deposits from water wind and ice (e.g., shale, sandstone, limestone).
Seismic zone An area of Earth's crust that experiences horizontal or vertical movement, often associated with earthquakes and volcanoes. Areas of high seismic activity are found along fault lines and on the edges of tectonic plates.
Services Economic activities by people in which no goods are produced (e.g., sales personnel, bank employees, teachers, doctors, bus drivers, accountants).
Sewage treatment Methods of dealing with raw human wastes before being returned to bodies of water. Methods may be physical, chemical, or biological, or a combination of these.
Softwood Wood produced by most coniferous trees (e.g., pine).
Soil Layer of unconsolidated material found at the Earth's surface that has been influenced by climate, relief, parent material, time, and organisms. Soil normally consists of weathered mineral particles, dead and living organic matter, and air spaces.
Soil capability A classification system for soils based on characteristics of the soil as determined by soil surveys. There are 7 classes, each of which indicates the degree of limitation imposed by the soil in its use for mechanized agriculture. They are used for making decisions on land improvement, for developing land-use plans, and for preparing equitable land assessments.
Solar energy Energy produced directly or indirectly from the sun.
Solar radiation Radiant heat from the sun, emitted in the form of short waves. It is measured in megajoules per square metre.
Soluble Able to be dissolved. Certain minerals are soluble in water and are carried down through the soil from one horizon to the next.
Stratosphere The layer of the atmosphere from 10 to 50 kilometres above Earth's surface.
Subduction The downward movement of an oceanic plate into the asthenosphere along converging plate boundaries. Eventually the plate melts into the molten mass.
Subsistence farming A type of agriculture in which livestock is raised and crops are cultivated for consumption rather than for sale.
Sustainable development A level of development that ensures potential for future generations whereby the environment and its resources are not overwhelmed by human activity.
Tectonics The internal forces that form the features of Earth's crust.
Temperate Refers to the "middle" zones of Earth's surface, between the tropics and the polar regions.
Tertiary period The first period of the Cenozoic Era (65 million years ago to the beginning of the glacial periods about one million years ago), during which mammals developed.
Thermal energy Electricity produced by burning fossil fuels, such as coal, oil, and natural gas.
Time zone A geographical area within which clocks are set to a standard time. Time zones occupy approximately 15 degrees of longitude.
Topographic map A map that displays the relief of the land through the use of contour lines. Base elevation is sea level. Canada has national coverage in topographic maps at scales ranging from 1: 25 000 to 1: 250 000.
Tropic of Cancer An imaginary line drawn 23°30′ degrees north of the equator indicating the northernmost extent of the apparent seasonal movement of the sun.
Tropic of Capricorn An imaginary line drawn 23°30′ south of the equator indicating the southernmost extent of the apparent seasonal movement of the sun.
Troposphere The layer of air directly above Earth's surface where most of the important weather phenomena take place. It contains more than 95% of Earth's air and extends an average of 10 kilometres upwards, although the range is from 7 to 17 kilometres, depending upon latitude. Temperatures decrease with altitude.
Tsunami A seismic wave caused by an earthquake.
Tundra The climate, vegetation, or soil of the arctic and sub-arctic regions between the forested areas and those with permanent snow and ice. Mosses, lichens, and permafrost are characteristics of the area.
Urban Referring to a city or town. In Canada, an area that contains at least 1000 people with a population density of at least 400 people per square kilometre.
Urbanization The process of change in an area from a rural to an urban landscape.
Water table The level beneath Earth's surface below which the rock and soil are saturated. The depth of the water table varies, depending upon type of rock, availability of water, slope and human influences.
Watt The power that produces energy at the rate of one joule per second.
Weather station A location equipped with instruments to record atmospheric conditions. In Canada, continuous data is relayed to Environment Canada for analysis and forecasting purposes.
Wetland Land whose water table is at or very near the surface (e.g., bogs, swamps, marshes, and areas of shallow water). These areas are valuable for migrating birds and act as "filters" for water before it enters rivers or streams.
Wholesale The business of selling products and services in large quantities, not to the final consumer, but to retail businesses that then sell them to consumers.
Wind chill factor A measurement that combines the effect of low temperature and the speed of the wind. A high wind chill factor can cause frostbite or hypothermia.
Wisconsin ice sheet The most recent continental ice sheet that began to recede about 15 000 years ago. It covered much of North America with ice up to 2000 metres thick.
Zonal soil The most predominant of the three major soil orders reflecting the influence of climate and natural vegetation (e.g., chernozem, podzol). Soils in this group are well developed and have distinct horizons.

ECONOMICS AND TRADE

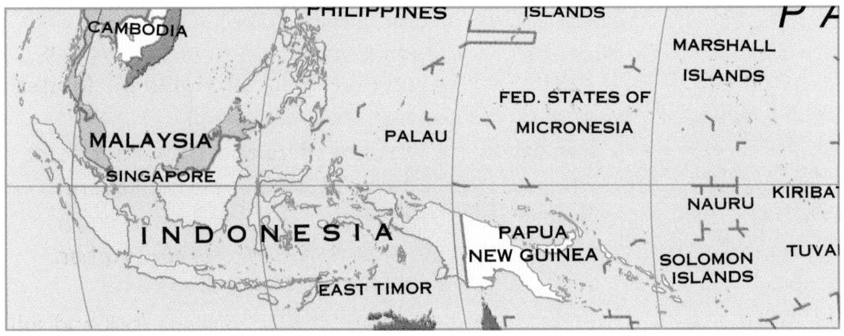

Part of Pacific Rim Thematic map, pp.164-165

HISTORY AND SOCIAL STUDIES

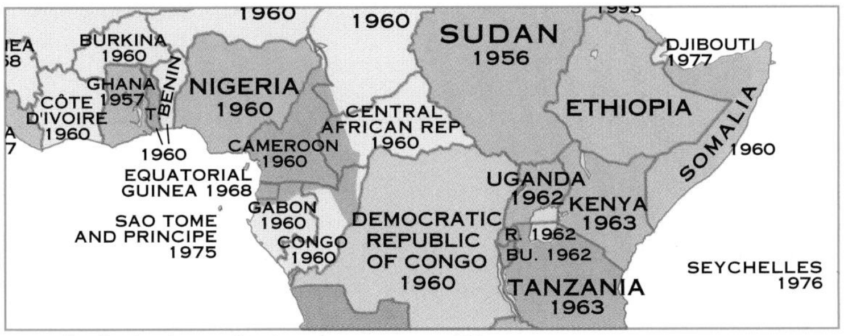

Part of Colonization and Indepedence map, p.131

ENVIRONMENT

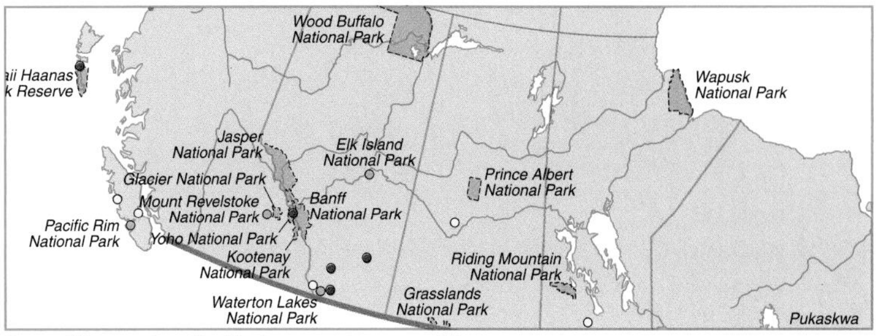

Part of Protecting the Environment map, p.55

TOURISM

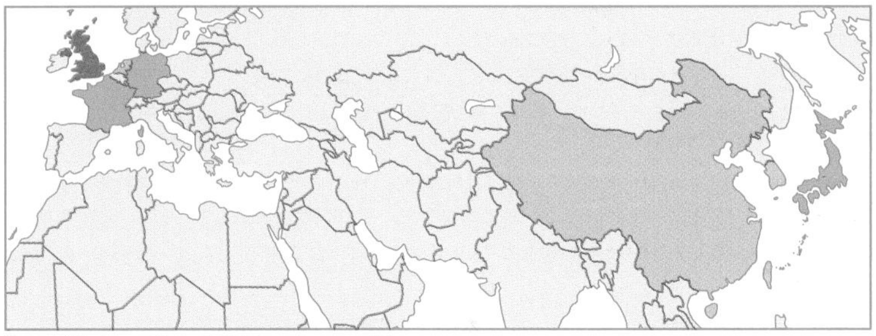

Part of International Visitors map, p.49

WEATHER AND CLIMATE

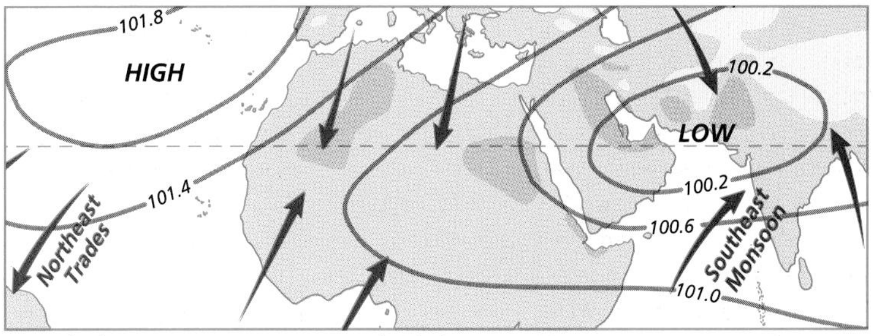

Part of July Temperature, Pressure and Winds map, p.82

How to use the Gazetteer

All the names on the maps in this atlas, except some of those on the special topics maps, are included in the gazetteer.
The names are arranged in alphabetical order. Where the name has more than one word, the separate words are considered as one word to decide the position of the name in the index:

White Bay
White Bear
Whitefish
White Hill
Whitehorse

Where there is more than one place with the same name, the country name is used to decide the order:

Los Angeles Chile
Los Angeles U.S.A.

If both places are in the same country, the county or state or province name is also used:

Fuzhou Fujian China
Fuzhou Jiangxi China

Each entry in the index starts with the name of the place or feature, followed by the name of the country, state, or territory in which it is located. This is followed by the number of the most appropriate page on which the name appears, usually the largest scale map. Next comes the alphanumeric reference, followed by the latitude and longitude.

Names of physical features, such as rivers, capes, and mountains, are followed by a description. The descriptions are usually shortened to one or two letters; these abbreviations are provided below. Town names are followed by a description only when the name may be confused with that of a physical feature:

Lake Louise *town*

To help distinguish the different parts of each entry, different styles of type are used:

province /state name (if included)
page number
place name
latitude/longitude
description (if any)
country name
alphanumeric gridreference

Deer Lake *town* Ont. Canada **64 B4** 52.37N 94.02W

The **alphanumeric grid reference** can be used to find the general location of a feature on a map. Page 170 in the atlas describes how to use the numbers and letters in the frame of the maps to locate a place or feature.

The **latitude and longitude reference** gives a more exact description of the position of the feature. Each name in the index has a different latitude and longitude reference, so the feature can be located accurately. Page 170 of the atlas describes lines of latitude and longitude, and explains how they are numbered and divided into degrees and minutes.

Abbreviations

Ala.	Alabama
Alta.	Alberta
b., **B.**	bay, Bay
B.C.	British Columbia
Bosnia.	Bosnia-Herzegovina
c., **C.**	cape, Cape
C.A.R.	Central African Republic
Carib. Sea	Caribbean Sea
Colo.	Colorado
Czech Rep.	Czech Republic
d.	internal division e.g., state, province
Del.	Delaware
des.	Desert
Dem. Rep. Congo	Democratic Republic of Congo
Dom. Rep.	Dominican Republic
Equat. Guinea	Equatorial Guinea
est.	estuary
f.	physical feature e.g., valley, plain, geographic district
Fed. States of Micronesia	Federated States of Micronesia
Fla.	Florida
g., **G.**	Gulf
Ga.	Georgia
i., **I.**, *is.*, **Is.**	island, Island, islands, Islands
Ill.	Illinois
Ind.	Indiana
l., **L.**	lake, Lake
La.	Louisiana
Liech.	Liechtenstein
Lux.	Luxembourg
Man.	Manitoba
Mass.	Massachusetts
Med. Sea	Mediterranean Sea
Minn.	Minnesota
Miss.	Mississippi
Mt.	Mount
mtn., **Mtn.**	mountain, Mountain
mtns., **Mtns.**	mountains, Mountains
N.B.	New Brunswick
Neth. Ant.	Netherlands Antilles
Nev.	Nevada
Nfld. and Lab.	Newfoundland and Labrador
N.C.	North Carolina
N. Korea	North Korea
N. Mex.	New Mexico
N.S.	Nova Scotia
N.Y.	New York
N.W.T.	Northwest Territories
Oc.	Ocean
Ont.	Ontario
Oreg.	Oregon
Pa.	Pennsylvania
P.E.I.	Prince Edward Island
pen., **Pen.**	peninsula, Peninsula
Phil.	Philippines
P.N.G.	Papua New Guinea
pt., **Pt.**	point, Point
Qué.	Québec
r., **R.**	river, River
Rep. of Ire.	Republic of Ireland
research stn.	research station
Resr.	Reservoir
R.S.A.	Republic of South Africa
Russian Fed.	Russian Federation
Sask.	Saskatchewan
Serb. and Mon.	Serbia and Montenegro
Sd.	Sound
S.C.	South Carolina
S. Korea	South Korea
str., **Str.**	strait, Strait
Tex.	Texas
U.A.E.	United Arab Emirates
U.K.	United Kingdom
U.S.A.	United States of America
Va.	Virginia
Vt.	Vermont
W. Va.	West Virginia
Wyo.	Wyoming
Y.T.	Yukon Territory

A

B

C

Caubvick, Mount Canada **68 G5** 58.50N 63.40W
Cauca *r.* Colombia **117 J2** 8.57N 74.30W
Caucaia Brazil **122 F6** 3.45S 38.45W
Caucasus *mts.* Asia/Europe **139 H2** 43.53N 40.00E
Causapscal Canada **68 F3** 48.21N 67.14W
Cavan Canada **64 Z3** 44.12N 78.28W
Caxias Brazil **122 E6** 4.53S 43.20W
Caxias do Sul Brazil **123 D4** 29.14S 51.10W
Cayenne French Guiana **122 D7** 4.55N 52.18W
Cayman Brac *i.* Cayman Is. **117 I4** 19.44N 79.48W
Cayman Is. C. America **117 H4** 19.00N 81.00W
Cayos Miskito *is.* Nicaragua **117 H3** 14.30N 82.40W
Cayuga Canada **66 E2** 42.57N 79.51W
Cebu Philippines **155 G6** 10.17N 123.56E
Cebu *i.* Philippines **155 G6** 10.15N 123.45E
Cedar *r.* U.S.A. **113 H5** 41.15N 91.20W
Cedar City U.S.A. **112 D4** 37.40N 113.04W
Cedar Falls *town* U.S.A. **64 B1** 42.31N 92.27W
Cedar Lake Man. Canada **60 D2** 53.24N 100.11W
Cedar Lake Ont. Canada **66 F6** 46.01N 78.27W
Cedar Rapids *town* U.S.A. **113 H5** 41.59N 91.31W
Cedar Springs *town* Canada **66 B2** 42.17N 82.02W
Cedros *i.* Mexico **112 C2** 28.15N 115.15W
Celaya Mexico **116 D5** 20.32N 100.48W
Celebes Sea Indonesia **155 G4** 3.00N 122.00E
Cenderawasih G. Indonesia **155 J3** 2.30S 135.20E
Central, Cordillera *mts.* Bolivia **122 C5** 20.00S 65.00W
Central, Cordillera *mts.* Colombia **122 B7** 5.00N 75.20W
Central, Cordillera *mts.* Peru **122 B6** 7.00S 79.00W
Central African Republic Africa **128 F5** 6.25N 20.12E
Central Butte Canada **60 C1** 50.48N 106.30W
Central Range *mts.* P.N.G. **155 K3** 5.00S 142.30E
Central Russian Uplands Russian Fed. **139 G3** 54.27N 36.28E
Central Saanich Canada **57 W2** 48.35N 123.28W
Central Siberian Plateau *f.* Russian Fed. **143 M4** 66.00N 108.00E
Centreville Canada **73 I4** 49.01N 53.54W
Cerralvo *i.* Mexico **116 C5** 24.17N 109.52W
Cerro de Pasco Peru **122 B5** 10.43S 76.15W
Ceuta N. Africa **138 C1** 35.53N 5.20W
Chad Africa **128 E6** 15.07N 18.13E
Chad, Lake Africa **128 E6** 13.27N 14.24E
Chadan Russian Fed. **152 G8** 51.20N 91.39E
Chagai Hills Afghanistan/Pakistan **146 E3** 29.17N 63.23E
Chaghcharan Afghanistan **146 E4** 34.28N 65.03E
Chagos Archipelago Indian Ocean **134 J2** 7.00S 72.00E
Chah Bahar Iran **146 E3** 25.18N 60.38E
Chakonipau, Lake Canada **68 E5** 56.24N 68.36W
Chaleur Bay Canada **68 F2** 47.58N 65.55W
Challenger Deep Pacific Oc. **80 F4** 11.20N 143.15E
Chaman Pakistan **146 E4** 30.55N 66.28E
Chamberlain Canada **60 C1** 50.51N 105.33W
Chamberlain Lake U.S.A. **68 E2** 46.13N 69.17W
Champlain, L. U.S.A. **113 L5** 44.45N 73.20W
Champlain, Lake Canada/U.S.A. **65 G2** 44.23N 73.22W
Chandalar *r.* U.S.A. **74 D3** 66.36N 145.51W
Chandeleur Is. U.S.A. **113 I2** 29.50N 88.50W
Chandigarh India **147 F4** 30.42N 76.48E
Chandler Canada **68 F3** 48.21N 64.41W
Chandrapur India **147 F2** 19.57N 79.21E
Changchun China **153 N6** 43.50N 125.20E
Changde China **153 K3** 29.03N 111.35E
Chang Jiang *r.* China **153 M4** 31.23N 121.48E
Changsha China **153 K3** 28.10N 113.00E
Changzhi China **153 K5** 36.09N 113.12E
Changzhou China **153 L4** 31.45N 119.57E
Channel Islands English Channel **138 C2** 49.20N 2.37W
Channel-Port-aux-Basques Canada **69 H2** 47.33N 59.01W
Chanthaburi Thailand **154 C6** 12.38N 102.12E
Chao Phraya *r.* Thailand **154 C6** 13.35N 100.37E
Chapais Canada **68 D3** 49.47N 74.51W
Chapala, Lago de *l.* Mexico **116 D5** 20.00N 103.00W
Chapleau Canada **65 E2** 47.51N 83.24W
Chaplin Canada **60 C1** 50.28N 106.40W
Chardzhev Turkmenistan **146 E4** 39.05N 63.34E
Chari *r.* Cameroon/Chad **128 E6** 12.48N 14.34E
Chariton *r.* U.S.A. **64 B1** 40.50N 93.00W
Charles City U.S.A. **64 B1** 43.04N 92.40W
Charleston S.C. U.S.A. **113 K3** 32.48N 79.58W
Charleston W.Va. U.S.A. **113 J4** 38.23N 81.20W
Charleville Australia **158 D3** 26.24S 146.14E
Charlo Canada **72 B4** 48.01N 66.26W
Charlotte U.S.A. **113 J4** 35.05N 80.50W
Charlottesville U.S.A. **113 K4** 38.02N 78.29W
Charlottetown Canada **72 D3** 46.16N 63.09W
Charlton Island Canada **65 F4** 52.02N 79.35W
Charters Towers *town* Australia **158 D3** 20.04S 146.19E
Chase Canada **56 G2** 50.49N 119.41W
Chatham Canada **66 B2** 42.24N 82.11W
Chatham Is. Pacific Oc. **159 H1** 44.00S 176.35W
Chatham Strait U.S.A. **56 C4** 56.38N 134.24W
Chatsworth Canada **66 D4** 44.28N 80.55W
Chattahoochee *r.* U.S.A. **113 J3** 30.52N 84.57W
Chattanooga U.S.A. **113 I4** 35.01N 85.18W
Chautauqua, Lake U.S.A. **66 E2** 42.13N 79.28W
Chavigny, Lac *l.* Canada **68 D5** 58.16N 75.17W
Cheboksary Russian Fed. **139 H3** 56.09N 47.13E
Cheboygan U.S.A. **113 J6** 45.40N 84.28W
Chedabucto Bay Canada **72 E2** 45.22N 61.27W
Cheektowaga U.S.A. **66 F2** 42.54N 78.45W
Cheju do *i.* S. Korea **153 N4** 33.20N 126.30E
Chelyabinsk Russian Fed. **139 J3** 55.11N 61.24E
Chelyuskin, C. Russian Fed. **143 M5** 77.20N 106.00E
Chemainus Canada **57 V2** 48.55N 123.43W
Chemainus *r.* Canada **57 V2** 48.54N 123.45W
Chemnitz Germany **138 E3** 50.50N 12.56E
Chengde China **153 L6** 40.48N 118.06E
Chengdu China **152 I4** 30.37N 104.06E
Chennai India **147 G2** 13.06N 80.16E
Chenzhou China **153 K3** 25.45N 113.00E
Cherepovets Russian Fed. **139 G3** 59.08N 37.55E
Cherkasy Ukraine **138 G2** 49.26N 32.05E
Cherkessk Russian Fed. **139 H2** 44.13N 42.03E
Chernihiv Ukraine **138 G3** 51.29N 31.19E
Chernivtsi Ukraine **138 F2** 48.19N 25.56E
Cherskiy Russian Fed. **143 S4** 68.43N 161.24E
Cherskogo Range *mts.* Russian Fed. **143 Q4** 65.50N 143.00E
Chesapeake B. U.S.A. **113 K4** 38.00N 76.00W
Chëshskaya Bay Russian Fed. **139 H4** 67.23N 46.29E
Chesley Canada **66 C4** 44.18N 81.06W
Chester Canada **72 C2** 44.33N 64.15W
Chesterfield Inlet Canada **74 I3** 63.49N 92.46W
Chéticamp Canada **72 E3** 46.37N 60.52W
Chetwynd Canada **56 F3** 55.42N 121.38W
Cheyenne U.S.A. **112 F5** 41.08N 104.50W
Chiang Mai Thailand **154 B7** 18.48N 98.59E
Chiang Rai Thailand **154 B7** 19.56N 99.51E
Chibougamau Canada **68 D3** 49.55N 74.22W
Chibougamau *r.* Canada **68 D3** 49.42N 75.58W
Chicago U.S.A. **113 I5** 41.50N 87.45W
Chic-Chocs, Monts *mts.* Canada **72 B4** 48.47N 66.15W
Chichagof Island U.S.A. **74 E2** 57.50N 135.51W
Chiclayo Peru **122 B6** 6.47S 79.47W
Chico U.S.A. **112 B4** 39.46N 121.50W
Chicoutimi-Jonquière Canada **68 E3** 48.25N 71.14W
Chidley, Cape Canada **68 F6** 60.26N 64.20W
Chifeng China **153 L6** 41.17N 118.56E
Chignecto Bay Canada **72 C2** 45.30N 65.00W
Chihuahua Mexico **116 C6** 28.40N 106.06W
Chilanko Forks *town* Canada **56 E3** 52.07N 124.05W
Chilcotin *r.* Canada **56 F2** 51.44N 122.24W
Chile S. America **123 B3** 33.00S 71.00W
Chilko *r.* Canada **56 F3** 52.01N 123.42W
Chilko Lake Canada **56 E2** 51.26N 124.06W
Chillán Chile **123 B3** 36.37S 72.10W
Chilliwack Canada **57 Z3** 49.10N 121.57W
Chiloé, Isla de Chile **123 B2** 43.00S 73.00W
Chilpancingo Mexico **116 E4** 17.33N 99.30W
Chimborazo *mtn.* Ecuador **122 B6** 1.10S 78.50W
Chimbote Peru **122 B6** 8.58S 78.34W
China Asia **152 H4** 33.00N 103.00E
Chinchaga *r.* Canada **59 B3** 58.49N 118.22W
Chindwin *r.* Myanmar **147 H3** 21.27N 95.15E
Chinook U.S.A. **60 B1** 48.36N 109.14W
Chipman Canada **72 C3** 46.10N 65.52W
Chiriquí, G. of Panama **117 H2** 8.00N 82.20W
Chirripó *mtn.* Costa Rica **117 H2** 9.31N 83.30W
Chisasibi Canada **68 C4** 53.49N 78.59W
Chişinau Moldova **138 F2** 47.02N 28.50E
Chita Russian Fed. **143 N3** 52.03N 113.35E
Chitradurga India **147 F2** 14.14N 76.22E
Chitral Pakistan **147 F4** 35.53N 71.47E
Chittagong Bangladesh **147 H3** 22.20N 91.49E
Chitungwiza Zimbabwe **129 G3** 18.01S 31.04E
Chon Buri Thailand **154 C6** 13.24N 100.59E
Chongjin N. Korea **153 N6** 41.55N 129.50E
Chongqing China **153 J3** 29.31N 106.35E
Chonju S. Korea **153 N5** 35.50N 127.05E
Choybalsan Mongolia **153 K7** 48.02N 114.32E
Christchurch New Zealand **159 G1** 43.32S 172.37E
Christian Island Canada **66 D4** 44.52N 80.14W
Christina *r.* Canada **59 D3** 56.39N 111.02W
Christmas I. Indian Ocean **154 D1** 10.30S 105.40E
Chuckchi Pen. Russian Fed. **143 U4** 66.00N 174.30W
Chugach Mountains U.S.A. **74 D3** 61.07N 146.09W
Chukchi Sea Arctic Oc. **143 U4** 69.30N 172.00W
Chukchi Sea Russian Fed./U.S.A. **74 A3** 69.12N 171.31W
Chukotat *r.* Canada **68 C6** 60.48N 77.52W
Chumphon Thailand **154 B6** 10.35N 99.14E
Chunchon S. Korea **153 N5** 37.53N 127.45E
Churapcha Russian Fed. **143 P4** 61.55N 132.14E
Churchill Canada **60 F3** 58.44N 94.05W
Churchill *r.* Man. Canada **60 F3** 58.11N 94.23W
Churchill *r.* Nfld. and Lab. Canada **69 G4** 53.16N 60.14W
Churchill, Cape Canada **61 F3** 58.45N 93.16W
Churchill Falls *town* Canada **68 G4** 53.31N 63.51W
Churchill Lake Canada **60 B2** 55.59N 108.19W
Church Point Canada **57 V1** 48.18N 123.34W
Chute-des-Passes Canada **68 E3** 49.52N 71.17W
Chuuk *i.* Fed. States of Micronesia **162 K7** 7.23N 151.46E
Chuxiong China **152 I3** 25.03N 101.33E
Ciego de Avila Cuba **117 I5** 21.51N 78.47W
Cienfuegos Cuba **117 H5** 22.10N 80.27W
Cilacap Indonesia **154 D2** 7.44S 109.00E
Cincinnati U.S.A. **113 J4** 39.10N 84.30W
Circle U.S.A. **74 D3** 65.52N 144.02W
Cirebon Indonesia **154 D2** 6.46S 108.33E
City of Toronto *d.* Canada **64 X2** 43.42N 79.20W
Ciudad Bolívar Venezuela **122 C7** 8.06N 63.36W
Ciudad Camargo Mexico **116 C6** 27.41N 105.10W
Ciudad Delicias Mexico **116 C6** 28.10N 105.30W
Ciudad de Valles Mexico **116 E5** 22.00N 99.00W
Ciudad Guayana Venezuela **122 C7** 8.22N 62.40W
Ciudad Ixtepec Mexico **116 E4** 16.32N 95.10W
Ciudad Juárez Mexico **116 C7** 31.42N 106.29W
Ciudad Madero Mexico **116 E5** 22.19N 97.50W
Ciudad Obregón Mexico **116 C6** 27.28N 109.55W
Ciudad Victoria Mexico **116 E5** 23.43N 99.10W
Claire, Lake Canada **59 C3** 58.36N 112.06W
Clairmont Canada **59 B2** 55.16N 118.49W
Clare U.S.A. **65 D1** 43.49N 84.46W
Claremont U.S.A. **65 G1** 43.22N 72.20W
Clarence Strait U.S.A. **56 C3** 55.52N 132.49W
Clarenville-Shoal Harbour Canada **69 I3** 48.05N 53.38W
Claresholm Canada **59 C1** 50.01N 113.35W
Clarington Canada **64 Y2** 43.55N 78.34W
Clarke City Canada **72 B5** 50.11N 66.41W
Clark Fork *r.* U.S.A. **57 G2** 48.08N 116.10W
Clark Point Canada **66 C4** 44.05N 81.45W
Clarks Harbour Canada **72 C1** 43.27N 65.39W
Clarkson Canada **64 W2** 43.31N 79.38W
Clarksville U.S.A. **113 I4** 36.31N 87.21W
Clayton U.S.A. **112 F4** 36.27N 103.12W
Clear, Cape Rep. of Ireland **138 C3** 51.25N 9.31W
Clear Creek *town* Canada **66 D2** 42.35N 80.33W
Clear Hills Canada **59 B3** 56.45N 119.36W
Clearwater Canada **56 G2** 51.38N 119.59W
Clearwater *r.* Canada **59 D3** 56.41N 111.21W
Clearwater *r.* U.S.A. **64 A2** 47.53N 96.15W
Clermont-Ferrand France **138 D2** 45.46N 3.05E
Cleveland U.S.A. **113 J5** 41.30N 81.41W
Cleveland, Mount U.S.A. **57 H2** 48.56N 113.59W
Climax Canada **60 B1** 49.12N 108.23W
Cline River *town* Canada **59 B2** 52.12N 116.29W
Clinton B.C. Canada **56 F2** 51.06N 121.36W
Clinton Ont. Canada **66 C3** 43.37N 81.32W
Clinton U.S.A. **65 C1** 41.51N 90.12W
Clipperton I. Pacific Oc. **163 U8** 10.17N 109.13W
Cloquet U.S.A. **64 B2** 46.43N 92.27W
Cloridorme Canada **72 C4** 49.10N 64.51W
Cloud Peak *mtn.* U.S.A. **112 E5** 44.23N 107.11W
Clovis U.S.A. **112 F3** 34.14N 103.13W
Cluff Lake Mine *town* Canada **60 B3** 58.21N 109.30W
Cluj-Napoca Romania **138 F2** 46.46N 23.36E
Clyde Canada **59 C2** 54.08N 113.38W
Clyde River *town* Canada **75 L4** 70.23N 68.34W
Coal *r.* Canada **56 E4** 59.39N 126.58W
Coaldale Canada **59 C1** 49.43N 112.37W
Coal River *town* Canada **56 E4** 59.40N 126.55W
Coast Mountains Canada **56 E3** 52.40N 127.48W
Coast Range *mts.* U.S.A. **112 B5** 40.00N 123.00W
Coaticook Canada **68 E2** 45.08N 71.48W
Coats Island Canada **75 J3** 62.41N 82.53W
Coats Land *f.* Antarctica **167 G1** 78.51S 30.12W
Coatzacoalcos Mexico **116 F4** 18.10N 94.25W
Cobar Australia **158 D2** 31.31S 145.48E
Cobble Hill *town* Canada **57 V2** 48.41N 123.36W
Cobequid Bay Canada **72 D2** 45.18N 63.54W
Cobequid Mountains Canada **72 D2** 45.29N 63.45W
Cobham *r.* Canada **60 F2** 53.14N 93.58W
Cobija Bolivia **122 C5** 11.01S 68.45W
Cobourg Canada **66 F3** 43.58N 78.10W
Cochabamba Bolivia **122 C5** 17.26S 66.10W
Cochin India **147 F1** 9.55N 76.14E
Cochrane Alta. Canada **59 C1** 51.11N 114.28W
Cochrane Ont. Canada **65 E3** 49.04N 81.03W
Cochrane *r.* Canada **60 D3** 58.59N 101.48W
Cochrane Chile **123 B2** 47.20S 72.30W
Cockburn Town Turks and Caicos Is. **117 J5** 21.30N 71.30W
Coco *r.* Honduras **117 H3** 14.58N 83.15W
Coco, I. de *i.* Pacific Oc. **121 B7** 5.32N 87.04W
Cod, C. U.S.A. **113 L5** 42.08N 70.10W
Codó Brazil **122 E6** 4.28S 43.51W
Coeur d'Alene U.S.A. **57 G1** 47.41N 116.47W
Coffs Harbour Australia **159 E2** 30.19S 153.05E
Coiba, I. Panama **117 H2** 7.23N 81.45W
Coihaique Chile **123 B2** 45.35S 72.08W
Coimbatore India **147 F2** 10.59N 76.57E
Coimbra Portugal **138 C2** 40.13N 8.25W
Cold Lake *town* Canada **59 D2** 54.28N 110.12W
Coldwater Canada **66 E4** 44.43N 79.39W
Colima Mexico **116 D4** 19.14N 103.41W
Colima *mtn.* Mexico **116 D4** 19.32N 103.36W
Collier B. Australia **158 B4** 16.10S 124.15E
Collingwood Canada **66 D4** 44.30N 80.13W
Cologne Germany **138 D3** 50.56N 6.57E
Colombia S. America **122 B7** 5.00N 75.00W
Colombo Sri Lanka **147 F1** 6.56N 79.50E
Colón Panama **117 I2** 9.21N 79.54W
Colorado *r.* Argentina **123 C3** 39.50S 62.02W
Colorado *d.* U.S.A. **112 E4** 39.00N 106.00W
Colorado *r.* U.S.A. **112 G2** 28.30N 96.00W
Colorado *r.* U.S.A./Mexico **112 D3** 31.45N 114.40W
Colorado Plateau *f.* U.S.A. **112 D4** 36.00N 111.00W
Colorado Springs *town* U.S.A. **112 F4** 38.50N 104.40W
Columbia U.S.A. **113 J3** 34.00N 81.00W
Columbia *r.* U.S.A. **112 B6** 46.10N 123.30W
Columbia, Cape Canada **74 K5** 83.07N 70.30W
Columbia, Mount Canada **59 B2** 52.08N 117.25W
Columbia Mountains Canada **56 F3** 53.00N 121.00W
Columbus Ga. U.S.A. **113 J3** 32.28N 84.59W
Columbus Ohio U.S.A. **113 J4** 39.59N 83.03W
Colville U.S.A. **56 G2** 48.33N 117.55W
Colville *r.* U.S.A. **74 C4** 70.20N 150.32W
Colville Lake *town* Canada **74 F3** 66.59N 126.00W
Colwood Canada **57 W1** 48.26N 123.29W
Comandante Ferraz *research stn.* Antarctica **167 G2** 62.05S 58.24W
Commanda Canada **66 E5** 45.57N 79.36W
Comodoro Rivadavia Argentina **123 C2** 45.50S 67.30W
Comorin, Cape India **134 J3** 8.04N 77.35E
Comoros Africa **129 H3** 11.50S 44.17E
Conakry Guinea **128 B5** 9.31N 13.42W
Concepción Chile **123 B3** 36.50S 73.03W
Conception, Pt. U.S.A. **112 B3** 34.27N 120.26W
Conception Bay Canada **73 I3** 47.32N 53.07W
Conception Bay South *town* Canada **69 I2** 47.25N 52.34W
Conchos *r.* Chihuahua Mexico **116 D6** 29.34N 104.30W
Conchos *r.* Tamaulipas Mexico **116 E6** 25.00N 97.30W
Concord U.S.A. **113 L5** 43.13N 71.34W
Concordia Argentina **123 D3** 31.25S 58.00W
Conestogo Lake Canada **66 D3** 43.42N 80.42W
Congo Africa **128 E4** 2.24S 15.10E
Congo *r.* Congo/Dem. Rep. Congo **128 E4** 1.47S 16.32E
Congo, Democratic Republic of Africa **128 F4** 3.43S 22.17E
Congo Basin Dem. Rep. Congo **128 E4** 1.25S 20.23E
Conklin Canada **59 D2** 55.38N 111.05W
Conneaut U.S.A. **66 D1** 41.56N 80.34W
Connecticut *d.* U.S.A. **113 L5** 41.30N 73.00W
Conrad U.S.A. **60 B1** 48.09N 111.55W
Con Son *is.* Vietnam **154 D5** 8.30N 106.30E
Consort Canada **59 D2** 52.01N 110.46W
Constanta Romania **138 F2** 44.11N 28.37E
Constantine Algeria **128 D8** 36.23N 6.38E
Consuelo Peak *mtn.* Australia **158 D3** 24.57S 148.10E
Consul Canada **60 B1** 49.17N 109.32W
Contwoyto Lake Canada **74 G3** 65.42N 110.29W
Cook Is. Pacific Oc. **162 O5** 15.00S 160.00W
Cookstown Canada **64 W3** 44.11N 79.42W
Cook Str. New Zealand **159 G1** 41.15S 174.30E
Cooktown Australia **158 D4** 15.29S 145.15E
Coon Rapids *town* U.S.A. **64 B2** 45.10N 93.19W
Cooper Creek *r.* Australia **158 C3** 28.33S 137.46E
Copenhagen Denmark **138 E3** 55.40N 12.34E
Copper Cliff *town* Canada **65 E2** 46.27N 81.06W
Coppermine *r.* Canada **74 G3** 67.43N 115.13W
Coquimbo Chile **123 B4** 30.00S 71.25W
Coquitlam Canada **57 X3** 49.14N 122.52W
Coquitlam Lake Canada **57 X3** 49.25N 122.47W
Coral Harbour Canada **75 J3** 64.12N 83.19W
Coral Sea Pacific Oc. **159 E4** 13.00S 150.00E
Coral Sea Islands Territory Australia **159 E4** 15.00S 153.00E
Córdoba Argentina **123 C3** 31.25S 64.11W
Córdoba Mexico **116 E4** 18.55N 96.55W
Córdoba Spain **138 C1** 37.53N 4.46W
Córdoba, Sierras de *mts.* Argentina **123 C3** 30.30S 64.40W
Cordova U.S.A. **74 D3** 60.34N 145.38W
Corfu *i.* Greece **138 E1** 39.36N 19.47E
Corinne Canada **60 C1** 50.03N 104.37W
Corinth Greece **138 F1** 37.56N 22.55E
Corixa Grande *r.* Brazil/Bolivia **122 D5** 17.30S 57.55W
Cork Rep. of Ireland **138 C3** 51.54N 8.28W
Corner Brook *town* Canada **69 H3** 48.54N 57.47W
Cornwall Ont. Canada **65 G2** 45.02N 74.43W
Cornwall P.E.I. Canada **72 D3** 46.14N 63.13W
Cornwallis Island Canada **74 I4** 75.08N 94.56W
Coro Venezuela **117 K3** 11.27N 69.41W
Coronada B. Costa Rica **117 H2** 9.00N 83.50W
Coronation Canada **59 D2** 52.06N 111.26W
Coronation Gulf Canada **74 G3** 68.08N 112.32W
Corpus Christi U.S.A. **112 G2** 27.47N 97.26W
Corrientes Argentina **123 D4** 27.30S 58.48W
Corrientes, C. Mexico **116 C5** 20.25N 105.42W
Corry U.S.A. **66 E1** 41.55N 79.39W
Corsica *i.* France **138 D2** 42.20N 8.29E
Cortland U.S.A. **65 F1** 42.36N 76.11W
Çorum Turkey **139 G2** 40.33N 34.57E
Corumbá Brazil **122 D5** 19.00S 57.25W
Corunna Canada **66 B2** 42.53N 82.27W
Costa Rica C. America **117 H3** 10.00N 84.00W
Cotabato Philippines **155 G5** 7.14N 124.15E
Côte d'Ivoire Africa **128 C5** 7.35N 4.22W
Cotopaxi *mtn.* Ecuador **122 B6** 0.40N 78.30W
Coulonge *r.* Canada **68 C2** 45.52N 76.45W
Council Bluffs U.S.A. **112 G5** 41.14N 95.54W
Coupeville U.S.A. **57 X1** 48.13N 122.42W
Courtenay Canada **56 E2** 49.41N 124.59W
Cowan, L. Australia **158 B2** 32.00S 122.00E
Cowansville Canada **68 D2** 45.12N 72.45W
Cowichan *r.* Canada **57 V2** 48.46N 123.39W
Cowichan Bay *town* Canada **57 V2** 48.44N 123.38W
Cowichan Lake Canada **57 U2** 48.50N 124.12W
Cox's Bazar Bangladesh **147 H3** 21.27N 91.59E
Cox's Cove *town* Canada **73 F4** 49.07N 58.05W
Cozumel I. Mexico **116 G5** 20.30N 87.00W
Craig U.S.A. **56 C3** 55.26N 133.03W
Cranberry Junction Canada **56 D3** 55.35N 128.36W
Cranberry Portage Canada **60 D2** 54.35N 101.23W
Cranbrook Canada **57 H2** 49.32N 115.45W
Crandon U.S.A. **65 C2** 45.34N 88.54W
Credit Canada **64 W2** 43.03N 79.35W
Cree *r.* Canada **60 C3** 58.42N 105.39W
Cree Lake Canada **60 C3** 57.31N 106.29W
Creemore Canada **66 D4** 44.19N 80.05W
Creighton Canada **60 D2** 54.44N 101.58W
Crescent City U.S.A. **112 B5** 41.46N 124.13W
Creston Canada **57 G2** 49.06N 116.31W
Creston U.S.A. **113 H5** 41.04N 94.20W
Crete *i.* Greece **138 F1** 35.28N 24.41E
Crimea *pen.* Ukraine **139 G2** 45.20N 34.05E
Cristóbal Colón *mtn.* Colombia **122 B8** 10.53N 73.48W
Croatia Europe **138 E2** 45.02N 15.14E
Croker, Cape Canada **66 D4** 44.57N 80.58W
Crooked I. The Bahamas **117 J5** 22.45N 74.00W
Crooked Island Passage The Bahamas **117 J5** 22.45N 74.40W
Crooked Lake Canada **73 G4** 48.25N 56.15W
Crossfield Canada **59 C1** 51.25N 114.02W
Cross Lake Canada **60 E2** 54.45N 97.32W
Cross Lake *town* Canada **60 E2** 54.35N 97.51W
Croswell U.S.A. **66 B3** 43.17N 82.37W

F

G

H

L

M

Marcy, Mount U.S.A. **65 G2** 44.07N 73.57W
Mar del Plata Argentina **123 D3** 38.00S 57.32W
Marden Canada **64 V2** 43.35N 80.18W
Margaree Forks *town* Canada **72 E3** 46.20N 61.07W
Margarita *i.* Venezuela **122 C8** 11.00N 64.00W
Marianas Trench *f.* Pacific Oc. **80 F4** 12.30N 145.30E
Marianna U.S.A. **113 I3** 30.45N 85.15W
Marias *r.* U.S.A. **60 B** 47.55N 110.29W
Marías, I. Mexico **116 C5** 21.25N 106.30W
Mariato Pt. Panama **117 H2** 7.12N 80.52W
Maria van Diemen, C. New Zealand **159 G2** 34.29S 172.39E
Maribor Slovenia **138 E2** 46.32N 15.40E
Marie Byrd Land *f.* Antarctica **167 D1** 75.12S 126.40W
Marie Galante *i.* Guadeloupe **117 L4** 15.54N 61.11W
Mariestad Sweden **138 E3** 58.43N 13.50E
Marília Brazil **123 D4** 22.13S 50.20W
Marine City U.S.A. **66 B2** 42.43N 82.30W
Marinette U.S.A. **65 D2** 45.05N 87.39W
Maringá Brazil **123 D4** 23.36S 52.02W
Mariupol' Ukraine **139 G2** 47.06N 37.33E
Marjayoûn Lebanon **150 A3** 33.22N 35.35E
Markdale Canada **66 D4** 44.19N 80.38W
Markham Canada **64 X2** 43.53N 79.15W
Marlette U.S.A. **66 A3** 43.20N 83.05W
Marne *r.* France **138 D2** 48.49N 2.25E
Maroni *r.* French Guiana **122 D7** 5.30N 54.00W
Maroochydore Australia **159 E3** 26.43S 153.04E
Marotiri *i.* French Polynesia **163 Q4** 27.55S 143.26W
Maroua Cameroon **128 E6** 10.37N 14.19E
Marquesas Is. Pacific Oc. **163 R6** 9.00S 139.30W
Marquette U.S.A. **113 I6** 46.33N 87.23W
Marrakesh Morocco **128 C8** 31.39N 7.58W
Marsabit Kenya **128 G5** 2.20N 37.59E
Marseille France **138 D2** 43.18N 5.23E
Marshall U.S.A. **64 B2** 44.27N 95.47W
Marshall Is. Pacific Oc. **162 L8** 10.00N 167.00E
Marshfield U.S.A. **65 C2** 44.40N 90.10W
Mars Hill *town* U.S.A. **72 B3** 46.31N 67.52W
Martaban Myanmar **154 B7** 16.34N 97.34E
Martaban, Gulf of Myanmar **154 B7** 16.20N 96.57E
Martapura Indonesia **154 C3** 4.20S 104.22E
Martensville Canada **60 C2** 52.17N 106.40W
Martinique *i.* Windward Is. **117 L3** 14.40N 61.00W
Martinsville U.S.A. **113 K4** 36.43N 79.53W
Martin Vaz Is. Atlantic Oc. **121 H4** 20.30S 28.51W
Mary Turkmenistan **146 E4** 37.34N 61.52E
Maryborough Australia **159 E3** 25.32S 152.36E
Maryland *d.* U.S.A. **113 K4** 39.00N 76.30W
Mary's Harbour Canada **69 I4** 52.16N 55.47W
Marystown Canada **73 H3** 47.04N 54.56W
Marysville Canada **72 B2** 45.59N 66.35W
Masai Steppe *f.* Tanzania **128 G4** 4.47S 36.53E
Masaka Uganda **128 G4** 0.19S 31.44E
Masan S. Korea **153 N5** 35.10N 128.35E
Masbate Philippines **155 G6** 12.21N 123.36E
Masbate *i.* Philippines **155 G6** 12.00N 123.30E
Maseru Lesotho **129 F2** 29.19S 27.29E
Mashhad Iran **146 D4** 36.18N 59.35E
Masirah *i.* Oman **146 D3** 20.16N 58.58E
Masirah, Gulf of Oman **146 D2** 19.47N 58.22E
Mason City U.S.A. **113 H5** 43.10N 93.10W
Massachusetts *d.* U.S.A. **113 L5** 42.20N 72.00W
Massawa Eritrea **146 B2** 15.36N 39.27E
Massena U.S.A. **65 G2** 44.56N 74.53W
Masset Canada **56 C3** 54.01N 132.09W
Massey Canada **66 B6** 46.13N 82.05W
Massif Central *mts.* France **138 D2** 45.16N 3.25E
Masvingo Zimbabwe **129 G2** 20.04S 30.48E
Maşyāf Syria **150 B4** 35.04N 36.20E
Matabele Upland Zimbabwe **127 F3** 18.30S 30.00E
Matadi Dem. Rep. Congo **128 E4** 5.49S 13.29E
Matagami Canada **68 C3** 49.46N 77.38W
Matagami, Lac *l.* Canada **68 C3** 49.55N 77.44W
Matamoros Mexico **116 E6** 25.50N 97.31W
Matane Canada **68 F3** 48.51N 67.32W
Matanzas Cuba **117 H5** 23.04N 81.35W
Matapédia Canada **72 B3** 47.59N 66.57W
Matapédia *r.* Canada **72 B3** 47.58N 66.57W
Matapédia, Lac *l.* Canada **72 B4** 48.33N 67.34W
Matara Sri Lanka **147 G1** 5.58N 80.29E
Mataram Indonesia **154 F2** 8.36S 116.07E
Matā-Utu Wallis and Futuna Is. **162 N5** 13.17S 176.07W
Matheson Canada **65 E3** 48.32N 80.28W
Matimekosh Canada **68 F4** 54.56N 67.03W
Mato Grosso, Plateau *f.* Brazil **122 D5** 15.00S 55.00W
Matsqui Canada **57 Y3** 49.06N 122.21W
Matsu Is. Taiwan **153 M3** 26.12N 120.00E
Matsuyama Japan **153 O4** 33.50N 132.47E
Mattagami *r.* Canada **65 E3** 50.42N 81.31W
Mattawa Canada **66 F6** 46.18N 78.43W
Maturín Venezuela **122 C7** 9.45N 63.16W
Maui *i.* Hawaiian Is. **163 P9** 20.45N 156.15W
Mauke *i.* Cook Is. **163 P5** 19.49S 157.41W
Maumee *r.* U.S.A. **65 E1** 41.42N 83.28W
Maumere Indonesia **155 G2** 8.35S 122.13E
Mauritania Africa **128 B6** 19.51N 11.35W
Mauritius Indian Ocean **127 I2** 20.10S 58.00E
Mawson *research stn.* Antarctica **167 K2** 67.36S 62.53E
Maya *r.* Russian Fed. **143 P4** 60.25N 134.28E
Mayaguana *i.* The Bahamas **117 J5** 22.30N 73.00W
Mayagüez Puerto Rico **117 K4** 18.13N 67.09W
Maya Mts. Belize **116 G4** 16.30N 89.00W
Mayerthorpe Canada **59 C2** 53.58N 115.10W
Maykop Russian Fed. **139 H2** 44.36N 40.07E
Mayne Island Canada **57 W2** 48.52N 123.16W
Mayo Canada **74 E3** 63.37N 135.54W
Mayotte *i.* Africa **129 H3** 12.59S 45.09E
Mazar-e Sharif Afghanistan **146 E4** 36.43N 67.07E
Mazatlán Mexico **116 C5** 23.11N 106.25W
Mazyr Belarus **138 F3** 52.03N 29.15E
Mbabane Swaziland **129 G2** 26.20S 31.09E
Mbandaka Dem. Rep. Congo **128 E4** 0.00S 18.17E
Mbeya Tanzania **129 G4** 8.53S 33.26E
Mbuji-Mayi Dem. Rep. Congo **128 F4** 6.06S 23.36E
McAdam Canada **72 B2** 45.36N 67.20W
McArthur *r.* Australia **158 C4** 15.49S 136.38E
McBride Canada **56 F3** 53.18N 120.10W
McClintock Channel Canada **74 H4** 71.30N 103.00W
McClure Strait Canada **74 G4** 74.30N 117.00W
McCook U.S.A. **112 F5** 40.15N 100.45W
McCreary Canada **60 E1** 50.46N 99.30W
McFarlane *r.* Canada **60 C3** 59.13N 107.57W
McGivney Canada **72 B3** 46.22N 66.34W
McGrath U.S.A. **2 B4** 62.52N 155.37W
McGregor Bay *town* Canada **66 C6** 46.01N 81.46W
McKinley, Mount U.S.A. **74 C3** 63.05N 150.20W
McLennan Canada **59 B2** 55.42N 116.56W
McLeod *r.* Canada **59 C2** 54.09N 115.43W
McLeod Lake *town* Canada **56 F3** 54.59N 123.02W
McMurdo *research stn.* Antarctica **167 B1** 77.51S 166.37E
Mead, L. U.S.A. **112 D4** 36.10N 114.25W
Meadow Lake *town* Canada **60 B2** 54.08N 108.25W
Meadville U.S.A. **65 E1** 41.39N 80.09W
Meaford Canada **66 D4** 44.36N 80.36W
Mealy Mountains Canada **69 H4** 53.36N 58.36W
Meander River *town* Canada **59 B3** 59.03N 117.42W
Mecca Saudi Arabia **146 B3** 21.25N 39.47E
Medan Indonesia **154 B4** 3.35N 98.39E
Medanosa, Punta *c.* Argentina **123 C2** 48.08S 65.55W
Medellín Colombia **122 B7** 6.15N 75.36W
Medicine Hat Canada **59 D1** 50.03N 110.41W
Medina Saudi Arabia **146 B3** 24.31N 39.32E
Medina U.S.A. **66 F3** 43.13N 78.23W
Mediterranean Sea Africa/Europe **134 C6** 38.00N 10.00E
Meelpaeg Reservoir Canada **69 H3** 48.15N 56.36W
Meerut India **147 F3** 29.02N 77.45E
Meharry, Mt. Australia **158 A3** 23.01S 118.42E
Meiktila Myanmar **154 B8** 20.50N 95.53E
Meizhou China **153 L2** 24.20N 116.15E
Meknès Morocco **128 C8** 33.53N 5.30W
Mekong *r.* Asia **154 D6** 10.00N 106.20E
Mekong, Mouths of the Vietnam **154 D6** 10.00N 106.20E
Melaka Malaysia **154 C4** 2.11N 102.16E
Melbourne Australia **158 D2** 37.45S 144.58E
Meldrum Bay *town* Canada **65 E2** 45.55N 83.07W
Mélèzes, Rivière aux *r.* Canada **68 E5** 57.38N 70.12W
Melfort Canada **60 C2** 52.50N 104.37W
Melilla N. Africa **138 C1** 35.18N 2.57W
Melita Canada **60 D1** 49.16N 100.59W
Melitopol' Ukraine **139 G2** 46.51N 35.22E
Melrose Canada **72 D2** 45.16N 62.03W
Melville Canada **60 D1** 50.56N 102.49W
Melville, Lake Canada **69 H4** 53.37N 59.39W
Melville I. Australia **158 C4** 11.30S 131.00E
Melville Island Canada **74 H4** 75.14N 109.26W
Melville Peninsula Canada **75 J3** 68.09N 84.12W
Memberamo *r.* Indonesia **155 J3** 1.45S 137.25E
Memphis U.S.A. **113 H4** 35.05N 90.04W
Mendawai *r.* Indonesia **154 E3** 3.17S 113.20E
Mendoza Argentina **123 C3** 33.00S 68.52W
Menihek Canada **68 F4** 54.27N 66.34W
Menihek Lakes Canada **68 F4** 54.10N 66.32W
Menominee *r.* U.S.A. **65 D2** 45.06N 87.38W
Menomonee Falls *town* U.S.A. **65 C1** 43.10N 88.06W
Menomonie U.S.A. **64 C2** 44.53N 91.55W
Menongue Angola **129 E3** 14.38S 17.41E
Menorca *i.* Spain **138 D2** 40.06N 3.51E
Mentawai Is. Indonesia **154 B3** 2.50S 99.00E
Mentok Indonesia **154 D3** 2.04S 105.12E
Menzies, Mount Antarctica **167 K2** 73.26S 61.59E
Merasheen Island Canada **73 H3** 47.30N 54.15W
Merauke Indonesia **155 K2** 8.30S 140.22E
Merced U.S.A. **112 B4** 37.17N 120.29W
Mercy, Cape Canada **75 L3** 64.53N 63.32W
Mergui Myanmar **154 B6** 12.27N 98.37E
Mergui Archipelago Myanmar **154 B6** 11.38N 97.41E
Mérida Mexico **116 G5** 20.59N 89.39W
Mérida Spain **138 C1** 38.56N 6.20W
Mérida Venezuela **122 B7** 8.24N 71.08W
Mérida, Cordillera de *mts.* Venezuela **117 J2** 8.00N 71.30W
Meridian U.S.A. **113 I3** 32.21N 88.42W
Meron, Har *mtn.* Israel **150 A3** 32.59N 35.25E
Merowe Sudan **128 G6** 18.27N 31.51E
Merritt Canada **56 F2** 50.06N 120.46W
Mesopotamia *f.* Iraq **146 C4** 35.42N 42.19E
Messina Italy **138 E1** 38.11N 15.33E
Meta *r.* Colombia/Venezuela **122 C7** 6.10N 67.24W
Métabetchouan Canada **68 E3** 48.25N 71.53W
Metchosin Canada **57 V1** 48.21N 123.33W
Metlakatla U.S.A. **56 D3** 55.07N 131.34W
Metz France **138 D2** 49.07N 6.11E
Mexicali Mexico **116 A7** 32.26N 115.30W
Mexico C. America **116 D5** 20.00N 100.00W
Mexico, G. of N. America **116 F5** 25.00N 90.00W
Mexico City Mexico **116 E4** 19.25N 99.10W
Meymaneh Afghanistan **146 E4** 35.56N 64.45E
Mezen Russian Fed. **139 H4** 65.50N 44.16E
Mezen *r.* Russian Fed. **139 H4** 65.52N 44.11E
Mezquital *r.* Mexico **116 C5** 21.58N 105.30W
Miami U.S.A. **113 J2** 25.45N 80.10W
Miass Russian Fed. **139 J3** 54.58N 60.05E
Mica Creek *town* Canada **56 G3** 52.03N 118.34W
Michigan *d.* U.S.A. **113 I5** 45.00N 85.00W
Michigan, Lake U.S.A. **65 D1** 43.02N 87.18W
Michipicoten Island Canada **65 D2** 47.41N 85.48W
Michipicoten River *town* Canada **65 D2** 47.57N 84.50W
Michurinsk Russian Fed. **139 H3** 52.55N 40.30E
Midale Canada **60 D1** 49.23N 103.25W
Middle Arm Canada **73 G4** 49.42N 56.06W
Middle Bay *town* Canada **69 H3** 51.28N 57.29W
Middle Maitland Canada **66 C3** 43.53N 81.18W
Middlesbrough U.K. **138 C3** 54.34N 1.14W
Middleton Canada **72 C2** 44.56N 65.04W
Middletown U.S.A. **65 G1** 41.27N 74.25W
Midland Canada **66 E4** 44.44N 79.53W
Midland U.S.A. **112 F3** 32.00N 102.05W
Midmay Canada **66 C4** 44.02N 81.07W
Midway Is. Hawaiian Is. **162 N9** 28.15N 177.25W
Mikhaylovskiy Russian Fed. **152 D8** 51.41N 79.47E
Mikkwa *r.* Canada **59 C3** 58.21N 114.54W
Milan Italy **138 D2** 45.28N 9.11E
Mildura Australia **158 D2** 34.14S 142.13E
Miles City U.S.A. **112 E6** 46.24N 105.48W
Milford U.S.A. **72 A2** 44.58N 68.38W
Milk *r.* U.S.A. **112 E6** 47.55N 106.15W
Milk River *town* Canada **59 C1** 49.09N 112.05W
Millbrook Canada **64 Z3** 44.08N 78.27W
Mille Lacs *l.* U.S.A. **113 H6** 46.15N 93.40W
Mille Lacs, Lac des *l.* Canada **65 C3** 48.50N 90.22W
Millennium I. Kiribati **163 Q6** 10.00S 150.30W
Miller Lake *town* Canada **66 C5** 45.06N 81.26W
Millinocket U.S.A. **72 A2** 45.40N 68.43W
Mills Lake Canada **56 G5** 61.32N 118.22W
Milltown Canada **69 I2** 47.54N 55.47W
Milo U.S.A. **72 A2** 45.15N 68.59W
Milton N.S. Canada **72 C2** 44.04N 64.45W
Milton Ont. Canada **64 W2** 43.31N 79.53W
Milverton Canada **66 D3** 43.32N 80.56W
Milwaukee U.S.A. **113 I5** 43.03N 87.56W
Mīnāb Iran **146 D3** 27.09N 57.04E
Minaki Canada **64 B3** 49.59N 94.41W
Minas Channel Canada **72 C2** 45.09N 65.07W
Minatitlán Mexico **116 F4** 17.59N 94.32W
Mindanao *i.* Philippines **155 H5** 7.30N 125.00E
Minden Canada **66 F4** 44.56N 78.44W
Mindoro *i.* Philippines **154 G6** 13.00N 121.00E
Mindoro Str. Pacific Oc. **154 G6** 12.30N 120.10E
Mingan, Îles de Canada **68 G3** 50.12N 63.48W
Minipi Lake Canada **69 G4** 52.27N 60.47W
Minneapolis U.S.A. **113 H5** 44.55N 93.18W
Minnedosa Canada **60 E1** 50.15N 99.51W
Minnesota *d.* U.S.A. **113 H6** 46.00N 95.00W
Minnesota *r.* U.S.A. **64 B2** 44.55N 93.11W
Minnitaki Lake Canada **64 C3** 50.00N 91.53W
Minot U.S.A. **112 F6** 48.16N 101.19W
Minsk Belarus **138 F3** 53.53N 27.34E
Minto Canada **72 B3** 46.06N 66.05W
Minto, Lac *l.* Canada **68 D5** 57.30N 74.27W
Minto, Mount Antarctica **167 B2** 71.47S 169.48E
Miquelon Canada **68 C3** 49.24N 76.27W
Miquelon *i.* St. Pierre and Miquelon **73 G3** 46.58N 56.21W
Miramichi Canada **72 C3** 47.02N 65.27W
Mirbāţ Oman **146 D2** 17.02N 54.43E
Miri Malaysia **154 E4** 4.28N 114.00E
Mirim, Lagoa *l.* Brazil **123 D3** 33.10S 53.30W
Mirny *research stn.* Antarctica **167 L2** 66.33S 93.01E
Mirnyy Russian Fed. **143 N4** 62.25N 114.10E
Mirond Lake Canada **60 D2** 55.05N 102.45W
Mirpur Khas Pakistan **147 E3** 25.32N 69.04E
Miscou Island Canada **72 C3** 47.57N 64.30W
Misehkow *r.* Canada **65 C3** 51.26N 89.11W
Miskolc Hungary **138 F2** 48.06N 20.48E
Misoöl *i.* Indonesia **155 I3** 1.50S 130.10E
Misquah Hills U.S.A. **64 C2** 47.44N 91.23W
Misratah Libya **128 E8** 32.21N 15.04E
Missinaibi *r.* Canada **65 E3** 50.45N 81.31W
Missinipe Canada **60 C2** 55.35N 104.47W
Mission Canada **57 Y3** 49.09N 122.19W
Mississauga Canada **64 W2** 43.35N 79.37W
Mississippi *d.* U.S.A. **113 I3** 33.00N 90.00W
Mississippi *r.* U.S.A. **113 I2** 28.55N 89.05W
Mississippi Delta U.S.A. **113 I2** 29.00N 89.10W
Missoula U.S.A. **112 D6** 46.52N 114.00W
Missouri *d.* U.S.A. **113 H4** 39.00N 93.00W
Missouri *r.* U.S.A. **113 H4** 38.40N 90.20W
Mistanipisipou *r.* Canada **69 G3** 51.31N 61.52W
Mistassibi *r.* Canada **68 D3** 48.53N 72.15W
Mistassini Canada **68 D3** 48.54N 72.12W
Mistassini *r.* Canada **68 D3** 48.42N 72.22W
Mistassini, Lac *l.* Canada **68 D3** 51.01N 73.34W
Mistinibi, Lac *l.* Canada **68 G5** 56.04N 63.58W
Mistissini Canada **68 D3** 50.13N 73.48W
Misty Fiords National Monument Wilderness U.S.A. **56 D3** 55.37N 130.41W
Mitchell *r.* Australia **158 D4** 15.12S 141.40E
Mitchell Canada **66 C3** 43.28N 81.12W
Mitchell U.S.A. **112 G5** 43.40N 98.01W
Mitchell, Mt. U.S.A. **113 J4** 35.57N 82.16W
Mitchell's Brook *town* Canada **69 I2** 47.08N 53.33W
Mittimatalik Canada **75 K4** 72.35N 77.46W
Mitumba, Chaine des *mts.* Dem. Rep. Congo **129 F3** 11.46S 26.06E
Miyazaki Japan **153 O4** 31.58N 131.50E
Mobile U.S.A. **113 I3** 30.40N 88.05W
Mobile B. U.S.A. **113 I3** 30.30N 87.50W
Mobridge U.S.A. **112 F6** 45.31N 100.25W
Moçambique Mozambique **129 H3** 15.05S 40.41E
Moe Australia **158 D2** 38.12S 146.20E
Mogadishu Somalia **128 H5** 2.04N 45.20E
Mohawk *r.* U.S.A. **65 G1** 42.46N 73.44W
Moisie Canada **68 F3** 50.11N 66.06W
Moisie *r.* Canada **68 F3** 50.14N 66.05W
Moldova Europe **138 F2** 46.59N 28.55E
Molodezhnaya *research stn.* Antarctica **167 J2** 67.40S 45.51E
Molson Lake Canada **60 E2** 54.15N 96.56W
Moluccas *is.* Indonesia **162 H6** 2.00S 128.00E
Molucca Sea Pacific Oc. **155 H4** 2.00N 126.30E
Mombasa Kenya **128 G4** 3.59S 39.40E
Monaco Europe **138 D2** 43.44N 7.26E
Mona I. Puerto Rico **117 K4** 18.06N 67.54W
Mona Passage Dom. Rep. **117 K4** 18.10N 68.00W
Monashee Mountains Canada **56 G2** 51.17N 118.54W
Monclova Mexico **116 D6** 26.55N 101.20W
Moncton Canada **72 C3** 46.04N 64.47W
Mongolia Asia **152 I7** 46.30N 104.00E
Mongu Zambia **129 F3** 15.15S 23.08E
Monkton Canada **66 C3** 43.35N 81.05W
Monroe U.S.A. **113 H3** 32.31N 92.06W
Monrovia Liberia **128 B5** 6.20N 10.46W
Montague Canada **72 D3** 46.10N 62.39W
Montana *d.* U.S.A. **112 D6** 47.00N 110.00W
Montego Bay *town* Jamaica **117 I4** 18.27N 77.56W
Montemorelos Mexico **116 E6** 25.12N 99.50W
Montería Colombia **122 B7** 8.45N 75.54W
Monterrey Mexico **116 D6** 25.40N 100.20W
Montes Claros Brazil **122 E5** 16.45S 43.52W
Montevideo Uruguay **123 D3** 34.55S 56.10W
Montgomery U.S.A. **113 I3** 32.22N 86.20W
Mont-Joli *town* Canada **68 E3** 48.35N 68.12W
Mont-Laurier *town* Canada **68 D2** 46.33N 75.30W
Montmagny Canada **68 E2** 46.59N 70.34W
Montpelier U.S.A. **113 L5** 44.16N 72.34W
Montpellier France **138 D2** 43.37N 3.53E
Montréal Canada **68 D2** 45.32N 73.39W
Montreal *r.* Canada **65 F2** 47.08N 79.29W
Montreal Lake Canada **60 C2** 54.18N 105.39W
Montreal Lake *town* Canada **60 C2** 54.02N 105.49W
Montreal River *town* Canada **65 D2** 47.14N 84.38W
Montrose U.S.A. **112 E4** 38.29N 107.53W
Monts, Pointe des *pt.* Canada **72 B4** 49.18N 67.22W
Montserrat *i.* Leeward Is. **117 L4** 16.45N 62.14W
Monywa Myanmar **154 B8** 22.05N 95.13E
Moore, L. Australia **158 A3** 29.30S 117.30E
Moorhead U.S.A. **112 G6** 46.51N 96.44W
Moose *r.* Canada **65 E3** 51.20N 80.31W
Moose Factory *town* Canada **65 E3** 51.15N 80.38W
Moosehead Lake U.S.A. **68 E2** 45.42N 69.35W
Moose Jaw Canada **60 C1** 50.26N 105.33W
Moose Jaw *r.* Canada **60 C1** 50.33N 105.17W
Moose Mountain Creek *r.* Canada **60 D1** 49.13N 102.13W
Moosomin Canada **60 D1** 50.09N 101.41W
Moosonee Canada **65 E3** 51.16N 80.40W
Mopti Mali **128 C6** 14.30N 4.11W
Mora Sweden **138 E4** 61.00N 14.32E
Morden Canada **60 E1** 49.12N 98.07W
Moree Australia **159 D3** 29.29S 149.53E
Morelia Mexico **116 D4** 19.40N 101.11W
Morena, Sierra *mts.* Spain **138 C1** 37.57N 6.06W
Moresby Island Canada **57 W2** 53.06N 132.07W
Morgan City U.S.A. **113 H2** 29.41N 91.13W
Morioka Japan **153 Q5** 39.43N 141.10E
Morocco Africa **128 C8** 31.57N 5.40W
Moro Gulf Philippines **155 G5** 6.30N 123.20E
Morogoro Tanzania **128 G4** 6.47S 37.40E
Mörön Mongolia **152 I7** 49.36N 100.08E
Morondava Madagascar **129 H2** 20.18S 44.17E
Moroni Comoros **129 H3** 11.39S 43.14E
Morotai *i.* Indonesia **155 H4** 2.10N 128.30E
Morris Canada **60 E1** 49.21N 97.23W
Morris Jesup, Cape Greenland **166 I1** 83.63N 32.51W
Morriston Canada **64 V1** 43.27N 80.07W
Morro, Punta *c.* Chile **123 B4** 27.06S 71.00W
Morrosquillo, G. of Colombia **117 I2** 9.30N 75.50W
Moscow Russian Fed. **139 G3** 55.45N 37.38E
Mosjøen Norway **138 E4** 65.51N 13.12E
Mosquitos, Gulf of Panama **117 H2** 9.00N 81.00W
Mosquitos Coast *f.* Nicaragua **117 H3** 13.00N 84.00W
Mossoró Brazil **122 F6** 5.10S 37.20W
Mostar Bosnia **138 E2** 43.20N 17.49E
Mosul Iraq **146 C4** 36.18N 43.05E
Mouchalagane *r.* Canada **68 E3** 51.59N 69.26W
Moulmein Myanmar **154 B7** 16.30N 97.40E
Moundou Chad **128 E5** 8.36N 16.05E
Mount Brydges *town* Canada **66 C2** 42.54N 81.30W
Mount Clemens *town* U.S.A. **66 B2** 42.36N 82.53W
Mount Desert Island U.S.A. **72 A2** 44.21N 68.32W
Mount Forest *town* Canada **66 D3** 43.59N 80.44W
Mount Gambier *town* Australia **158 D2** 37.51S 140.50E
Mount Isa *town* Australia **158 C3** 20.50S 139.29E
Mount Jewett *town* U.S.A. **66 F1** 41.44N 78.38W
Mount Kenya Kenya **128 G4** 0.08S 37.18E
Mount Pearl *town* Canada **69 I2** 47.31N 52.48W
Mount Pleasant *town* U.S.A. **65 D1** 43.36N 84.46W
Mount Revelstoke National Park Canada **59 B1** 51.05N 118.02W
Mount Vernon *town* U.S.A. **57 Y1** 48.25N 122.20W
Mozambique Africa **129 G2** 20.09S 34.14E
Mozambique Channel Africa **129 H2** 20.15S 40.16E
Mtwara Tanzania **129 H3** 10.19S 40.09E
Muar Malaysia **154 C4** 2.01N 102.35E

N

Nyasa, Lake Africa **129 G3** 9.59S 34.05E
Nyiragongo *mtn.* Dem. Rep. Congo **128 F4** 1.52S 29.25E
Nyurba Russian Fed. **143 N4** 63.18N 118.28E

O

Oahe, L. U.S.A. **112 F6** 45.45N 100.20W
Oahu *i.* Hawaiian Is. **163 P9** 21.30N 158.00W
Oak Bay *town* Canada **57 W1** 48.27N 123.18W
Oak Harbor U.S.A. **57 X1** 48.18N 122.38W
Oakland U.S.A. **112 B4** 37.50N 122.15W
Oakville Canada **64 W1** 43.27N 79.40W
Oates Land *f.* Antarctica **167 B2** 70.13S 157.04E
Oaxaca Mexico **116 E4** 17.05N 96.41W
Ob *r.* Russian Fed. **142 I4** 66.50N 69.00E
Ob, G. of Russian Fed. **142 J4** 68.30N 74.00E
Oba Canada **65 D3** 49.04N 84.06W
Obed Canada **59 B2** 53.33N 117.13W
Obi *i.* Indonesia **155 H3** 1.45S 127.30E
Occidental, Cordillera *mts.* Chile **122 C5** 20.00S 69.00W
Occidental, Cordillera *mts.* Colombia **122 B7** 5.00N 76.15W
Occidental, Cordillera *mts.* Peru **122 B5** 14.00S 74.00W
Ocean Falls *town* Canada **56 E3** 52.21N 127.41W
October Revolution *i.* Russian Fed. **143 L5** 79.30N 96.00E
Odense Denmark **138 E3** 55.24N 10.23E
Oder *r.* Germany/Poland **138 E2** 49.54N 18.19E
Odessa Ukraine **138 G2** 46.28N 30.39E
Odessa U.S.A. **112 F3** 31.50N 102.23W
Ogasawara-shoto *is.* Japan **162 J9** 27.00N 142.10E
Ogbomosho Nigeria **128 D5** 8.08N 4.14E
Ogden U.S.A. **112 D5** 41.14N 111.59W
Ogdensburg U.S.A. **65 G2** 44.41N 75.30W
Ogilvie *r.* Canada **74 E3** 65.50N 137.13W
Ogilvie Mountains Canada **74 D3** 65.14N 140.00W
Ogoki *r.* Canada **65 D3** 51.40N 85.58W
O'Higgins, L. Chile **123 B2** 48.53S 73.10W
Ohio *d.* U.S.A. **113 J5** 40.00N 83.00W
Ohio *r.* U.S.A. **113 I4** 37.07N 89.10W
Oil City U.S.A. **113 K5** 41.26N 79.30W
Ojinaga Mexico **116 D6** 29.35N 104.26W
Ojos del Salado *mtn.* Chile/Argentina **123 C4** 27.05S 68.05W
Okak Islands Canada **69 G5** 57.27N 61.20W
Okanagan Lake Canada **56 G2** 49.58N 119.30W
Okanogan U.S.A. **56 G2** 48.22N 119.35W
Okanogan *r.* U.S.A. **112 B6** 47.45N 120.05W
Okavango Delta *f.* Botswana **129 F3** 19.42S 23.02E
Okayama Japan **153 O4** 34.40N 133.54E
Okeechobee, L. U.S.A. **113 J2** 27.00N 80.45W
Okefenokee Swamp *f.* U.S.A. **113 J3** 30.40N 82.40W
Okha Russian Fed. **143 Q3** 53.35N 142.50E
Okhotsk Russian Fed. **143 Q3** 59.20N 143.15E
Okhotsk, Sea of Russian Fed. **143 Q3** 55.00N 150.00E
Okinawa *i.* Japan **153 N3** 26.30N 128.00E
Oki-shoto *is.* Japan **153 O5** 36.10N 133.10E
Oklahoma *d.* U.S.A. **112 G4** 35.00N 97.00W
Oklahoma City U.S.A. **112 G4** 35.28N 97.33W
Okotoks Canada **59 C1** 50.44N 113.59W
Oktyabr'skiy Russian Fed. **139 I3** 54.28N 53.31E
Öland *i.* Sweden **138 E3** 56.57N 17.02E
Olbia Italy **138 D2** 40.55N 9.30E
Olcott U.S.A. **64 Y1** 43.20N 78.42W
Old Crow Canada **74 E3** 67.36N 139.54W
Olds Canada **59 C1** 51.48N 114.06W
Old Wives Lake Canada **60 C1** 50.05N 106.00W
Olean U.S.A. **113 K5** 42.05N 78.26W
O'Leary Canada **72 C3** 46.42N 64.15W
Olekminsk Russian Fed. **143 O4** 60.25N 120.00E
Olenek Russian Fed. **143 N4** 68.38N 112.15E
Olenek *r.* Russian Fed. **143 O5** 73.00N 120.00E
Olga, Lac *l.* Canada **68 C3** 49.47N 77.10W
Oliver Canada **59 B1** 49.10N 119.34W
Olomane *r.* Canada **72 E5** 50.14N 60.38W
Olongapo Philippines **154 G7** 14.52N 120.16E
Olsztyn Poland **138 F3** 53.47N 20.29E
Olympia U.S.A. **112 B6** 47.02N 122.53W
Olympic National Park U.S.A. **56 F1** 47.39N 123.31W
Olympus, Mount U.S.A. **56 F1** 47.45N 123.47W
Olympus, Mt. Cyprus **139 G1** 34.55N 32.52E
Omaha U.S.A. **112 G5** 41.15N 96.00W
Oman Asia **146 D2** 18.15N 53.34E
Oman, Gulf of Asia **146 D3** 25.37N 56.49E
Omdurman Sudan **128 G6** 15.38N 32.28E
Omemee Canada **64 Y3** 44.18N 78.33W
Omineca Mountains Canada **56 E4** 57.27N 126.24W
Omolon Russian Fed. **143 S4** 65.13N 160.34E
Omolon *r.* Russian Fed. **143 R4** 68.50N 158.30E
Omsk Russian Fed. **142 J3** 55.00N 73.22E
Onega, Lake Russian Fed. **139 G4** 62.10N 34.47E
Oneida Lake U.S.A. **65 G1** 43.11N 75.52W
Oneonta U.S.A. **65 G1** 42.27N 75.04W
Ongole India **147 G2** 15.32N 80.02E
Ono-i-Lau *i.* Fiji **162 N4** 19.00S 178.30W
Onondaga Canada **64 V1** 43.07N 80.07W
Ontario *d.* Canada **65 C3** 51.51N 88.00W
Ontario, Lake Canada/U.S.A. **65 F1** 43.31N 77.57W
Ootsa Lake Canada **56 E3** 53.50N 126.13W
Ootsa Lake *town* Canada **56 E3** 53.49N 126.07W
Opasquia Canada **64 B4** 53.15N 93.34W
Opeongo Lake Canada **66 F5** 45.41N 78.22W
Opinaca *r.* Canada **68 C4** 52.44N 76.09W
Opinaca, Réservoir Canada **68 C4** 52.40N 76.00W
Opiscotéo, Lac *l.* Canada **68 E4** 53.22N 68.23W
Opole Poland **138 E3** 50.40N 17.56E
Oporto Portugal **138 C2** 41.11N 8.36W
Opportunity U.S.A. **57 G1** 47.39N 117.14W
Oradea Romania **138 F2** 47.04N 21.57E
Oran Algeria **128 C8** 35.42N 0.38W
Orange Australia **158 D2** 33.19S 149.07E
Orange *r.* Namibia/R.S.A. **129 E2** 28.36S 16.28E
Orange, Cabo *c.* Brazil **122 D7** 4.25N 51.32W
Orangeburg U.S.A. **113 J3** 33.28N 80.53W
Orangeville Canada **64 V2** 43.55N 80.06W
Orcadas *research stn.* S. Atlantic Ocean **167 G2** 60.44S 44.44W
Orcas Island Canada **57 X2** 48.40N 122.56W
Orchila *i.* Venezuela **117 K3** 11.52N 66.10W
Ord, Mt. Australia **158 B4** 17.19S 125.30E
Ordu Turkey **139 G2** 40.59N 37.53E
Örebro Sweden **138 E3** 59.16N 15.14E
Oregon *d.* U.S.A. **112 B5** 44.00N 120.00W
Orel Russian Fed. **139 G3** 52.58N 36.05E
Orenburg Russian Fed. **139 I3** 51.46N 55.05E
Oriental, Cordillera *mts.* Colombia **122 B7** 5.00N 74.30W
Oriental, Cordillera *mts.* Bolivia/Peru **122 B5** 14.00S 70.00W
Orillia Canada **66 E4** 44.36N 79.25W
Orinoco *r.* Venezuela **122 C7** 9.00N 61.30W
Orinoco Delta *f.* Venezuela **122 C7** 9.00N 61.30W
Oristano Italy **138 D1** 39.56N 8.35E
Orizaba Mexico **116 E4** 18.51N 97.08W
Orkney Islands U.K. **138 C3** 59.06N 3.20W
Orlando U.S.A. **113 J2** 28.33N 81.21W
Orléans France **138 D2** 47.55N 1.54E
Ormoc Philippines **155 G6** 11.01N 124.36E
Oromocto Canada **72 B2** 45.50N 66.29W
Oromocto Lake Canada **72 B2** 45.32N 67.01W
Orono U.S.A. **72 A2** 44.54N 68.40W
Oroville U.S.A. **59 B1** 48.56N 119.26W
Orsha Belarus **138 G3** 54.30N 30.26E
Orsk Russian Fed. **139 I3** 51.07N 58.33E
Oruro Bolivia **122 C5** 18.05S 67.00W
Osaka Japan **153 P4** 34.40N 135.30E
Osa Pen. Costa Rica **117 H2** 8.20N 83.30W
Osgoode Canada **65 G2** 45.06N 75.37W
Oshakati Namibia **129 E3** 17.45S 15.43E
Oshawa Canada **64 Y2** 43.54N 78.51W
Oshkosh U.S.A. **65 C2** 44.01N 88.32W
Osijek Croatia **138 E2** 45.35N 18.42E
Oskaloosa U.S.A. **64 B1** 41.18N 92.39W
Oslo Norway **138 E3** 59.55N 10.46E
Osorno Chile **123 B2** 40.35S 73.14W
Osoyoos Canada **56 G2** 49.02N 119.29W
Ossa, Mt. Australia **158 D1** 41.52S 146.04E
Ossokmanuan Lake Canada **68 F4** 53.16N 64.41W
Östersund Sweden **138 E4** 63.11N 14.39E
Ostrava Czech Rep. **138 E2** 49.51N 18.17E
Oswego U.S.A. **65 F1** 43.27N 76.31W
Otish, Monts Canada **68 E4** 52.28N 70.40W
Otoskwin *r.* Canada **65 C3** 51.55N 88.53W
Ottawa Canada **65 G2** 45.25N 75.40W
Ottawa *r.* Canada **65 F2** 45.28N 74.16W
Ottawa Islands Canada **68 B5** 59.30N 80.30W
Otter Rapids *town* Canada **65 E3** 50.10N 81.39W
Ottumwa U.S.A. **64 B1** 41.03N 92.25W
Otway, Cape Australia **158 D2** 38.51S 143.33E
Ouachita *r.* U.S.A. **113 H3** 31.52N 91.48W
Ouachita Mts. U.S.A. **113 H3** 34.40N 94.30W
Ouagadougou Burkina **128 C6** 12.22N 1.31W
Ouargla Algeria **128 D8** 31.56N 5.20E
Ouesso Congo **128 E5** 1.36N 16.04E
Ouest, Pointe de l' *pt.* Canada **72 C4** 49.51N 64.31W
Oulu Finland **138 F4** 65.01N 25.30E
Outardes *r.* Canada **68 E3** 49.07N 68.23W
Outardes Quatre, Réservoir Canada **68 E3** 50.11N 69.12W
Outer Hebrides *is.* U.K. **138 C3** 57.53N 7.21W
Outlook Canada **60 C1** 51.29N 107.03W
Oviedo Spain **138 C2** 43.22N 5.50W
Owatonna U.S.A. **64 B2** 44.06N 93.14W
Owensboro U.S.A. **113 I4** 37.46N 87.07W
Owen Sound Canada **66 D4** 44.36N 80.55W
Owen Sound *town* Canada **66 D4** 44.34N 80.56W
Owen Stanley Range *mts.* P.N.G. **155 L2** 9.30S 148.00E
Owl *r.* Canada **61 F3** 57.49N 92.52W
Oxbow Canada **60 D1** 49.14N 102.12W
Oxford Canada **72 D2** 45.43N 63.53W
Oxford U.K. **138 C3** 51.45N 1.15W
Oxford House *town* Canada **60 F2** 54.53N 95.21W
Oxford Lake Canada **60 F2** 54.52N 95.47W
Oxnard U.S.A. **112 C3** 34.12N 119.11W
Oxtongue Lake *town* Canada **66 F5** 45.21N 78.56W
Oyen Canada **59 D1** 51.21N 110.28W
Ozark Plateau U.S.A. **113 H4** 36.00N 93.35W

P

Pachuca Mexico **116 E5** 20.10N 98.44W
Pacific Ocean 162-163
Pacific Rim National Park Canada **56 E2** 48.42N 124.52W
Padang Indonesia **154 C3** 0.55N 100.21E
Padangpanjang Indonesia **154 C3** 0.30N 100.26E
Padre I. U.S.A. **112 G2** 27.00N 97.20W
Pagadian Philippines **155 G5** 7.50N 123.30E
Pagan *i.* N. Mariana Is. **162 J8** 18.08N 145.46E
Painesville U.S.A. **66 C1** 41.43N 81.15W
Paisley Canada **66 C4** 44.18N 81.17W
Pakanbaru Indonesia **154 C4** 0.34N 101.30E
Pakesley Canada **66 D5** 45.55N 80.31W
Pakistan Asia **146 E3** 28.01N 64.37E
Pakokku Myanmar **154 B8** 21.21N 95.07E
Pakxé Laos **154 D7** 15.05N 105.50E
Palana Russian Fed. **143 R3** 59.05N 159.59E
Palangkaraya Indonesia **154 E3** 2.18S 113.55E
Palatka Russian Fed. **143 R4** 60.08N 150.56E
Palau Pacific Oc. **155 I5** 7.00N 134.25E
Palawan *i.* Philippines **154 F5** 9.30N 118.30E
Palembang Indonesia **154 C3** 2.59S 104.50E
Palermo Italy **138 E1** 38.07N 13.21E
Palestine *f.* Asia **150 A2** 31.40N 35.10E
Pali India **147 F3** 25.46N 73.26E
Palikir Fed. States of Micronesia **162 K7** 6.55N 158.10E
Palk Strait India/Sri Lanka **147 F1** 9.36N 79.18E
Palma de Mallorca Spain **138 D1** 39.35N 2.40E
Palmas, C. Liberia **127 C5** 4.30N 7.55W
Palmer *research stn.* Antarctica **167 F2** 64.46S 64.05W
Palmer Land *f.* Antarctica **167 F2** 69.37S 66.18W
Palmerston Canada **66 D3** 43.50N 80.52W
Palmerston I. Cook Is. **162 O5** 18.04S 163.10W
Palmerston North New Zealand **159 G1** 40.21S 175.37E
Palmira Colombia **122 B7** 3.33N 76.17W
Palmyra I. Pacific Oc. **162 O7** 5.52N 162.05W
Palopo Indonesia **154 G3** 3.01S 120.12E
Palu Indonesia **154 F3** 0.54N 119.52E
Pamirs *mts.* Asia **147 F4** 38.39N 72.48E
Pampa U.S.A. **112 F4** 35.32N 100.58W
Pampas *f.* Argentina **123 C3** 35.00S 63.00W
Pamplona Spain **138 C2** 42.49N 1.39W
Panache, Lake Canada **66 C6** 46.16N 81.20W
Panaji India **147 F2** 15.30N 73.50E
Panama C. America **117 H2** 9.00N 80.00W
Panamá, G. of Panama **117 I2** 8.30N 79.00W
Panama, Isthmus of *f.* C. America **109 K2** 9.00N 80.00W
Panama Canal Panama **117 I2** 9.21N 79.54W
Panama City Panama **117 I2** 8.57N 79.30W
Panama City U.S.A. **113 I3** 30.10N 85.41W
Panay *i.* Philippines **155 G6** 11.10N 122.30E
Panevėžys Lithuania **138 F3** 55.44N 24.23E
Pangkalanbuun Indonesia **154 E3** 2.43S 111.38E
Pangkalpinang Indonesia **154 D3** 2.05S 106.09E
Pangman Canada **60 C1** 49.39N 104.39W
Pangnirtung Canada **75 L3** 66.03N 65.48W
Pangody Russian Fed. **142 J4** 65.48N 74.27E
Papeete French Polynesia **163 Q5** 17.30S 149.31W
Papua, G. of P.N.G. **155 K2** 8.50S 145.00E
Papua New Guinea Australia **155 L2** 6.00S 148.00E
Paracel Is. S. China Sea **154 E7** 16.20N 112.00E
Paradise Hill *town* Canada **60 B2** 53.32N 109.27W
Paradise River *town* Canada **69 H4** 53.26N 57.14W
Paraguay *r.* Argentina/Paraguay **123 D4** 27.30S 58.50W
Paraguay S. America **123 D4** 23.00S 58.00W
Paraíba *r.* Brazil **123 E4** 21.45S 41.10W
Paramaribo Suriname **122 D7** 5.52N 55.14W
Paraná Argentina **123 C3** 31.45S 60.30W
Paraná *r.* Argentina **123 D3** 34.00S 58.30W
Paranã *r.* Brazil **123 D4** 12.30S 48.10W
Paranaíba *r.* Brazil **122 D5** 20.00S 51.00W
Paranapanema *r.* Brazil **123 D4** 22.30S 53.03W
Pardo *r.* Brazil **123 D4** 21.56S 52.07W
Parecis, Serra dos *mts.* Brazil **122 C5** 13.30S 60.00W
Parent Canada **68 D2** 47.55N 74.37W
Parepare Indonesia **154 F3** 4.03S 119.40E
Paria Pen. Venezuela **117 L3** 10.45N 62.30W
Paris Canada **66 D3** 43.11N 80.24W
Paris France **138 D2** 48.52N 2.21E
Parkes Australia **158 D2** 33.09S 148.10E
Park Falls *town* U.S.A. **65 C2** 45.56N 90.26W
Parkhill Canada **66 C3** 43.09N 81.41W
Parksville Canada **56 E2** 49.19N 124.19W
Parma Italy **138 E2** 44.48N 10.19E
Parnaíba Brazil **122 E6** 2.58S 41.46W
Parnaíba *r.* Brazil **122 E6** 3.00S 42.00W
Pärnu Estonia **138 F3** 58.23N 24.30E
Parrsboro Canada **72 C2** 45.24N 64.20W
Parry, Cape Canada **74 F4** 70.12N 124.31W
Parry, Lac *l.* Canada **68 D5** 59.43N 75.19W
Parry Islands Canada **74 G4** 76.50N 111.03W
Parry Sound *town* Canada **66 D5** 45.21N 80.02W
Pasadena Canada **73 G4** 49.02N 57.36W
Pasadena U.S.A. **112 C3** 34.10N 118.09W
Pascagama *r.* Canada **68 D3** 48.38N 75.34W
Pasig Philippines **154 G6** 14.30N 120.54E
Pasquia Hills Canada **60 D2** 53.05N 103.12W
Pasto Colombia **122 B7** 1.12N 77.17W
Patagonia *f.* Argentina **123 C2** 45.00S 68.00W
Paterson U.S.A. **113 L5** 40.55N 74.10W
Pathfinder Resr. U.S.A. **112 E5** 42.25N 106.55W
Patna India **147 G3** 25.35N 85.16E
Patos, Lagoa dos *l.* Brazil **123 D3** 31.00S 51.10W
Patos de Minas Brazil **122 E5** 18.35S 46.32W
Patras Greece **138 F1** 38.14N 21.45E
Patten U.S.A. **72 A2** 45.59N 68.27W
Pattullo, Mount Canada **56 D4** 56.10N 129.39W
Paulatuk Canada **74 F3** 69.20N 123.47W
Paulo Afonso Brazil **122 F6** 9.25S 38.15W
Pavlodar Kazakhstan **142 J3** 52.21N 76.59E
Payne, Lac *l.* Canada **68 D5** 59.33N 74.35W
Peace *r.* Canada **59 D3** 58.54N 111.50W
Peace Point *town* Canada **59 C3** 59.10N 112.23W
Peace River *town* Canada **59 B3** 56.15N 117.17W
Peachland Canada **56 G2** 49.47N 119.45W
Peale, Mt. U.S.A. **112 E4** 38.26N 109.14W
Pearl *r.* U.S.A. **113 I3** 30.15N 89.25W
Peary Channel Canada **74 H4** 79.30N 100.30W
Peawanuck Canada **65 D4** 55.01N 85.23W
Pechora *r.* Russian Fed. **142 H4** 68.10N 54.00E
Pechora G. Russian Fed. **142 H4** 69.00N 56.00E
Pecos U.S.A. **112 F3** 31.25N 103.30W
Pecos *r.* U.S.A. **112 F2** 29.45N 101.25W
Pécs Hungary **138 E2** 46.05N 18.13E
Pedro Juan Caballero Paraguay **123 D4** 22.30S 55.44W
Peel *d.* Canada **64 W2** 43.46N 79.45W
Peel *r.* Canada **74 E3** 68.03N 134.26W
Peerless Lake *town* Canada **59 C3** 56.40N 114.34W
Peers Canada **59 B2** 53.40N 116.00W
Pefferlaw Canada **64 X3** 44.18N 79.16W
Pegasus B. New Zealand **159 G1** 43.15S 173.00E
Peggy's Cove *town* Canada **72 D2** 44.31N 63.54W
Pegu Myanmar **154 B7** 17.18N 96.28E
Peipus, Lake Estonia/Russian Fed. **138 F3** 58.38N 27.28E
Pekalongan Indonesia **154 D2** 6.54S 109.37E
Pelee Island Canada **66 B1** 41.45N 82.36W
Pelee Point Canada **66 B1** 41.54N 82.30W
Peleng *i.* Indonesia **155 G3** 1.30S 123.10E
Pelican Narrows *town* Canada **60 D2** 55.12N 102.54W
Pelleluhu Is. P.N.G. **155 K3** 1.09S 144.23E
Pelly *r.* Canada **56 C5** 62.20N 134.00W
Pelly Bay *town* Canada **74 J3** 68.39N 89.44W
Pelly Mountains Canada **56 C5** 61.30N 132.00W
Pelotas Brazil **123 D3** 31.45S 52.20W
Pemadumcook Lake U.S.A. **72 A2** 45.40N 68.54W
Pemba Mozambique **129 H3** 12.59S 40.32E
Pemba Island Tanzania **128 G4** 5.25S 39.46E
Pemberton Canada **56 F2** 50.20N 122.49W
Pembina *r.* Canada **59 C2** 53.12N 115.59W
Pembina *r.* U.S.A. **60 E1** 48.58N 97.14W
Pembroke Canada **65 F2** 45.49N 77.06W
Peña Nevada, Cerro *mtn.* Mexico **116 E5** 23.49N 99.51W
Penas, Golfo de *g.* Chile **123 B2** 47.20S 75.00W
Penetanguishene Canada **66 E4** 44.46N 79.56W
Peninsular Malaysia *d.* Malaysia **154 C4** 5.00N 102.00E
Pennant Point Canada **72 D2** 44.26N 63.39W
Pennfield Canada **72 B2** 45.07N 66.44W
Pennines *hills* U.K. **138 C3** 54.23N 2.18W
Pennsylvania *d.* U.S.A. **113 K5** 41.00N 78.00W
Penobscot *r.* U.S.A. **72 A2** 44.35N 68.53W
Pensacola U.S.A. **113 I3** 30.30N 87.12W
Pensacola Mountains Antarctica **167 F1** 85.24S 73.42W
Pentecôte *r.* Canada **68 F3** 49.45N 67.09W
Penticton Canada **56 G2** 49.30N 119.35W
Penza Russian Fed. **139 H3** 53.12N 45.01E
Penzhina, G. of Russian Fed. **143 S4** 61.00N 163.00E
Peoria U.S.A. **113 I5** 40.43N 89.38W
Percé Canada **68 F3** 48.31N 64.14W
Pereira Colombia **122 B7** 4.47N 75.46W
Péribonca *r.* Canada **68 D3** 48.44N 72.04W
Perija, Sierra de *mts.* Venezuela **117 J2** 9.00N 73.00W
Perito Moreno Argentina **123 B2** 46.35N 71.00W
Perlas Pt. Nicaragua **117 H3** 12.23N 83.30W
Perm' Russian Fed. **139 I3** 58.01N 56.14E
Perpignan France **138 D2** 42.42N 2.54E
Perth Australia **158 A2** 31.58S 115.49E
Perth Canada **65 F2** 44.54N 76.15W
Perth-Andover Canada **72 B3** 46.44N 67.42W
Peru S. America **122 B5** 10.00S 75.00W
Peru-Chile Trench *f.* Pacific Oc. **81 K3** 18.00S 75.00W
Perugia Italy **138 E2** 43.07N 12.23E
Pescara Italy **138 E2** 42.27N 14.12E
Peshawar Pakistan **147 F4** 34.01N 71.40E
Petah Tiqwa Israel **150 A3** 32.05N 34.53E
Petawawa Canada **65 F2** 45.54N 77.17W
Peterborough Canada **66 F4** 44.18N 78.20W
Peter Pond Lake Canada **60 B2** 55.59N 108.48W
Petersburg U.S.A. **74 E2** 56.49N 132.56W
Petersville U.S.A. **2 B4** 62.33N 150.50W
Petitcodiac Canada **72 C2** 45.55N 65.11W
Petit Mécatina *r.* Canada **69 H3** 50.40N 59.25W
Petit Mécatina, Île du *i.* Canada **72 F5** 50.34N 59.18W
Petitot *r.* Canada **59 A4** 60.15N 123.29W
Petoskey U.S.A. **65 D2** 45.22N 84.58W
Petrolia Canada **66 B2** 42.52N 82.08W
Petrolina Brazil **122 E6** 9.22S 40.30W
Petropavlovsk Kazakhstan **142 I3** 54.53N 69.13E
Petropavlovsk-Kamchatskiy Russian Fed. **143 R3** 53.03N 158.43E
Petrozavodsk Russian Fed. **138 G4** 61.48N 34.19E
Pevek Russian Fed. **143 T4** 69.40N 170.16E
Phan Thiêt Vietnam **154 D6** 10.56N 108.06E
Phatthalung Thailand **154 C5** 7.38N 100.05E
Phayao Thailand **154 B7** 19.10N 99.55E
Phet Buri Thailand **154 B6** 13.01N 99.55E
Philadelphia U.S.A. **113 K4** 39.55N 75.10W
Philippines Asia **155 G6** 13.00N 123.00E
Philippine Trench *f.* Pacific Oc. **80 F4** 10.30N 126.46E
Phitsanulok Thailand **154 C7** 16.50N 100.15E
Phnom Penh Cambodia **154 C6** 11.35N 104.55E
Phoenix U.S.A. **112 D3** 33.30N 111.55W
Phoenix Is. Kiribati **162 N6** 4.00S 172.00W
Phôngsali Laos **154 C8** 21.40N 102.06E
Phrae Thailand **154 C7** 18.07N 100.09E
Phuket Thailand **154 B5** 8.00N 98.28E
Pic *r.* Canada **65 D3** 48.39N 86.17W
Pickering Canada **64 X2** 43.51N 79.03W
Pickle Lake *town* Canada **65 C3** 51.27N 90.12W
Picton Canada **65 F1** 43.59N 77.09W
Pictou Canada **72 D2** 45.39N 62.44W
Pictou Island Canada **72 D2** 45.49N 62.31W
Picture Butte Canada **59 C1** 49.52N 112.46W
Piedras Negras Mexico **116 D6** 28.40N 100.32W
Pierre U.S.A. **112 F5** 44.23N 100.20W
Pietermaritzburg R.S.A. **129 G2** 29.36S 30.23E
Pietersburg R.S.A. **129 F2** 23.54S 29.27E
Pigeon *r.* Canada/U.S.A. **65 C3** 48.01N 89.44W

Q

R

T

Tônlé Sab *l.* Cambodia **154 C6** 12.50N 104.00E
Toowoomba Australia **159 E3** 27.35S 151.54E
Topeka U.S.A. **113 G4** 39.03N 95.41W
Torbay Canada **73 I3** 47.40N 52.45W
Torch *r.* Canada **60 D2** 53.51N 103.05W
Tori-shima *i.* Japan **162 J10** 30.28N 140.18E
Torngat Mountains Canada **68 F5** 59.48N 64.28W
Tornio Finland **138 F4** 65.50N 24.11E
Toronto Canada **64 X2** 43.40N 79.23W
Torrens, L. Australia **158 C2** 31.00S 137.50E
Torreón Mexico **116 D6** 25.34N 103.25W
Torres Str. Pacific Oc. **158 D4** 10.30S 142.20E
Tórshavn Faroe Is. **138 C4** 62.00N 6.47W
Toruń Poland **138 E3** 53.01N 18.37E
Tottori Japan **153 O5** 35.32N 134.12E
Toubkal, Jbel *mts.* Morocco **128 C8** 31.03N 7.57W
Toulnustouc *r.* Canada **72 A4** 49.45N 68.17W
Toulon France **138 D2** 43.08N 5.56E
Toulouse France **138 D2** 43.37N 1.26E
Toungoo Myanmar **154 B7** 18.55N 96.25E
Tours France **138 D2** 47.23N 0.42E
Townsville Australia **158 D4** 19.13S 146.48E
Towori G. Indonesia **155 G3** 2.00S 122.30E
Toyama Japan **153 P5** 36.42N 137.14E
Trabzon Turkey **139 G2** 40.59N 39.44E
Tracadie-Sheila Canada **72 C3** 47.30N 64.55W
Tracy Canada **72 B2** 45.41N 66.41W
Trail Canada **56 G2** 49.06N 117.43W
Trangan *i.* Indonesia **155 I2** 6.30S 134.15E
Transantarctic Mountains Antarctica **167 B1** 78.00S 150.00E
Transylvanian Alps *mts.* Romania **138 F2** 45.15N 22.25E
Traralgon Australia **158 D2** 38.12S 146.34E
Traverse City U.S.A. **113 I5** 44.46N 85.38W
Tremblant, Mont Canada **65 G2** 46.15N 74.34W
Trento Italy **138 E2** 46.04N 11.08E
Trenton Canada **72 D2** 45.37N 62.39W
Trenton U.S.A. **113 L5** 40.15N 74.43W
Trent-Severn Waterway Canada **66 E4** 44.28N 79.09W
Trepassey Canada **69 I2** 46.40N 53.02W
Tres Picos *mtn.* Argentina **123 C3** 38.13S 61.50W
Trieste Italy **138 E2** 45.39N 13.46E
Trincomalee Sri Lanka **147 G1** 8.37N 81.13E
Trindade *i.* Atlantic Oc. **121 H4** 20.30S 29.15W
Trinidad Bolivia **122 C5** 15.00S 64.50W
Trinidad *i.* S. America **117 L3** 10.20N 61.10W
Trinidad U.S.A. **112 F4** 37.11N 104.31W
Trinidad & Tobago S. America **117 L3** 10.30N 61.20W
Trinity Canada **69 I3** 48.59N 53.55W
Trinity Bay Canada **69 I2** 47.47N 53.37W
Tripoli Lebanon **150 A4** 34.26N 35.52E
Tripoli Libya **128 E8** 32.52N 13.08E
Tristan da Cunha *i.* Atlantic Oc. **80 A2** 38.00S 12.00W
Triton Canada **69 I3** 49.31N 55.37W
Trobriand Is. P.N.G. **155 M2** 8.35S 151.05E
Trois-Pistoles Canada **68 E3** 48.05N 69.12W
Trois-Rivières *town* Canada **68 D2** 46.21N 72.35W
Troitsko-Pechorsk Russian Fed. **139 I4** 62.43N 56.10E
Tromsø Norway **138 E4** 69.39N 18.57E
Trondheim Norway **138 E4** 63.25N 10.22E
Trout *r.* Canada **56 G5** 61.17N 119.52W
Trout Creek *town* Canada **66 E5** 45.59N 79.21W
Trout Lake N.W.T. Canada **56 F5** 60.34N 121.23W
Trout Lake Ont. Canada **64 B3** 51.15N 93.06W
Trout Lake *town* Alta. Canada **59 C3** 56.30N 114.33W
Trout Lake *town* N.W.T. Canada **56 F5** 60.25N 121.14W
Troy U.S.A. **66 A2** 42.36N 83.09W
Troyes France **138 D2** 48.18N 4.05E
Trujillo Peru **122 B6** 8.06S 79.00W
Truro Canada **72 D2** 45.22N 63.13W
Trutch Canada **56 F4** 57.44N 122.57W
Tsaratanana, Massif du *mts.* Madagascar **129 H3** 13.44S 48.59E
Tsetserleg Mongolia **152 I7** 47.26N 101.22E
Tsiigehtchic Canada **74 E3** 67.28N 133.45W
Tsimlyansk Reservoir Russian Fed. **139 H2** 47.46N 42.14E
Tsumeb Namibia **129 E3** 19.14S 17.43E
Tsushima *i.* Japan **153 N4** 34.30N 129.20E
Tuamotu Is. Pacific Oc. **163 Q5** 17.00S 142.00W
Tuban Indonesia **154 E2** 6.55S 112.01E
Tubruq Libya **128 F8** 32.04N 23.57E
Tubuai *i.* Pacific Oc. **163 Q4** 23.23S 149.27W
Tuchitua Canada **74 F3** 60.56N 129.11W
Tucson U.S.A. **112 D3** 32.15N 110.57W
Tucumcari U.S.A. **112 F4** 35.11N 103.44W
Tucuruí Brazil **122 E6** 3.42S 49.44W
Tucuruí Resr. Brazil **122 E6** 4.35S 49.33W
Tuguegarao Philippines **155 G7** 17.36N 121.44E
Tukangbesi Is. Indonesia **155 G2** 5.30S 124.00E
Tuktoyaktuk Canada **74 E3** 69.26N 133.00W
Tuktut Nogait National Park Canada **74 F3** 68.33N 121.03W
Tula Russian Fed. **139 G3** 54.12N 37.37E
Tulita Canada **74 F3** 64.55N 125.31W
Tulsa U.S.A. **112 G4** 36.07N 95.58W
Tumbler Ridge *town* Canada **56 F3** 55.07N 121.01W
Tungsten Canada **74 F3** 61.53N 128.03W
Tunis Tunisia **128 E8** 36.46N 10.16E
Tunisia Africa **128 D8** 34.52N 9.24E
Tunja Colombia **122 B7** 5.33N 73.23W
Tunulic *r.* Canada **68 F5** 58.27N 66.44W
Tupelo U.S.A. **113 I3** 34.15N 88.43W
Tupper Canada **56 F3** 55.31N 120.03W
Tura Russian Fed. **143 M4** 64.05N 100.00E
Turgeon *r.* Canada **65 F3** 50.00N 78.57W
Turin Italy **138 D2** 45.04N 7.41E
Turkana, Lake Ethiopia/Kenya **128 G5** 3.59N 35.57E
Turkestan Kazakhstan **152 B6** 43.17N 68.16E
Turkey Asia/Europe **139 G1** 39.19N 34.21E
Turkey *r.* U.S.A. **64 C1** 42.45N 91.04W
Turkmenbashi Turkmenistan **146 D5** 40.02N 52.59E
Turkmenistan Asia **146 D5** 40.50N 58.26E
Turks and Caicos Is. C. America **117 J5** 21.30N 71.50W
Turks Is. Turks and Caicos Is. **117 J5** 21.30N 71.10W
Turku Finland **138 F4** 60.27N 22.15E
Turneffe Is. Belize **116 G4** 17.30N 87.45W
Turner Valley *town* Canada **59 C1** 50.41N 114.17W
Turpan China **152 F6** 42.55N 89.06E
Turquino *mtn.* Cuba **117 I5** 20.05N 76.50W
Tuscaloosa U.S.A. **113 I3** 33.12N 87.33W
Tuticorin India **147 F1** 8.48N 78.08E
Tutuila *i.* American Samoa **162 N5** 14.18S 170.42W
Tuvalu Pacific Oc. **162 M6** 7.24S 178.20E
Tuxtla Gutiérrez Mexico **116 F4** 16.45N 93.09W
Tver Russian Fed. **139 G3** 56.50N 35.54E
Twenty Mile Creek Canada **64 X1** 43.11N 79.22W
Twillingate Canada **69 I3** 49.34N 54.29W
Twin Falls *town* Canada **68 F4** 53.33N 64.20W
Twin Falls *town* U.S.A. **112 D5** 42.34N 114.30W
Twisp U.S.A. **56 F2** 48.21N 120.07W
Two Hills *town* Canada **59 D2** 53.43N 111.44W
Tyler U.S.A. **113 G3** 32.22N 95.18W
Tynda Russian Fed. **143 O3** 55.11N 124.34E
Tyre Lebanon **150 A3** 33.15N 35.14E
Tyrrhenian Sea France/Italy **138 E1** 40.13N 10.15E
Tyumen' Russian Fed. **139 J3** 57.09N 65.28E

U

Ubangi *r.* C.A.R./Dem. Rep. Congo **128 E4** 0.25S 17.44E
Uberaba Brazil **123 E5** 19.47S 47.57W
Uberlândia Brazil **122 E5** 18.57S 48.17W
Ubon Ratchathani Thailand **154 C7** 15.15N 104.50E
Ucayali *r.* Peru **122 B6** 4.00S 73.30W
Ucluelet Canada **56 E2** 48.56N 125.33W
Udachnyy Russian Fed. **143 N4** 66.30N 112.43E
Udaipur India **147 F3** 24.35N 73.47E
Uddevalla Sweden **138 E3** 58.21N 11.57E
Udon Thani Thailand **154 C7** 17.29N 102.45E
Uele *r.* Dem. Rep. Congo **128 F5** 4.08N 22.26E
Uelen Russian Fed. **143 U4** 66.07N 169.52W
Uel'kal' Russian Fed. **143 U4** 65.36N 179.26W
Ufa Russian Fed. **139 I3** 54.44N 55.58E
Uganda Africa **128 G5** 2.34N 32.37E
Uglegorsk Russian Fed. **143 Q2** 49.01N 142.04E
Ugol'nyye Kopi Russian Fed. **143 T4** 64.49N 177.34E
Uinta Mts. U.S.A. **112 D5** 40.45N 110.30W
Ujung Pandang Indonesia **154 F2** 5.09S 119.28E
Ukhta Russian Fed. **139 I4** 63.33N 53.46E
Ukiah U.S.A. **112 B4** 39.09N 123.12W
Ukraine Europe **138 G2** 49.23N 31.18E
Ulaangom Mongolia **152 G7** 49.59N 92.00E
Ulan Bator Mongolia **153 J7** 47.54N 106.52E
Ulan-Ude Russian Fed. **143 M3** 51.55N 107.40E
Uliastay Mongolia **152 H7** 47.42N 96.52E
Ulithi *i.* Fed. States of Micronesia **155 J6** 10.00N 139.40E
Uluru *mtn.* Australia **158 C3** 25.20S 131.01E
Umboi *i.* P.N.G. **155 L2** 5.35S 148.00E
Ume *r.* Sweden **138 F4** 63.46N 20.19E
Umeå Sweden **138 F4** 63.50N 20.17E
Umingmaktok Canada **74 H3** 67.38N 107.56W
Umiujaq Canada **68 C5** 56.33N 76.25W
Umuarama Brazil **123 D4** 24.00S 53.20W
Ungava, Péninsule d' Canada **68 D6** 60.46N 74.25W
Ungava Bay Canada **68 F5** 59.16N 67.29W
Union City U.S.A. **66 E1** 41.54N 79.50W
United Arab Emirates Asia **146 D3** 23.30N 52.20E
United Kingdom Europe **138 C3** 54.35N 1.53W
United States of America N. America **112 F4** 39.00N 100.00W
Unity Canada **60 B2** 52.26N 109.08W
Upernavik Greenland **75 M4** 72.48N 56.09W
Upolu *i.* Samoa **162 N5** 13.55S 171.45W
Upper Arrow Lake Canada **56 G2** 50.23N 117.55W
Upper Blackville Canada **72 C3** 46.37N 65.53W
Upper Humber *r.* Canada **73 G4** 48.58N 57.54W
Upper Liard Canada **74 F3** 60.04N 128.56W
Upper Musquodoboit Canada **72 D2** 45.08N 62.57W
Upper Salmon Reservoir Canada **73 G4** 48.21N 56.14W
Uppsala Sweden **138 E3** 59.51N 17.38E
Upsalquitch *r.* Canada **72 B3** 47.54N 66.58W
Ural *r.* Kazakhstan/Russian Fed. **139 I2** 46.55N 51.46E
Ural'sk Kazakhstan **139 I3** 51.11N 51.24E
Ural'skiy Khrebet *mts.* Russian Fed. **139 J4** 66.50N 63.48E
Uranium City Canada **60 B3** 59.31N 108.43W
Urengoy Russian Fed. **142 J4** 65.59N 78.30E
Urgench Uzbekistan **146 E5** 41.32N 60.39E
Urmia, Lake Iran **146 C4** 37.57N 45.17E
Uruapán Mexico **116 D4** 19.26N 102.04W
Urubamba *r.* Peru **122 B5** 10.43S 73.55W
Uruguaiana Brazil **123 D4** 29.45S 57.05W
Uruguay S. America **123 D3** 33.00S 55.00W
Uruguay *r.* Uruguay **123 D3** 34.00S 58.30W
Ürümqi China **152 F6** 43.43N 87.38E
Usak Turkey **138 F1** 38.40N 29.24E
Ushuaia Argentina **123 C1** 54.47S 68.20W
Usol'ye-Sibirskoye Russian Fed. **143 M3** 52.48N 103.40E
Ussuriysk Russian Fed. **143 P2** 43.48N 131.59E
Ust-Ilimsk Russian Fed. **143 M3** 58.05N 102.40E
Ust-Kamchatsk Russian Fed. **143 S3** 56.14N 162.28E
Ust-Kamenogorsk Kazakhstan **152 E8** 50.00N 82.40E
Ust-Kut Russian Fed. **143 M3** 56.40N 105.50E
Ust-Maya Russian Fed. **143 P4** 60.25N 134.28E
Ust'-Nera Russian Fed. **143 Q4** 64.32N 143.08E
Ust-Olenek Russian Fed. **143 N5** 72.59N 120.00E
Ust Urt Plateau Kazakhstan/Uzbekistan **139 I2** 43.29N 56.11E
Utah *d.* U.S.A. **112 D4** 39.00N 112.00W
Utara I. Indonesia **154 C3** 2.42S 100.05E
Utica Miss. U.S.A. **66 A2** 42.38N 83.02W
Utica N.Y. U.S.A. **113 K5** 43.06N 75.05W
Utikuma Lake Canada **59 C2** 55.48N 115.30W
Uttaradit Thailand **154 C7** 17.20N 100.05E
Uummannaq Greenland **75 L4** 76.34N 68.51W
Uummannaq Greenland **75 M4** 70.41N 52.07W
Uvs Nuur *l.* Mongolia **152 G8** 50.30N 92.30E
Uxbridge Canada **64 X3** 44.07N 79.06W
Uzbekistan Asia **146 E5** 42.39N 60.19E
Uzhhorod Ukraine **138 F2** 48.37N 22.17E

V

Vaal *r.* R.S.A. **129 F2** 29.05S 23.39E
Vaasa Finland **138 F4** 63.06N 21.38E
Vachon *r.* Canada **68 E6** 60.11N 71.30W
Vadodara India **147 F3** 22.16N 73.14E
Vaiaku Tuvalu **162 M6** 8.31S 179.13E
Vaitupu *i.* Tuvalu **162 M6** 7.28S 178.41E
Valdai Hills Russian Fed. **138 G3** 56.59N 32.52E
Valdés, Pen. Argentina **123 C2** 42.30S 64.00W
Valdes Island Canada **57 V3** 49.04N 123.38W
Valdez U.S.A. **74 D3** 61.07N 146.16W
Valdivia Chile **123 B3** 39.46S 73.15W
Val-d'Or *town* Canada **68 C3** 48.06N 77.47W
Valdosta U.S.A. **113 J3** 30.51N 83.51W
Valemount *town* Canada **56 G3** 52.51N 119.16W
Valencia Spain **138 C1** 39.29N 0.21W
Valencia Venezuela **122 C8** 10.14N 67.59W
Valera Venezuela **122 B7** 9.21N 70.38W
Valladolid Spain **138 C2** 41.39N 4.43W
Valledupar Colombia **122 B8** 10.10N 73.16W
Valletta Malta **138 E1** 35.54N 14.30E
Valley *r.* Canada **60 E1** 51.39N 99.56W
Valley City U.S.A. **112 G6** 46.57N 97.58W
Valleyview Canada **59 B2** 55.04N 117.17W
Val Marie Canada **60 C1** 49.14N 107.43W
Val-Paradis *town* Canada **68 C3** 49.09N 79.18W
Valparaíso Chile **123 B3** 33.05S 71.40W
Valparaiso U.S.A. **65 D1** 41.28N 87.03W
Vals, C. Indonesia **155 J2** 8.30S 137.30E
Van Turkey **139 H1** 38.30N 43.22E
Van Buren U.S.A. **72 B3** 47.10N 67.56W
Vancouver Canada **57 W3** 49.16N 123.08W
Vancouver Island Canada **56 E2** 49.28N 125.39W
Vanderhoof Canada **56 E3** 54.01N 124.01W
Vänern *l.* Sweden **138 E3** 59.05N 13.36E
Vanimo P.N.G. **155 K3** 2.42S 141.20E
Vanino Russian Fed. **143 Q2** 49.03N 140.14E
Vanua Levu *i.* Fiji **162 M5** 16.33S 179.15E
Vanuatu Pacific Oc. **162 L5** 16.00S 167.00E
Varanasi India **147 G3** 25.20N 83.04E
Varna Bulgaria **138 F2** 43.12N 27.54E
Västerås Sweden **138 E3** 59.37N 16.33E
Vatnajökull *f.* Iceland **138 B4** 64.28N 16.37W
Vättern *l.* Sweden **138 E3** 58.05N 14.21E
Vaughan Canada **64 W2** 43.47N 79.33W
Vauxhall Canada **59 C1** 50.04N 112.06W
Vava'u Group *is.* Tonga **162 N5** 19.40S 174.30W
Växjö Sweden **138 E3** 56.53N 14.49E
Vaygach *i.* Russian Fed. **142 H5** 70.00N 59.00E
Vegreville Canada **59 C2** 53.29N 112.03W
Velhas *r.* Brazil **122 E5** 17.10S 44.49W
Velikiye Luki Russian Fed. **138 G3** 56.20N 30.31E
Vellore India **147 F2** 12.56N 79.07E
Vel'sk Russian Fed. **139 H4** 61.03N 42.05E
Venezuela S. America **122 C7** 7.00N 65.20W
Venezuela, G. of Venezuela **122 B8** 11.30N 71.00W
Venice Italy **138 E2** 45.26N 12.20E
Ventspils Latvia **138 F3** 57.23N 21.36E
Veracruz Mexico **116 E4** 19.11N 96.10W
Verde *r.* Brazil **123 D4** 21.18S 51.50W
Verde *r.* U.S.A. **112 D3** 33.22N 112.20W
Verkhoyansk Russian Fed. **143 P4** 67.25N 133.25E
Verkhoyansk Range *mts.* Russian Fed. **143 O4** 66.00N 130.00E
Vermilion Canada **59 D2** 53.21N 110.51W
Vermillion Bay *town* Canada **64 B3** 49.51N 93.25W
Vermont *d.* U.S.A. **113 L5** 44.00N 72.30W
Vernadsky *research stn.* Antarctica **167 F2** 65.15S 64.16W
Verner Canada **65 E2** 46.25N 80.07W
Vernon Canada **56 G2** 50.16N 119.17W
Verona Italy **138 E2** 45.26N 10.59E
Verwood Canada **60 C1** 49.31N 105.37W
Vestfjorden *f.* Norway **138 E4** 67.40N 13.54E
Vesuvius Italy **138 E2** 40.50N 14.26E
Victoria *d.* Australia **158 D2** 37.20S 144.10E
Victoria *r.* Australia **158 B4** 15.12S 129.43E
Victoria Canada **57 W1** 48.25N 123.22W
Victoria *r.* Canada **73 G4** 48.44N 56.42W
Victoria Seychelles **132 H2** 4.38S 55.28E
Victoria U.S.A. **112 G2** 28.48N 97.00W
Victoria, Lake Africa **128 G4** 0.59S 32.51E
Victoria, Mt. Myanmar **154 A8** 21.11N 93.56E
Victoria, Mt. P.N.G. **155 L2** 8.55S 147.35E
Victoria de las Tunas Cuba **117 I5** 20.58N 76.59W
Victoria Falls Zambia/Zimbabwe **129 F3** 17.49S 25.42E
Victoria Island Canada **74 G4** 70.42N 110.00W
Victoria Lake Canada **69 H3** 48.18N 57.19W
Victoria Land *f.* Antarctica **167 B2** 74.23S 159.55E
Victoriaville Canada **68 E2** 46.03N 71.58W
Viedma Argentina **123 C2** 40.45S 63.00W
Viedma, L. Argentina **123 B2** 49.40S 72.30W
Vienna Austria **138 E2** 48.12N 16.23E
Vientiane Laos **154 C7** 18.01N 102.48E
Vietnam Asia **154 D6** 15.00N 108.00E
Vieux-Fort Canada **69 H3** 51.25N 57.49W
Vieux Poste, Pointe du *c.* Canada **72 E5** 50.06N 61.47W
Vigo Spain **138 C2** 42.14N 8.43W
Vijayawada India **147 G2** 16.33N 80.39E
Viking Canada **59 D2** 53.05N 111.47W
Vilcabamba, Cordillera *mts.* Peru **122 B5** 12.40S 73.20W
Villahermosa Mexico **116 F4** 18.00N 92.53W
Villarrica Paraguay **123 D4** 25.45S 56.28W
Villavicencio Colombia **122 B7** 4.09N 73.38W
Vilnius Lithuania **138 F3** 54.40N 25.16E
Vilyuy *r.* Russian Fed. **143 O4** 63.37N 119.00E
Vilyuysk Russian Fed. **143 O4** 63.46N 121.35E
Viña del Mar Chile **123 B3** 33.02S 71.35W
Vinh Vietnam **154 D7** 18.42N 105.41E
Vinnytsya Ukraine **138 F2** 49.14N 28.30E
Vinson Massif *mtn.* Antarctica **167 F1** 78.28S 85.11W
Virden Canada **60 D1** 49.51N 100.56W
Virginia *d.* U.S.A. **113 K4** 37.30N 79.00W
Virgin Is. (British) C. America **117 L4** 18.30N 64.30W
Virgin Is. (U.S.A.) C. America **117 L4** 18.30N 65.00W
Visby Sweden **138 E3** 57.38N 18.18E
Viscount Melville Sound Canada **74 H4** 73.50N 108.00W
Vishakhapatnam India **147 G2** 17.42N 83.22E
Vistula *r.* Poland **138 E3** 54.18N 18.55E
Viti Levu *i.* Fiji **162 M5** 18.00S 178.00E
Vitim *r.* Russian Fed. **143 N3** 59.30N 112.36E
Vitória Brazil **123 E4** 20.19S 40.21W
Vitória da Conquista Brazil **122 E5** 14.53S 40.52W
Vitoria-Gasteiz Spain **138 C2** 42.51N 2.39W
Vitsyebsk Belarus **138 G3** 55.12N 30.10E
Vityaz Depth Pacific Oc. **80 G5** 43.30N 150.00E
Vizcaíno, Sierra *mts.* Mexico **116 B6** 27.20N 114.30W
Vizianagaram India **147 G2** 18.08N 83.31E
Vladikavkaz Russian Fed. **139 H2** 43.02N 44.41E
Vladimir Russian Fed. **139 H3** 56.08N 40.24E
Vladivostok Russian Fed. **143 P2** 43.09N 131.53E
Vlorë Albania **138 E2** 40.28N 19.30E
Volga *r.* Russian Fed. **139 H2** 45.47N 47.34E
Volga Uplands Russian Fed. **139 H3** 48.59N 44.23E
Volgograd Russian Fed. **139 H2** 48.44N 44.30E
Vologda Russian Fed. **139 G3** 59.13N 39.54E
Volos Greece **138 F1** 39.22N 22.57E
Volta, Lake Ghana **128 D5** 6.23N 0.05E
Volta Redonda Brazil **123 E4** 22.31S 44.05W
Volzhskiy Russian Fed. **139 H2** 48.49N 44.45E
Vorkuta Russian Fed. **142 I4** 67.27N 64.00E
Voronezh Russian Fed. **139 G3** 51.38N 39.12E
Vosges *mts.* France **138 D2** 47.46N 6.41E
Voss Norway **138 D4** 60.38N 6.27E
Vostok *research stn.* Antarctica **167 L1** 79.21S 108.04E
Vostok I. Kiribati **163 P5** 10.05S 152.23W
Votkinsk Russian Fed. **139 I3** 57.03N 53.58E
Votkinsk Reservoir Russian Fed. **139 I3** 57.23N 55.12E
Voyageurs National Park U.S.A. **64 B3** 48.28N 92.44W
Vulcan Canada **59 C1** 50.24N 113.16W
Vung Tau Vietnam **154 D6** 10.21N 107.04E
Vyatka Russian Fed. **139 H3** 58.36N 49.41E

W

Wa Ghana **128 C6** 10.04N 2.30W
Wabag P.N.G. **155 K2** 5.27S 143.42E
Wabasca *r.* Canada **59 C3** 58.18N 115.23W
Wabasca-Desmarais Canada **59 C2** 55.57N 113.50W
Wabash *r.* U.S.A. **113 I4** 38.25N 87.45W
Wabassi *r.* Canada **65 D3** 51.46N 86.18W
Wabowden Canada **60 E2** 54.54N 98.38W
Wabush Canada **68 F4** 52.51N 66.49W
Waco Canada **68 F3** 51.26N 65.37W
Waco U.S.A. **112 G3** 31.33N 97.10W
Waddington, Mount Canada **56 E2** 51.21N 125.18W
Wadena Canada **60 D1** 51.57N 103.48W
Wadena U.S.A. **64 B2** 46.33N 95.06W
Wadi Halfa Sudan **128 G7** 21.48N 31.20E
Wad Medani Sudan **128 G6** 14.22N 33.30E
Wagga Wagga Australia **158 D2** 35.07S 147.24E
Wahpeton U.S.A. **112 G6** 46.16N 96.36W
Waigeo *i.* Indonesia **155 I3** 0.05N 130.30E
Waingapu Indonesia **154 G2** 9.30S 120.10E
Waini Pt. Guyana **122 D7** 8.24N 59.48W
Wainwright Canada **59 D2** 52.50N 110.51W
Wainwright U.S.A. **74 C4** 70.39N 159.51W
Wakaw Canada **60 C2** 52.38N 105.44W
Wakefield U.S.A. **65 C2** 46.28N 89.56W
Wake I. Pacific Oc. **162 L8** 19.17N 166.36E
Wakkanai Japan **153 Q7** 45.26N 141.43E
Waldemar Canada **64 V2** 43.53N 80.16W
Walhalla U.S.A. **60 E1** 48.55N 97.55W
Walkerton Canada **66 C4** 44.08N 81.09W
Wallace U.S.A. **57 G1** 47.30N 116.00W
Wallaceburg Canada **66 B2** 42.35N 82.23W
Wallis and Futuna *is.* Pacific Oc. **162 N5** 13.16S 176.15W
Walvis Bay Namibia **129 E2** 22.58S 14.30E
Wandering River *town* Canada **59 C2** 55.12N 112.28W
Wangaratta Australia **158 D2** 36.23S 146.21E
Wapikopa Lake Canada **65 C4** 52.55N 88.10W
Wapiti *r.* Canada **59 B2** 55.08N 118.18W
Wapsipinicon *r.* U.S.A. **64 C1** 41.46N 90.20W
Wapusk National Park Canada **61 F3** 57.51N 93.22W

X

Y

Z

ACKNOWLEDGEMENTS

The Pearson School Atlas represents another stage in my 25-year association with Prentice Hall/Pearson Publishers. I have been blessed with gifted editors and production personnel who have brought this resource to reality. In this current edition, the assistance, direction, and support of Kelly Ronan have been exemplary. I have been surrounded by individuals and organizations who have contributed to my personal and professional development as a geographer, teacher, consultant, and author – the ROGES, the (former) Professional Development Committee of OSSTF, the Geography Consultants of Ontario, especially George Thompson, the consultative staff of Ontario Agri-Food Education, and my Agriculture in the Classroom colleagues across Canada.

Robert Morrow

Topographic map extracts on pages 58, 62, 63, 67, 70, 71, 76, 77, 169 and 175
© Produced under licence from Her Majesty the Queen in Right of Canada, with permission of Natural Resources Canada.

Photographs on pages 6-7 and 14-15 *Masterfile*
Satellite images on pages 57 and 173 *Science Photo Library*
Satellite images on pages 61, 65, 69, 73, 75, 129, 139, and 159 *NASA Visible Earth*
Satellite images on pages 117, 122 and 123 *data courtesy of the U.S. Geological Survey, EROS Data Center, Sioux Falls, SD*
Data for the map at bottom right page 111 *Stockholm Environment Institute at the University of York, UK*

The publisher of this book has made every reasonable effort to trace the ownership of data and to make full acknowledgement for their use. If any errors or omissions have occurred, they will be corrected in future editions, providing written notification has been received by the publisher.

The following lists give the references and sources used in the preparation of the thematic maps, graphs and statistical tables in the atlas :

CANADA THEMATIC

pages 4-5 Canada and the World Atlas
pages 6-7 Canada and the World Atlas
pages 8-9 Canada and the World Atlas, Environment Canada
pages 10-11 Canada and the World Atlas
page 12 Environment Canada
page 13 Environment Canada, NASA (National Aeronautics and Space Administration)
pages 14-15 Canada and the World Atlas
pages 16-17 Canada and the World Atlas
pages 18-19 Canada and the World Atlas, Statistics Canada, Organization for Economic Co-operation and Development (OECD)
pages 20-21 Natural Resources Canada, Petroleum Economist, The Times Atlas of the World 10th Comprehensive edition
pages 22-23 Canada Electricity Association, National Energy Board, Natural Resources Canada, ATCO Power, BC Hydro, Columbia Power Corporation, Energy Ottawa, Great Lakes Power, Hydro Québec, Manitoba Hydro, Maritime Electric, New Brunswick Power, Newfoundland and Labrador Hydro, Nova Scotia Power, Ontario Power Generation, Sask Power, TransAlta, Yukon Energy
pages 24-25 Canada and the World Atlas, Statistics Canada, UNCTAD/WTO International Trade Centre
pages 26-27 Canada and the World Atlas, Fisheries and Oceans Canada, Statistics Canada, Food and Agricultural Organization of the United Nations (FAO)
pages 28-29 Canada and the World Atlas, Natural Resources Canada, FAO
pages 30-31 Statistics Canada
pages 32-33 Statistics Canada, BC Finance and Economic Review 2002, Alberta Economic Development, The Saskatchewan Economy, Manitoba Financial Report 2002,Ontario Ministry of Finance, Institut de la statistique Québec, Department of Finance New Brunswick, Ministry of Finance Nova Scotia, Prince Edward Island Statistics
pages 34-35 Canada and the World Atlas, Statistics Canada 2001 Census
pages 36-37 Canada and the World Atlas, Statistics Canada 2001 Census
pages 38-39 Canada and the World Atlas
pages 40-41 The National Atlas of Canada
pages 42-43 Statistics Canada 2001 Census, Clean Air Strategic Alliance, World Bank World Development Indicators(WDI) 2002, National Sewage Report Card
pages 44-45 Statistics Canada 2001 Census, Citizenship and Immigration Canada (CIC)
pages 46-47 Transport Canada, Statistics Canada
pages 48-49 Canada Tourism
pages 50-51 UN Statistics Division, World Trade Organization
pages 52-53 Environment Canada, Carbon Dioxide Information Analysis Center
pages 54-55 Environment Canada, National Parks Canada, UNESCO (United Nations Educational, Scientific and Cultural Organization

CANADA REGIONAL

pages 56 to 77 All Physical and Political maps on these pages are created from databases © Collins Bartholomew Ltd.

WORLD THEMATIC

pages 82-83 United Nations Environment Programme (UNEP)
pages 84-85 National Oceanic and Atmospheric Administration (NOAA)
page 87 FAO
page 88 The Times Atlas of the World 10th Comprehensive Edition, United Nations Population Division (UNDP), World Urbanization Prospects 2001
page 89 UNICEF (United Nations Children's Fund), World Bank WDI 2002
pages 90-91 UNDP World Urbanization Prospects 2001
page 92 World Bank WDI 2002, UN Statistics Division
page 93 World Trade Organization
pages 94-95 International Energy Agency, BP Statistical Review 2002
pages 96-97 UN Statistics Division, United Nations Framework Convention on Climate Change (UNFCCC)
pages 98-99 UN Human Development Reports 2002, World Bank WDI 2002, FAO State of Food Insecurity 2002, UNAIDS Report 2002
page 100 UN Human Development Reports 2002, UN Statistics Division
page 101 UNHCR Yearbook 2001
page 102 World Bank WDI 2002
page 103 UN Human Development Reports 2002
page 104 International Labour Organization, IDBAmerica, Year Book of Australia 2002
page 106 UN Human Development Reports 2002
page 107 The Commonwealth, North Atlantic Treaty Organization, Organization of American States, League of Arab States, African Union, Association of Southeast Asian Nations, South Pacific Forum, Colombo Plan, Organization of the Oil Exporting Countries, Organisation for Economic Cooperation and Development, European Union, The Caribbean Community, Latin American Integration Association, Andean Community, Economic Community of West Africa, Economic and Monetary Community of Central Africa, Southern African Development Community, North American Free Trade Agreement

WORLD REGIONAL

pages 108 to 167 All Political, Physical and Physical and Political maps on these pages are created from databases © Collins Bartholomew Ltd.
page 108 UNPD Urbanization Prospects 2001, UN Demographic Yearbook 1999
page 110 Canada and the World Atlas
page 111 World Tourism Organization, US Census Bureau, World Trade Organization, SEI/SIDA
page 114 USGS Land Cover Data Base, World Climate Data
page 115 US Census Bureau, US Department of Commerce, World Trade Organization
page 116 UN Urbanization Prospects 2001, UN Demographic Yearbook
page 118 USGS Land Cover Data Base, World Climate Data
page 119 World Tourism Organization, Canada and the World Atlas, UN Statistics Division
page 120 UN Urbanization Prospects 2001, UN Demographic Yearbook 1999
pages 122-123 UN Urbanization Prospects 2001, UN Demographic Yearbook 1999
page 124 USGS Land Cover Data Base, World Climate Data
page 125 World Tourism Organization, The Times History of the World, UN Statistics Division
page 126 UN Urbanization Prospects 2001, UN Demographic Yearbook 1999
pages 128-129 UN Urbanization Prospects 2001, UN Demographic Yearbook 1999
page 130 USGS Land Cover Data Base, World Climate Data
page 131 World Tourism Organization, The Times History of the World, UN Statistics Division
pages 132-133 UN Urbanization Prospects 2001, UN Demographic Yearbook 1999
page 136 UN Urbanization Prospects 2001, UN Demographic Yearbook 1999
page 137 The Times Atlas of European History
pages 138-139 Urbanization Prospects 2001, UN Demographic Yearbook 1999
page 140 USGS Land Cover Data Base, World Climate Data
page 141 World Tourism Organization, UN Statistics Division
pages 142-143 UN Urbanization Prospects 2001, UN Demographic Yearbook 1999
page 144 USGS Land Cover Data Base, World Climate Data
page 145 Canada and the World Atlas, UN Statistics Division
pages 146-147 UN Urbanization Prospects 2001, UN Demographic Yearbook 1999
page 148 USGS Land Cover Data Base, World Climate Data
page 149 World Tourism Organization, UNHCR Yearbook 2001, UN Statistics Division
page 150 UN Urbanization Prospects 2001, UN Demographic Yearbook 1999, BP Statistical Review 2002
page 151 The Times History of the World, World Factbook 2002
pages 152-153 UN Urbanization Prospects 2001, UN Demographic Yearbook 1999
pages 154-155 UN Urbanization Prospects 2001, UN Demographic Yearbook 1999
page 156 USGS Land Cover Data Base, World Climate Data
page 157 World Tourism Organization, The Times History of the World, UN Statistics Division
pages 158-159 UN Urbanization Prospects 2001, UN Demographic Yearbook 1999
page 160 USGS Land Cover Data, World Climate Data
page 161 World Tourism Organization, The Times History of the World, UN Statistics Division, Australian Bureau of Statistics, Statistics New Zealand
pages 164-165 UN Statistics Division

CANADA STATISTICS

pages 176-185 Statistics Canada, CIC, Fisheries and Oceans Canada, Natural Resources Canada, Industry Canada, Elections Canada

WORLD STATISTICS

(In this section, the data is provided for the latest date in which meaningful comparisons among the largest number of countries is possible.)

pages 186-193 UN Statistical Division, World Bank WDI 2002, UNESCO, CIA Factbook 2002

National Library of Canada Cataloguing in Publication

Morrow, Robert, 1942-
Pearson school atlas / Robert Morrow.

Includes index.
ISBN 0-13-039311-8 (bound).--ISBN 0-13-122506-5 (pbk.)

1. Atlases, Canadian. I. Title.

G1021.M87 2003 912 C2003-901252-2

ISBN 0-13-039311-8 (Hardcover) ISBN 0-13-122506-5 (Paperback)

Publishers: Mark Cobham, Susan Cox
Product Managers: Melanie Trevelyan, David LeGallais
Managing Editor: Elynor Kagan
Developmental Editor: Kelly Ronan
Coordinating Editor: Angelie Kim
Production Coordinator: Zane Kaneps
Cover Design: Alex Li
Cartography: Collins Bartholomew Ltd- Moira Jones, Mark Steward, Neal Jordan-Caws
Reviewers: *Aboriginal content:* Shawn Bernard, Patrick Loyer; *Middle-East content:* Martin Bunton, Christopher Friedrichs, Derek Penslar, James Whidden; *Geographic content:* Bruce Clark, Dennis Desrivieres, Lloyd Greenham, John Wallace

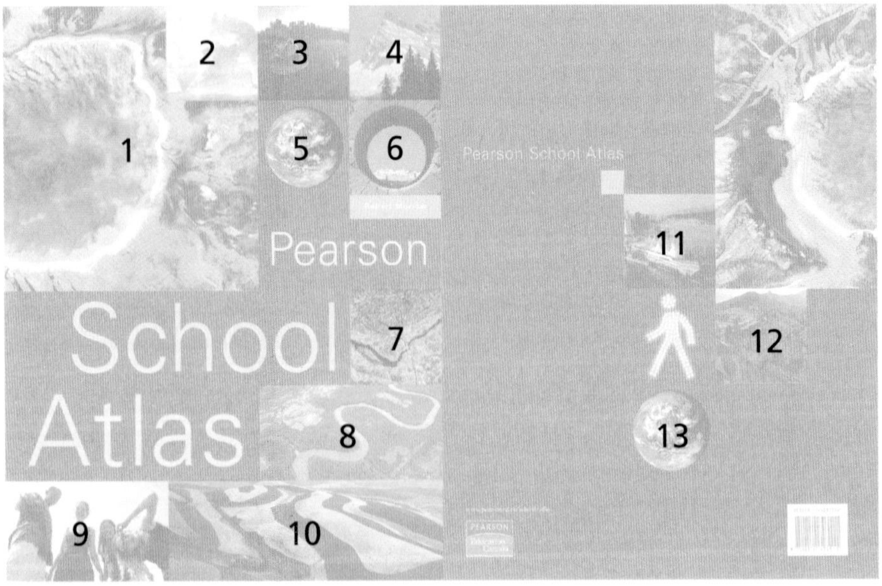

1. Grand Prismatic Spring, Yellowstone © Charles O'Rear/CORBIS
2. Iceberg, Newfoundland – © Grant V. Faint/ImageBank/GettyImages
3. Sydney – © Romilly Lockyer/ImageBank/GettyImages
4. Alberta – Corel
5. Earth showing Western Hemisphere – PhotoDisc/GettyImages
6. Morocco – © Darrell Gulin/ImageBank/Gettyimages
7. Ottawa (satellite shot) – DigitalVision
8. New Brunswick Landscape – © Carl & Ann Purcell/CORBIS
9. Teenagers – © Vicky Kasala/ImageBank/GettyImages
10. Contour Strip Farmed Wheat Fields, Washington – © Joseph Sohm; ChromoSohm Inc./CORBIS
11. Vancouver – Corel
12. Nepal – Corel
13. Earth showing Western Hemisphere – PhotoDisc/GettyImages

4 5 RRD 08

Manufactured in the United States.

PEARSON
Education
Canada

OCEANS: AREA

1.	Pacific Ocean	155 557 000 km^2
2.	Atlantic Ocean	76 762 000 km^2
3.	Indian Ocean	68 556 000 km^2
4.	Southern Ocean	20 327 000 km^2
5.	Arctic Ocean	14 056 000 km^2

COUNTRIES: TOTAL AREA

1.	Russia	17 075 200 km^2
2.	Canada	9 984 670 km^2
3.	United States	9 629 091 km^2
4.	China	9 596 960 km^2
5.	Brazil	8 511 965 km^2

COUNTRIES: POPULATION (2002 EST.)

1.	China	1 284 303 705
2.	India	1 045 845 226
3.	United States	280 562 489
4.	Indonesia	231 328 092
5.	Brazil	176 029 560

LAKES: AREA

1.	Caspian Sea	374 000 km^2
2.	Lake Superior	82 100 km^2
3.	Lake Victoria	62 940 km^2
4.	Lake Huron	59 500 km^2
5.	Lake Michigan	57 016 km^2

LAKES: DEPTH

1.	Lake Baikal	1637 m
2.	Lake Tanganyika	1435 m
3.	Caspian Sea	946 m
4.	Lake Nyasa (or Malawi)	706 m
5.	Lake Issyk Kul	700 m

RIVERS: LONGEST

1.	Nile	6690 km
2.	Amazon	6296 km
3.	Mississippi-Missouri	5970 km
4.	Yangtze	5797 km
5.	Ob	5567 km

RIVERS: FLOW (AT MOUTH)

1.	Amazon	174 894 m^3 per second
2.	Congo	38 969 m^3 per second
3.	Negro	34 979 m^3 per second
4.	Orinoco	25 187 m^3 per second
5.	La Plata-Paraná	22 895 m^3 per second

ISLANDS: AREA

1.	Greenland	2 175 597 km^2
2.	New Guinea	820 033 km^2
3.	Borneo	743 107 km^2
4.	Madagascar	587 042 km^2
5.	Baffin	507 451 km^2

CANADIAN FACTS

1. **Largest island:** Baffin Island (507 451 km^2)
2. **Longest river:** Mackenzie River (4241 km)
3. **Largest lake:** Lake Huron (36 000 km^2 within Canada)
4. **Highest mountain:** Mount Logan (5951 m)
5. **Highest lake:** Lake Chilko (1171 m)
6. **Northernmost point:** Cape Columbia, Ellesmere Island
7. **Southernmost point:** Middle Island, Lake Erie
8. **Westernmost point:** Mount St. Elias, Yukon
9. **Easternmost point:** Cape Spear, Newfoundland and Labrador
10. **Largest national park:** Wood Buffalo (44 807 km^2)

CANADIAN WEATHER EXTREMES

1. **Highest temperature:** 45.0°C; Midale and Yellow Grass, SK (July 5, 1937)
2. **Lowest temperature:** -63°C; Snag, YT (Feb. 3, 1947)
3. **Greatest precipitation in one day:** 489.2 mm; Ucluelet, BC (Oct. 6, 1967)
4. **Greatest snowfall in one day:** 118.1 cm; Lakelse Lake, BC (Jan. 17, 1974)
5. **Greatest precipitation in one year:** 8122.6 mm; Henderson Lake, BC (1931)
6. **Least precipitation in one year:** 12.7 mm; Arctic Bay, NU (1949)
7. **Highest air pressure:** 107.96 kPa; Dawson, YT (Feb. 2, 1989)
8. **Lowest air pressure:** 94.2 kPa; St. Anthony, NL (Jan. 20, 1977)
9. **Highest wind speed:** 201.1 km/h; Cape Hopes Advance, QC (Nov. 18, 1931)
10. **Foggiest place:** Grand Bank, NL (average of 120 days a year)

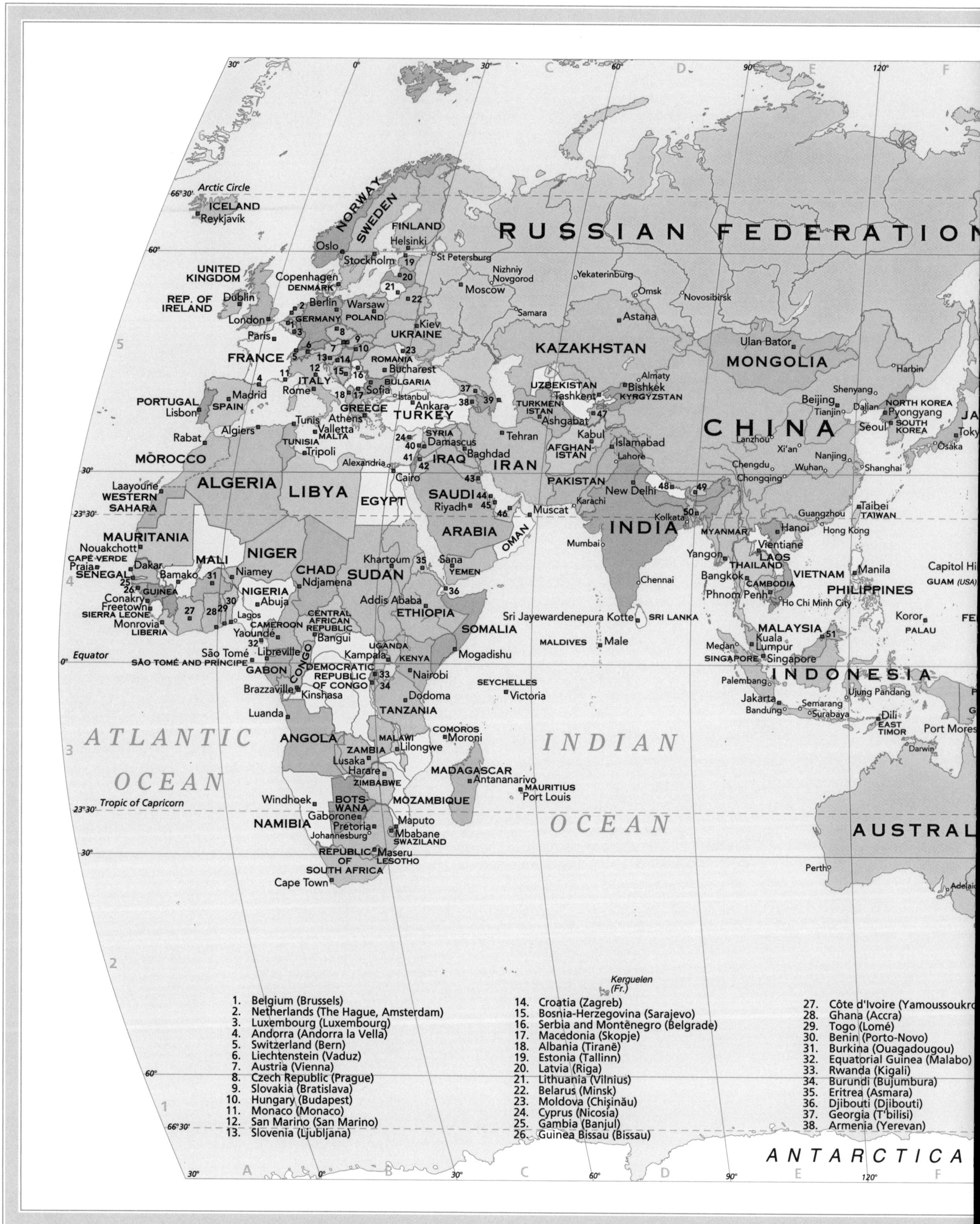
A
B
C
D
E
F
30°
0°
60°
90°
120°
66°30'
23°30'
Arctic Circle
Equator
Tropic of Capricorn
ICELAND
Reykjavík
NORWAY
SWEDEN
FINLAND
Oslo
Helsinki
Stockholm
St Petersburg
RUSSIAN FEDERATION
UNITED KINGDOM
Copenhagen
DENMARK
REP. OF IRELAND
Dublin
London
Berlin
Warsaw
GERMANY
POLAND
Nizhniy Novgorod
Moscow
Samara
Yekaterinburg
Omsk
Novosibirsk
Astana
Kiev
UKRAINE
Paris
FRANCE
ROMANIA
Bucharest
BULGARIA
Sofia
ITALY
Rome
Madrid
PORTUGAL
Lisbon
SPAIN
GREECE
Athens
Istanbul
Ankara
TURKEY
Tunis
Valletta
MALTA
Algiers
Rabat
TUNISIA
Tripoli
MOROCCO
ALGERIA
LIBYA
EGYPT
Alexandria
Cairo
Laayoune
WESTERN SAHARA
SYRIA
Damascus
IRAQ
Baghdad
IRAN
Tehran
KAZAKHSTAN
UZBEKISTAN
Tashkent
Bishkek
KYRGYZSTAN
Almaty
TURKMENISTAN
Ashgabat
Kabul
AFGHANISTAN
Islamabad
Lahore
PAKISTAN
New Delhi
Karachi
INDIA
Mumbai
Kolkata
Chennai
Sri Jayewardenepura Kotte
SRI LANKA
MALDIVES
Male
MONGOLIA
Ulan Bator
CHINA
Beijing
Tianjin
Dalian
Shenyang
Harbin
NORTH KOREA
Pyongyang
Seoul
SOUTH KOREA
Tokyo
Osaka
Lanzhou
Xi'an
Nanjing
Shanghai
Chengdu
Chongqing
Wuhan
Guangzhou
Hong Kong
Taibei
TAIWAN
Hanoi
MYANMAR
Yangon
Vientiane
LAOS
THAILAND
Bangkok
CAMBODIA
Phnom Penh
VIETNAM
Ho Chi Minh City
Manila
PHILIPPINES
Capitol Hill
GUAM (USA)
Koror
PALAU
MALAYSIA
Kuala Lumpur
Medan
SINGAPORE
Singapore
INDONESIA
Palembang
Jakarta
Bandung
Semarang
Surabaya
Ujung Pandang
Dili
EAST TIMOR
Port Moresby
Darwin
AUSTRALIA
Perth
Adelaide
SAUDI ARABIA
Riyadh
Muscat
OMAN
YEMEN
Sana
Khartoum
SUDAN
CHAD
Ndjamena
NIGER
Niamey
MALI
Bamako
MAURITANIA
Nouakchott
CAPE VERDE
Praia
SENEGAL
Dakar
GUINEA
Conakry
Freetown
SIERRA LEONE
Monrovia
LIBERIA
NIGERIA
Abuja
Lagos
CAMEROON
Yaoundé
CENTRAL AFRICAN REPUBLIC
Bangui
Addis Ababa
ETHIOPIA
SOMALIA
Mogadishu
São Tomé
SÃO TOMÉ AND PRÍNCIPE
Libreville
GABON
CONGO
Brazzaville
DEMOCRATIC REPUBLIC OF CONGO
Kinshasa
UGANDA
Kampala
KENYA
Nairobi
SEYCHELLES
Victoria
TANZANIA
Dodoma
Luanda
ANGOLA
COMOROS
Moroni
MALAWI
Lilongwe
ZAMBIA
Lusaka
Harare
ZIMBABWE
MADAGASCAR
Antananarivo
MAURITIUS
Port Louis
Windhoek
BOTSWANA
Gaborone
MOZAMBIQUE
NAMIBIA
Pretoria
Johannesburg
Maputo
Mbabane
SWAZILAND
REPUBLIC OF SOUTH AFRICA
Maseru
LESOTHO
Cape Town
ATLANTIC OCEAN
INDIAN OCEAN
Kerguelen (Fr.)
ANTARCTICA
1. Belgium (Brussels)
2. Netherlands (The Hague, Amsterdam)
3. Luxembourg (Luxembourg)
4. Andorra (Andorra la Vella)
5. Switzerland (Bern)
6. Liechtenstein (Vaduz)
7. Austria (Vienna)
8. Czech Republic (Prague)
9. Slovakia (Bratislava)
10. Hungary (Budapest)
11. Monaco (Monaco)
12. San Marino (San Marino)
13. Slovenia (Ljubljana)
14. Croatia (Zagreb)
15. Bosnia-Herzegovina (Sarajevo)
16. Serbia and Montenegro (Belgrade)
17. Macedonia (Skopje)
18. Albania (Tiranë)
19. Estonia (Tallinn)
20. Latvia (Riga)
21. Lithuania (Vilnius)
22. Belarus (Minsk)
23. Moldova (Chişinău)
24. Cyprus (Nicosia)
25. Gambia (Banjul)
26. Guinea Bissau (Bissau)
27. Côte d'Ivoire (Yamoussoukro
28. Ghana (Accra)
29. Togo (Lomé)
30. Benin (Porto-Novo)
31. Burkina (Ouagadougou)
32. Equatorial Guinea (Malabo)
33. Rwanda (Kigali)
34. Burundi (Bujumbura)
35. Eritrea (Asmara)
36. Djibouti (Djibouti)
37. Georgia (T'bilisi)
38. Armenia (Yerevan)

SCALE 1 : 70 000 000

0 800 1600 2400 3200 km

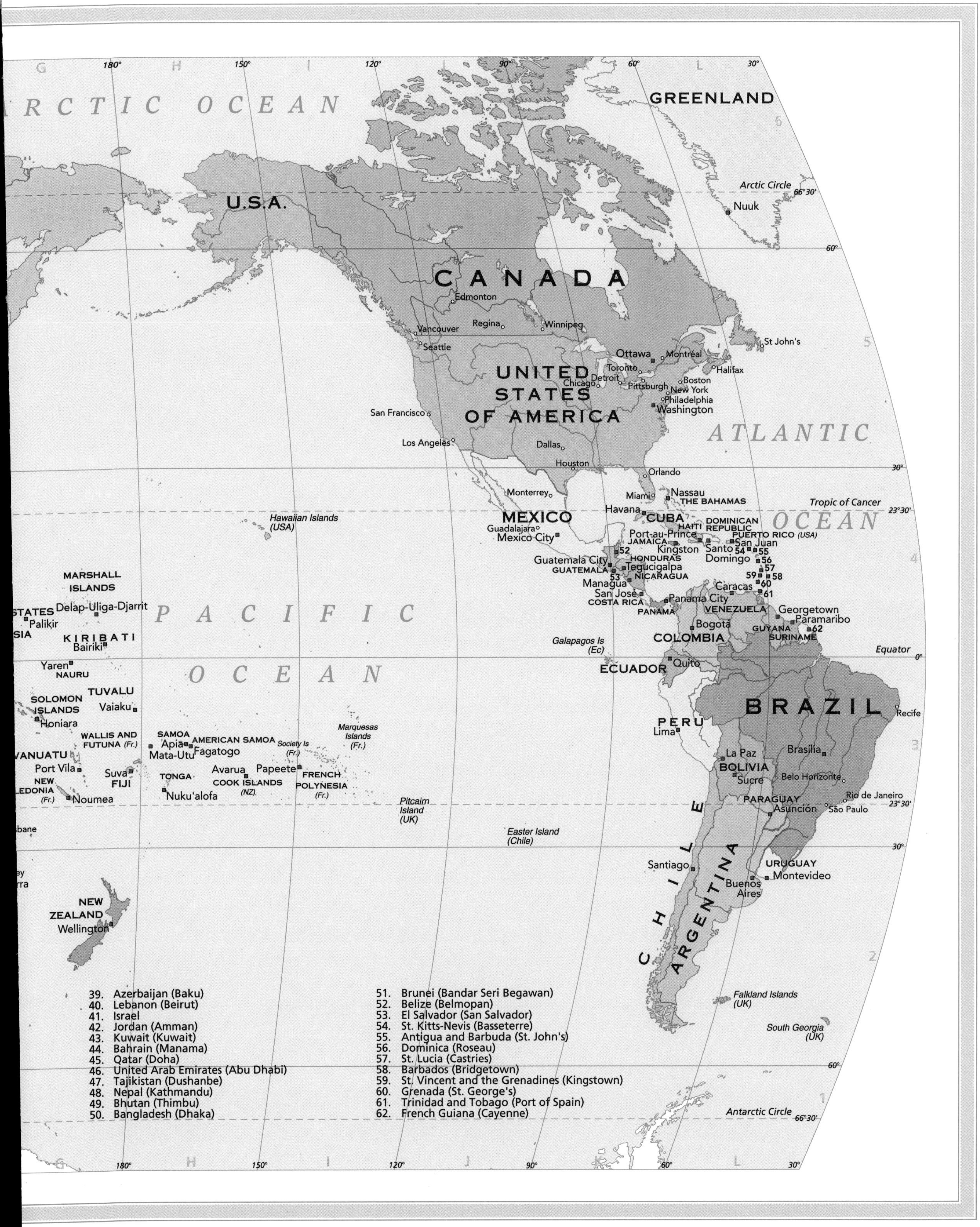
ARCTIC OCEAN
GREENLAND
Arctic Circle 66°30'
Nuuk
U.S.A.
CANADA
Edmonton
Regina
Winnipeg
Vancouver
Seattle
St John's
Ottawa
Montréal
Halifax
Toronto
Detroit
Chicago
Boston
New York
Pittsburgh
Philadelphia
Washington
UNITED STATES OF AMERICA
San Francisco
Los Angeles
Dallas
Houston
Orlando
ATLANTIC OCEAN
Monterrey
Miami
Nassau
THE BAHAMAS
Tropic of Cancer 23°30'
Havana
CUBA
MEXICO
Guadalajara
Mexico City
HAITI
DOMINICAN REPUBLIC
PUERTO RICO (USA)
Port-au-Prince
JAMAICA
Kingston
Santo Domingo
San Juan
Guatemala City
GUATEMALA
HONDURAS
Tegucigalpa
NICARAGUA
Managua
San José
COSTA RICA
PANAMA
Panama City
Caracas
VENEZUELA
Georgetown
Paramaribo
GUYANA
SURINAME
Bogotá
COLOMBIA
Galapagos Is (Ec)
Equator 0°
Quito
ECUADOR
Hawaiian Islands (USA)
MARSHALL ISLANDS
Delap-Uliga-Djarrit
Palikir
KIRIBATI
Bairiki
PACIFIC OCEAN
Yaren
NAURU
TUVALU
Vaiaku
SOLOMON ISLANDS
Honiara
WALLIS AND FUTUNA (Fr.)
Mata-Utu
SAMOA
Apia
AMERICAN SAMOA
Fagatogo
Society Is (Fr.)
Marquesas Islands (Fr.)
VANUATU
Port Vila
Suva
FIJI
TONGA
Nuku'alofa
Avarua
COOK ISLANDS (NZ)
Papeete
FRENCH POLYNESIA (Fr.)
NEW CALEDONIA (Fr.)
Noumea
Pitcairn Island (UK)
Easter Island (Chile)
BRAZIL
Recife
PERU
Lima
Brasília
La Paz
BOLIVIA
Sucre
Belo Horizonte
Rio de Janeiro
São Paulo
PARAGUAY
Asunción
CHILE
ARGENTINA
Santiago
URUGUAY
Montevideo
Buenos Aires
NEW ZEALAND
Wellington
Falkland Islands (UK)
South Georgia (UK)
Antarctic Circle 66°30'
39. Azerbaijan (Baku)
40. Lebanon (Beirut)
41. Israel
42. Jordan (Amman)
43. Kuwait (Kuwait)
44. Bahrain (Manama)
45. Qatar (Doha)
46. United Arab Emirates (Abu Dhabi)
47. Tajikistan (Dushanbe)
48. Nepal (Kathmandu)
49. Bhutan (Thimbu)
50. Bangladesh (Dhaka)
51. Brunei (Bandar Seri Begawan)
52. Belize (Belmopan)
53. El Salvador (San Salvador)
54. St. Kitts-Nevis (Basseterre)
55. Antigua and Barbuda (St. John's)
56. Dominica (Roseau)
57. St. Lucia (Castries)
58. Barbados (Bridgetown)
59. St. Vincent and the Grenadines (Kingstown)
60. Grenada (St. George's)
61. Trinidad and Tobago (Port of Spain)
62. French Guiana (Cayenne)

Times projection